The Ancient Indus Valley

New Perspectives

ABC-CLIO's
Understanding Ancient Civilizations Series

The Ancient Indus Valley

New Perspectives

JANE R. McINTOSH

A B C ⬥ C L I O

Santa Barbara, California • Denver, Colorado • Oxford, England

Library of Congress Cataloging-in-Publication Data
McIntosh, Jane.
  The ancient Indus Valley : new perspectives / Jane McIntosh.
    p. cm. —(Understanding ancient civilizations series)
  Includes bibliographical references and index.
  ISBN 978-1-57607-907-2 (hard copy : alk. paper) — ISBN 978-1-57607-908-9
  (ebook) 1. Indus civilization. I. Title.
DS425.M338 2008
934—dc22

                                                                  2007025308

12 11 10 09 08   1 2 3 4 5 6 7 8 9 10

Production Editor: Anna A. Moore
Editorial Assistant: Sara Springer
Production Manager: Don Schmidt
Media Editor: Jed DeOrsay
Media Resources Coordinator: Ellen Brenna Dougherty
Media Resources Manager: Caroline Price
File Manager: Paula Gerard

ABC-CLIO, Inc.
130 Cremona Drive, P.O. Box 1911
Santa Barbara, California 93116-1911

This book is also available on the World Wide Web as an ebook.
Visit www.abc-clio.com for details.

This book is printed on acid-free paper ∞

Manufactured in the United States of America

Contents

PART 3: CURRENT ASSESSMENT

Series Editor's Preface

In recent years there has been a significant and steady increase of academic and popular interest in the study of past civilizations. This is due in part to the dramatic coverage, real or imagined, of the archaeological profession in popular film and television, as well as to extensive journalistic reporting of spectacular new finds from all parts of the world. Because archaeologists and other scholars, however, tend to approach their study of ancient peoples and civilizations exclusively from their own disciplinary perspectives and to publish just for their professional colleagues, there has long been a lack of general factual and other research resources available for the nonspecialist. The *Understanding Ancient Civilizations* series is intended to fill that need.

Volumes in the series are principally designed to introduce the general reader, student, and nonspecialist to the study of specific ancient civilizations. Each volume is devoted to a particular archaeological culture (e.g., the ancient Maya of southern Mexico and adjacent Guatemala) or cultural region (e.g., Israel and Canaan), and each seeks to achieve, with careful selectivity and astute critical assessment of the literature, an expression of a particular civilization and an appreciation of its achievements.

The keynote of the *Understanding Ancient Civilizations* series is to provide, in a uniform format, an interpretation of each civilization that will express its culture and place in the world, as well as the qualities and background that make it unique.

Series titles include volumes on the archaeology and prehistory of the ancient civilizations of Egypt, Greece, Rome, and Mesopotamia, as well as the achievements of the Celts, Aztecs, and Inca, among others. Others are in the planning stage.

I was particularly fortunate in having Kevin Downing from ABC-CLIO contact me in search of an editor for a series about archaeology. It is a simple statement of the truth that there would be no series without him. I was also lucky to have Simon Mason, Kevin's successor at ABC-CLIO, continuing to push the production of the series. Given the scale of the project and the schedule for production, he deserves more than a sincere thank you.

JOHN WEEKS

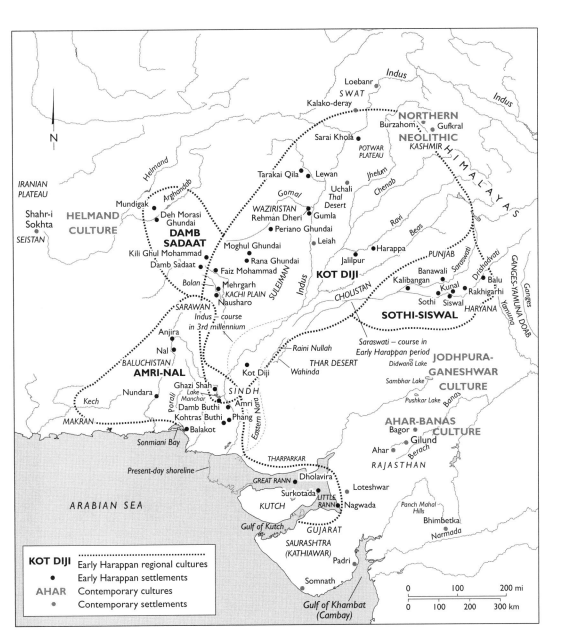

Map 1. The Indus region in the Early Harappan period. This map shows the regional cultures of the Early Harappan period and contemporary cultures of the region.

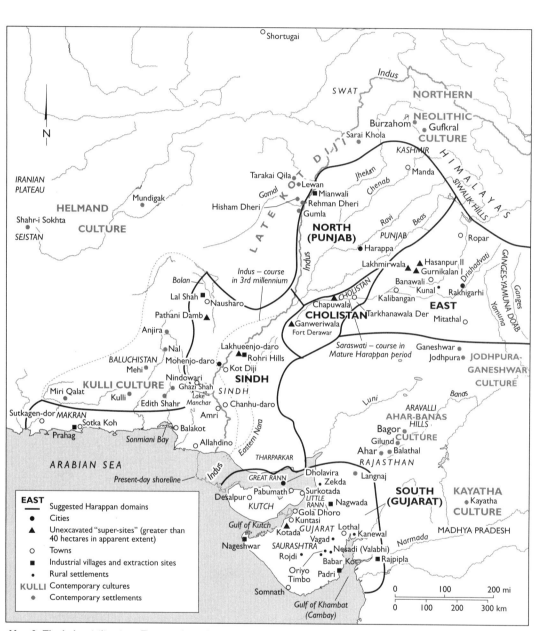

Map 2. The Indus civilization. This map shows the Indus region during the Mature Harappan period, including the the domains of the Indus civilization, the best known settlements, and contemporary cultures.

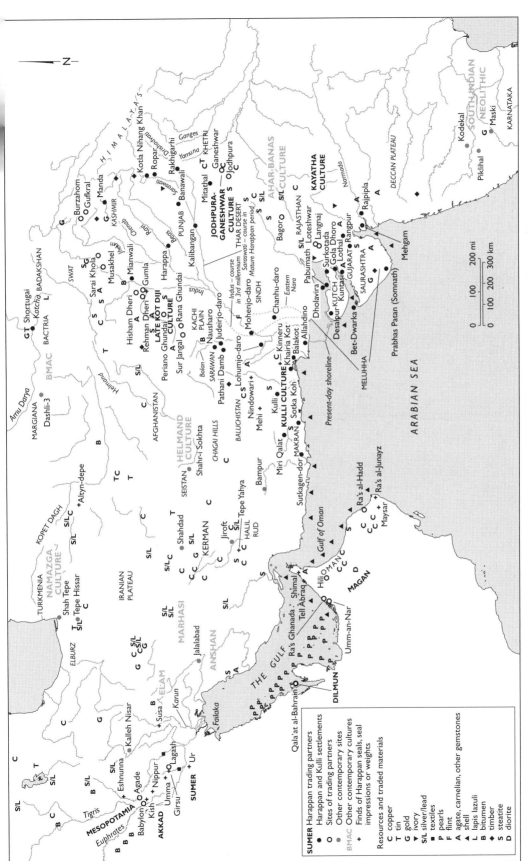

Map 3. Harappan trade. The map indicates the extent of Harappan trading contacts, contemporary cultures, and the sources of the principal traded commodities.

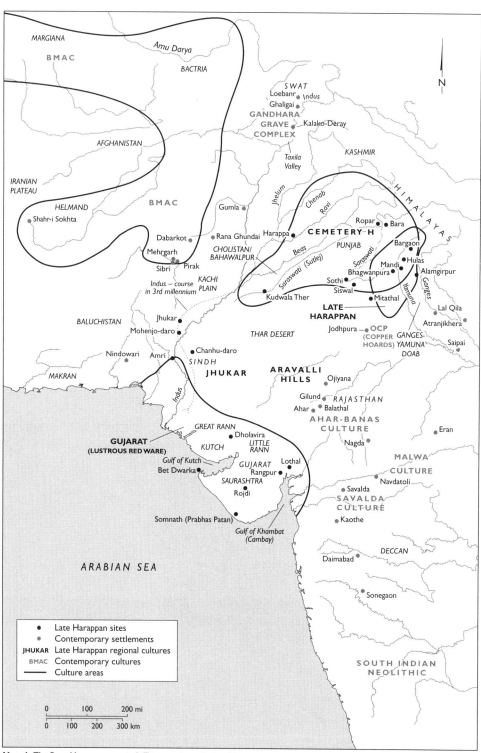

Map 4. The Post-Harappan period. *This map shows the Post-Harappan regional cultures and contemporary cultures of the period.*

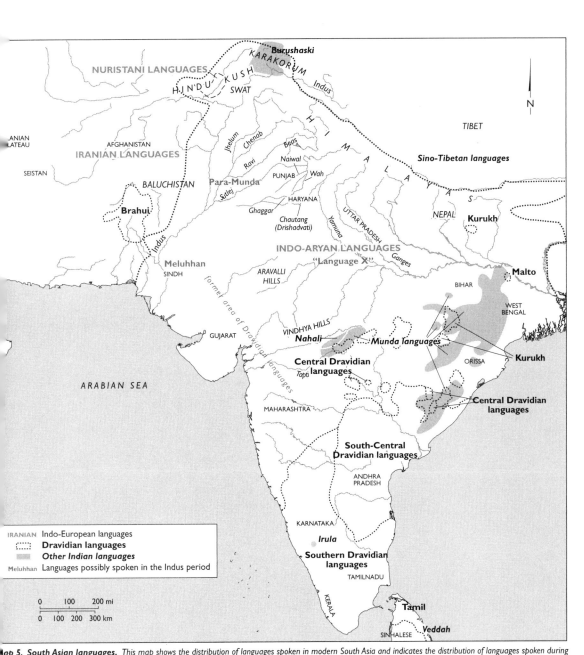

Map 5. South Asian languages. *This map shows the distribution of languages spoken in modern South Asia and indicates the distribution of languages spoken during the Harappan period.*

PART I

Introduction

Introduction

THE INDUS IN ITS SETTING

The Indus Valley, a region of great fertility, defines the eastern edge of the zone in which Near Eastern agriculture developed, based on wheat, barley, sheep, goats, and cattle. To its west lies Baluchistan, the mountainous eastern edge of the Iranian plateau, an area with which it has always been closely linked. Networks of trade routes across the Iranian plateau have often provided distant communications with the civilizations of the Near East, while the Arabian Sea, into which the Indus flows, has allowed seaborne connections with the Gulf and the Near East, with Arabia and East Africa, and with south India, eastern India, and Southeast Asia. The Indus is fed by the five rivers from which the Punjab takes its name, powerful tributaries that water a region of forests and grassland, supporting agriculture along their banks and sustaining pastoral communities elsewhere. These rivers rise in the Himalayas, which form a formidable but not impenetrable barrier between the Indian subcontinent and the lands to its east: the deserts and steppe of Central Asia, as well as China and Southeast Asia beyond. Southeast of the Punjab lay the valleys of the Ganges and Yamuna, which have constituted the center of Indian civilization since the first millennium BCE. This, however, is only a recent configuration, since in the third millennium the ancestor of the Yamuna River may have been a tributary of a major river, the Saraswati, that flowed parallel to the Indus across what is now the Great Indian (Thar) Desert. The desert region and the Aravalli Hills to its south separated the Indus-Saraswati Valley from the central part of peninsular India: They were home, then as now, to hunter-gatherer and pastoral communities. In the west, the Indus entered the Arabian Sea south of its present delta; where today there are the marshy Ranns and the Kutch and Saurashtra peninsulas, in the third millennium there were sea and islands. Agriculture, pastoralism, and fishing have supported the inhabitants of this region for millennia.

Also in the third millennium the Indus Basin was the focus of settlement in the subcontinent, other areas being home to small farming communities, pastoral tribes, and hunter-gatherers. While the rewards of farming in the region were immense, it was and still is tectonically active as the Himalayas inexorably push upward: Earthquakes and major changes in the course of the rivers are therefore an ever present threat, as are devastating floods. The loss of the Saraswati in the second millennium played a major part in the decline of the Indus civilization (also known as the Harappan civilization after one of its principal cities, Harappa). In the third millennium this civilization flourished over an area far larger than those of its contemporaries in Mesopotamia and Egypt. But while both of the latter continued to evolve in the second millennium, the Indus civilization disintegrated, and the focus in later times shifted to the Ganges Valley. Nevertheless the Indus civilization left a lasting legacy, setting the pattern for many later aspects of life in the subcontinent, many of which have endured to the present day.

A LOST CIVILIZATION

While the civilizations of Egypt, Mesopotamia, and China left enduring monuments and historical records and were remembered in later times, the Indus civilization was forgotten. Thus, when the European antiquarians began to investigate Asia's past in the late eighteenth and nineteenth centuries, only the later traces of India's ancient history commanded their attention: the cities of the Mauryan Empire, where some centuries earlier the Buddha had lived, and the megalithic monuments of the south, with their striking similarity to prehistoric European tombs. The discovery of the Indus civilization in the 1920s, when excavations began at Mohenjo-daro and Harappa, therefore took Europe by storm. The cities' well laid-out streets and fine houses with bathrooms surprised and impressed archaeologists and the public alike, while the discovery of seals bearing an enigmatic script intrigued them. The contemporaneity of the Indus cities with Mesopotamia's civilization was quickly established. Excavations by Sir Mortimer Wheeler in the 1940s brought further publicity.

Partition in 1947 redrew the map, with the greater part of the known Harappan civilization falling within newly formed Pakistan: The situation acted as a spur to the Indian government to investigate its remaining Harappan regions: Gujarat and the Indo-Gangetic divide. Survey work in Cholistan, on the Pakistan side of the border, revealed the importance of the now dry Saraswati River in Indus times. Recent work by collaborative international teams at the two best-known and largest cities, Harappa and Mohenjo-daro, using the most up-to-date techniques, have greatly enhanced understanding of the civilization, while the investigation of new sites, such as the city of Dholavira and a number of small rural settlements, has extended our knowledge in new directions.

A LAND OF UNSOLVED MYSTERIES

Though much is now known about the Indus civilization, the failure to decipher the script has left many questions unanswered, including the very identity of the Indus people. Uniquely among all the ancient and more recent civilizations, it appears to have developed and thrived without warfare or violent competition, either internally or externally. There are no palaces, and very few structures can be identified as having had a religious function; yet the civilization seems to have been highly organized, with good-quality artifacts widely distributed, even in villages. Its merchants traded Harappan products

The discovery in the 1920s of Mohenjo-daro and Harappa revealed the hitherto unsuspected existence of the Indus civilization. Here at Mohenjo-daro, houses more than four thousand years old still stand several stories high. Though now bare brick, the walls were originally covered with gleaming plaster. (Munir Khan/Harappa.com)

over a vast area, from Central Asia to Mesopotamia, and yet almost nothing is known of what they brought home. And, after six or seven centuries, urban life suddenly collapsed, a process whose reasons are still hotly debated, not least because of the controversy over the arrival of the speakers of the Indo-Aryan languages that now dominate the subcontinent, a subject that stirs up deep partisan feelings among some scholars.

PART 2

Indus Civilization

CHAPTER 2

Location of the Indus Civilization and Its Environmental Setting

LOCATION

The region in which the Indus civilization developed lies at the intersection of two major zones: the dry Iranian plateau and the largely tropical South Asian peninsula, watered by the monsoons. These belonged originally to two different landmasses separated by a vast stretch of ocean. In the geologically recent past, the peninsula broke away from the southern continent of Gondwanaland and around thirty-five million years ago crashed into Asia (Laurasia), being driven against it, slipping beneath it, and causing the edges of both plates to buckle and rise, forming the Himalayas. A trough was created at the junction of the plates and gradually filled with eroded material, forming the Indo-Gangetic plain. The collision zone is still active, with the result that periodically earth tremors are experienced in and beyond the mountains, altering the landscape and often causing massive destruction. Areas rise or sink, and rivers change their courses. The annual flooding and alluviation also promote changes in the course of the major rivers and have impacted the coastline.

The Indus River rises in the Himalayas, as do the other rivers that form the Punjab. These come together at the Panjnad to form the massive lower course of the Indus, flowing through Sindh, a region that is largely desert beyond the alluvial stretches along the river. Other tributaries join the Indus from the mountains of Baluchistan, which separate the Indus plains from the Iranian plateau, and the mighty river fans out into a delta in the Arabian Sea. To the east of the Punjab other rivers rise from the Himalayas and the Siwalik Hills: These include the Ganges, flowing east to a huge delta in the Bay of Bengal, and the Yamuna, now the companion of the Ganges but in antiquity probably contributing to a major river that flowed southwest. Identified as the Saraswati River eulogized in early Indian literature, this is now reduced to a series of small seasonal rivers periodically flowing into the largely dry Ghaggar-Hakra riverbed. The ancient Saraswati may have spent its waters in an inland delta in the Great Indian (Thar) Desert that borders the Indus region to the south, or it may have continued to the sea, joining the Indus delta or flowing into the Gulf of Kutch in Gujarat. Gujarat was the southern province of the Indus civilization: Today Kutch is separated from the Indian mainland by the marshy Ranns, but in Indus times the latter were probably open water. *Rabi* (winter)

A satellite photograph of the Indus Basin showing the cultivated areas along the Indus River, the mountains that frame it to the north and west, the desert to its east, the fringe created by the Aravalli Hills, and the salt wastes and shallow seas that surround Kutch; to its south, only the northern part of Saurashtra is visible. East of the Punjab in the north, traces may be seen of the dry beds of the once-mighty Saraswati River. (NASA)

cultivation is the main practice in most of the greater Indus region, as it is in the lands farther west, with wheat and barley as the principal crops. In many areas where cultivation is not possible, grasslands offer pastures for feeding substantial numbers of domestic animals; forests in upland areas and various minerals, such as metal ores and gemstones, are also exploited.

Beyond the desert to the south and into the lands of the Ganges to the east, the environment of the subcontinent changes. The most dramatic difference is a substantial increase in rainfall, particularly during the southwest monsoon from June to September; there is also far less seasonal variation in temperature, and in the Ganges Valley there was originally dense forest that presented a major barrier to agricultural settlement. Here *kharif* (summer) cultivation is the norm and the staple crops are rice and a variety of millets: Most of these grains, however, did not come under cultivation until the late third millennium or later. At the time of the Indus civilization, the peninsula and eastern South Asia were sparsely occupied by groups living by hunting, gathering, and fishing or by farming often dominated by animal husbandry. Economically the people of the Indus were linked with regions to their west, in Baluchistan and the Iranian plateau, with whom there were longstanding communications and trade; but in the Indus period links were also established and developed with the cultures of the Gulf, initially with those of Oman but also with the emerging empires of southern Mesopotamia and with the lands between the two civilizations. Seaborne trade continued to be of great importance to the subcontinent from the first millennium BCE onward.

THE ENVIRONMENTAL SETTING

The Indo-Iranian Borderlands

The eastern edge of the arid Iranian plateau rises to form the mountains of Baluchistan, whose northeast members are continuous with the much higher ranges of the Himalayas. Several ranges of high mountains border the Indus Valley: In the north, the Sulaiman Range runs nearly due south, extending into the Indus plain as the Marri-Bugti Hills. Farther south, the Kirthar Range also runs nearly due north-south, and between the Kirthar Range and the Marri-Bugti Hills lies the Kachi plain, a substantial extension of the alluvial plain. The valley of the Bolan River, which flows through the Kachi plain, creates one of the major passes giving access from the Indus plains to the Baluchi highlands and the Iranian plateau beyond. A number of smaller rivers and mountain torrents also break through the mountains and provide east-west routes: Of these the most important is the Gomal River in the north of the Sulaiman Range. To the west the mountains are lower and heavily dissected by valleys and streams, those in the north mainly flowing west while those of southern Baluchistan flow north-south. These rivers create narrow valleys and plateaus with limited areas of cultivable soil. A few valleys have more extensive areas of arable land, including the Bannu Basin and Gomal Valley in the north, the Quetta Valley in the center, and the Las Bela plain in the south.

The region is semiarid, with limited and often unreliable winter rainfall over most of the region, brought by westerly winds. Agriculture therefore relies heavily on other sources of water: springs and wells in some areas, and, more widely, hill runoff when rain and snowmelt feed seasonal streams and rivers. This water is often captured and stored for later use or diverted onto fields, using a variety of small dams (bunds and gabarbands): although hard to date, some of these dams seem likely to have been constructed as early as in the pre-Indus period. Given the scarcity of water, cultivation in the region is therefore of less importance than pastoralism: keeping sheep, goats, and cattle. Many pastoralists spend their summers at home in Baluchistan and migrate with their animals to the Indus region during the cold winter months, a pattern that stretches back into antiquity. A wide range of wild game lives in the hills, including gazelle, markhor and other wild goats, wild sheep (urial), boar, and onager, as well as predators such as wolf, bear, leopard, and in the past probably Asiatic lion. The native vegetation is largely of the steppe or scrub type, with scattered trees such as acacia, tamarisk, and euphorbia, as well as juniper, jujube (zizyphus), almond, pistachio, and other edible species in some parts. Native grasses include a variety of wild barley. Both trees and other vegetation were more abundant in antiquity.

The mountains of the Indo-Iranian borderlands, particularly the Chagai Hills and those of the Sarawan region, are the source of many useful minerals, some exploited since remote antiquity: salt, steatite, agate and other semiprecious stones, alabaster, copper, and others.

The narrow Makran coast bordering the Arabian Sea is a bleak and inhospitable region, waterless except for occasional oases and rivers. The Kech-Dasht Valley in the west is the main focus of settlement and also provides a major route into the interior. East of the Makran is Las Bela, also a fertile plain, watered by the Porali and Hingol Rivers. Other rivers also provide paths from the coast into the mountains for most of the year when they are dry, and they are navigable after the rains. Fish furnish the main source of food for those dwelling on the coast; dates are the main crop in areas where cultivation is possible. The indented coast provides numerous small natural harbors and anchorages and is sheltered from the full impact of the monsoon winds. Maritime trade is important, as it was to the Indus people who established a number of coastal settlements in strategic locations. Seaborne relations with the people of the Oman peninsula, on the western side of the Gulf of Oman, may have been established by the early third millennium.

Punjab

The Indus River rises in the heights of the Himalayas in a spring near the Manasarover Lake in Tibet, the source also of the Sutlej River, which becomes a tributary of the Indus far downstream. Flowing west and then south, fed by spring snowmelt and summer monsoon rain, its waters swelled by mountain streams and tributaries, including the Kabul River, the Indus descends steeply and passes through the dissected terrain of the Potwar plateau and the low hills of the Salt Range. To their south it enters the plains and becomes navigable. It skirts the western edge of the alluvial plain; between it and the mountains of the Sulaiman Range runs the Derajat, a low treeless plain, through which run routes that link the Indus plain with passes into the mountains. The alluvial plain extends eastward from the Indus, eventually running into that of the Ganges. A number of rivers cross the northern part of the plain: today five, the Jhelum, Chenab, Ravi, Beas, and Sutlej, gradually converge with each other and eventually join with the Indus at the Panjnad east of the Marri-Bugti Hills. Whereas the rivers are well entrenched in the north, farther into the plains they have broader, shallower beds and are apt to change their course. Within the areas flooded by the rivers, which vary in width from a few hundred meters to 10 kilometers or more, deposits of alluvium provide rich fertile soils that are extensively cultivated and that supply the agricultural needs of the region. The natural vegetation of the alluvial valleys includes grasses and some trees, such as acacia and sissoo, now much reduced by clearance but probably forming a dense forest in antiquity. Apart from the Thal Desert (the central part of the Sindh Sagar doab between the Indus and the Jhelum Rivers), the slightly higher ground of the interfluve areas is mainly grassland, providing abundant pasture for large numbers of cattle and other animals. The foothills and lower slopes of the Himalayas to the north are densely forested, including many species useful for timber, and in antiquity the forest cover was far greater. The mountains were also the source of minerals, including bitumen from the Mianwali district, steatite from various areas, salt from the Salt Range, and various gems and other stones from Kashmir. Small amounts of gold can be panned from the Indus sediments, and gold and a little silver and lead are also available in Kashmir and in some other parts of the Himalayas.

The Punjab receives some winter rainfall and some rain in the summer from the southwest monsoon, with winter rainfall highest in the west, decreasing eastward as the monsoon rainfall increases. The principal crop is wheat, grown in the winter through the spring, while large numbers of cattle and smaller numbers of sheep and goats are raised on the rich pastures of the interfluve savannah. The region abounds in wildlife today, and a wider range of species lived here in the past, including perennial and migratory birds (such as grouse, partridge, jungle fowl, peafowl, and cranes), deer, gazelle, onager, boar, rhino, elephant, and predators such as tigers and bears, while the rivers are home not only to fish but also to crocodiles and the *bulhan*, or blind Indian dolphin. In the adjacent hills live wild sheep and goats (urial and markhor).

Sindh

The rivers that join the Indus at the Panjnad are all substantial, perennial watercourses, carrying large volumes of water, with the result that the Indus is swelled to a mighty river south of the Panjnad. After this meeting, the river turns westward and eventually splits, its main branch running in a southwesterly direction roughly parallel to the Kirthar Hills of southern Baluchistan, with an eastern branch, the Eastern Nara, running parallel. While the Indus enters the Arabian Sea south of the mountains of Baluchistan in a fan of distributaries, the Nara debouches into the Rann of Kutch. The gentle gradient of lands in Sindh is sufficient to maintain a rapid flow of water in the Indus but inadequate to prevent the river from meandering. The river's course has changed in detail on many occasions, as the annual floods cause it to cut new channels or as meanders are cut off to form oxbow lakes, and there have also been several major changes in its course since the end of the Pleistocene. The Indus and the Eastern Nara Rivers flow through land that receives little rainfall and is essentially desert, overlaid by alluvial deposits renewed by the annual inundation; in places these deposits are hundreds of meters thick. During the winter months, when there is little rain, the Indus is confined to its bed, often flowing along a levee. However, swollen in the spring by snowmelt in the Himalayas and in the summer by the rains of the southwest monsoon, the waters carried by the river increase five-, eight-, or even twelve-fold; massive floods on the latter scale now occur on average every five to fifteen years. The floodwaters overflow the levee banks and spread out over a wide area on both sides of the river, depositing first their heavy sediments on the levee banks and adjacent areas, then progressively finer sediments as the waters spread away from the river. Beyond the annually inundated active floodplain are areas that often also receive floodwater. Periodically the river breaks through the levee banks and cuts a new channel through the alluvium of its flood plain. One or both banks may be affected, so the annual provision of water and alluvial silts in any particular area is not entirely reliable, although the fluctuations do not cause prolonged hardship, due to the fertility of the soil and the abundance of the crops grown there (mainly wheat but also barley, pulses, and other crops). These are winter sown; some summer crops are also cultivated, including cotton and sesame. The most favored places for cultivation are patches of deep sediment left behind in channels carved out by the floodwaters: These can generally be sown directly, without breaking the soil with a plow. These fertile patches change their location annually and therefore must be searched for; other areas, watered and provided with fresh alluvium by the inundation, are plowed before planting, after the waters have receded. Cattle and water buffaloes are the main livestock kept by Sindhi farmers, whereas the fringes of the plain (the western piedmont and the margins of the Thar Desert) provide grazing for sheep and goats and, in the west, for wild sheep, wild goats, and onagers.

Oxbow lakes, where meanders of the river have been bypassed, are fertile habitats for wildlife. Seasonal lakes are also formed in levees abandoned by the river. Around the lakes grow reeds and palms as well as grasses. Many species of fish, shellfish, turtles, crocodiles, and birds abound in the lakes and rivers, and fishing is a major occupation of a number of groups in the region. Wild water buffalo, swamp deer, and wild boar were once also found in these wetland locations. Vegetation along the rivers is restricted to plants that can tolerate being immersed annually by the inundation, but substantial gallery forest grows in the meander plain of the river, beyond the active flood plain. Though reduced over the last century, the natural vegetation of the region includes a range of trees, such as acacia, pipal, sissoo, neem, tamarisk, and jujube. These forests and grassland have been home to tigers and lions, rhinos and elephants, peafowl, and other birds including the francolin.

Settlements are concentrated where water is available but where their inhabitants are not threatened by the annual inundation, such as on the banks of oxbow lakes and islands. Indus cities were often constructed on an artificial platform, to raise them above the danger of flooding, or were protected with massive brick walls.

To the west of the Indus River a piedmont plain edges the Kirthar Range of the mountains of Baluchistan and Sindh Kohistan to its south; through this run passes leading to the Baluchi uplands. In the summer this zone is watered by seasonal streams and torrents pouring down the mountainsides that deposit alluvium along their foot. The majority of these western watercourses peter out on the plain, but some may in the past have flowed into the Indus. North of the Kirthar Range and west of the Marri-Bugti Hills lies the Kachi plain, a substantial extension of the Indus plain into the mountains of Baluchistan. The Bolan River flows through the center of the plain and is the main access route to the west from the central Indus region. The valley is also watered by rivers flowing from the mountains on both sides, of which the Mula and the Nari are the most important. Unlike Sindh, this plain is also watered by rainfall, mainly in the summer from the southwest monsoon but also in the winter. Cultivation is now mainly in the summer *(kharif)* though some winter *(rabi)* cultivation also takes place: In the Indus period, *rabi* cultivation predominated, making use in some cases of small-scale irrigation using bunds (small dams) and small channels. The Kachi plain is a region transitional between the mountains of Baluchistan and the more challenging Indus plains, and it was occupied by farmers (at Mehrgarh) by the eighth millennium BCE.

In winter, when the Indus keeps to its bed, it is navigable by large boats; during the summer floods it is often too turbulent for navigation but at other times during the summer country boats with a shallow draught can be used on it. West of the Indus, a smaller river, the Western Nara, flows along an abandoned former bed of the Indus, the Sindh Hollow, and empties into Lake Manchar, a substantial lake on the west side of the Indus. Less violent than the Indus, the Western Nara can be used for navigation for part of the inundation season, as well as for irrigation. Lake Manchar increases in extent by around 10,000 hectares during the inundation and is a bountiful source of fish and birds. Its inhabitants have developed methods of coping with the floods by living in boats or in huts raised above the waters on platforms or by moving from houses to platforms during the floods. Lake Manchar today is considerably larger than it was in Indus times.

The main resource of the Indus Valley is its alluvium for agriculture. But, unlike the rivers of Mesopotamia and Egypt, the Indus also has important mineral resources. In central Sindh its current course passes through a major outcrop of limestone, the Rohri and Sukkur Hills, which have extensive deposits of high-quality flint, exploited by the region's inhabitants since Palaeolithic times. Alum, gypsum, and building stone are also available and in the Kachi plain there is bitumen, used by the early inhabitants of Mehrgarh to waterproof baskets.

To the east of the Indus and Eastern Nara is an arid region, somewhat higher than the Indus plain, giving way to the Great Indian, or Thar, Desert. The desert fringes and the arid Tharparkar region to the southwest receive some summer rainfall from the southwest monsoon, transforming these areas into a rich grassland into which cattle, goats, and sheep from the Indus Valley are driven for summer pasture. The limited rain falling on the desert accumulates in hollows to form seasonal lakes and pools, which provide water for people and animals.

Gujarat

The Tharparkar forms a corridor, used particularly in the summer when it is grassland, between the Indus Valley and the southern region of Gujarat. This region receives more rainfall than the desert and Indus Valley but still only around 400–800 millimeters per year, falling during the summer monsoons. *Kharif* dry farming is the norm today in the region, along with animal husbandry utilizing the thickets of scrubby vegetation, such as acacia, euphorbia, and caper, and grasses. Large numbers of cattle and goats are kept, as well as some sheep, both by farmers and by pastoral nomads who may move to Sindh during the driest months in the spring. Water buffaloes are also important in northern Gujarat and are kept in smaller numbers elsewhere. On the higher ground there is forest, often including the economically valuable teak, and in antiquity the forest cover was much greater. The area is home to many herbivores, such as wild water buffalo, boar, blackbuck, spotted deer, onager, and nilgai, and probably in the past bison (gaur), as well as elephants, rhinos, and lions. It also attracts many flocks of migratory and perennial birds, such as waterfowl, particularly in the Ranns but also in pools created by the rivers. The indented coastline has mudflats and deep estuaries, treacherous to those unfamiliar with their perils but offering good natural harbors. Fishing was and is a major activity in the Gujarat region and along the coast to its north. Fish caught in these waters include pomfret, mullet, grunt, shark, Bombay duck, sole, and many other species, as well as cuttlefish and a great range of shellfish, the shells from the latter being particularly esteemed as a raw material for making bangles and other artifacts. Pearl oysters are also known in the Gulf of Kutch.

The northern and northeast edge of the region is occupied by the Great and Little Ranns of Kutch, sandy salt mudflats that become marshes when they are flooded during the summer months. In the Indus period it seems likely that the Ranns were open water throughout the year. Settlement here is concentrated on patches of high ground, islands during the Indus period, on the largest of which, Kadir Island, was situated the major Indus city of Dholavira.

South of the Great Rann is the Kutch peninsula, a great island in Indus times. A substantial area of grassland south of the Great Rann provides rich pastures for large numbers of cattle, and pastoralism is the main way of life on the peninsula, which has little agriculture due to its low rainfall and lack of perennial rivers. Compensating for these dry conditions to some extent are underground water sources retained in sandstone, which mitigate the effects of periodic droughts.

The Little Rann curves round the east and south of Kutch and separates it from Saurashtra (Kathiawar), a large peninsula, much of which is taken up by a hilly plateau, surrounded by a belt of fertile alluvial soils. The many streams and small rivers draining the high ground carry a little water year round but are torrential and destructive after the monsoon rains. Saurashtra's soils are predominantly the water-retentive black cotton soils, suitable for dry farming, and crops are also irrigated from wells.

The Little Rann continues into the Nal Depression, an area of low-lying ground extending to the Gulf of Khambhat (Cambay), which fills with water during the monsoon season. In its center is the Nal Lake, a seasonal body of water. Pollen evidence shows this to have been a freshwater lake in the Indus period, greater in extent than the present-day lake. The important Indus town of Lothal is situated near the southern end of the Nal Depression.

The adjacent lands of the Indian mainland were also important to the Indus people. The North Gujarat plain is fertile but arid sandy alluvium with thorn forest. The Indus people apparently avoided the plain for settlement, and it has been argued that they did so because it was inhabited by well established hunter-gatherer groups with whom the Indus people enjoyed mutually beneficial relations. To the south, the coast of the Gulf of Khambhat is also alluvial, but the soils are salty and the plain is dissected by a number of seasonal river valleys, including the deeply entrenched Narmada and Tapti Rivers; it receives more rainfall than the areas to its north and west, tending to heavy flooding in the monsoon period. Fertile black cotton soils occur in parts of the region, and there is some cultivation but much of the region is grassland. The coastal strip is backed by the mountains of the Western Ghats.

Gujarat has important deposits of gemstones, particularly agate, which were obtained from the rivers and plateaus of Saurashtra and were mined at Rajpipla on the Narmada. Steatite and alabaster were also available. There was some copper in North Gujarat, and a little tin may have been obtained in North Gujarat and the Panch Mahal Hills to the east.

The Aravallis and the Thar Desert

A number of seasonal rivers flow into the Ranns or enter the sea through the Gulf of Khambhat. The most northerly is the Luni River, which flows into the northeast corner of the Great Rann. It originates among the Aravalli Hills, as do the Banas, which flows into the Little Rann; the Sabarmati, which empties into the Gulf of Khambhat; and other rivers. The Aravallis are a range of low hills situated on the southern edge of the Thar Desert. The vegetation of this area includes drought-resistant acacia and tamarisk. The area receives adequate rain in the summer to support agriculture in the lowland areas and to provide pasture on the uplands. The monsoon rains also fill the beds of seasonal streams, rivers, and lakes. It was home in Indus times to groups who lived mainly by fishing, hunting, and gathering. These hills are rich in minerals, including steatite, and were one of the main sources of the copper used by the Indus people; they may also have provided tin, gold, silver, and lead.

North and northwest of the Aravallis lies the Thar Desert, a rocky plateau of ancient alluvial clays overlain by shifting sand dunes and by patches of hills. Although potentially fertile, the soils depend on rainfall, which is generally low, with less than 100 millimeters in some parts. Fossil channels of ancient watercourses have been detected in parts of the Thar Desert, some blocked by sand dunes to form lakes. During the summer months these fill with runoff water from the hills and dunes but soon become saline and dry up. This region supports some wild fauna such as blackbuck, Indian gazelle, and desert foxes, and it is exploited today by pastoralists and in antiquity by hunter-gatherers; it may have been more hospitable in the past than it is today.

The Indo-Gangetic Divide and the Saraswati River Valley

Between the northeastern edge of the Thar Desert and the Himalayas lies the flat, fertile alluvial plain of the Indo-Gangetic divide, the region between the Punjab rivers and the Ganges. In its southern part, the Yamuna and Ganges rivers descend from the Himalayas to run in parallel south and east to their confluence at Allahabad and thence to the river's great delta on the Bay of Bengal. The Ganges-Yamuna doab (the land between the rivers) is an area of high rainfall; in antiquity this was covered by thick forests, including sissoo and sal, and by dense thickets, including acacia, all providing useful timbers. The abundant and varied flora and fauna, including Indian jungle fowl (the wild ancestor of the domestic chicken), supported hunter-gatherer communities, particularly around lakes. The Indus people moved into the northern part of the doab, penetrating as far east as the western bank of the Ganges, probably using fire to clear limited areas of forest, but, until the development in the first millennium BCE of iron tools for effective forest clearance, farmers from the north were unable to penetrate farther into the Ganges region. In the regions once settled by Indus farmers, winter-grown wheat is the main crop today, using irrigation.

Farther north, numerous streams and rivers descend from the Siwalik Hills, a low range forming part of western edge of the Himalayas and bordered by sal forest, and gradually converge to form a single river, known today as the Ghaggar or Hakra, now generally dry beyond the modern settlement of Hanumangarh. In antiquity it was called the Saraswati, a name confined today to one of the small rivers rising in the Siwaliks. These rivers are dry for most of the year but carry water seasonally, bringing alluvium to the plains between the Sutlej and Drishadvati (modern Chautang) Rivers. However, the existence of dry ancient riverbeds and the heavy concentration of Indus and other prehistoric sites along the existing and dried-up rivers indicate that in the past the rivers carried far more water and extended their flow farther west, perhaps as far as the Arabian Sea. While the rivers carry water only during the monsoon season, groundwater is also available from wells. Floodwaters from the Sutlej River to the north also sometimes fill portions of the dry riverbeds, creating lakes. The eastern area, with its numerous seasonal watercourses, is prime agricultural land, growing mainly wheat during the winter. Farther west the perennial vegetation is desert scrub with some trees, such as euphorbia and acacia. However, during the rains that fall in small quantities in both winter and summer, the region is transformed into rich grassland offering excellent pasture both for domestic herds of cattle, camel, and sheep, often brought here from Sindh during the annual Indus floods, and for wild game such as Indian gazelle, blackbuck, and, in the past, onager. Other local fauna in antiquity included wild boar, tigers, and lions. Modern irrigation permits some productive cultivation, and there is also considerable high-risk and low-yielding rain-fed agriculture in the river valleys.

THE CHANGING LANDSCAPE

Many aspects of the South Asian environment have been stable throughout the postglacial period but there have also been major changes, both natural and human induced. There is considerable debate as to whether the rainfall, the temperature, and the pattern of the monsoon winds in Indus times differed from those of today. Tectonic movements bringing earthquakes and landslides have been responsible for major alterations to the pattern of the landscape, and the activities of rivers have frequently sculpted changes on a smaller scale. Human exploitation, particularly for cultivation and animal husbandry, has wrought not only considerable destruction of vegetation and fauna, but also associated environmental degradation, while the natural drainage has been altered in some areas by the building of dams and the cutting of canals.

The "Lost Saraswati" River

The most dramatic change took place in the region south of the Indus River, where there is evidence that a great river system flowed in the Harappan period. Through ground survey and methods of remote sensing such as satellite photography, many stretches of dry riverbed have been traced in the Thar Desert and in the Indo-Gangetic divide, often as much as 10 kilometers wide, showing that they once held substantial rivers. The shells of freshwater molluscs found in their banks tell the same story. Today a number of small seasonal rivers rising in the Siwalik Hills occupy a narrow channel running for a short distance in some of these dry riverbeds. A massive concentration of Harappan and other prehistoric settlements has been discovered along the dry riverbeds, and it is clear that the drainage of the region has a complicated history. Many names are attached to different parts of the drainage, including the Hakra and the Ghaggar; so, for the sake of clarity, scholars frequently refer to the whole ancient system as the lost Saraswati. In the *Vedas*, the earliest sacred literature of the subcontinent, there are references to the Saraswati as a mighty river, but by the early first millennium BCE the Saraswati was said to disappear into the sand and to flow underground to join the Yamuna farther south.

Dating ancient river courses is a knotty problem, although the date of settlements along their banks is helpful, and establishing the sequence and significance of changes is a formidable task. There is not yet full agreement on the history of the Saraswati, and continuing work often brings changes to the generally accepted picture. At present it is thought (see Maps, 2, 4, and 5) that, during the Indus period and in earlier times, the rivers rising in the Siwalik Hills—including the Naiwals, the river still known as the Saraswati, the Ghaggar, the Wah, and the Drishadvati (now known as the Chautang)—were augmented by the waters of the Yamuna, flowing in the current bed of the Drishadvati, and of the Sutlej, now a tributary of the Indus, then flowing in the one of the western riverbeds that combine to form the Hakra. Both the Sutlej and the Yamuna are major rivers that rise in the Himalayas and that are swelled by snowmelt and monsoon rains; during the Indus period, the waters of these rivers combined to form a great waterway that flowed through the now arid region of Cholistan in the Thar Desert. The Beas River, which now joins the Sutlej, in Indus times flowed west to merge with the other rivers of the Punjab a little east of their confluence with the Indus. The precursor of what is now the Yamuna system was a minor river fed by a series of streams rising in the Himalayan foothills east of the Drishadvati.

In the Indus period the Saraswati river system may have been even more productive than that of the Indus, judging by the density of settlement along its course. In the Bahawalpur region, in the western portion of the river, settlement density far exceeded that elsewhere in the Indus civilization. Several sizable cities lay within this dense concentration, including the metropolis of Ganweriwala whose location is equidistant from the other great Indus cities of Harappa and Mohenjo-daro. Indus settlements are also densely concentrated along other parts of the river's course; while there are some fifty sites known along the Indus, the Saraswati has almost a thousand. Although this is a somewhat distorted figure since erosion and alluviation have between them probably destroyed or deeply buried many settlements in the Indus Valley itself, there can be little doubt that the Saraswati system did yield a great proportion of the Indus people's agricultural produce.

The course of the Saraswati west of Bahawalpur is still uncertain. Recent work has uncovered evidence of a possible inland delta near Fort Derawar, and it has been suggested that the Saraswati may have ended here, running into the sand in a fan of distributaries. There is also some evidence that the Saraswati split into two beds near Fort Derawar. For a stretch of around one hundred and fifty miles to the southwest no relics of ancient river channels can be traced, although the widespread presence of alluvium in the desert indicates that at some time, probably in the much earlier past, a river flowed in this region (which is beyond the reach of present or past Indus alluviation). However, what may have been the continuation of the Saraswati reappears as two rivers, now seasonal, flowing through the Thar Desert: the Raini Nullah and the Wahinda. To their west a continuation is offered by the bed now occupied by the Eastern Nara, a tributary of the Indus: It is not known whether this channel was fed by the Indus or by the Saraswati in the Harappan period. This river may have joined the Indus at the head of its delta to reach the Arabian Sea through what is now the Great Rann. Alternatively, the Eastern Nara may have flowed separately into the Great Rann.

During the second millennium BCE, there were significant alterations to the regional drainage, probably as the result either of a major tectonic event that shifted the course of the major rivers before they descended to the plains or of slightly altered gradients on the extremely flat plains. Some evidence indicates that changes occurred first to the Yamuna/Drishadvati. The main river (Yamuna) shifted its course eastward early in the second millennium, eventually reaching its current bed by the first millennium, while the Drishadvati bed retained only a small seasonal flow; this seriously decreased the volume of water carried by the Saraswati. The Sutlej gradually shifted its channel northward, eventually being captured by the Indus drainage. At first it was an independent tributary of the Indus, but in more recent times it joined the Beas before they both flowed into the Indus. The loss of the Sutlej waters caused the Saraswati to be reduced to the series of small seasonal rivers familiar today. Surveys show a major reduction in the number and size of settlements in the Saraswati region during the second millennium.

The Changing Course of the Indus

The lower Indus drainage has also had a complex history. While the river is prone to change along most of its course, today the central section of its bed is anchored by the gorge in the Rohri-Sukkur Hills, the Sukkur gap, through which it flows. As recently as the time of Alexander the Great (fourth century BCE), however, it skirted these hills to the west. Throughout its Holocene history the Indus has had a major tributary, the Eastern Nara, which, over time, has also changed both its course and the place of its confluence with the Indus. The progressive creation of a substantial delta on the Arabian Sea, reducing the rivers' gradient and increasing their length, has been a major cause of the rivers' changing course. While there is still debate about which of the palaeochannels traced in Sindh was occupied by which river at which time, a likely sequence of changing courses has been established.

In the early Holocene period, the Indus probably followed the course of the Jacobabad and Shahdadkot palaeochannels, flowing east to the south of the Marri-Bugti Hills and south along the eastern edge of the Kirthar Range. It then swung west and flowed along the Sanghar palaeochannel, joining the Eastern Nara, and the combined river flowed into the Arabian Sea a little northwest of Kutch. It may have held this course until around 4000 BCE, but by the Indus period it was flowing in the more gently curving Warah palaeochannel east of its earlier course. This crossed the course of the modern Indus a little south of Mohenjo-daro and flowed south in the Samaro-Dhoro palaeochannels, being joined by the Eastern Nara well to the south. It is possible that during both periods the river occupying the bed of the Eastern Nara was the lower course of the Saraswati rather than a branch of the Indus as it is today. Further alterations in the rivers' course occurred by or after 2000 BCE, and by the fourth century, when Alexander visited the region, the river was closer to its modern course.

In 1819 an earth tremor in Kutch created a huge natural dam 75 miles long and up to 16 miles wide that disrupted the flow of the Eastern Nara branch of the Indus. After seven years, however, the river's floodwaters created a breach and the Nara resumed its flow to the sea. Dramatic short-term events on this scale are likely to have taken place also in the past, and some scholars hypothesize that a similar event caused Mohenjo-daro to be swamped by floodwaters, initiating its decline: This theory finds little support, however.

The Arabian Sea Coast

It is thought that the Harappan settlements in the inhospitable Makran coastal region, such as Sutkagen-dor and Balakot, were located to engage in sea trade and the exploitation of coastal resources. Now well inland, these were closer to the coast in Harappan times when, according to the results of geological studies, the Makran coastline ran north of its present-day location. Intriguing evidence from Amri on the Indus, now well inland, suggests the possibility that an arm of the sea stretched much farther inland in the early third millennium: Molluscs in Early Harappan levels are almost all marine species, but by the Harappan period riverine species were increasing and were as common as marine species by the Late Harappan period. This may relate to other evidence that suggests that the sea level around 3000 BCE was between 2 and 5 meters higher in this region than today's level and that it fell dramatically after around 2200–2000 BCE. The region has also been subject to considerable tectonic uplift in the postglacial period.

From the Karachi region, the coastline in the early postglacial period seems to have run roughly east to around the mouth of the Luni River in Gujarat. The mouth of the Indus lay well to the east of its present location. Throughout most of the Holocene period the Indus River has been building a massive delta, its annual deposition of silts at its mouth pushing the coastline progressively west and southwest. In modern times, however, a major dam and a number of major canals have been built for irrigation, removing significant volumes of water upstream and reducing the quantity of silt deposited at the river mouth, with the result that today the delta is being eroded away slightly faster than it is being replaced by annual alluviation.

The Harappan Indus delta was therefore emptying into what is now the swampy Ranns of Kutch. At that time, however, this was open water, separating mainland South Asia from a large island that is now Kutch. Tectonic activity may have raised the region since Harappan times, and the Indus and other rivers also deposited silt, filling in the area of the Ranns. To the south, the Saurashtra peninsula may also have been separated from the mainland by a tidal channel that ran through what is now the Nal Depression; this has been filled in through time by alluvium deposited by rivers of Rajasthan and Gujarat. On the other hand, pollen evidence shows that Nal Lake in its center was a freshwater lake in Harappan times.

Climate Changes

Pollen evidence from the saline Sambhar, Didwana, and Lunkaransar Lakes and from the freshwater Pushkar and Gajner Lakes in Rajasthan has been interpreted as showing that the temperatures and summer rainfall during the middle Holocene period were higher than those of today and that rainfall rose considerably around 3000 BCE, continued at the elevated level until the early second millennium, and then declined. Settlement around 3000 BCE in Kashmir, a region that for long periods of the past was too cold for human habitation, suggests the onset of a period of warmer, wetter conditions in the third millennium BCE. Opinions on these matters, however, are divided, and many scholars hold the view that temperature, rainfall, and monsoon patterns changed little during the Holocene period. Wetter conditions recorded in the lakes of Rajasthan, for example, could be the result of the rivers then flowing through the region rather than of an increase in rainfall. Nevertheless, a number of fluctuations in temperature and rainfall, as evidenced at certain times in various parts of the world, are thought to reflect global climate changes, due to factors such as changes in the tilt of the earth in its solar orbit and occasional major catastrophes such as massive volcanic eruptions. Evidence from many areas indicates that warmer and wetter conditions than those of today pertained globally in the mid-Holocene period. Thereafter, the picture is more complicated, with increased rainfall in some areas coinciding with decreases in others. However, warmer, drier conditions seem to have been widespread during the second millennium.

ENVIRONMENTAL DEGRADATION

The present-day vegetation in South Asia is the product of millennia of human activity and exploitation. Trees have been felled for timber, for use in constructing buildings and ships, for making furniture, tools, and other artifacts, or for fuel for domestic and industrial purposes. Forests have been cleared to open up land for settlement and cultivation. Modern tree cover is therefore far less dense and far less widespread than in ancient times, and the moist deciduous forests of trees growing up to 120 feet tall that once covered most of the greater Indus region have widely been replaced by dry deciduous forest, with shorter trees, and by scrubby thorn forest, associated with poorer soil fertility, lower water retention, reduced plant cover and diversity, and greatly reduced fauna. Forest regeneration has been inhibited by grazing herds of domestic animals, which have also had a marked effect on other vegetation. Firing the enormous quantity of baked bricks used in constructing Indus cities could have decreased the extent of vegetation cover, although studies have shown that even the present-day scrubby vegetation of the region could have provided a sustainable source of fuel adequate for the purpose. Manufacturing charcoal for the fuel used in smelting copper may have had a more significant impact: During the Harappan period at Lothal, charcoal was made from a variety of trees from the local deciduous forests, but by the latest Harappan levels it was being made only from scrubby acacia, and animal dung was also in use as fuel, suggesting that tree felling had significantly affected the local forest cover by this time.

Deforestation and overgrazing over the millennia have caused considerable erosion, increasing runoff and hence increasing the volume and speed of water in the Indus, in turn increasing the risk of excessive and devastating floods. These activities have also brought about environmental degradation and a reduction in moisture retention by soils and plants, as well as the reduction or local extinction of much of the native fauna. This process may have begun by the Indus period: Evidence of environmental strain by the second millennium BCE has been found in some areas such as the Kachi plain. Nevertheless the severe degradation of much of the flora and fauna of the subcontinent is by and large a more recent development.

In ancient Mesopotamia and in parts of South Asia in historical and recent times, regular irrigation over a prolonged period caused salinization, eventually turning land into a salt waste where cultivation became increasingly

A view of Mohenjo-daro through the morning mist. The modern environment of the Indus Valley bears little resemblance to that in Harappan times. Agriculture, animal grazing, and forest clearance have taken their toll on the once-lush natural vegetation and abundant, diverse fauna. The river has repeatedly changed its course and canals and dams have been added. (J. M. Kenoyer, Courtesy Department of Archaeology and Museums, Government of Pakistan)

difficult and eventually impossible. Although this cycle would also have taken place in the ancient Indus Valley if artificial irrigation had been employed, there is no evidence from the Indus period either of large-scale irrigation or of salinization there: The annual river floods and limited rainfall seem to have been adequate to support agriculture in the plains.

REFERENCES

Agrawal, D. P., and J. S. Kharakwal. 2003. *Archaeology of South Asia. II. Bronze and Iron Ages in South Asia.* New Delhi: Books International.

Allchin, Bridget. 1984. "The Harappan Environment." In *Frontiers of the Indus Civilization,* edited by B. B. Lal and S. P. Gupta, 445–454. New Delhi: Books and Books.

Allchin, Bridget, and Raymond Allchin. 1968. *The Birth of Indian Civilization. India and Pakistan Before 500 B.C.* Harmondsworth, UK: Penguin.

Allchin, Bridget, and Raymond Allchin. 1982. *The Rise of Civilization in India and Pakistan.* Cambridge, UK: Cambridge University Press.

Allchin, Bridget, and Raymond Allchin. 1997. *Origins of a Civilization.* New Delhi: Viking Penguin India.

Allchin, Bridget, Andrew Goudie, and Karunarkara Hegde. 1987. *The Prehistory and Palaeogeography of the Great Indian Desert.* New York: Academic Press.

Bhan, Kuldeep K. 1989. "Late Harappan Settlements of Western India, with Special Reference to Gujarat." In *Old Problems and New Perspectives in the Archaeology of South Asia,* edited by Jonathan Mark Kenoyer, 219–242. *Wisconsin Archaeological Reports.* Vol. 2. Department of Anthropology. Madison: University of Wisconsin Press.

Chakrabarti, Dilip K. 1997. *The Archaeology of Ancient Indian Cities.* New Delhi: Oxford University Press.

Chakrabarti, Dilip K. 1999. *India: An Archaeological History. Palaeolithic Beginnings to Early Historic Foundations.* New Delhi: Oxford University Press.

Chitalwala, Y. M. 1982. "Harappan Settlements in the Kutch-Saurashtra Region: Patterns of Distribution and Routes of Communication." In *Harappan Civilization. A Contemporary Perspective,* edited by Gregory L. Possehl, 197–202. New Delhi: Oxford & IBH Publishing Co.

Fagan, Brian. 2004. *The Long Summer. How Climate Changed Civilization.* London: Granta Books.

Farmer, B. H. 1993. *An Introduction to South Asia.* 2nd ed. London and New York: Routledge.

Johnson, Gordon. 1995. *Cultural Atlas of India.* Oxford: Andromeda.

Kenoyer, Jonathan Mark. 1998. *Ancient Cities of the Indus Valley Civilization.* Karachi: Oxford University Press and American Institute of Pakistan Studies.

Lawler, Andrew. 2007. "Climate Spurred Later Indus Decline." *Science* 316: 979.

Misra, V. N. 1984. "Climate, a Factor in the Rise and Fall of the Indus Civilization—Evidence from Rajasthan and Beyond." In *Frontiers of the Indus Civilization,* edited by B. B. Lal and S. P. Gupta, 461–489. New Delhi: Books and Books.

Misra, V. N. 1994. "Indus Civilization and Rgvedic Sarasvati." In *South Asian Archaeology 1993,* edited by Asko Parpola and Petteri Koskikallio, 511–526. Helsinki: Suomalainen Tiedeakatemia.

Misra, V. N. 1995. "Climate Change and the Indus Civilization." In *The "Lost" Saraswati and the Indus Civilization,* edited by S. P. Gupta, 125–163. Jodhpur, India: Kusumanjali Prakashan.

Mughal, M. Rafique. 1982. "Recent Archaeological Research in the Cholistan Desert." In *Harappan Civilization. A Contemporary Perspective,* edited by Gregory L. Possehl, 85–95. New Delhi: Oxford & IBH Publishing Co.

Mughal, M. Rafique. 1984. "The Post-Harappan Phase in Bahawalpur District, Pakistan." In *Frontiers of the Indus Civilization,* edited by B. B. Lal and S. P. Gupta, 499–503. New Delhi, India: Books and Books.

Mughal, M. Rafique. 1999. *Indus Age: The Beginnings.* New Delhi: Oxford University Press.

Mughal, M. Rafique. 2002. *The Indus Civilization. A Contemporary Perspective.* Walnut Creek, CA: AltaMira Press.

Philip, George, Ltd. 1991. *Philip's Atlas of the World.* London: George Philip Ltd.

Possehl, Gregory L. 1992. "The Harappan Cultural Mosaic: Ecology Revisited." In *South Asian Archaeology 1989,* edited by Catherine Jarrige, 237–241. Madison, WI: Prehistory Press.

Raikes, R. L. 1984. "Mohenjo Daro Environment." In *Frontiers of the Indus Civilization,* edited by B. B. Lal and S. P. Gupta, 455–460. New Delhi: Books and Books.

Ratnagar, Shereen. 2000. *The End of the Great Harappan Tradition. Heras Memorial Lectures 1998.* New Delhi: Manohar.

Ratnagar, Shereen. 2004. *Trading Encounters. From the Euphrates to the Indus in the Bronze Age.* New Delhi: Oxford University Press.

Schwartzberg, Joseph E., ed. 1992. *A Historical Atlas of South Asia.* 2nd impression, with additional material. New York and Oxford: Oxford University Press.

Singh, Gurdip. 1971. "The Indus Valley Culture (Seen in the Context of Post-Glacial Climate and Ecological Studies in North-west India)." *Archaeology and Physical Anthropology in Oceania* 6 (2): 177–189.

Spate, O. H. K., and A. T. A. Learmonth. 1967. *India and Pakistan: A General and Regional Geography,* 3rd ed. London: Methuen & Co.

Thapar, B. K. 1982. "The Harappan Civilization: Some Reflections on Its Environments and Resources and Their Exploration." In *Harappan Civilization. A Contemporary Perspective,* edited by Gregory L. Possehl, 3–13. New Delhi: Oxford & IBH Publishing Co.

Wilkinson, T. J. 2002. "Indian Ocean: Cradle of Globalization. Scholar Voices." [Online article; retrieved 10/2/02.] www.accd.edu/sac/history/keller/IndianO/Wilkin.html.

Yash Pal, B. Sahai, R. K. Snood, and D. P. Agrawal. 1984. "Remote Sensing of the 'Lost' Saraswati River." In *Frontiers of the Indus Civilization,* edited by B. B. Lal and S. P. Gupta, 491–497. New Delhi: Books and Books.

Historical and Chronological Setting

HISTORY OF THE INVESTIGATION OF SOUTH ASIA'S PAST

Antiquarians

Early European visitors to India in the sixteenth and seventeenth centuries often took an interest in its monuments, sometimes making careful records of their observations. The spirit of inquiry that characterized eighteenth-century polymaths, from London to Calcutta, led them in many directions, including science, natural history, philosophy, languages, and the human condition. Great interest was taken in the intellectual, cultural, scientific, and religious heritage of India, a land considered by some scholars to be the original source of Western knowledge and thought. It was within this intellectual climate that Sir William Jones founded the Asiatic Society of Bengal in 1784.

Studies of classical literature, including that relating to Alexander's expedition in northern India and to the subsequent diplomatic mission by the Greek envoy Megasthenes to the court of Emperor Chandragupta Maurya, provided some information on early Indian history, and light was shed on later periods by the writings of Chinese pilgrims who visited Buddhist sites in India. In addition, there was a great deal of Indian literature, from the sacred texts of the *Vedas* through the mythological accounts of former times, such as the *Ramayana*, to the many sources of the historical period, such as the *Arthashastra*, the Machiavellian advice of Chandragupta's minister Kautilya, in addition to Buddhist, Jain, and Hindu sacred literature. All this literature provided source material for scholars interested in understanding Indian history and culture and in assessing India's contribution to world civilization.

Jones himself made the significant observation that Sanskrit, the language of India's early sacred texts, bore strong similarities both to the language of the *Avesta*, Iran's early sacred texts, and to those of Europe, including not only Greek and Latin, but also the Celtic and Germanic languages, and he suggested that they all sprang from a common source. This discovery of the Indo-European language family was to have profound intellectual consequences: The speakers of Indo-European languages came to be regarded as a single race, the Aryans, seen by many as culturally superior and, pervertedly, by the Nazis as a master race; and the wide distribution of the Indo-European languages brought to the fore theories of migration as the principal explanation for cultural change and development.

The members of the Asiatic Society, along with other inquiring minds among the European officials and soldiers in India, took a magpie interest in Indian antiquities, reporting accidental discoveries of ancient remains during agricultural or building work and occasionally doing a little digging themselves; describing monuments, such as rock-cut temples and the south Indian megaliths; noting local people's beliefs about them; and attempting to identify historical sites, such as Chandragupta's capital at Pataliputra. Regional surveys investigated everything relating to local life, from agriculture, topography, and natural history to religion and customs, not neglecting antiquities. The inhabitants of south India were found to be speakers of non-Indo-European languages, dubbed Dravidian by Robert Caldwell. By the 1830s the copying and study of inscriptions and the study of coins were also well in train, due in great part to the endeavors of James Prinsep, assay master of the Calcutta Mint. By the 1840s both Brahmi and Kharoshthi, the scripts of later first-millennium India, had been deciphered, opening up considerable resources of historical data.

There was also a growing feeling among the British that they had a duty to preserve and record the antiquities of the areas they governed. In 1848 a number of individuals were given a mandate to explore different parts of India and to record and report on the monuments there: These designees included Alexander Cunningham, who in 1861 was made archaeological surveyor and in 1871 was appointed director-general of the newly established Archaeological Survey of India, a post he held until 1885. Though wide-ranging, his investigations were focused on Buddhist monuments and on Early Historic cities known from the accounts of the early Chinese pilgrims, as well as Indian and classical sources; they involved surveys, descriptions, and excavations. He also collected and studied antiquities, particularly coins, and took note of local traditions and ethnography. In the 1850s, he visited the ruins of the Indus city of Harappa. Although he recognized that the mounds were made by people, being the ruins of a vast accumulation of brick structures, he was far from suspecting their great antiquity, instead accepting the view expressed by other visitors that the site was a fortress less than fifteen hundred years old. However, he noticed and published a number of curious remains from the site, including an inscribed Indus seal that he believed was an import, because he knew of nothing comparable from India. Sadly by the 1870s Harappa had suffered massive destruction at the hands of railway contractors who had plundered it for bricks.

Cunningham's assistants and successors also concentrated on historical monuments, though there were also some investigations of megalithic tombs, structures that intrigued scholars because they bore strong similarities to the imposing megalithic monuments of Western Europe. In 1863 Robert Bruce Foote had discovered Palaeolithic tools in southern India. Finds of Neolithic and earlier tools were also made elsewhere. Foote compared Indian artifacts to those of Europe, recognizing Palaeolithic, Neolithic, and Iron Age remains; he also deduced that the south Indian ash mounds had been associated with Neolithic cattle keeping. Other scholars, notably A. C. L. Carlleyle and Vincent Smith, interpolated a period of microlith users and a Copper Age into the chronological scheme. Prehistoric paintings were discovered in the Vindhya Hills and elsewhere and were attributed to people who used stone tools, though their date was not established. Occasional finds were made of Harappan material (for example by W. T. Blanford in 1875 in the Rohri Hills and in 1877 at Sutkagen-dor) and were noted as being of skilled workmanship. Nevertheless, the notion of India as the source of civilization had been so completely abandoned that urban society was thought to have emerged here only in the mid first millennium BCE, a time by which Mesopotamia's civilizations had fallen to the might of Persia, when the heroic but barbarous petty kingdoms whose conflicts have been immortalized in the great Indian epic, the *Mahabharata,* gave rise to towns in the Ganges Valley, some of which were visited by the Buddha.

The Marshall Era

In 1890 the post of director-general was abolished and the responsibility for archaeological work was transferred to regional government. When in 1899 Lord Curzon was appointed viceroy of India, he took critical stock of the resultant patchy and generally unsatisfactory level of archaeological activity, recommending the revival of the post of director-general to oversee and coordinate the work, and in 1902 John (later Sir John) Marshall took up the post. Among his innovations were a conservation policy, the publication of annual reports, and the training of Indians as senior officers of the Archaeological Survey, posts few Indians had previously occupied. He also insisted on the employment of such scientific excavation techniques as he had learned in his brief earlier career as a classical archaeologist: While in many ways an advance on previous work, these techniques left much to be desired. In particular, although the three-dimensional position of objects was noted, all recording was by arbitrary levels taken from the local ground surface. Although the greater part of Marshall's work still focused on historical sites, in the south megalithic tombs continued to attract attention and several ash mounds were also excavated, and in the northwest, including Kashmir, prehistoric material was also being discovered.

Marshall was familiar with the material, including the curious seal, that Cunningham had recovered at Harappa, and he instituted work there in 1920 under the direction of D. R. Sahni. The understanding of the nature of the remains found there was seriously compromised by the havoc wrought by the railway engineers who had earlier plundered the site for bricks. Mohenjo-daro was known as the site of a poorly preserved Buddhist stupa, situated on the mound's summit, but during explorations here R. D. Banerji had picked up a flint scraper, suggesting the mound had far greater antiquity; he therefore began excavations here in 1922. Mohenjo-daro also yielded seals inscribed with unknown characters, comparable to those from Harappa, and, like Harappa, the site was found to have a great depth of deposits belonging to a huge ancient brick-built city. Marshall was on leave at this time, and so it was not until the summer of 1924 that he studied the seals and other novel material and the architectural remains from these two sites. Based on the stratigraphy of the sites, with Indus deposits well below those of the historical period, on the use

UNKNOWN INDIAN PICTURE-WRITING: A NEW PROBLEM IN PALÆOGRAPHY.

PHOTOGRAPHS BY THE ARCHÆOLOGICAL SURVEY OF INDIA, WESTERN CIRCLE. BY COURTESY OF SIR JOHN MARSHALL, DIRECTOR-GENERAL OF ARCHÆOLOGY IN INDIA.

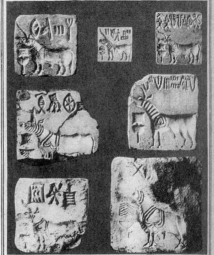

ENGRAVED WITH A PICTOGRAPHIC SCRIPT UNLIKE ANY PREVIOUSLY KNOWN INDIAN ALPHABET, BUT SOMEWHAT RESEMBLING MYCENÆAN PICTOGRAPHS: PREHISTORIC SEALS FROM MOHENJO-DARO AND HARAPPA.

BEARING FIGURES OF BULLS AND MYSTERIOUS PICTOGRAPHIC SYMBOLS, SOME RESEMBLING ROMAN NUMERALS: PREHISTORIC INDIAN SEALS FROM HARAPPA AND MOHENJO-DARO WITH AN UNKNOWN FORM OF PICTURE-WRITING.

MADE PERHAPS TO AMUSE LITTLE PREHISTORIC PEOPLE IN THE INDUS VALLEY TWO OR THREE THOUSAND YEARS AGO: TERRA-COTTA ANIMALS, BIRDS, AND OTHER TOYS FROM MOHENJO-DARO.

USED WITH A PREHISTORIC MORTAR: A PESTLE OF BLACK HÆMATITE.

A page from the *Illustrated London News* showing a selection of artifacts recovered in the first season's excavations at Mohenjo-daro. These include seals (top), figurines (center), a pestle (center right), a pot (bottom left), and shell inlay pieces. The *ILN* was instrumental in making the public rapidly aware of the exciting discoveries in the Indus. (*Illustrated London News*)

of copper but not iron, and on the mysterious writing on the seals that was clearly unrelated to the Brahmi script of the later centuries BCE, he concluded that the Indus cities predated the Mauryan period. Eager to obtain better information on their possible age from the wider archaeological community, he published these finds in the September 20 edition of *Illustrated London News* and was gratified by an immediate response from Mesopotamian scholars who found parallels between the material and architecture from Mohenjo-daro and Harappa and that from third-millennium BCE Susa and Sumerian cities. Though considerably refined since Marshall's day, the synchronism and cultural links between these civilizations have stood the test of time.

Excavations continued at the two cities, including a major season at Mohenjo-daro in 1925–1926 directed by Marshall himself. The difficult working conditions took their toll on the health of several of the excavators, who over the following years included K. N. Dikshit, M. S. Vats, D. R. Sahni, and Ernest Mackay, the latter a veteran of Near Eastern excavation. These investigations brought to light large residential areas with well-built houses, straight streets, and fine drains, the brick-built pool known as the Great Bath on the higher mound at Mohenjo-daro, and at Harappa a large building labeled the Granary, an unjustified appellation that has stuck. Finds included bead jewelry, copper tools, several of the best-known seals, the sculpted torso known as the Priest-King, and the bronze figurine known as the Dancing-girl. Soundings at Mohenjo-daro were cut down to the water table, the height of which prevented the lowest levels of the site being investigated. Mackay also excavated part of a smaller Indus settlement, the town of Chanhu-daro, where he uncovered considerable evidence of craft activities such as bead and seal manufacture, including a workshop with a furnace: This work was funded by the Boston Museum of Fine Arts, which was permitted to retain the material found there. At Harappa, a cemetery (Cemetery H) was found, containing burials with pottery different from that in the city. Vats undertook an interesting analysis of the iconography of the Cemetery H pottery in the light of Vedic ritual practices. No cemetery was located at Mohenjo-daro (nor has any subsequently been discovered), but Mackay uncovered a number of skeletons in the streets of Mohenjo-daro, belonging to a late period of occupation.

Marshall saw this civilization as the Indus valley's distinctive indigenous development, comparable with but not related to the contemporary Sumerian civilization in the Tigris-Euphrates Valley, though there were strong links between them. The relationship of the Indus civilization to the Vedic Aryans, the people who had composed India's earliest surviving literature, was already being considered and in several publications R. P. Chanda, one of Marshall's officers, set forth arguments that the Indus civilization had possessed a non-Vedic culture, that its cities had been destroyed by the Vedic Aryans, but that Indus religion survived this destruction and underlay much of later Indian beliefs and practices. Marshall in his 1931 publication on the Indus civilization endorsed these views. Gordon Childe a few years later noted that the distinctive features of the Indus civilization included the elaborate drains and planned urban layout, the scarcity of any architecture that could be identified as a palace or temple, the absence of monumental tombs, and the apparent lack of warfare.

Mohenjo-daro and Harappa lie nearly 400 miles apart, as Marshall observed, drawing attention also to the striking uniformity of architecture and artifacts from the two cities. By the mid-1930s, excavations and survey work

Sir John Marshall. It was during his term of office as director-general of the Archaeological Survey of India that the Indus civilization was discovered and the cities of Mohenjo-daro and Harappa excavated. (*Illustrated London News*)

had revealed Indus sites as far afield as Kotla Nihang Khan in east Punjab and Rangpur in Saurashtra, where Vats believed the Indus occupation to have been later than that at Mohenjo-daro or Harappa. Aurel Stein explored the dried-up riverbeds of Bahawalpur, revealing a number of Indus sites. It was becoming clear that the Indus civilization was considerably larger in extent than the other states of this time: Old Kingdom Egypt and the Akkadian and Ur III empires in Mesopotamia.

Other investigations began to reveal the antecedents of the Indus civilization. Aurel Stein located many earlier sites in Baluchistan, such as Periano Ghundai, briefly excavating a number of them as well as the settlement of Dabarkot, which yielded some Indus period remains, and a number of sites, including Kulli, where he identified the Kulli complex, related to the Indus civilization. Harold Hargreaves dug at Nal, an early settlement in southern Baluchistan, while at Amri in Sindh, N. G. Majumdar excavated the first town in the Indus plains known to have belonged to the pre-Indus period. He also identified a degenerate phase of the civilization at a number of sites, including Jhukar, after which the period in Sindh is now known.

The short inscriptions on the Indus seals and on a few copper bars from Mohenjo-daro that Banerji at first compared to Indian punch-marked coins attracted considerable interest, and an attempt at decipherment of the script was made as early as 1925, by Colonel L. A. Waddell. In the years that followed, further efforts were made, based on comparisons between Indus signs and those of the Sumerian, Minoan, Etruscan, Hittite, and Brahmi scripts, and even Easter Island *rongo-rongo*. None produced a successful result. A question of key importance in decipherment of the script was what language it rendered: Marshall was of the opinion that the languages spoken in the Indus civilization were likely to have been members of the Dravidian family.

Wheeler

In 1944 Sir Mortimer Wheeler was seconded to India as director-general of the Archaeological Survey. One of his main objectives was training the rising generation of Indian archaeologists in the field methods that he had perfected in Britain and France. These involved excavation by natural cultural layers, rather than by the artificial levels favored by Marshall and his contemporaries, and the careful recording of stratigraphy. He therefore ran a number of training excavations at key sites that could be expected to further the understanding of India's past, including the great Indus city of Harappa.

On his first visit, Wheeler was struck by the AB mound at Harappa, which he immediately interpreted as a fortified citadel, evidence that the Indus civilization was not unwarlike, as had previously been supposed. His impression was confirmed by excavation at several points around its perimeter, which revealed the remains of a massive mud brick wall with towers and impressive gateways.

These excavations included a deep trench cut down to natural soil, providing a stratigraphic record of the history of the city's occupation that was of key importance. The first occupation here included sherds resembling the pottery found in northern Baluchistan at sites such as Rana Ghundai, recently excavated by E. J. Ross. Pottery from different regions in Baluchistan had recently been studied by Stuart Piggott, who had identified several regional styles and who had compared these wares with pottery from the Indus civilization on the one hand and with that from Iran and West Asia on the other.

Above this early occupation at Harappa was constructed a massive brick rampart as protection against floods, together with a wall that went through a number of phases of modification and rebuilding, during which in Wheeler's view it acquired a more defensive character. Wheeler also excavated a cemetery at Harappa, R–37, associated with the main occupation of the city, and he demonstrated that a time interval, represented by a considerable buildup of deposits, separated this cemetery from the burials in Cemetery H. Some of the latter were cut through derelict architecture; structurally poor buildings containing Cemetery H material also abutted the west side of the citadel mound. Wheeler saw the Cemetery H culture as intrusive and enthusiastically adopted a suggestion made by Childe that its makers may have been the Aryan invaders of India, thought by then to have arrived around 1500 BCE. With characteristic vigor, he developed a theory (already suggested by V. S. Agrawala of the Archaeological Survey) that the Indo-Aryans were largely responsible for the demise of the Indus cities, quoting Vedic descriptions of the sack of Dasa fortresses and arguing that "[it] may be no mere chance that at a late period of Mohenjo-daro men, women and children appear to have been massacred there . . . On circumstantial evidence, Indra [the Aryan god of war] stands accused" (Wheeler 1947).

An early visit to Mohenjo-daro had allowed Wheeler to identify a fortified citadel there also. After the partition of India and Pakistan in 1947, Wheeler was for some years an archaeological adviser to the government of Pakistan and in 1950 conducted excavations at Mohenjo-daro, which yielded enough evidence of solid brickwork, including towers, to convince him that his identification was correct. He also fully uncovered the foundations of a large structure on the mound, previously identified as a *hammam* (steam bath), interpreting it as a Great Granary. These discoveries and interpretations allowed Wheeler and Piggott to formulate a picture of the Indus civilization that has dominated popular understanding of the civilization to this day. Mohenjo-daro and Harappa were seen as the twin capitals of a great state, ruled probably by priest-kings. Cities were thought to follow a standard plan, with a fortified citadel containing public buildings and a residential lower town, its streets constructed to a cardinally orientated grid plan resembling that of much later Hellenistic cities and towns. Great granaries were presumed to store grain that was raised in tribute or as taxes to be distributed to state employees, as in contemporary Mesopotamia. A highly efficient and well maintained system of drains and sanitation was a standard feature of Indus cities. Standardization was also apparent in the Indus artifacts, such as the bead necklaces, stone and metal tools, and finely made pottery. Piggott thought these artifacts showed "competent dullness . . . a dead level of bourgeois mediocrity in almost every branch of the visual arts and crafts" (Piggott 1950, 200), though Wheeler commented favorably on the technical skills and aesthetic qualities apparent in some objects, such as the steatite seals with their lively depictions of animals. The overall picture was of a civilization in which considerable technical competence and a high standard of living were offset by cultural stagnation and the stifling effects of rigid bureaucracy and an authoritarian regime, continuing apparently unchanged for nearly a millennium.

Wheeler expected to find and looked for features that were familiar from other civilizations and that were thought to be among their defining characteristics: monumental public architecture such as temples; defensive works and weaponry; royal burials and palaces. The structures on the citadel mounds, such as the Granary and Great Bath at Mohenjo-daro, could reasonably be

Sir Mortimer Wheeler, a charismatic figure, excavated at Harappa and Mohenjo-daro in the mid-twentieth century. His forcefully and convincingly expressed views on the Indus civilization cast a long shadow: only slowly are contrary interpretations, based on more recent work, beginning to penetrate public consciousness. (Getty Images)

interpreted as public and religious buildings. The massive brick-walled citadels and their impressive gateways matched the expected defenses and fortifications. Metal objects, such as spearheads, daggers, arrowheads, and axes, were potentially weapons, though Wheeler noted that "a majority may have been used equally by the soldier, the huntsman, the craftsman, or even by the ordinary householder" (Wheeler 1968, 73). Other features that were characteristic of the early civilizations of Egypt and Mesopotamia were absent, however: No palaces or royal graves had been discovered, for example, and no obvious temples. Despite these differences, Wheeler argued that the Indus people had adopted the idea of civilization from the Sumerians, along with key features such as writing.

After Partition

Exploration. The postwar years saw a great increase in knowledge of the Indus civilization. The partition of India in 1947 assigned the known Indus sites, including both Mohenjo-daro and Harappa, to newly formed Pakistan, giving a spur to Indian investigations in the areas remaining on Indian soil. This resulted in the discovery of many sites in Gujarat and the northern Ganges-Yamuna region, some of which were excavated. Of particular importance was the "port" town of Lothal in Gujarat, excavated by S. R. Rao, which had a concentration of craft workshops, producing many typical Indus objects such as beads and metalwork, and substantial storehouses. An enigmatic large brick basin on the east side of the town was initially interpreted as a dock and is still not understood. Excavations outside the town also uncovered a number of burials; since only the R–37 cemetery at Harappa was previously known, these provided welcome new information on Indus burial practices. A third cemetery was uncovered at Kalibangan, another town discovered during the explorations in India and excavated during the 1960s. Here B. B. Lal and B. K. Thapar, both of whom had worked with Wheeler, revealed not only an Indus provincial town with characteristic citadel and planned lower town, but also the unplanned Early Indus settlement that it had replaced. The earlier town was surrounded by a substantial mud brick rampart. An unusual discovery associated with the town was a field plowed in two directions, strikingly similar to modern practice. On the other side of the new border, Kot Diji, excavated by F. A. Khan, Pakistan's director of archaeology, and Amri, where new excavations were undertaken by the French archaeologist, Jean-Marie Casal, also yielded Early Indus material and shed light on the transition from regional urban communities to the full-fledged Indus civilization. A deep sounding by George Dales showed that there were similarly ancient deposits at Mohenjo-daro, but the high water table prevented their excavation. Continuing investigations in adjacent Baluchistan revealed additional sites that were clearly earlier than the Mature Indus civilization, as well as others that seemed contemporary with it. More light was shed on Indus towns by Walter Fairservis's excavations at Allahdino, a very small settlement but one with many of the features of an urban center. Fairservis was also one of the foremost scholars attempting to understand how the Indus civilization developed and functioned.

Dating and Development. The chronology of the Indus civilization had been established to some extent using material paralleled in historically dated Mesopotamia. This chronology showed that the Mature Indus period had begun by around 2500 BCE and had continued into the early second millennium, perhaps as late as 1500 BCE, but no dates could be put on the earlier settlements of the Indus region and Baluchistan or on the cultures that succeeded the Mature Indus period, known from Jhukar in Sind and Cemetery H at Harappa. In 1949, however, the situation changed dramatically when the physicist Willard Libby invented radiocarbon dating, winning a Nobel Prize and starting a revolution in archaeological knowledge and understanding. This technique allows surviving organic materials, such as bone, wood, and shell, to be dated directly, rather than relying on stratigraphy, on comparison or association with dated artifacts, or on other indirect or contextual methods. The advent of radiocarbon dating made it possible to date cultures individually instead of tying their chronology to those of the few that had historical dates. This enabled archaeologists to build a clear picture of how cultures related to each other in time and, by freeing them from the overriding concern with chronology, encouraged them to look at wider issues. By the late 1950s, India had established a radiocarbon laboratory under D. P. Agrawal, first at the Tata Institute of Fundamental Research in Bombay (Mumbai), moving later to the Physical Research Laboratory in Ahmedabad.

It now became apparent that farming settlements had existed by the fifth millennium BCE in the Indo-Iranian borderlands. In the 1970s, excavations began on a large settlement area at Mehrgarh on the Bolan River from which fourth-millennium material had been collected. The river had cut down through deposits accumulated over thousands of years, and in the section thus exposed an area with earlier levels of settlement was observed. These proved to date back to the seventh or eighth millennium BCE, showing that farming had developed in this area at around the same time as in much of West Asia. Still the only farming settlement of such antiquity known in South Asia, Mehrgarh has been a major focus of research and may help answer the vexed question whether agriculture originated in the Near East and spread from there into neighboring regions or developed independently in multiple centers.

Pastoralists from Baluchistan were active in the Indus Basin during the fourth-millennium, but it was only toward the end of the millenium that farmers began to settle there. Several regional groups were identified: Amri-Nal in Sindh, southern Baluchistan, and parts of Gujarat; Damb Sadaat in central Baluchistan; Kot Diji in the large central and northern region, including Cholistan; and Sothi-Siswal in the east, including the site of Kalibangan. (Rather confusingly, these contemporary regional groups are often referred to as phases, a term more generally used to denote consecutive subperiods.) The emergence of the Mature Harappan civilization, initially thought to have been a sudden dramatic event, has more recently been established to have taken place over a period of around a century, between 2600 and 2500 BCE. The driving force behind this transformation is still the subject of considerable speculation.

Sometime in the earlier second millennium, the area again became the home of various regional groups lacking many features that had characterized the Indus civilization, such as cities, writing, sanitation, and long-distance trade. The groups were distinguished from each other by their artifact styles, particularly their pottery, which often resembled that current in the same region in Early Indus times. Refining the date of this change has proved challenging, though it is of great importance in understanding what actually occurred. It now seems that it was a gradual process rather than a sudden collapse, taking place over the period 2000 to 1900 or 1800 BCE, and that the depopulation in the heartland was not matched in the outer regions, Gujarat and the east, which actually saw an increase in settlement numbers.

Recent Work

In the half century that has elapsed since Wheeler's vigorous writings crystallized the public's perception of the Indus civilization, a great deal of new data have accumulated that have shed much clearer light on the antecedents, internal workings, external relations, and decline of the Indus civilization. In addition, seismic shifts have taken place in archaeological paradigms, both with respect to the Indus civilization and in archaeology in general.

Focus on the Cities. The excavations at Harappa and Mohenjo-daro under Marshall's aegis in the 1920s and 1930s were vast undertakings, executed at a time when the techniques of field archaeology were in their infancy. It is therefore unsurprising that these excavations are considered inadequate by recent standards and that they fail to answer many of the questions now seen as important. Although other cities and towns have been excavated in the years since the civilization was discovered, Mohenjo-daro and Harappa still seem to have been outstandingly important, holding the key to understanding many aspects of life in the Indus Valley five thousand years ago. From the 1980s, therefore, work was undertaken at Mohenjo-daro and Harappa by German, Italian, and American teams in collaboration with Pakistani scholars, with the aim of reassessing the evidence from the early excavations, using up-to-date equipment and approaches, including experimental archaeology and ethno-archaeology. At Mohenjo-daro archaeologists from Aachen Technical University and from IsMEO in Rome have painstakingly studied the field notes and photographs from the original excavations and have created their own photographic and documentary record of the remaining architecture, working out the relationship of the artificial levels of the Marshall era to the city's actual layout and stratigraphy. At Harappa, HARP (the joint Pakistan–American Harappa Archaeological Research Project) has also undertaken some excavation: One result has been the discovery of an occupation prior to the Early Indus (Kot Diji) settlement, perhaps dating back as far as 3500 BCE. At both cities, much has been discovered about urban architecture, including details of the massive mud brick platforms that provided protection from the ever present dangers of flooding. Surveys have been conducted to determine the extent of the cities, revealing that the visible mounds were only a part of the urban area. The investigations have also given new insights into the organization and functioning of these cities and in particular of their industrial activities. Complementary data have come from studies in other regions, particularly Gujarat where major new evidence has also been provided by the excavations of Ravi Singh Bisht at Dholavira, a city that has both striking similarities to Mohenjo-daro and Harappa and significant differences.

Settlement. The number of known Indus sites has grown hugely: from thirty-seven in 1947 to more than a thousand today. The first excavations in the Indus Valley had revealed the cities of Mohenjo-daro and Harappa, and subsequently a number of towns were investigated. Recently, still more cities have been identified, such as Ganweriwala in the Cholistan Desert. Although excavations at Kalibangan had revealed the world's earliest plowed field, little was known of the country dwellers, the farmers and pastoralists who must have constituted the bulk of the population. In recent years much has been done to rectify this situation. Several villages and pastoralists' camps have been excavated; some small settlements of specialist artisans have also been investigated.

Regional surveys have built up a general picture of the distribution of Indus sites and their relationship to the landscape. For example, Harappa was found to be virtually the only Indus site in the western Punjab, suggesting that Harappa's situation could relate to its importance in trade, particularly in timber from the Himalayas, and pointing to the essential role of pastoral nomads, then as now, in providing links between settled communities. Studies by Greg Possehl of the pattern of settlement in the Saurashtra region revealed major changes in land use through time, with the Indus settlements concentrated along the rivers and a great increase in settlement in the post-Harappan period as farmers began to occupy the interfluve areas. Intensive surveys by Rafique Mughal in Cholistan, where Stein and others had previously located a number of sites, revealed a great concentration of settlements along the dried-up course of the Ghaggar-Hakra (the lost Saraswati) river, showing that this region, though now desert, was one of the most densely settled areas in Indus times, perhaps the agricultural heartland of the civilization.

Foreign Trade. Investigations outside the Greater Indus region have provided new insights into the overseas trade of the Indus people. A full-fledged Indus settlement was excavated at Shortugai in Afghanistan, 1,000 kilometers from the Indus, a trading outpost controlling the flow of material from the lapis mines of Badakhshan. The Indus people seem to have founded Shortugai to enable them to monopolize the supply to the outside world of lapis, a beautiful blue stone that was highly prized. Metal ores may also have been obtained from the region.

Excavations have been conducted at Shahr-i Sokhta, Tepe Yahya, and a number of other cities that flourished in the fourth and early third millennia across the Iranian plateau, revealing trading networks that brought lapis to the Near East before the Indus civilization established its monopoly; other goods also flowed along these routes, such as chlorite and metal ores. Much attention during the 1970s to 1990s focused on the civilization of the Helmand Valley and on the cultures of Central Asia. Knowledge of the urban cultures of the Iranian plateau is constantly expanding: Most recently a state has been discovered in the Kerman region with a major settlement at Jiroft, possibly the legendary state of Aratta known to the Sumerians.

Other states mentioned in the early Mesopotamian texts have also been identified and their cultures subjected to detailed investigation. The Indus civilization has been identified as the land of Meluhha, while Bahrain and Oman are believed to be the regions referred to as Dilmun and Magan, important places for trade and the supply of raw materials. Investigations in these areas have shed light on the contribution of the Gulf cultures to international trade and industry, as well as filling out the picture of these societies themselves. The Indus civilization has been shown to have been a major player in Gulf trade, its merchants establishing trading outposts in Mesopotamia itself. What still remains a mystery, however, is what the Indus people were importing from the Near East.

Even more distant connections have been revealed by recent work. By 2000 BCE a number of African crops were being cultivated in parts of the Greater Indus region. These may have reached the Harappans via Oman, which could have acquired them by coastwise trade through southern Arabia. Or there is the intriguing possibility that the experienced sailors of the Indus had themselves reached East Africa.

The Enigmatic Script. Since its discovery, the Indus script has baffled and intrigued scholars and lay people alike. New light has been thrown on the script's origins by discoveries of early inscribed items in the Ravi phase (3300/3500–2800 BCE) at Harappa. Many attempts have been made to decipher the script: Some are based on tenuous resemblances between some of its signs and those in other scripts or on guesses at the pictorial value of the signs; others are apparently drawn purely from imagination. Since the 1960s there have been a number of scholarly studies, notably by the teams led by the Russian scholar Yuri Knorozov and the Finnish archaeologist Asko Parpola and by the Indian scholar Iravatham Mahadevan, involving computer and other analyses of the structure of the script. Parpola and Mahadevan have also compiled concordances reproducing the seals and other inscribed materials from major collections in South Asia and elsewhere, essential raw material for studying the script. Significant progress has been made in determining the type of script, its direction of writing, and some other features—but decipherment seems as elusive as ever. Indeed, in a new study, Steve Farmer has even questioned whether the signs actually belong to a script.

Problems of the Decline. Many investigations have focused on the causes of the Indus urban collapse. A study of the supposed massacre victims at Mohenjo-daro has shown that they should be interpreted more prosaically as burials in deserted buildings, and the chronology of the decline effectively rules out the Vedic Aryans as destroyers of the cities. However, the Indo-Aryans' entry into the subcontinent remains a subject of often heated debate: They are widely believed to have moved into the northwest during the second millennium but are archaeologically elusive.

Explanations for the collapse of the cities have shifted to other possible causes, such as natural disasters. Robert Raikes suggested that a massive flood devastated Mohenjo-daro; however, the evidence is open to several interpretations and the theory has not stood the test of time. Satellite photography has been used to chart changes in the course of the rivers in the Indus Basin. Vedic and later texts indicate that the Saraswati dried up between the early second and early first millennia BCE: investigations into the chronology of this major environmental change have provided evidence to suggest that it played a major part in the civilization's collapse. Recently, however, the collapse itself has been subject to scrutiny: Increased information about late Mature Harappan and Posturban period sites has shown that, while there was a decline in occupation in the Indus heartland, settlement numbers increased in Gujarat and the Indo-Gangetic divide. Rather than a collapse, the early second millennium saw an abandonment of many urban features coupled with development in other areas.

Prospects. Partly due to the absence of readable texts, the Indus civilization, despite the progress achieved in the eighty-odd years since its discovery, remains enigmatic. Speculation surrounds the nature of its social and political organization, its religion, and religion's role in the operation of the state; and an important school of thought doubts that the Indus civilization was a single unified state because the architectural diversity of the excavated sites has undermined the early impression of cultural uniformity. Many questions are unanswered and many of these are likely to remain so. Numerous studies have focused on the reasons behind the civilization's demise whereas others have sought evidence of the prime movers that led to the rise of the state. However, investigations in some of the most fruitful areas for evidence of the crucial period of development, in the northwest, have been halted in recent years by the growth of Islamic extremism, by the rise and fall of the Taliban, and by the unsettled political conditions that have followed the invasion of Afghanistan in 2001–2002.

STUDYING THE INDUS CIVILIZATION

The Languages and Scripts

Much is known about the people of many early civilizations through their writings: These reveal not only the names and actions of kings and other leading figures but also much about the organization of society, laws, religious beliefs, education, economic organization, mythology, scientific understanding, and many other aspects of life. The Indus civilization, in contrast, has no deciphered writings, and the surviving texts are too short and cover too small a range of uses to provide any such information even if they were to be deciphered. Thus many aspects of the Indus civilization are unknown.

Among these is the very language of the Indus people. The majority of present-day inhabitants of the Indian subcontinent speak languages belonging to the Indo-European family. The most recent of these is English, spoken as a second language by most educated South Asians; the majority of them are Indo-Aryan languages that have been spoken by an increasing number of people since the second millennium BCE. But in the Indus period, Indo-European languages were probably not spoken by any group resident in South Asia, though this is strongly contested by a minority of scholars. Dravidian languages are spoken today by the inhabitants of southern India and by some groups elsewhere in the subcontinent, including Brahui in Baluchistan; these are the modern representatives of the language family to which, according to some scholars, the Indus language most probably belonged. However, languages of the Austro-Asiatic language family, today spoken by a few small tribal groups in India as well as over much of Southeast Asia, were probably also spoken in South Asia during the Indus period, and an early Austro-Asiatic language is an alternative candidate for the Indus language. There are other, less likely candidates among the minority languages of the subcontinent: Tibeto-Burman languages are spoken in the Himalayas and belong to the Sino-Tibetan family; Burushaski, a language isolate, is spoken in the western Karakoram; and there were probably other languages in the Indus period that have left no living descendants.

Archaeological and Historical Methods of Age Determination

Crucially, an understanding of the past depends on being able to date, and thus order and relate, the materials produced in the past and the developments that took place. Stratigraphy and typology are essential tools for establishing relative dates, but absolute dating depends on the use of a number of scientific dating techniques, applicable only to certain materials. When written sources exist, historical materials can at times offer a precise local chronology, though many factors may introduce distortion or chronological uncertainty. An extra dimension of difficulty is added when, as with the Indus civilization, historical dates are derived from external sources, in this case Mesopotamia.

Archaeological Dating. When a site is excavated, objects and structures are generally found in a stratigraphic sequence of deposits of soil and other materials that have resulted from past human activities and occupation and from natural processes. The stratigraphic succession gives a relative chronology of the styles of artifact and architecture; recognizing known types of objects and structures in excavated deposits enables researchers to assign relative dates to the deposits; thus typology and stratigraphy collaborate in providing a relative chronology that can be placed in real time by dating some of the artifacts or deposits by historical or scientific means. Pottery—fragile but durable, widely used, with enormous potential for variation in form, manufacture, and decoration—is particularly useful as a typological dating tool, and pottery styles provide much of the dating for prehistoric sites in the Indian subcontinent. Pottery is not so useful for dating subperiods within the duration of the Indus civilization due to the Indus standardization of pottery styles; also, the longevity of certain styles (such as Siswal ware, which was used from Early Indus to Posturban times) makes them difficult to use as chronological markers.

Carbon-14 (radiocarbon) dating was the first radiometric dating technique to be developed, and today many scientific dating techniques are available.

This section of a trench at Harappa represents five hundred years of human activity: the successive layers of occupation within it run from the time of first settlement at the site until the beginning of the Early Indus period around 2800 BCE. In the foreground is the edge of a storage pit dug by the earliest settlers. (Harappa Archaeological Research Project, Courtesy Department of Archaeology and Museums, Government of Pakistan)

Frequently these techniques are used to date the context in which archaeological material has been found rather than the material itself, making it vital to ensure that the material is securely linked to its context. Contamination of samples by younger or older material is also a potential problem. When a large number of dates can be obtained from a site, inconsistent dates can be weeded out, but when, as is common, only two or three dates are obtained (often due to financial constraints), it can be difficult to distinguish between dates that are wrong and those that are unexpected but accurate.

Due to statistical limitations on accurate measurement, most scientific dating techniques also have a degree of imprecision, which similarly can be reduced by dating a number of samples from the same context. Scientific dating techniques are nevertheless invaluable because they provide dates that are not reliant on potentially flawed historical or cultural assumptions.

Radiocarbon dating is the most commonly used technique because it can be applied to a range of organic material, including bone, which is often recovered from excavations. While alive, organisms take up the radioactive isotope carbon-14 (which makes up a tiny fraction of the carbon in the atmosphere), but uptake ceases after death, and the carbon then decays at a known rate: The amount remaining in the organism is therefore proportional to the time that has elapsed since its death. Because the proportion of radiocarbon in the atmosphere has fluctuated slightly in the past, dates in radiocarbon years (conventionally written ce and bce) have to be corrected to calendar dates (written CE and BCE) by reference to a calibration curve derived mainly from dendrochronology (tree ring dating).

Pottery, that almost ubiquitous material, cannot be dated by radiocarbon, but some success has been achieved in dating it by thermoluminescence (TL), although this technique is still relatively imprecise (around 10 percent of the sample's age). A number of other techniques dependent on the decay of radioactive material (radiometric techniques) are also available, but radiocarbon is the main one that has been used to date South Asian material.

Historical Dating. Although no historical materials survive from the Indus civilization itself, the Harappans were in trading communications with the literate civilizations of the Near East, Sumer and Akkad, from which there is a great deal of historical material. The first indication of the antiquity of the Indus civilization came from Mesopotamia where a few Harappan objects had been found associated with Akkadian and Ur III material. Indus artifacts, such as carnelian beads and seals, are now known from contexts ranging from the Royal Cemetery at Ur to the Kassite period (approximately mid third to later second millennia BCE). The sparse later material may have survived in Mesopotamia long after it was imported, and the majority of Indus objects come from contexts predating the Isin-Larsa period (early second millennium BCE). Although they contribute nothing to the internal chronology of the Indus civilization, historical dates from Mesopotamia are of great value in charting the development and changing patterns of trading relations through the Gulf, in which the Harappans played an important part.

The chronology of first-millennium Mesopotamia is well established; in earlier periods, however, there are major uncertainties. The internal chronologies of a number of long "floating" sequences of events are secure, but they are separated by periods of uncertain duration, one of which, unfortunately, falls between the Akkadian and Ur III empires in the middle of the period when the Indus and Mesopotamian civilizations were in trading contact. Several points in these chronologies are fixed by the observation of datable astronomical events such as the movements of the planet Venus. However, there are generally several possible occurrences of these events within the relevant time span, with the result that there are currently three different and plausible chronologies for Mesopotamia in the second and later third millennia BCE (known respectively as the High, Middle, and Low Chronologies). The Middle Chronology is most frequently adopted, for the convenience of having consistency among the writings of different scholars: Following this chronology, the dates for the period that runs from the beginning of the Akkadian Empire to the fall of the Ur III Empire, when trade flourished between southern Mesopotamia and the Indus, are 2334 to 2004 BCE; the High and Low Chronologies would shift the dates backward or forward by about half a century.

South Asia's earliest historical date is the Persian conquest of the northwest around 530 BCE, when the Early Historic cities were flourishing in the Ganges Valley and beyond. In addition, a number of Indian historical sources cover the period from the sixth century BCE onward, providing reasonably secure dates for a number of rulers, religious figures (including the Buddha), and events. Indian oral literature, later committed to writing, survives from earlier times, going back around a millennium. The earliest is the *Rigveda*, a religious text that seems most likely to refer mainly to the second half of the second millennium BCE. This places it some centuries later than the date, around 1900 BCE, of the decline of Indus urbanism, but makes it contemporary with some of the Posturban Harappan cultures of the northwest.

Sources for Studying the Indus Civilization

For nonliterate cultures and for those, like the Indus civilization, whose writings are undeciphered, archaeological excavation and reconnaissance are the main sources of material used to reconstruct and interpret the past, but the skills of many other disciplines are also utilized. In South Asia, ethnography is particularly valuable, shedding considerable light on industrial and economic practices. Historical sources, though absent from the Indus civilization itself, are abundant in Mesopotamia and provide some useful information on trade; later South Asian oral and written history also offers valuable insights into what may have survived from the Indus period into later times.

Archaeological Sources. Archaeology makes it possible to reconstruct many details of the daily life of individuals and communities in the past and to gain some understanding of how human societies have developed. To this end archaeologists make use not only of the archaeological techniques of field survey, excavation, and typological analysis, but also of techniques adapted from other disciplines, such as aerial photography, ethnoarchaeology, and archaeozoology, and of the technical expertise of other fields, such as physics, chemistry, soil science, medicine, and linguistics. The artifacts made by the Indus people, including pottery and jewelry, and their works of art, such as the rare statues and the abundant figurines and seal carvings, give some insight into their aesthetic sense and artistic ability, as well as providing some information about vanished aspects of their lives, such as clothing, and slight clues to their religion. Typology and chemical and physical analyses of artifacts offer insights into the practical and social uses to which these objects were put as well as into the movement of goods and materials and the relationships between communities. Detailed studies of artifact distributions and their relationship to architecture and other features can contribute a great deal of information on past activities, such as the methods employed in craft manufacture or the practices related to death and burial, as well as shedding some light on social organization: Such studies recently at Mohenjo-daro and Harappa have seen considerable success.

Domestic architecture, unusually well known in the Indus civilization, can reveal many aspects of daily life, while the relative paucity and considerable diversity of Indus public architecture fuels much speculation about the ritual practices and social and political organization for which these buildings were required. The early scholarly concentration on cities and towns has been balanced by some recent investigations of smaller sites. Extensive surveys have shed considerable light on regional settlement patterns and changes in the landscape, particularly in the river systems, contributing significantly to an understanding of both the development and heyday of the Indus civilization and its later transformation from an urban civilization into smaller-scale farming societies spread over a more extensive area. Taphonomic agents, such as alluviation and erosion, however, have destroyed or concealed settlements in many areas, skewing the picture. Pollen analysis has produced a limited amount of information on past environment. Plant remains have also yielded some data on the economy of the Indus civilization, its successors, and its predecessors, and animal remains have provided a great deal more.

The analysis of human bones and other remains can reveal details of people's physical lives, such as their diet and the environmental stresses, diseases, or injuries they suffered. Such analysis may also give insights into population history in particular establishing the extent to which outsiders have been involved in shaping major developments in the subcontinent. Unfortunately, most of the burial places of the Indus people have eluded discovery, and physical anthropological data are therefore relatively limited.

Other Sources. Mesopotamian texts refer to sea trade with a number of cultures, among whom the one known as Meluhha has been confidently identified with the Indus civilization. Some light has therefore been shed on the development, nature, and conduct of international trading relations, in which the Indus civilization was a major participant, Indus traders traveling to Mesopotamia and even taking up residence there.

Later Indian texts can also be useful in providing clues to aspects of life in the Indus civilization. The earliest extant texts, the *Vedas*, were composed by Indo-Aryans, who are recognized by the majority of scholars as having been outsiders who entered the subcontinent during the second millennium. Comparisons between Vedic practices and those attested in later texts, therefore, may allow some earlier practices to be sifted out, and attempts can then be made to identify evidence of these among Indus material.

Ethnographic observation of groups operating in circumstances similar to those of the past may provide additional insights into economic practices, manufacturing techniques, the use of particular tools, the function of certain architectural features, and so on; this is particularly relevant in South Asia, which has many unbroken traditions of domestic, industrial, and other activities and whose population includes many pastoralists, as well as tribal groups who pursue a way of life similar in some ways to that of the hunter-gatherers who occupied the region in antiquity.

REFERENCES

Allchin, Bridget, ed. 1994. *Living Traditions. Studies in the Ethnoarchaeology of South Asia.* New Delhi: Oxford & IBH Publishing Co.

Bisht, Ravi Singh. 1997. "Dholavira Excavations: 1990–94." In *Facets of Indian Civilization. Recent Perspectives. Essays in Honour of Professor B. B. Lal,* edited by Jagat Pati Joshi, 107–120. New Delhi: Aryan Books International.

Chakrabarti, Dilip K. 1988. *A History of Indian Archaeology.* New Delhi: Munshiram Manoharlal.

Chanda, R. P. 1926. *The Indus Valley in the Vedic Period. Memoirs of the Archaeological Survey of India.* SI 31. Calcutta: Archaeological Survey of India.

Chanda, R. P. 1929. *Survival of the Prehistoric Civilization of the Indus Valley. Memoirs of the Archaeological Survey of India.* SI 41. Calcutta: Archaeological Survey of India.

Childe, Gordon. 1926. *The Aryans: A Study of Indo-European Origins.* London: Kegan Paul, Trench, Trubner & Co.

Childe, Gordon. 1934. *New Light on the Most Ancient East: The Oriental Prelude to European Prehistory.* London: Kegan Paul, Trench, Trubner & Co.

Crystal, David. 1987. *The Cambridge Encyclopedia of Language* Cambridge, UK: Cambridge University Press.

Cunningham, Alexander. 1875. "Harappa." *Archaeological Survey of India: Report for the Years 1872–3* 5: 105–108.

Dales, George F. 1964. "The Mythical Massacre at Mohenjo Daro." *Expedition* 6 (3): 36–43. Reprinted 1979 in *Ancient Cities of the Indus,* edited by Gregory L. Possehl, 293–296. New Delhi: Vikas Publishing House.

Dales, George F. 1974. "Excavations at Balakot, Pakistan, 1973." *Journal of Field Archaeology* 1 (1/2): 3–22.

Dales, George F. 1979. "Excavations at Balakot." In *South Asian Archaeology 1977,* edited by M. Taddei, 241–274. Naples: Istituto Universitario Orientale, Seminario di Studi Asiatici.

Fairservis, Walter A. 1961. "The Harappan Civilization: New Evidence and More Theory." *Novitates* 2055: 1–35. Reprinted 1979 in *Ancient Cities of the Indus,* edited by Gregory L. Possehl, 49–65. New Delhi: Vikas Publishing House.

Fairservis, Walter A. 1967. "The Origins, Character and Decline of an Early Civilization." *Novitates* 2302: 1–48. Reprinted 1979 in *Ancient Cities of the Indus,* edited by Gregory L. Possehl, 66–89. New Delhi: Vikas Publishing House.

Fairservis, Walter A. 1982. "Allahdino: An Excavation of a Small Harappan Site." In *Harappan Civilization. A Contemporary Perspective,* edited by Gregory L. Possehl, 106–112. New Delhi: Oxford & IBH Publishing Co.

Farmer, Steve, Richard Sproat, and Michael Witzel. 2004. "The Collapse of the Indus-script Thesis: The Myth of a Literate Harappan Civilization." [Online article; retrieved 1/12/07.] www.safarmer.com/fsw2.pdf.

Gadd, C. J. 1932. "Seals of Ancient Indian Style Found at Ur." *Proceedings of the British Academy* 18: 3–22. Reprinted 1979 in *Ancient Cities of the Indus,* edited by Gregory L. Possehl, 115–122. New Delhi: Vikas Publishing House.

Gadd, C. J., and Sidney Smith. 1924. "The New Links between Indian and Babylonian Civilizations." *Illustrated London News,* October 4, 614–616. Reprinted 1979 in *Ancient Cities of the Indus,* edited by Gregory L. Possehl, 109–110. New Delhi: Vikas Publishing House.

Hargreaves, Harold. 1929. *Excavations in Baluchistan 1925. Sampur Mound, Mastung and Sohr Damb, Nal. Memoirs of the Archaeological Survey of India.* SI 35. Calcutta: Archaeological Survey of India.

Jansen, Michael, and Gunter Urban, eds. 1984. *Reports on Fieldwork Carried out at Mohenjo-daro, Pakistan 1982–83 by the IsMEO-Aachen University Mission: Interim Reports I.* Aachen and Rome: RWTH and IsMEO.

Jansen, Michael, and Gunter Urban, eds. 1987. *Reports on Fieldwork Carried out at Mohenjo-daro, Pakistan 1983–84 by the IsMEO-Aachen University Mission: Interim Reports II.* Aachen and Rome: RWTH and IsMEO.

Jarrige, Catherine, Jean-Francois Jarrige, Richard H. Meadow, and Gonzague Quivron. 1995. *Mehrgarh: Field Reports 1974–1985, from Neolithic Times to the Indus Civilization.* Karachi: Department of Culture and Tourism of Sindh, Department of Archaeology and Museums, French Ministry of Foreign Affairs.

Kenoyer, Jonathan Mark. 1989. "Old Problems and New Perspectives in the Archaeology of South Asia." *Wisconsin Archaeological Reports.* Vol. 2. Department of Anthropology. Madison: University of Wisconsin Press.

Knorozov, Yuri. 1976. "The Characteristics of the Language of the Proto-Indian Inscriptions." In *The Soviet Decipherment of the Indus Valley Script: Translation and Critique,* edited by Arlene R. K. Zide and Kamil V. Zvelebil, 55–59. Series Practica, 156. The Hague and Paris: Janua Linguarum.

Lal, B. B. 1970–1971. "Perhaps the Earliest Ploughed Field So Far Excavated Anywhere in the World." *Puratattva* 4: 1–3.

Lal, B. B. 1984. "Some Reflections on the Structural Remains at Kalibangan." In *Frontiers of the Indus Civilization,* edited by B. B. Lal and S. P. Gupta, 55–62. New Delhi: Books and Books.

Lambrick, H. T. 1964. *Sind: A General Introduction.* Hyderabad: Sindhi Adabi Board.

Mackay, Ernest J. H. 1931. "Further Links between Ancient Sind, Sumer and Elsewhere." *Antiquity* 5 (20): 459–473. Reprinted 1979 in *Ancient Cities of the Indus,* edited by Gregory L. Possehl, 123–129. New Delhi: Vikas Publishing House.

Mackay, Ernest J. H. 1935. *The Indus Civilization.* London: Luzac and Co.

Mackay, Ernest J. H. 1938. *Further Excavations at Mohenjo Daro.* New Delhi: Government of India.

Mackay, Ernest J. H. 1943. *Chanhu-daro Excavations 1935–36.* New Haven, CT: American Oriental Society.

Mahadevan, Iravatham. 1972. "Study of the Indus Script through Bi-lingual Parallels." Paper read at the Second All-India Conference of Dravidian Linguists, Sri Venkateswara University. Reprinted 1979 in *Ancient Cities of the Indus,* edited by Gregory L. Possehl, 261–267. New Delhi: Vikas Publishing House.

Mahadevan, Iravatham. 1977. *The Indus Script: Texts, Concordance and Tables. Memoirs of the Archaeological Survey of India,* 77. New Delhi: Archaeological Survey of India.

Mahadevan, Iravatham. 1982. "Terminal Ideograms in the Indus Script." In *Harappan Civilization. A Contemporary Perspective,* edited by Gregory L. Possehl, 311–317. New Delhi: Oxford & IBH Publishing Co.

Majumdar, N. G. 1934. *Explorations in Sind. Memoirs of the Archaeological Survey of India.* SI 48. Calcutta: Archaeological Survey of India.

Marshall, John. 1924. "First Light on a Forgotten Civilization." *Illustrated London News,* September 20, 528–532 and 548. Reprinted 1979 in *Ancient Cities of the Indus,* edited by Gregory L. Possehl, 105–107. New Delhi: Vikas Publishing House.

Marshall, John. 1926a. "Harappa and Mohenjo Daro." *Annual Report of the Archaeological Survey of India, 1923–4:* 47–54. Reprinted 1979 in *Ancient Cities of the Indus,* edited by Gregory L. Possehl, 181–188. New Delhi: Vikas Publishing House.

Marshall, John. 1926b. "Mohenjo-daro." *Illustrated London News,* February 27: 346–349. Reprinted 1976 in *The Great Archaeologists,* edited by Edward Bacon, 228–230. London: Martin Secker and Warburg.

Marshall, John. 1931. *Mohenjo Daro and the Indus Civilization.* London: Arthur Probsthain.

McIntosh, Jane. 1999. *The Practical Archaeologist.* 2nd ed. New York: Facts on File.

McIntosh, Jane. 2005. *Ancient Mesopotamia. New Perspectives.* Santa Barbara, CA: ABC-CLIO.

Mehta, D. P., and Gregory L. Possehl. 1993. "Excavation at Rojdi, District Rajkot." *Indian Archaeology—A Review 1992–3:* 31–32.

Mehta, R. N. 1984. "Valabhi—A Station of Harappan Cattle-Breeders." In *Frontiers of the Indus Civilization,* edited by B. B. Lal and S. P. Gupta, 227–230. New Delhi: Books and Books.

Mughal, M. Rafique. 1973. *The Present State of Research on the Indus Valley Civilization.* Karachi: Karachi, Dept. of Archaeology and Museums, Ministry of Education and Culture, Govt. of Pakistan.

Mughal, M. Rafique. 1982. "Recent Archaeological Research in the Cholistan Desert." In *Harappan Civilization. A Contemporary Perspective,* edited by Gregory L. Possehl, 85–95. New Delhi: Oxford & IBH Publishing Co.

Mughal, M. Rafique. 1984. "The Post-Harappan Phase in Bahawalpur District, Pakistan." In *Frontiers of the Indus Civilization,* edited by B. B. Lal and S. P. Gupta, 499–503. New Delhi: Books and Books.

Mughal, M. Rafique. 1990. "The Harappan Settlement Systems and Patterns in the Greater Indus Valley (circa 3500–1500 B.C.)." *Pakistan Archaeology* 25: 1–90.

Mughal, M. Rafique. 1997. *Ancient Cholistan: Archaeology and Architecture.* Lahore: Ferozsons.

Parpola, Asko. 1994. *Deciphering the Indus Script*. Cambridge, UK: Cambridge University Press.

Piggott, Stuart. 1946. "The Chronology of Prehistoric Northwest India." *Ancient India* 1: 8–26.

Piggott, Stuart. 1950. *Prehistoric India*. Harmondsworth, UK: Penguin.

Possehl, Gregory L. 1979a. "Pastoral Nomadism in the Indus Civilization." In *South Asian Archaeology 1977*, edited by M. Taddei, 537–551. Naples: Istituto Universitario Orientale, Seminario di Studi Asiatici.

Possehl, Gregory L. 1979b. "Lothal: A Gateway Settlement of the Harappan Civilization." In *Ancient Cities of the Indus*, edited by Gregory L. Possehl, 212–218. New Delhi: Vikas Publishing House.

Possehl, Gregory L. 1980. *The Indus Civilization in Saurashtra*. New Delhi: B. R. Publishing Corporation.

Possehl, Gregory L. 1986. *Kulli: An Exploration of Ancient Civilization in South Asia*. Durham, NC: Carolina Academic Press.

Possehl, Gregory L. 1989. *Radiocarbon Dates for South Asian Archaeology*. Philadelphia: University of Pennsylvania Museum of Archaeology and Anthropology.

Possehl, Gregory L. 1999. *Indus Age: The Beginnings*. Philadelphia: University of Pennsylvania Press.

Possehl, Gregory L. 2002. "Fifty Years of Harappan Archaeology: The Study of the Indus Civilization since Indian Independence." In *Indian Archaeology in Retrospect. II. Protohistory. Archaeology of the Harappan Civilization*, edited by S. Settar and Ravi Korisettar, 1–41. Indian Council of Historical Research. New Delhi: Manohar.

Rao, S. R. 1979 and 1985. *Lothal: A Harappan Port Town (1955–62)*. 2 vols. *Memoirs of the Archaeological Survey of India*. SI 78. New Delhi: Archaeological Survey of India.

Renfrew, Colin, and Paul Bahn. 2004. *Archaeology: Theories Methods and Practice*. 4th ed. London: Thames and Hudson.

Sayce, A. H. 1924. "Remarkable Discoveries in India." *Illustrated London News*, September 27, 526. Reprinted 1979 in *Ancient Cities of the Indus*, edited by Gregory L. Possehl, 108. New Delhi: Vikas Publishing House.

Stein, Marc Aurel. 1929. *An Archaeological Tour in Gedrosia*. *Memoirs of the Archaeological Survey of India*. SI 43. Calcutta: Archaeological Survey of India.

Stein, Marc Aurel. 1931. *An Archaeological Tour in Waziristan and Northern Baluchistan*. *Memoirs of the Archaeological Survey of India*. SI 42. Calcutta: Archaeological Survey of India.

Stein, Marc Aurel. 1942. "A Survey of Ancient Sites along the Lost Saraswati River." *The Geographical Journal* 99: 173–182.

Thapar, B. K. 1975. "Kalibangan: A Harappan Metropolis beyond the Indus Valley." *Expedition* 17 (2): 19–32. Reprinted 1979 in *Ancient Cities of the Indus*, edited by Gregory L. Possehl, 196–202. New Delhi: Vikas Publishing House.

Vats, M. S. 1940. *Excavations at Harappa*. New Delhi: Government of India.

Waddell, L. A. 1925. *The Indo-Sumerian Seals Deciphered: Discovering Sumerians of Indus Valley as Phoenicians, Barats, Goths and Famous Vedic Aryans, 3100–2300 B.C.* London: Luzac and Co.

Wheeler, R. E. Mortimer. 1947. "Harappa 1946: The Defences and Cemetery R–37." *Ancient India* 3: 58–130.

Wheeler, R. E. Mortimer. 1950. *Five Thousand Years of Pakistan: An Archaeological Outline.* London: Royal India and Pakistan Society.

Wheeler, R. E. Mortimer. 1953. *The Indus Civilization.* Cambridge, UK: Cambridge University Press.

Wheeler, R. E. Mortimer. 1955. *Still Digging.* London: Michael Joseph.

Wheeler, R. E. Mortimer. 1966. *Civilizations of the Indus Valley and Beyond.* London: Thames and Hudson.

Wheeler, R. E. Mortimer. 1968. *The Indus Civilization.* 3rd ed. Cambridge, UK: Cambridge University Press.

Zide, Arlene R. K., and Kamil V. Zvelebil, eds. 1976. *The Soviet Decipherment of the Indus Valley Script: Translation and Critique.* Series Practica, 156. The Hague and Paris: Janua Linguarum.

CHAPTER 4

Origins, Growth, and Decline of the Indus Civilization

EARLY SOUTH ASIA (CA. 2 TO 1 MILLION–7000 BCE)

Hunters, Gatherers, and Fishers

The archaeological record of early human occupation in South Asia is very patchy, generally being represented only by isolated stone tools, often disturbed from their original context. Various finds of stone tools suggest that people were present in several areas of South Asia before 1 million years ago and perhaps as early as 2 or 1.8 million. Part of a fossil hominid skull is known from the Narmada region, dated around 300,000 years ago; it probably represents *Homo heidelbergensis*, who lived then in Africa, Europe, and West Asia but may be a form intermediate between that and *Homo erectus*, who occupied parts of East and Southeast Asia at that time. Modern humans *(Homo sapiens)* probably reached South Asia from Africa via Arabia around 70,000 years ago. Working floors, and a scatter of material in caves and open-air sites, are the most usual remains of human occupation, but occasionally traces of windbreaks or huts have been found, made of perishable materials, boulders, and posts.

From around 30,000 years ago, however, the evidence from South Asia becomes much more abundant and varied, giving a much fuller picture of its inhabitants' way of life. Their tools were made from fine, long stone blades struck from a core, using a variety of techniques that continued in use not only into Indus times but even up to the present day: These include heating the raw material and the use of inverse indirect percussion. Stone working debris at the great factory site in the Rohri Hills, where suitable flint was abundant and easily extracted, bears witness to the use of these techniques. This flint outcrop had also been exploited by earlier groups, as had other sources of good-quality raw material.

A fascinating direct insight into the way of life of these hunter-gatherers comes from the paintings that began during the late Palaeolithic, a time when art was flourishing in a number of parts of the world, and these became more common in the subsequent Mesolithic period. Such paintings can be seen in caves such as those at Bhimbetka in Central India.

In addition to the vivid painted scenes, the remains of food and of the tools used to process foods show that early South Asians were hunting game such as birds, antelope, wild goats, sheep, and cattle; fishing; and collecting lizards, shellfish, and various plant foods. Some changes in the nature and distribution

53

of these resources took place after about 10,000 BCE as temperatures rose, the ice sheets retreated in northern parts of the globe, and rainfall increased worldwide, but many of the economic patterns established during the previous twenty thousand years endured.

In many parts of the world, the plants on which animal and human foragers depend are available at different times of year in different areas. Many hunter-gatherers, therefore, move seasonally to exploit plant foods as they become available and to follow the herds of game animals as they move between seasonal pastures. At certain times of the year, favored areas attract groups of foragers to come together, meeting not only to take advantage of the seasonal abundance of resources but also to engage in social activities. The evidence indicates that such seasonal movement and aggregation were the pattern of life in many parts of South Asia at this time. In the northwest, the availability of vegetation was influenced by marked differences between very hot summer and very cold winter temperatures, with associated aridity. Many groups are likely to have spent their winters on the margins of the Indus plains and their summers in the mountains of Baluchistan or in Gujarat, their movements dictated by the availability of grazing for the animals that they hunted and by the contrasts between summer and winter temperatures. This pattern of movement continued after the adoption of animal husbandry and continues to the present day, the same environmental constraints governing the pattern of life despite major changes in global temperature, the environment, and human economies.

A similar pattern of seasonal movements occurred elsewhere in the subcontinent, between upland and lowland regions, between coastal and inland locations, and between other areas with complementary resources. Marine and freshwater fish, shellfish, water plants, and wildfowl were often important, favoring the occupation of coasts and lakeshores. In some tropical regions, local resource abundance and the relative lack of seasonal temperature extremes allowed some hunter-gatherer communities to occupy permanent or semipermanent settlements.

South Asia's many hunter-gatherer groups exploited a range of environments, from desert to tropical rainforest and from coast to mountain plateau. The Central Indian rock paintings provide a revealing supplement to the material remains uncovered by archaeologists, which are often little more than the tiny stone tool components (microliths) that were mounted singly or together in bone or wooden handles to create a variety of tools such as arrows, knives, and harvesting tools. The paintings show many scenes of people using such tools: men brandishing a fistful of arrows, shooting them from a bow, or hotly pursuing game with a many-barbed spear. Other scenes, however, depict tools of organic materials, which have not survived. Women use nets to catch fish and wooden digging sticks to extract small creatures from their burrows, men and women carry home game or fruit in bags slung from their heads, others climb trees with bags or baskets to collect honey or fruit, and the whole family sits down in a tent, the "x-ray" view of their stomachs showing they are eating fish.

A hunting scene, one of many rock paintings found at Bhimbetka in central India. Hunter-gatherers began creating these vivid scenes of their daily lives more than ten thousand years ago. (Namit Arora)

The rock paintings also show other sides of life that are generally beyond the reach of archaeological detection. There are scenes of dancing men, dressed in loin clothes and often wearing streamers on their legs, arms, and heads, who move together in a long line or execute complicated individual steps, either singing to accompany themselves or accompanied by musicians. Many clues, from style, technology, and other sources, have been pieced together to date the individual paintings, since the decoration of these caves continued into recent times.

In contrast to most parts of the world, in South Asia the shift to farming did not bring about the end of the hunter-gatherer way of life. On the contrary, a symbiotic relationship developed between hunter-gatherers and farming communities, and even today there are tribal groups whose livelihood depends on the exploitation of wild resources such as honey, which they trade with their neighbors for grain or manufactured goods. In Indus times a mutually beneficial relationship between hunter-gatherers and settled communities seems to have been important.

EARLY FARMERS IN NORTHWEST SOUTH ASIA (7000–4300 BCE)

The Beginnings of Farming

In the millennia following the end of the last Ice Age, farming began in many parts of the world. One of the earliest regions to adopt farming was the Near East. There, during the final millennia of the last glacial period, hunter-gatherers in some areas began to occupy sedentary settlements, exploiting storable foods such as nuts and cereals. What impelled these groups to plant cereals rather than just harvesting them is still much debated. Hunter-gatherers do not lack the knowledge to practice farming; on the contrary, they are intimately familiar with the plants and animals on which they depend and often actively promote the growth of preferred plants by planting, weeding, and using fire to clear competing vegetation. Farming is not generally an easier way of life than hunting and gathering for, although farming increases the productivity of an area from a human perspective, in general the energy input is higher than for hunting and gathering, and there are considerable risks in reducing the range of food sources exploited. There must, therefore, have been a compelling incentive that led communities to take up agriculture.

One possible explanation is that farming began as a way of supporting a growing population. Nomadic people space their children at around four-year intervals, limiting the number of infants that need to be carried around. Settled communities are not constrained in this way, so they tend to have a greater number of children, more closely spaced (although sedentism also generally increases mortality from disease), and this brings about population growth. Other triggers have been suggested to explain the shift to food production: Climatic fluctuations may have encouraged communities to sow crops to offset declining natural food sources, or social demands may have created the need for food surpluses to provide feasts that cemented social bonds.

Whatever factors provided the initial stimulus, the combination of agriculture, food storage, and sedentism promoted population growth and the accumulation of possessions. It became necessary to develop good inter-community relationships as a buffer against the risks of agricultural failure and as a means of obtaining commodities from other regions, including such things as seashells and attractive varieties of stone, for making tools and ornaments. Once agriculture developed, it tended to spread by various means. In many cases farmers established new settlements in adjacent areas as their original settlements expanded in size. In other cases, hunter-gatherer communities acquired domestic plants and animals from their farming neighbors by trading or raiding. Hunter-gatherers might turn to farming independently or in response to influences from farming communities, and the presence of agricultural settlements in an area might create pressures on land or resources that pushed hunter-gatherers into adopting some aspects of food production.

Early Farmers in the Indo-Iranian Borderlands

By 7000 BCE, farming communities existed throughout the regions of the Near East where rain-fed agriculture was possible, including the western Iranian plateau and the southern Zagros Mountains. The farmers cultivated wheat, barley, rye, and a variety of pulses, and some were beginning to herd sheep and goats or raise pigs or cattle.

Mehrgarh. Around the same time, there was also a community practicing agriculture, as well as hunting and gathering, at Mehrgarh on the arid Kachi plain in Pakistan, a triangular extension of lowland alluvium west of the Indus plains. Excavations there uncovered a settlement going back to about 7000 BCE. The villagers lived in rectangular houses built of mud bricks, divided internally into two or four rooms, and there were also doorless, compartmented buildings for storage. They used stone blades, grindstones, bone tools, and baskets lined with bitumen, and they produced a few unfired clay figurines though they did not make pottery. The dead were interred between the houses, accompanied by grave goods, including stone tools, jewelry made of shell,

Some of the exposed remains of the long-lived settlement at Mehrgarh, occupied by farmers and pastoralists from around 7000 to 2500 BCE. The houses and other buildings here were constructed of mudbrick. (Corbis)

steatite, lapis lazuli, turquoise, and calcite, and sometimes by young goats. One grave yielded a bead of native copper, probably produced by cold hammering. A number of the steatite beads seem to have been heated, to change their color from black to white. In the later part of period I, burials were often placed in a chamber excavated in the side of a pit, with a low wall built alongside to seal it.

Mehrgarh is still the only farming settlement of this antiquity known from the Indo-Iranian borderland region. A few other aceramic (pre-pottery) farming sites, such as Kili Ghul Mohammad near modern Quetta and Gumla on the plains of the Gomal River, may date back to the sixth millennium BCE, although their chronology is not secure. Settlements contemporary with Mehrgarh I may still lie buried beneath comparable alluvial deposits or later settlements, or they may have been destroyed by natural forces. At present, therefore, it is impossible to say whether Mehrgarh was an isolated community or part of a large network of farming settlements in this region. In addition, although by the sixth or even seventh millennium there were farming communities to the south and east of the Caspian Sea and in northern Afghanistan, almost nothing is known of the regions between the Indo-Iranian borderlands and western Iran in the seventh millennium. This makes it difficult to understand the wider context of the evidence of farming at Mehrgarh.

Excavations over eleven years by a team of many specialists have resulted in Mehrgarh's becoming one of the best studied villages in South Asia. The abundance of evidence from this site goes some way to compensate for its isolation. At the time of the earliest settlement, the people of the village hunted gazelle, blackbuck, water buffalo, various deer, onager, wild sheep, wild cattle, and other game, and they gathered plants such as dates and jujube (*Zizyphus*); they also raised domestic goats and grew barley and some emmer and einkorn wheat. During the summer months, when temperatures in the area were often above 38 degrees Centigrade (100 degrees Fahrenheit) during the coolest part of day, the villagers may have retreated to the cooler uplands of Baluchistan. At least some, if not all, members of the community must have moved, taking their goats into Baluchistan to find summer grazing (probably in the Quetta region where modern pastoralists from the Kachi plain take their animals during the summer) and following the wild animals that also migrated in search of summer pasture. On the other hand, the presence of dates, harvested in the summer, implies that some of the community spent part of the summer at Mehrgarh.

Agricultural Origins. It is still unclear how northwest South Asia, represented by Mehrgarh, relates to the West Asian center of agricultural development. Did farming colonists bring in wheat, barley, and goats, did indigenous Baluchi hunter-gatherers acquire these through their long-range exchange networks and gradually turn to farming or were these plants and animals domesticated by the Baluchis from local wild stock? The question has been intensively studied and many pieces of evidence have been accumulated, but a definitive answer is still not possible.

On balance, studies of the plant remains and animal bones from Mehrgarh and genetic studies of domestic plants and animals suggest that the site's first domesticates were introduced from the Near East, not locally domesticated. The wild ancestors of emmer and einkorn wheat were present in the Near East, where they were domesticated, but were not found farther east; so wheat, at least, was brought into South Asia. Barley, the main crop of Mehrgarh in period I, might have been locally domesticated: There is disagreement on whether wild barley was present in Baluchistan (though it was probably found farther north, in Afghanistan). Some recent genetic studies, however, suggest that the Near Eastern domestic plants were domesticated once only: wheat (emmer and einkorn), pea, chickpea, and lentil in southeast Anatolia and barley in the Jordan Valley.

Wild goats were part of the native fauna of Baluchistan. While a few of the goats at Mehrgarh were wild, the majority seem to have been domestic from the earliest levels onward. Recent genetic studies indicate that goats were domesticated in several places, giving rise to distinct lineages. One center was in the Near East, from which domestic goats spread at an early date, probably around 8000 BCE: This lineage is by far the most common and widespread. Another center was farther east, somewhere in South or East Asia (the regions to which the lineage is confined), with the spread through this region dating no earlier than around 2000 BCE and possibly as late as 1000 CE. These data might support either of the conflicting theories: introduction from the Near East or local domestication in Baluchistan.

One suggested scenario is that the people of Mehrgarh were settlers of West Asian ancestry, who had gradually spread east through northern Iran. However, the eminent physical anthropologist Kenneth Kennedy, who has studied both the bones from burials at Mehrgarh and other early South Asian skeletons, has found no more differences among them than one would expect within a population. This suggests that the people of Mehrgarh were probably of South Asian stock. On the other hand, recent human genetic studies show that, while mitochondrial DNA, transmitted in the female line, indicates little or no contribution to the gene pool from outside the subcontinent, South Asian Y-chromosomes cluster with those from Near Eastern and European populations, suggesting a movement, largely composed of men, from West Asia into both Europe and South Asia: This might have been associated with the spread of farming.

Alternatively, it is possible that wheat, and perhaps barley and goats, reached the village through trade across the Iranian plateau from the Near East. Other evidence demonstrates the existence of trade networks across this vast area, stretching from the Zagros Mountains in the west through the southwest regions of Central Asia, and into Baluchistan. Commodities from far afield were present at Mehrgarh: lapis and turquoise beads from Turkmenia and northern Afghanistan, and shells from the Arabian Sea, 500 kilometers to the south. The people involved in this trade would individually have travelled relatively short distances, with exchanges generally taking place between kins-folk, for example as marriage gifts. Innumerable short steps of this kind, how-ever, could move goods over vast distances. A mechanism, therefore, existed by which West Asian domestic plants and animals could ultimately have reached Mehrgarh and its region. In the earliest village there, agriculture and hunting and gathering were practiced side by side, agriculture becoming the main way of life only in later periods.

The evidence from a single site, however well investigated, is not enough to establish the pattern of development in a region. The question of the origin of agriculture in the Indo-Iranian borderlands, therefore, is still unanswered. The introduction of wheat through trade, along with the local domestication of goats and barley, might seem to be an attractive explanation for the presence of these domesticates at Mehrgarh, but this then focuses attention on the problem of understanding the stimuli behind the shift to agriculture in this region.

The Consolidation of Agriculture. Subsequent developments are rather better understood. Throughout period I at Mehrgarh, cattle and sheep increased in im-portance, and by the end of the period (around 5500 or 5000 BCE), the people of the village had come to rely mainly on domestic cattle, sheep, and goats for their meat, rather than on hunted game. Genetic studies show that the world's do-mestic cattle belong to two separate lineages: one including both European cattle and the African zebu, the other containing the Indian zebu (*Bos indicus*). The lat-ter is probably descended from *Bos namadicus*, the wild cattle of Pleistocene South Asia, which may have been the variety of wild cattle being hunted at Mehrgarh. Studies of the bones of cattle from Mehrgarh show the progressive diminution in size that is a characteristic of domestication in many species. (Size diminution alone, however, is not sufficient evidence of domestication because it also occurred during the postglacial period in a number of species that were not domesticated.) As time went on, cattle became progressively important in the economy of Mehrgarh's inhabitants.

Local domestication is less certain in the case of sheep. Cytogenetic studies indicate that there was more than one focus of sheep domestication in Asia, and size diminution through time in the sheep present at Mehrgarh is consistent with the domestication of wild sheep in this region. However, studies seem to indicate that all modern sheep derive from one wild ancestor, the Asiatic moufflon (*Ovis orientalis*), which is not found east of the Zagros Mountains; wild sheep in Baluchistan are urial (*Ovis vignei*). It is therefore possible that do-mestic sheep were obtained from the west through the exchange networks.

Naked six-row barley was the main crop in early Mehrgarh, but hulled six-row and two-row barley and several varieties of wheat were also grown in small quantities. A wild cereal, goats-face grass (*Aegilops squarrosa*), hybridized with the cultivated emmer wheat, produces a free-threshing bread wheat (*Triticum aestivum vulgare*). Goats-face grass probably grew as a weed in the fields of Mehrgarh, so it is possible that *T. aestivum* evolved there, though plant studies indicate that the most likely source area for the original hybridization is the southwest Caspian region.

Traces of a cotton thread were detected inside a bracelet of copper beads from a grave dating to the end of period I, currently the earliest known evidence of cotton textile in the world.

Farming Communities of the Northwest. By the mid-sixth or early fifth millennium, a number of farming settlements are known in Baluchistan, including Kili Ghul Mohammad, Anjira, Siah Damb, and Rana Ghundai. Some, such as Anjira, were pastoral camps; others, such as Mehrgarh (period II), were larger communities also practicing cultivation. Mehrgarh continues to provide the most comprehensive information on the period. Domestic cattle there increased in importance at the expense of other animals, and sheep became more numerous than goats. A number of charred cotton seeds identified there suggest either cotton cultivation or the use of the wild cotton plant. Small-scale irrigation is apparently implied by some of the varieties of cereals under cultivation. A large number of compartmented storage buildings (granaries) indicate the increasing importance of cereal cultivation at Mehrgarh and perhaps imply some social complexity. Some of the cells contained impressions of grains, and in one two sickles were found, made of three small blades set in bitumen, originally with wooden handles. A substantial buttressing wall around earlier deposits created a terrace on which the granaries were built, and this must have required community cooperation in its construction.

An increased range of craft activities took place in the settlements of this period, notably the manufacture of the first local pottery vessels. These were made in a variety of simple ways: by coating both faces of a reed core with clay, by moulding clay in a bitumen-lined basket, or by covering the inside of an old basket with clay and firing it, destroying the basket and producing a distinctive type of pottery known as basket-marked ware. Pots were also built up from slabs and pieces of chaff-tempered clay and sometimes coated with a red slip: this ware is known also from contemporary sites across the Iranian plateau. Later in the period some of the pottery was made on the tournette (turntable or slow wheel). A number of fireplaces and working surfaces of hard clay or brick paving, used for industrial activities, were found at Mehrgarh. Objects made at the site included bone, stone, and flint tools, pots and unfired clay figurines, and beads and other ornaments of shell, steatite, and ivory, and probably leather goods, woven textiles, and baskets. Several crucibles containing copper slag bear witness to the beginning of metallurgy, though only a small ingot, a bead, and a ring in copper survive. It is possible that Mehrgarh was providing a regional focus for industry and trade, where many communities met seasonally to engage in exchange and social activities such as arranging and celebrating marriages.

Contemporary Cultures. A number of hunter-gatherer settlements are known in Baluchistan, in coastal regions, and inland along the Luni River in the Thar

Desert, as well as in the rest of the subcontinent. In the northwest, there are a few sites, such as Tharro Hill, in the coastal area from the Makran to the Indus delta, where surface-collected material suggests farming settlement and inter-action between farmers and hunter-gatherers. Abundant natural resources and relatively low population densities probably meant that there were no incentives to embark on major changes in the pattern of existence. Nevertheless, in the hunter-gatherer settlement of Bagor in Rajasthan, the faunal remains include the bones of cattle, sheep, goat, and pig, which may have been domestic animals, although there is some disagreement on this. Sheep and goat together made up more than half the animals present throughout the duration of the settlement (into early historical times). If indeed they were domestic animals, which seems quite likely, they were probably acquired initially, by trading or raiding, from the farming communities in neighboring Baluchistan. Thereafter, domestic animals may have been raised by the people of Bagor, because herding fits in well with a hunter-gatherer existence, seasonal movement being a significant feature of both. Similar evidence comes from Loteshwar in northern Gujarat, a hunter-gatherer settlement with domestic sheep and goats as well as wild animals, that may be as early as the sixth millennium.

LATER SETTLEMENTS (4300–3200 BCE)

Chalcolithic Villages in Baluchistan

By around 4300 BCE (Togau phase), the number of settlements known in Baluchistan and in the adjacent lowlands had greatly increased, and often they were larger than earlier sites. These settlements included Periano Ghundai in the Zhob Valley, Mundigak in the Kandahar region, Faiz Mohammad in the Quetta Valley, Togau in the Sarawan region, and Sheri Khan Tarakai in the Bannu Basin. Occupation also continued at Mehrgarh (period III) and other existing settlements.

Pottery, which had developed rapidly, was of fine quality, and many vessels were shaped on a wheel, allowing a degree of mass production, though others were handmade. Often the pots were painted with abstract or geometric designs. The widely distributed Togau ware vessels were decorated with stylized figures of caprids, birds, and other animals; somewhat similarly decorated wares were also being produced in contemporary Iran and Turkmenia. The geometric patterns are reminiscent of those created in later woven fabric and carpets, suggesting that there was also a flourishing textile industry: A spindle whorl found at Sheri Khan Tarakai supports this. Mehrgarh had become a center of craft production by the early fourth millennium: There workshops turned out large quantities of fine pottery, beads of lapis lazuli, turquoise, shell, and carnelian, shell bangles, and bone and stone tools, including tiny drills made of phtanite (a hard green chert containing traces of iron oxide) for perforating beads. A deep deposit of debris at the site included the remains of circular kilns, ash, and pottery wasters. A range of industrial activities has also been found at other sites of the period.

The development of kilns used to fire pottery at high temperatures gave the people of Baluchistan advanced pyrotechnological skills, which they also employed in other industrial activities. The majority of beads at Mehrgarh were made of steatite in a variety of shapes but standardized in size. They were converted to a white color by heating, and faint traces on their surface show that they were coated with a copper-based glaze, creating a type of faience: This would have required a controlled kiln temperature of around 1000 degrees Centigrade. The people of Mehrgarh and Baluchistan also smelted copper ores, which were available in Afghanistan, and cast objects in copper. These are rarely found since the metal was valuable, and broken tools or ornaments could be melted down for reuse. Gold was also worked, as is shown by the find of a tubular gold bead.

The well-established agricultural economy now included not only the original varieties of domestic cereal but also oats (*Avena*), a new variety of barley, and two developed varieties of bread wheat (*T. aestivum compactum*, club wheat, and *T. aestivum sphaerococcum*, shot wheat). The latter was to become the variety of wheat most commonly cultivated in South Asia.

Burials of this period have been excavated only at Mehrgarh. There was no longer any funerary architecture, but the rites were more varied, including both single and multiple inhumations and some secondary burials of collected bones. Grave goods were rare, usually consisting only of jewelry, worn mainly by adult women. Interestingly, the physical characteristics of the people buried in the period III cemetery suggest the presence of representatives of a new population, with affinities across the Iranian plateau and in the Near East, despite the strong cultural continuity from earlier periods.

Expansion

The fourth millennium saw a further substantial increase in the density of settlement in Baluchistan (Kechi Beg phase) and the expansion of people from this region into the Indus Basin, particularly Cholistan (Hakra phase).

During the later fourth millennium, settlements were developing across the Iranian plateau at important nodes in the long-distance trade routes and in areas where highly prized raw materials were to be found. These formed a network that conducted trade in local and exotic materials, particularly lapis lazuli. Much of West Asia, from Mesopotamia to Turkmenia and the Indus region, was linked into an interaction sphere in which innovations and ideas as well as actual commodities circulated freely.

Baluchistan. About a hundred and fifty sites are attributed to the Kechi Beg phase in Baluchistan, many more than are known in the preceding period. These include both existing settlements, such as Mundigak, Gumla, Rana Ghundai, and Mehrgarh, and new sites, such as Damb Sadaat in the Quetta Valley and Adam Buthi in southern Baluchistan. Settlement extended eastward in the coastal region to the Sonmiani bay where Balakot was established as a coastal village, probably by about 4000 BCE.

Some villages, including Sheri Khan Tarakai, were now around 15 to 20 hectares in extent, although the majority, such as the type-site Kechi Beg, were still less than 5 hectares. Houses were generally of mud brick, often with stone foundations. As in earlier times, it is likely that at least some of the inhabitants of these villages were involved in seasonal transhumance between upland and lowland regions. Water buffalo were among the fauna exploited at Sheri Khan Tarakai, though it is not known whether they were domesticated or hunted. The fauna at Balakot included hunted animals, though surprisingly, despite the settlement's proximity to the sea, marine resources were of little importance. Grape pips at Mehrgarh imply that this local fruit was now being exploited, though whether it was cultivated is not clear. Simple irrigation was probably practiced in parts of the northwest: At Mehrgarh there is a ditch or canal that may have been used for this purpose.

Craft traditions continued to develop. Differences in the styles of pottery suggest the existence of regional groups, their distinctiveness determined to a considerable extent by the topography of this mountainous region, but there are also strong similarities between the wares, including the frequent use of geometric decoration. Other designs included animals, such as cranes and caprids and especially snakes. Often the animals had become stylized into simple zigzags. Although most designs were painted in one or several colors, some were molded as raised ridges or snakes.

At Sheri Khan Tarakai, craft products included many terra-cotta figurines. The majority of these were very stylized humans in the form of cylinders with facial features and appliqué breasts, attached to exaggerated buttocks and splayed legs in a standing or sitting position; others were bottle shaped. A few figurines depicted bulls, and all bore painted features and decorations. Similar human and bull figurines have been found in smaller numbers at other sites, including Mehrgarh.

A marked reduction in the use of flint and heavy-duty stone tools reflects the growing importance of metal as a material for making tools. Microliths were now used mainly as insets forming the cutting edge of sickles. Copper was also made into pieces of jewelry, such as beads and pins. An increasing variety of materials were being used for beads, including agate and jasper.

Cholistan and the Western Punjab. Although sporadic earlier finds suggest some, probably seasonal, movement from Baluchistan into the adjacent areas of the Indus Basin, this period (fourth millenium) saw the first substantial settlement on the plains. The newcomers moved into territory previously inhabited only by hunter-gatherers. The main concentration of sites is in the valley of the Saraswati in the Cholistan region. Here surface survey has led to the identification of around a hundred sites with sherds of Hakra pottery, which included various handmade black-slipped, painted, mud appliqué, and basket-marked wares. These settlements were apparently made on virgin soil. Since none have been excavated, it is not possible to ascertain their nature, but it seems likely (on the basis of the density and nature of the material found there) that some were temporary camps occupied by pastoralists, probably during the rainy season when the region was covered in grass, and that others were farming settlements with mud brick houses. Farther east, however, the excavated site of Kunal has provided more information. The settlement was first occupied in the Hakra phase when a low artificial mound of soil was created there. Semisubterranean houses were built on the mound, with their floors sunk through the mound into the top of the ground surface and with superstructures of wattle and daub. There was perhaps also a Hakra period settlement at Rakhigarhi on the Drishadvati River.

Farther north, two other sites also furnish more information: Jalilpur and Harappa, both on or near the Ravi River in the Punjab. Terra-cotta net sinkers at Jalilpur show that fishing was important to the people of this settlement, but domestic sheep, goats, and cattle also played an important role in their economy. The remains of mud brick houses with beaten earth floors were found, though the excavations were too limited to reveal any details of their plans.

Settlement began at Harappa by 3300 BCE and perhaps as early as 3500. Houses there were constructed of wooden posts with reed and clay roofs, and bell-shaped pits lined with clay were used to store wheat and barley. One house, abandoned with most of its contents, had a number of pottery vessels set on the floor, along with other domestic material such as beads, terra-cotta and shell bangles and spindle whorls, and bone and stone tools. Manufacturing debris, such as broken agate and jasper drills, shows that the beads were made in the settlement; some were of terra-cotta and others of materials from distant sources such as carnelian, lapis lazuli, steatite, and amazonite. They included microbeads less than a centimeter in diameter, probably perforated with a copper wire. Some of the steatite examples were unaltered; others were fired white or coated in blue-green glaze.

Among the most interesting finds at Harappa are a number of sherds bearing a sign incised before firing or scratched on afterward. In one case there were three signs in a line. Some of these resembled signs used later in the Indus script, suggesting that they represent an early stage in the development of Indus writing. There were also carved bone button seals, something also known from Mehrgarh where they were made in terra-cotta as well: These bore geometric designs. Another exciting find was the impression on a terra-cotta bead of a piece of plain weave cloth.

The pottery at Harappa, called Ravi ware by the excavators, was quite similar to the Hakra wares of Cholistan. It was all handmade until the end of the period, when it began to be made on the slow-wheel. The remains of a kiln for firing the pottery, built of mud bricks, was found in the settlement. The pots included cooking vessels and bowls, but also pedestaled vessels that were to become one of the most distinctive forms in the Indus pottery repertoire. Many were decorated with polychrome designs, including geometric patterns and birds; some of the motifs were to become very characteristic of later Kot Dijian and Mature Harappan pottery. Hakra and Ravi pottery included a variety of wares that recall earlier or contemporary styles in Baluchistan and the Kachi plain. In contrast to Baluchistan, Hakra sites yielded a large number of microliths, although copper was also used. Stone

A hand-made pot from the Ravi period at Harappa, when the settlement was first occupied. The design of intersecting circles was one that continued to be popular through the Early and Mature Harappan periods. (Harappa Archaeological Research Project, Courtesy Department of Archaeology and Museums, Government of Pakistan)

pestles and ring stones, beads and bangles, and terra-cotta figurines were also found at these sites. Human and bull figurines from Harappa resembled those from Baluchistan.

Kohistan and Gujarat. Regions farther to the southwest also saw settlement expansion in this period. In the piedmont region fringing the lower Indus plain, several settlements, including Amri and Ghazi Shah, were established in localities raised above the Indus alluvium, generally with access to thermal springs and seasonal streams running off the Kirthar Range. This region, like Cholistan and Punjab, offered excellent seasonal pastures for domestic animals.

Farther south, the earliest occupations at Padri and Somnath probably belong to this period. The inhabitants of these settlements used pottery that differed from Kechi Beg and Hakra wares, and it seems likely that they were representatives of a local culture, with hunter-gatherer antecedents, rather than related to the cultures of Baluchistan. However, there is a strong possibility that this region was visited seasonally by pastoralists from the Indo-Iranian borderlands, resulting in contacts and the cultural exchange of materials and ideas.

THE EARLY INDUS (EARLY HARAPPAN) PERIOD (3200–2600 BCE)

Early Indus Developments

The late fourth and early third millennia saw the spread of farming communities into the Indus Basin and eventually as far as the upper Ganges-Yamuna doab: Permanent settlements were established both in areas that had previously only been visited seasonally by pastoralists and in new areas. Some communities shifted their home location from upland to plain, although the pastoral sector still travelled seasonally between regions. This move must reflect the development among highland communities of the technology, knowledge, and confidence to exploit the new environmental zones offered by the Indus Basin and to overcome their limitations. This was part of an enduring process, whereby pastoralists seeking seasonal grazing gained familiarity with new regions that later enabled their kin or other members of the community to move in and colonize these regions with permanent agricultural settlements.

In arid Baluchistan, dry farming was possible only in river valley bottoms, and water conservation was vital for high agricultural productivity. The inhabitants of many settlements built simple dams (bunds and gabarbands) to impound or divert water that flowed off the surrounding higher ground in the spring when the melting of highland snows filled generally dry streams with seasonal torrents. This water could then be used for irrigation later in the year when temperatures rose and the ground became parched. As population increased, this technological expertise aided the settlement of new regions, made necessary by competition for the limited land suitable for farming in the arid highland region. The economic importance of cattle, the dominant domestic animal, also put pressure on arable land because they need to graze or obtain fodder from land suitable for cultivation, unlike sheep and goats, which can find adequate grazing in the scrub vegetation on uncultivated land. It is possible that these economic pressures were increased by climatic factors, since some global data suggest that the fourth millennium was more arid than previous millennia and that this aridity peaked in the period around 3200–3000 BCE.

Settlement in the Indus Basin was attractive because it offered a vast expanse of well-watered fertile land for arable agriculture and even wider expanses for grazing animals. Wild game, fish, and plants offered additional resources, and there were sufficient timber and plentiful mud for construction, as well as fuel for domestic and industrial activities. Unlike other foci of urban development, such as the Euphrates Valley, the Indus Basin and its environs were well-endowed with mineral resources, including flint in the Rohri Hills in Sindh, agate and carnelian in Gujarat, gold dust on the upper Indus, and steatite, copper, and perhaps tin in nearby Rajasthan, as well as the stone and metal ores available in the Indo-Iranian borderlands.

But the region had significant drawbacks too. Mosquitoes could carry malaria, and other fevers were also a feature of life on the plains. The jungle housed not only game such as gazelle and jungle fowl, but also deadly predators and dangerous wild animals, such as tigers, snakes, and the formidable elephant. The instability of the Indus was also a major problem, with the constant threat of floods and changes in the river's course. Existing technology, designed to conserve water, had to be changed and developed to deal with an excess of water.

While this period is called Pre-Harappan by some scholars, the interchangable terms "Early Indus" or "Early Harappan" are generally preferred, because they reflect this period's cultural continuity with the following Indus civilization.

Regional Groups. The Early Indus period saw greater variety in craft products in settlements than in earlier periods and growing regional diversity, particularly in pottery styles. Differences in the pottery from different areas suggest the existence of regional groups, some of which are linked to groups in Baluchistan, probably reflecting the links between highland and lowland maintained by seasonal transhumant pastoralists. In the period from around 3200 to 2600 BCE, three major traditions seem to have emerged in the greater Indus region, named after important sites: the Amri-Nal, Kot Diji, and Sothi-Siswal traditions (often called phases), respectively in the south, center/north, and east. Another tradition, known as Damb Sadaat, existed in central Baluchistan. Stylistic differences in their pottery and other artifacts distinguish them, but there were also very considerable cultural similarities between groups.

Whether, as some suggest, these regional pottery groupings can be identified with ethnic groups is uncertain; taking a broad view of the Indus Basin and adjacent regions, there seem likely to have been a number of contemporary cultures in these regions by the early third millennium, with a variety of ancestries. These included traditional hunter-gatherers (such as the inhabitants of Bhimbetka in Madhya Pradesh) who had no apparent contact with farming communities; hunter-gatherers who had modified their lifestyle to include some animal husbandry, following contact with farming groups, as at Bagor; and other settled hunter-gatherers, such as the Jodhpura-Ganeshwar culture in the Aravallis Hills. There were settled farmers and pastoralists of hunter-gatherer ancestry, some of whom, such as the Southern Neolithic culture in Karnataka, raised locally domesticated plants and animals; others such as the Ahar-Banas culture in Rajasthan and the Northern Neolithic in Kashmir, had acquired some domesticates from their farming neighbors in the Indus region and adjacent highlands. In the greater Indus region, there were indigenous groups who had been living in closer association with pastoralists or settlers from the northwest since at least the later fourth millennium, when they were represented by settlements such as Padri and Somnath in Gujarat, Jalilpur in Punjab, and Kunal in the Saraswati plains. These groups were integrated to varying degrees with new settlers from the Indo-Iranian borderlands: The three lowland Early Indus traditions reflected this hybrid ancestry. Other farming communities still occupied their ancestral lands in the highlands.

Industry. Though the Early Harappan period was not a time of great innovation, there were many developments in the existing technologies, such as a range of fine pottery and figurines that display great liveliness and imagination. These are often more realistic than in earlier periods and cover a wider range of subject matter, and the human figures are shown in a greater variety of postures. For example, one female figurine from Harappa is standing, holding a bowl, and wearing a skirt; details of her skirt's weave and her jewelry were painted on. Features were not only modeled or shown in paint but also incised or added by appliqué. The widest range of figurine types was found at the adjacent sites of Mehrgarh VII and Naushaoro I. Many depict women, scantily clad but generally lavishly adorned with jewelry and head ornaments or with a variety of hair styles. These are frequently referred to as Mother Goddesses. Some male figures are also known at Mehrgarh, generally wearing turbans. Humped bulls are still the main animal figurines, but now others are also depicted, including ram figurines at Harappa that had holes for wheels. Goddesses and cattle are important in the folk religion of the subcontinent today and in historical times, providing good evidence of cultural continuity; so these models may have had some religious significance.

Wheel-made pottery predominated, although handmade wares were still produced as well. Some pottery was also formed in molds. Pots were fired in updraft kilns but also in open-air bonfire kilns. Two small kilns for firing figurines and terra-cotta bangles were found in the AB mound at Harappa. Terra-cotta bangles found here were decorated with pinched, incised, or painted patterns, and their firing conditions were controlled to produce a red (oxidized) or gray (reduced) color. An increasing number of bangles were also made of marine shell.

Steatite was used now not only for beads and other ornaments but also for seals. The practice of glazing some steatite objects developed further and gave rise to the production of faience. This is attested to in the later Kot Diji levels at Harappa, where microbeads and a variety of larger beads began to be made from frit (ground-up silica and glazing material made into a paste and formed into beads that were then fired).

Copper artifacts were probably becoming more common, since many tools and ornaments have survived. Small objects of gold are found in larger numbers, including pendants, beads, and small gold discs from Harappa that had apparently been sewn onto clothing. Other common artifacts include stone beads, shell and terra-cotta bangles, and stone tools, as well as coiled basketry, known from an impression on a ground surface at Harappa.

Some settlements show signs of specialization in particular crafts or other industrial activities, such as the procurement of raw materials. For example, huge quantities of figurines were produced at Mehrgarh in this period, suggesting mass production. Lewan, a village in the Bannu Basin in northern Baluchistan, specialized in the production of stone tools, including querns, axes, and hammers, which were traded over a wide area. A degree of specialization had begun earlier, for example at Mehrgarh, but it was becoming more pronounced in this period.

Some settlements of this period, including Rehman Dheri in the Gomal Valley and Kalibangan in the Ghaggar (Saraswati) Valley, were surrounded by a substantial wall; in the river valleys these seem likely to have been flood defenses. A large platform was constructed at Mehrgarh, associated with

An Early Harappan figurine found at Harappa. The subject is clothed, which is unusual; she wears a painted skirt and carries a bowl. Painted bangles cover her arms, and she is also wearing a necklace with pendants. Her hair is arranged in a tiered hairstyle tied at the back. (Richard H. Meadow, Courtesy Department of Archaeology and Museums, Government of Pakistan)

a buttressed wall. Houses were generally of mud brick, often with stone foundations. Within some sites, standardization was already often present in the form of standardized brick sizes; at Harappa these were in the ratio 1:2:4, while at Kalibangan the ratio was 1:2:3.

Economy. Evidence for subsistence is scarce from Early Indus sites. Animal bones, where available, show that cattle, sheep, and goat were regularly kept, especially cattle (which made up around 90 percent of the fauna at Jalilpur, for example), along with water buffalo in some Indus Basin settlements, including Kalibangan. Often wild animals were also hunted, including birds, fish, and various kinds of deer. Rehman Dheri is one of the few settlements from which plant material has been recovered: Wheat was the main crop there, though later barley was more important. Wheat and barley were also grown at Kalibangan on the upper Saraswati where a plowed field was uncovered: The field had been plowed in two directions, presumably for raising two crops that matured at different times, a practice known in modern northern India. The plow was probably drawn by bullocks, which were also used to draw carts, known from terra-cotta models at Jalilpur and cart ruts at Harappa. The small settlement of Phang in the Kirthar Range seems to have made use of a gabarband for irrigation, and small-scale irrigation works were probably employed in other highland regions; settlements were also often located to make use of other water sources for raising crops, such as springs, hillwash, and mountain streams.

Burials. Limited evidence of burial practices exists, but in Gujarat two burials at Nagwada may be associated with a "cenotaph" (a pit containing pottery but no bones). This was to be a feature of some of the later Harappan cemeteries too. At Mehrgarh a cemetery of nineteen graves was excavated immediately above the latest period of the settlement: These consisted of small boxes built of mud bricks, containing the remains of infants, generally without grave goods though three beads were recovered. These graves resemble one found at Nal, but in neither site was there datable material associated with the graves, which could be of a later date, though this is thought unlikely at Mehrgarh. In contrast, at Periano Ghundai four cremation burials were found, one in a vessel of Bhoot ware; another cremation was found at Moghul Ghundai, also in the Zhob Valley.

Precursors to Writing. Among the finds from Damb Sadaat phase settlements were a number of stamp seals bearing geometric designs, such as stepped crosses or zigzags, resembling contemporary objects from some Central Asian and Iranian sites such as Shahr-i Sokhta. Several steatite button seals were found in a Kot Diji level at Harappa: these also bore geometric designs, though they differed from the stepped square patterns of the Damb Sadaat tradition. A similar seal had also been found in the Ravi phase at Harappa. A particularly fine example of a button seal from Harappa bore a four-pointed star and five whorls, one inside the star and the others in the corners of the seal. Slight blue-green traces indicate that originally the seal had been glazed. A carved ivory pendant from the early Kot Diji phase at Rehman Dheri was decorated on one face with a pair of deer similar to those in pottery designs and on the other with two scorpions and a frog. Both faces also had a T-shaped sign, and there was also an arrow and a sign like the letter *I* on the deer side.

At Harappa the Early Indus period saw the continued use of potters' marks, incised on pottery before firing, and of signs used in other contexts. One mold fragment from a later Early Indus deposit bore three signs, probably representing a

Potters' marks were often incised on the base of pots before firing, perhaps to identify the products of individual potters when large numbers of vessels were fired together in a bonfire kiln. While most of the marks are simple and of a universal nature, a few were later used as signs in the Indus script. (Harappa Archaeological Research Project, Courtesy Department of Archaeology and Museums, Government of Pakistan)

further stage in the development of the script and perhaps giving the owner's name. Often the signs resemble later signs in the Indus script, and sometimes two such signs are associated in the same order as in the later script. Similar signs or potters' marks occur on pots from Rehman Dheri of this or the Transition period (2600–2500). The impression of a square seal on a circular piece of clay was also found in the Kot Diji phase at Harappa, suggesting that the idea of using a seal as a mark of authority or in an organizational context was now developing. Discovered in a hearth where it had presumably been discarded, it bore several signs and two designs like ladders. Harappa also yielded a broken seal with a design apparently showing an elephant. This seal and the seal impression comprised the two elements of the later Mature Indus seals: an inscription and a design, generally of an animal.

The evolution of a repertoire of local signs and the use of stamp seals seem likely to reflect developments in the organization of society, perhaps relating to a growing need to indicate ownership in a society no longer entirely organized along kinship lines and to allow some control over the movement of commodities. The presence of a cubical stone weight in Kot Dijian Harappa, on the same weight standard as that of the Mature Harappan period, is similarly suggestive of organizational developments.

Amri-Nal

Amri-Nal sites are known over southern Baluchistan, including the Makran region, southwest Sindh, and Gujarat, but few have been excavated to any great extent, and only Amri and Balakot have yielded a significant amount of information. The Kechi Beg period had seen separate traditions in different parts of southern Baluchistan and on the fringes of the southern Indus plain; after the initial settlement of these regions, however, the distinctions between these small groups began to break down, perhaps in response to the new environment where few geographical barriers separated one area from another. By 2900 BCE, for example, the material at Balakot resembled that from Amri. Amri pottery was a fine red or buff ware decorated with bands of geometric patterns and its forms included tall jars and open bowls; Nal pottery was characterized particularly by a range of fine straight-sided bowls and canisters, decorated with distinctive patterns combining precisely arranged geometric elements and realistic animals. While Amri pottery was more common in Kohistan and Nal pottery in Baluchistan, both were found at sites throughout the region.

The settlement at Amri had houses of mud brick with external fireplaces but also several compartmented buildings that may have been granaries. In

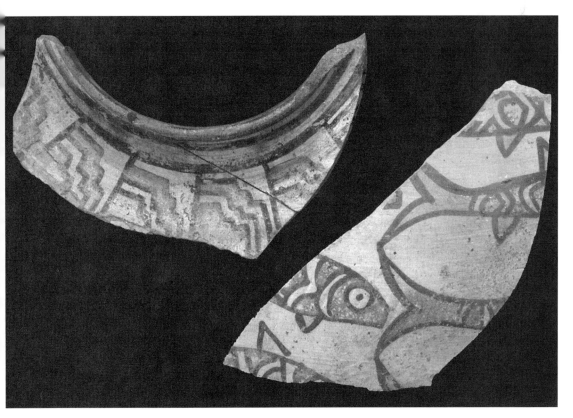

Colorful geometric patterns and animal designs cover the entire surface of Nal pottery, dating from the Early Harappan period in southern Baluchistan. These potsherds are from the large settlement of Niai Buthi. (J. M. Kenoyer, Courtesy Department of Archaeology and Museums, Government of Pakistan)

Baluchistan, house foundations were generally of stone, with mud brick walls above. The burned remains of rafters from a sloping roof were found at Nal (although it is not clear whether this came from an Early Indus or a later house). A number of settlements may have been surrounded by stone walls, though again it is not certain whether these belong to the Amri-Nal or a succeeding period.

A concentration of chert flakes and cores, debris from stone working, may represent an artisan's quarter of the settlement at Amri. Nal has evidence of metalworking of uncertain date.

A number of new settlements appeared during this period in Gujarat. These may include Dholavira, later to be a major Indus city, where the earliest levels of occupation contain pottery that may belong to the Amri-Nal tradition, though it was said by the excavator to resemble the pottery from Padri. Burials probably of this period are known at Surkotada and Nagwada, the latter associated with pottery of Amri-Nal type. At other settlements of this period, such as Somnath (Prabhas Patan), Loteshwar, and Padri, different pottery, including Anarta ware, suggests the continuation of indigenous traditions distinct from that of Amri-Nal, known from the earlier occupations at Padri and Loteshwar. At Somnath remains were found of structures built probably of wattle and daub. Copper artifacts were present in a number of these settlements.

A number of these sites were located on or near the seacoast. This period saw a general increase in coastal settlements, including a number in Makran. Some of the latter did not have Amri-Nal materials but an assemblage known as Dasht.

Kot Diji

Kot Diji sites are known over a wide area, with concentrations in central and northern Baluchistan and Cholistan, and more scattered sites in Punjab, as far north as Swat, and in Sindh, including Kot Diji itself, which lies east of where the Indus flowed at that time, and Jhukar further west. A few Kot Diji sites are known in Kohistan, among the concentration of Amri-Nal sites, and some settlements have pottery of both traditions. In parts of Cholistan, the sites related to this period found during field surveys seem to decrease in number and increase in size, suggesting greater permanence of settlement as farming villages replaced pastoral camps. None of the Cholistan sites has been excavated, so the information available from them is limited.

The site of Kohtras Buthi in the Kirthar Range has the remains of two stone walls, below the settlement, which was built on a ridge: the walls were possibly defensive, since they effectively protected the vulnerable flank of the settlement. A number of Kot Diji sites were of substantial size, including Rehman Dheri in the Gomal Valley, which had a wall built of clay slabs, possibly entirely surrounding the 19-hectare settlement although it has been traced only in one part. The houses there were also built of clay slabs, which were locally available as a building material, being cut from dry riverbeds. Some houses were circular, others rectangular. In the early phase of settlement, houses contained silos for storing grain, while in later phases storage jars were used.

Kot Diji was smaller, around 2 hectares. It also had the remains of a wall, perhaps originally surrounding the whole site, built some time after the first occupation of the site but early in the settlement's history. At a later stage in the Kot Diji period, the wall was abandoned and the settlement expanded, with houses built over the remains of the wall. Houses in the upper levels had stone foundations and mud brick walls. Kot Diji was located adjacent to the Rohri Hills, a key source of high-quality flint that had been exploited since Palaeolithic times.

In Punjab there was continuity of settlement from the Hakra period at Jalilpur and Ravi phase at Harappa. At the latter site, the Kot Diji phase is dated around 2800–2600 BCE and remains of this period have been unearthed covering the AB ("citadel") mound and the adjacent E mound and extending on to mound ET, indicating a considerable expansion of the settlement, which grew to around 25 hectares by the end of the period, when the two mounds were each surrounded by a substantial mud brick wall. Within the walls the settlement, which was beginning to develop into an urban center, was laid out in cardinally orientated streets with houses and craft debris.

Kot Diji pottery—fine red or buff ware with black painted decoration—bore some similarities to that of Amri. However, many of the vessel shapes were different, and the decoration on Kot Diji pottery included a number of distinctive elements, such as floral motifs, a fish scale pattern, and a "horned deity" (a head with enormous buffalo horns, thought to relate to the "proto-Shiva" of Indus iconography). The range of Kot Diji vessels included large porous water containers with grooved surfaces (Bhoot ware). Another class of pottery, Wet ware, common to both Kot Diji and areas of Baluchistan, was also probably used to store water: The characteristic appearance of these was achieved by applying a thick slip that was then partially removed with a damp cloth, leaving a rough, cloth-patterned surface. The pottery uncovered in the early deposits at Harappa show a clear line of development from the Ravi to Kot Diji styles.

Damb Sadaat

Material from the Kot Diji sites in Waziristan (northern Baluchistan) differs somewhat from that in other Kot Diji regions. In the adjacent area of central Baluchistan, particularly the Quetta Valley, the material is thought to be different enough to be treated as a separate tradition, known as Damb Sadaat. The sites of the Kachi plain, Mehrgarh (periods VI–VII) and Naushargo (period I), lay within the general area of Kot Diji sites but were not typical, more closely resembling the Damb Sadaat tradition in their material.

Pottery from Damb Sadaat sites, such as Mundigak, Damb Sadaat, and Faiz Mohammad, had a number of similarities with Kot Diji pottery, including the presence of Wet wares, but it also included very different features, such as its distinctive repertoire of geometric, animal, and plant motifs. Faiz Mohammad Grey ware was manufactured in two stages, being fired first in oxidizing conditions and then refired in reducing conditions in high-temperature kilns to produce its gray color. Technologically it resembles Emir Grey ware, a type of

A fine steatite button seal from the Kot Diji period at Harappa. The geometric design has widespread parallels stretching as far as Central Asia. Traces of blue-green material show that the surface was originally glazed. (Harappa Archaeological Research Project, Courtesy Department of Archaeology and Museums, Government of Pakistan)

pottery that was found in east Iranian sites, though the two wares were differently decorated. Faiz Mohammad Grey ware shares motifs with local Quetta ware, which was decorated with plants and animals and geometric motifs such as zigzags and stepped-square patterns. The latter are paralleled in regions to the northwest, including Bactria and Turkmenia, where compartmented seals and figurines similar to those of Damb Sadaat are also known.

Sothi-Siswal

The Early Indus period saw the spread of occupation over the eastern portion of the Saraswati system, extending as far as the Ganges-Yamuna doab in the southeast. The main concentration of sites was in the valley of the Drishadvati River: These included the type-sites Sothi and Siswal after which the tradition is named (known variously as Sothi, Siswal, or Sothi-Siswal). A small settlement was established at Rakhigarhi, also on the Drishadvati, where houses were oriented in the cardinal directions and a baked brick public drain was constructed. The settlement of Kalibangan was situated in the triangle of land at the confluence of the Drishadvati and Saraswati Rivers. It was about 4.5 hectares in extent: A substantial mud brick wall several meters wide, with a defensible gate in the north side, enclosed a roughly rectangular mound, of which a small part has been excavated, revealing mud brick houses apparently built along streets orientated in the cardinal directions. Courtyards formed the center of the houses, which were furnished with ovens; one also had a baked brick drain. A wall also surrounded Banawali, situated on the Saraswati River. This was probably designed for flood defense because there is evidence that it eventually collapsed due to water damage, after an attempt to reinforce it with a subsidiary wall alongside.

Sothi-Siswal pottery included a fine red ware and some coarser wares, often similar to those from Kot Diji Cholistan; some Kot Diji wares were also present. Floral and animal motifs were common. Sothi-Siswal pottery is found in Early Indus sites in this region, but it also continued in use alongside Indus pottery in the Mature Harappan period and is found in sites of the Posturban period. The chronology of the Sothi-Siswal tradition is not well established: Only Kalibangan has been dated by radiocarbon, and its dates are not internally consistent.

Neighbors and Trade

There is plentiful evidence of internal trade within and between the regions of the Early Indus period, particularly evident in the presence of marine shells in sites far inland such as Harappa, Kalibangan, and Banawali. At Harappa, different types of chert from sources in Baluchistan and Sindh were brought to the site for making tools and ornaments. The resources present at this and other sites reflect trade links in many directions, carrying gemstones, marine shells, copper ore, stone, and other utilitarian and luxury commodities. The trade networks that had linked Baluchistan with the Iranian plateau and Turkmenia extended to encompass the Indus region too. Pastoralists engaged in seasonal movements between highland and lowland pastures provided regular contacts between hill and plain and links with the new patterns of movement emerging in the plains themselves.

Neighbors to the South. A number of Sothi-Siswal settlements, such as Kunal and Kalibangan, obtained copper from the Aravalli Hills to the south. Here communities of the Jodhpura-Ganeshwar culture, who exploited wild resources, also mined copper, which they cast in flat molds into axes, fishhooks, arrowheads, and other small objects. They made various types of red pottery, some of which was made on the slow-wheel and showed affinities with Early Harappan pottery.

Farther southwest, on the Banas and Berach Rivers in southern Rajasthan, the people of the Ahar-Banas culture, established in the region before 3000 BCE, were also exploiting the copper ores of the Aravallis by the early third millennium, making axes and other artifacts of copper. Though only copper artifacts have been found at Ahar, there were stone tools at other sites such as Gilund. These people raised a variety of crops, including wheat and barley.

The presence of these cereals implies some contact with communities farther north but, unlike the Jodhpura-Ganeshwar culture, the Ahar-Banas people seem not to have traded with the Early Harappans.

Neighbors to the West. Farming settlements had been established in western Iran and Turkmenia for millennia, and contacts across the region had supplied Mehrgarh and other sites with small quantities of turquoise and lapis lazuli. While much of the Iranian plateau and Turkmenia was mountain or desert, making agriculture possible only in limited areas, the region was rich in timber, metal ores, attractive varieties of stone such as chlorite, and other minerals.

During the fourth millennium, Elam, in southwest Iran, was closely linked to developments in Mesopotamia, sharing the cultural advances that took place there, including the emergence of accounting and writing systems by 2900 BCE. The growing demand for Iranian minerals promoted trade, which in turn encouraged the eastward spread of Near Eastern goods and ideas. In the late fourth millennium, Elam shifted its focus of attention eastward, away from Mesopotamia and toward the towns that had developed in key locations on the Iranian plateau, where there was not only land suitable for cultivation but also access to local minerals or an important situation with respect to the trade routes. It seems that Elam at this time no longer merely participated in the trading networks but also established trading outposts in many of the towns to give more direct control over the movement of goods. The presence of Elamites is attested by the discovery of a number of seals and sealings bearing Proto-Elamite writing and numbers, concerned with such administrative matters as the supplying of agricultural produce, at settlements such as Tepe Sialk, Tepe Yahya, and Tal-i Malyan (Anshan). The abandonment of writing and the return to the use of the traditional uninscribed stamp seals reflects the withdrawal of the Elamite presence from these towns around 2800 BCE.

In subsequent centuries the Iranian towns continued to flourish and grow and to take part in a trading network linking Mesopotamia, Elam, other Zagros cultures, Turkmenia, Baluchistan, and the Indus region. Among the most distinctive manufactured goods in circulation at the time were carved stone vessels in the so-called Intercultural Style, which were made at Tepe Yahya and possibly at other sites in the Kerman region, including Jiroft (Konar Sandal).

One of the few regions favorable to settlement in the eastern part of the Iranian plateau was Seistan, adjacent to Baluchistan. Here the Helmand and Arghandab Rivers flowed into a marshy inland delta debouching into the Hamun-i Helmand, a vast lake. The Helmand Basin was inhabited by farmers who used irrigation to grow wheat and barley, grapes, melons, and other crops, including flax. They also raised cattle, camels, sheep, and goats; hunted local game; and caught fish and waterfowl. Strong similarities in artifacts such as pottery and figures between the Helmand Basin and Chalcolithic sites in southeast Turkmenia may indicate the arrival during the later fourth millennium BCE of some settlers from the latter region, where irrigation agriculture was well developed and where in the Hari Rud delta there was substantial depopulation at this time. By 3200 BCE, a small town had developed at Shahr-i Sokhta (period I) on a terrace of the alluvial plain, south of Hamun-i Helmand. This settlement of around 15 hectares had an Elamite presence, indicated by the discovery of a tablet inscribed in the Proto-Elamite script and a number of sealings.

After the Elamite withdrawal around 2800 BCE, Shahr-i Sokhta (period II) continued to grow, becoming increasingly important as the center of a thriving agricultural region with many small villages. Its prosperity also depended in part on its role as a break-of-bulk center for lapis lazuli, which was brought here as raw nodules from which Shahr-i Sokhta artisans removed extraneous material, exporting only pieces of pure lapis. A huge cemetery outside the town contained a considerable variety of burials, including some in brick-built chambers, well furnished with fine jewelry, pottery, stone vessels, and metal-work. Routes linked the region to southern Turkmenia, Baluchistan, and Kerman, respectively to the north, east and southwest of Shahr-i Sokhta.

The Northern Neolithic. In Kashmir, the earliest settlements with evidence of agriculture and animal husbandry appeared around 3000 BCE, mainly concentrated on the Pleistocene alluvial terraces *(karewas)*. Villages such as Gufkral and Burzahom were made up of partially underground huts: These were pits with plastered walls that were accessed by means of steps or ladders and that probably had conical superstructures supported by central posts. The inhabitants of these villages hunted a range of wild animals but they also kept domestic dogs, sheep, and goats, and cultivated wheat, barley, and various pulses. Although the animals may have been local domesticates, the crops were probably acquired from their western neighbors. These settlements show a shift from a largely hunter-gatherer economy to one dominated by farming by the middle of the Neolithic period. The people of the Northern Neolithic culture made rather coarse gray pottery with mat impressions on the base and tools of bone and polished stone. These included rings of jadeite and distinctive rectangular and half-moon–shaped knives that resemble the harvesting knives used by the Neolithic people of northern China, who also lived in semi-subterranean houses. Burials of dogs at Burzahom were also reminiscent of Chinese and Manchurian practices. Physically, however, the people of Kashmir were related to those of South Asia rather than China or Central Asia, though they may have spoken a Sino-Tibetan language.

Similar pit houses were the norm in other northern areas, in settlements such as Kalako-deray and Loebanr in Swat, and Sarai Khola, Leiah, and possibly Uchali in the northern Punjab. The Swat people used bone tools that are also reminiscent of tools used in northern China. Although each area had somewhat different local traditions, which can be seen in such things as the style of pottery they made, there were also general similarities, suggesting contacts between them. The existence of long-distance contacts is underlined by the discovery of jade beads at Loebanr, since jade came from Central or East Asia. Two Kot Diji pots found at Burzahom, one containing carnelian and agate beads, show that the people of the north were also in contact with Early Indus people, probably when the latter sought raw materials in the mountains.

THE TRANSITION (2600–2500/2450 BCE)

The Early Indus period had seen the agricultural settlement of large parts of the Indus Basin and the emergence of a few settlements that were probably towns. In a short period of around a century or a century and a half from 2600 BCE, these settlements and the society of their inhabitants underwent a radical transformation, resulting in the emergence of the Indus civilization, a complex and highly organized society. Many changes, for example in craft specialization, were more of degree than of kind, but there were also significant innovations and transformations, such as the emergence of writing and the beginning of sea trade. While the transition was complete in some areas by 2500 BC, in others, such as the eastern region, it is probable that the Mature Harappan period started later.

More than three-fifths of Early Indus settlements, such as Balakot, were abandoned during the transition: In Cholistan, for example, only four out of the thirty-seven sites identified continued to be occupied. Many of the excavated towns were destroyed by fire: These included Kot Diji, Amri, Nausharo, and Gumla, though at Kalibangan an earthquake was the probable reason for the town's destruction and abandonment. When these settlements were reoccupied, both local and Mature Harappan pottery styles were in use for a while, suggesting the introduction into the local culture of a new tradition developed elsewhere. At Kunal, a number of hoards were found: One was a collection of silver and gold objects including two silver tiaras and a silver bangle; others contained beads of semiprecious stone and copper and stone tools. Some of these towns were replaced by new settlements in the same location, sometimes in a short period of time, sometimes after two or three generations, but most of the earlier settlements were not reoccupied. Instead, there were a great many new foundations, including more than a hundred and thirty in Cholistan. Those established in Sindh possibly included the great city of Mohenjo-daro. (There is disagreement on the date of the waterlogged earliest levels there, known only from small soundings, though the pottery from the earliest levels is probably of the Kot Diji period.) An important exception to the general pattern was Harappa, which, far from being abandoned, enjoyed continuous development from the Kot Diji period into the Mature Harappan period (also known as the Mature Indus period), during which features characteristic of the Indus civilization gradually emerged.

Many of the new settlements seem to have been constructed according to a plan, with wide, cardinally orientated streets, brick wells and drains, and well-appointed houses using bricks made to a standard size. In the larger settlements, baked brick was frequently used for construction as well as mud brick. Often these settlements had a surrounding wall; for example, a substantial mud brick wall was constructed around Nausharo, which seems to have taken over from Mehrgarh, now abandoned, as the regional center of the Kachi plain. Kalibangan was transformed from a single-walled settlement into a town with an elevated mound (citadel), divided into two walled sectors, and a lower walled town to its east, an arrangement found in a number of other

Indus settlements. In the small settlement of Kunal, the previous pit houses were replaced by rectangular houses of mud brick, some with clay-lined grain silos, and rubbish pits and jars for waste water were provided in the streets. Mohenjo-daro was constructed in part on massive clay and mud brick plat-forms, as a defense against the prevalent risk of flooding. Platforms were also constructed at Harappa and the town underwent considerable growth. At Dholavira in Gujarat, which had seen a small earlier occupation, a massive wall was built to enclose a new planned settlement whose residential area later expanded onto open ground north of the walled settlement. These three settle-ments suggest the emergence during the transition of regional centers, a higher tier in the settlement hierarchy. Another such center was founded at Ganweriwala, sited in the Saraswati Valley equidistant between Mohenjo-daro and Harappa; unfortunately, because this has not been excavated, nothing is known of it except that it attained a size of 80 hectares or more during the fol-lowing Mature Harappan period. Rakhigarhi, located a similar distance from both Harappa and Ganweriwala, was to become the fifth regional center. The excavations there have not distinguished a separate transitional phase, but there is a marked contrast between the Sothi-Siswal settlement and the huge walled settlement of the subsequent Mature Harappan period.

At the same time other signs of greater complexity were emerging. Within these cities and towns the range and sophistication of craft activities greatly in-creased, and there are indications of developing specialization. The development of special craft objects, of exotic or rare materials or of fine or time-consuming workmanship, and the appearance of artifacts ideologically endowed with spe-cial significance reflect increasing status differentiation. New styles and varieties of artifacts appeared, including metal vessels, and bronze came into widespread use. At the same time the various regional styles of pottery and other artifacts were superseded by standardized Mature Harappan products after 2500 BCE. Some regions were less closely integrated: The inhabitants of Saurashtra and the North Gujarat plain (Sorath Harappan) and southern Baluchistan (Kulli culture) maintained their own character, showing some significant differences from the classic Mature Harappan culture in Sindh and other core regions. The rest of the borderlands formed no part of the Indus realms. Kot Dijian material continued in use (Late Kot Diji period) in northern Baluchistan, where Rehman Dheri flour-ished as a regional urban center, and was quite distinct from the culture of the plains. Mundigak became part of the Helmand culture, and the major route through Central Baluchistan, which had linked the Iranian plateau and Turkmenia with the Indus plains, was abandoned.

One of the key developments of this period was the emergence of a writing system. Seals with simple designs had been used in the Early Indus period, when there had also been marks made on pottery: Both are likely to have been connected with administrative or organizational functions. During the transi-tion period, however, this simple range of signs developed into what is gener-ally taken to be a complete writing system. This script was used on seals that now bore an inscription and an image, drawn usually from a limited repertoire of animal representations. An intermediate stage in this development may be seen at Kunal, where six square stamp seals of gray stone were found. These bore a geometric motif but resembled typical Mature Harappan seals in being square with a boss on the back. The development of seals and writing suggests the emerging need for more complex administration and record keeping.

Explaining the Transition

Many features characteristic of the Indus civilization were known by the Early Harappan period in some towns: cardinally orientated streets, baked bricks, substantial walls, skilled and partially specialized craftsmanship, and the rudimentary use of signs to indicate ownership or for administrative purposes. In addition to villages and pastoral camps, there were a number of towns, probably providing goods, services, and organization for the villages in their area. But their influence did not extend far, and regional styles of pottery and other artifacts indicate the existence of a number of different groups and traditions. These interacted with each other and with neighboring cultures in India, Kashmir, and the Iranian plateau. Over a few generations, the majority of settlements were destroyed or abandoned or rebuilt on a greatly expanded scale and to a grander plan, with wide streets, brick drains and wells, and substantial surrounding walls, and the number of settlements increased enormously, most of them being new foundations. In addition to camps, villages, and towns, there were now cities. Urban settlements housed artisans in a widened range of crafts, often practicing more specialized craft skills and engaging full-time in these activities. The simple seals and potters' marks had developed into a writing system, used on seals that were widespread. Regional artifact styles had been largely superseded by uniform and high-quality products throughout the Indus basin, reflecting cultural and possibly political unity. Overland interactions with neighboring cultures increased in some directions, with integrated trade and procurement networks, which were added to and in some areas replaced by overseas trade to Oman and other lands bordering the Gulf.

An understanding of how and why these changes took place is still elusive. The evidence of fiery destruction at many sites has been interpreted by some scholars as the reflection of warfare, although there is no other evidence to support this, such as weaponry among the artifact assemblage. Evidence of violent death might be sought among funerary remains but these are too limited to be helpful.

An alternative explanation is that the deliberate destruction of old settlements and the creation of new ones following certain principles, such as the cardinal orientation of streets and the emphasis on water supply and sanitation, reflect the widespread adoption of a new ideology, which was to underlie the unity and considerable uniformity of the Indus civilization. In this scenario, rather than reflecting enemy action, the destruction by fire of the settlements was an act of ritual or ideological purification. Indeed some scholars suggest that the Indus civilization was not a single state but a collection of smaller independent polities unified by this shared ideology, a hypothesis that has its attractions.

While the widespread rebuilding and relocation of settlements are peculiarities of the Indus Basin, many of the other developments, such as craft specialization, the implied emergence of a social hierarchy, and writing, are features that generally characterize the civilizations that emerged in various parts of the world from the late fourth millennium onward. These features reflect the growth of urban societies based on the production of an agricultural surplus and involved in trade and internal distribution networks to obtain and circulate essential and luxury goods, some of which were emblems of power for the emerging elite or symbols of prestige for the urban centers and their gods.

The stimuli behind the transformation of the cultures of the Indus Basin into an integrated urban civilization are still as much the subject for debate and speculation as they were when the civilization was first discovered.

THE MATURE INDUS CIVILIZATION (2600–1900/1800 BCE)

Whatever the mechanism that brought about the emergence of the Indus civilization, there is no doubt that the society that had crystallized around 2500 BCE was significantly different from that of the Early Harappan period, in scale, organizational and social complexity, cultural uniformity, and ideology or ethos.

The Mature Harappan culture (Indus civilization) was concentrated in the Indus and Saraswati Valleys and stretched from Gujarat in the south and the Makran coast and the Kachi plain in the west to the foothills of the Himalayas and the northern edge of the Ganges-Jamuna doab in the north and east. In the eastern Indus region, Sothi-Siswal material continued in use alongside Mature Harappan artifacts throughout the Indus civilization, suggesting that this region was less strongly integrated into the Indus system or had less wholeheartedly adopted the Indus ideology, and the same was true of local traditions in Saurashtra and northern Gujarat. In inland southern Baluchistan, the Kulli complex, at settlements such as Edith Shahr and Nindowari, was related to but not fully part of the Indus civilization, although to its south, in the Makran coastal region of Baluchistan, settlements such as Sutkagen-dor were Indus towns. The rest of the highland region, however, was no longer politically integrated with the Indus region.

Cities of the Indus

It is possible that Mohenjo-daro was the principal metropolis of the Indus civilization. Centrally located in Sindh between the Indus and Eastern Nara Rivers, with the Punjab to its northeast, the Saraswati to its south and east, Gujarat to its southwest, and the Kachi plain to its west, it was well placed to control communications throughout the Indus realms. It was also the largest settlement by far, its known area exceeding that of Harappa by half as much again. Among the workshops scattered throughout the city or concentrated in the suburbs, there were representatives of all types of industrial activity, and the houses yielded artifacts of every kind manufactured by the Indus people, including many inscribed seals. On its citadel was constructed a unique feature, the Great Bath, a large watertight basin set in the center of a complex of rooms and plausibly interpreted as a religious structure, related to a water-centered cult.

Harappa was also a great city, with a similar range of industries and similar signs of affluence. It lay near the edge of the Indus lands in the Punjab where it could control access to the resources of the Himalayas. The other major cities that have been identified were also situated toward the edges of the Indus domains: Rakhighari in the east, Ganweriwala in the center of the Saraswati Valley, and Dholavira in Gujarat. Of these Ganweriwala is known only from surface traces, and excavations at Rakhighari have been limited, but extensive investigations at Dholavira have provided valuable evidence of the development of the city through time, its size gradually increasing and its citadel becoming more complex. Where Mohenjo-daro relied on a large number of wells for domestic water, Dholavira had massive reservoirs. Many other differences as well as similarities between these cities underline two principal characteristics of Indus civilization: on the one hand a strong and uniform cultural pattern that produced the same range of artifacts, the same types of houses, the same civic arrangement of separate walled mounds, in each city and town; on the other hand, a huge diversity in the way the urban layout was effected and in other fundamental aspects of life.

Probably most striking is the range of religious structures and presumably practices to be found in Indus cities in different areas, perhaps reflecting the diverse origins of the Indus people. Although the Great Bath at Mohenjo-daro was unique, bathrooms were ubiquitous, suggesting that ritual bathing played a part in the lives of Indus people as it has in the lives of later South Asians. A possible temple has also been identified at Mohenjo-daro, perhaps housing a sacred tree. In contrast, in a number of cities there were fire altars and places of animal sacrifice, sometimes only in a public place while in other cases there were also domestic shrines of this type. One might surmise that the Indus civilization was a federal and multicultural state, united by a common ideology that brought together a patchwork of communities with different cultural, and quite probably ethnic, backgrounds.

Town and Country

In addition to the five cities, many towns shared features of the urban layout such as the division into separate walled mounds or areas, the efficient drainage system, and the well-built houses. Often these towns had substantial industrial areas, producing a range of artifacts, and they were well supplied with the high-caliber standardized craft products characteristic of the Indus civilization. These included fine pottery, tools of high-quality flint, a range of generally simple metal artifacts, many charming terra-cotta figurines of humans and animals, inscribed seals, and a great variety of personal ornaments made of shell, gemstones, metals, and several manufactured materials including faience. In addition there must have been many fine products in materials that have perished but of which a few tantalizing traces survive, such as wood and textiles.

A small stone-lined tank in the castle (the upper half of the citadel) at Dholavira. This may have been used for bathing, perhaps in a ritual context. The round stone on the bottom may have been a seat or to help the bather step into and out of the basin. On one side is an inlet chute to supply the water. (Namit Arora)

There were also smaller settlements that specialized in particular craft activities based on locally procured materials, such as Nageshwar in Gujarat, which was devoted to the production of artifacts from local marine shells, fished in the nearby waters of the Gulf of Kutch.

The majority of the Indus people, however, were farmers or pastoralists. Few of their settlements have been excavated, but these few indicate that even the ordinary farmer probably had access to good-quality craft products. Arable farmers dwelt in small permanent villages, and there were also temporary seasonal settlements occupied by pastoralists in the areas where they took their animals for seasonal grazing. It is likely that, as today, pastoralists also acted as carriers for the transport of goods.

While the agriculture of the Indus civilization was based mainly on barley, wheat, and pulses as in earlier times, other crops, notably rice and various millets, were also grown in some regions of the Indus realm, particularly Gujarat and the eastern periphery, and especially after 2000 BCE.

Trade and Communications

Some communications within the Indus-Saraswati region were over land, using bullock carts for short journeys and the animals of pastoral nomads as beasts of burden over longer distances. Bulky goods, however, were more easily transported by water, along the rivers and around the coasts. Many of the raw materials needed by the Indus people could be obtained in the regions controlled by the Indus civilization: flint from the Rohri Hills, carnelian and agate from southern Gujarat, gold dust from the upper reaches of the rivers, timber from the Punjab and Gujarat, and clays from most areas, while textiles could be made from the cotton grown by the farmers, possibly wool from the pastoralists' sheep, and probably the hair from their goats, as well as leather. Other materials were obtained from the inhabitants of neighboring regions: copper and possibly tin ores from the Jodhpura-Ganeshwar culture of the Aravalli Hills; ivory, honey, and other forest products from the hunter-gatherers who ranged through the arid areas to the south of the Indus-Saraswati region; and probably other materials from settled neighbors such as the Kayatha culture.

In the early third millennium, the inhabitants of the Indus region had participated in the trading networks that operated across the Iranian plateau. With the emergence of the Indus civilization, however, came a major change. Seagoing boats were now constructed and Indus merchants sailed through the Gulf to trade directly with the inhabitants of Oman and eventually with Bahrain and the cities of southern Mesopotamia. While there is little evidence of the ships themselves and nothing is known of their antecedents, the fact that Indus merchants are known to have traveled to Mesopotamia, while Mesopotamian ships did not venture outside the confines of the Gulf, suggests that the development of seaworthy vessels was an Indus innovation.

The Indus people also established a trading outpost at Shortugai in Afghanistan, allowing them to monopolize the supply of lapis lazuli to Mesopotamia. Many settlements in this region and in northern Iran have yielded Indus material. But while the Mesopotamian texts attest to the importation of a range of Indus raw materials, and Indus beads are well known from Mesopotamian excavations, it is difficult to establish just what the Indus people obtained in exchange.

Neighbors to the West

Late Kot Diji. The northern parts of the Indo-Iranian borderlands, the Gomal Valley, with the towns of Rehman Dheri and Gumla, and the Bannu Basin, with settlements such as Taraqai Qila and Lewan, were not incorporated into the Indus realms. Here a late version of the Kot Diji material was in use and Mature Harappan pottery was absent, although there were other types of Indus artifacts, such as toy carts, beads, and, most significantly, weights. Some interaction must therefore have occurred between the Indus civilization and the inhabitants of these regions, presumably for trade. The same may be true of Sarai Khola in the Taxila Valley.

Helmand Culture. During the transitional phase of Harappan development, the Kandahar Valley, with its large town of Mundigak, had become incorporated into the flourishing culture of the Helmand Basin (Seistan), which by this time may have been a state. Helmand's city at Shahr-i Sokhta grew to around 150 hectares by 2400 BCE, including a cemetery, separate from the rest of the city, which covered 21 hectares. Mundigak became the state's second center, dominating the eastern part of state; it grew to around 60 hectares in size.

Craft production was now concentrated in a substantial artisans' quarter of around 30–40 hectares in the west and south of Shahr-i Sokhta. Here many materials were worked including copper, alabaster, chlorite, flint, and marine shell. Pottery, thrown on the fast wheel and generally undecorated, was made on an industrial scale in factory workshops, associated with fifty to a hundred kilns. Metal was also worked on an industrial scale. In contrast, other crafts were undertaken in small workshops of one or two rooms. High-value imported materials such as turquoise were made into jewelry in different workshops from those working local materials. Shahr-i Sokhta continued to play an important part in international trade, having links with Turkmenia to its north and Oman to its south, but the earlier connections between this region and the Indus valley were apparently severed.

Monumental buildings were constructed on high mounds of mud brick masonry in both cities, the House of the Foundations in the Eastern Residential quarter and the large enclosure building in the Central Quarters at Shahr-i Sokhta, and at Mundigak the "temple" and the "palace," whose terraced summit had a façade of mud brick pillars surmounted by a brick frieze. Mud brick was generally used in the architecture of the two sites, though the Mundigak temple had limestone foundations. Domestic architecture was also in mud brick: many substantial houses had six or eight rooms. The many compartmented seals found at Shahr-i Sokhta seem to have been used principally to stamp sealings used to "lock" doors.

Kulli. In contrast to the Helmand culture, which had little evidence of links with the Indus region, the Kulli culture in southern Baluchistan was closely integrated with the Harappan civilization. Kulli pottery shared many forms with the Harappan repertoire but also included distinctive shapes such as canisters and maintained the earlier tradition of painted zoomorphic decoration. The designs now included wide-eyed elongated animals, especially zebus, as well as fish, bird, and plant motifs such as pipal leaves. The Kulli people also made distinctive human and animal figurines, particularly bulls with painted decoration. Some imported Indus material was present, including model carts. Finds of an Indus weight at Mehi and Indus seals at Nindowari underline the close degree of interaction between the Indus civilization and the Kulli culture.

Several of the major Kulli sites had substantial architecture. At Nindowari, a terraced series of platforms led up to a monumental platform at the summit with a drain in it. Similar structures were built at Edith Shahr. A number of the larger settlements were fortified. Unlike the Indus settlements, the architecture in this region was of stone walls and stone-flagged floors, reflecting the locally available building material, though boulders used at Kulli itself were brought there from 3 kilometers away. Curiously, some of the rooms had their doorways in the corner, a structurally unsound arrangement. Nindowari and Kulli had structures that may have been granaries. In one room at Nindowari, 173 animal and 28 human figurines were found: This was perhaps a shrine.

A staircase at Kariya Buthi, a Kulli settlement on the Hab River. Kulli towns were often built on elevated and terraced ground; staircases gave access to the higher areas of the settlement. The Kulli culture played an important role in Harappan trade. (Ute Franke-Vogt)

Generally the settlements of the Kulli culture were located to take advantage of the limited available agricultural land, which was cultivated using various types of irrigation works such as dams and gabarbands. Dates and fish were of considerable importance, but pastoralism was probably the main way of life. Kulli settlements were also well placed with respect to the routes traversing this terrain, linking the coast with the highlands and the Kachi and Indus plains. Some were also located near sources of minerals such as copper ore. It is possible that the Kulli people supplied the Harappans with raw materials and were carriers for Harappan trade during their seasonal pastoral movements.

While the Kulli material is characteristic of the inland areas of southern Baluchistan, the classic Mature Harappan culture was spread along the coastal region where a number of important sites were established, notably Sutkagendor, the most westerly Indus town, which may have been a fortified outpost controlling or guarding coastal traffic, since it had strong walls with towers and a fortified gateway. It is likely that these sites were established as outposts related to the Harappans' Gulf sea trade.

Neighbors to the South

Jodhpura-Ganeshwar. The Harappans obtained some and probably a significant proportion of the copper ore they used from the Khetri region of the Aravalli hills, south of Cholistan. This region was occupied by a culture named after two of its settlements: Jodhpura and Ganeshwar. The people of the Jodhpura-Ganeshwar culture were in the main hunters, gatherers, and fishers, but they also exploited local copper ore. Other metal ores available in the Aravallis and the adjacent Tosham region included lead, zinc, and tin, and it is possible that the tin was also exploited, although there is no evidence of this. Evidence of copper mining and smelting in this region goes back as far as the late fourth millennium, and by the Early Harappan period the Jodhpura-Ganeshwar people were manufacturing large quantities of small copper objects, which they traded with neighboring groups. As in the Early Harappan period, the Jodhpura-Ganeshwar red pottery shows signs of Harappan influence.

Ahar-Banas. The Ahar-Banas culture continued in the area to the southwest of the Jodhpura-Ganeshwar culture, with whom they were in communication. Limited, and possibly indirect, contact with the Harappans is shown by the presence at Ahar of six Indus beads, one of lapis lazuli and five of carnelian. The Ahar-Banas people lived in settlements, such as Ahar, Balathal, and Gilund, made up of substantial rectangular houses of stone, wattle and daub, and mud brick, with flat thatched or earth-covered roofs; at Balathal, stone was quarried locally to build house foundations. Larger houses were divided into several rooms and often there was a kitchen area with a built hearth (*chulah*) and a saddle quern. The Ahar-Banas people practiced farming, growing millets, wheat, barley, and pulses; raising cattle and other animals; and exploiting local wild resources such as deer, peafowl, fish, and snails. The importance of cattle is reflected in their production of cattle figurines.

Kayatha. Other farming settlements appeared during the later third millennium farther to the south, in Madhya Pradesh, east of Gujarat and north of the Narmada River. These belonged to the Kayatha culture, best-known from the settlement at Kayatha. People here made microliths and blades of chalcedony and also used copper axes, bangles, and other objects, either locally made or obtained from the Jodhpura-Ganeshwar culture. They made various styles of plain and painted pottery, possibly inspired by Harappan pottery. Caches of carnelian, agate, and steatite beads probably reflect contacts with the Harappans in Gujarat to the west, perhaps related to the exploitation of local carnelian and agate sources. After 2100 BCE, some of the pottery styles present there, such as white-painted Black-and-Red ware, indicate contacts with the Ahar-Banas culture. Terra-cotta figurines of bulls are also known at Kayatha from this period.

Hunter-Gatherers. Bagor in Rajathan had been occupied for several millennia by hunter-gatherers who also herded domestic sheep, goats, and cattle. After 2800 BCE they began making pottery, which had some similarities to the ceramics of their neighbors, the Ahar-Banas and Kayatha cultures, though the Bagor pots were of much poorer quality. Two arrowheads, a ribbed spearhead, and an awl, all of copper, and a necklace of beads, including some of banded agate and carnelian, are known from a burial of this period. The arrowheads were probably made by the Jodhpura-Ganeshwar culture but may have reached the inhabitants of Bagor through trade with the Harappans in Gujarat, perhaps along with the beads, in exchange for the kind of goods to which hunter-gatherers had access, such as game and ivory. Similar evidence comes from Langnaj, a hunter-gatherer settlement in northern Gujarat, where a copper knife and dentalium beads suggest contacts with the Harappans.

Southern Neolithic. Recently discovered evidence from Karnataka in South India indicates that there were settled communities in this region by the early third millennium, occupying cleared and leveled sites on granite hills, where they constructed round huts of timber posts, wattle, and daub. They also constructed large wooden stockades (ash mounds) on open ground, where they penned locally domesticated cattle, periodically setting fire to the pens to destroy the dung, perhaps to prevent disease. The central importance of cattle is reflected in the large numbers of terra-cotta figurines of cattle and the depictions of cattle in the rock art of the region, which is mainly Neolithic in date. These people began to cultivate local food plants, including several varieties of millet and pulse, as well as growing or gathering tubers; through time, the latter declined in importance in favor of millets. They made poorly fired gray pottery and stone tools, including many ground stone axes. Some of the settlements were in the important gold-bearing regions, suggesting that local gold may have been utilized at this time. If so, it is possible that gold from this region eventually reached the Indus civilization.

Mysteries of the Indus State

A prominent feature of most civilizations is evidence of the ruling elite: palatial residences, rich burials, unique luxury products, and propaganda such as monumental inscriptions and portrait statuary or reliefs. Strikingly, these are all absent from the Indus civilization. This poses the questions of how the Indus state was organized politically, whether there were rulers, and, if so, why they are archaeologically invisible. Another striking contrast between the Indus and other ancient civilizations is the apparent absence from the Indus civilization of any evidence of conflict. Though the cities were surrounded by massive walls, these seem to have been defenses against flooding rather than against hostile people, as well as barriers to control the flow of people and goods, and they were probably designed also to impress. Weapons are absent, as are signs of violent destruction during the civilization's heyday. An entirely peaceful state seems anomalous in the history of world civilization.

Writing is another characteristic feature of civilizations. The Harappans used inscribed seals, and a small range of other objects also bear signs from their script. The paucity of these inscribed materials and the brevity of the inscriptions means that the script has not been deciphered: neither the meaning of the signs nor the language they convey can yet be worked out. It is generally assumed that a greater range of Harappan texts existed on perishable materials, such as palm leaves, and that these included the records used by the Harappan authorities in the running of the state. However, a recent suggestion that no such records had once existed and that the Harappan signs do not actually constitute a script raises further intriguing questions about how the Indus state could have functioned.

THE POSTURBAN (LATE HARAPPAN) PERIOD (1900/1800–1300 BCE)

The Indus civilization flourished for around five hundred to seven hundred years, and in the early second millennium it disintegrated. This collapse was marked by the disappearance of the features that had distinguished the Indus civilization from its predecessors: writing, city dwelling, some kind of central control, international trade, occupational specialization, and widely distributed standardized artifacts. In the post-Indus period, local materials were used for objects like stone tools, and the cultural uniformity of the Mature Indus civilization gave way to a number of regional groupings, often using material reminiscent of that belonging to the Early Indus phase in each area. While there was considerable depopulation in the Indus heartland, settlements increased in number in Gujarat, and Late Harappan communities were established in areas well outside those occupied by the Mature Harappan people, particularly in the east. While sea trade now only reached the inhabitants of Gujarat, the wide distribution of many cultural elements (such as features of ceramic form and decoration, and distinctive stamp seals) indicates that there was considerable interregional communication, and movements of individuals and groups both within the subcontinent and between it and the regions to its north and west.

Urban Decay

At Mohenjo-daro, the last period of occupation of the city shows a serious decline in civic standards, with poorly constructed houses, pottery kilns in what had previously been residential areas, the neglect of civic amenities such as drains, and corpses thrown into abandoned houses or streets instead of being buried with due rites. Important public buildings such as the Great Bath went out of use. Some stone sculptures were deliberately broken. A similar situation is known in many cities and towns, and others were abandoned altogether. The central region saw a massive reduction in the density of settlement, and, throughout the greater Indus region, the majority of settlements were villages and campsites, with a few small towns, though in both Gujarat and the east the number of settlements increased dramatically. This seems to imply either that emigration from the center

A burial urn from the Late Harappan cemetery at Harappa (Cemetery H). The painted frieze around the urn's shoulder shows the characteristic blend of earlier Harappan motifs, like the peacock, with new designs, such as wavy lines. The depiction of the peacock, apparently in flight, is also quite different from the way it was represented in the Harappan style. (Harappa Archaeological Research Project, Courtesy Department of Archaeology and Museums, Government of Pakistan)

to the outer regions occurred or that there were conditions favoring population growth in the peripheries and a demographic crash in the center, or both.

At the same time many of the characteristic features of urban life and organization declined and disappeared. Writing was no longer used, though occasionally signs were scratched as graffiti on pottery. Cubical weights became rare or ceased to be used, indicating that metrical controls were no longer needed.

One reason for this urban decay may have been the poor health of the citizens. Studies of the skeletons from Mohenjo-daro's upper levels show that many individuals had suffered and often died from disease, including malaria. Both malaria and cholera are likely to have been associated particularly with life in the Indus towns and cities, with their abundance of clean and foul water in wells, water tanks, and drains.

Economic Developments

In the early second millennium, many cities in southern Mesopotamia declined or were abandoned, due mainly to the salinization of the soil. The focus of power shifted farther north, to the Babylon region (northern Babylonia), and traders greatly reduced the scale of their operations in the Gulf, eventually turning instead to trade routes through the Iranian plateau and sources of raw materials in Anatolia and the Mediterranean. Whether the steep decline in Mesopotamian trade could have seriously affected the economy of the Indus civilization, however, is unknown. Other factors in the decline of the civilization may have included the beginning of the drying up of the Saraswati River, which sustained the densest area of Harappan settlement. This is reflected in the depopulation of Cholistan during the early second millennium and the increase in settlements in the regions to the east.

At much the same time there were significant agricultural developments. Mature Harappan agriculture had been based on the West Asian group of domesticates, which were utilized across the huge area from the Indus region to Western Europe: wheat, barley, and pulses, sheep, goat, and cattle. By the late third or very early second millennium, new crops were coming under cultivation in the Indus realms: rice and several varieties of millet. These were better suited for cultivation in much of India than wheat and barley, and so they both changed the productivity of some of the areas already under cultivation and opened up new areas for productive agriculture.

Late Harappan Cultures in the West

Jhukar. In the early second millennium, a number of settlements in Sindh were abandoned, including Balakot, Allahdino, and Mohenjo-daro. The latest surviving levels at Mohenjo-daro saw squatter occupations in some dilapidated houses. Among the objects found there are a few stray artifacts that seem alien in style: a copper shaft hole axe-adze of Iranian or Central Asian design and several daggers with midribs and holes where they had been riveted to metal handles. Similar objects are known at Chanhu-daro, Amri, and Jhukar, including shaft hole axes, copper pins with decorated heads, and round or occasionally square compartmented stamp seals bearing geometric designs, including one resembling a radiating sun or Catherine wheel. These indicate that there were significant contacts between Sindh and the cultures west of the mountains in Iran and Turkmenia, whether through trade or the arrival of immigrants. These objects were associated with a style of pottery named after the site of Jhukar, a buff ware with painted designs, with similarities to the Early Indus Amri ware. This pottery can be seen to have developed from that of the Harappan period, as can many of the artifacts at these and other contemporary sites in Sindh, though there seems to have been a steady decline in their quality. Though there was no break between the Mature Harappan and Jhukar occupations in these settlements, there was a marked decline in the standard of living, with inferior houses built from salvaged bricks and no attempt to follow the earlier planned street layouts. Hoards of concealed jewelry and metal objects have been found at Mohenjo-daro and Chanhu-daro, suggesting a prevalent feeling of insecurity. In the latter town, unfinished craft objects suggest the hasty abandonment of activities in the face of danger. There are, however, no signs of the violent destruction that have been found in many sites farther west, in Baluchistan and eastern Iran.

Gujarat. In Gujarat the transition to Late Harappan began early, perhaps by 2100 BCE. This region had always maintained a degree of local distinctiveness: for example, pottery styles characteristic of the Early and pre-Harappan periods, such as Prabhas ware, continued in use alongside Mature Harappan pottery. Sites like Lothal had been fully integrated members of the Indus ecumene; others, such as Somnath, less so. By the end of the third millennium, however, even previously well integrated sites such as Lothal were beginning to drop out of the Mature Harappan way of life. Instead of high-quality flint brought in from the Rohri Hills in Sindh, stone tools were now made of local stone such as jasper and agate. Mature Harappan pottery declined in quantity and was replaced by an increased quantity of traditional local wares, such as Prabhas ware, and by new wares, in particular Lustrous Red ware, a bright red ceramic that became dominant in Gujarat sites like Rangpur during the early second millennium and that was later also used farther afield in the Deccan, reflecting trade, population movement, or both.

Other typical Mature Harappan material, such as stone weights, inscribed seals, and even beads, disappeared. In contrast, copper continued in use, perhaps reflecting the development of close trading relations with the Chalcolithic cultures to the east of Gujarat, Ahar-Banas, Jodhpura-Ganeshwar, and Malwa. Significantly, a number of the copper objects are of types known not in the Indus civilization but in the Chalcolthic cultures of Rajasthan and the Deccan.

The regional city of Dholavira declined and was then abandoned. It was re-occupied after perhaps fifty years as a small settlement of poor-quality houses that lasted for about a century before again being deserted. At many sites, such as Rangpur, brick architecture was abandoned in favor of other styles of con-struction: wattle and daub with a wooden framework, or stone foundations on which walls were built of mud, and in most cases thatched roofs. The construc-tion of bathrooms and drains ceased. The warehouses at Lothal went out of use. Nevertheless, this did not reflect a decline so much as a change of empha-sis, away from the urban aspects of the Indus civilization and toward a more rural way of life. This is well illustrated by Rojdi, a large farming village, where period IC (ca. 1900–1700 BCE) saw a great expansion of the settled area (perhaps a tripling in size), apparently involving planned rather than haphaz-ard development, and the construction of a substantial wall with a large gate strengthened by buttresses.

In addition to the expansion of some previously occupied settlements, the earlier half of the second millennium saw a very considerable increase in the number of settlements in Gujarat. This probably reflects the change to new crops: Mature Harappan agriculture had used wheat and barley as the staple crops and in Gujarat native millets had also been important; now bajra and jowar, drought-resistant millets that were high yielding, free threshing, and well suited to the environment of Saurashra, became increasingly important. Rice may also have been cultivated at some sites, such as Rangpur.

Trade. The Late Harappan period saw the abandonment of Harappan settle-ments in the Makran, such as Sutkagen-dor, due to falling sealevels, which also affected some sites in Gujarat, including Lothal and Kuntasi. Patterns of sea trade through the Gulf altered as Mesopotamia experienced political and economic upheavals from around 2000 BCE, causing a major retraction in its trade. Gujarat no longer acted as the entry point for sea trade on behalf of the whole Indus region. This did not mean the complete cessation of sea trade, however. Bet Dwarka, a settlement now under water off the coast of Saurashtra, may have been established in the early second millennium as a port serving the communities of Saurashtra or Gujarat as a whole.

Neighbors to the East and South

Ahar-Banas Culture. Sizable communities had developed in the Ahar-Banas culture in western Rajasthan by the early second millennium, and some may by this time have been towns. Substantial traces of copper slag show that the inhabitants of Ahar were engaged in large-scale industrial activities. A stone and mud brick wall was built around the inner part of the Balathal settlement, thought to contain the residence of the settlement's leader. Elsewhere in the settlement was a complex of residential rooms and workshops, including a kiln, and another complex that may have been used for storage and food processing as well as housing. Ojiyana, a recently discovered site, was surrounded by a substantial wall within which was a network of streets oriented east-west.

Lustrous Red ware and white-painted Black-and-Red ware are among the styles of pottery found in the Ahar-Banas settlements, along with a large number of figurines of zebu cattle; Lustrous Red ware demonstrates a link with the Late Harappan settlements to the southwest in Gujarat, for example at Rangpur. The range of crops under cultivation by the Ahar-Banas people now included rice, jowar, and bajra, as in Gujarat.

Gilund, currently under excavation, included a substantial building subdivided by crosswalls into rectangular cells that contained pits and clay bins: The building seems to have been used for storage and may have been a community facility under the control of the town's leader. One bin contained more than a hundred clay impressions of seals, which suggest some degree of bureaucratic control and management. The impressions are remarkably similar to the geometric designs of seals used by the people of the Bactria-Margiana Archaeological Complex (BMAC), providing startling new support for the indications of contacts and perhaps the movement of people from this Central Asian culture. Others resemble Jhukar seals from Chanhu-daro and different seals from Pirak and Nindowari. Button seals in Jhukar style have also been recovered from Gilund. This gives added support to the picture of considerable cultural interactivity, exchanges, and probably the movement of small groups of people throughout the region from Central Asia to Central India.

Malwa and the Deccan. Settlements of farmers—growing wheat, ragi, and pulses; raising cattle, sheep, goats, and pigs; and hunting local game such as deer—were established at Navdatoli and other sites in Malwa during the late third millennium. This Malwa culture also included Nagda and other sites of the earlier Kayatha culture, as well as Eran farther to the east. The distinctive dark-painted pottery included jugs with long spouts and channel-spouted bowls. Stone tools and beads were very common, and there were also tools and ornaments in copper, including axes resembling those made by the Jodhpura-Ganeshwar culture. Rectangular and circular houses were accompanied by smaller buildings for storing agricultural produce. Substantial mud brick walls surrounded some of the settlements, including Nagda and Eran.

Farther south in Maharashtra, settlements of the Savalda culture may also have been established during the late third millennium. The best-known settlement is Daimabad, a farming village whose inhabitants grew wheat, barley, and pulses. At another site, Kaothe, which may be a seasonal pastoralists' camp, bajra probably of this period has been found, showing that this was also grown. The Savalda occupation at Daimabad was succeeded by a period in which Late Harappan material was prominent, including red pottery in typical Harappan shapes, two button seals said to bear Indus signs, and a burial in a grave lined with mud bricks in the standard Indus ratio. A hoard of four solid cast copper figures—a buffalo, an elephant, a rhino, and a man driving a chariot—may belong to this period, although they were discovered outside the site in circumstances that made their context impossible to establish, and they have no parallels in the Indus civilization. Copper slag indicates that there was a local metallurgical industry, which continued through the next phase, in which Late Harappan material disappeared. Finally around 1800 BCE Daimabad became incorporated into the Malwa culture, which now extended south as far as Sonegaon.

Southern Neolithic. The cattle-keeping farmers of the south, in Karnataka and Andhra Pradesh, had grown a range of local crops during the third millennium. From around 1800 BCE, however, they also began cultivating wheat, barley, hyacinth bean, ragi, and bajra, as well as cotton and linseed, suggesting that they were in trading contact with the Malwa culture to their north. Malwa-style urn burials at Watgal confirm this link. It is probable that the technology of copper working was also introduced from farther north, since from this period onward a few copper artifacts began to appear in Southern Neolithic settlements. A small number of gold objects show that the important local sources of this metal were by now being exploited.

Developments in the Northwest

Helmand. Around 2200 BCE, Shahr-i Sokhta and Mundigak went into decline, both shrinking very significantly in area. Both suffered attacks during this period: Mundigak was temporarily abandoned, then briefly reoccupied before being finally abandoned. At Shahr-i Sokhta, the Burnt Building, a large mud brick structure built around a courtyard, which was perhaps a palace, was destroyed by fire: A bronze spearhead and an unburied body have been found among the debris. The settlement was reoccupied by squatters but abandoned around 1800 BCE. This coincided with a similar decline in Turkmenia where prosperous Bronze Age towns such as Altyn-depe and Namazga also shrank very considerably, as did the area of the Namazga culture to which they belonged.

The decline in Seistan and Turkmenia coincided with a global climatic change that is thought to have taken place around 2200 BCE. Evidence from sources as far apart as the Oman seabed, Tell Leilan in northern Mesopotamia, and the Greenland ice sheets seems to indicate that a period of severe drought across a region from the eastern Mediterranean through much of Asia took hold around 2200 BCE and lasted for around three hundred years. Its effects were felt globally, with frequent El Niños in South America affecting the monsoon rains and bringing drought to many parts of Asia. Reduced rainfall would have been critical in marginal regions like Seistan, where agricultural potential was precariously balanced; the Indus region, dependent less on monsoon rainfall than on snowmelt-fed rivers, was largely unaffected at first, although in the longer term some Indus regions may have suffered.

Bactria-Margiana Archaeological Complex (BMAC). In the same period, from around 2200 BCE, however, a new culture, the Bactria-Margiana Archaeological Complex, or BMAC, was developing in northern Afghanistan. This may reflect a migration eastward from the Namazga settlement area in southern Turkmenia. The new settlements appeared first in the Murghab delta in Margiana and gradually extended into other oases of the region. They were established along small rivers, where their inhabitants reared domestic animals and used floodwater and canal irrigation to raise crops. Associated material shows a high level of craftsmanship, with fine-quality, undecorated wheel-thrown pottery and with abundant metalwork, including many weapons and stone and bronze filigree seals. A fortified settlement dominated each region: These were either rectangular or square, around a hectare in area, and enclosed in a massive mud brick wall with towers. This culture spread into adjacent regions to the west and south, occupying the areas formerly of the Helmand culture and the urban cultures of Turkmenia. At the Indus trading outpost of Shortugai, Bactrian material was present during the last period of Indus occupation, when lapis lazuli processing ceased; in the subsequent period the settlement became part of the BMAC. By 1700 BCE the distinctive BMAC material was no longer present in its core region in the Amu-Darya (Oxus) region but was known in areas farther west and east, including Baluchistan and India.

Baluchistan and the Kachi Plain. The Indo-Iranian borderlands seem to have experienced considerable disruption in the early to middle second millennium. A number of settlements were destroyed by fire, including Rana Ghundai and Dabarkot, the latter apparently on four occasions. Gumla was destroyed and abandoned, and later burials were dug into its ruins. Many settlements in Baluchistan were apparently abandoned in the second millennium, and much of the material of this period recovered from the region is in the form of stray objects or burials with material that is linked stylistically with the BMAC and regions to its north. Burials near the earlier settlement of Mehrgarh (Mehrgarh South Cemetery) fitted this pattern, containing plain gray pottery and metal objects paralleled in north Afghanistan or southern Turkmenia. Material from a small settlement at nearby Sibri was similar, including BMAC-style compartmented seals and flat violin-shaped figurines.

The best-known site of this period, however, is Pirak. Here a large settlement was established around 1700 BCE. The houses were very different from those of the Indus Valley; they were rectangular, often multiroomed, structures of mud brick, and lines of niches were set into the inside of the walls. A brick platform held the hearth, and reed matting covered the floor. Silos were used to store the grain grown there, which comprised wheat, barley, jowar, and rice.

Material from the settlement included handmade pottery decorated with painted bands of geometric patterns, compartmented seals like those from the

BMAC, many copper or bronze objects, and terra-cotta figurines depicting camels and horses. In the succeeding period, the figurines also show horses with human riders. Many bones of both horses and camels have also been recovered from the settlement. Domestic Bactrian camels were kept in earlier times in Turkmenia and at Shahr-i Sokhta. Horses had been domesticated in the Eurasian steppe around 4000 BCE but did not reach the Indo-Iranian region until the second millennium; the Pirak specimens are the earliest securely dated and indubitable evidence of these domestic animals in the subcontinent. Despite the new features at Pirak, however, there was also material showing continuity with local traditions.

Gandhara Grave Complex. In the valleys of Swat and the extreme northwest, where long-established routes led through the mountains to northern Iran and Central Asia, the period after 2000 BCE saw the emergence of distinctive new burial rites associated with settlements such as Ghaligai, Loebanr, and Kalakoderay. Collectively these are known as the Gandhara Grave Complex. The funerary rites are distinguished by their diversity and by their regional and chronological variation. They included cremation and complete and fractional inhumation. Complete bodies were placed on their backs with their knees bent, in pits capped with stone slabs and sometimes lined with drystone walling. People were generally buried singly or in pairs. Children were sometimes interred in small slab cists. Cremated bones were placed in pottery cists or urns, some with pinched and cut-out decoration in the form of a face, or directly in the grave. The associated grave goods included pottery, violin-shaped human figurines, and metal objects, especially pins with elaborate heads. Many of these were closely similar to artifacts from sites in northern Iran, the BMAC, and the Caucasus, and it is thought that this reflects the arrival of numerous small groups of immigrants over the course of the second millennium. This is supported by the presence of horses in a few graves and by depictions of horses on pottery.

Despite these foreign elements, there was also continuity, with settlements of pit houses whose inhabitants practiced mixed farming, though at some sites rice was now grown as well as wheat and barley, and grapes as well as pulses. Links continued with the Taxila Valley to the south, and with Kashmir where rice cultivation also began and a few copper objects now appeared.

Late Harappans in the North and East

Cemetery H. In the late levels at Harappa, there were some signs of urban decay, though these were less marked than at Mohenjo-daro. Drains were no longer properly maintained. Some buildings were constructed of reused bricks. Concealed hoards of valuables suggest a degree of urban unrest. Other signs of urban decline include animals left unburied in the streets and a corpse left (or concealed?) in a building rather than decently interred. Nevertheless there continued to be a thriving occupation at Harappa. Many buildings were constructed of new bricks. Contemporary with this period was the use of Cemetery H where in the lower level (period II) graves contained extended inhumations with both typical Harappan pottery and some innovations: new shapes and a new style of decoration. In the upper level of the cemetery, however, a new rite appears: urns containing the collected bones of individuals who had generally been cremated, along with pottery in a new style, named Cemetery H after the graveyard. Physical analysis of these bones suggests that they belonged to people different from the earlier inhabitants of the city. Cemetery H pottery appears to be a hybrid style in which both new and Harappan forms were made, often largely plain, with a single band or frieze of painted decoration. Many of the motifs used in the decoration, such as peacocks, animals, and pipal leaves, were familiar, while others, such as stars, dotted rings, wavy lines, and people with long streaming locks of wavy hair, were new. Parallels for some of the shapes and designs occur in the general BMAC area, in northern Iran and northern Afghanistan. Cemetery H pottery is also found associated with the Late Harappan occupation at Harappa (period 5, 1900–1300 BCE), a time when occupation of the city seems to have increased in density, producing overcrowding. Cemetery H pottery is widely distributed in the eastern Punjab and farther east, and it is known as far north as Swat; Harappa lies near the western edge of its distribution.

This period also saw a marked decrease in the use of imported materials, such as marine shells, turquoise, and lapis lazuli, in the northern and eastern Harappan regions. At the same time, however, faience became increasingly common as a material for manufacturing jewelry in these regions and in the villages of the Late Harappan settlers farther east, in the Ganges-Yamuna doab. A bead from a hoard at Harappa, dated around 1700 BCE, was made of brown glass, the earliest known example of glass in South Asia. A new form of kiln appeared at Harappa in the Cemetery H period, another indication that technology was developing rather than declining.

Sothi-Siswal/Late Harappan. The Late Harappan period in the eastern region saw a gradual spread of settlement south and east into the Ganges-Yamuna doab, though none crossed the Ganges to its eastern bank. Settlements in this eastern region included some sites, such as Mitathal and Ropar, that had been occupied earlier (Mitathal, for instance, had been founded in the Early Harappan period) and others, such as Bara, that were new foundations. This spread went hand in hand with a gradual decline in the density of settlement from west to east. One of the principal factors in this southeastward ripple of settlement was the decline in the waters carried by the rivers of the Saraswati system; another was the increasing importance of rice, which, unlike wheat and barley, was well suited to cultivation in the lands being colonized.

The pottery produced in Late Harappan settlements in this region is said to display features of form, decoration, and fabric derived from many sources, including Mature Harappan, Sothi-Siswal, Jodhpura-Ganeshwar, Cemetery H, and Jhukar wares and even Iranian wares. Other materials in these settlements include copper artifacts. Houses were generally rectangular and were constructed of mud bricks.

OCP/Copper Hoards. Early archaeological investigations in Rajasthan and the Ganges-Yamuna doab often uncovered small sherds of a friable badly damaged ware that was described as Ochre-Colored Pottery (OCP), from which an

Although there were signs of civic decay at Harappa in the Posturban period, it was still a time of innovation and vibrancy, as is demonstrated by the production of glass, a considerable technological advance. This bead is the earliest glass object known from the subcontinent. (Harappa Archaeological Research Project, Courtesy Department of Archaeology and Museums, Government of Pakistan)

otherwise unknown culture took its name. A number of caches of distinctive copper artifacts, including antenna-hilted swords, anthropomorphic axes, swords with a hooked tang and a midrib, and barbed and tanged harpoons, were also found in the doab, and they were attributed to a Copper Hoard culture. It was only in the later twentieth century, however, that excavations demonstrated that eastern OCP and copper hoards were made by the same people in the doab, who could now be chronologically pinned down to the early to mid second millennium. The copper hoards' artifacts are often of high-arsenic copper, the arsenic either being a deliberate alloy or, more probably, present as an impurity in the copper ore: This contrasts with other contemporary and earlier copper artifacts in South Asia, indicating a source other than the Aravallis.

OCP is a red ware with red slip and often painted decoration. Its antecedents lay in the red wares of the Jodhpura-Ganeshwar culture, showing that its makers included the indigenous cultures of the region, which had a long tradition of manufacturing copper artifacts. OCP sites can be divided into two groups. The western OCP was known at sites such as Jodhpura, Siswal, Mitathal, and Bara, occupied by late Jodhpura-Ganeshwar or Late Harappan groups, and their pottery showed a mixture of traits derived from both Jodhpura-Ganeshwar red ware and Late Harappan pottery as well as Cemetery H pottery and the Sothi-Siswal ceramic tradition that had endured from the Early Harappan period. Many of these settlements had evidence of extensive copper smelting.

To the east of Rajasthan, a somewhat different style of OCP was found from around 2000 BCE onward in western Uttar Pradesh at sites such as Lal Qila, Atranjikhera, and Saipai, along with objects made of copper. These were settlements of rectangular postbuilt wattle-and-daub houses. Their inhabitants practiced arable agriculture, growing rice, wheat, and barley and raising cattle, sheep, goats, pigs, and buffaloes.

While some settlements had only OCP pottery, others such as Ambikheri and Bargaon had a mixture of OCP and Late Harappan material. Some scholars do not recognize a significant distinction between the OCP and Late Harappan wares, instead seeing OCP as one of several varieties of Late Harappan pottery. The impression these settlements give is of a patchwork of farming communities whose diverse ancestry was often reflected in their choice of styles of artifact but who were otherwise similar and well integrated.

The Harappan Legacy

The Harappan civilization disintegrated as a coherent entity in the early second millennium, with the loss of the features that had characterized city dwelling, such as writing and sophisticated hydraulic engineering. Its breakup also marked the point of change where the Indus Valley ceased to be the center of Indian civilization, a role that passed to the Ganges Valley, where in the first millennium a new city-based culture emerged. But, though the Ganges cities developed a new script and many other wholly novel features, many aspects of life there and in other parts of the subcontinent were inherited from the economic, technological, cultural, religious, and social achievements of the Indus civilization.

REFERENCES

Agrawal, D. P. 1982. "The Technology of the Indus Civilization." In *Indian Archaeology. New Perspectives,* edited by R. K. Sharma, 83–112. New Delhi: Agam Kala Prakashan

Ajithprasad, P. 2002. "The Pre-Harappan Cultures of Gujarat." In *Indian Archaeology in Retrospect. II. Protohistory. Archaeology of the Harappan Civilization,* edited by S. Settar and Ravi Korisettar, 129–157. Indian Council of Historical Research. New Delhi: Manohar.

Allchin, Bridget. 1995. "The Potwar Project 1981 to 1993: A Concluding Report on the British Archaeological Mission to Pakistan's Investigations into Hominid and Early Human Cultures and Environments in the Northern Punjab, Pakistan." *South Asian Studies* 11: 149–156.

Allchin, Bridget, and Raymond Allchin. 1982. *The Rise of Civilization in India and Pakistan.* Cambridge, UK: Cambridge University Press.

Allchin, F. R. 1984. "The Northern Limits of the Harappan Culture Zone." In *Frontiers of the Indus Civilization,* edited by B. B. Lal and S. P. Gupta, 51–54. New Delhi: Books and Books.

Allchin, F. R. 1996. *The Archaeology of Early Historic India.* Cambridge, UK: Cambridge University Press.

Allchin, Raymond, and Bridget Allchin. 1997. *Origins of a Civilization.* New Delhi: Viking Penguin India.

Anon. 2006. "Bactria-Margiana Archaeological Complex." *Wikipedia.* [Online article; retrieved 1/20/06.] en.wikipedia.org/wiki/BMAC.

Athreya, Sheela. 2003. "Was *Homo heidelbergensis* in South Asia?" [Online article; retrieved 2/23/07] anthropology.tamu.edu/faculty/athreya/research.htm.

Badr, A., K. Müller, R. Schäfer-Pregl, H. El Rabey, S. Effgen, H. H. Ibrahim, C. Pozzi, W. Rohde, and F. Salamini. "On the Origin and Domestication History of Barley (*Hordeum vulgare*)." *Molecular Biology and Evolution* 17 (4): 499–510. [Online article; retrieved 10/2/05.] mbe.oxfordjournals.org/cgi/content/abstract/17/4/499?ijkey= 0eebb13bc0e0bb98daf670030f112393f9de2317&keytype2=tf_ipsecsha.

Barber, Elizabeth J. W. 1991. *Prehistoric Textiles.* Princeton, NJ: Princeton University Press.

Bellwood, Peter. 2004. *First Farmers: The Origins of Agricultural Societies.* Oxford: Blackwell Publishing.

Bellwood, Peter, and Colin Renfrew, eds. 2002. *Examining the Farming/Language Dispersal Hypothesis.* Cambridge, UK: McDonald Institute for Archaeological Research.

Bradley, Daniel G., David E. MacHugh, Patrick Cunningham, and Ronan T. Loftus. 1996. "Mitochondrial Diversity and the Origins of African and European Cattle." *Proceedings of the National Academy of Sciences* 93 (10): 5131–5135. [Online article; retrieved 10/2/05.] www.pnas.org/cgi/content/abstract/93/10/5131?ijkey=9573438 6357c9a02987d9146d70095a46e8ddd66&keytype2=tf_ipsecsha.

Brooks, R. R. R., and V. S. Wakankar. 1976. *Stone Age Painting in India.* New Haven, CT: Yale University Press.

Chakrabarti, Dilip K. 1999. *India: An Archaeological History. Palaeolithic Beginnings to Early Historic Foundations.* New Delhi: Oxford University Press.

Chakrabarti, Dilip K. 2004. "Prelude to the Indus Civilization." In *Indus Civilization. Sites in India. New Discoveries,* edited by Dilip K. Chakrabarti, 23–33. Mumbai: Marg Publications.

Chattopadhyaya, Umesh C. 2002. "Researches in Archaeozoology of the Holocene Period (including the Harappan Tradition in India and Pakistan)." In *Indian Archaeology in Retrospect. II. Protohistory. Archaeology of the Harappan Civilization,* edited by S. Settar and Ravi Korisettar, 365- 419. Indian Council of Historical Research. New Delhi: Manohar.

Costantini, Lorenzo. 1984. "The Beginning of Agriculture in the Kachi Plain: the Evidence of Mehrgarh." In *South Asian Archaeology 1981,* edited by Bridget Allchin, 29–33. Cambridge, UK: Cambridge University Press.

Dales, George F. 1974. "Excavations at Balakot, Pakistan, 1973." *Journal of Field Archaeology* 1 (1/2): 3–22.

Dales, George F. 1979. "Excavations at Balakot." In *South Asian Archaeology 1977,* edited by Maurizio Taddei, 241–74. Naples: Istituto Universitario Orientale, Seminario di Studi Asiatici.

Dales, George F., and Jonathan Mark Kenoyer. 1993. "The Harappa Project 1986–9: New Investigations at an Ancient Indus City." In *Harappan Civilization,* 2nd ed, edited by Gregory L Possehl, 469–520. New Delhi: Oxford University Press.

Dani, A. H., and B. K. Thapar. 1996. "The Indus Civilization." In *History of Civilizations of Central Asia. 1. The Dawn of Civilization: Earliest Times to 700 B.C.,* edited by A. H. Dani and V. M. Masson, 283–318. Paris: UNESCO.

Fagan, Brian. 2004. *The Long Summer: How Climate Changed Civilization.* London: Granta Books.

Fairservis, Walter. 1982. "Allahdino: An Excavation of a Small Harappan Site." In *Harappan Civilization. A Contemporary Perspective,* edited by Gregory L. Possehl, 106–112. New Delhi: Oxford & IBH Publishing Co.

Fairservis, Walter. 1984. "Archaeology in Baluchistan and the Harappan Problem." In *Frontiers of the Indus Civilization,* edited by B. B. Lal and S. P. Gupta, 277–287. New Delhi: Books and Books.

Franke Vogt, Ute. 2000. "The Archaeology of Southeastern Balochistan." [Online article; retrieved 6/14/05.] www.harappa.com/baluch/index.html.

Fuller, Dorian. 2003. "Lost Farmers and Languages in Asia: Some Comments to Diamond and Bellwood." *Science* May 28. [Online article; retrieved 4/1/07.] sciencemag.org/cgi/eletters/300/5619/597#689?ck=nck.

Fuller, Dorian. 2005."Archaeobotanical and Settlement Survey, South Indian Neolithic." [Online article; retrieved 10/2/05.] www.ucl.ac.uk/archaeology/staff/profiles/fuller/India.html.

Glover, Ian C., and Charles F. W. Higham. 1996. "New Evidence for Early Rice Cultivation in South, Southeast and East Asia." In *The Origins and Spread of Agriculture and Pastoralism in Eurasia,* edited by David R. Harris, 413–441. Washington, DC: Smithsonian Institution.

Grigson, Caroline. 1985. "*Bos indicus* and *Bos namadicus* and the Problem of Autochthonous Domestication in India." In *Recent Advances in Indo-Pacific Prehistory,* edited by V. N. Misra and Peter Bellwood, 425–428. New Delhi: Oxford & IBH Publishing Co.

Habib, Irfan. 2002. *The Indus Civilization: A People's History of India. 2.* Aligarh, India: Tulika and Aligarh Historians Society.

Harris, D. R. 1998. "The Spread of Neolithic Agriculture from the Levant to Western Central Asia." In *The Origins of Agriculture and Crop Domestication,* edited by A. B. Damania, J. Valkoun, G. Willcox, and C. O. Qualset, 65-82. Aleppo: ICARDA. [Online article; retrieved 4/1/07.] www.ipgri.cgiar.org/publications/HTMLPublications/47/ch07.htm.

Hiendleder, S., K. Mainz, Y. Plante, and H. Lewalski. 1998. "Analysis of Mitochondrial DNA Indicates That Domestic Sheep Are Derived from Two Different Ancestral Maternal Sources: No Evidence for Contributions from Urial and Argali Sheep." *The Journal of Heredity* 89 (2): 113–120. [Online article; retrieved 10/2/05.] jhered.oxfordjournals.org/cgi/content/abstract/89/2/113?ijkey=7f97dbe464c27a9b4de7dd54d9d22bf33d26b43c&keytype2=tf_ipsecsha.

Hiendleder, Stefan, Bernhard Kaupe, Rudolf Wassmuth, and Axel Janke. 2002. "Molecular Analysis of Wild and Domestic Sheep Questions Current Nomenclature and Provides Evidence for Domestication from Two Different Subspecies." *Proceedings:*

Biological Sciences 269 (1494): 893–904. [Online article; retrieved 10/10/05.] www.jour-nals.royalsoc.ac.uk/(eu1muq45ol1mi3455njupvjf)/app/home/contribution.asp?referrer=parent&backto=issue,4,15;journal,92,208;linkingpublicationresults,1:102024,1.

Hole, Frank. 2006. "Neolithic Age in Iran." London: Circle of Ancient Iranian Studies. [Online article; retrieved 4/1/07.] www.cais-soas.com/CAIS/Archaeology/Pre-History/neolithic_Iran.htm.

Hooja, Rima, and Vijai Kumar. 1997. "Aspects of the Early Copper Age in Rajasthan." In *South Asian Archaeology 1995,* edited by Raymond and Bridget Allchin, 323–334. New Delhi: Oxford & IBH Publishing Co.

Jarrige, Jean-Francois. 1979. "Excavations at Mehrgarh-Pakistan." In *South Asian Archaeology 1975,* edited by J. E. van Lohuizen de Leeuw, 76–87. Leiden: E. J. Brill.

Jarrige, Jean-Francois. 1982."Excavations at Mehrgarh: Their Significance for Understanding the Background of the Harappan Civilization." In *Harappan Civilization. A Contemporary Perspective,* edited by Gregory L. Possehl, 79–84. New Delhi: Oxford & IBH Publishing Co.

Jarrige, Jean-Francois. 1984a. "Towns and Villages of Hill and Plain." In *Frontiers of the Indus Civilization,* edited by B. B. Lal and S. P. Gupta, 289–300. New Delhi: Books and Books.

Jarrige, Jean-Francois. 1984b. "Chronology of the Earlier Periods of the Greater Indus as Seen from Mehrgarh, Pakistan." In *South Asian Archaeology 1981,* edited by Bridget Allchin, 21–29. Cambridge, UK: Cambridge University Press.

Jarrige, Jean-Francois. 1985. "Continuity and Change in the North Kachi Plain (Baluchistan, Pakistan) at the Beginning of the Second Millennium B.C." In *South Asian Archaeology 1983,* edited by Janine Schotsmans and Maurizio Taddei, 35–68. Naples: Istituto Universitario Orientale, Dipartimento di Studi Asiatici.

Jarrige, Jean-Francois, and Monique Lechevallier. 1979. "Excavations at Mehrgarh, Baluchistan: Their Significance in the Prehistorical Context of the Indo-Pakistan Borderlands." In *South Asian Archaeology 1977,* edited by M. Taddei, 463–535. Naples: Istituto Universitario Orientale, Seminario di Studi Asiatici.

Jarrige, Jean-Francois, and Richard Meadow. 1980. "The Antecedents of Civilization in the Indus Valley." *Scientific American* 243 (2): 122–133.

Jarrige, Jean-Francois, and Marielle Santoni. 1979. *Fouilles de Pirak.* Paris: Diffusion de Boccard.

Joshi, Jagat Pati, ed. 2004. "Bhagwanpura: A Late Harappan Site in Haryana." In *Indus Civilization. Sites in India. New Discoveries,* edited by Dilip K. Chakrabarti, 44–51. Mumbai: Marg Publications.

Kennedy, Kenneth A. R. 1982. "Skulls, Aryans and Flowing Drains: The Interface of Archaeology and Skeletal Biology in the Study of the Harappan Civilization." In *Harappan Civilization. A Contemporary Perspective,* edited by Gregory L. Possehl, 289–295. New Delhi: Oxford & IBH Publishing Co.

Kennedy, Kenneth A. R. 2000. *God-Apes and Fossil Men. Palaeoanthropology of South Asia.* Ann Arbor: University of Michigan Press.

Kennedy, Kenneth A. R., and Gregory Possehl, eds. 1984. *Studies in the Archaeology and Paleoanthropology of South Asia.* Oxford: Oxford University Press.

Kenoyer, Jonathan Mark. 1998. *Ancient Cities of the Indus Valley Civilization.* Karachi: Oxford University Press and American Institute of Pakistan Studies.

Kenoyer, Jonathan Mark, and Richard H. Meadow. 1998. "The Latest Discoveries: Harappa 1995–98." [Online article; retrieved 6/14/05.] www.harappa.com/indus2/index.html.

Kenoyer, Jonathan Mark, and Richard H. Meadow. 2001. "Harappa 2000–2001." [Online article; retrieved 6/14/05.] www.harappa.com/indus3/index.html.

Kenoyer, Jonathan Mark, and Richard H. Meadow. 2005. "Harappa 1995–2001." [Online article; retrieved 6/14/05.] www.harappa.com/indus5/index2.html.

Khan, Farid, J. Robert Knox, and Ken D. Thomas. 1988. "Prehistoric and Protohistoric Settlements in Bannu District." *Pakistan Archaeology* 23: 99–148.

Khatri, J. S., and M. Acharya. 1994–1995. "Kunal: A New Indus-Saraswati Site." *Puratattva* 25: 84–86.

Khatri, J. S. and M. Acharya. 2002. "Kunal—The Earliest Pre-Harappan Settlement." In *Facets of Indian Civilization. Recent Perspectives. Essays in Honour of Professor B. B. Lal*, edited by Jagat Pati Joshi, 88–91. New Delhi: Aryan Books International.

Lahiri, Nayankot and D. P. Sharma. 2004. "Harappan Settlers of the Ganga-Yamuna Doab." In *Indus Civilization. Sites in India. New Discoveries*, edited by Dilip K. Chakrabarti, 52–56. Mumbai: Marg Publications.

Lal, B. B. 1971. "Perhaps the Earliest Ploughed Field So Far Excavated Anywhere in the World." *Puratattva* 4 (1970–1971): 1–3.

Lal, B. B. 1984. "Some Reflections on the Structural Remains at Kalibangan." In *Frontiers of the Indus Civilization*, edited by B. B. Lal and S. P. Gupta, 55–62. New Delhi: Books and Books.

Lawler, Andrew. 2007. "Climate Spurred Later Indus Decline." *Science* 316: 979.

Lechevallier, Monique. 1984. "The Flint Industry of Mehrgarh." In *South Asian Archaeology 1981*, edited by Bridget Allchin, 41–51. Cambridge, UK: Cambridge University Press.

Lechevallier, Monique, and Gonzague Quivron. 1981."The Neolithic in Baluchistan: New Evidence from Mehrgarh." In *South Asian Archaeology 1979*, edited by Herbert Hartel, 71–92. Berlin: Deitrich Reimer Verlag.

Lechevallier, Monique, and Gonzague Quivron. 1985. "Results of the Recent Excavations at the Neolithic Site of Mehrgarh, Pakistan." In *South Asian Archaeology 1983*, edited by Janine Schotsmans and Maurizio Taddei, 69–90. Naples: Istituto Universitario Orientale, Dipartimento di Studi Asiatici.

Loftus, R. T., D. E. MacHugh, D. G. Bradley, P. M. Sharp, and P. Cunningham. 1994. "Evidence for Two Independent Domestications of Cattle." *Proceedings of the National Academy of Sciences* 91: 2757–2761. [Online article; retrieved 10/3/05.] www.pnas.org/cgi/content/abstract/91/7/2757?ijkey=7c6ddea6cc44276f45a5cd256 62fc0f1f5dbf572&keytype2=tf_ipsecsha.

Lovell, N. C., and Kenneth A. R. Kennedy. 1989. "Society and Disease in Prehistoric South Asia." In *Old Problems and New Perspectives in the Archaeology of South Asia*, edited by Jonathan Mark Kenoyer, 89–92. *Wisconsin Archaeological Reports.* Vol. 2. Department of Anthropology. Madison: University of Wisconsin Press.

Luikart, Gordon, Ludovic Gielly, Laurent Excoffier, Jean-Denis Vigne, Jean Bouvet, and Pierre Taberlet. 2001. "Multiple Maternal Origins and Weak Phylogeographic Structure in Domestic Goats." *Proceedings of the National Academy of Sciences of the United States of America* 98 (10): 5927–5932. [Online article; retrieved 10/2/05.] www.pnas.org/cgi/content/full/98/10/5927.

Lukacs, John R. 1989. "Biological Affinities from Dental Morphology: The Evidence from Neolithic Mehrgarh." In "Old Problems and New Perspectives in the Archaeology of South Asia," edited by Jonathan Mark Kenoyer, 75–88. *Wisconsin Archaeological Reports.* Vol. 2. Department of Anthropology. Madison: University of Wisconsin Press.

MacHugh, David E., and Daniel G. Bradley. 2001. "Livestock Genetic Origins: Goats Buck the Trend." *Proceedings of the National Academy of Sciences of the United States of America* 98 (10): 5382–5384. [Online article; retrieved 10/2/05.] www.pnas.org/cgi/content/extract/98/10/5382.

Mackay, Ernest J. H. 1943. *Chanhu-daro Excavations 1935–36.* New Haven, CT: American Oriental Society.

Marshall, John. 1931. *Mohenjo Daro and the Indus Civilization.* London: Arthur Probsthain.

Masson, V. M. 1976. "The Bronze Age in Khorasan and Transoxiana." In *History of Civilizations of Central Asia. 1. The Dawn of Civilization: Earliest Times to 700 B.C.,* edited by A. H. Dani and V. M. Masson, 225–246. Paris: UNESCO.

Mathpal, Y. 1985. "The Hunter-Gatherer Way of Life Depicted in the Mesolithic Rock Paintings of Central India." In *Recent Advances in Indo-Pacific Prehistory,* edited by V. N. Misra and Peter Bellwood, 177–183. New Delhi: Oxford & IBH Publishing Co.

Meadow, Richard. 1981. "Early Animal Domestication in South Asia: A First Report of the Faunal Remains from Mehrgarh, Pakistan." In *South Asian Archaeology 1979,* edited by Herbert Hartel, 143–179. Berlin: Deitrich Reimer Verlag.

Meadow, Richard. 1982. "From Hunting to Herding in Prehistoric Baluchistan." In *Anthropology in Pakistan,* edited by Stephen Pastner and Louis Flam, 145-153. Ithaca, NY: Cornell University Press.

Meadow, Richard. 1984. "Notes on the Faunal Remains from Mehrgarh, with a Focus on Cattle (*Bos*)." In *South Asian Archaeology 1981,* edited by Bridget Allchin, 34–40. Cambridge, UK: Cambridge University Press.

Meadow, Richard. 1989. "Continuity and Change in the Agriculture of the Greater Indus Valley: The Palaeoethnobotanical and Zooarchaeological Evidence." In *Old Problems and New Perspectives in the Archaeology of South Asia,* edited by Jonathan Mark Kenoyer, 61–74. *Wisconsin Archaeological Reports.* Vol. 2. Department of Anthropology. Madison: University of Wisconsin Press.

Meadow, Richard. 1993. "Animal Domestication in the Middle East: A Revised View from the Eastern Margin." In *Harappan Civilization,* 2nd ed, edited by Gregory L Possehl, 295–315. New Delhi: Oxford University Press.

Meadow, Richard. 1996. "The Origins and Spread of Agriculture and Pastoralism in Northwestern South Asia." In *The Origins and Spread of Agriculture and Pastoralism in Eurasia,* edited by David R. Harris, 390–412. Washington, DC: Smithsonian Institution.

Meadow, Richard H., and Jonathan Mark Kenoyer. 2003. "Recent Discoveries and Highlights from Excavations at Harappa: 1998–2000." [Online article; retrieved 6/14/05.] www.harappa.com/indus4/e1.html.

Meadows, J. R. S., K. Li, J. Kantanen, M. Tapio, W. Sipos, V. Pardeshi, V. Gupta, J. H. Calvo, V. Whan, B. Norris, and J. W. Kijas. 2005. "Mitochondrial Sequence Reveals High Levels of Gene Flow between Breeds of Domestic Sheep from Asia and Europe." *Journal of Heredity,* 96 (5): 494–501. August 31. [Online article; retrieved 10/3/05.] jhered.oxfordjournals.org/cgi/content/abstract/96/5/494.

Misra, V. N. 1973. "Bagor: A Late Mesolithic Settlement in North-west India." *World Archaeology* 5 (1): 92–100.

Misra, V. N. 1998. "Balathal: A Chalcolithic Settlement in Mewar, Rajasthan, India: Results of First Three Seasons' Excavation." *South Asian Studies* 13: 251-275.

Moulherat, C., M. Tengberg, J.-F. Haquet, and B. Mille, 2002. "First Evidence of Cotton at Neolithic Mehrgarh, Pakistan: Analysis of Mineralized Fibres from a Copper Bead." *Journal of Archaeological Science* 29: 1393–1401.

Neumayer, E. 1983. *Prehistoric Indian Rock Paintings*. New Delhi: Oxford University Press.

Ozkan, H., A. Brandolini, R. Schäfer-Pregl, and F. Salamini. 2002. "AFLP Analysis of a Collection of Tetraploid Wheats Indicates the Origin of Emmer and Hard Wheat Domestication in Southeast Turkey." *Molecular Biology and Evolution* 19 (10): 1797–1801. [Online article; retrieved 10/3/05.] mbe.oxfordjournals.org/cgi/content/full/19/10/1797.

Parekh, V. S., and V. H. Sonawane. 1991. "Excavations at Loteshwar, District Mahesana." *Indian Archaeology—a Review 1990–1*:12–16.

Parihar, Rohit. 2001. "Promise of the Past." *India Today.* [Online article; retrieved 1/31/06.] www.indiatoday.com/webexclusive/dispatch/20010702/ruben.html.

Pedrosa, Susana, Metehan Uzun, Juan-Josè Arranz, Beatriz Gutièrrez-Gil, Fermìn San Primitivo, and Yolanda Bayûn. 2005. "Evidence of Three Maternal Lineages in Near Eastern Sheep Supporting Multiple Domestication Events." *Proceedings: Biological Sciences* 272 (1577): 2211–2217. [Online article; retrieved 10/10/05.] www.journals.royalsoc.ac.uk/(eu1muq45ol1mi3455njupvjf)/app/home/contribution.asp?referrer=parent&backto=issue,14,15;searcharticlesresults,1,3.

Possehl, Gregory L. 1993. "The Date of Indus Urbanization: A Proposed Chronology for the Pre-urban and Urban Harappan Phases." In *South Asian Archaeology 1991,* edited by Adalbert J. Gail and Gerd J. R. Mevissen, 231-250. Stuttgart: Franz Steiner Verlag

Possehl, Gregory L. 1999. *Indus Age: The Beginnings.* New Delhi: Oxford University Press.

Possehl, Gregory L. 2002. *The Indus Civilization. A Contemporary Perspective.* Walnut Creek, CA: AltaMira Press.

Possehl, Gregory L. 2003. "Cache of Seal Impressions Discovered in Western India Offers Surprising New Evidence for Cultural Complexity in Little-known Ahar-Banas Culture, circa 3000–1500 B.C." [Online article; retrieved 1/15/06.] www.museum.upenn.edu/new/research/possehl/ahar-banas.shtml.

Possehl, Gregory L. 2004. "Rojdi: A Sorath Harappan Settlement in Saurashtra." In *Indus Civilization. Sites in India. New Discoveries,* edited by Dilip K. Chakrabarti, 80–88. Mumbai: Marg Publications.

Ratnagar, Shereen. 2000. *The End of the Great Harappan Tradition. Heras Memorial Lectures 1998.* New Delhi: Manohar.

Ratnagar, Shereen. 2001. *Understanding Harappa. Civilization in the Greater Indus Valley.* New Delhi: Tulika.

Ratnagar, Shereen. 2004. *Trading Encounters. From the Euphrates to the Indus in the Bronze Age.* New Delhi: Oxford University Press.

de Saizieu, Blanche Bartelemy, and Anne Bouquillon. 1993. "Steatite Working at Mehrgarh during the Neolithic and Chalcolithic Periods: Quantitative Distribution, Characterization of Material and Manufacturing Processes." In *South Asian*

Archaeology 1993, edited by Asko Parpola and Petteri Koskikallio, 47–70. Helsinki: Suomalainen Tiedeakatemia.

Samzun, Anaick, and P. Sellier. 1985. "First Anthropological and Cultural Evidences for the Funerary Practices of the Chalcolithic Population of Mehrgarh, Pakistan." In *South Asian Archaeology 1983,* edited by Janine Schotsmans and Maurizio Taddei, 91–120. Naples: Istituto Universitario Orientale, Dipartimento di Studi Asiatici.

Sarianidi, V. 1996. "Food-producing and Other Neolithic Communities in Khorasan and Transoxiana: Eastern Iran, Soviet Central Asia and Afghanistan." In *History of Civilizations of Central Asia. 1. The Dawn of Civilization: Earliest Times to 700 B.C,.* edited by A. H. Dani and V. M. Masson, 109–126. Paris: UNESCO.

Shaffer, Jim G. 1978. *Prehistoric Baluchistan.* New Delhi: B. R. Publishing Corporation.

Sharif, M., and B. K. Thapar. 1976. "Food-producing Communities in Pakistan and Northern India." In *History of Civilizations of Central Asia. 1. The Dawn of Civilization: Earliest Times to 700 B.C.,* edited by A. H. Dani and V. M. Masson,127–152. Paris: UNESCO.

Shinde, V. 1998. "Pre-Harappan Padri Culture in Saurashtra: The Recent Discovery." *South Asian Studies* 14: 173–182.

Stringer, Chris, and Peter Andrews. 2005. *The Complete World of Human Evolution.* London: Thames and Hudson.

Thapar, B. K. 1975. "Kalibangan: A Harappan Metropolis beyond the Indus Valley." *Expedition* 17 (2): 19–32. Reprinted 1979 in *Ancient Cities of the Indus,* edited by Gregory L. Possehl, 196–202. New Delhi: Vikas Publishing House.

Thomas, P. K. 1975. "Role of Animals in the Food Economy of the Mesolithic Culture of Western and Central India." In *Archaeozoological Studies,* edited by A. T. Clason, 322–328. Amsterdam: North-Holland/Elsevier.

Tosi, M., S. Malek Shahmirzadi, and M. A. Joyenda. 1976. "The Bronze Age in Iran and Afghanistan." In *History of Civilizations of Central Asia. 1. The Dawn of Civilization: Earliest Times to 700 B.C.,* edited by A. H. Dani and V. M. Masson, 191–224. Paris: UNESCO.

Uerpmann, Hans-Peter. 1996. "Animal Domestication: Accident or Intention?" In *The Origins and Spread of Agriculture and Pastoralism in Eurasia,* edited by David R. Harris, 227–237. Washington, DC: Smithsonian Institution.

Vidale, Massimo. 1995. "Early Beadmakers of the Indus Tradition. The Manufacturing Sequence of Talc Beads at Mehrgarh in the Fifth Millennium B.C." *East and West* 45: 45–80.

Zohary, Daniel, and Maria Hopf. 2000. *Domestication of Plants in the Old World. The Origin and Spread of Cultivated Plants in West Asia, Europe and the Nile Valley.* 3rd ed. Oxford: Oxford University Press.

V CHAPTER 5
Economics

SUBSISTENCE PATTERNS

The economy of the Indus civilization was based on animal husbandry, particularly of zebu cattle, and on arable agriculture, growing cereals, pulses, and other plants. These were supplemented by the exploitation of wild resources, such as fish. Pastoralism and agriculture differed in their relative importance in each of the great diversity of environments that composed the Indus realms: In the valleys and plains of the Indus and Saraswati Rivers, their tributaries, and other smaller rivers mixed farming was highly profitable; rain and other local water resources also supported farming in other regions, such as Baluchistan, sometimes with the help of irrigation. Animals were taken at certain times of year to graze on the expanses of seasonal pastures in Gujarat and Punjab and in the uplands of Baluchistan. Coastal settlements took advantage of marine resources such as shellfish, which provided not only food but also shells, an important resource for making ornaments.

The archaeological evidence for Indus agriculture is extremely patchy. The preservation of plant remains is often poor, depending on local conditions, the type of plant, and chance. Whereas cereal cultivation has left evidence in the form of carbonized grain and impressions of stalks and grains in pottery and bricks, and pulses also preserve well, roots and tubers and many fruits and vegetables produce few or no hard parts that survive as archaeological traces, so evidence of their cultivation is rare. This problem is compounded by variations in the standards of recovery in archaeological excavations and by problems of identification. Animal bones, generally better preserved than plant remains and more frequently recovered from sites, also present identification problems: In addition to the well-known difficulties in distinguishing sheep from goats, Richard Meadow, a leading archaeozoologist, has drawn attention to the strong similarities, for example, between sheep/goat and blackbuck/gazelle, and among cattle, water buffalo, and nilgai (1996, 404). Evidence from the few sites that have well reported economic data cannot necessarily be regarded as representative of the Indus civilization as a whole, for reasons such as environmental differences. The picture of Harappan agriculture is therefore very fragmentary, having been put together from very restricted sources, filled out by comparison with traditional agricultural practices in the region.

Agriculture in the Mature Harappan period, as in its antecedent cultures in the Indo-Iranian borderlands, was based on wheat, barley, pulses, sheep, goats, and cattle, the same assemblage of crops and animals as the cultures to the west in the Iranian plateau, southern Central Asia, and West Asia, most of which had originally been domesticated in West Asia. Each region of Asia had other local plants and animals, notably zebu cattle in South Asia. With a few exceptions, such as sesame and cotton in South Asia, the crops followed a regime of autumn sowing and spring harvest across the entire region from Anatolia to central India: This is known as *rabi* cultivation in South Asia. Around the early second millennium, however, major new crops were added that required spring or summer sowing and autumn harvesting: *kharif* cultivation. These crops were to set the pattern for agriculture over much of the subcontinent in later times, although *rabi* crops have continued to dominate in the northwest, and in many regions both *rabi* and *kharif* crops are grown.

ARABLE AGRICULTURE

Crops

Rabi Crops. Wheat and barley were the staple cereals of *rabi* cultivation. The Harappans cultivated various types of wheat: a little emmer and einkorn, along with three kinds of bread wheat, of which shot wheat (*Triticum aestivum sphaerococcum*) was the most common in the Mature Harappan period. Barley was more important than wheat at some sites, including the Indus outpost at Shortugai on the Amu Darya and the Baluchi site of Miri Qalat. The Harappans grew three or four varieties of barley, including both naked and hulled types. This range of crop varieties allowed them to exploit the different properties of the various types of land suitable for cultivation. At Rojdi in Gujarat, barley was very poorly represented in the extensive collection of botanical remains and was not cultivated after period A (2500–2200 BCE), and in the Kachi plain bread wheat was more important than barley. Oats (*Avena* sp.) were present at Mehrgarh in the fourth millennium and have also been recovered from Pirak and Late Harappan Hulas. Oats seem generally to have been present in early archaeological contexts as a weed of cultivation that invaded stands of wheat and barley, rather than being deliberately cultivated: This fits with their sporadic appearance in South Asian botanical samples.

A number of other crops were cultivated during the *rabi* season, the majority—including lentil, pea (or field pea, *Pisum sativum* var. *arvense*), chickpea, and *Linum*—probably originally domesticated in West Asia. Peas are known from sites such as Kalibangan, Chanhu-daro, and Harappa, chickpea at Kalibangan, and lentils at Nausharo and Rojdi, though peas were not cultivated at the latter site until the Late Harappan period when all three were also cultivated at Hulas; chickpeas are also known at Pirak. Lentils and peas were among the plants cultivated at Shortugai, the Indus outpost in northern Afghanistan. Another pulse, also possibly derived from the west, was grasspea (chickling vetch, *Lathyrus sativus*). Although remains of this plant are known

A pit from the Ravi period at Harappa containing seeds of wheat and barley. These were the main staples of agriculture in the northwest until the last centuries of the Mature Harappan period. (Harappa Archaeological Research Project, Courtesy Department of Archaeology and Museums, Government of Pakistan)

from a number of Harappan sites and at Late Harappan Hulas, it was probably not grown for human consumption, since it is poisonous to humans if eaten in large quantities. Its recent consumption has been as a famine or desperation food, and it may have been grown for animal feed.

Millets. During the third millennium, a number of indigenous cereals were brought under cultivation by the Indus civilization or by contemporary South Asian cultures. Little millet (*Panicum sumatrense*) was common at Mature Harappan Rojdi, Oriyo Timbo, and Babar Kot in Gujarat, and present at Harappa around 3000 BCE, and browntop millet (*Brachiaria ramosa)* was also grown at Rojdi. A small amount of *Setaria* sp. was cultivated at Surkotada and Rojdi: This may have been *S. verticillata*, bristley foxtail millet, also domesticated in South India during the third millennium, or *S. pumila,* yellow foxtail millet, both native species. Foxtail millet (*Setaria italica*), known in the Late Harappan period, is thought possibly to be a local domesticate but was more probably introduced. It was a major crop in China, having been brought under cultivation in the seventh millennium BCE, and was being grown as far west as Tepe Gaz Tavila in southeast Iran by the sixth millennium. Seeds of another indigenous millet, Job's tears (*Coix lacrima-jobi*), have been found at Harappa and at the contemporary Ahar-Banas settlement of Balathal, in both cases as beads, a common use for these seeds.

Broomcorn (or common) millet (*Panicum miliaceum*) was probably brought under cultivation in southern Central Asia (as well as in China) and might have reached the Indus civilization via their trading outpost at Shortugai, which was situated in the region adjacent to southern Turkmenia, where broomcorn millet was an important crop. A wild ancestor of broomcorn millet exists in South Asia, so it may alternatively have been a local domesticate. Several species of *Panicum* were present at Rojdi, and it is possible that broomcorn millet was among them. The first certain occurrence of this millet in South Asia is at Pirak, in the early second millennium.

During the early second millennium, a number of plants of African origin appeared in Gujarat and were incorporated into the range of crops grown by the local Harappans. These included three kinds of millet: jowar (sorghum or Guinea corn, *Sorghum bicolor),* bajra (pearl millet, *Pennisetum typhoides*), and ragi (finger millet, *Eleusine coracana).* Abundant ragi was reported at Rojdi during the earlier part of the Mature Harappan period, from about 2500 BCE onward, as well as possible ragi phytoliths in bricks and sherds at Harappa, but its presence this early is unlikely. Dorian Fuller (2001, personal communication), an archaeobotanist with a detailed knowledge of South Asian plants, cautions that it is likely that some claimed occurrences of ragi are based on a misidentification of *Setaria* spp., *Echinochloa colona* (Sawa millet), or *Brachiaria ramosa* (browntop millet), all native South Asian millets; a native weedy grass (*Eleucine indica*) was also abundant at Rojdi. Later there was ragi in Cemetery H levels at Harappa and in Late Harappan Hulas to the east, and Fuller himself has identified a grain of ragi at Hallur in South India, dated after 1800 BCE.

Bajra may have been present in late third-millennium Babar Kot in Saurashtra; it is known later at Rangpur and also reached South India after 1800 BCE. Jowar was a major crop at Rojdi during the early second millennium, and, in the Posturban period, jowar is also reported at Pirak and at Late Harappan Hulas. The timing of the appearance of these higher-yielding African millets in Gujarat coincides with the period of considerable increase in settlements in the region and the expansion of cultivation into areas of moisture-retentive soils. Other local millets, kodon (*Paspalum scrobiculatum*) and sawa millet, were also added to the range of crops in the period after 2000 BCE.

Although the evidence is very uncertain, it is possible that some African crops were under cultivation in Oman (ancient Magan) during the third millennium, and sorghum and another African millet may also have been cultivated in the Yemen at this time, though their identification is not certain. These plants are assumed to have spread due to contacts across the Red Sea between southwest Arabia and East Africa, regions between which there were close communications in later times. Unfortunately the third-millennium archaeology of both areas is poorly known, and the earliest record of these crops in

Africa greatly postdates their appearance elsewhere, although there is much earlier evidence of their exploitation as wild plants. It is also possible that some of these plants were part of the original flora of the Yemen and were taken into cultivation there. From southwest Arabia the domestic plants probably spread via local exchange networks through the southern coastal region of Arabia as far as Oman. Alternatively, the crops may have been carried as provisions by seafarers plying the sea lanes of this coast, who on their return home handed over the residue as novelties that were used in experiments. If these commodities were carried by organized sea traders, the latter may have come from either Oman or the Indus.

Rice. Rice is indigenous to parts of South and East Asia, including the Indus region and the Ganges Valley. The history of its cultivation is complex and probably involved a number of different centers of domestication. Genetic evidence has recently established that rice was brought into cultivation in at least two separate areas: domestication of a perennial wild rice in East Asia produced the short-grained *japonica* variety whereas domestication, probably in several regions of South Asia, of an annual wild rice gave rise to the long-grained *indica* variety, which also spread through Southeast Asia and China.

Rice cultivation began in the middle Ganges region during the third millennium and somewhat later in eastern India. The cultures growing rice in Southeast Asia had close cultural connections with the inhabitants of eastern India, Bangladesh, and intervening regions, indicated by shared artifact types such as cord-marked pottery and distinctive shouldered axes.

Rice grew wild in Gujarat. Charred rice husks and impressions of rice husks and leaves in Harappan pottery have been found in this region, at Lothal and Rangpur. These have been studied by Naomi Miller, who has established that they are unlikely to reflect rice cultivation. Instead it is probable that rice was among the wild plants consumed by grazing cattle resulting in rice husks being present in their dung, which was used for fuel and a tempering agent in pottery. Rice husks and phytoliths have also been found in pottery and bricks at Harappa. Rice, probably wild, is known from Early Harappan Balu in Haryana and Kunal. In Swat rice appears at Ghaligai before 2000 BCE as grain impressions in sherds of Late Kot Diji pottery: These may have been from either domestic or wild rice. By the early second millennium, however, rice was certainly being grown in the eastern Indus region. It was among the cultivated plants at the Late Harappan site of Hulas, where both wild and cultivated *indica* rice were identified.

Japonica rice was grown in China's Yangtze Valley by the sixth millennium BCE, and its cultivation spread from there to other parts of China and into Southeast Asia. From northern China, rice cultivation spread to Manchuria and Korea. It was possibly from here that rice cultivation reached Kashmir, a region that had a number of links with China: Rice began to be grown at Gufkral in Kashmir during the first half of the second millennium. Rice, apparently *japonica,* was the principal crop of the settlement at Pirak in the Kachi plain, an arid region where irrigation would have been required.

Other Food Plants. South Asia had a number of native pulses that were locally domesticated. These included green gram (*Vigna radiata*) and black gram (*Vigna mungo*), which were grown at a number of Mature Harappan sites and at contemporary Balathal in Rajasthan. Horsegram (*Macrotyloma uniflorum*) was domesticated in South India during the same period and is known from Late Harappan Hulas. During the early second millennium, two further pulses, of African origin, were added: hyacinth bean (*Lablab purpureus*) and cowpea (*Vigna unguiculata*), the latter being grown at Hulas and both appearing in South India after 1800 BCE. All varieties of pulse were more important in peripheral regions such as Gujarat than in the Indus Valley heartland.

Very few other Harappan cultivated plants have been recovered. There is evidence, however, of the widespread cultivation of a species of *Brassica,* brown mustard (Indian rape), and of gourds in the Mature Harappan period, and later of ivy gourd, while okras were grown at Balathal in the neighboring Ahar-Banas region. Jujube (ber, *Zizyphus jujuba*), an edible red berry, was known at Mehrgarh from the earliest period, though it was probably gathered rather than cultivated; this may also have been true of its later use. Melons were cultivated at Shahr-i Sokhta in adjacent Seistan and probably by the Harappans. Other fruits that may have been grown or collected locally include caper, mango, and sugarcane, and adjacent regions may also have supplied fruits, vegetables, and nuts, including cucumbers, pistachios, almonds, and walnuts, all known from sites farther west; walnuts have also been recovered from Hulas, along with the fruit of the pipal tree (*Ficus religiosa*).

The stones of dates, a high-calorie fruit that is three-quarters sugar, were found in early Mehrgarh; date palms occurred wild in Baluchistan and they may have been cultivated from early times. Many date stones were recovered from Nausharo and at Mohenjo-daro, and it is likely that dates were transported to parts of the Indus region where they were not grown.

Grapes were being grown in the Kachi plain by the early third millennium, as well as in adjacent Baluchistan and Seistan. Grape pips were found at Mehrgarh and Nausharo and later at Pirak I; they were also common at Shortugai, the Indus outpost in northern Afghanistan.

Herbs and spices, such as garlic, turmeric, ginger, cumin, and cinnamon, are likely to have been grown or collected too, but the only trace yet identified is of coriander at Miri Qalat in Baluchistan.

Sesame, native to South Asia, was probably the principal plant grown for its oil: It is known from a number of Harappan sites, including Chanhu-daro and Harappa, and contemporary sites in the Indo-Iranian borderlands such as Miri Qalat. By 2250–2200 BCE, sesame was under cultivation in Mesopotamia, presumably first brought there by Harappan traders. Castor, another Indian oilseed, was cultivated at Late Harappan Hulas.

Fibers. Oil could also be obtained from linseed (*Linum usitatissimum*), which was found at Miri Qalat and a number of Harappan sites, including Nausharo and Rojdi. Alternatively it may have been grown for its fiber, flax. The latter was being used to manufacture linen cloth during this period on the Iranian plateau; however, no linen has been identified from Harappan sites. There is evidence of cotton cloth at Mohenjo-daro and probably Harappa: The production of cotton textiles may have meant that linen was of no interest to the Harappans. Cotton may have been cultivated at Mehrgarh by the fifth millennium, though, like *Linum*, it may also have been grown for its oil-rich seeds. In the Mature Harappan period it was grown in both the Indus Valley and Baluchistan. Locally available plants, such as indigo and turmeric, were probably used as dyes; indigo is among the plants recovered from Rojdi, and the use of madder root is attested to by the presence at Mohenjo-daro of cloth dyed red with madder.

Water and Irrigation

Irrigation Works. In Baluchistan the sparse winter rainfall, though important, could not be relied on to water the crops raised in the generally limited areas of suitable soil. Water could be obtained from wells and springs in some cases, but by the early third millennium, if not before, the inhabitants of the region also developed small-scale dams (bunds and gabarbands) to retain some of the water that flowed in seasonal streams and small rivers (*nais*) after the rains. In some cases, for example at Early Indus Diwana on the upper Hab River, a dam was designed to impound water, which could be released or channeled onto fields as required. In other cases dams and channels led the floodwater into embanked fields, where they deposited silt and provided enough soil moisture for the growing crops. One type of dam consisted of small walls built to jut out into the bed of a stream or river so that some of its water was diverted onto the ground behind the wall, depositing fertile silt that formed a small field. Settlements in the Kulli area (southern Baluchistan) seem invariably to be associated with dams; this area also received some unreliable summer rainfall.

On the edges of the Kachi plain and along the western piedmont of Sindh, as in Baluchistan, small dams and occasional small channels were created to retain and distribute the seasonal runoff from mountain streams and rivers. These *nais* carried their greatest flow in July and August but also brought minor floods in January and February from the limited winter rainfall, which also provided supplementary water during the growing season. Some *nais*, fed by springs, had a small perennial flow.

The Kachi plain is a hot arid region where agriculture relied on the limited winter rainfall, heavier but not always reliable monsoon rains, and the water provided by the Bolan, Mula, and Nari Rivers. Here also dams and channels were necessary to make best use of the water supplies, and only in this area of the lowlands have irrigation channels been found.

Canal irrigation is attested to at Shortugai, the Indus outpost in northern Afghanistan at the confluence of the Amu Darya and Kokcha Rivers: A canal has been traced that drew off water from the Kokcha. This might be taken to indicate that the Indus people brought canal irrigation technology with them when they settled here; however, the Namazga culture in adjacent southern Turkmenia, from whom it is likely that the inhabitants of Shortugai acquired the broomcorn millet that they cultivated, had long experience of canal irrigation that may have inspired the inhabitants of Shortugai.

Water Supply. Unlike the situation in the mountains and foothills of the Indo-Iranian borderlands, there is little evidence that major irrigation works were used or required over most of the Indus region. Groundwater, rivers, lakes, streams, and especially floodwaters sufficed.

The Indus floods in Sindh came largely in July and August, providing water throughout the summer for *kharif* crops while winter crops were sustained by the water retained in streams, channels, lakes, and dhands (seasonal lakes), supplemented by water brought down in January or February by the *nais* flowing off the mountains of Baluchistan. The Indus plains had a variety of zones suitable for agriculture. The margins of dhands and oxbow lakes, the latter formed by abandoned meanders of the Indus, allowed cultivation from year to year. The active flood plain of the rivers provided excellent arable land, its fertility renewed annually by the silts deposited by the floodwaters, the coarse sediments closest to the river being richest in nutrients. Patches of deeper sediment reflected the unpredictable distribution of channels cut by the river's floodwaters: These had to be searched for, but they provided the best agricultural land, cultivable without plowing. In western Sindh, Lake Manchar flooded an enormous area during the inundation, and the retreating floodwaters left fertile ground highly suitable for cultivation: Today this is around 8,000 hectares in extent. While the productivity of the Indus in Sindh is very high, it is not reliable. About one year in four brings abnormally high or low quantities of water; the river floods unevenly, depending on where it breaks its banks; and it changes its course frequently. This combination of high but unpredictable productivity must have made it advantageous to develop storage practices and facilities.

Farther north in the Punjab, farming was confined to the alluvial soils in the valleys, annually flooded by the five rivers, with large areas of uncultivated higher ground between them. This region received monsoon rain in the summer, and some winter rainfall, particularly in the western portion. The area southeast of the Punjab, the eastern part of the ancient Saraswati system, is prime agricultural land well watered by numerous seasonal watercourses and by heavy summer monsoon rains. Although today the numerous rivers and streams carry only seasonal flow in their upper reaches and are dry farther west, in the Indus period this river system carried far more water and flowed at least to the Fort Derawar area in Cholistan, if not beyond, with perennial flow in the larger rivers. Dense settlement along branches of the Saraswati River indicates that it was one of the most productive regions of the Harappan realms and underlines the significance of the progressive reduction in the volume of water carried by the Saraswati River system in the Late Harappan period. Agriculture was supported by the floodwaters of the rivers, with their burden of alluvium; since the rivers were fed by water from the Siwaliks rather than the Himalayas, the volume of water they carried was considerably less than that in the Indus and its tributaries, with proportionally less violent floods. In Cholistan, water for agriculture could also be obtained from shallow wells tapping the high water table of the river valleys, and there was also some summer and winter rainfall.

Complex irrigation systems have been sought, but it seems likely that none were required, agricultural settlement being confined to the riverine environments where simple means of water provision were adequate, in contrast with the highlands where water conservation was essential. In some parts of the Indus realms, particularly Sindh, small channels were probably dug to bring water from dhands or streams into fields and to carry away excess water from swampy areas. Neither irrigation nor drainage channels have been located, but this does not mean that they did not exist. The annual deposition of alluvium filled in many irregularities of the plain's surface, which would have included artificial channels, and the unpredictable distribution of the inundation waters meant that the location of fields would often have changed. These factors mean that new channels would have had to be dug each year, rather than cleaning out old ones, and would have made it inappropriate to invest effort in constructing major irrigation canals. Any surviving traces of such channels must by now be deeply buried beneath four millennia's alluvium.

Most Harappan farming settlements in Gujarat were located in Saurashtra. In the Mature Harappan period, these were confined to locations along the rivers and streams, and particularly along the Nal Depression, which retained floodwater through the winter months. Only in the Late Harappan period did farming settlements spread onto the moisture retentive, black cotton soils in other parts of Saurashtra, where *kharif* crops could be raised, watered by rainfall brought by the summer monsoon. The number of settlements in the region expanded at least fourfold in this period. Kutch, to the north of Saurashtra, was an island in the Indus period. Today the brackish subsoil water and poor rainfall provide little support for arable agriculture, but in Indus times, when a considerable flow of river water entered the Ranns, the underground water was probably sweet and could have been accessed for irrigation by digging wells.

Wells and reservoirs also supported the inhabitants of Dholavira on Khadir Island in the Great Rann. Wells here and in other regions could provide ample water for growing crops. Drawing water from them would have been a labor-intensive activity, requiring considerable animal power, though in areas subject to summer flooding only shallow wells were needed to reach the high water table. A masonry well at Allahdino may have been used for irrigation: It was situated on higher ground, from which the water could run down to the fields. The fine examples of wells in Indus towns show the high level of Harappan competence in constructing them. In the central region, Sindh, the Indus-Ganges doab, and perhaps the western Saraswati, the floods filled numerous hollows (dhands), which for some months acted as reservoirs from which to draw water to irrigate the crops; many held water until December and some as late as February. The Indus people probably used lifting gear such as the shadoof to raise irrigation water from these and from streams and channels. One sherd of Indus pottery from Mohenjo-daro bears a scratched picture of such a device, a simple T-shaped arrangement of an upright and a horizontal pole, with a bucket on one side and a counterweight on the other.

More than seven hundred wells were sunk at Mohenjo-daro when the city was built. Over the centuries houses were rebuilt and street levels rose; new courses of bricks were therefore added to the wells to keep their tops at the same height with respect to the street. The removal of earth and debris during the excavation of the city has left many wells standing like towers high above the exposed remains of earlier streets. (J. M. Kenoyer, Courtesy Department of Archaeology and Museums, Government of Pakistan)

Agricultural Practices

Rabi and Kharif. Early agriculture in the Indo-Iranian borderlands was based on a range of crops—wheat, barley, peas, lentils, chickpeas, and flax—which were sown in November or December and harvested in April or May: *rabi* cultivation. *Rabi* crops required the cooler temperatures of the winter season, and the warmth available in the spring was adequate to ripen them. These were the crops that were introduced by farming colonists to the Indus Basin. A possible exception to this regime was cotton, which had been exploited and probably cultivated for millennia. Cotton is now grown as a summer (*kharif*) crop, planted in June and harvested from November onward. However, although winter frosts inhibit its growth, they do not kill it: cotton can therefore also be grown as a perennial bush, and it is thought that this was the method of cultivation in Harappan times, the bushes being grown on the edges of the active flood plain of the rivers. Jujube, a wild fruit that had been exploited or cultivated since the early occupation at Mehrgarh, could be gathered at any time during the winter months, from October to February.

One may surmise that initially the farming settlers in the greater Indus region adapted their *rabi* cultivation of traditional plants to the new constraints and opportunities of the Indus Basin, notably the far greater availability of water and cultivable land. After a time, however, they also began to make use of other plants native to the region; their willingness to experiment with these probably reflects the presence in the population of a significant number of people descended from the hunter-gatherers who had originally lived in the region and who had a long established familiarity with these plants. One local cereal, little millet, which was cultivated in Mature Harappan Gujarat, could be grown as a *rabi* crop (as it is today in Tamilnadu) and may therefore have initially been incorporated into the established *rabi* regime.

On the other hand, little millet could also be planted in the early monsoon period, around June or July, for harvest in October. The Harappans in the Indus Basin would have been aware that many other native species required summer temperatures to grow and the shortening days of autumn to reach maturity. These plants could take advantage of the moisture offered by the summer floods and monsoon rainfall, the latter being particularly relevant in Gujarat. During the Mature Harappan period, perhaps in its early days, a number of these were taken into cultivation; by around 2000 BCE these included *Setaria*, brown-top millet, green and black gram, sesame, and possibly broomcorn millet and rice. These native *kharif* crops were then supplemented by imported species: jowar, bajra, ragi, hyacinth bean, and cowpea ultimately from Africa, and perhaps rice, foxtail millet, and broomcorn millet from regions to the north and east. If, as seems possible, contacts took place with South India, where several South Asian millets and *kharif* pulses were cultivated, this may also have encouraged the gradual adoption of *kharif* cultivation in the Harappan realms.

The introduction of jowar, ragi, and bajra and the local domestication or introduction of domesticated rice were significant in altering the pattern of cultivation in the subcontinent: All achieved an enduring importance as staples, in contrast to indigenous millets. For the first time, serious alternatives to wheat and barley were available. The changing popularity of different varieties of millet in the sequence at Rojdi and the abandonment of barley cultivation after the first period (Rojdi A, 2500–2200 BCE) probably reflect a period of experimentation in which a pattern of agriculture, tailored to local conditions, gradually evolved from the "one-size-fits-all" uniform assemblage of West Asian crops, which would have produced less impressive results in Gujarat than in the Indus plains. A shift from *rabi* cultivation alone to *rabi* supplemented by some *kharif* cultivation occurred at Harappa in period 3C (ca. 2200–1900 BCE). By the Late Harappan period, the mosaic of differing local crop mixes and *rabi–kharif* balances was well developed in some previously settled regions, such as Gujarat, while in others, such as the Kachi plain, and in new areas such as the Deccan and the Ganges-Yamuna doab it was still evolving. It is possible that climatic changes also played a part in this evolution: the period 2200–1900 BCE is thought to have seen reduced rainfall.

The addition of *kharif* crops brought a number of advantages. They provided a means to reduce the risks involved in cultivation in the Indus region, where yields could be high but there were ever present dangers of crop failure due to drought, excessive flooding, or changes in the course of the rivers. The ability to plant a summer crop if spring harvests were poor therefore offered an important insurance against food shortages. Most of the millets were drought resistant, fast growing, and well suited to cultivation on poorer soils and in high temperatures, features that made them particularly attractive for cultivation in Gujarat, while rice could be grown in areas too wet for other cereals to thrive. New crops increased the diversity available in the diet. Finally, *kharif* crops enabled double-cropping to be practiced, allowing two crops to be obtained from the land during a single year. Alternatively, and less labor intensively, cultivation might be rotated and land might be fallowed between crops. Double-cropping gave great potential for increasing agricultural productivity, and some scholars argue that double-cropping was an essential feature of agriculture by the later part of the Mature Harappan period. For example, an increasing population in the Kachi plain was associated in the early second millennium with combined *rabi* cultivation of cereals and pulses and *kharif* cultivation of rice and jowar.

The incorporation of *kharif* crops into the Harappan agricultural system had a further advantage that had far-reaching consequences. While the West Asian crops are well suited to the northwest part of the subcontinent where they were first grown and where they are still today the main staples, *kharif* crops are better adapted for cultivation in the rest of South Asia. Wheat and barley were introduced to much of the subcontinent, for instance appearing in South Indian Neolithic sites before 1800 BCE, but it was the native and introduced *kharif* crops that were to become the principal cultigens of these regions. Millets became the staple crop in Gujarat, the Deccan, and the south; this is reflected in the appearance in the Late Harappan period of many settlements on the previously uncultivated water-retentive black cotton soils of the north Gujarat plain and Saurashtra, which were ideal for the summer rain-fed cultivation of millets.

Unlike millets, rice demanded a substantial supply of water throughout the growing season. It could be grown in naturally flooded areas or in permanently bunded fields containing impounded water (wet rice cultivation), or it could be raised in areas where sufficient water came from high summer rainfall (dry rice cultivation). Summer rainfall was coupled with the water brought down in the summer by seasonal streams and rivers from the surrounding mountains, which was often retained in simple dams; this combination enabled growers to raise rice in the Kachi plain, where it was the main crop at Posturban Pirak. The Kachi plain was the only area of the greater Indus region in which there is evidence of irrigation. In addition, the Kachi plain was closely linked to Baluchistan, where small-scale dams had been used for water conservation since at least the Early Indus period. The farmers in this area, then, were experienced in the use of irrigation and therefore adapted to the incorporation of rice cultivation in the spectrum of agricultural practices. The construction of a canal alongside the settlement at Pirak shows the continuation of irrigation technology in the region.

The evidence for rice as a crop is limited in the Indus region as a whole, though it may have been present at Harappa. It could be cultivated in the river valleys and elsewhere by sowing it in the dhands created by floodwater being retained in depressions. The margins of Lake Manchar would have provided ideal conditions, as they do today. However, in the Ganges-Yamuna doab and in areas to the east, summer monsoon rainfall was adequate to provide water for growing rice, and this is reflected in the cultivation of rice in Late Harappan sites in this region, such as Hulas, and in the spread of farming communities into the Ganges Valley in the first millennium.

Ground Preparation and Tools. The only direct evidence of the practices of Indus agriculture comes from the plowed fields at Kalibangan, belonging to the Early Harappan period, and at the Indus outpost of Shortugai. The field at Kalibangan was about 140 meters square and had been plowed in two directions at right angles, a practice still used in the region. In modern times, closely spaced strips are first plowed in one direction and are sown with horsegram. More widely spaced strips, plowed at right angles to the first furrows, are sown with mustard seed. This matches the arrangement in the Kalibangan field, where furrows 30 centimeters apart were plowed first, followed later by furrows 1.9 meters apart. The small field at Shortugai may have been used for growing flax, judging by the large number of *Linum* seeds scattered across it.

A terra-cotta model plow (ard) was found at Banawali, giving an idea of the form of the Harappan plow. It had a narrow, pointed share to gouge through the ground surface and a curved shaft by which it was drawn along. The model can give no idea of the scale of the original: It is possible, therefore, that it was small enough to have been drawn by a man, though it is more likely that a yoke for a plow team of two oxen would have been attached to the shaft.

Plowing was probably practiced mainly in permanently cultivated areas, such as in Sindh outside the active floodplains of the Indus and in the Saraswati Valley. New deposits of silt, exposed as the floods subsided from the

Indus floodplain and from the margins of seasonal lakes such as dhands and Lake Manchar, could be sown directly, without preparation. The black cotton soils of Gujarat, used for *kharif* cultivation, also did not require plowing: Deep cracks that opened during the dry season adequately turned and broke up the soil, and a new cultivable surface developed as the ground absorbed the summer rains and swelled up, sealing the cracks again. The ground needed only to be harrowed before sowing. No direct evidence of an Indus harrow survives, but there has been some speculation that the Indus sign of a vertical line with a series of shorter lines at right angles to it may represent a harrow.

In lands where it was used, the plow enabled larger areas to be cultivated than was possible with hand tools such as digging sticks and hoes, and it made use of animal traction, reducing the human effort involved in ground preparation. Ratnagar (2001) argues that farmers in the Indus period were likely to have been less interested in achieving high productivity than in ensuring reliability: minimizing the risk rather than maximizing yields. Nevertheless, an increase in agricultural efficiency by using animal labor is likely to have increased productivity and therefore produced a surplus that enabled some sectors of the community to engage in part-time or full-time nonfarming activities such as craft production and trading expeditions. Yields would also be higher if the seeds were carefully sown rather broadcast. The crisscross plowed furrows at Kalibangan would have required careful sowing along the furrows in order to maintain the clear separation between the two crops grown in the field; this suggests that sowing rather than broadcasting was practiced even in Early Indus times. In Mesopotamia, where a seeder plow was used, a field could be sown using less than half the seed that would be required for broadcasting, and the ratio of sown to harvested seed could be as high as one to fifteen.

Apart from the plow, very little is known about the agricultural tools or cultivation techniques used by the Harappans. Gypsum crystals found on a sherd at Kalibangan may have been used as a fertilizer. Harvesting was probably undertaken with a flint blade or flint-edged sickle. At sites in the Kachi plain, early sickles were made of flint microliths fastened with bitumen into a handle probably of wood. By the fourth millennium this was the only use made of microliths at Mehrgarh, and they continued in use into the Post-Harappan period, being present at Pirak. Fuller (2001) suggests that variations in the plant remains at Rojdi and Harappa may reflect changes in the practices of crop processing, with some degree of centralization in threshing and winnowing in the Harappan period, resulting in only processed grain being stored, while in the Late Harappan period whole grain was stored and processed only as required. This suggestion has been supported by Weber (2001).

ANIMAL HUSBANDRY

Animals played a major role in Indus agriculture. The main domestic animals were cattle, but sheep, goats, and other animals were also kept, their relative importance relating to local environmental conditions and no doubt to other factors.

Raising livestock was a useful investment against crop failure. In good years, when crop yields were high, grazing would also be good and the number of animals that were kept could be increased, surplus agricultural produce being available as fodder if the grazing ran out. In lean years, when grazing was limited, the additional animals could either be killed for food or used to obtain other foodstuffs, for example, by trading with pastoralists, by giving the animals as gifts to kin in other areas in the expectation of useful return gifts, or perhaps by exchanging them for grain stored by those in authority, though the evidence of central storage is limited and dubious.

Millets are nowadays often grown for fodder as well as for human consumption. While it is likely that the fodder needs of the Harappan domestic animals were largely met by grazing them on natural vegetation in areas beyond the cultivated land and by taking them to areas of seasonal pasture, it is possible that some use was made of fodder crops. Charcoal evidence from the latest Harappan levels at Lothal in Gujarat gives some indication of local environmental deterioration, which may imply reduced availability of grazing, at least locally. In addition, bullocks kept for plowing were probably provided with fodder, particularly during the plowing season. In Mesopotamia, as much as one-tenth of the crop could have been used to maintain the plow team, though, of course, this amount could be reduced if, as in some South Asian villages, a single plow team was maintained by and for a whole village.

Bovids

Cattle. Cattle were the main domestic animals of the Indus farmers, their bones constituting half or even three-quarters of those found in Indus sites in Gujarat and often around half elsewhere. This set a pattern that has continued up to the present day when South Asia has the highest density of cattle in the world (182 per square mile). Cows were probably kept for their milk and bullocks for drawing plows and carts, threshing, and raising water, while a few bulls would be maintained for breeding, one bull being enough to service all the cows of a village. Bones recovered from Indus sites show that many cattle were also killed for meat: they bear butchery marks and are often burnt. It is perhaps worth emphasizing that the weight of meat obtained from a cow or bullock is very much greater than that provided by a sheep or goat: A ratio of around 50 percent cattle in the faunal sample therefore implies that the bulk of meat consumed came from cattle. Cattle dung was probably used for fuel and mixed with mud as a daub applied to wattle walls.

Both the humped zebu (*Bos indicus*) and the humpless *Bos taurus* may have been kept because both appear as figurines in the Indus civilization and in earlier and later times. Distinguishing the skeletal remains of these species is difficult, though in cases where it was possible Caroline Grigson (1984), who has examined the bones from Harappa, concluded that only *Bos indicus* was present. It is thought likely that there were a number of different breeds of cattle in third-millennium South Asia, including smaller and larger varieties. A short-horned bovid depicted on seals may have been either the humpless bull or the gaur (Indian bison).

The unicorn frequently shown on seals is also often identified as a bovid, perhaps the humpless bull whose representation with a single horn may be due to an artistic convention (which was common in the Near East) for depicting bovids that actually had two horns. Alternatively, it may be intended as a mythical, probably composite, beast. The latter is perhaps more likely because figurines of unicorns have also been found and because the individual features of the unicorn on the seals, such as the very long horn and the pricked ear, do not match any known bovid. Alternatively, it may be a local copy of a foreign (e.g., Near Eastern) depiction of a humpless bull, if this were the case it would provide evidence that the humpless bull was not present in the Indus civilization.

The use of bullocks for traction is vividly illustrated by the many terra-cotta models of carts drawn by a pair of bullocks. They would also have been used to draw plows and probably provided the muscle power needed to draw water from wells for irrigation. Model yokes have been found at Nausharo. Other uses for cattle included threshing grain and carrying goods as pack animals.

Although it is likely milk was used, there is no evidence for this of the types known from contemporary cultures: in Mesopotamia, artistic representations of milking and textual references to milk and milk products; in Europe, vessels designed for milking and for processing milk into cheese, as well as occasional examples of an insufflator (a tube used to blow into the vagina or rectum of the animal to stimulate the milk letdown reflex). Studies of the age and sex structure of cattle and caprine populations at prehistoric sites can also reveal evidence that reflects the keeping of these animals for milk as well as for meat and other purposes, but, as far as I am aware, no such studies have been published on Indus domestic animals.

Bison. Another bovid that may have been exploited by the Harappans is the gaur (Indian bison, *Bibos gaurus*). Wild gaur now inhabit hilly areas in peninsular India but may also have been found in Gujarat and Rajasthan and possibly even the Indus Valley in prehistoric times. No bones from Indus settlements have been identified positively as gaur, but there are representations on a number of seals of a bovid with the short horns and shoulder ridge of the gaur.

Buffalo. Water buffaloes (*Bubalus bubalis*) were probably herded because there are buffalo bones at earlier sites such as Rehman Dheri and Mehrgarh period I, and they were also present at the Ahar-Banas site of Ahar. Bones definitely from domestic buffalo are known at Mature Indus sites, including Balakot and Dholavira. However, wild buffalo were probably also still hunted. Buffaloes occur as images on Indus seals, where they appear to be wild. Buffalo milk is richer than cows' milk, having a higher butterfat content, so it is likely that it was made into ghee.

Unlike cattle, domestic water buffaloes were generally kept in or near the village rather than taken elsewhere for seasonal grazing or used as pack animals. They require daily access to water (river buffalo) or mud (swamp buffalo, the variety present at Balakot) to keep their skins moist.

This seal depicts a bovid, either a short-horned bull or the Indian bison (gaur). Cattle, and particularly the humped zebu cattle, were the most important domestic animals kept by the Harappans. (J. M. Kenoyer, Courtesy Department of Archaeology and Museums, Government of Pakistan)

Caprines

Though cattle were the principal Harappan domestic animals, farmers also kept a few goats and sheep; caprines were also among the small numbers of livestock kept by town and city dwellers. Specialist pastoralists may have raised larger flocks of sheep and goats in some regions.

Domestication in sheep (as in many species) had led to or coincided with a diminution in size from that of the wild progenitor. Such small sheep continued into Indus times, being known, for example, from Dholavira, Nausharo, and Sibri, and they were still present in Kachi sites in the second millennium. Much larger domestic sheep at Harappa, however, may show that selective breeding was taking place to increase size. Sheep were kept in far larger numbers than goats at Harappa in the Punjab, a common practice in many communities because goats are less tractable, though often a small number of goats are kept with a flock of sheep, as they are said to calm the sheep and are also useful in leading the flock to pasture. Goats, however, have the advantage of being able to browse on a wider range of plants, so they can find food in more challenging terrain: This probably explains the more equal proportions of sheep and goats at Dholavira and Naushro, sites in relatively arid environments.

Sheep and goats were kept for meat and perhaps for their milk. It is usually assumed that sheep were also kept for their wool. There is, however, no direct evidence that this was so. Wool is present in wild sheep as a short undercoat, grown to protect against winter weather and shed in the spring. Sheep bred for longer wool appeared in the Near East during the fourth millennium and spread into Europe during the third millennium. The wool of these sheep was still molted in the spring and could be combed out or plucked from the animal or collected after it was shed. In Mesopotamia there is both pictorial and documentary evidence of woolly sheep and woolen textiles from the late fourth millennium onward; in Europe, aside from the very rare surviving textiles, the evidence is in the form of combs for removing the wool from the sheep; flat spindle whorls for spinning wool; a change in the age and sex structure of flocks (an increase in adults, often including some wethers [castrated rams], which provide the best and most abundant wool); and a substantial increase in the proportion of sheep among the domestic stock that were kept. As far as I am aware, none of these features has been actively looked for in the Indus realms; so the question remains open. It is perhaps significant, however, that the excavators of Mehrgarh believe leather to have been the main material used for clothing in the periods leading up to the Indus civilization, suggesting that neither wool nor cotton was in use for textiles before the Harappan period. The detailed analysis of the faunal remains at Balakot showed that most male sheep were culled at a young age, a pattern suggesting that sheep were kept for meat rather than for wool production. A similar picture may obtain from Dholavira, where a significant proportion of the caprines were killed before or as they reached maturity; though the faunal report did not divide the bones by sex as well as age, it is likely that the sheep kept into adulthood, around 40 percent of the total, were breeding females. Furthermore, trade between the Indus and Mesopotamia has always seemed unbalanced, the Indus receiving nothing obvious in return for its exports. If, however, the Harappans did not themselves produce wool, the woollen textiles that Mesopotamia produced on an industrial scale and exported widely may well have been a commodity that was highly prized by and valuable to the Harappans. Another possibly significant pointer, though only negative evidence, is the discovery in the second-millennium Deccan site of Nevasa of threads used to string beads, made of cotton, silk, and flax but not wool. Barber, an expert on prehistoric textiles, places South Asia well outside the area in which wool was used for making textiles in the third millennium (1991, map 1.8, 34).

Pastoralism

For millennia, upland and lowland areas had been linked by the seasonal movements of pastoralists, driving their flocks and herds between summer and winter pastures. Herders also moved within the Indus region itself, grazing their animals on the areas of high ground and seasonal grassland. A study of the distribution of Indus settlements shows significant clusters of towns and villages in some regions, separated by large tracts in which few or no settlements have been located despite intensive fieldwork. Pastoralists, and perhaps also hunter-gatherers, moved within these tracts, grazing their animals and providing the vital links that held together the civilization. Good pastures existed on the higher ground in the interfluve areas of the Punjab, used to graze the animals of farmers settled in the valleys of the Punjab rivers. In prehistoric and recent times, these pastures received an influx of animals from the adjacent northern highlands during the winter months, but throughout the Indus period communications between the northern borderlands and the Indus region appear to have been severely limited; so the Late Kot Diji inhabitants of the highlands probably took their animals to other pastures west of the mountains. In summer, from around March to October, the pastures of the Kulli region in southern Baluchistan may still have been utilized by Indus pastoralists, though the majority of animals were probably grazed in the summer in eastern Sindh, particularly on the seasonal grasslands of the Tharparkar, Kutch, particularly the grassland immediately south of the Great Rann, Saurashtra, and the western Saraswati Valley. Winter grazing was available on the Kachi plain, in Sindh, Punjab, and Gujarat. The inhabitants of the mountains would thus have spent their summers near home and travelled to seasonal pastures in the winter, while in the greater Indus region it was the winter months that saw the herders at home and the spring and summer when they moved to other pastures, though the distances they had to travel were often quite short.

Pastoralists may have been separate tribes, as was often the case in other regions and as is sometimes the case today in the subcontinent. A symbiotic relationship exists between these pastoralists and settled farmers in the regions that they visit, each providing the other with their produce. The farmers supply grain, vegetables, and fruits, as well as stubble grazing after the fields have been harvested, while the pastoralists provide meat, leather, wool, and goat hair, as well as dung to fertilize the fields and milk products like cheese and yogurt. Similar arrangements may have existed in Harappan times.

On the other hand, the ancestors of those who had settled on the Indus plains had belonged to communities that practiced transhumance in the Indo-Iranian borderlands, with a settled base in which at least some members of the community lived year-round and with temporary camps in the areas to which part of the community, probably often only the young men, moved seasonally to obtain pasture for their animals. Settled farmers and pastoralists were in this case members of the same families. Today the majority of cattle are kept by people who are primarily settled farmers, and the specialist pastoralists are mainly shepherds, keeping sheep. The modern zebu is adapted to a diet with marked seasonal variations in the quality and quantity of grazing, living today mainly on scrub vegetation on uncultivated wasteland areas. In good years the grazing and water available in the area around a village are adequate to maintain the village animals, and it is only in bad years, occurring perhaps every five to six years, that migration in search of grazing and water is necessary.

It is likely that in the Indus period there were both specialist pastoralists and farmers who spent part of their year in transhumance. In the latter case the animals belonged to the farmers and could be exploited directly, and those who took them to pasture would return seasonally to their place in the settled family. Specialist pastoralists, on the other hand, would have had an elaborate pattern of traditionally established or negotiated relationships with settled farmers whereby milk, dung, and other animal products were exchanged for grain, access to grazing, and perhaps manufactured goods. In practice the distinctions are likely to have been blurred, since many pastoralists are likely to have had a settled base where the elderly and women with very young children lived year-round, growing a few crops. Settled farmers may have made arrangements with pastoralists whereby the latter took charge of some of the farmers' livestock during the period when the animals needed to be taken to seasonal pastures away from the settlement. In Mesopotamia, where this system was well developed, contracts for such arrangements survive from this period: The pastoralist received in payment a proportion of the annual yield of wool and lambs from the flock. In addition to the private arrangements between individuals or families, pastoralists in Mesopotamia also entered into such contracts with temple or secular authorities. The elusive rulers of the Indus state may have employed similar means to maintain large herds and flocks that could not be supported on pastures in the vicinity of the cities.

A few settlements have been found that can be linked to pastoralists, although they are hard to locate, given their ephemeral nature. At Nesadi (Valabhi) in Saurashtra, pastoralists dwelt in circular huts with rammed earth floors, occupying the settlement during the winter months, as their successors do today. At this time of year there was abundant lush grazing in the region, which not only provided fodder for the domestic cattle of the inhabitants but also attracted wild animals such as deer, which the pastoralists hunted. In the summer, this campsite was under seasonal (monsoon) floods, the pastoralists having moved away to higher ground.

Another probable pastoralists' campsite, from the Late Harappan period, was uncovered at Oriyo Timbo in Gujarat. This site was probably occupied seasonally by a community whose main economic strategy was the herding of cattle, sheep, and goats but who may also have practiced a limited amount of cultivation. No structural remains were found there, with the exception of hearths, and it is therefore probable that temporary huts were constructed on arrival each year. The main surviving traces of the settlement's occupants are sherds of Lustrous Red ware pottery, querns, and grinding stones. Analysis of the cattle and caprine bones show that the animals were killed in the hot season, March to July, indicating the time of year when this camp was occupied.

Other Domestic Animals

A number of other domestic animals were kept by the Harappans. These probably did not include domestic pigs; wild boar were common throughout the Indus Valley and adjacent lowlands and were among the abundant game hunted by the Harappans.

Dogs. Bones of the domestic dog (*Canis familiaris*) have been found in many Harappan sites, as have a number of dog figurines. These indicate that there were several different breeds, including a squat animal resembling a bulldog and a rangy beast like an Afghan hound. Another type had pointed ears, while a fourth had an upright tail. Collars are shown around the necks of some of the figurines, reinforcing their domestic status. One dog is shown tied to a post and may represent a guard dog.

A number of Harappan figurines depict various breeds of dogs. Often they are shown wearing collars, like this charming animal, clearly a domestic pet. (Richard H. Meadow, Courtesy Department of Archaeology and Museums, Government of Pakistan)

The *dhole,* or red dog (*Cuon alpinus,* immortalized in Kipling's *Jungle Book* tale "Red Dog"), was probably captured (as orphaned puppies?) and perhaps tamed. The dhole is indigenous to the entire Indian subcontinent as well as to other parts of Asia. Dhole bones have been identified at Rojdi, and a dhole may have been presented as a gift (referred to as tribute in the text) to Ibbi-Sin, the last king of the Sumerian Ur III dynasty (ca. 2028–2004 BCE). Wolves may also have been tamed: Wolf bones have been recovered from Surkotada and Lothal.

Cats. It is possible that cats were kept by the Harappans: A number of felid species are native to the region, including *Felis lybica,* the ancestor of the domestic cat, and the rather larger *Felis viverrina,* the fishing cat. Paw prints made by the latter were found in a brick at Chanhu-daro that had been laid out to dry when the cat ran across, pursued by a dog. While cats may not have been deliberately domesticated, they are often commensal with humans in farming settlements where they are attracted by the rodents that feed on stored domestic grain. Unconfirmed bones of domestic cat (*Felis catus*) have been identified at Rojdi.

Birds. The chicken (*Gallus gallus*) may have been domesticated in South Asia, where its ancestor, the wild Indian red jungle fowl, was indigenous to the Ganges Valley and to parts of the greater Indus region. Recent genetic work, however, suggests that all modern domestic chickens were descended from birds domesticated in Thailand, though some genetic variations may indicate contributions from other birds, making it still possible that Indian chickens were locally domesticated. Chicken bones have been found on many Harappan sites, including the cities of Mohenjo-daro and Harappa, the towns of Ropar and Kalibangan in the east, and Lothal, Rojdi, and Surkotada in the west.

A variety of other birds were exploited by the Harappans. Cranes are captured and kept as pets by the people of the Bannu Basin in modern Pakistan, and the representation of cranes on fourth-millennium pottery from this region, at Taraqai Qila and other sites, has been tentatively interpreted by Dr. Farid Khan (1991) as suggesting that the practice may also have taken place in ancient times, using the perforated stones found there as weights in a bola to capture the birds. This is an imaginative but not improbable suggestion.

Peacocks were a popular theme on Harappan and Cemetery H pottery. These handsome birds are native to the subcontinent, living near water in areas of deciduous forest. Peafowl are frequently commensal with humans, being attracted to cultivated ground and the edges of settlements where their food, such as insects and seeds, is easy to obtain. Although their bones have been identified only at Rojdi, it is likely they were more widely caught, both for their meat and for their feathers. Like cranes, they might also have been kept as pets. The *haia* bird, mentioned in a Mesopotamian text, may have been a peacock and, if so, may have been one of the variety of live animals taken to Sumer by Indus traders, perhaps as diplomatic gifts. The text reads:

May your birds all be peacocks! May their cries grace royal palaces! (ECSL2006, lines 229–230).

A terra-cotta from Harappa depicts a man carrying a duck, ducks decorate some ivory gaming counters from Mohenjo-daro, and there is also one Indus sign of a duck within a circle (a pond?). It is possible that the Harappans kept ducks, though the hunting of wild duck as game seems more probable.

Hares. Hares were common in the Indus region and may have been kept as children's pets but could also provide meat. They are known as terra-cotta figurines and are one of the small group of signs commonly occurring on copper tablets; they also occur among the miniatures at Harappa.

Mongooses. Another species that was present at a number of sites, including Mohenjo-daro, Harappa, Rangpur, Surkotada, and Kuntasi, was an ichneumon, the Indian gray mongoose *(Herpestes edwardsi)*. It is possible that mongooses were kept by the Harappans as a protection against snakes. Bones of a mongoose, probably imported from the Indus, were found in early second-millennium Bahrain (Dilmun).

Elephant. The fauna of the greater Indus region included the Indian elephant *(Elephas maximus)*. Ivory, which probably came mainly from the elephant, was extensively used by the Harappans: At Mohenjo-daro it was more common than bone as a material for making artifacts. Elephant bones have been recovered from a number of sites throughout the Indus region, from Lothal and Surkotada in Gujarat, to Mohenjo-daro and Chanhu-daro in Sindh, and to Harappa and Kalibangan in the east; although elephants could have been hunted for their meat, these bones may suggest that tame elephants were employed as work animals, to haul logs, for example. Further suggestive evidence of tame elephants comes from representations on seals of elephants apparently wearing a cloth over their back, and a clay model of elephant's head with painted designs on its forehead: Elephants are similarly decorated with paint on festive days in modern South Asia.

Camel. The two-humped Bactrian camel was domesticated in southern Central Asia, originally for meat and fur, and figurines show that it was used there to draw carts and as a beast of burden by the midthird millennium. A skeleton identified as a domestic camel was found at Mohenjo-daro, from a level belonging to the Posturban period. Similarly, camel bones identified at Harappa, Surkotada, Kanewal, Kalibangan, and perhaps Rojdi were all from the upper levels of these settlements, and none is likely to be earlier than 2000 BCE. A single representation of a camel at Kalibangan also confirms that the Harappans were familiar with the creature, not surprisingly given the existence of the Indus colony of Shortugai in camel country. Shortugai has also yielded a rather schematic terra-cotta figurine of a camel. Camels were probably of no local significance during the Indus civilization, and those present might have belonged to traders from eastern Iran or Turkmenia, where they were in common use. In the Posturban period at Pirak, domestic camel bones and figurines of camels are present from period I, dated after 1700 BCE. The Bactrian camel did not come into widespread use in South Asia and disappeared from the region before the end of the second millennium, and it was the Arabian camel that eventually became established there as an important draft and pack animal, but not before the midfirst millennium BCE and probably much later.

However, the bones from Harappan settlements have mostly been identified as the one-humped Arabian camel (dromedary). This is problematic since domestic Arabian camels are not otherwise known outside their Arabian homeland much before 1000 BCE: Doubts have therefore been expressed about this identification. On the other hand, there were large numbers of bones from (almost certainly wild) Arabian dromedaries, favored as a raw material for tools, at Umm an-Nar, Ra's Ghanada, and Tell Abraq in Oman. Since the Harappans had close trading ties with the people of the Oman peninsula, it is possible that meat and bones from hunted wild dromedaries or even live captive animals were brought to the Indus region through trade. The concentration in Gujarati sites of around half the alleged Harappan camel bones would support this suggestion.

Equids. There is considerable controversy about the presence of the domestic horse in early South Asia, made contentious by being bound up in the Indo-Aryan debate (see chapter 11). Bones said to come from the domestic horse have been found at a number of Harappan sites. From detailed studies of these equid bones, however, the eminent archaeozoologist Richard Meadow concluded that none definitely came from a domestic horse, and the balance of probability is that all the equid bones in Harappan and pre-Harappan contexts in India and Pakistan came from the onager (*Equus hemionus,* also known as the steppe ass). This wild equid is indigenous to northern South Asia, unlike the ancestor of the horse, *E. przewalskii,* which is native to the steppe region from the Ukraine to Mongolia. Morphologically, the two species are similar and it is often difficult to distinguish their bones.

The onager is apparently too intractable to be domesticated, although there are claims that young onager can be tamed. Wild onager could provide meat and skins for leather: This is probably the reason for the presence of equid bones on Indus sites.

Horses were domesticated on the European fringes of the Eurasian steppe around 4000 BCE, probably being used initially for meat; good evidence of domestic horses is known by 3000 BCE in Kazakhstan. Evidence from the steppe and adjacent regions indicate that the horse was used as a pack and particularly as a draft animal and that, as such, it spread out from the steppe into southern and Eastern Europe and parts of Asia, being used particularly to draw war chariots, invented around 2100 BCE. Horse riding probably began around the same time but was not an efficient mode of transport until the invention of supportive saddles and sophisticated bridles during the first millennium BCE. Horses reached South Asia from steppe cultures north of the Caspian, by way of Turkmenia, Bactria, and perhaps Seistan. The earliest indubitable evidence of the domestic horse in the subcontinent comes from Pirak, well after the Mature Harappan period: There horse bones and horse figurines

All equid bones from Harappan sites are likely to come from the onager (khur or steppe ass), which was probably hunted, given its reputation as a creature too intractable for domestication. (Andreas Loban)

are known in period I (from 1700 BCE), while in period II there were also figurines of horse riders. Horses appear at a number of second- and early first-millennium sites in South Asia, ranging from the Gandhara Graves in the north to the South Indian megaliths. Second-millennium sherds from Birkot Ghundai in the Swat valley unmistakably depict horses; in contrast, there are no Harappan depictions of horses (for discussion of a fraudulent attempt to create one, see Witzel and Farmer 2000).

AQUATIC RESOURCES

The history of the exploitation of aquatic resources is obscured by the frustrating paucity of well-reported faunal collections from prehistoric sites in the greater Indus region. However, at the exemplary site of Mehrgarh the remains of fish were rare despite the proximity of the Bolan River, and the reported remains from other Neolithic and Chalcolithic sites in the Indo-Iranian borderlands do not suggest a tradition of exploiting riverine resources. The absence of fish in the coastal settlement of Balakot during the pre- and Early Harappan periods suggests that the pastoralists from Baluchistan who settled there had no interest in the locally available marine resources. In contrast, the presence of seashells at inland sites such as Mehrgarh, brought there through exchange networks, indicates that from early times there were coastal communities who did exploit marine resources. Similarly, fish were regularly caught by hunter-gatherer communities in the subcontinent, as is vividly shown in the rock art at Bhimbetka and other Central Indian sites. Fish bones were among the faunal remains at Bagor, and in the Hakra period site of Jalilpur on the Ravi River terra-cotta net sinkers indicate that fishing was practiced. In all probablility, the pre- and Early Harappan inhabitants of Gujarat exploited marine resources: Although faunal remains have not been reported from their settlements, the coastal location of sites such as Padri and Somnath and the island situation of Dholavira are suggestive, as is the presence of fishhooks at Padri.

Early riverine and coastal communities in the greater Indus region are likely to have developed boats and the other technology needed for exploiting marine and freshwater resources. It is probable that the Early Harappan farming settlers gradually acquired from indigenous communities the skills, knowledge, and technology to exploit the sea, rivers, and lakes, and by the Harappan period fishing was integrated with other aspects of the economy. For example, the Harappan inhabitants of Balakot, in contrast to their earlier shunning of the sea, developed an economy based heavily on the exploitation of marine fish and shellfish.

Fish and Fishing

An important source of food for the Harappans was fish: Large numbers of fish bones have been recovered from the Harappan settlements whose faunal remains have been studied. Some bones came from fish 2 meters or more in length, and it is likely that fish were an important source of protein. At Balakot fish provided around half the faunal component of the diet. The faunal remains from the coastal settlement of Balakot and from Harappa far inland near the Ravi River have been examined in detail, providing a complementary picture of the exploitation of marine and freshwater resources.

A large selection of marine fish were exploited at Balakot, including requiem sharks, stingrays, wolf herring, sea bream, mullet, and drum, but the villagers concentrated on a few species, particularly marine catfish, mackerel, and various types of grunt, the latter around 90 percent of the fish caught. The range of fish varied seasonally, with few species being available in winter but many coming in close to shore in the summer and autumn to spawn, making them easy to catch. The grunt, however, spawns during the winter and could be easily caught with stationary nets set up in the shallow waters of Sonmiani Bay where Balakot is located. A similar range of marine fish was found at Allahdino, along with freshwater catfish. The Harappans probably used similar techniques to those of modern fishers in the region, who catch some fish close to the shore and others farther out to sea, using fixed nets particularly for large fish and cast nets for smaller ones; some nets are also set on the sea bottom to catch crabs and other crustacea. Modern fishers also practice trolling: crisscrossing an area of sea towing a series of lures and hooks from the boat.

Farther south in Kutch, fish might also have been caught, as today, using tidal traps into which the fish swam when the tide was up and in which they were caught as the tide went out. Analyses of the types and condition of the shellfish from coastal settlements confirm that fishing also took place from off-shore boats.

The remains from Harappa show that the range of freshwater fish was more restricted than that available from the sea. Here the main species exploited were four types of catfish, though various types of carp, snakeheads, and spiny eels were also important. The distribution of the remains at Harappa shows that some households consumed large quantities of fish while others ate little. At Nausharo in the Bolan Valley, carp and catfish were also the species of fish caught.

The banks of the main Indus River were too friable and the current too swift to make it safe to fish there, but fish such as carp and catfish were caught in the backwaters and smaller channels, where water flow was slow, particularly during the winter and spring. The Saraswati was far less turbulent, and it is probable that the inhabitants of many of the settlements along its banks would have caught fish from it. Channels cut for irrigation or drainage might also have yielded fish. Fishing could also have taken place in the rivers and streams of Baluchistan; the pools that form in the dry season on the Hab River in the Kulli province are today a rich source of fish. Fishing was also a major occupation in the oxbows and lakes of the Indus Basin, particularly Lake Manchar, but also in the seasonal dhands whose fishstocks were replenished by the annual flood-waters. During the inundation itself, however, no fishing was possible.

Nets were the principal fishing device, used on the side channels, oxbows, and lakes. The bottom of the nets were weighted down with terra-cotta net sinkers, similar to large beads but exhibiting a characteristic wear pattern from the chaffing of the string used to secure them in place along the edge of the net. These have been found in many Indus settlements, from the great city of Harappa to the small village of Kanewal. A sherd of pottery from Harappa depicts a fishing scene, in which a man stands among fish, holding one or several nets, while along the foot of the scene runs a large net presumably surrounding an area of water in which the fish have been trapped.

During the period immediately after the inundation when the rivers were still high and turbulent, fish could be caught in the shallow areas along the banks of the main rivers, using hook and line. While simple hooks had been in use since earlier times, the Harappans were probably responsible for developing the barbed fishhook, which also had a looped end to which the line was fastened. Copper fishhooks have been found at Mohenjo-daro, Harappa, Padri, and Chanhu-daro. An example of exceptional size from Padri in Saurashtra suggests that very large marine fish were being taken, presumably from substantial boats.

Examination of the cut marks on fish bones at Balakot shows that they were butchered with knives probably of copper rather than stone. The heads were removed, probably to be boiled up in a soup or stew until the meat fell off. The virtual absence of all bones but the vertebrae at Allahdino suggests that the

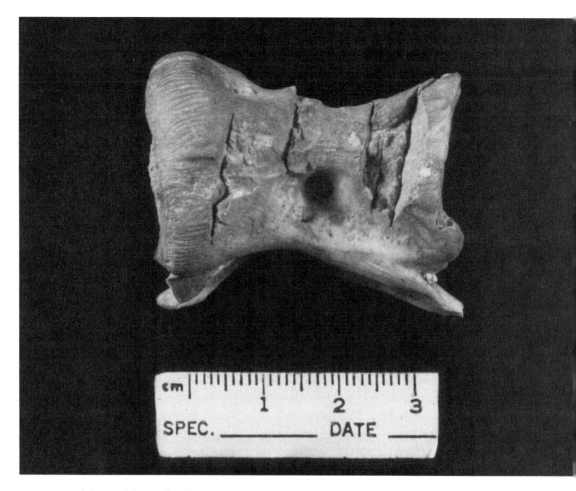

A bone of the sua fish *(Protonibea diacanthus)*, from the coastal settlement of Balakot where fishing was important. This fish comes inshore to spawn during the summer monsoon period when it is readily caught, even today, by fishermen using traditional methods. Cut marks on this bone reveal details of butchery which can be compared with modern butchery practices to suggest patterns of exploitation. (William R. Belcher)

fish were butchered before they were brought to the site by nonresident fishers; in contrast, the full representation of bones at Balakot indicates that this was a fishing settlement where the catch was processed.

Preserved Fish

As well as being eaten fresh, fish were dried or salted so that they could be eaten later or elsewhere. At the tiny site of Prahag, west of Balakot along the Makran coast, where sherds of Harappan and local pottery are known, evidence was found of fish processing on a large scale. Skate, jack, grunt, marine catfish, drum, and small shark appear to have been caught locally, probably from boats using a hook and line. They were then cut open and the heads and tails removed, as well as part of the vertebral column of the skates and sharks; they may then have been preserved by salting or drying. Dolphins were also caught, and the people of this region also ate sheep, goats, and gazelle, perhaps reserving the dried fish for export. Bones of marine catfish and jack at Harappa show that preserved fish was transported even this far inland, more than 850 kilometers from the coast. Similarly, abundant bones of shark, marine catfish, drum, sea bream, and jack at Miri Qalat in Baluchistan, 120 kilometers of difficult terrain distant from the sea, also provide evidence of a flourishing trade in preserved marine fish: In modern Baluchistan dried fish are used not only for human food but also as fodder for animals. Probably only a limited range of species were distributed in this way. Grunt (*Pomadasys hasta*), the predominant fish at Balakot, are often preserved by salting in modern times.

The settlement of Padri in Saurashtra has been suggested by its excavator, Vasant Shinde, to have been a salt-making village in the Harappan period. Salt making is one of the local industries there today, and the flat area on the southern side of the Harappan village was ideally suited for this purpose because it was submerged at high tide but protected from lesser tides by a high natural barrier. This allowed seawater to be captured and left to evaporate in small embanked plots, a process taking a little over a week. Shinde suggests that the well-made, sturdy, nonporous storage jars found at Padri were designed for transporting salt. If so, preserving fish and perhaps other meat may have been one of the main purposes for which this industry was intended.

Molluscs

Shellfish were taken in considerable quantities by coastal communities. The shells were processed to make a variety of objects, particularly bangles, and this may have been the main reason for their collection, the edible molluscs being a bonus of the shell-working industry. The internal shells ("bones") of cuttlefish, found, for instance, at Othmanjo Buthi in Sindh, could have been used as an abrasive device for sanding wood or could have been ground up and made into an abrasive paste. Some settlements, such as Nageshwar on the northern coast of Saurashtra, probably existed for the specialized purpose of exploiting marine molluscs for manufacturing shell objects.

The shells were obtained in various ways. Nageshwar is situated on a freshwater lake with easy access to extensive shallow bays in the sheltered waters of the Gulf of Kutch from which abundant supplies of *Turbinella pyrum* (chank) and *Chicoreus ramosus* (spiny murex) shells could be obtained. Although these could be gathered in the shallow coastal waters, the fishers of Nageshwar seem generally to have gone into deeper water on rafts or small boats to obtain shells that were free from the boring activities of *Cliona* sponges and other marine organisms to which those near the shore were prey. Farther north, the shellfish collectors of Balakot and other settlements on the coast of Sindh and Makran obtained some of their shells, such as the bivalve *Meretrix casta*, from intertidal pools and from the shallows at low tide. Other types of mollusc had to be dived for from boats on reefs in shallow coastal waters. Here the fishers might encounter hazards such as moray eels, Portuguese man-of-wars and other dangerous jellyfish, and poisonous sea snakes and fishes. Fishing and diving for shells probably took place mainly before and after the monsoon, in April to June and in October to January. In addition to chank and spiny murex, these regions yielded *Lambis truncata sebae* and *Fasciolaria trapezium* shells, all used for making objects found throughout the Indus realms, as well as various species whose circulation was more restricted, such as clam shells (*Tivela damaoides*), which were worked at Balakot to make shell bangles worn by people in the local area and at other sites along the Makran coast but not farther afield. In addition, at Balakot *Terebralia palustris* molluscs, which live in mangrove swamps and brackish water, were collected in large quantities and were probably the main source of shellfish for food; they were not used for making shell objects.

WILD RESOURCES

The farming communities of the Indus and neighboring regions had always continued to exploit some wild resources alongside those derived from arable agriculture and pastoralism, and it seems that this practice increased and broadened in the Mature Harappan period.

Animals

To some extent hunting was a by-product of agriculture, birds and herbivores being killed to protect crops and predators to protect livestock, but game could also be a valuable addition to the diet. Many types of game animal such as chinkara and other gazelles, onager, wild sheep (urial), wild goats (Persian wild goat, markhor, and ibex), blackbuck, and other antelopes lived in the hills and grazed in the scrub and grasslands of the plains, while the well-watered areas along the rivers and lakeshores were home to nilgai, wild boar, water buffalo, wild cattle, elephant, chital, barasingha, and other deer. Several varieties of turtle, crocodiles, and dolphins, as well as molluscs and fish, could be taken from rivers and lakes. Wildfowl were also available around water, and particularly on Lake Manchar and in Gujarat. There were also other birds that made good eating, such as francolin, partridge, pheasant, jungle fowl, grouse, and peafowl. Even lizards were caught and eaten.

While some of the animals were probably hunted by villagers and city dwellers, game may also have been brought in by hunter-gatherers. Although the fourth-millennium farming settlers may have absorbed or displaced the hunter-gatherers who lived in the areas that they began to cultivate, hunter-gatherer groups continued to flourish elsewhere. For example, the Indus people never colonized the north Gujarat plain, probably because of its well-established hunter-gatherer population. The Harappans traded with hunter-gatherer communities such as those in Gujarat, Rajasthan, and the Aravalli hills, thus gaining access to wild products including those of more distant areas visited by hunter-gatherers in the course of their seasonal movements to exploit different resources. In some modern Indian communities, hunter-gatherers are employed to guard crops and deal with marauding wild animals, a role they could have had in the Indus realms as well. A mosaic of practices probably lies behind the variations in the fauna represented on different sites: For example, few bones of wild animals have been found at Rangpur and Surkotada in Gujarat, but they are common at Lothal, Dholavira, Kanewal, and Rojdi in the same region. The well-reported faunal remains from Rojdi give a particularly full picture: Wild animals eaten by its inhabitants included chausingha, hog deer, chital, barasingha, sambar, nilgai, blackbuck, and chinkara (Indian gazelle). Kanewal yielded a similar range of animals, and Dholavira had not only gazelle, deer, and blackbuck, but also onager and hare. At Nausharo on the Kachi plain, game included chinkara, wild boar, and onager, while at Harappa and Mohenjo-daro there were also hog deer, chital, and several other species of deer. Harappa and Balakot also had nilgai, and there were also gazelle at Balakot. Bird bones, turtle, and tortoise were common in most Harappan sites.

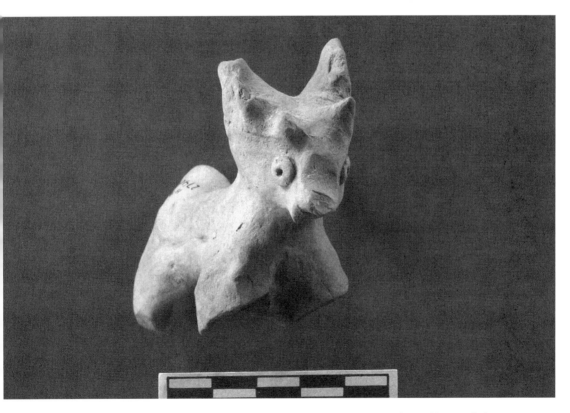

A deer figurine from Harappa. Deer and many other wild animals were hunted by people living within the Indus realms, perhaps by specialist hunters, though Harappan city-dwellers may also have hunted for food and farmers for meat and to protect their crops. (Richard H. Meadow, Courtesy Department of Archaeology and Museums, Government of Pakistan)

Other valuable commodities could be obtained from wild animals. Some game may have been taken for their pelts, for use in making clothing, or as covers and rugs. These may have included desert foxes, leopards, tigers, and Asiatic lions; wolf bones have been found at a number of sites, jackal bones in several settlements in Gujarat, and those of a black bear at Amri. Crocodile skins might also have been valued. Rhinoceroses were hunted for their horns and hides: Rhino bones are known from a large number of settlements, including Harappa, Nausharo, Kalibangan, Lothal, Surkotada, and Kanewal. Elephants were killed for their ivory, although there may also have been an unknown number of domestic elephants. Boars' tusks were also usable as a type of ivory and boars' bristles for fine brushes such as those used for painting pottery. Porcupine quills could be used to make piercing instruments such as needles and awls. Antlers made a useful raw material for manufacturing tools and handles: The antlers of Kashmir stag and sambar were utilized at Harappa and Mohenjo-daro, along with those of chital and hog deer at the latter site.

Edible Plants

Wild plants were also important: as well as providing grazing for domestic animals, some, such as *Chenopodium,* were undoubtedly exploited as human food. It may have been through familiarity with the range of local flora that some summer-growing plants were brought under cultivation, introducing the innovation of *kharif* agriculture. In this way rice, some millets and pulses, and a number of vegetables are likely to have first been incorporated into the diet and then added to the range of crops. Fruits such as jujube, almond, and pistachio were gathered. It has been suggested that wild plants were collected particularly when cultivated crops were unable to supply the full needs of the community, either because of bad harvests or because of population increase in the region. At Rojdi, about a quarter of the plant food came from wild sources; more than a dozen species of wild plants were utilized at Harappa; and the balance between wild and domestic plant foods was likely to have been regionally and locally variable.

Timber

The forests of the Himalayas, Baluchistan, and the Gujarati hills, as well as the jungles of well watered lowlands in the Indus Basin, were the source of timber used as a building material, for fuel, for many domestic purposes, and for export. Useful species included sissoo, acacia, and tamarisk, which were widely available. Sissoo was used for roof beams at Mohenjo-daro, while acacia was found at Lothal and Rangpur, used for making tools and furniture as well as in construction. The main use of tamarisk was for fuel, though it could be used for making many objects and structural elements; it is attested to at Rangpur. Rosewood was available on the plains, as well as in peninsular India: It was used for one of the wooden coffins found at Harappa and was also employed for making furniture, tools, and the wheels of carts. In the east the forests also held sal trees. The trees at higher altitudes in the mountains included deodar and pine, known from Harappa and Mohenjo-daro and used in buildings and for other purposes; both are fragrant woods, as is sissoo. Elm, also growing at high altitudes, was used for construction at Harappa. Another mountain species, the birch, is not attested to, but in later times it was used for fuel and its bark was an important writing material. Teak, generally useful and particularly suitable for shipbuilding because it is water-resistant, grew on the high ground in Gujarat, and in lower parts of the region *baru* grass (*Sorghum halepensis*) yielded tough tubular stems up to 5 meters long that were suitable for making smaller boats. Ebony was available in the forests of the Western Ghats but has not been found in Harappan sites, though it may be referred to in Mesopotamian texts as an import from the Indus (*sulum meluhhi*, "black wood of Meluhha," alternatively identified as rosewood). Mangrove, also possibly similarly mentioned (*kusabku meluhhie*, "Meluhhan seawood," alternatively identified as teak), was available along the west coast and may have been used in boatbuilding and for fuel. Native fruit trees included jujube, almond, and pistachio; a wooden mortar set in a grinding platform at Harappa was of jujube wood. Bamboo was available in the Makran and its wood was found at Harappa. Date palms grew in the Makran and in Sindh: As well as their fruit, they yielded wood, leaves for making baskets, mats, and roofs, and fiber for ropes and cords.

REFERENCES

Allchin, Bridget. 1984. "The Harappan Environment." In *Frontiers of the Indus Civilization*, edited by B. B. Lal and S. P. Gupta, 445–454. New Delhi: Books and Books.

Allchin, Bridget, and Raymond Allchin. 1982. *The Rise of Civilization in India and Pakistan*. Cambridge, UK: Cambridge University Press.

Anon. 2006a. "Sorghum." *Wikipedia* [Online information; retrieved 2/1/06.] en.wikipedia.org/wiki/sorghum.

Anon. 2006b. "Pearl Millet." *Wikipedia* [Online information; retrieved 2/1/06.] en.wikipedia.org/wiki/Pearl_millet.

Anon. 2006c. "Proso Millet." *Wikipedia* [Online information; retrieved 2/1/06.] en.wikipedia.org/wiki/Proso_millet.

Anon. 2006d. "Foxtail Millet." *Wikipedia* [Online information; retrieved 2/1/06.] en.wikipedia.org/wiki/Foxtail_millet.

Anon. 2006e. "Finger Millet." *Wikipedia* [Online information; retrieved 2/1/06.] en.wikipedia.org/wiki/Finger_millet.

Anon. 2006f. "Job's Tears." *Wikipedia* [Online information; retrieved 2/1/06.] en.wikipedia.org/wiki/ Job%27s_Tears.

Anthony, David. 1998. "Current Thoughts on the Domestication of the Horse in Asia." *South Asian Studies* 13: 315–318.

Barber, Elizabeth J. W. 1991. *Prehistoric Textiles*. Princeton, NJ: Princeton University Press.

Belcher, William R. 1993. "Riverine and Marine Fish Resource Utilization of the Indus Valley Tradition." *Journal of Pakistan Archaeologists Forum* 2 (I–II): 241–279.

Belcher, William R. 1994. "Riverine Fisheries and Habitat Exploitation of the Indus Valley Tradition: An Example from Harappa, Pakistan." In *South Asian Archaeology*

1993, edited by Asko Parpola and Petteri Koskikallio, 71–80. Helsinki: Suomalainen Tiedeakatemia.

Belcher, William R. 1997. "Marine and Riverine Resource Use during the Indus Valley Tradition: A Preliminary Comparison of Fish Remains from Balakot and Harappa." In *South Asian Archaeology 1995,* edited by Raymond and Bridget Allchin, 173–185. New Delhi: Oxford & IBH Publishing Co.

Belcher, William R. 2005. "A Baluchi Fishing Village." [Online article; retrieved 4/24/00.] www.harappa. com/fisher/index.html. Accessed June 14, 2005.

Bellwood, Peter. 2004. *First Farmers. The Origins of Agricultural Societies.* Oxford: Blackwell Publishing.

Besenval, Roland, and Jean Desse. 1995. "Around or Lengthwise? Fish Cutting-up Areas on the Baluchi Coast (Pakistani Makran)." *The Archaeological Review,* 4 (1/2): 133–149.

Bhan, Kuldeep K. 1989. "Late Harappan Settlements of Western India, with Special Reference to Gujarat." In *Old Problems and New Perspectives in the Archaeology of South Asia,* edited by Jonathan Mark Kenoyer, 219–242. *Wisconsin Archaeological Reports.* Vol. 2. Department of Anthropology. Madison: University of Wisconsin Press.

Bhan, Kuldeep K. 2004. "In the Sand Dunes of North Gujarat." In *Indus Civilization. Sites in India. New Discoveries,* edited by Dilip K. Chakrabarti, 96–105. Mumbai: Marg Publications.

Bokonyi, Sandor. 1998. "Horse Remains from the Prehistoric Site of Surkotada, Kutch, Late 3rd Millennium B.C." *South Asian Studies* 13: 297–307-.

Bose, A. B. 1975. "Pastoral Nomadism in India: Nature, Problems and Prospects." In *Nomads and Pastoralists in South Asia,* edited by Lawrence S. Leshnik and Gunter D. Sontheimer, 1–15. Wiesbaden: Otto Harrassowitz.

Chakrabarti, Dilip K. 1999. *India: An Archaeological History. Palaeolithic Beginnings to Early Historic Foundations.* New Delhi: Oxford University Press.

Chakrabarti, Dilip K. 2004. "Introduction." In *Indus Civilization. Sites in India. New Discoveries,* edited by Dilip K. Chakrabarti, 6–22. Mumbai: Marg Publications.

Chattopadhyaya, Umesh C. 2002. "Researches in Archaeozoology of the Holocene Period (Including the Harappan Tradition in India and Pakistan)." In *Indian Archaeology in Retrospect. II. Protohistory. Archaeology of the Harappan Civilization,* edited by S. Settar and Ravi Korisettar, 365–419. Indian Council of Historical Research. New Delhi: Manohar.

Dales, George F. 1982. "Adaptation and Exploitation at Harappan Coastal Settlements." In *Anthropology in Pakistan,* edited by Stephen Pastner and Louis Flam, 154–165. Ithaca, NY: Cornell University Press.

Deshpande, Shweta Sinha, and Vasant Shinde. 2005. "Gujarat between 2000 and 1400 BCE." *South Asian Studies* 21: 121–135.

Edens, Christopher. 2002. "Before Sheba." In *Queen of Sheba. Treasures from Ancient Yemen,* edited by St John Simpson, 80–87. London: British Museum Press.

Electronic Corpus of Sumerian Literature (ECSL). 2006. "Enki and the World Order." [Online information; retrieved 5/21/06] etcsl.orinst.ox.ac.uk/cgibin/etcsl.cgi? text=t.1.1.3&charenc=j#.

Fairservis, Walter A. 2002. "Views of the Harappans—The Transitional Years." In *Facets of Indian Civilization. Recent Perspectives. Essays in Honour of Professor B .B. Lal,* edited by Jagat Pati Joshi, 167–173. New Delhi: Aryan Books International.

Francfort, H. P. 1984. "The Harappan Settlement at Shortugai." In *Frontiers of the Indus Civilization*, edited by B. B. Lal and S. P. Gupta, 301–310. New Delhi: Books and Books.

Franke Vogt, Ute. 2000. "The Archaeology of Southeastern Balochistan." [Online article; retrieved 6/14/05.] www.harappa.com/baluch/index.html.

Fuller, Dorian. 2001. "Harappan Seeds and Agriculture: Some Considerations." *Antiquity* 75 (288): 410–414.

Fuller, Dorian. 2003. "Lost Farmers and Languages in Asia: Some Comments to Diamond and Bellwood." *Science* May 8. [Online article; retrieved 4/2/07.] www.sciencemag.org/cgi/eletters/300/5619/597#689?ck=nck.

Fuller, Dorian, Ravi Korisettar, and P. C. Venkatasubbaiah. 2001. "Southern Neolithic Cultivation Systems: A Reconstruction Based on Archaeobotanical Evidence." *South Asian Studies* 17: 171–187.

Fuller, Dorian, Ravi Korisettar, P. C. Venkatasubbaiah, and Martin K. Jones. 2004. "Early Plant Domestications in Southern India Some Preliminary Archaeobotanical Results." *Vegetation History Archaeobotany* 13 (2): 115–129. May 25. [Online article; retrieved 1/2/06.] www.ucl.ac.uk/archaeology/staff/profiles/fuller/pdfs/vha.pdf.

Fumihito, A., T. Miyake, S. Sumi, M. Takada, S. Ohno, and N. Kondo. 1994. "One Subspecies of the Red Junglefowl (*Gallus gallus gallus*) Suffices as the Matriarchic Ancestor of All Domestic Breeds." *Proceedings of the National Academy of Sciences* 91: 12505–12509. [Online article; retrieved 10/2/05.] www.pnas.org/cgi/content/abstract/91/26/12505?maxtoshow=&HITS=10&hits=10&RESULTFORMAT=&searchid=1128268038916_1885&stored_search=&FIRSTINDEX=20&minscore=5000&journalcode=pnas.

Glover, Ian C., and Charles F. W. Higham. 1996. "New Evidence for Early Rice Cultivation in South, Southeast and East Asia." In *The Origins and Spread of Agriculture and Pastoralism in Eurasia*, edited by David R. Harris, 413–441. Washington, DC: Smithsonian Institution.

Grigson, Caroline. 1984. "Some Thoughts on Unicorns and Other Cattle Depicted at Mohenjo-daro and Harappa." In *South Asian Archaeology 1981*, edited by Bridget Allchin, 166–169. Cambridge, UK: Cambridge University Press.

Hegde, K. T., K. K. Bhan, V. H. Sonawane, K. Krishnan, and D. R. Shah. 1992. *Excavations at Nageshwar, Gujarat. A Harappan Shellworking Site on the Gulf of Kutch.* Baroda: Department of Archaeology and Ancient History, M. S. University of Baroda.

Hesse, Brian. 2000. "Animal Husbandry and Human Diet in the Ancient Near East." In *Civilizations of the Ancient Near East*, edited by Jack M. Sasson, 203–222. Peabody, MA: Hendrickson Publishers. (Reprint of 1995 edition. New York: Scribner's.)

Jarrige, Jean-Francois. 1997. "From Nausharo to Pirak: Continuity and Change in the Kachi/Bolan Region from the 3rd to the 2nd Millennium B.C." In *South Asian Archaeology 1995*, edited by Raymond and Bridget Allchin, 11–35. New Delhi: Oxford & IBH Publishing Co.

Kenoyer, Jonathan Mark. 1984. "Shell Industries at Moenjodaro, Pakistan." In *Reports on Fieldwork Carried Out at Mohenjo-daro, Pakistan 1982–83 by the IsMEO-Aachen University Mission: Interim Reports I*, edited by Michael Jansen and Gunter Urban, 99–115. Aachen and Rome: RWTH and IsMEO.

Kenoyer, Jonathan Mark. 1998. *Ancient Cities of the Indus Valley Civilization*. Karachi: Oxford University Press and American Institute of Pakistan Studies.

Khan, Farid. 1991 "The Antiquity of Crane-catching in the Bannu Basin." *South Asian Studies* 7: 97–99.

Killick, Robert, and Jane Moon, eds. 2005. *The Early Dilmun Settlement at Saar.* Ludlow: Archaeology International.

Kipling, Rudyard. 2005. *The Second Jungle Book.* London: Dodo Press.

Kohler-Rollefson, Ilse. 1996. "The One-humped Camel in Asia: Origin, Utilization and Mechanisms of Dispersal." In *The Origins and Spread of Agriculture and Pastoralism in Eurasia,* edited by David R. Harris, 282–294. Washington, DC: Smithsonian Institution.

Lal, B. B. 1971. "Perhaps the Earliest Ploughed Field So Far Excavated Anywhere in the World." *Puratattva* 4 (1970–1971): 1–3.

Leshnik, Lawrence. 1973. "Land Use and Ecological Factors in Prehistoric North-West India." In *South Asian Archaeology,* edited by Norman Hammond, 67–84. Cambridge, UK: Cambridge University Press.

Meadow, Richard H. 1979. "Prehistoric Subsistence at Balakot: Initial Consideration of the Faunal Remains." In *South Asian Archaeology 1977,* edited by Maurizio Taddei, 274–315. Naples: Istituto Universitario Orientale, Seminario di Studi Asiatici.

Meadow, Richard H. 1984. "A Camel Skeleton from Mohenjo-Daro." In *Frontiers of the Indus Civilization,* edited by B. B. Lal and S. P. Gupta, 133–139. New Delhi: Books and Books.

Meadow, Richard H. 1988. "The Faunal Remains from Jalilpur 1971." *Pakistan Archaeology* 23: 204–220.

Meadow, Richard H. 1989. "Continuity and Change in the Agriculture of the Greater Indus Valley: The Palaeoethnobotanical and Zooarchaeological Evidence." In *Old Problems and New Perspectives in the Archaeology of South Asia,* edited by Jonathan Mark Kenoyer, 61–74. *Wisconsin Archaeological Reports.* Vol. 2. Department of Anthropology. Madison: University of Wisconsin Press.

Meadow, Richard H., ed. 1991. *Harappa Excavations 1986–1990.* Madison, WI: Prehistory Press.

Meadow, Richard H. 1993. "Animal Domestication in the Middle East: A Revised View from the Eastern Margin." In *Harappan Civilization,* 2nd ed., edited by Gregory L. Possehl, 295–315. New Delhi: Oxford University Press.

Meadow, Richard H. 1996. "The Origins and Spread of Agriculture and Pastoralism in Northwestern South Asia." In *The Origins and Spread of Agriculture and Pastoralism in Eurasia,* edited by David R. Harris, 390–412. Washington, DC: Smithsonian Institution.

Meadow, Richard H., and Ajita Patel. 1998. "A Comment on 'Horse Remains from Surkotada' by Sandor Bokonyi." *South Asian Studies* 13: 308–315.

Mehta, D. P., and Gregory L. Possehl. 1993. "Excavation at Rojdi, District Rajkot." *Indian Archaeology—a Review 1992–3:* 31–32.

Mehta, R. N. 1984. "Valabhi—A Station of Harappan Cattle-Breeders." In *Frontiers of the Indus Civilization,* edited by B. B. Lal and S. P. Gupta, 227–230. New Delhi: Books and Books.

Miller, Naomi. 1984. "The Use of Dung as Fuel: An Ethnographic Example and an Archaeological Application." *Paleorient* 10 (2): 71–79.

Miller, Naomi, and T. L. Smart. 1984. "Intentional Burning of Dung as Fuel: A Mechanism for the Incorporation of Charred Seeds into the Archaeological Record." *Journal of Ethnobiology* 4 (1): 15–28.

Misra, V. N. 1998. "Balathal: A Chalcolithic Settlement in Mewar, Rajasthan, India: Results of First Three Seasons' Excavation." *South Asian Studies* 13: 251–275.

Momin, K. N. 1984. "Village Harappans in Kheda District of Gujurat." In *Frontiers of the Indus Civilization*, edited by B. B. Lal and S. P. Gupta, 231–234. New Delhi: Books and Books.

Patel, Ajita. 1997. "The Pastoral Economy of Dholavira: A First Look at Animals and Urban Life in Third Millennium Kutch." In *South Asian Archaeology 1995*, edited by Raymond and Bridget Allchin, 101–113. New Delhi: Oxford & IBH Publishing Co.

Possehl, Gregory L. 1979. "Pastoral Nomadism in the Indus Civilization." In *South Asian Archaeology 1977*, edited by Maurizio Taddei, 537–551. Naples: Istituto Universitario Orientale, Seminario di Studi Asiatici.

Possehl, Gregory L. 1980. *The Indus Civilization in Saurashtra*. New Delhi: B. R. Publishing Corporation.

Possehl, Gregory L. 1986. *Kulli: An Exploration of Ancient Civiliation in South Asia*. Durham, NC: Carolina Academic Press.

Possehl, Gregory L. 1992. "The Harappan Cultural Mosaic: Ecology Revisited." In *South Asian Archaeology 1989*, edited by Catherine Jarrige, 237–241. Madison, WI: Prehistory Press.

Possehl, Gregory L. 1994. "Govindbhai-no Vadi." In *Living Traditions. Studies in the Ethnoarchaeology of South Asia*, edited by Bridget Allchin, 193–204. New Delhi: Oxford & IBH Publishing Co.

Possehl, Gregory L. 1999. *Indus Age: The Beginnings*. New Delhi: Oxford University Press.

Possehl, Gregory L. 2002. *The Indus Civilization. A Contemporary Perspective*. Walnut Creek, CA: AltaMira Press.

Ratnagar, Shereen. 1992. "A Bronze Age Frontier: Problems of Interpretation." *53rd Session Thematic Symposium "Frontiers in Indian History." Indian History Congress. Symposia Papers: 2*. New Delhi: Indian History Congress.

Ratnagar, Shereen. 2000. *The End of the Great Harappan Tradition. Heras Memorial Lectures 1998*. New Delhi: Manohar.

Ratnagar, Shereen. 2001. *Understanding Harappa. Civilization in the Greater Indus Valley*. New Delhi: Tulika.

Ray, Himanshu Prabha. 2003. *The Archaeology of Seafaring in Ancient South Asia*. Cambridge, UK: Cambridge University Press.

Rissman, Paul C., and Y. M. Chitalwala. 1990. *Harappan Civilization and Oriyo Timbo*. New Delhi: Oxford & IBH Publishing Co., and American Institute of Indian Studies.

Schwartzberg, Joseph E., ed. 1992. *A Historical Atlas of South Asia*, 2nd impression, with additional material. New York and Oxford: Oxford University Press.

Sherratt, Andrew. 1997. *Economy and Society in Prehistoric Europe. Changing Perspectives*. Princeton, NJ: Princeton University Press.

Shinde, Vasant. 1991. "Excavation at Padri, District Bhavnagar." *Indian Archaeology—a Review 1990–1:* 8–10.

Shinde, Vasant. 1992a. "Padri and the Indus Civilization." *South Asian Studies* 8: 55–66.

Shinde, Vasant. 1992b. "Excavation at Padri, District Bhavnagar." *Indian Archaeology—a Review 1991–92*: 21–22.

Shinde, Vasant. 1998. "Pre-Harappan Padri Culture in Saurashtra: The Recent Discovery." *South Asian Studies* 14: 173–182.

Shinde, Vasant. 2004. "Saurashtra and the Harappan Sites of Padri and Kuntasi." In *Indus Civilization. Sites in India. New Discoveries,* edited by Dilip K. Chakrabarti, 64–70. Mumbai: Marg Publications.

Sopher, David. 1975. "Indian Pastoral Castes and Livestock Ecologies. A Geographical Analysis." In *Nomads and Pastoralists in South Asia,* edited by Lawrence S. Leshnik and Gunter D. Sontheimer, 183–208. Wiesbaden: Otto Harrassowitz.

Tosi, Maurizio, S. Malek Shahmirzadi, and M. A. Joyenda. 1976. "The Bronze Age in Iran and Afghanistan." In *History of Civilizations of Central Asia. 1. The Dawn of Civilization: Earliest Times to 700 B.C.,* edited by A. H. Dani and V. M. Masson, 191–224. Paris: UNESCO.

Weber, Steven A. 1991. *Plants and Harappan Subsistence. An Example of Stability and Change from Rojdi.* New Delhi: Oxford & IBH Publishing Co., and American Institute of Indian Studies.

Weber, Steven A. 2001. "Seeds of Urbanism Revisited." [Online article; retrieved 2/25/06.] www.ucl.ac.uk/archaeology/staff/profiles/fuller/pdfs/AntiquityWeber%20debate.pdf.

Whyte, Robin Orr. 1975. "The Nature and Utilization of Grazing Resources in India." In *Nomads and Pastoralists in South Asia,* edited by Lawrence S. Leshnik and Gunter D. Sontheimer, 220–234. Wiesbaden: Otto Harrassowitz.

Wilkinson, Tony J. 2002. "Agriculture and the Countryside." In *Queen of Sheba. Treasures from Ancient Yemen,* edited by St John Simpson, 102–109. London: British Museum Press.

Witzel, Michael, and Steve Farmer. 2000. "Horseplay in Harappa." *Frontline* October 13. [Online article; retrieved 4/2/07.] www.safarmer.com/frontline/horseplay.pdf.

Zohary, Daniel, and Maria Hopf. 2000. *Domestication of Plants in the Old World. The Origin and Spread of Cultivated Plants in West Asia, Europe and the Nile Valley.* 3rd ed. Oxford: Oxford University Press.

CHAPTER 6

Resources, Trade, and Communications

INTRODUCTION

The Indus civilization, in addition to possessing the prerequisite of high agricultural productivity, was unusual in being well-endowed with local supplies of minerals and other important natural resources. In the greater Indus region, there were limestone and exceptionally good flint in the Rohri Hills; agate and carnelian in Gujarat; bitumen in the Bolan Valley; widespread sources of clay for potting and mud for construction; timber and woody shrubs for building and fuel from forests along the rivers and in the adjacent hills; and gold in the upper reaches of the Indus. Although agriculture and pastoralism were the mainstays of the Indus economy, some settlements were situated to manage economically important resources such as seashells or timber.

The society was organized so that regionally available raw materials, such as marine shells and Rohri Hills flint, were distributed throughout the Harappan realms. High-quality manufactured goods, such as fine pottery, were similarly widely distributed, and both raw materials and manufactured goods reached not only towns and cities such as Mohenjo-daro, Harappa, and Dholavira, but even small settlements. Some settlements such as Manda in the Himalayas seem to have owed their existence to the need to obtain resources (such as timber); in others, such as Lothal in Gujarat, manufacturing, procurement, and distribution played major roles, well beyond the needs of their inhabitants and hinterland. The existence of a standardized system of weights and measures implies an integrated network of internal communications and control over trade and probably an overall authority. Numerous seals of a standard design reflect some regulation of distribution and suggest the existence of merchants acting as government officials. A few sealings bearing the imprint of such seals have been found, sometimes preserving an impression of the material of the packages to which they had been attached; in some cases these were associated with buildings that were probably warehouses.

The rivers provided a principal transport network, particularly for bulky goods such as timber. Overland transport over short distances utilized bullock carts. The seasonal movements of pastoralists enabled the latter to play a major role as carriers in the internal trade network; hunter-gatherers, similarly mobile, were probably important in providing links with areas outside the Indus region.

Adjacent areas could furnish the Indus realms with other natural resources such as stone and gemstones, copper ore from Rajasthan, and timber from adjacent uplands. Some resources, however, had to be obtained from more distant regions, including the Iranian plateau, Turkmenia, Oman, Mesopotamia, and possibly south India. The establishment of a Harappan town at Shortugai in northern Afghanistan, the presence of resident Indus merchants in southern Mesopotamia, and the prominence of Indus material in Gulf settlements show the importance attached to this trade and the active role played by the Harappans in long-distance trade. However, surprisingly little evidence of foreign trade has been found in sites of the Indus civilization itself.

INTERNAL TRADE AND COMMUNICATIONS

An Integrated Polity

One of the features of the Indus civilization that most struck early researchers was its apparent uniformity: The material found in sites throughout the Indus realms seemed entirely uniform, with no regional or chronological variation. Closer familiarity with the Indus material and the establishment of a sequence of development at a few sites, such as Harappa, have dispelled this impression of complete invariability: Some changes through time have been established and some regional variations defined. Nevertheless, there remains a considerable degree of uniformity in the material found throughout the Indus realms, reflecting a culturally integrated polity with strongly developed internal distribution networks.

To a large extent, the people of the Indus realms would have been self-sufficient in food (although the larger towns and the cities would have needed to draw foodstuffs from their hinterland to support their large populations, which included large numbers of nonfarming citizens). Foodstuffs were nevertheless transported between different regions of the Indus realm: The vast majority have left no trace, but date stones at Mohenjo-daro and the bones of dried marine fish at Harappa provide tangible evidence that this occurred.

The raw materials of different regions were also transported to other parts of the Indus realms. Whereas in earlier times, local sources of flint were exploited by the inhabitants of each region, during the Harappan period the very high-quality brownish gray flint of the Rohri Hills was intensively extracted and distributed to every part of the Indus polity, either as a raw material or in the form of finished artifacts: For example, most of the stone tools at Balakot were acquired in finished form.

Shells, used particularly as the main material for making bangles, were gathered in large quantities on the Makran and Gujarat coasts. Some were processed locally and distributed either as blanks or as finished objects while others were transported intact to major settlements where they were cleaned and worked. Often individual workshops concentrated on producing a particular type of shell artifact or on working a particular variety of shell. Similarly, there were lapidary workshops both near the sources of agate, carnelian, and other gemstones and in major settlements far from these sources.

Two tiny bullet cores from which microblades were struck. These were made of the fine flint found in the Rohri Hills, which was quarried by the Harappans and distributed throughout the Indus realms. (Paolo Biagi)

Pottery for everyday use was probably manufactured in every settlement and certainly in all the towns and cities. The highly organized nature of the Indus civilization is clear from the fact that even these simple everyday wares were manufactured in pottery workshops by specialized potters, rather than being made in the home. Although pottery throughout the Harappan polity shared many features, these local wares are more variable and there are some regional or local styles. In contrast, some special wares seem to have been produced in one or a few centers for widespread distribution: for example, black-slipped storage vessels were made at Harappa (and possibly only there) and were also used in external trade. Often, individual workshops concentrated on particular types.

Craft production and the distribution of manufactured goods probably reflect several layers of organization. At the level of the individual community, many everyday commodities were locally produced and probably distributed among individuals and families by mutual exchanges of goods for goods or services. Cross-cutting this was the pattern of kinship-based exchange that had operated for millennia in this region (as in many other regions of the world in preurban times). By this means individuals and families in one community were supplied with the products of another, either of their own manufacture or obtained from other producers. Such goods changed hands in the context of such family events as marriages. The distribution of goods by such kinship-based exchanges forms an archaeologically detectable pattern: Their quantity steadily declines as the distance from their source increases. Though important in the cementing of kinship ties, such a system cannot account for the widespread distribution and universal availability of the Indus craft products. There was therefore a third layer, some mechanism that ensured the reliable and efficient supply and distribution of craft products: This seems to imply the existence of some form of bureaucracy and central control of production and distribution. A number of towns, such as Lothal and Gola Dhoro in Gujarat and Chanhu-daro in Sindh, produced large quantities of craft objects, such as shell bangles, beads in many materials, steatite seals, and metalwork, far in excess of local needs, for wider distribution, while Mohenjo-daro, Harappa, and probably the other cities were centers of production of a wide range of crafts, and some small settlements specialized in a single craft, such as the shellworking site at Nageshwar.

Weights and Measures

Another insight into the organized nature of the internal distribution network is provided by the existence of a standardized system of weights and measures, used throughout the Indus realms. Weights, made of stone such as chert, were generally cubical in shape, but fine jasper or agate weights in the form of truncated spheres also occurred, as well as a few pierced conical weights and knobbed conical weights resembling the pawn in a chess set. They are known

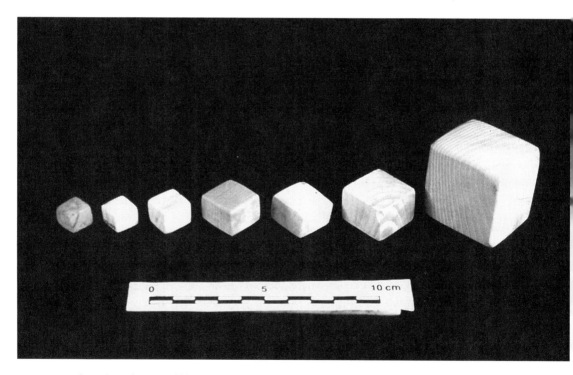

A graduated series of Harappan weights made of chert. These were found in the small but highly organized settlement of Allahdino. (J. M. Kenoyer, Courtesy Department of Archaeology and Museums, Government of Pakistan)

to have been made at Harappa and Chanhu-daro. Small cubical weights, ranging from one to sixty-four times the smallest unit of 0.871 grams, were present in all sizes of settlements, while major towns and cities also had heavier weights, up to 10.865 kilograms (12,800 units).

Four engraved batons—of shell, ivory, terra-cotta, and copper—marked into units show that there was also a system for measuring length.

In Mesopotamia, comparable standardized systems of weights and measures, on a different standard, were in use by the twenty-third century BCE. These were the result of the standardization of a number of different preexisting systems by the newly unifed Akkadian state, and further official standardization was required under the Ur III dynasty after a period of political disintegration had undermined the application of a official standardized system. In contrast, the Indus system of weights and measures was apparently standardized from the start, again suggesting the unity of the Indus state and the existence of a central authority.

Mesopotamian weights were regularly used in administrative contexts. The copious Sumerian administrative documents that survive refer to the weights of goods received or issued, in taxation or payment of dues, in payment for services, and in official trading. The Sumerians used weighed amounts of silver and, less frequently, grain as a standard by which to calculate the value of other goods, as a medium of exchange between different commodities, and as a means of paying directly—all functions fulfilled at a much later date by coins. In documents referring to foreign trade, merchants setting out on official expeditions were issued with weighed commodities for exchange, and on their return the weight and value of the goods they delivered was recorded. That the Indus weight system was also involved in such trading transactions is amply demonstrated by the occasional discovery of Indus weights in foreign places with which the Indus people traded, such as Mesopotamia, Susa, Dilmun (Bahrain), and Magan (Oman). In Dilmun, a major entrepot, weights on the Mesopotamian and Indus standards were used side by side, presumably in transactions involving the conversion of values between the two systems.

It is highly probable that the Indus weights, like those of Mesopotamia, were used by those in authority in regulating the issue and receipt of goods and in measuring the quantities of goods received in taxation or issued in official payment. Kenoyer (1998, 99) notes that groups of weights have often been found near the gateways of Indus cities, suggesting that they were used by officials who were regulating the flow of goods into the city and collecting dues on them. Whatever their precise use, the very existence of a system of weights standardized throughout the Indus region implies official control and the regulation of the movement of commodities.

Seals

One of the most characteristic finds from Indus settlements is the square stamp seal. Usually made of steatite (soapstone) and hardened by firing, each seal bore an inscription, usually short, and a picture, generally of a single animal, although scenes also occurred. The use of a design on the seal would have allowed their recognition by all concerned parties, such as carriers and warehouse workers, whereas the writing could be understood only by (the probably limited number of) literate individuals. The seals had a semicircular perforated boss on the back so that they could be carried on a cord or fastened to a belt or wrist strap.

Seals may have had a number of uses. In the context of trade and the movement of goods, they could be used in two ways. First, they could have acted simply as tokens establishing an individual's identity or credentials. In this context they may have been issued as badges of authority to merchants traveling on official business and to other individuals who needed to show their authority or prove their credentials. In historical times, tokens bearing an official seal were used as passes in a system controlling road traffic. If the Indus realms were not a united state but a series of smaller polities, the seals might similarly have been used as identifiers by individuals who passed between the polities on the business of trade and resource procurement. Personal seals could also have been used by individuals to establish their identity in private transactions.

Second, seals could have been used to create impressions in soft media, such as clay or wax, attached to goods. Such sealings could serve to identify packaged goods as the property of the state or of a particular individual or as deriving from a particular place. The presence of an unbroken clay sealing could also act as a guarantee that the sealed package had not been opened or tampered with before it reached the intended recipient. Doors, to houses or storerooms, could similarly be sealed, a practice attested at the Helmand city of Shahr-i Sokhta and in Mesopotamian literary sources, though not known from any Harappan site. In Mesopotamia, where documents were written on clay tablets, seals were also impressed on a variety of documents to identify the individuals or officials involved in, acting as witnesses to, or attesting to the accuracy of an agreement or transaction. If comparable documents were created by the Harappans, they were made of perishable materials of which no trace remains.

The patterns left on the reverse of the surviving sealings show that they were attached to cords or sacking used to package bales of goods. It is likely that these sealings were part of a system for controlling and recording goods and their distribution, and sanctioning their issue. A few sealings are also known from sites outside the Harappan realms, including one probably from Umma in Sumer that had been used to cover the knot on a cord fastening a piece of cloth over the mouth of a jar. Sealings at Lothal also include examples from jars.

Far more Indus seals have been found than sealings, possibly indicating that they were used predominantly as tokens. On the other hand, sealings were ephemeral: Made of unbaked clay, they would have been broken when the sealed packages were opened, after which they would have been treated as rubbish; the majority, therefore, are likely to have returned to dust. Most of the few clay sealings that do survive come from Lothal, where they were preserved by a warehouse fire. Sealings might also have been of wax, in which case they would have disintegrated long ago; use on wax would have produced less wear on the seals, many of which appear little used.

Three clay tags, each bearing two different seal impressions, from the Mature Indus period at Harappa. These were probably attached to consignments of goods sent to Harappa. Some seal impressions show both the animal design and the inscription; others, like these, only the inscription. (Harappa Archaeological Research Project, Courtesy Department of Archaeology and Museums, Government of Pakistan)

The Resources of the Greater Indus Region

The principal resource of the Indus realms was its agricultural wealth, since land suitable for growing crops and raising livestock was plentiful and well distributed. Other foodstuffs, such as fish and other aquatic resources, wildfowl, game, and wild plants, were also abundant and important. Apart from food, the people of the Indus civilization also required tools, shelter, clothing, and a number of commodities that had social, and probably political or religious, significance.

The mountains and hills of the Indus region, including the high ground in Gujarat and the ranges of the Himalayas and Baluchistan, were heavily forested, and there were also forests in parts of the river valleys. Small trees and shrubs for fuel, used for domestic and industrial purposes, were universally available and could be supplemented by burning cattle dung, which is rich in fiber. Timber was also extensively used in construction, along with the ubiquitous clay, which was either applied as daub or molded into bricks: some of these were used after drying in the sun, and others were fired. Clay was also used for making pottery and terra-cottas.

Other raw materials were localized in their distribution. A substantial outcrop of exceptionally good flint in the Rohri-Sukkur region of the middle Indus Valley provided flint for tools used throughout the Indus realms. The flint was quarried and worked in situ into cores or tool blanks, which were then distributed to Indus settlements to be made into finished tools. In some cases the flint was worked into finished blades at the Rohri site. Other kinds of stone were employed for building and for making a limited number of sculptures. Limestone was also obtained from the Rohri Hills and probably from sources in Gujarat. Alum, gypsum, and building stone are also available in Sindh, and basalt in the Kirthar Range bordering Sindh and extensively in Gujarat. Alabaster was to be found in Gujarat and the Marri-Bugti Hills of Baluchistan. Steatite, of great importance for manufacturing seals, personal ornaments, and other small objects, was available on the upper Indus and in the Makran and Gujarat.

Items of jewelry, particularly bangles and strings of beads, were very important in Indus dress. Many bangles were manufactured from seashells fished or gathered by coastal communities in Gujarat and the Makran. A flourishing exchange network had brought seashells to inland sites in earlier times, but the volume of such shells circulating in the Indus period was vastly greater. Beads were made from a great variety of materials, the majority from gemstones such as agate, carnelian (chalcedony), jasper, and onyx, which could be obtained from the rivers of Kutch and Saurashtra and from southern Gujarat, in particular the Rajpipla mines on the Narmada River. Some gemstones were also available in other regions, including amethyst from the Sutlej Valley in the Punjab. Metals were also used, and of these gold may have been obtained in the greater Indus region: Gold dust can be panned from the upper reaches of the Indus and Jhelum, and there was also some gold in the Alech Hills of Saurashtra. Small deposits of other metals are known but may not have been exploited in Harappan times: copper and a little tin in northern Gujarat, and a little copper and silver in parts of the Punjab.

Ivory from the elephants that inhabited much of the Indus realm, and particularly Gujarat and the eastern Punjab, was so abundant that it was often used for making tools. It was also made into figurines, jewelry, and small objects such as dice. Rhino horn was also available. Bone and horn were ubiquitous, from both domestic and wild animals, and there was also antler from the latter. Animal skins were probably made into leather, for many purposes, probably including clothing and perhaps sails. Woven textiles were also made from locally grown fibers: certainly cotton and probably linen (flax).

Salt, used in cooking and for preserving food such as fish, was probably made by evaporating seawater in coastal salt pans. One site where salt may have been made has been located at Padri in Saurashtra. Rock salt could also be obtained from various areas, including southeast Sindh.

Bitumen is known around Sibi in the Kachi plain and in the Mianwali area of Punjab. It may have been exploited, since a large quantity of bitumen was employed in the construction of the Great Bath at Mohenjo-daro. The use of bitumen to waterproof baskets at Mehrgarh, thousands of years earlier, suggests familiarity with the Kachi sources.

Oysters are known to occur off the Sindh and Gujarat coast, though they are of the winnow variety that produces only small, inferior pearls. A Mesopotamian reference to fish eyes (usually taken to be pearls) from the Indus region might indicate that the Harappans made use of their local pearls, but it is possible that the term "fish eyes" in this context meant beads of banded agate.

Mechanisms of Distribution

The closely integrated nature of the Indus realms implies the existence of efficient communications networks, utilizing inland routes over land and by river and along the coast by sea.

Land Transport. Local transport was on foot or by bullock cart. Terra-cotta models provide a clear picture of the wooden carts with solid wooden wheels that were widely used for land transport over short distances. These are virtually identical to those of modern farmers of the Indus region. Some consisted simply of a solid wooden platform above the axle, others had an open framework. In some cases the platform may have had permanent sidepieces but

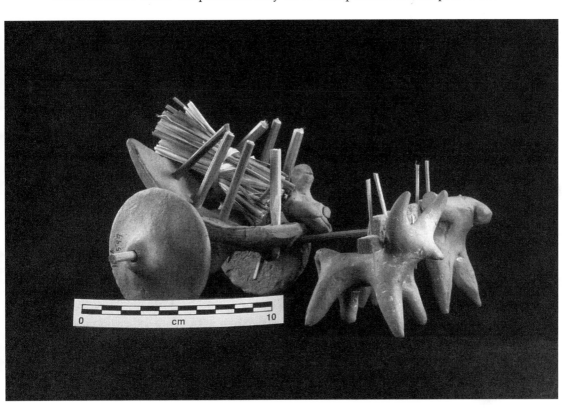

Terra-cotta models show that the Harappans used a range of wooden carts with solid wheels, drawn by oxen, to transport goods and sometimes people over short distances. Modern wooden components have been added to this model to replace those used by the Harappans, which have long since decayed away. (Sharri R. Clark and Laura J. Miller, Courtesy Department of Archaeology and Museums, Government of Pakistan)

many just had holes into which wooden stakes could be slotted when required to form sides supporting a load. These carts were drawn by oxen or bullocks, of which there are also terra-cotta models. A different style of cart, with a short chassis, a roof, and high sides, was probably a vehicle in which people traveled. A small platform in front of the cab provided a seat for the driver.

Land transport over long distances probably generally employed pack animals, though small valuable commodities could be carried by people on foot. In modern South Asia, pastoralists play an important role in providing links between settled communities and in transmitting goods from place to place as they move in their seasonal round. Seasonal movement was an important part of the pastoral economy in Harappan times, and it seems highly probable that people taking their animals through different parts of the Indus realms would have acted as carriers, moving goods from source to consumer and participating in a complex network of connections among pastoral groups from different regions, enabling the produce of one region to be transported to others. While the camels and horses available to more recent pastoralists were not present in Indus times, cattle can transport heavy loads and even sheep can be used as pack animals. While many goods probably moved within private transactions, pastoralists may also have been entrusted with the carriage of official consignments of goods by representatives of those in authority.

Many of the routes traveled today were probably also used in the past because many of the constraints are likely to be timeless in their effect. Thus routes from the mountains into the Indus regions are channeled through the existing passes; where rivers have followed the same course, suitable crossing points are likely to have been in use for millennia; in arid stretches, routes pass through places that water can reliably be found; and other features of the terrain similarly dictate the following of certain routes. On the other hand, many of the rivers of the greater Indus region have changed their course or the volume of water flowing in them has changed, affecting the routes along and across them. Volcanic activity has not only altered mountain landscape but has also affected other regions, such as Gujarat. Deforestation has created routes through regions that were once impenetrable. Changes in sea level and the buildup of alluvial deposits have altered the coastline. For instance, though land routes now cross the Ranns of Kutch in the dry season, in the Indus period access to Kutch must have been by boat across open water. Thus, although information on modern routes is helpful in reconstructing those of the past, it must be used with caution and combined with data on the topographical and ecological situation in the Indus period.

Water Transport. Although land transport was important, particularly over short distances and between lowland and highland regions, water transport along the rivers and streams would have been easier for long-distance transport, particularly of heavy or bulky goods. Most of the major settlements were linked by a network of waterways that were navigable for at least part of the year. The Indus is navigable from where it enters the plains in Punjab, south of the Salt Range. Coastal communications by sea would have linked communities within Gujarat, and those of Gujarat with those of the Makran coast.

The development of watercraft was stimulated by the needs of fishers and the colonization of areas where water transport was required, such as the islands of Gujarat and the shores of Lake Manchar. During the rainy season, when a huge area surrounding Lake Manchar is submerged by floods, modern inhabitants of the region abandon their homes on its shores and take to houseboats, or they live year round on houseboats, a way of life that may have existed in Indus times. Modern communities also live on houseboats on the Indus in Sindh. Boats like these with a shallow draft can be used on the Indus except during the most turbulent period of the summer inundation; other branches of the modern Indus, such as the Western Nara, are navigable for most of the year. While the course of the Indus and its branches and tributaries have changed since Harappan times, there is no reason to suppose that it was any less navigable then than now. The Saraswati system must also have offered water transport.

Two illustrations, on a clay tablet and a stone seal from Mohenjo-daro, show a flat-bottomed boat with a cabin on its deck, resembling modern Indus houseboats. It has a high stern, high bow, and a pair of steering oars or paddles. Although the illustrations are too schematic for certainty, it would appear that these vessels were constructed of bundles of reeds lashed with cords. The material used may have been baru grass (*Sorghum halepensis*), which grows in Gujarat and is used today for boats in the region. The cabin appears to have had four outer posts of reed bundles within which was a flatroofed structure, possibly of fabric, supported on four thin poles. Such boats could have been used both on the rivers and at sea, and they had the advantage of being able to operate in shallow water, making them easy to load and unload without a quay or dock. Their life expectancy, however, would be limited to a few months. This could be extended by caulking with bitumen, which was available to the Harappans from sources in the Kachi plain and possibly on the upper Indus; however, traditional South Asian ship construction in recorded times did not use bitumen.

A rough graffito on a sherd, also from Mohenjo-daro, may depict the same type of craft or a sailing boat with a mast and perhaps a furled sail; lines at one end may be a steering oar. A clay model from Lothal represents a boat with a mast, attachments for a sail, and a steering oar. It seems to have had a keel, a flat bottom, and high bows, with a lower stern. Such a ship could have been used both for coastal sailing and for seafaring in the Gulf where its shallow draft would have been advantageous. Although the model gives no indication of the material from which such vessels would have been built, teak, a preferred timber for shipbuilding, grows in Gujarat, where the Harappan seagoing ships would have been constructed, as does *Thespesia populnea* (country teak), a wood used particularly for the keels of ships. It is likely that Harappan ships would have been built of these timbers, which were also among the Harappan exports to Mesopotamia where they were also destined for shipbuilding. Teak vessels had a life expectancy of many decades, possibly as much as eighty years. Although there is no evidence of the method of construction, it is possible that they were made of planks stitched together, as are many modern South Asian boats. Vessels constructed in this way are very resilient. Other country craft include boats made of hollowed logs, and such vessels may also have been used by the Harappans for coastal or river travel and fishing, though only plank-built vessels would have been suitable for carrying any volume of cargo.

The growth of sea fishing and the collection of marine molluscs in the Harappan period would have encouraged the development of seagoing ships, and these are known to have existed by the twenty-fourth century BCE (when they were mentioned in Akkadian texts), if not before. On the western coast of South Asia, the efficient exploitation of marine resources requires the use of offshore boats; globally, areas with such resources have tended to develop seagoing boats and the skills and knowledge to venture out to sea, whereas areas with rich resources near to land generally do not. The topography of Gujarat, with Kutch probably an island year-round, many permanent creeks and seasonal waterways, as well as many natural anchorages, would also have favored the development of boats at an early date. The presence of hunter-gatherer communities in this area before 3000 BCE suggests that boats at least for inshore use existed by this period, and the great development in the exploitation of marine resources in the Harappan period implies the corresponding development of boatbuilding, boat design, and navigation skills.

A prismatic seal from Mohenjo-daro bearing one of the few Harappan depictions of watercraft: a flat-bottomed boat with a central cabin, resembling modern houseboats used on the Indus River. (J. M. Kenoyer, Courtesy Department of Archaeology and Museums, Government of Pakistan)

One of the Mohenjo-daro illustrations shows two birds on the boat's deck. Birds may have been kept for navigation: in recent times birds have been released from boats at sea so that their flight could indicate the direction of land. Many other natural clues, such as types of fish and coastal land animals, and the shapes of land and rocks, must have been utilized to aid navigation. For example, in the classical text *The Periplus of the Erythraean Sea,* the approach to the Indus estuary was identified by changes in the color of the water and the presence of large numbers of sea snakes. In addition to the position of the stars and the sun, cloud patterns, currents, wave patterns, and wind directions would have provided information on position and the direction of travel.

SOUTH ASIAN TRADE AND EXCHANGE

Although the resources of the greater Indus region were rich and varied, it lacked a number of important raw materials, notably copper. Metal tools played an important part in Harappan industry, such as stone carving and carpentry, and were also used in preference to traditional stone tools for some purposes. Some of the raw materials required by the Harappans could be obtained from neighboring areas. Finds of Harappan material in the settlements of adjacent foraging, fishing, or farming cultures reveal the extent of their trading links.

Hunter-Gatherers

Contacts between farmers and hunter-gatherer communities are attested from early times when hunter-gatherers at settlements such as Bagor in Rajasthan and Loteshwar in Gujarat acquired domestic sheep and goats by trading or raiding, perhaps as early as the sixth millennium BCE. The spread first of pastoral groups and later of farmers into the Indus plains and beyond into Gujarat and the Indo-Gangetic divide brought farmers and hunter-gatherers into closer contact, and in many areas this led to acculturation. For example, hunter-gatherer communities in Saurashtra in the late fourth millennium began to make pottery that was distinct from the Kechi Beg wares of the contemporary inhabitants of Baluchistan, adopting the technology but inventing their own styles; this phenomenon is paralleled in other parts of the world, for example, in Europe, when hunter-gatherers and farmers came into close contact. Later this region had several different styles of Harappan pottery (Sindhi and Sorath), but its inhabitants were no longer pursuing a hunter-gatherer way of life. However, in some other regions, such as the adjacent north Gujarat plain, farming settlements did not become established and here hunter-gatherers continued their established way of life, often moving with the seasons to exploit the resources of different econiches.

In most parts of the world, the development of farming ultimately spelled the end of hunting and gathering as a way of life, due to competition for land and the destruction of the parts of the environment on which hunter-gatherers depended. This was not the case in the Indian subcontinent, where hunter-gatherer groups have continued to exist up to the present day. Instead of being submerged, they adapted their self-sufficient lifestyle, moving gradually into mutually beneficial interdependence with settled communities. Since hunter-gatherers had a mobile way of life, exploiting regions that could not support agriculture, they could provide the desirable products of jungle and desert that were otherwise difficult or impossible for settled groups to obtain, such as honey, wax, ivory, resin, wild silk, and plant fibers for making cord. Agate and other gemstones for making beads may also have been obtained by hunter-gatherers. They could also act as carriers, transmitting the commodities of one settled region to the inhabitants of another; in exchange they could receive both foodstuffs, such as grain, and goods whose manufacture was beyond their own technological capabilities, such as copper knives. At the time of the Indus civilization, this relationship was in its infancy but was nevertheless becoming an established pattern.

For example, the site of Langnaj in north Gujarat was a hunter-gatherer camp that was occupied over a long period. At the time of the Indus civilization, the bones that were excavated there show that meat from hunted wild animals was being supplemented by that from domestic animals. Similarly, Harappan steatite and dentalium beads, copper knives, and pottery were present alongside the foragers' own repertoire of stone tools.

At Bagor, farther to the east, people living by hunting, gathering, and herding began to make pottery after 2800 BCE. They acquired manufactured goods from groups settled in neighboring regions as well as technological knowledge: They had copper objects probably made in the Aravallis to their northwest, and from the greater Indus region beyond they acquired Harappan beads of banded agate and carnelian and Harappan-style copper arrowheads; their pottery loosely copied that of the Ahar-Banas and Kayatha cultures to their southwest.

The extent to which hunter-gatherers were integrated into Harappan society probably varied regionally. In some areas, such as Saurashtra, hunter-gatherers may have been occupational specialists comparable with transhumant pastoralists or the people who gathered and worked marine shells, and were probably regarded as members of Harappan society. Such foragers are difficult to identify or distinguish archaeologically from other Harappans. In contrast, in other areas, such as the north Gujarat plain, hunter-gatherers were culturally distinct and were among the many groups with whom the Harappans traded.

Neighbors to the South

Rajasthan and the Deccan. The Harappans enjoyed good trading relations with a number of other cultures on their borders. Of particular importance was their trade with the people of the Aravallis, the Jodhpura-Ganeshwar culture, who gained much of their livelihood from fishing, hunting, and gathering. The Khetri region of the Aravalli Hills is one of the richest sources of copper in the subcontinent. Often the copper ore occurs in association with arsenic: When smelted, arsenical copper ore produces a useful natural alloy that is harder than pure copper. These hills also yielded steatite, used for the majority of Indus seals. Other minerals occurring there include turquoise, sodalite (a mineral resembling lapis lazuli), zinc, gold, silver, and lead, though there is no evidence that these were extracted there during the Indus period. Tin deposits are known in the Khetri belt, particularly in the Tusham Hills in Haryana, at the northeast end of the Khetri belt, not far south of the eastern region of the Harappan civilization. However, although a number of Harappan metal artifacts were made of bronze (tin-copper alloy), the majority were of copper or copper-arsenic alloy. Tin was not used in the post-Harappan period when this eastern region was a focus of settlement, and in the first millennium BCE tin was imported. All these data suggest that this local source of tin was not known in ancient times.

The Harappans made very extensive use of copper. Many ordinary tools were made of copper, and they were widely distributed, indicating that the Harappans had access to large quantities of copper, in contrast, for example, to the people of Mesopotamia. What proportion of this copper came from the Aravalli sources is unclear. A number of factors makes it difficult to identify the source of metal ores used by any culture; these include the variation in trace element concentrations within ore bodies, and the practice of melting down old objects for reuse, thereby potentially mixing metal from different sources. Spectrographic analysis has shown that artifacts at many Harappan sites, including Mohenjo-daro and Harappa, contained nickel and arsenic. However, these are present in both the Aravalli copper ores and those of Oman, an area with which the Harappans also traded. It is likely that the Harappans used copper from a number of sources, of which the Aravallis may have been the most important.

As early as the Early Indus period, a trading relationship had developed between the Indus farmers and the people of the Aravallis, who had been exploiting the region's copper since the late fourth millennium. The Jodhpura-Ganeshwar people seem to have mined and smelted the copper ore themselves and to have exchanged the smelted copper with Harappans who traveled to the region to trade. In return, the people of the Aravallis obtained manufactured goods and other Indus produce, probably including objects made from the copper they had previously supplied, since Harappan arrowheads were found at Kulhadeka-Johad near Ganeshwar in the Khetri mine area and at Jodhpura. The trade network probably operated along a riverine route, particularly through Kalibangan, located some 250 kilometers to the north of Ganeshwar along the Kantali River, which was tributary to the Drishadvati in antiquity. In the Early Indus period when copper artifacts were relatively rare, Kalibangan had an unusually large number (fifty), including characteristic Jodhpura-Ganeshwar arrowheads. Kalibangan was therefore probably engaged in the importation of copper and copper artifacts from the Aravallis from the Early Indus period onward. In the Mature Harappan period, the route through Kalibangan (which has yielded twelve hundred Harappan copper objects) was probably used to bring copper to Harappa. Rakhigarhi, Mitathal, and Banawali to the northwest of Ganeshwar may also have been involved in the importing of copper in the Mature Harappan period. Another route may have led west from the Aravallis to Kot Diji and thence to Mohenjo-daro.

Given the volume of Aravalli copper used by the Indus civilization, the trade must have been substantial and well organized. Not enough work has been done in the region, however, to give a picture either of how this trade operated or of the mining and smelting activities of the Jodhpura-Ganeshwar people.

The Ahar-Banas culture to the southwest of the Aravallis had relatively little connection with the Harappans. Exchange networks had introduced wheat and barley to this region, and these were grown alongside local crops. Six Harappan beads were discovered at Ahar; while these might be evidence of direct communications between Ahar-Banas and the Harappans, it is more probable that the beads were acquired at one remove, through exchange with hunter-gatherers or with other cultures that traded with the Harappans.

The Kayatha culture farther to the south, however, may well have had trading links with the Harappans of Gujarat to their west. Tin and gold occur in the region, though it is not known whether these were exploited. The region also contains sources of the agate and carnelian prized by the Harappans, who may have come there in person to obtain the stones or who may have acquired them by trading with the Kayatha culture. The latter obtained beads made of these materials from the Harappans.

Southern India. Whether the Harappans traveled farther south is unknown. South India has one of the world's largest gold reefs, as well as precious and semiprecious stones such as amethyst, beryl, and amazonite. Gold from Karnataka in south India has a natural admixture of silver, and so the electrum objects known from the Indus civilization may indicate that gold from there was being imported and worked by the Harappans. South Indian Neolithic gold and Deccan amethyst may have been exploited and traded, ultimately reaching the Indus through exchange networks; there is no evidence of direct contacts between this region and the Indus. However, communications of some sort, operating through the regions between the northwest and southern India, are suggested by a number of data: the appearance of sheep and goats in South India during the later third millennium; a surface find of a Mesopotamian cylinder seal at Maski, near the Hutti gold reef (known to have been exploited in early times, since gold is present at Neolithic sites such as Piklihal, Maski, and Kodekal); the discovery of a Harappan bronze chisel at Piklihal; and the recent discovery of a stone axe inscribed with four signs in the Indus script from Mayiladuthurai in Tamilnadu. Hunter-gatherers were probably involved in the chain of communications. It is possible, though unlikely, that the Harappans themselves traveled to Karnataka to exploit its gold and minerals.

Neighbors to the North and West

The mountainous regions to the north and west of the Indus realms, the Indo-Iranian borderlands and the Himalayas, were rich in resources useful to the Harappans: notably timber, metal ores, and other minerals. The Indo-Iranian borderlands had been culturally integrated with the Indus Basin during the Early Harappan and preceding periods, but major changes had occurred with the cultural unification of the Indus civilization. Many earlier settlements were abandoned. The Kot Diji areas of the northern borderlands developed their own separate Late Kot Diji culture, though they continued to trade with the Harappans. Harappan artifacts such as beads, terra-cotta cakes, and toy carts might have been acquired haphazardly in individual transactions, when, for example, pastoralists from this region migrated to the plains during the winter, but the presence of an Indus weight in the Late Kot Diji settlement of Gumla shows that this trade was organized. Harappan pottery was present in some settlements such as Periano Ghundai, Rana Ghundai, and Sur Jangal: Often the Harappan material was concentrated in a small part of the settlement. Very little Mature Harappan material was found in the town of Rehman Dheri, the major settlement of the region, but it was common in the small site of Hisham Dheri immediately to its north, perhaps suggesting the latter might have been a caravanserai or trading settlement where Harappan traders came to conduct local business.

Among the important resources of this region was salt, from the Salt Range where a Late Kot Diji settlement is known at Musakhel. The Salt Range also had copper ore and gypsum. Farther north in Swat, where the important Late Kot Diji settlement of Sarai Khola was located, there was alabaster; this could also have been obtained farther south, from the western Bugti Hills.

To the east of the Late Kot Diji culture area, in Kashmir, there were settlements of the Northern Neolithic culture, such as Gufkral and Burzahom. In the early third millennium, these sites had been in contact with settlements in the northern borderlands and the Indus plains, and these contacts continued. The presence of traded Indus material, such as the cache of nine hundred agate and carnelian beads at Burzahom, reflects the importance to the Harappans of Himalayan timber, exploited over a broad front. The Harappans may also have obtained minerals from this area, including gold, silver, lead, copper, steatite, agate, and amazonite, and possibly jade from Khotan in China, a material obtained and used by the Kashmir people themselves.

Kulli. In contrast to the northern borderlands, southern Baluchistan, home to what is known as the Kulli culture, remained closely linked with the Indus civilization. Opinions are divided whether the Kulli material and settlements represent a separate culture or merely a highland regional subculture of the Indus civilization. Indus seals and weights have been found in several Kulli settlements, confirming the close economic and cultural relationship between the Indus civilization and the Kulli region.

The people of the Kulli culture, presumably the descendants of the Amri-Nal farmers and pastoralists of the region, seem to have combined pastoralism with sophisticated irrigation agriculture. They occupied large walled settlements generally situated on bluffs, which often had an elevated area with monumental platforms that may have served some religious purpose. Distinctive Kulli material included many figurines of bulls and women, as well as certain forms and decorative motifs in the pottery, such as straight-sided canisters and zoomorphic designs. However, many of their pottery vessels resembled those of the Harappans, and other characteristic Harappan artifacts, such as model carts, were known in Kulli sites. Conversely, a few Kulli objects were found in Harappan settlements in adjacent regions, such as Nausharo and Lohumjo-daro; these included two steatite boxes at Mohenjo-daro that resemble ones from Mehi.

Several Harappan seals with the unicorn design were found at Nindowari and weights at Mehi and Kinneru, indicating that the Kulli culture was involved in the Harappan trade networks. Southern Baluchistan, and particularly the Sarawan region, was a source of minerals including substantial copper deposits (eastern Las Bela), as well as agate, steatite (Makran and Zhob district), jasper, carnelian (Hab Valley), and chert, the latter probably exploited from the Harappan settlement of Bakkar Buthi. Dates and perhaps other fruit were also probably traded from this region, as they are today.

The Kulli region lay astride the land routes that linked the Harappan settlements of the Makran coast with those of the Kachi plain and Sindh, of particular importance during the summer months when communications by sea were difficult or impossible. A number of towns in the Hab Valley seem to have been related to controlling the access routes between Sindh and the Kulli interior. Since pastoralism played a major part in the Kulli economy, the region's transhumant herders and shepherds, moving down from the hills in the winter, are likely to have acted as carriers for the Harappans.

Since at least the seventh millennium, the Kachi plain had benefited from its location on a major route through the Bolan pass into the interior of Baluchistan and from there through the Quetta and Kandahar Valleys to Seistan or beyond, through the Khojak pass, to Afghanistan and Central Asia. The political changes that accompanied the emergence of the Harappan civilization, however, seem to have closed this route beyond the Quetta Valley. Northwestern Baluchistan, with the important town of Mundigak, became incorporated into the Helmand culture and no longer traded with the Indus region. Small quantities of Harappan material in the Quetta Valley show that a limited amount of interaction occurred with the people of what had earlier been the Damb Sadaat region. Traffic through the Bolan pass would now have come almost exclusively from southern Baluchistan, passing through the Quetta Valley: The use of this route is indicated by the presence of Kulli material in Nausharo in the Kachi plain. Another route from the Kulli area led through the Mula Valley to the plains at Pathani Damb, site of a Mature Harappan town that may have been of considerable size.

Procurement Centers

One of the hallmarks of the Indus civilization was the establishment of outposts beyond the main area of Harappan settlement, designed to control the produce of key regions. These included Manda, Ropar, and Kotla Nihang Khan in the north, located in the Himalayan foothills on the Chenab and Sutlej Rivers, near where each became navigable. These settlements were well placed to control the exploitation and distribution of timber such as pine, ebony, sissoo, and sal from the Himalayan foothills and deodar from higher in the mountains.These were carried downriver to other Harappan regions and also exported overseas. Gold dust may also have been available on the upper Sutlej. Another Harappan settlement in the north was located near Mianwali bordering the Late Kot Diji territory south of the Salt Range and may have been concerned with salt procurement. At the opposite end of the greater Indus region was the outpost of Mehgam on the southern Gujarat mainland, a site linked to the exploitation of gemstones. The most distant (and surprising) outpost was at Shortugai in Afghanistan, discussed later in this chapter.

The Indus town of Lothal in Saurashtra lay on the border between the agricultural lands of the Indus civilization and the sparsely inhabited north Gujarat plain, home to hunter-gatherer groups, and was not far from the sea. A substantial part of this small town was given over to the manufacture of various Indus products such as beads and objects of copper, shell, and ivory. The volume of these goods produced was quite out of proportion to the needs of the town's modest resident population and the inhabitants of its hinterland. The greater part of its products, therefore, must have been made for use elsewhere. Some, it seems likely, were intended for trade with the hunter-gatherer inhabitants of north Gujarat and the desert regions to the south of the Indus realm. Others may have been made for export overseas.

OVERLAND TRADE ACROSS THE IRANIAN PLATEAU

Resources

From the earliest period of settlement at Mehrgarh in the seventh millennium, far-reaching trade networks had given the village's inhabitants access to the products of other regions, such as seashells from the Makran coast, turquoise from Kyzyl Kum in Central Asia, and lapis lazuli probably from Badakshan in Afghanistan. By the fifth millennium, lapis and turquoise were also reaching Susiana and Mesopotamia at the western end of the Iranian plateau, showing that trading networks operated right across these regions. These became more developed in the fourth millennium, with a number of trading towns growing up in the Iranian plateau, particularly at nodes in the trade routes, some procuring raw materials, some working local or imported materials, and most reaping the benefits of transit trade. Two major routes traversed the Iranian plateau between east and west: One (later a part of the famous Silk Road) ran north of the desert interior and crossed the Zagros Mountains through the Diyala Valley to reach Assyria and Babylonia; the other ran to the south of the desert, passing through Anshan to Elam and from there into southern Mesopotamia. Key materials involved in this trade included chlorite from Kerman, copper from a number of sources including the arsenic-rich deposits at Anarak in western Iran, tin from Afghanistan and the south Caspian, silver from Iran, steatite from southern Iran, turquoise from Central Asia, and gold from western Iran. A major source of minerals, including copper, alabaster, steatite, diorite, and aragonite, lay in the Chagai Hills of western Baluchistan, equally accessible to the cultures of the Indo-Iranian borderlands and those of Seistan. Lapis lazuli from Badakshan or perhaps Chagai found its way to centers throughout the trade network, small amounts reaching Baluchistan, Elam, and the Gulf, while considerable quantities were imported into southern Mesopotamia, where it was used to decorate many valuable objects.

Early Trade Networks

Elam, a state comprising Susiana and Anshan in southwest Iran, played a major role in this trade in the early third millennium, establishing trading stations in a number of Iranian towns, including Shahr-i Sokhta in Seistan. By around 2800 BCE, Elam no longer played a dominant role in eastern Iran, and from around 2300 it was incorporated into the empires of southern Mesopotamia, although the trading towns and trade network continued to flourish. The products of these towns enjoyed a wide circulation: For example, chlorite bowls (*série ancienne*) manufactured at Tepe Yahya, mainly during the mid-third millennium, are known from towns and cities in Mesopotamia and Elam, on the Iranian plateau, and in the Gulf region; one fragment was recovered from the lowest excavated levels at Mohenjo-daro, and others have been found at Nausharo, Dholavira, and near Sutkagen-dor in the Makran.

Towns in the Indo-Iranian borderlands and Early Indus settlements in the river plains were active participants in this trade network. Trade routes through the major valleys of the borderlands linked the Indus Basin to Seistan and Afghanistan and beyond them to the Iranian plateau and Central Asia.

In the later third millennium, however, a major shift in trading patterns occurred. Mesopotamia, a major consumer of raw materials from the Iranian plateau and beyond, shifted most of its interest to new sources and suppliers in the Gulf, and communications between the Indus region and Seistan ceased. This had the major effect of denying the Harappans access to the important and varied mineral resources of the Chagai Hills. Trade within the Iranian plateau continued, reaching as far west as Susa, but it no longer provided the international highway between Mesopotamia and the Indian subcontinent.

Little Harappan material is known from Iranian sites, and the few objects found could have been acquired by trade with third parties such as Magan and Elam. The known finds include etched carnelian beads at Tepe Hissar, Shah Tepe, Jalalabad, Kalleh Nisar, and Tepe Yahya; a sherd bearing a Harappan seal impression was also found at Tepe Yahya. Harappan etched carnelian and long barrel carnelian beads were found at Susa, as well as a cylinder seal with a Harappan bull-and-manger design and some Indus script signs, and a round seal with a bull and six Harappan signs.

The Lapis Trade

Lapis lazuli, an exceptionally beautiful type of blue stone, was one of the principal materials procured through these trade networks. It was one of the most highly prized raw materials in the ancient world, often used in conjunction with gold and other precious materials to create exceptional ornaments and works of art.

For a long time it was thought that the Sar-i Sangh and other mines at Badakshan in Afghanistan were the sole source of the lapis lazuli known in antiquity to the inhabitants of the great swathe of territory from Egypt to India. Recently, however, a deposit of visually similar and chemically related material was discovered in the Chagai Hills, south of Seistan in western Baluchistan. Opinions are divided on whether this should also be called lapis lazuli. Scientific analyses of lapis lazuli from ancient sites are rare, and so the source of the material from which ancient lapis lazuli objects were made is generally unknown. One exception is the material from Shahr-i Sokhta, not far from Chagai. Analyses have shown this to include lapis derived from three sources: Chagai, Badakshan, and a more distant source in the Pamirs, less than a third of the samples that were analyzed coming from Chagai. Shahr-i Sokhta had a major role as a break-of-bulk center for the lapis trade: There raw nodules were worked to remove the cortex (outer rind) and impurities, and the lapis was prepared for export, either as pure clean nodules or as finished items such as beads. It seems strange that Shahr-i Sokhta did not confine its procurement of lapis to that from the nearby Chagai hills rather than exploiting more distant sources. It may be that the Chagai hills source was discovered during the third millennium and that its exploitation was therefore a recent addition to the long-established trade in lapis from Badakshan. Shahr-i Sokhta was on a major route to Afghanistan and Turkmenia, and it had very close cultural ties with the inhabitants of southeast Turkmenia who exploited the Badakshan lapis source and from whom the people of Shahr-i Sokhta obtained large quantities of turquoise.

The people of the Indo-Iranian borderlands and Indus Basin had gained access to lapis by trade, probably along the route that led from the Kachi plain through the Bolan pass to Quetta and Mundigak, where it joined the major trade route to southern Turkmenia and Afghanistan. This route had linked the people of the Indo-Iranian borderlands with the farming communities of Afghanistan, Turkmenia, and the South Caspian since at least the seventh millennium BCE, and it was the route by which turquoise from Kyzyl Kum reached South Asia. Regular communications, probably by camel caravan, are likely to have existed between the cultures of Helmand and southern Turkmenia along this route throughout the third and second millennia.

During the period of the Indus civilization, however, it seems that communications between the Indus and Seistan were severed, and the Bolan route ceased to be used beyond Quetta. Which culture initiated this situation is unknown. The people of the Indus region no longer had access to the resources of the Chagai Hills, and turquoise and lapis lazuli no longer reached them via the route to the Bolan pass.

Instead the Harappans traded with Afghanistan and Central Asia via a more northerly route. This route started in the Punjab; it passed through Late Kot Diji territory along the Gomal River, or followed the Indus north through Swat and then along the Kabul River through the Khyber pass into northern Afghanistan, where there were copper, silver, and lead sources. The importance to the

Harappans of resources from the north is indicated by the fact that, rather than merely sending traders to the region, they established an Indus trading outpost at Shortugai, at the confluence of the Kokcha and Amu Darya Rivers in Afghanistan, to facilitate their procurement of local resources. As well as lapis lazuli, these resources included tin and gold. In addition, turquoise and jadeite could be obtained from the neighboring Namazga culture in the Kopet Dagh area of southern Turkmenia. Trade with the latter is confirmed by the presence of Harappan material, including etched carnelian beads, ivory rods and dice, and two Harappan seals at Altyn-depe, one of the principal Namazga towns. Many Harappan carnelian beads were also found in looted graves in northern Afghanistan, and one etched carnelian bead and a figurine of a bull were found in the BMAC palace at Dashli-3. A few Namazga artifacts were found in Harappan sites, including animal-headed bronze pins. The Namazga culture was connected, via a trade route running south of the Elburz mountains, to Tepe Hissar and Shah Tepe, both of which have yielded a few Indus carnelian beads.

A group of seven Bronze Age (probably Harappan) sites has been located in the region, of which only Shortugai has been excavated. It was a typical Indus settlement despite being 625 miles (1,000 kilometers) distant from the Indus region. Artifacts there include the standard Harappan types such as terra-cotta cakes, cart models and figurines, and typical Harappan pottery, as well as bangles made of chank seashell. A seal with a rhino design was also found here. Houses were of the usual Harappan design, using bricks of standard size. The inhabitants of the settlement practiced farming, using irrigation, and craft activities, including smelting and working copper and making beads. Carnelian and lapis lazuli were the main materials worked.

Shortugai was strategically located to control access to the mineral resources of the region. The metal ores, particularly tin, were probably of particular interest to the Harappans. Lapis, though highly prized by Near Eastern cultures, was less highly regarded by the Harappans, who preferred other materials; relatively little lapis has been found in Harappan sites. It seems, however, that the Harappans valued it for its export potential, and that they monopolized its supply to the cultures of the Gulf and Mesopotamia.

GULF TRADE

The cultures who bordered the (Arabian/Persian) Gulf had a long history of intercommunity contacts, mainly by sea, going back to the fifth millennium when pottery in the style of Mesopotamian Ubaid wares was distributed as far south as Oman. Coastal fishing communities were probably regularly in contact with those in adjacent areas and across the mouth of the Gulf, and those of the Arabian Sea coast of Oman may also have been in contact with others along Arabia's southern coasts.

The mid-third millennium saw a radical change in the patterns of trade in the great area from West Asia to the Indus. Although trade with neighbors and between the cultures of the Iranian plateau continued, Mesopotamian and

Harappan participation in the trading networks right across the Iranian plateau, which depended on the use of pack animals, virtually ceased, and was replaced by trade using water transport. Though not without its risks, such as storms and perhaps pirates, this was generally an easier and more efficient means of transporting goods, particularly bulky or heavy materials. Direct seaborne communications through the Gulf were now established between the Indus civilization and Mesopotamia, the main Near Eastern consumer of imported raw materials. This link enabled the Harappans to conduct direct commercial relations with Mesopotamia, giving them direct control over the management of their trade rather than depending on intermediaries (as the land traffic had) and thereby improving both their returns on their exports and their ability to control the supply of imports. Sea trade also gave the Harappans access to the resources and markets of the cultures in the Gulf. The establishment of new Harappan settlements along the Makran coast reflected the development of this maritime trade.

Harappans in the Makran

The Makran is arid, inhospitable terrain, where fishing is the main livelihood. Land travel along the coast is difficult, and communications are easier by sea. The dissected Makran coast offers many sheltered inlets suitable for boats to anchor, some giving access to seasonal rivers that are navigable routes into the interior after the rains; at other times of the year, the dry beds of these watercourses provide paths for foot traffic. Communities must have been exploiting the resources of the Makran coast by the seventh millennium BCE, when seashells were traded to the inland settlement of Mehrgarh, and a number of settlements are known there in the Early Harappan period.

The Harappans established several towns in the Makran, their existence explicable only in relation to overseas trade. Sutkagen-dor was a small town with substantial stone walls and gateways. Sotka Koh, 100 miles to its east, seems also to have had a walled sector. It is likely the towns were fortified as strongholds to protect goods, reflecting their location in territory directly exposed to the presence of outsiders. Both were situated at the mouth of seasonal rivers providing routes into the interior (Sutkagen-dor on the Dasht, Sotka Koh on the Shadi Kaur), while farther east an unexcavated site at Pir Shah Jurio lies 3 miles inland from the mouth of the Hab. Sutkagen-dor, now 35 miles inland, is located near Gwadar bay, a major anchorage since historical times, while Sotka Koh is currently 9 miles inland from a modern fishing village at Pasni, also important as a port. However, in Harappan times when the sea level was higher, they were probably on or near the sea. There is a local tradition of a harbor at Sutkagen-dor. The settlement had strong stone walls up to 24 feet thick at their base, with bastions or towers on the west and east sides and a narrow gate in the southwestern corner, enclosing a citadel containing mud brick houses; an unwalled lower town lay to the north and east, and it has been suggested that there was a wharf along one edge of the settlement. The unexcavated town of Sotka Koh was similar in size to Sutkagen-dor: Part of a wall remains there, associated with an unwalled settlement. Another such site at Khairia Kot, on the west side of Las Bela in west Sonmiani bay, now 25 miles from the coast, might also have been a port. In contrast, Balakot, farther to the east on east Sonmiani bay, was a fishing settlement, apparently not involved in trade (only one import was found there, a pot similar to those at Umm-an-Nar in Oman). Allahdino on the Malir River, probably near the coast in Harappan times, was also not a port, but may have been a commerical center where goods were stored for distribution or forwarding.

It seems likely that shiploads of goods from Oman and from trade through the Gulf were brought to Sutkagen-dor and Sotka Koh in the Makran, with no restriction on the time of year when sailing could take place in the sheltered waters of the Gulf. In these settlements, the goods may have gone through customs' control and were probably divided into smaller packages for onward distribution overland, carried by human porters or pack animals (cattle or sheep).

The establishment of Harappan trading towns on the Makran coast probably altered the local patterns of communications. This is illustrated by the settlement of Miri Qalat, which had earlier (periods II–III) been linked to the Iranian plateau and northern Baluchistan. Finds there in period III included proto-Elamite pottery. However, Harappan material there in period IV, along with large quantities of fish from the coast (three days' journey to the south), suggests that in the Mature Harappan period Miri Qalat was drawn into the Harappan sphere of influence.

Gujarat

Although today the coast of South Asia extends southeast from Las Bela, in Harappan times the Indus River debouched into what is now the Ranns of Kutch, and its delta was far less developed; at the same time sealevels were higher, with the result that the coast in Harappan times ran east from around Karachi before turning south around what is now the mouth of the Luni River. The Ranns of Kutch were open water, probably at least 4 meters deep, and Kutch was an island. Saurashtra was attached to the mainland by a far narrower neck of land than today, and this was probably flooded for part or all of the year. The Gulf of Khambat was wider than today and ran farther inland.

In Harappan times, therefore, Gujarat had an extensive coastline. Many coastal settlements in Gujarat, such as Pabumath, were anchorages for fishing vessels and probably for seagoing trading ships. As in more recent times, port settlements, such as Kuntasi, were often located at the mouths of rivers or slightly inland along them. The best-known is Lothal, near the Sabarmati River. In the third millennium, a river channel, now dry, flowed along the west side of the settlement and was navigable to the Gulf of Khambat; since Harappan times, however, the estuary of the Sabarmati and the associated coast have been extended by heavy silt deposition, and today Lothal is 12 miles from the sea.

Though a small town, Lothal was a major industrial center, with two bead workshops, a copper smithy, shell and ivory workshops, and kilns. Some workshops produced goods of local materials for distribution to other parts of the Indus realms, while other products may have been for overseas trade. As discussed earlier, Lothal was a gateway settlement through which goods and

materials from neighboring hunter-gatherer and farming groups were channeled into the Harappan internal trade network, in exchange for Harappan
manufactured goods.

A large brick basin was constructed along the eastern side of the town, This
was thought by its excavator, S. R. Rao, to have been a dock into which boats,
up to 20 meters long and 6 meters wide, could have come to unload. The basin
is around 22 by 37 meters and 4–4.5 meters deep, revetted with a thick wall
built of baked brick, four bricks thick. The basin's sides are vertical, and there
are no steps giving access to the basin. A channel entering the north of the
basin through a wide gap linked it to the river estuary at high tide, and in the
basin's south was another channel that Rao interpreted as an outlet or spillway: Grooves show that this was originally fitted with sluice gates. There was
also a broad shallow gap in the southern end of the east side; this might have
been an additional spillway, although it is also possible that it resulted from
later brick robbing given that the edges are irregular. Rao interpreted the gap
as a later entrance into the basin, although this is problematic. Postholes along
the side of the basin may once have held mooring posts.

A view of the basin at Lothal, commonly known as the dock. It undoubtedly held water, probably seawater given that marine shells have been found in it; it had an inlet channel linking it with
the river flowing past the settlement and an outlet channel with a sluice gate. Little else can be
said about it with certainty and its purpose has yet to be convincingly established. (Namit
Arora)

Serious objections have been raised to the interpretation of this basin as a dock; for example, the approach channel, which turns twice through 90 degrees, seems excessively awkward, and the positioning of the dock on the opposite side of the town from the river also seems to create needless access difficulties. Several scholars have suggested that the basin could have been a reservoir for drinking water or for irrigation, and others have countered this with the valid objections that its water would have been contaminated by the town's drains, one of which flowed into the basin, and that the local water supplies were perfectly adequate for agriculture, without a special reservoir. Marine shells have been found in the basin, indicating that it was filled with seawater. The purpose of the basin therefore remains a mystery. Modern practices in the region suggest that docks were probably unnecessary: Vessels could be drawn up on beaches or could anchor in shallow water at high tide over mudflats, from which they could be unloaded when the tide went out. Boats unloading at inland ports could be drawn up by the riverbank with basic moorings or at most a simple quay: For instance, a sloping quay was used at the port of Kuntasi. Large vessels could be moored offshore and their cargos conveyed to land in smaller boats.

A possible alternative function suggested itself to me when reading about the problems of beaching ships to repair them (Ray 2003). It is perhaps possible that the Lothal basin was a dry dock. It was located on the opposite side of the town from the river and was therefore protected from tidal surges, and it had inlet and outlet sluices that would have enabled users to control the flow of water into and out of the basin. A ship could have been floated into the basin, the water drained, the repairs made, and water allowed back in to refloat the vessel. This is a preliminary hypothesis at present as I have not yet had the opportunity to investigate its feasibility.

However, there is no doubt that, even without a dock, Lothal was engaged in trade. A substantial warehouse was found in the citadel area of the town immediately adjacent to the "dock." This consisted of a podium with a checkerboard originally of sixty-four square mud brick blocks (of which twelve remain), separated by narrow aisles, probably originally with a roof of perishable material. This building was destroyed by fire at some point in its career, preserving some of the contents. Around seventy burned clay tags were found in this building, with the imprint of cloth, cords (including knots), or matting on their backs, evidence of the packages to which they had originally been fastened. A seal had been impressed on the front of these tags; twelve bore the impression of the same seal, and the majority bore the unicorn device, suggesting official control of the materials stored there. None of the seals found in Lothal had been used on these sealings, which implies that the packages had been sealed elsewhere before being brought to Lothal. The twelve impressions of the same seal suggest either a very substantial shipment from a single source or a regular consignment of goods from a single source over a period of time.

One substantial house in the settlement was identified by Rao as perhaps belonging to a merchant. It contained two seals, eight gold pendants, and some sherds of Reserved Slip ware.

Kuntasi (Bibi-no-Timbo), a smaller settlement on the opposite side of Saurashtra from Lothal, has also been identified as a port. It is situated in an area of poor agricultural potential and limited freshwater, indicating that its location was dictated by other criteria. In the Harappan period, it was on a tidal creek and accessible from the sea at high tide. Anchorstones were found on the surface of the site before excavation and others within the settlement. A rectangular stone platform was identified as a jetty. Beside this was an industrial complex, including copper-working furnaces and kilns for firing beads and pottery. Beyond lay rooms that may have been used for storage, some with clay bins. The settlement had a strong stone fortification wall with a substantial gateway and a watchtower overlooking the river. A number of large houses with courtyards were excavated inside the settlement, and there was probably other housing outside the walls. Among the finds from Kuntasi were Harappan weights, implying commercial activity. An uninscribed stamp seal bearing a geometric pattern was found in the storage area of the industrial complex. This unusual seal was apparently similar to one known from an early context at Harappa. The unusual quantity of beads of lapis lazuli found in this settlement probably reflects its role in overseas trade given that lapis lazuli was a material not much used by the Harappans themselves but an important

A number of these circular stones with a central perforation were found in or beside the "dock" at Lothal and are often interpreted as anchors. This is possible, although similar stones were used as architectural elements in Harappan cities. (Namit Arora)

Harappan export to Mesopotamia. It has also been suggested that Kuntasi was a trading center for materials collected by local hunter-gatherers. Kuntasi was therefore similar to Lothal in many ways, though on a smaller scale. The excavator, Dhavalikar, would date the beginning of Kuntasi's role as a port and industrial center to the period 2200–2000 BCE. A land route may have connected Kuntasi with Lothal via Rangpur.

A number of the settlements in Gujarat were heavily fortified. In part this may reflect the local use of stone in architecture; however, as in the case of the coastal sites in Makran, it may also reflect the position of the region at the interface between the Harappan polity and the outside world, necessitating at least security and at worst defensibility. A stone warehouse was reported at Prabhas Patan, a coastal settlement at the mouth of the Hiran River in Saurashtra. Desalpur, a small settlement in Kutch, had a stone and rubble wall and may have been a port. Surkotada, also on Kutch and inland from Pabumath, was a small settlement raised on an earthen platform, surrounded by a substantial mud and mud brick wall with rubble facing, bastions, and an elaborate gateway. Both Desalpur and Surkotada appeared to lack most of the aspects of a town and are more likely to have been settlements designed mainly as strongholds.

Many of the other sites in Kutch were also fortified. The most impressive is the city of Dholavira, situated on Khadir Island in what is now the Ranns of Kutch. This grew from a small town with a substantial brick and stone wall into a city of at least 60 hectares, which was a center for craft production, including metal working and the manufacture of beads, pottery, and shell artifacts. The meager local water sources were inadequate to supply the residents so huge rockcut water tanks were constructed. Its unfavourable location for water and for agriculture suggests that the economic justification for its location lay elsewhere: it was probably related to trade, internal communications, and industry since it was well placed to control overseas trade, communications between Gujarat and the rest of the Harappan realm, and the channelling of gemstones and beads, shells and shell products, ivory and other produce of Gujarat into the internal distribution network.

Maritime Conditions

The coastal Harappans came to play a major role in seafaring in the Gulf and the Arabian Sea. From Sutkagen-dor westward, the South Asian coast benefited from the sheltered sailing conditions of the Gulf. East and south of this area, however, ships were exposed to the perilous currents and storms of the Arabian Sea and to the strongly seasonal pattern of the winds. During the winter months, between October/November and March/April, the gentle northeast monsoon winds blow from India toward the Arabian Peninsula and ultimately East Africa. If the Harappans had the knowledge and skill to use these monsoon winds, they may have sailed directly between Gujarat and the Oman coast in the winter; the settlement of Ra's al-Hadd, where Harappan material, including a seal and an ivory comb, has been found, is today the natural landfall for ships using the monsoon winds. Marine conditions bring an abundance of fish into Arabian coastal waters during the late summer and winter, making this the main fishing season. This was therefore the time of year when contacts across the Gulf of Oman would have been at their peak, and this would have been the time when fishers and traders crossed between the Indus region and the lands of Arabia and the Gulf, especially the Oman peninsula.

In contrast, in summer, between May and September, the violent and stormy southwest monsoon winds make seafaring dangerous: there was therefore no easy route for seafarers from the Gulf to reach Gujarat at this time of year. Seafaring during the summer would probably have been confined to the calmer waters of the Gulf and to creeks and backwaters in the Indus delta and Gujarat.

Magan and the Harappans

Confirmation of the seasonal pattern of seafaring, at least in Oman, has come from the sites of the eastern Omani coast, such as Ra's al-Junayz (Ra's al-Jinz) and Ra's al-Hadd, which were occupied only during the winter months, September to March, when they were used as a base for fishing and shellworking. The seasonal inhabitants of these settlements brought with them copper tools, pottery, and plant foods from the interior. Such coastal settlements in Oman and United Arab Emirates (UAE) have yielded stone net sinkers, fishhooks of shell or copper, and shell lures.

From the Makran coast, it is a short, easy sea crossing, around 30–40 hours under sail, to Oman on the western side of the Gulf, known as Magan to the Mesopotamians, and seaborne relations between these areas may have been established by the early third millennium BCE; fishing sites on the Oman coast are known by the fifth millennium. Magan and the Makran probably belonged during the earlier third millennium (Hili period in Magan) to a cultural interaction sphere in which ideas and small quantities of each region's local materials were exchanged and in which links were created and maintained by fishers exploiting the marine resources of the southern end of the Gulf during the winter months. Later trade between them is demonstrated by the presence of a few imported objects in Kulli sites and Kulli material in burial cairns on Umm-an-Nar in Magan.

By 2500 BCE (Umm-an-Nar period in Magan), the inhabitants of the Indus region and Gujarat had also become involved in this interaction sphere, as fishers but also as traders, establishing settlements in the Makran to give them control over the key Gulf of Oman crossings. The volume and variety of traded goods increased under their influence, and their artifacts inspired native industries in Magan. Although shells used for making bangles and other objects were available along the Makran and Gujarat coasts, the Harappans may have obtained some of their supply of spiny murex (*Chicoreus ramosus*) and *Fasciolaria trapezium* from the east and north coasts of Oman as well. Oman may also have furnished the Harappans with turtles for meat, shells, and leather. However, the main attraction of Magan to the Harappans was its extensive copper deposits.

The settlement of Ra's al-Junayz, on the east coast of Oman, was one of those engaged in trade with the Indus: It has yielded large storage vessels and other Harappan pots, a copper stamp seal with a Harappan design and inscription, a few Harappan beads, and a Harappan ivory comb, as well as a copper flat axe in the Harappan style.

A quantity of bitumen was found there, stored in particular rooms of some of the houses, dated to the second half of the third millennium. The bitumen was in several forms. Rectangular or plano-convex blocks of solid bitumen were shown by analysis probably to have derived from Mesopotamia where there were major deposits, particularly at Hit on the middle Euphrates. These blocks had been imported as an essential raw material for shipbuilding and maintenance. In addition, bitumen-coated sherds of Mesopotamian pottery, the only Mesopotamian ware found there, bear witness to the import of bitumen as a liquid. Bitumen was also present in the form of slabs or small three-sided pieces, both bearing impressions of mats and reed bundles. Barnacles and impressions of barnacles were found on the opposite, smooth face of the bitumen slabs. Analysis of the composition of these slabs shows that they were a mixture of bitumen with tallow or fish oil (to increase plasticity), gypsum (to increase hardness and water resistance), and tempering material such as chopped reeds and palm leaf fragments. This mixture was used to caulk boats built of tightly bound reed bundles tied or sewn together and covered with reed mats. Simple reed boats had a life expectancy of some months, which was greatly increased by caulking to make them waterproof. Bitumen caulking was probably also used on boats built of wooden planks. Additionally, the caulking protected the boat's hull from barnacles, which could be removed more easily from the bitumen skin, applied 2–5 centimeters thick. The bitumen coating was periodically removed and could then be heated, cleaned up, and reapplied. Evidence of this practice comes not only from the bitumen pieces removed and stored at Ra's al-Junayz but from the presence, inside some of these pieces, of broken fragments of barnacle shell, evidently incorporated during an earlier reuse of this bitumen; an Ur III period text from Mesopotamia also refers to the practice. An Iranian pot that had been used to heat bitumen was found at the earlier Omani coastal site of RH-5 (Qurum) near Muscat. Umm-an-Nar off the west coast of Magan also yielded bitumen blocks, bitumen caulking recovered from boats, and jars coated with bitumen.

Much of the Oman peninsula is desert or mountains, the latter rich in copper and attractive stone, particularly diorite, olivine-gabbro, and chlorite. As well as coastal fishing, the inhabitants of the region practiced pastoralism and agriculture in inland oases and wadis. Most of their inland settlements were also sited to exploit the copper deposits, of which there were more than a hundred: The copper ore was smelted near the mines, then refined and made into ingots in the adjacent settlements. These inland sites were linked to coastal settlements that engaged in trade and industry, particularly copper smelting and working. Interestingly, despite the abundance of copper and the evident importance of its exploitation, copper objects were not common in Magan sites and those that were in circulation were generally small and technologically simple: fishhooks, chisels, flat axes, spear- and arrowheads, and small pieces of jewelry, such as rings and pins. This may imply that one of the main reasons for mining and smelting copper was for export, in exchange for valued Harappan, Mesopotamian, and Dilmunite goods and materials. A few copper or bronze vessels may have been imports from the Indus.

The best-known of these inland settlements is Maysar 1 in Wadi Samad, which, like most settlements of the Magan interior, comprised a village and a fortified tower, the latter probably used for storage, as a place of refuge when danger threatened, and as the residence of the local chief. The settlement's inhabitants cultivated the surrounding land using irrigation and engaged in a number of craft activities including the manufacture of (*série tardive*) chlorite vessels, which were probably traded to other parts of the Gulf and Mesopotamia. Numerous furnaces, crucibles, crushing stones, and copper slag and many bun-shaped ingots attest to the importance of working copper from nearby mines. Some of the pottery vessels produced at Maysar show similarities to Harappan pottery in form and decoration. A triangular prismatic seal decorated with animals in Harappan style, a local imitation of a Harappan prototype, emphasizes the link with Harappan traders.

The latter may have penetrated the interior or may have confined their presence to coastal settlements, but their influence was substantial. Harappan pottery is known in considerable amounts from settlements on or near the coast, for example, making up a third of the pottery excavated at Asimah. The majority were large storage jars, sometimes bearing Harappan signs or graffiti. Indus beads were placed in a number of burials, for instance at Umm-an-Nar and Hili. Many local wares, both in coastal and in inland settlements, show Harappan inspiration. Other Harappan-influenced material found in Magan settlements include flat copper axes, and local metallurgy and seal cutting owed much to Harappan technology. One axe, from Tell Abraq, resembles an example from Mohenjo-daro that had been finished with a smooth outer shell made by dipping the cast object into molten copper. An unusual pear-shaped seal from Ra's al-Junayz was inscribed with a stick man closely resembling one of the signs in the Indus script. Harappan weights have been found at Tell Abraq, dated around 2300 BCE, and at early second-millennium Shimal. Two of these were made of the usual banded chert; the third, from Abraq, was of jasper, a material rarely used; but all are likely to have been manufactured in the Indus realms. The presence of Harappan weights in Magan implies that the Harappans needed to control quantities in their exchanges there.

In recent times the Oman peninsula has exported dates and dried fish, pearls, and mother-of-pearl to South Asia, and these may have been among its exports in Harappan times too. Copper, however, was probably the principal commodity sought by the Harappans there. The high nickel-content copper objects found at Lothal have been taken to imply that the copper from which they were made was derived from Magan, copper ores from which contain nickel and arsenic; however, this was also true of copper from the Aravallis in Rajasthan, also exploited by the Harappans. Hundreds of sherds of large Harappan black-coated storage jars are known from coastal sites like Ra's al-Junayz, Ra's al-Hadd, and Ra's Ghanada, as well as some inland sites, such as Asimah. These may suggest that, in return for their copper, the people of Magan received grain or other foodstuffs, as well as small personal items such as carnelian and lapis lazuli beads and ivory combs. Tin, used at Umm-an-Nar for alloying with copper, may also have come from or through the Harappans. Analyses of the composition of bronze items from four tombs suggest that they were made of imported bronze rather than of copper locally alloyed with imported tin, so the alloy may also have been brought in by the Harappans. Zebu cattle, bred in South Asia, were introduced into Oman during the third millennium, and they too may have been imported in the context of the copper trade.

Magan and the Harappans were also involved in a trade route that stretched as far as Africa. Ra's al-Junayz, 45 nautical miles south from Sotka Koh, is located on the most easterly point of Oman: This is the main landmark for ships crossing from Pakistan to the Arabian peninsula, and from here the route follows the southern Arabian coast to Yemen, from which it is a short distance across the Red Sea to Djibouti and Ethiopia. Incense may have traveled east along this route: it was the principal commodity of southwest Arabia in later times and was being imported in considerable quantities by the Egyptians by the late third millennium. It was also by this route that African crops, notably jowar (sorghum), ragi (finger millet), and bajra (bulrush millet), were introduced to the Indian subcontinent. The existence of links between Africa and the trade networks that passed through the Gulf is underlined by the discovery of copal resin from Zanzibar in a later third-millennium burial at the Mesopotamian city of Eshnunna.

The Eastern Gulf

By the twenty-fourth century BCE and probably earlier, the Harappans were also sailing right through the Gulf to Mesopotamia. The most direct and easiest sea route north followed the eastern shore of the Gulf. This is an inhospitable land. The mountains of southern Iran run parallel with and close to the coast, leaving only a narrow strip of coastal land, accessible from the interior of the Iranian plateau only through a few passes, and offering few resources to support human habitation. Settlements, such as Siraf, were established in some periods at points where a good anchorage existed, though such sheltered spots are few in number. One such place was Bushehr where a pass cut through the mountains by the Shapur River allowed a route to be established linking Anshan to the coast via Shiraz, but this was probably little used in the third millennium. Elam, the major state in the southwest of the Iranian plateau, had access to the sea at the head of the Gulf via the navigable River Karun but developed its main trade networks overland. Around 2300 BCE, Elam was conquered by Sargon of Akkad and remained largely in the orbit of the southern Mesopotamian states until 2004 BCE, when the Elamites sacked Ur. A number of Harappan seals, beads, and ivory inlays and a Harappan weight were found at Susa, the Elamite capital, and gaming boards of similar design are known from Susa and Lothal.

East of Anshan in the interior of southern Iran were various small polities, notably Shahdad and Tepe Yahya in Kerman, Jiroft in the Halil Rud Basin, Bampur and other towns in Iranian Baluchistan, and the Helmand culture in Seistan. These lay on routes running mainly east–west through the Iranian plateau, but a route to the seacoast around modern Minab and Bandar Abbas, opposite the northern tip of Oman, connected them with the sea. Trade between these towns and Magan took place during the earlier third millennium, but the people from the Iranian plateau do not seem to have sailed farther afield. During the Mature Harappan period, when the Harappans dominated the Makran coastal region, the volume of this Iran-Magan trade became negligible.

The Western Gulf

The western shore of the Gulf is mainly desert but settlements thrived in oases such as Hofuf and in coastal locations suitable for fishing. Islands off the western shore also offered opportunities for settlement. During the early third millennium, there was a flourishing culture on Tarut Island, and by the middle of the millennium Bahrain, which had earlier seen settlement followed by abandonment, was reoccupied and rapidly built up a flourishing economy based on agriculture, animal husbandry, hunting, and particularly fishing. A town was established on the coast at Qala'at al-Bahrain, where there was a good natural harbor. The island's main agricultural product was dates, which came to be famed in the Near East for their quality. The surrounding waters yielded not only fish but also oysters from which "fish-eyes"(pearls) and mother-of-pearl could be obtained. The island is blessed with springs of freshwater that also bubble up offshore, and it has fine natural harbors, including one at Qala'at al-Bahrain. It was therefore a natural port of call for seafarers sailing through the Gulf who would put in to replenish their stocks of water. This led to the island's eventually developing a major role as a trading entrepot where goods from Mesopotamia, the Indus, and other places could be exchanged or obtained.

Trading relations also existed between Magan and Dilmun (the Mesopotamian name for the eastern Arabian littoral and Bahrain). For example, Umm-an-Nar pottery has been found in Bahrain.

Persian Gulf Seals. During the later third millennium, the people of Dilmun began to make round (Persian Gulf) seals, with simple motifs representing mainly animals or a human foot and with a high domed boss with a central groove. These continued in use into the early second millennium. A number of similar round seals bearing Harappan motifs, particularly of a short-horned bull, and occasionally Harappan script have also been found, particularly in Bahrain and at Ur, but also from Failaka, Babylon, Girsu, and Susa and from Mohenjo-daro and Chanhu-daro in the Indus realms. Some of these seals had recognizably Harappan sign sequences, but in other cases the inscriptions included some signs or sign combinations unknown in the Indus region, suggesting that they rendered non-Harappan names or words. These may perhaps have been the

A two-room house in the settlement of Saar on Bahrain (ancient Dilmun). A bench with a basin, and a hearth and tannur can be seen along the two outer walls of the inner room. Saar dates mainly to the early second millennium BCE, when Dilmun was a prosperous entrepot for Gulf trade that provided a link between the Harappans and the Mesopotamians (who were no longer in direct contact). Dilmun's increased wealth from trade is reflected in the appearance of such stone-built houses. (London-Bahrain Archaeological Expedition)

property of Dilmunites who were closely engaged in Harappan trade. No other script was used on Persian Gulf seals and the majority were uninscribed. The relative chronology of classic Persian Gulf seals and those with Harappan motifs and inscriptions is unknown: however, it is possible that the Harappans introduced the Dilmunites to the idea of using stamp seals.

No written records are known from Dilmun, although familiarity with Mesopotamia's use of writing might have encouraged the development of literacy. Crawford (1998) notes that the round stamp seals of Dilmun would have been suitable for use with ink on a medium such as parchment. Since none of the non-Harappan Gulf seals, however, bore inscriptions, literacy is unlikely to have played an important part in local life.

Mesopotamian Traders in the Gulf

At the head of the Gulf lay Mesopotamia. Sumer, its southern region, saw the development in the early third millennium of city-states along the branches of the Euphrates. At that time the waters of the Gulf extended much farther north than today, and the city of Ur lay near the sea. The rivers of the region were navigable, providing a link from the sea to the cities of Akkad, the region north of Sumer. The independent city-states of Sumer and Akkad were united into a single state by Sargon of Akkad between 2334 and 2316 BCE. This empire broke up around 2200, but the region was reunified under the Ur III dynasty (2112–2004 BCE). Sumer had developed writing during the late fourth millennium and by 2500 BCE was creating copious records of economic transactions, legal documents, political statements, letters, and literature, so a considerable amount of information survives on Mesopotamian involvement in Gulf trade.

This seems to have ebbed and flowed. During the fifth millennium (Ubaid period), characteristic Ubaid pottery is known right through the Gulf, from Bahrain and Saudi Arabia to Qatar and UAE. This distribution may reflect active trade with these regions by the Sumerians, but it is more likely that contacts between people from different parts of the Gulf, probably in the course of fishing expeditions, led to the exchange and spread of this desirable pottery; faunal remains in the settlements of the period in the eastern province of Arabia were composed largely of fish. In the fourth millennium (Uruk period), the Sumerians turned their attentions northward, trading with northern Mesopotamia and Anatolia. Fishing communities in the Gulf, however, probably continued to interact with their neighbors.

Magan. In the early third millennium, finds of pottery show that the Sumerians established trading relations with settlements on the UAE coast of Magan, such as Umm-an-Nar, whose inhabitants obtained copper and diorite through their connections with the interior. The Sumerians may also have penetrated the interior in this period. They continued to trade with Magan throughout the third millennium, receiving copper, timber, red ochre, turtles, diorite, and olivine-gabbro in return for wool, textiles and garments, oil, hides, large quantities of barley, and bitumen. By around 2500 BCE, Umm-an-Nar, situated on an island just off the western coast of Magan, was a major trading entrepot. Crawford (1998, 126) suggests that the underrepresentation of women and children among the burials at Umm-an-Nar may reflect the role of this settlement as a specialist center for traders and sailors without families. A building with seven narrow rooms in this settlement may have been a warehouse for storing goods for trade and commodities received in trade. Mesopotamian material was found only in coastal settlements, in contrast to Harappan material, known throughout Magan, suggesting that Mesopotamian traders were confined to the coast.

A few texts suggest that the Akkadian kings were not entirely satisfied with these trading arrangements: Perhaps the quantities of desired materials made available to them were inadequate. Old Babylonian (early second-millennium) copies of Akkadian inscriptions refer to an expedition by Manishtushu (2269–2255 BCE), in which he defeated a coalition of thirty-two "cities" and quarried black stone from their hills: The invaded region might have been Magan, though part of Iran is also possible. Inscriptions of his successor, Naram-Sin (2254–2218 BCE), refer to the latter's successful campaign in

Magan. Among the objects Naram-Sin dedicated to the temple was a *série récente* chlorite vessel, probably booty from Magan. Naram-Sin also followed his victory there by quarrying diorite.

Sargon of Akkad claimed that boats from Magan sailed to his capital city, Agade, and twenty-first-century BCE documents discovered in the merchant quarter at the Sumerian city of Ur may refer to boats from this region, though the phrase "boats of Magan" may mean Sumerian vessels designed for the trip to Magan or of the same type as vessels used in Magan. Ur III period archives from Umma and Girsu also refer to delegates from Magan, among other foreigners, but it seems unlikely that sailors from Magan were major players in the sea trade.

Dilmun. By the late fourth millennium, the Mesopotamians were trading with a land they called Dilmun. This name probably referred to different areas of the Gulf at different times. In the early third millennium, it was probably applied to the island of Tarut and to the Eastern Province of the adjacent Arabian mainland. In the later third millennium it seems to have referred also to the Island of Bahrain, which by the early second millennium had become the main center. At this time the people of Dilmun also established a major outpost on the island of Failaka off the southern coast of Mesopotamia.

Tarut had trading relations with Mesopotamia, Magan, various parts of Iran, and Baluchistan in the earlier third millennium. At this time it was a producer of chlorite vessels in what is known as the Intercultural Style (*série ancienne*). Other major production centers were Tepe Yahya, situated very close to a large deposit of chlorite, and probably Jiroft to its north. These vessels were widely traded in the Gulf, Mesopotamia, and the Iranian plateau. Dilmun was referred to in the twenty-fifth and twenty-fourth centuries BCE as a intermediary supplier of timber and copper. Although there are references to Dilmun in the subsequent periods, during the later third millennium its role as an entrepot seems to have declined, and the Mesopotamians dealt directly with Magan through its western coastal centers, such as Umm-an-Nar, and with the Harappans who came themselves to Sumer. It was only after the fall of Ur III that Dilmun again operated as a major entrepot.

As agricultural land in the region was limited, imported grain became important to the local economy. Large shipments of grain from Mesopotamia are recorded: one, for example, contained 187,500 imperial gallons (714,000 liters) of grain. Mesopotamia also supplied Dilmun with other foodstuffs, wool, and silver. Pearls and mother-of-pearl were exported from Dilmun to Mesopotamia along with the fine dates that were cultivated on Bahrain.

The Indus and Mesopotamia

Although Sumerian and Akkadian traders were active in the Gulf, there is no evidence that they ever reached farther south than the western coast of Magan. Harappan material, however, began to appear in Mesopotamia in the early days of the Indus civilization: Carnelian beads, for example, are known from some of the graves in the Royal Cemetery at Ur, dated between 2600 and 2450

BCE. Initially such exotica may have reached the Sumerians indirectly either by trade through the Iranian plateau or via their trade with the people of Magan, with whom the Harappans were now in regular contact. By the late twenty-fourth century, however, the Harappans were sailing through the Gulf right up to ports in southern Mesopotamia, for it was at this time that Sargon of Akkad boasted that ships from Dilmun, Magan, and Meluhha docked at the quays of his capital, Agade, which lay far up the Euphrates river.

Meluhha, it is now generally agreed, was the name by which the Indus civilization was known to the Mesopotamians: Meluhha was the most distant of the trio of foreign lands, and the imports from Meluhha mentioned in Sumerian and Akkadian texts, such as timbers, carnelian, and ivory, match the resources of the Harappan realms. The Meluhhans were said to have had large boats, and indeed substantial, seaworthy craft would have been a prerequisite for trade over the distances involved. By the time of Sargon, therefore, if not before, the Indus people were plying the Gulf sea lanes and anchoring in Mesopotamian ports.

After the collapse of the Akkadian dynasty in 2193 BCE, there was a period of political disintegration, during which various Mesopotamian city-states reasserted their independence. One of the foremost was Lagash, under its great ruler Gudea (2141–2122 BCE), who made use of the established trade networks to acquire exotic materials, including wood and "translucent carnelian from Meluhha," for a great temple he was building in his capital city, Girsu (Electronic Text Corpus of Sumerian Literature, "The Building of Ningirsu's Temple," line 443). Southern Mesopotamia was again united in 2112 BCE by Ur-Nammu, who founded the Third Dynasty of Ur (Ur III), the second Mesopotamian empire. Although Ur III period texts do not refer to the arrival of ships from Meluhha, numerous pieces of evidence attest to the actual presence in Sumer of merchants from the Indus region at this time.

Harappans in Sumer and Akkad (Babylonia)

Harappan trade with Babylonia seems to have been established on a significant scale by Akkadian times. One Mesopotamian cylinder seal of this period identified its owner as a "Su-i-li-su, Meluhha interpreter." Another text, probably of this period, recorded that a Meluhhan called Lu-Sunzida paid a certain Urur, son of Amar-Luku, 10 shekels of silver as compensation for a broken tooth. It is probable that Harappan merchants were resident in Mesopotamia by this time, but one should not underestimate the difficulty of archaeologically identifying their presence: In a comparable situation in nineteenth-century BCE Kanesh in Anatolia, the presence of a substantial Assyrian merchant quarter in the town was known only from the cuneiform tablets found in the merchants' houses detailing their trading and other activities, while in other respects (architecture and artifacts) their remains were indistinguishable from those of their Anatolian neighbors. Small objects that have been occasionally found, such as dice, frequently in a worn or broken condition, might have been the personal possessions of Indus merchants, as would be the Harappan seals that have been found. The Akkadian levels in the city of

Eshnunna yielded Harappan material, including a cylinder seal with a design of Harappan animals (an elephant, a rhino, and a gharial), carnelian beads, and Harappan pottery. Possehl (1997) draws attention to a toilet of this period at Eshnunna, associated with Harappan-style drainage, suggestive of Harappan influence and probably of a Harappan presence in the city.

During the Ur III period, there are a number of references to Meluhhan people or sons of Meluhha *(du-mu me-luh-ha)* in various economic contexts. Evidence of the presence of Harappan merchants in Sumer at this time comes from a number of major cities, including Lagash and Girsu in the territory of Lagash, Ur, Kish, Eshnunna, and Umma. A village of Meluhhans *(e-duru me-luh-ha)*, presumably a trading colony managing the Sumerian end of the Indus trade network, existed on Lagash land in the twenty-first century BCE. Apart from its foreign inhabitants, the village seems to have been unremarkable, cultivating barley and paying its taxes in the usual way, and three individuals from the village were referred to by Sumerian names.

Many finds reflect the participation of Indus merchants in the local organization of trade. A clay sealing, probably found in the city of Umma, bore the impression of a seal with a bull and manger motif and a six-sign Harappan inscription. The sealing had been placed over the knot in a cord that fastened a piece of cloth to the neck of a jar. The city had direct trading connections with Meluhha, Dilmun, and Magan. A text from Umma recorded that a ship's agent from Meluhha had received rations of oil, while another of the period recorded an advance of silver (used, in effect, as currency) to a Meluhhan man. Around forty-five seals with Harappan connections were found in Sumerian cities, beginning in the Akkadian period, though the majority were of Ur III date. These included standard square Harappan seals and cylinder seals with Indus animal designs and inscriptions in the Harappan script, known from Ur, Susa, and Eshnunna. An unusual seal from Ur had a design of a bull without a manger and an inscription in cuneiform. There were also Indus-style square seals with the script unusually arranged, presumably to render non-Indus names or titles. Two seals were found in Kish, both with the bull and manger design and Harappan inscriptions. These seals and sealings suggest the involvement of Harappan merchants in the packaging of goods for dispatch to the Indus. A yellow carnelian Harappan cubical weight of 13.5 grams, identical to one from Chanhu-daro, was found in Ur III period Ur: similarly this suggests the involvement of the Harappan traders in transactions requiring the determination of value by weight.

Mesopotamia's Imports from the Indus

Some indication of the range of materials that the Sumerians and Akkadians imported from Meluhha can be gleaned from Mesopotamian texts. These included various types of timber, stone, and metal, as well as ivory and animals. Some of these were clearly of Indus origin; others were not products of the Indus region itself but were materials that the Harappans imported and traded on to Mesopotamia. In addition, texts refer to some goods that the Mesopotamians imported from Dilmun and that were clearly not produced there; many of these were originally from the Indus region.

Carnelian. Carnelian (red stone) was frequently mentioned in Mesopotamian texts, often as an import from Dilmun (which had no native carnelian), though in Gudea's inscriptions it was said to come from Meluhha. Although it is also found in parts of Iran, carnelian must have come mainly from the Harappans, who mined and worked it in considerable quantities. Their most distinctive carnelian products included exceptionally long beads and beads decorated with various so-called etched (actually bleached) designs, including eye patterns; identical carnelian beads have been found at Mesopotamian sites such as Kish, Ur, Nippur, Eshnunna, and even Assur in the north. Sometimes the Sumerians engraved these beads with cuneiform inscriptions, such as two that the Akkadian King Shulgi dedicated to the goddess Ningal as booty from his war against Susa. The Sumerians also imported unworked pieces of carnelian that were used by their own artisans. For example, there was a carnelian-working industry at Girsu; its products were small and rough compared with those imported from the Indus.

Lapis Lazuli. One of the most prized materials imported into Mesopotamia was lapis lazuli, referred to as a suitable material for adorning temples and known in Mesopotamia by the Uruk period. It was used for decorating precious objects, including the lyres and gaming boards placed as grave offerings in the Royal Cemetery at Ur, as well as being widely employed for small pieces of jewelry, such as beads and the heads of pins.

In the story of "Enmerkar and the Lord of Aratta," King Enmerkar of Uruk negotiates with the lord of Aratta (possibly Jiroft in the Halil-Rud Basin in Iran) to obtain lapis, and it is clear from this and other texts that lapis was being traded overland in the first two centuries of the third millennium. In later texts, however, lapis is said to come from Meluhha. The distribution of this material after 2500 BCE shows a complete change in the organization of its trade. It seems that the Harappans were using their trading station at Shortugai to monopolize the supply of lapis to the west. Lapis lazuli was occasionally used for beads by the Indus people themselves, but they preferred harder local stones like agate, and most of the lapis that the Harappans imported was traded to Mesopotamia. This may have had a serious impact on the east Iranian city of Shahr-i Sokhta, which had built a large-scale industry on the processing and supply of lapis. In the last two centuries of the third millennium, Shahr-i Sokhta ceased to make beads and process lapis lazuli, and around 2200 BCE it went into a decline.

Plants and Plant Products. Linguistic evidence suggests that sesame oil was among the Indus exports to Mesopotamia. It was known in Sumerian as *ilu/ili* and in Akkadian as *ellu/ulu,* terms that are strikingly similar to an early Dravidian name for sesame, *el* or *ellu.* The plant from which the oil came, however, was known by an unrelated name and was under cultivation in Mesopotamia by around 2250 BCE; it may have been introduced from the Indus or from Africa, to which it was also indigenous, via the Levant.

Timbers of various sorts were valued imports to southern Mesopotamia, which lacked substantial trees for construction. "Highland *mesu* wood," from which the Sumerians made boats, chariots, and furniture, was probably sissoo (*Dalbergia sissoo*), which grew in the Punjab and in other parts of the Indus Basin, as well as in Baluchistan. Another wood used for construction and furniture was called *kusabku*—sea wood. This might have been mangrove but this identification would be problematic, since mangrove, which grows in the saline waters of the Indus delta and other Indian river deltas and on the Pakistani Makran coast, is not suitable for fine use, such as the throne inlaid with lapis lazuli mentioned in one Sumerian text. However, teak, native to the hills of Gujurat, is much used for boatbuilding because it is water-resistant, and it may therefore be a good alternative identification of sea wood. Teak is a very fine timber that would have been highly suitable for making decorative furniture.

Many other kinds of Meluhhan timber are mentioned. One called *sulum meluhhi* (black wood of Meluhha) might have been ebony, native to the Western Ghats. No trace of ebony has yet been found at Indus sites themselves, but since wood does not generally survive, the few extant pieces cannot be representative of the full range of timbers used by the Harappans. Alternatively, *sulum meluhhi* may have been rosewood (*Dalbergia latifolia*), which is known from Harappa. The Mesopotamians also claimed to import Meluhha date palm as timber. This is puzzling because the date palm flourished in southern Mesopotamia itself; the name may perhaps refer to a different type of tree that bore a resemblance to the date palm.

A reference to reeds in the Sumerian text "Enki and the World Order" suggests that something resembling reeds was a noteworthy product of the Indus region. There are several possibilities. Reeds are said to have been imported by the Mesopotamians from Magan and used for containers, arrowshafts, and furniture; so the Magan reed was probably bamboo. The Harappans imported bamboo from the Makran for use in buildings, for oars and masts, and as a packing material at Lothal; so possibly the highland reeds were bamboo. Alternatively, the reference may be to sugarcane, which grew wild in the Punjab. Other timbers used by the Harappans, including deodar, tamarisk, pine, elm, and acacia, seem not to have been imported by the Sumerians.

Metals. Both Magan and Meluhha are referred to in the Mesopotamian texts as sources of copper. The Sumerians obtained some copper directly from Oman throughout the third millennium, but during the latter part Meluhha and Dilmun also acted as intermediaries and Sumer had no direct contact with Oman after about 2000 BCE. It is curious that the Harappans, who were conducting expeditions to Magan to obtain copper, presumably to meet a shortfall in the supply of more local (Aravalli and perhaps Baluchi) copper for their own needs, should also have been trading it on to the Sumerians who were themselves obtaining Magan copper. It is possible that the Harappans, who probably traded directly with the copper miners inland, may have obtained copper at a rate sufficiently favorable to allow them to make a profit by selling it to the Sumerians, who had only indirect access to Magan copper via coastal settlements.

Tin was a rare commodity in the ancient world, but one to which Sumer and Meluhha both had access. Its sources are uncertain. One reference, in an inscription of Gudea, suggests that some of Sumer's tin came from Meluhha. The Harappans may have obtained tin from the Aravallis, but more probably it came from Afghanistan, where it occurred close to the Indus outpost of Shortugai, along with gold.

Meluhha is given in the Mesopotamian texts as a source of gold dust, a commodity available from various parts of the Indus and neighboring regions. Gold dust was probably panned by the Harappans on the upper reaches of the Indus River, as it is today. The export of gold dust to Mesopotamia suggests that substantial quantities were available to the Indus people. This is borne out by the considerable number of pieces of gold jewelry found in Indus towns and cities.

Animals and Animal Products. Ivory from Indian elephants was used in great quantities by the Indus people. Curiously, although the Mesopotamians used ivory, their surviving texts record Meluhha as the source only of ivory birds.

A number of Indian animals were brought to Mesopotamia as gifts or exotic goods. These may have included water buffaloes, vividly depicted on a few Akkadian cylinder seals and mentioned in a few texts. In one, they were among the exotic animals invoked to give a flavor of the cosmopolitan nature of the Akkadian capital, Agade: the goddess Inanna ensured

> that monkeys, mighty elephants, water buffalo, exotic animals, as well as thoroughbred dogs, lions, mountain ibexes, and *alum* sheep with long wool would jostle each other in the public squares (Electronic Corpus of Sumerian Literature, "The Cursing of Agade," lines 21–24).

Transporting animals of the size and ferocity of water buffaloes to Mesopotamia would reinforce the suggestion that the Harappans must have possessed large ships. An Ur III text describes a red dog originally from Meluhha, probably a dhole (*Cuon alpinus*), which was given to King Ibbi-Sin as tribute from Marhasi (inland southwestern Iran).

Figurines of animals were also among the goods brought to Mesopotamia by the Harappans. These included ivory birds and carnelian monkeys, according to the texts, and model monkeys in several materials, including gold, have been found.

Mesopotamian Trade with the Indus

Sumerians in the Indus Realms? There is a considerable body of evidence, archaeological and textual, to show that Harappan traders were present in Sumer and Akkad. Did the Sumerians also go to the Indus to trade? Some scholars argue that there is evidence that they did. For example, it has been suggested that wooden coffins and reed shrouds used in some of the burials at Harappa reflect Sumerian funerary practices and may therefore be the burials of Sumerian traders. However, these might equally reflect innovations brought back to the Indus by Harappans who had lived in or visited Mesopotamia.

A few small Mesopotamian barrel-shaped weights of black stone are known from Harappa and Mohenjo-daro, and one each from Lothal and Dholavira, the latter of limestone and therefore perhaps made locally rather than being from Mesopotamia. These objects were found in a variety of contexts, though often associated with Harappan cubical weights. Ratnagar (2004, 312) argues that these may reflect the presence of Mesopotamian traders in Indus cities. However, they may alternatively have been used by Harappan merchants when packing goods for export. Such weights were in use in Mesopotamia only from around the end of the Ur III period (reign of Shu-Sin, 2037–2029 BCE) onward; they may therefore have been acquired in Dilmun, where both the Mesopotamian and the Harappan weight systems were in use and where Mesopotamian barrel-shaped weights have been found, rather than in Mesopotamia itself.

Written records were an integral part of the Mesopotamian economic system and it is inconceivable that Sumerian merchants, if they were present, would not have left records in the form of cuneiform tablets in the Harappan cities where they were based. Cylinder seals and sealings would also be likely to have been found; however, although a few cylinder seals are known from Harappan sites, all differ from standard Mesopotamian seals in style and execution, and they are more likely to be the property of Harappan merchants who had used them in Mesopotamia than to have belonged to Mesopotamian merchants operating in the Indus.

Neither these nor other suggested pieces of evidence (such as shared artistic motifs) provide a convincing indication that the Sumerians made their way to the Indus region, and it is probable that they did not.

Mesopotamian Exports. It is still not clear what the Indus civilization imported from Mesopotamia in exchange for all its exports. Mesopotamian texts give some indication of the range of goods that they exported to other lands: the surplus of local agricultural produce, such as barley, wheat, dates, leather and wool, dried fish, and goods manufactured from local materials such as fine woolen textiles, perfumed ointments and oils. There were also goods and materials imported from other regions, such as silver from Anatolia or Elam; such materials were imported in larger quantities than the Mesopotamians required and were traded on. Finally, goods manufactured in Mesopotamia from imported materials were also traded. Many of these exports, such as textiles and foodstuffs, have left no archaeological trace since they have long since been consumed or have perished. So, although it is known that Mesopotamia was exporting such goods, there is no way of determining whether the Indus people were customers for them.

Archaeological evidence, textual references, and knowledge of local resources and requirements make it possible to reconstruct the patterns of trade between Mesopotamia and the peoples of the Gulf. In exchange for their own raw materials and traded-on goods, the cultures of the Gulf received important everyday commodities, such as oil, grain, and textiles, that they could not produce themselves or that were locally in short supply, along with luxury goods from Mesopotamia and elsewhere, such as fine pottery. These cultures had many needs or desires that could not be met locally, and so it is not difficult to understand why they traded with Mesopotamia.

But the benefits derived by the Indus civilizaton from trade with the west are far harder to divine. No Sumerian texts refer to goods destined for Meluhha. From the commodities that Mesopotamia had to offer, there seems little that the Indus people could not obtain closer to home or produce themselves in abundance. Very few Mesopotamian objects have been found in Indus sites: a few pieces of jewelry and other small objects, curios rather than the stuff of an economically significant trade network. The Indus people had no need of Mesopotamian grain or other foodstuffs, and their industries were as technologically advanced as those of Sumer and Akkad. It is possible, however, that some commodities from Mesopotamia may have been thought superior to the local Indus versions and therefore valued and considered worth importing, just as in the nineteenth century BCE the Anatolians valued high-quality Babylonian textiles even though they produced textiles themselves. In the context of Indus-Mesopotamian trade, for example, Sumerian or Dilmun dates may have been preferred to dates from Baluchistan.

Similarly, there were few foreign raw materials to which the Harappans did not have more local access: Shells abounded on their own seacoast, gemstones for jewelry were available from Gujarat or the Deccan, copper came from the Aravallis, and so on. In some cases local supply may not have been able to keep pace with demand, necessitating the import of copper, for example, from Oman as well as from the Aravallis. A few raw materials, however, probably could not be obtained from the Indus region or its near neighbors.

Silver. One possibility was silver, although supplies of silver closer to the Indus than Mesopotamia may have been exploited. A potential source was in Rajasthan around Ajmer, although the paucity of silver at Kalibangan (relatively close to the source) compared with Mohenjo-daro and Harappa suggest that the Harappans did not exploit this small deposit. Another source was the Panjshir Valley in northern Afghanistan, where silver was later mined. This lay along one of the routes that may have connected Shortugai with the Indus region. Silver was much used by the Indus elite, being made into jewelry such as beads and bangles. Silver objects have been found in major cities, in Mohenjo-daro especially, where they include silver vessels, and in Harappa, but only rarely in other, less important sites.

The Harappans also used lead, mainly to alloy with copper or as a smelting flux, but also occasionally to make objects such as vessels or ornaments. Lead ore often contains a small amount of silver, and this was the case in the ores of Rajasthan and Afghanistan. Traces of lead in silver from Mohenjo-daro suggest that Harappan silver was extracted from a combined lead and silver ore.

The Mesopotamians imported silver from both Elam and Anatolia, and they often used it as a medium of exchange, in the form of rings or coils from which the required amount could be cut. The texts make it clear that a considerable amount of silver was obtained by the Mesopotamians for trade with the Gulf;

it is therefore quite possible that Mesopotamia was the immediate source of the silver used by the Harappans. Silver was not in use before the Early Indus period in the subcontinent and ceased to be used after the Indus decline. A Harappan weight discovered at Ur implies that the Harappans were weighing some commodity that they obtained for export. The size of weight, 13.5 grams, suggests that the material being weighed was a high-value commodity traded in small consignments; silver fits this description.

Textiles. The Harappans had cotton and leather to make clothing and other textiles, and they kept small numbers of sheep and goats, the latter producing hair that could be used as a fiber. However, as I argued in the previous chapter, the Harappan sheep may not have produced wool (except for the short, seasonally shed undercoat that characterized wild sheep). Even if Indus sheep did produce wool, the yearly yield would have been small, given the small numbers of sheep that were kept. Sumer, in contrast, was rearing tens of thousands of sheep annually and producing wool and woolen textiles on an enormous scale: for example, one Ur III "textile factory" at Lagash employed six thousand people. Many of these textiles were produced for the export market, and Sumerian textiles had an international reputation for fine quality. It is therefore likely that Mesopotamian woolen textiles were among the goods sought by the Harappans.

The Nature of Sumerian-Harappan Trade Relations

History and ethnography show many patterns of trade, exchange, and the acquisition of goods. Some involve gift giving in the context of activities involving kin or social partners; these may not require an equivalent return. In some other cases, goods and materials are obtained by force or the threat of force, and the donor may gain little or nothing in return. Goods may be exchanged for nonmaterial rewards, such as an increase in status or protection against foes. In a high proportion of cases, however, transactions are on a reciprocal basis, in which each party feels that they profit by the transaction, though the goods exchanged may seem to the outsider quite unequal in their value: glass beads for gold, for example.

The Sumerian and Harappan civilizations were comparable in their organizational and economic complexity. Furthermore, it seems that it was the Harappans who took the initiative in the trade between their countries, rather than the Sumerians, despite the fact that Sumer and Akkad had a great need to engage in trade to obtain the goods necessary for daily life (such as metals) and for other, prestige purposes, such as the embellishment of temples and the enhancement of royal status. The Harappans' export of timber to Babylonia is of great significance in this context. While small quantities of precious commodities like lapis lazuli or obsidian were easily moved over long distances, the transport of relatively low-value, high-bulk goods, of which timber is an excellent example, is likely to be undertaken only in the context of a well-developed trading network, between roughly equal partners, and for substantial profits. One would expect the society to whom the trade was of the greater importance to be the one that invested the labor in transporting such bulky goods. In later times, when the Mesopotamians obtained timber from the Levant and elsewhere, they undertook expeditions to fell and transport the timber themselves. The epic tale of "Gilgamesh and Huwawa" shows that this was the normal procurement method in early times also. Yet during the later third millennium, the Sumerians were content to rely on supplies brought to them by the Harappans. This implies that the Harappans had strong motives for trading and as traders were at least as organized and accomplished as the Mesopotamians, if not more so.

The trade in lapis lazuli seems to support this interpretation. The Harappans expended considerable efforts to acquire this stone, even establishing a special procurement center, yet this was almost entirely for trade with Mesopotamia, given that they themselves made little use of it.

These considerations, coupled with the attested presence of resident Harappans in Sumer, make it certain that the Harappans were trading with southern Mesopotamia for their own profit and that through this trade they acquired commodities important to them, despite the paucity of evidence for these imports. This contradicts the frequently expressed belief that the Harappans gained far less from the trade than the Sumerians. The Harappans were therefore clearly an impressive mercantile society engaged in substantial seaborne trade.

LATER DEVELOPMENTS IN LOCAL AND INTERNATIONAL TRADE

Late Mature Harappan Period

Some changes occurred in the Indus region during the final part of the Mature Harappan period, but at most sites there is insufficient chronological precision for change through time to be recognized. Harappa is an exception: in this city the period saw housing congestion and some consequent decline in civic standards as the city's population grew. In Gujarat there was a general decline in the city of Dholavira, marked particularly by the lack of maintenance in the citadel area, though continuing commercial activity is indicated by the presence of seals. More generally, the introduction of summer crops was beginning to effect a change in the agricultural regime that was to have enduring significance.

Major changes were occurring at this time in the west. After the collapse of the Ur III empire (which culminated in the Elamite sack of Ur in 2004 BCE), southern Mesopotamia split into a number of independent city-states, among which Isin was preeminent during the twentieth century BCE. Sumerian traders were usually private individuals, but until the end of the Ur III period the majority of the goods they transported were furnished by state (palace or temple) investment, though the merchants also carried small quantities of goods on their own behalf. Now, however, traders were largely self-financed or relied on private investment, and they had neither the means to finance long-distance expeditions nor the backup resources needed as insurance against major disasters. Mesopotamian trading expeditions and the vessels in which they were undertaken were therefore scaled down, and the texts now make it clear that these sailed only to Dilmun, three days' sailing from Ur and five to seven days back. However, there are far more references to Mesopotamian boats in this period, suggesting that a greater proportion of the commerce between Mesopotamia and Dilmun was in the hands of Mesopotamian merchants. By this period, Dilmunites had also settled on the island of Failaka, much closer to Mesopotamia. Relations between Failaka and Mesopotamia were close, and the island has yielded large quantities of Early Dilmun seals, in use from around 2000 BCE (Early Dilmun period, also known as City II).

As a result of these changes, Dilmun now became the intermediary, providing Mesopotamia with goods and raw materials from the Gulf and Meluhha and growing rich on the proceeds. Elam also traded with Dilmun, though this trade is less well documented. Copper in this period was said to come to Mesopotamia not from Magan but from Dilmun. Omani Wadi Suq ware on Bahrain demonstrates the existence of direct links between Magan and Dilmun. Numerous texts in the Ur temple archives record offerings from individual traders returning from successful expeditions to Dilmun where, in exchange for textiles and silver, they had obtained copper, ivory, lapis lazuli, beads of precious stones, and pearls, of which only the latter were the produce of Dilmun itself. The scale of the trade was still substantial: For example, one text refers to 13,000 Dilmun minas of copper. On the other hand, it is clear that only small quantities of small pieces of ivory were available; this may reflect differences in the volume of trade between Dilmun and Magan (the main copper source), and between Dilmun and the Indus (the most likely source of the ivory).

Dilmun was now a state, with its capital at the coastal city of Qala'at al-Bahrain. Qala'at, now grown to around 40 hectares, had substantial warehouses in its center and many of its houses had seals and weights. A building beside a gate in the city wall, where many seals and weights were found, may have been a customs house, though this is disputed. To the city's southwest, located inland but probably connected by an inlet of the sea to the sheltered Tubli Bay on the east coast, the prosperous village of Saar was founded around 2050 BCE, and there too seals and a few weights were found in some of the houses. The weights followed two systems: that of Mesopotamia and that of the Indus. This indicates that the conversion of weights and prices of goods between the two systems now took place in Dilmun. In Mesopotamian texts, the Indus weight system was referred to as the standard of Dilmun, emphasizing Sumer's loss of direct contact with the Harappans. This weight system was used also in Ebla, an important city-state in Syria. Texts from Mari, a city-state on the middle Euphrates, indicate that Mari also traded with Dilmun.

In the poem "Enki and Ninhursaga," dated around 2000 BCE, Dilmun was said to be visited by traders from Tukrish (northwestern Iran), Meluhha, Marhashi (the area west of Elam and north of Anshan), Magan, the Sealand (the far south of Mesopotamia), Zalamgar ("the tentlands"), Elam, and Ur. Significantly, Tukrish is given as the supplier of lapis lazuli, suggesting a loosening of the Harappan monopoly on Badakshan lapis and perhaps renewed

Iranian trade in lapis derived from Chagai. Several objects from Bahrain, such as a seal from Hamad town and copper objects in the temple at Barbar, show links with Turkmenia and Afghanistan, probably reflecting the growing international importance of the Bactria-Margiana Archaeological Complex (BMAC) and in particular its spread into Seistan. Further evidence of Dilmun's international contacts has been recovered through analysis of bitumen found in Bahrain; while the pieces of bitumen found at Qala'at al-Bahrain came only from Mesopotamian sources, other sites on the island yielded bitumen pieces mainly of Iranian origin.

In the early second millennium, the trade between Bahrain and Magan (Wadi Suq period) increased, since Dilmunite traders had replaced Mesopotamians in the north-bound copper trade. Early Dilmun pottery occurred in coastal sites, such as vessels from Abraq made of the same clay as some vessels from Saar. An Early Dilmun seal was found at the inland site of Mazyad in Buraimi. The expansion of Dilmun's role coincided with cultural changes in Magan, where the tower houses were abandoned and permanent settlements were reduced in number and extent, although many settlements continued to prosper. For example, on the western coast Umm-an-Nar was abandoned but Tell Abraq continued to flourish. Though direct Mesopotamian trade with Magan had ceased, trade with Dilmun still brought a limited amount of Mesopotamian material to the western coast, for example to Tell Abraq. Settlements on the south and east coast continued to trade with the Harappans, as probably did those on the west coast and inland. A Harappan pot and a chert weight, for example, were deposited in a grave at Shimal in the north. Several South Asian technological features were adopted in Magan at this time. It is possible that Harappan involvement in trade with Magan increased after 2000 BCE with the removal of Mesopotamian influence.

In the poem "Enki and Ninhursaga," Meluhha is referred to both as the supplier of its own goods and as the transporter of Magan timber, suggesting that its boats were larger than those of Magan or Dilmun. Though direct Harappan trade with Mesopotamia had ceased, the Mesopotamians obtained Indus goods through the Dilmun entrepot. From the Harappan perspective, the loss of direct access to Mesopotamian markets may have been satisfactorily offset by the reduction in the distance that Harappan ships had to sail to obtain the goods they desired. In any case, in the aftermath of the chaos that attended the end of the Ur III empire, the increasingly prosperous Early Dilmun culture was probably a more satisfactory trading partner than Sumer, and by the time that political order was reestablished in southern Mesopotamia, the new pattern of trade through Dilmun had become the norm.

Early Dilmun Seals. The early second millennium was marked by the development of a new style of Gulf seal. These Early Dilmun seals were still round but had two or three parallel lines and four dots decorating a rather lower boss on the reverse, and they had new designs on the obverse. These included two men drinking with straws from a jar, probably filled with beer; two or three gazelles; and a number of other pictorial subjects, as well as animal heads arranged in a wheel. These were used alongside the earlier Persian Gulf seals for a while, but the latter type went out of use by 1800 BCE. Very many Early Dilmun seals were found in Failaka and at Qala'at and Saar on Bahrain. Two economic documents, one from Susa, were impressed with Dilmun seals, demonstrating the commercial function of the latter.

An Early Dilmun seal was found on the surface of the Indus trading town of Lothal, perhaps indicating that Dilmun traders visited the Indus region or at least Gujarat. Unlike the Persian Gulf seals, about a third of which bore Indus inscriptions, none of the Early Dilmun seals were inscribed.

Posturban Harappan Period

The Indus Realms. The early second millennium saw new developments in the Indus region. By 1900 BCE many of the cities were in decline. The cultural (and probably political) unity of the Indus region was breaking down and with it the ability to organize large-scale trade and distribution networks. Imported goods, such as lapis and turquoise and even marine shells, became scarce in Indus sites in the north and east. Beads, made during the Mature Harappan period of many different materials, were now made from a decreased range of materials, including terra-cotta and sometimes copper, and mainly from materials that were locally available. The wide distribution of Rohri flint was replaced by the exploitation of local stone sources: For example, in Gujarat stone blades were now made of local agate, chalcedony, and jasper. Cubical weights were no longer commonly used, although in Gujarat weights of a different form, a truncated sphere, were still in use. The trade-related towns of the Makran were abandoned, as were the Kulli settlements. Gujarat, the gateway between the Indus and world overseas, saw a substantial increase in population but also a great increase in self-sufficiency in the remaining villages and small towns. Lothal, a major trade center in Harappan times, was reduced to a village of mud huts and the "dock" abandoned.

The inhabitants of Gujarat may have continued to trade with the cultures of the Gulf, but it was on a smaller scale and on a less organized basis. In particular, relations with the Oman peninsula are likely to have been unbroken. The Late Harappans of Gujarat seem to have obtained a steady supply of copper, either from Oman or, more probably, from the Aravalli Hills through cultural contacts and trade links that were developing with the cultures of Rajasthan and the Deccan, areas in which the Late Harappans may also have settled in later centuries. In the Late Harappan period, the presence of Lustrous Red ware shows that there were links between the Late Harappans of Gujarat and the Ahar-Banas culture. The introduction of wheat and barley, ragi and bajra, sheep and goats to south India by 1800 BCE reflects the growing communications among the communities of the western side of the subcontinent.

It is possible that sea level changes that had taken effect by around 2000 BCE had caused the coastline to recede along the Makran coast, resulting in the important towns of Sutkagen-dor and Sotka Koh losing their key role in sea trade. Sometime after 1800 BCE, the sea also receded from the port of Kuntasi

A spherical agate weight found in the late levels at Harappa. Since it does not conform to the Harappan weight standards, it was probably used in trade with external partners. (Harappa Archaeological Research Project, Courtesy Department of Archaeology and Museums, Government of Pakistan)

in Gujarat, reducing the settlement's importance, though the river running near the settlement still gave it some access to the sea. Industrial activity at the site declined at the same time, and the settlement was abandoned after 1700. On the other hand, a new port was established at Bet Dwarka in the northwest tip of Saurashtra, in a locality underwater both today and probably also in the third millennium, but exposed by the falling sea level of the early second millennium. The discovery of an Early Dilmun seal there reflects continued contacts with Dilmun.

In addition to the effects of falling sea level, the coastlines of Kutch and Saurashtra may have been affected by the accumulation of silt deposits from the Indus and other rivers, gradually changing the open waters of the Ranns into salt marshes and pushing the head of the Gulf of Khambat southward. The changing coastline may have been partially responsible for the abandonment of Lothal's role in overseas trade.

The city of Dholavira was apparently abandoned for some decades but was reoccupied around 1850 BCE in a much reduced form, its occupied area comprising the citadel and part of the Middle Town, surrounded by a wall of far lower quality than before. Clearly one of its principal roles, as a channel for local produce and communications to the rest of the Indus polity, was no longer applicable, nor was it prospering from overseas trade. Perhaps its period of abandonment related to sea level changes and to the growth of sediment in the Little Rann, making Khadir Island, on which it is located, no longer easily accessible by sea. This was in contrast to the situation in Saurashtra, where there was a marked increase in population and settlement numbers, and settlements such as Rojdi demonstrate increasing affluence, based largely, it would seem, on agricultural prosperity.

Mesopotamia and the Gulf. At the same time, further major changes were taking place at the other end of the erstwhile Gulf trading network. By the mid-eighteenth century BCE, the great Babylonian King Hammurabi created a new empire. But unlike earlier southern Mesopotamian states, this was centered on Babylon, whose focus of interest lay to the north. The Babylonians were now looking elsewhere for copper, to Anatolia, to southeast Iran, and to the island of Cyprus, while timber now came from the Levant, and other materials flowed in from new sources. Mesopotamia forgot the Indus, though not its products; by the first millennium, the term "Meluhha" meant Ethiopia, from which Mesopotamia imported many of the commodities that it had once received from the Harappans, such as ivory.

The cities of the south declined in importance, along with their seaborne trade. Salinization of the land, the result of centuries of irrigation, was also undermining the prosperity of southern Mesopotamian agriculture. A shadowy kingdom, Sealand, developed south of Hammurabi's realm, at the head of the Gulf. Almost nothing is known of it, but it is unlikely to have had the resources for more than desultry overseas trade. In the same period and probably mainly in consequence of the Mesopotamian situation, the prosperity of Bahrain declined, the major Barbar temple being abandoned and inferior houses constructed in settlements without planning control, while Failaka was drawn more closely into the Mesopotamian cultural area. Dilmun's overseas trade did not cease; Elam, at least, continued to trade with Dilmun. For example, a text from the reign of King Kutir-Nahhunte I (fl.1730) records that Dilmunites delivered 17.5 minas of silver to Susa. By 1700 BCE a number of settlements had been abandoned. It was not until the fifteenth century that the Kassite dynasty revived a major interest in Gulf trade, conquering Dilmun, and by this time things had greatly changed in the Indus region.

Changing Trade Patterns. The last centuries of the third millennium had seen the emergence in northern Afghanistan of the Bactria-Margiana Archaeological Complex (BMAC). Over subsequent centuries, it expanded west and south. It took over Shortugai and its region and ended the Indus lapis trade. It also expanded into Seistan, bringing it into the vicinity of the Indus realms. Distinctive BMAC material, such as stamp seals with geometric, floral, and avian designs, and local products reflecting BMAC designs began to appear in the Indus cities, now in decline, and beyond them in the villages and small towns of the Deccan where, for example, sealings with BMAC-style motifs were found at the Ahar-Banas settlement of Gilund. The stylistic similarities with BMAC material were particularly marked in Baluchistan and the Kachi plain, where in addition there were camel and horse figurines at Pirak after 1700 BCE. This must reflect a resumption of links between the Iranian plateau and South Asia across the passes of Baluchistan, making use of pack and draft animals.

The second millennium, therefore, although it did not see the complete abandonment of sea trade, saw a reversion to the earlier communications network operating between the northern part of the Indian subcontinent and its western neighbors, the Iranian plateau and southern Central Asia. At the same time, while the Harappans' close integration of the Indus regions was gone, relations were growing and developing between the various communities of the subcontinent.

REFERENCES

Agrawal, D. P. 1984. "The Metal Technology of the Harappans." In *Frontiers of the Indus Civilization,* edited by B. B. Lal and S. P. Gupta, 163–167. New Delhi: Books and Books.

Agrawala, R. C. 1984. "Aravalli, the Major Source of Copper for the Indus and Indus-related Cultures." In *Frontiers of the Indus Civilization,* edited by B. B. Lal and S. P. Gupta, 157–162. New Delhi: Books and Books.

Agrawala, R. C., and Vijay Kumar. 1982. "Ganeshwar-Jodhpura Culture: New Traits in Indian Archaeology." In *Harappan Civilization. A Contemporary Perspective,* edited by Gregory L. Possehl, 125–134. New Delhi: Oxford & IBH Publishing Co.

Allchin, F. R. 1984. "The Northern Limits of the Harappan Culture Zone." In *Frontiers of the Indus Civilization,* edited by B. B. Lal and S. P. Gupta, 51–54. New Delhi: Books and Books.

Asthana, S. 1979. "Indus-Mesopotamian Trade: Nature of Trade and Structural Analysis of Operative System." In *Essays in Indian Protohistory,* edited by D. P. Agrawal and Dilip K. Chakrabarti, 31–47. New Delhi: B. R. Publishing Corporation.

Asthana, S. 1982. "Harappan Trade in Metals and Minerals: A Regonal Approach." In *Harappan Civilization. A Contemporary Perspective,* edited by Gregory L. Possehl, 271–285. New Delhi: Oxford & IBH Publishing Co.

Asthana, S. 1984. "The Place of Shahdad in Indus-Iranian Trade." In *Frontiers of the Indus Civilization,* edited by B. B. Lal and S. P. Gupta, 353–361. New Delhi: Books and Books.

Astour, Michael C. 2000. "Overland Trade Routes in Ancient Western Asia." In *Civilizations of the Ancient Near East,* edited by Jack M. Sasson, 1401–1420. Peabody: Hendrickson Publishers. (Reprint of 1995 edition. New York: Scribner's).

Bass, George F. 2000. "Sea and River Craft in the Ancient Near East." In *Civilizations of the Ancient Near East,* edited by Jack M. Sasson, 1421–1431. Peabody, MA: Hendrickson Publishers. (Reprint of 1995 edition. New York: Scribner's).

Beech, Mark. 2003. "The Development of Fishing in the U.A.E.: A Zooarchaeological Perspective." In *Archaeology of the United Arab Emirates. Proceedings of the First International Conference on the Archaeology of the U.A.E,* edited by Daniel Potts, Hasan Al Naboodah, and

Peter Hellyer, 290–308. London: Trident Press. [Online article; retrieved 4/4/07.] www.kenzay-training.com/uae/download/archeology/007eniro.pdf.

Belcher, William R. 1997. "Ancient Harappa in 3-D." [Online article; retrieved 6/14/05.] www.harappa.com/3D/index.html.

Besenval, Roland. 1994. "The 1992–1993 Field Seasons at Miri Qalat: New Contributions to the Chronology of Protohistoric Settlement in Pakistani Makran." In *South Asian Archaeology 1993*, edited by Asko Parpola and Petteri Koskikallio, 81–92. Helsinki: Suomalainen Tiedeakatemia.

Bhan, Kuldeep. 1994. "Cultural Development of the Prehistoric Period in North Gujarat with Reference to Western India." *South Asian Studies* 10: 71–90.

Bhan, Kuldeep, V. S. Sonawane, P. Ajithprasad, and S. Pratapchandran. "Gola Dhoro." [Online article; retrieved 7/5/05.] www.harappa.com/goladhoro/index.html.

Boucharlat, Rémy. 2000. "Archaeology and Artifacts of the Arabian Peninsula." In *Civilizations of the Ancient Near East*, edited by Jack M. Sasson, 1335–1354. Peabody, MA: Hendrickson Publishers. (Reprint of 1995 edition. New York: Scribner's.)

Buchanan, Briggs. 1967. "A Dated Seal Impression Connecting Babylonia and Ancient India." *Archaeology* 20 (2): 104–107. Reprinted 1979 in *Ancient Cities of the Indus*, edited by Gregory L. Possehl, 145–147. New Delhi: Vikas Publishing House.

Casanova, Michèle. 1992. "The Sources of the Lapis-lazuli Found in Iran." In *South Asian Archaeology 1989*, edited by Catherine Jarrige, 49–56. Madison, WI: Prehistory Press.

Chakrabarti, Dilip K. 1997. *The Archaeology of Ancient Indian Cities*. New Delhi: Oxford University Press.

Chakrabarti, Dilip K. 2004a. "Prelude to the Indus Civilization." In *Indus Civilization. Sites in India. New Discoveries*, edited by Dilip K. Chakrabarti, 23–43. Mumbai: Marg Publications.

Chakrabarti, Dilip K. 2004b. "Internal and External Trade of the Indus Civilization." In *Indus Civilization. Sites in India. New Discoveries*, edited by Dilip K. Chakrabarti, 29–33. Mumbai: Marg Publications.

Chitalwala, Y. M. 1982. "Harappan Settlements in the Kutch-Saurashtra Region: Patterns of Distribution and Routes of Communication." In *Harappan Civilization. A Contemporary Perspective*, edited by Gregory L. Possehl, 197–202. New Delhi: Oxford & IBH Publishing Co.

Chitalwala, Y. M. 2004. "The Spread of the Harappan Civilization in Kutch and Saurashtra." In *Indus Civilization. Sites in India. New Discoveries*, edited by Dilip K. Chakrabarti, 89–95. Mumbai: Marg Publications.

Cleuziou, Serge. 2003. "Early Bronze Age Trade in the Gulf and the Arabian Sea: The Society behind the Boats." In *Archaeology of the United Arab Emirates. Proceedings of the First International Conference on the Archaeology of the U.A.E*, edited by Daniel Potts, Hasan Al Naboodah, and Peter Hellyer, 134–149. London: Trident Press. [Online article; retrieved 4/4/07.] www.kenzay-training.com/uae/download/archeology/003bronze.pdf.

Cleuziou, Serge, and Maurizio Tosi. 1994. "Black Boats of Magan: Some Thoughts on Bronze Age Water Transport in Oman and beyond from the Impressed Bitumen Slabs of Ra's al-Junayz." In *South Asian Archaeology 1993*, edited by Asko Parpola and Petteri Koskikallio, 744–761. Helsinki: Suomalainen Tiedeakatemia.

Crawford, Harriet. 1998. *Dilmun and Its Gulf Neighbours.* Cambridge, UK: Cambridge University Press.

Dales, George F. 1968. "Of Dice and Men." *Journal of the American Oriental Society* 88 (1): 14–23. Reprinted 1979 in *Ancient Cities of the Indus,* edited by Gregory L. Possehl, 138–144. New Delhi: Vikas Publishing House.

Dales, George F. 1982. "Adaptation and Exploitation at Harappan Coastal Settlements." In *Anthropology in Pakistan,* edited by Stephen Pastner and Louis Flam, 154–165. Ithaca: Cornell University Press.

de Cardi, Beatrice. 1984. "Some Third and Fourth Millennium Sites in Sarawan and Jhalawan, Baluchistan, in Relation to the Mehrgarh Sequence." In *South Asian Archaeology 1981,* edited by Bridget Allchin, 61–68. Cambridge, UK: Cambridge University Press.

Deshpande, Shweta Sinha, and Vasant Shinde. 2005. "Gujarat between 2000 and 1400 BCE." *South Asian Studies* 21: 121–135.

Dhavalikar, M. K. 1993. "Harappans in Saurashtra: The Mercantile Enterprise as Seen from Recent Excavation of Kuntasi." In *Harappan Civilization,* 2nd ed., edited by Gregory L. Possehl, 555–568. New Delhi: Oxford University Press.

Dhavalikar, M. K. 1996. *Kuntasi, a Harappan Emporium on West Coast.* Pune: Deccan College Post-Graduate and Research Institute.

Dhavalikar, M. K. 1997. "Meluhha—The Land of Copper." *South Asian Studies* 13: 275–279.

During Caspers, Elisabeth. 1984. "Sumerian Trading Communities Residing in Harappan Society." In *Frontiers of the Indus Civilization,* edited by B. B. Lal and S. P. Gupta, 363–370. New Delhi: Books and Books.

Edens, Christopher. 1993. "Indus-Arabian Interaction during the Bronze Age: A Review of Evidence." In *Harappan Civilization*, 2nd ed., edited by Gregory L. Possehl, 335–363. New Delhi: Oxford University Press.

Electronic Text Corpus of Sumerian Literature. 2002a. "The Building of Ningirsu's Temple." Cylinder A. [Online article; retrieved 1/30/02.] www-etcsl.orient.ox.ac.uk/section2/tr217.htm.

Electronic Text Corpus of Sumerian Literature. 2002b. "The Cursing of Agade." [Online article; retrieved 1/30/02.] www-etcsl.orient.ox.ac.uk/.

Electronic Text Corpus of Sumerian Literature. 2002c. "Enki and the World Order." [Online article; retrieved 1/30/02.] www-etcsl.orient.ox.ac.uk/.

Electronic Text Corpus of Sumerian Literature. 2002d. "Enmerkar and the Lord of Aratta." [Online article; retrieved 1/30/02.] www-etcsl.orient.ox.ac.uk/.

Electronic Text Corpus of Sumerian Literature. 2002e. "Enki and Ninhursaga." [Online article; retrieved 5/24/06.] www-etcsl.orient.ox.ac.uk/.

Electronic Text Corpus of Sumerian Literature. 2002f. "Gilgamesh and Huwawa." [Online article; retrieved 1/30/02.] www-etcsl.orient.ox.ac.uk/.

Fairservis, Walter. 1982. "Allahdino: An Excavation of a Small Harappan Site." In *Harappan Civilization. A Contemporary Perspective,* edited by Gregory L. Possehl, 106–112. New Delhi: Oxford & IBH Publishing Co.

Fairservis, Walter. 1984. "Archaeology in Baluchistan and the Harappan Problem." In *Frontiers of the Indus Civilization,* edited by B. B. Lal and S. P. Gupta, 277–287. New Delhi: Books and Books.

Fentress, Marcia. 1982. "From Jhelum to Yamuna: City and Settlement in the Second and Third Millennium B.C." In *Harappan Civilization. A Contemporary Perspective,* edited by Gregory L. Possehl, 245–260. New Delhi: Oxford & IBH Publishing Co.

Foster, Benjamin. 1977. "Commercial Activity in Sargonic Mesopotamia." In *Trade in the Ancient Near East. Papers Presented to the XXIII Rencontre Assyriologique Internationale,* edited by J. D. Hawkins, 31–43. London: British School of Archaeology in Iraq.

Fox, Robin. 1969. "Professional Primitives: Hunters and Gatherers of Nuclear South Asia." *Man in India* 49 (2): 139–160.

Francfort, Henri-Paul. 1984a. "The Harappan Settlement at Shortugai." In *Frontiers of the Indus Civilization,* edited by B. B. Lal and S. P. Gupta, 301–310. New Delhi: Books and Books.

Francfort, Henri-Paul. 1984b. "The Early Periods of Shortughai (Harappan) and the Western Bactrian Culture of Dashly." In *South Asian Archaeology 1981,* edited by Bridget Allchin, 170–175. Cambridge, UK: Cambridge University Press.

Franke Vogt, Ute. 2000. "The Archaeology of Southeastern Balochistan." [Online article; retrieved 6/14/05.] www.harappa.com/baluch/index.html.

Guha, Sudeshna. 1994. "Recognizing 'Harappan': A Critical Review of the Position of Hunter-gatherers within Harappan Society." *South Asian Studies* 10: 91–97.

Gupta, S. P. 1984. "Internal Trade of the Harappans." In *Frontiers of the Indus Civilization,* edited by B. B. Lal and S. P. Gupta, 417–424. New Delhi: Books and Books.

Habib, Irfan. 2002. *The Indus Civilization: A People's History of India. 2.* Aligarh: Tulika and Aligarh Historians Society.

Hesse, Brian. 2000. "Animal Husbandry and Human Diet in the Ancient Near East." In *Civilizations of the Ancient Near East,* edited by Jack M. Sasson, 203–222. Peabody, MA: Hendrickson Publishers. (Reprint of 1995 edition. New York: Scribner's.)

Hooja, Rima, and Vijai Kumar. 1997 "Aspects of the Early Copper Age in Rajasthan." In *South Asian Archaeology 1995,* edited by Raymond and Bridget Allchin, 323–334. New Delhi: Oxford & IBH Publishing Co.

Inizan, Marie-Louise. 1993. "At the Dawn of Trade, Carnelian from India to Mesopotamia in the Third Millennium: The Example of Tello." In *South Asian Archaeology 1991,* edited by Adalbert J. Gail and Gerd J. R. Mevissen, 121–134. Stuttgart: Franz Steiner Verlag.

Jarrige, Jean-Francois. 1985. "Continuity and Change in the North Kachi Plain (Baluchistan, Pakistan) at the Beginning of the Second Millennium B.C." In *South Asian Archaeology 1983,* edited by Janine Schotsmans and Maurizio Taddei, 35–68. Naples: Istituto Universitario Orientale, Dipartimento di Studi Asiatici.

Jarrige, Jean-Francois. 1986. "Excavations at Mehrgarh-Nausharo." *Pakistan Archaeology* 10-22: 63–131.

Joshi, Jagat Pati, and Madhu Bala. 1982. "Manda: A Harappan Site in Jammu and Kashmir." In *Harappan Civilization. A Contemporary Perspective,* edited by Gregory L. Possehl, 183–195. New Delhi: Oxford & IBH Publishing Co.

Kenoyer, Jonathan Mark. 1998. *Ancient Cities of the Indus Valley Civilization.* Karachi: Oxford University Press and American Institute of Pakistan Studies.

Killick, Robert, and Jane Moon, eds. 2005. *The Early Dilmun Settlement at Saar.* Ludlow: Archaeology International.

Knox, R. 1994. "A New Indus Valley Cylinder Seal." In *South Asian Archaeology 1993*, edited by Asko Parpola and Petteri Koskikallio, 375–378. Helsinki: Suomalainen Tiedeakatemia.

Kochha, N., R. Kochhar, and Dilip K. Chakrabarti. 1999. "A New Source of Primary Tin Ore in the Indus Civilization." *South Asian Studies* 15: 115–118.

Kramer, Samuel Noah. 1977. "Commerce and Trade: Gleanings from Sumerian Literature." In *Trade in the Ancient Near East. Papers presented to the XXIII Rencontre Assyriologique Internationale*, edited by J. D. Hawkins, 59–66. London: British School of Archaeology in Iraq.

Lahiri, Nayanjot. 1999. *The Archaeology of Indian Trade Routes up to c. 200 BC. Resource Use, Resource Access and Lines of Communication.* New Delhi: Oxford University Press.

Lamberg-Karlovsky, C. C. 1972. "Trade Mechanisms in Indus-Mesopotamian Inter-relations." *Journal of the American Oriental Society* 92 (2): 222–230. Reprinted 1979 in *Ancient Cities of the Indus,* edited by Gregory L. Possehl, 130–137. New Delhi: Vikas Publishing House.

Leshnik, Lawrence. 1968. "The Harappan 'Port' at Lothal: Another View." *American Anthropologist* 70 (5): 911–922. Reprinted 1979 in *Ancient Cities of the Indus,* edited by Gregory L. Possehl, 203–211. New Delhi: Vikas Publishing House.

Mahadevan, Iravatham. 2006. "A Note on the Muruku Sign of the Indus Script in Light of the Mayiladuthurai Stone Axe Discovery." [Online article; retrieved 5/16/06.] www.harappa.com/arrow/stone_celt_indus_signs.html.

Mainkar, V. B.1984. "Metrology in the Indus Civilization." In *Frontiers of the Indus Civilization,* edited by B. B. Lal and S. P. Gupta, 141–151. New Delhi: Books and Books.

McIntosh, Jane. 2005. *Ancient Mesopotamia: New Perspectives.* Santa Barbara, CA: ABC-CLIO.

Mulchandani, Anil. 1998. "A Walk through Lothal." [Online article; retrieved 1/14/06.] www.harappa.com/lothal/index.html.

Oppenheim, A. Leo. 1954. "The Seafaring Merchants of Ur." *Journal of the American Oriental Society* 74: 6–17. Reprinted 1979 in *Ancient Cities of the Indus,* edited by Gregory L. Possehl, 155–163. New Delhi: Vikas Publishing House.

Parpola, Asko. 1994. *Deciphering the Indus Script.* Cambridge, UK: Cambridge University Press.

Possehl, Gregory L. 1979a. "Lothal: A Gateway Settlement of the Harappan Civilization." In *Ancient Cities of the Indus,* edited by Gregory L. Possehl, 212–218. New Delhi: Vikas Publishing House.

Possehl, Gregory L. 1979b. "Pastoral Nomadism in the Indus Civilization." In *South Asian Archaeology 1977,* edited by Maurizio Taddei, 537–551. Naples: Istituto Universitario Orientale, Seminario di Studi Asiatici.

Possehl, Gregory L. 1986. *Kulli: An Exploration of Ancient Civilization in South Asia.* Durham, NC: Carolina Academic Press.

Possehl, Gregory L. 1997. "Seafaring Merchants of Meluhha." In *South Asian Archaeology 1995,* edited by Raymond Allchin and Bridget Allchin, 87–99. New Delhi: Oxford & IBH Publishing Co.

Possehl, Gregory L. 1999. *Indus Age: The Beginnings.* New Delhi: Oxford University Press.

Possehl, Gregory L.2003. "Cache of Seal Impressions Discovered in Western India Offers Surprising New Evidence for Cultural Complexity in Little-known Ahar-

Banas Culture, circa 3000–1500 B.C." [Online article; retrieved 1/15/06.] www.museum.upenn.edu/new/research/possehl/ahar-banas.shtml.

Postgate, J. N. 1992. *Early Mesopotamia. Society and Economy at the Dawn of History.* London: Routledge.

Potts, Daniel T. 1993. "Tell Abraq and the Harappan Tradition in Southeastern Arabia." In *Harappan Civilization,* 2nd ed., edited by Gregory L. Possehl, 323–333. New Delhi: Oxford University Press.

Potts, Daniel T. 1997. *Mesopotamian Civilization. The Material Foundations.* London: Athlone Press.

Potts, Daniel T. 2000. "Distant Shores: Ancient Near Eastern Trade with South Asia and Northeastern Africa." In *Civilizations of the Ancient Near East,* edited by Jack M. Sasson, 1451–1463. Peabody, MA: Hendrickson Publishers (Reprint of 1995 edition. New York: Scribner's.)

Potts, Timothy. 1994. *Mesopotamia and the East. An Archaeological and Historical Study of Foreign Relations ca. 3400–2000 BC.* Oxford University Committee for Archaeology Monograph 37. Oxford: Oxford University Committee for Archaeology.

Rao, S. R. 1963. "A 'Persian Gulf' Seal from Lothal." *Antiquity* 37 (2): 96–99. Reprinted 1979 in *Ancient Cities of the Indus,* edited by Gregory L. Possehl, 148–150. New Delhi: Vikas Publishing House.

Rao, S. R. 1968. "Contacts between Lothal and Susa." *Proceedings of the Twenty-sixth International Congress of Orientalists.* II, 25–37. Reprinted 1979 in *Ancient Cities of the Indus,* edited by Gregory L. Possehl, 174–175. New Delhi: Vikas Publishing House.

Rao, S. R. 1973. *Lothal and the Indus Civilization.* Bombay: Asia Publishing House.

Rao, S. R. 1979 and 1985. *Lothal: A Harappan Town (1955–62).* 2 vols. *Memoirs of the Archaeological Survey of India.* SI 78. New Delhi: Archaeological Survey of India.

Ratnagar, Shereen. 1982. "The Location of Harappa." In *Harappan Civilization. A Contemporary Perspective,* edited by Gregory L. Possehl, 261–264. New Delhi: Oxford & IBH Publishing Co.

Ratnagar, Shereen. 1992. *A Bronze Age Frontier. Problems of Interpretation. 53rd Session Thematic Symposium "Frontiers in Indian History." Indian History Congress. Symposia Papers: 2.* New Delhi: Indian History Congress.

Ratnagar, Shereen. 2001. *Understanding Harappa. Civilization in the Greater Indus Valley.* New Delhi: Tulika.

Ratnagar, Shereen. 2004. *Trading Encounters. From the Euphrates to the Indus in the Bronze Age.* New Delhi: Oxford University Press.

Ray, Himanshu Prabha. 2003. *The Archaeology of Seafaring in Ancient South Asia.* Cambridge, UK: Cambridge University Press.

Roaf, Michael. 1990. *Cultural Atlas of Mesopotamia and the Ancient Near East.* New York: Facts on File.

Santoni, Marielle. 1984. "Sibri and the South Cemetery of Mehrgarh: Third Millennium Connections between the Northern Kachi Plain (Pakistan) and Central Asia." In *South Asian Archaeology 1981,* edited by Bridget Allchin, 52–60. Cambridge, UK: Cambridge University Press.

Shaffer, Jim G. 1978. *Prehistoric Baluchistan.* New Delhi: B. R. Publishing Corporation.

Shaffer, Jim G. 1982. "Harappan Commerce: An Alternative Perspective." In *Anthropology in Pakistan,* edited by Stephen Pastner and Louis Flam, 166–210. Ithaca, NY: Cornell University Press.

Shinde, Vasant. 1992. "Padri and the Indus Civilization." *South Asian Studies* 8: 55–66.

Shinde, Vasant. 2004. "Saurashtra and the Harappan Sites of Padri and Kuntasi." In *Indus Civilization. Sites in India. New Discoveries,* edited by Dilip K. Chakrabarti, 64–70. Mumbai: Marg Publications.

Snell, Daniel C. 2000. "Methods of Exchange and Coinage in Ancient Western Asia." In *Civilizations of the Ancient Near East,* edited by Jack M. Sasson, 1487–1497. Peabody, MA: Hendrickson Publishers (Reprint of 1995 edition. New York: Scribner's.)

Srivastava, K. M. 2002. "An Inscribed Indus Seal from Bahrain." In *Facets of Indian Civilization. Recent Perspectives. Essays in Honour of Professor B. B. Lal,* edited by Jagat Pati Joshi, 92–102. New Delhi: Aryan Books International.

Thapar, B. K. 1975. "Kalibangan: A Harappan Metropolis beyond the Indus Valley." *Expedition* 17 (2): 19–32. Reprinted 1979 in *Ancient Cities of the Indus,* edited by Gregory L. Possehl, 196–202. New Delhi: Vikas Publishing House.

Tosi, Maurizio. 1993. "The Harappan Civilization beyond the Indian Subcontinent." In *Harappan Civilization,* 2nd ed., edited by Gregory L. Possehl, 365–377. New Delhi: Oxford University Press.

Tosi, Maurizio, S. Malek Shahmirzadi, and M. A. Joyenda. 1976. "The Bronze Age in Iran and Afghanistan." In *History of Civilizations of Central Asia. 1. The Dawn of Civilization: Earliest Times to 700 B.C,* edited by A. H. Dani and V. M. Masson, 191–224. Paris: UNESCO.

Vosmer, Tom. 2003. "The Naval Architecture of Early Bronze Age Reed-built Boats of the Arabian Sea." In *Archaeology of the United Arab Emirates. Proceedings of the First International Conference on the Archaeology of the U.A.E,* edited by Daniel Potts, Hasan Al Naboodah, and Peter Hellyer, 150–157. London: Trident Press. [Online article; retrieved 4/4/07.] www.kenzay-training.com/uae/download/archeology/003 bronze. pdf.

Weeks, Lloyd. 2003. "Prehistoric Metallurgy in the U.A.E.: Bronze Age–Iron Age Transitions." In *Archaeology of the United Arab Emirates. Proceedings of the First International Conference on the Archaeology of the U.A.E,* edited by Daniel Potts, Hasan Al Naboodah, and Peter Hellyer, 116–121. London: Trident Press. [Online article; retrieved 4/4/07.] www.kenzay-training.com/uae/download/archeology/003 bronze.pdf.

Weisgerber, Gerd. 1984. "Makan and Meluhha—Third Millennium BC Copper Production in Oman and the Evidence of Contact with the Indus Valley." In *South Asian Archaeology 1981,* edited by Bridget Allchin, 196–201. Cambridge, UK: Cambridge University Press.

Wilkinson, T. J. 2002. "Indian Ocean: Cradle of Globalization. Scholar Voices." [Online article; retrieved 10/2/02.] www.accd.edu/sac/history/keller/IndianO/Wilkin.html.

Yoffee, Norman. 1982. *Explaining Trade in Ancient Western Asia.* Malibu, CA: Undena.

Yoffee, Norman. 2000. "The Economy of Ancient Western Asia." In *Civilizations of the Ancient Near East,* edited by Jack M. Sasson, 1387–1399. Peabody, MA: Hendrickson Publishers. (Reprint of 1995 edition. New York: Scribner's.)

VII

Settlements

SETTLEMENTS AND SETTLEMENT PATTERNS

Although much is now known about Harappan settlements and settlement patterns, there is still much to learn. The great cities of Mohenjo-daro and Harappa were extensively excavated in the earlier twentieth century, but Marshall's poor grasp of stratigraphy and Wheeler's failure to publish his results have hampered understanding of what was found, although recent work in both cities has done much to rectify this situation. From neither city is the full picture of urban life available; Harappa in particular has been badly damaged by brick robbing, and part of what remains lies inaccessible beneath modern buildings, while a later stupa covers part of Mohenjo-daro's high mound, and the city's lowest deposits are waterlogged. Both cities included extensive suburban areas outside the excavated city center that are almost completely unexplored. Other important settlements, such as Rakhigarhi, have seen only limited investigation, and publication of the results of many important excavations has lagged woefully far behind their completion. The city of Dholavira has recently begun to provide important new information, but only a fraction of its residential areas has been investigated. Some small settlements such as Allahdino have been more fully excavated, and in recent years a number of rural and specialized industrial settlements have also been uncovered. Investigations, however, have been very patchy. The most intensively studied area has been Gujarat; in contrast, although surveys have identified dense settlement in Bahawalpur, almost no sites have been excavated there. It is particularly regrettable that the suggested city of Ganweriwala has not seen excavation.

Settlement Surveys

Much of the known evidence on settlement distribution, density, and size has come from surface surveys. In suitable areas these can provide a good indication of settlement distribution and density. One result of the drying up of the Saraswati River has been that sites along its branches have generally not been covered or disturbed by later settlement; in contrast, in other regions later settlement, agriculture, and other activities may have destroyed or masked Harappan sites. Some areas are not amenable to surveys, in particular Sindh, where thick alluvial deposits conceal the remains of former settlements unless, like those of Mohenjo-daro, they were substantial mounds visible above the alluvium. Conversely, changes in the course of the rivers has often eroded or

Mohenjo-daro's citadel is visible high above the modern alluvium because it is crowned by a large Buddhist stupa (relic mound) built around 200 CE. Excavation around the stupa led to the city's discovery. However, its presence means that, tantalizingly, the part of the citadel lying beneath it cannot be investigated. (Yousaf Fayyaz/Fotolia)

destroyed settlements. The coverage of the greater Indus region has also been uneven: While intensive surveys have been conducted along the former Saraswati River, and in Punjab and Gujarat, investigation of other regions has been much less comprehensive. The picture obtained from surveys is therefore far from complete.

The types of material collected from the surface of surveyed sites, mainly potsherds but also industrial debris such as kiln pieces, copper slag, or flint chips, give some clues to the variety of activities that took place at each. In some sites, the ruins of mounds survive, and surface examination can reveal some architectural clues. However, survey alone is limited in the information that it can yield about settlements. Sites found in survey are generally allocated, by size and by the materials they have yielded, to categories such as campsite, settled village, town, and city. However, excavations have demonstrated that the size of a settlement is not an adequate guide to its complexity. There is an expectation that small sites were villages or pastoralists' camps, but some on excavation have proved to be specialist industrial, trade, or administrative centers, while a number of larger settlements were villages rather than towns. For example, the prosperous farming village of Rojdi eventually grew to 7.5 hectares whereas the important industrial and trading town of Lothal was less than 5 hectares. Other considerations may also affect the surface extent of sites. Those occupied over a long period, and especially those that were relocated within a short distance, can result in a spread of material over an area far larger than that occupied at any one time; this effect is exemplified by the long-lived settlement of Mehrgarh, which moved its area of occupation several times. Manure containing domestic debris may be spread onto fields around a settlement, giving a false impression of the latter's extent, and later disturbance and reuse of building materials can produce a similar result. Seasonal occupation by pastoralists outside a town may also result over the centuries in a spread of occupation debris over an area far greater than that occupied in any one year.

Settlement Patterns

The Harappan Regions. The most densely settled region seems to have been Cholistan, in the lower part of the Saraswati Valley. The many settlements identified here range from less than 2 to more than 100 hectares. This suggests that a dense network of farming settlements existed in this area, with many towns, satellite industrial villages, and at least one city, Ganweriwala. But this picture must remain hypothetical until excavations are undertaken in sample sites to verify what has been proposed.

Farther east, surveys in the upper valleys of the Sutlej, Saraswati, and Drishadvati Rivers also show a considerable density of settlement, though less concentrated than in Cholistan, with sites of a range of sizes. A number of the larger sites (most in the range of 10–30 hectares) have been excavated to some extent. These include Mitathal and the massive site of Rakhigarhi (80 hectares) in the east, Banawali in the center of this area, and Kalibangan at the confluence of the Drishadvati and the Saraswati.

In contrast, in the Punjab very few sites have been located, despite extensive fieldwork. This probably reflects the overwhelming importance of pastoralism in this generally arid region where cultivation would have been confined to the banks of the rivers: the Chenab, Jhelum, Ravi, Beas, and Indus. The only major settlement in this region appears to have been Harappa. Beyond these regions to the northeast, there were only a few outlying settlements, such as Ropar in the Siwalik Hills, located to exploit Himalayan timber.

The highlands west of the Punjab had been closely integrated with the Indus region in the Early Harappan period but did not form part of the Mature Harappan realms. Though politically separate, the northern highlands were probably friendly territory through which Harappan traders could pass to reach southern Central Asia and the Harappan outpost of Shortugai. Some pastoralists from this region may have brought their animals into the Indus region during the winter.

The situation was somewhat different in southern Baluchistan, where the people of the Kulli culture enjoyed a close relationship with the Harappans. To their south lay the Makran coastal region, whose inhabitants had previously depended on marine resources. This region was settled by the Harappans to facilitate maritime trade through the Gulf. Excavations have been conducted in the fortified settlements of Sutkagen-dor and Sotka Koh, and other coastal trade posts have also been located, situated at the mouth of rivers that offered routes through the mountains. There were also towns and villages, such as Balakot and Prahag, concerned with fishing and the shell industry.

Harappan sites were also located in the foothills of Baluchistan where seasonal streams provided water for agriculture and routes into the highlands. These included Ghazi Shah near the foot of the Kirthar Range. Pastoralists on their annual migrations from upland summer to lowland winter pastures passed through this border region, and some border settlements, such as 100-hectare Pathani Damb at the foot of the Kirthars controlling the Mula pass, may have functioned as customs' and warehousing centers for goods being transported by these pastoralists.

Encircled by these regions was Sindh, a region that on ecological grounds should have been densely settled with farming communities but where alluvial deposits are likely to have skewed the discovery of ancient sites toward the larger and therefore more visible settlements. Nevertheless, a few smaller sites have been located and excavated, including Allahdino whose tiny 1.4-hectare extent contrasts with its evident importance and organization. There are also sites of intermediate size, including Chanhu-daro on the Indus, and 25-hectare Judeirjo-daro on the interface with the Kachi plain, as well as the vast settlement of Mohenjo-daro, now reckoned at 250 hectares. The importance of the Indus as a highway also influenced settlement location in this region.

South of Sindh lies Gujarat, the southernmost Harappan province, and probable location of the Indus delta in Harappan times. The northern part, Kutch, was at that time an island and the southern part, Saurashtra, was separated from the mainland by the Nal Depression, possibly filled with water. Most of the farming settlements of the region were located in Saurashtra. These were relatively few in number; pastoralism was of more importance than arable agriculture in the region at that time. (The situation changed markedly in the early second millennium when the cultivation of *kharif* crops saw the expansion of farming settlement into rainfall-dependent areas.) Pastoral camps have been found in Saurashtra and in the seasonal grasslands of north Gujarat, home mainly to hunter-gatherers. This is the only region where rural settlements, such as Nesadi, Rojdi, and Kanewal, have been excavated. Other settlements, in the coastal regions and islands of Gujarat, were related to land and sea trade and to industry, such as shellworking and bead-making. The city of Dholavira, the regional center, was at least 60 hectares; towns such as Lothal, Surkotada, Kuntasi, and Gola Dhoro were only a few hectares but were internally complex. The value of access to sea routes and marine resources is underlined by the existence of specialist settlements designed to exploit them, such as the shell processing settlement at Nageshwar and the salt production site at Padri.

Settlement Location. Regional factors determined the density of permanent settlements in the Harappan zones, with farming settlements concentrated in the Saraswati Valley and, it is assumed, in Sindh and being confined to the more restricted areas of suitable land in the Punjab and Gujarat. The archaeologically less visible, often temporary, camps of pastoralists and hunter-gatherers must have filled the apparent settlement gaps in many regions.

Other factors also influenced the location of settlements throughout the Indus realms. Access to water is an important consideration in settlement siting the world over. The majority of Harappan settlements were located near water sources such as streams and aquifers, but the Harappans were competent hydraulic engineers, sinking wells (as at Mohenjo-daro) and building reservoirs (as at Dholavira) where local surface water supplies were inadequate. They dealt with the problems of river flooding, annually variable in its location and force and a potential deterrent to settlement in some areas, by constructing many settlements with massive flood defenses in the form of platforms and walls.

Good communications and access to raw materials are also worldwide considerations in settlement location, but these seem to have been unusually important to the Harappans. Towns and cities were situated at strategic locations to facilitate and control communications, both within the Indus realms and with the outside world. Such settlements included those in Makran, founded to manage trade with and through the Gulf. Many villages and towns were focused on the large-scale procurement and processing of raw materials, such as shells at Nageshwar and Balakot or gemstones for beads at Lothal, and a number of such settlements were established on the borders or outside the Harappan polity, such as Manda in the Himalayas to procure timber and the distant settlement of Shortugai to obtain lapis and metals.

CITIES, TOWNS, AND VILLAGES

Planned Settlements

Harappan urban settlements, of whatever size, from 250-hectare Mohenjo-daro to 1.4-hectare Surkotada, generally shared a number of features: the use of bricks of uniform proportions (1:2:4) and usually size (7 by 14 by 28 centimeters for houses, 10 by 20 by 40 centimeters for city walls); efficient provision of water and sanitation; workshops and other industrial facilities; well-appointed housing; cardinally orientated streets; and the use of baked brick, particularly for bathrooms, drains, and wells. Generally, walls surrounded the settlement or separate parts of it, some freestanding while others provided revetment for foundation platforms; and there was usually a separately walled sector (a "citadel"), often on a raised mound, within which were located many of the settlement's public buildings. Evidence is accumulating that the settlements also had unwalled suburbs.

These features, however, were expressed in very different ways, both from one settlement to another and from region to region. Stone, for example, was rarely used in architecture except in Gujarat, where it was common; Mohenjo-daro and Chanhu-daro were unusual in their very extensive use of baked bricks for building houses. Citadels were sometimes separate mounds, in other cases a subsection of the area within the settlement wall, and the structures present in this area were different in almost every settlement. Water facilities also varied markedly; for example, Mohenjo-daro had seven hundred wells, whereas Harappa, near a river, had only a few, and Dholavira had huge reservoirs. Settlements varied in the degree to which they were planned: In some (for example, Kalibangan), the north-south orientation of the main streets resulted in a grid plan; in others (for example, Banawali), there is much less apparent order; and a few did not even adhere to cardinal orientation.

Also characteristic of Indus towns and cities were several negative features, notably the apparent paucity or absence of substantial administrative and reli-

A view across the northern part of the citadel at Mohenjo-daro. The layout of Mohenjo-daro shows the planning typical of many Harappan settlements, in which geometry and cardinal orientation played major parts. Mohenjo-daro may have been laid out as a pristine settlement, but these features are also seen in Dholavira which was built in several stages over hundreds of years. (Yousaf Fayyaz/Fotolia)

gious buildings and of readily identifiable elite residences. Few large-scale storage facilities have been identified. Cemeteries are also rare, although their presence outside some settlements suggests that the current situation reflects accidents of discovery. The same might perhaps be said of other negative features, given the small proportion of the settlement investigated in most cases.

Cities

It has been suggested that the Harappan polity was made up of a number of "domains" (Possehl 1982, 19), each dominated by a city. Three of these, Mohenjo-daro (Sindh), Harappa (Punjab), and Dholavira (Gujarat) have been extensively investigated; of the other two identified cities, Ganweriwala (Cholistan) has seen no excavation while Rakhigarhi (East) is still in the early stages of investigation. A number of other sites of comparable size have been located, including 100-hectare Pathani Damb in the Kachi plain. Three huge surface scatters of Sothi-Siswal and Mature Harappan material were found at Gurnikalan I (144 hectares), Hasanpur II (100 hectares), and Lakhmirwala (225 hectares) within 30 kilometers of each other on old beds of the Naiwal River, a tributary of the Saraswati; two of them were also occupied in later times. The coexistence of three cities so close together would seem implausible, though it is perhaps possible that they were successive settlements. Sothi-Siswal material is hard to date in vacuo, since it was used continuously from Early Harappan to post-Harappan times. Other massive surface spreads of settlement debris have been found in the Saraswati Valley, Sindh, and elsewhere. Without excavation, however, it is impossible to determine anything useful about these sites.

Although the evidence is limited, it is likely that the cities were the administrative, religious, economic, and social centers of their respective domains and that a significant proportion of their residents were engaged in nonsubsistence activities. The central location of Mohenjo-daro, its size, and its unique features, particularly the Great Bath, suggest that this city may have been the capital of the Harappan polity, but this is by no means proven and Harappa may have enjoyed equal importance. Both cities had some unique types of inscribed materials, which are likely to have had administrative significance, and they shared other types not found in any other site.

Mohenjo-daro. Mohenjo-daro is the best-known and best studied Indus city. Its history is uncertain. The high water table has prevented excavation of its lowest levels, but it is likely that it was a new foundation in the Transition or early Mature Harappan period. Test bores have shown that the occupation evidence continues for at least 7 and perhaps 15 meters below the present ground surface, but there is no evidence of settlement preceding the construction of the city. On the contrary, Jansen (2002) notes that the ancient location of the Indus west of the city posed annual risks of flooding that would have made it impossible to occupy the site before the construction of the platforms on which the city was built above flood level, a mammoth undertaking. Most of the exposed architecture belongs to the later part of the Mature Harappan period.

Later occupation (Jhukar period) was uncovered in some parts of the city: Poor-quality housing, corpses thrown into disused buildings and streets, and kilns and industrial waste in former public and residential buildings attest to the decline in civic standards in this period.

Mohenjo-daro lies in a central location in the Indus realms, between the great northern settlement of Harappa and the southern city of Dholavira, and close to the great north-south highway of the Indus River, which integrated the land from the Himalayas to the sea. From Mohenjo-daro routes stretched into the upland region of southern Baluchistan, closely tied to the Indus lowlands, while to its east lay the rich valley of the Saraswati. It was therefore ideally situated to control communications throughout the Indus realm and was perhaps founded specifically for this purpose. Its workshops housed the full range of craft activities practiced by the Indus people and produced some objects unique to the city. Many inscribed materials, including seals, copper tablets, and stoneware bangles, hint at a well developed bureaucracy organized from this center. Its unique Great Bath highlights the settlement's importance and suggests its role in serving the entire Indus realms.

The city, as it is known today, consists of a western citadel mound and an eastern Lower Town, separated by a deep depression that may have been a major thoroughfare. The citadel was created by constructing an enormous platform of sand and silt within a 6-meter-thick mud brick retaining wall. Several enlargements of the platform brought it eventually to a height of 7 meters and an extent of 200 by 400 meters. Each of the structures of the citadel had its own additional platform, including the Great Bath, a religious installation likely to have had statewide importance, the "granary," and a pillared hall. Bathrooms and residential buildings were also present on the citadel.

A number of residential areas were investigated in the Lower Town, which was also constructed on an artificial mound; parts of the retaining wall have been identified. Two or three main streets and a number of minor ones ran north-south with streets and lanes running east-west from them, separating the city into a number of residential blocks, with two-story and even perhaps three-story houses. Most of the houses had a series of rooms off a courtyard, but some were small buildings with only two or three rooms. Workshops were identified in some of the houses, as well as areas of concentrated industrial activity in some parts of the periphery. In addition there were a few structures that were probably not ordinary houses; one was identified as a possible temple and another as a possible caravanserai. Around seven hundred wells were constructed as part of the original plan of the city, and it seems none were added later. As the street and house level rose, new courses of bricks were added to raise the wellheads. An excellent network of drains was present throughout the city, and a number of cesspits were also found.

The mounds alone cover a substantial area, but recent investigations have shown the city also to have had extensive suburbs, particularly south and east of the Lower Town, but also to the north, now buried under the alluvium of the surrounding plain. Several rescue excavations uncovered baked bricks and baked brick structures, including a well, and elsewhere an extensive industrial area was found. Traces of baked brick architecture have also been found in the modern bed of the Indus River, almost 2 kilometers to the east. The city was probably more than 250 hectares in extent, and it may have housed as many as a hundred thousand people.

Harappa. Located in the north of the Indus realms, Harappa's position enabled it to control the routes through the mountains; the exploitation of their resources, including metals and timber; and the channelling of these into the Indus realms. Like Mohenjo-daro, Harappa's excavated mounds have revealed a range of industrial activity, some impressive public and private architecture, and a great quantity and variety of inscribed objects, some unique to this city. Unlike Mohenjo-daro, however, the settlement has a long history, and, unlike many Early Harappan settlements, it was not rebuilt to a new plan during the Transition Period but grew organically.

The first settlement at Harappa was established in the fourth millennium, and by the early third it was an important and innovative town, more than 25 hectares in extent, with many flourishing industries foreshadowing those of the Mature Harappan period. Already the settlement consisted of two areas (AB and E). A street excavated in mound E was orientated north-south. It was possibly in this region that the transformation of the Early Indus culture into that of the Mature Harappan civilization occurred and from here that the changes spread into other regions.

What remains of the city today consists of a number of mounds around a central depression, which may have held water as a reservoir in the Mature Harappan period. The highest mound (AB, the citadel mound), on the west, was massively plundered for baked bricks during the nineteenth century CE, and little is known of the structures that once stood on it. The rest of the settlement also suffered brick robbing, so the architecture is known only from the mud brick foundations of baked brick walls, wall stubs, robber trenches, and walls overlooked by the robbers.

The remains of a substantial wall surround mound AB. When Cunningham visited it in the 1850s, before the site was plundered for railway ballast, he observed a flight of stairs ascending to the summit from each side of the citadel. East of this mound and south of the depression lies mound E and its later eastward extension, mound ET. Mound E was walled at the beginning of the Mature Harappan period. During the twenty-fifth century BCE, civic standards on mound E declined, the streets developing potholes and accumulating rubbish, and houses falling down. In the subsequent phase of urban renewal, Mound ET, which had been occupied since the Transition period, was surrounded by a wall, joined onto that of mound E. At the intersection, a massive gateway was built, giving access for carts as well as foot traffic, and a major street ran from this gateway north along the eastern side of mound E's perimeter wall.

New houses were constructed on solid mud brick platforms. The walls were repaired around 2250 BCE, with a massive bastion being added on the southeastern corner of mound E. Toward the end of period 3C (ca. 2000/1900 BCE) a corbelled culvert was constructed, the open end of which passed through the gateway, probably limiting traffic to pedestrians; this replaced an earlier covered drain that had passed under the wall by the gateway and had become clogged.

It is mainly in these mounds that remains of the city have been excavated, including houses and industrial areas. To the south of the mounds are two cemeteries, one (R-37) dating from the Mature Harappan period, the other (Cemetery H) from the Late Harappan period. Also to the south was a small mound with houses and bathing platforms.

The modern town of Harappa lies in the northeast, overlying further Harappan structures and preventing their investigation. Observations in this area, however, indicate that this mound was not walled in Harappan times. In the area between the north of mound AB and the river (mound F), a number of Harappan buildings have been excavated, including the so-called Granary and a number of working platforms inside buildings. Here, too, craft activities seem to have been undertaken. This area also had a massive perimeter wall, 14 meters thick, parts of which have been traced along the north and west sides of the mound. As at Mohenjo-daro, surveys and casual finds of bricks and artifacts at Harappa show that during the Mature Harappan period a huge area outside the walled mounds was also occupied, giving the city an area of around 150 hectares, with a population of perhaps sixty thousand.

The upper deposits document the slow transition to the Late Harappan occupation when the urban layout was no longer respected, overcrowded housing being constructed in streets and former open areas.

Dholavira. At the opposite end of the Indus realms, Dholavira on Khadir Island in Kutch was around 60 hectares in extent (perhaps 100 hectares including suburbs) and had a population greatly in excess of that supported by the whole island today. This was made possible by the creation of substantial reservoirs. The city was well placed to control communications and the movement of local raw materials and overseas imports between the southern domain and the rest of the Harappan realms.

Settlement probably began in this locality around 3000 BCE. During the Early Indus period, a small town developed, surrounded by a wall of stones and clay mortar. At the beginning of the Mature Harappan period, a bipartite citadel was constructed over the remains of the earliest settlement, and the area immediately to its north was cleared of housing and paved to form an esplanade where public events may have taken place. Beyond this lay a walled residential area (the Middle Town), with cardinally oriented streets and with jars and sumps instead of drains. At least sixteen massive water storage tanks were constructed along the inner faces of an outer wall that surrounded the whole city. The geometric layout of the city is particularly striking: It is formed of a number of rectangles, each divided into smaller rectangles or squares, and the excavator (Bisht 1999) points out various regularities in the proportions of these.

Following a major earthquake, perhaps around 2200 BCE, the city was rebuilt and expanded to the east (Lower Town), and the city walls were extended to include this new residential area. Possible suburban occupation is also reported outside the walls, as well as a cemetery. Stone was used for the house foundations, topped by mud brick walls, and for facing the city walls. Many workshops were located in the residential areas. Unusually, Dholavira's houses seem not to have had bathrooms.

After about 2000 BCE, the city saw a decline and was eventually abandoned. After an interval, a small part of the city was reoccupied by people who constructed houses from stone rubble robbed from the earlier city. The reservoirs were no longer maintained but were used as rubbish dumps. After another period of desertion, the site was again reoccupied for a while by people who lived in round huts.

Ganweriwala. Located in Bahawalpur in the fertile Saraswati Valley, Ganweriwala covers 80 hectares and was divided into citadel and lower town. It was identified as a city on the basis of its size, but this needs to be tested by excavation.

Rakhigarhi. Although excavations have taken place at Rakhigarhi, situated on what was then the north bank of the Drishadvati, only brief accounts of the discoveries have been published. The site, which covered at least 80 and perhaps more than 100 hectares, today exists as five mounds, unfortunately covered to a

The enormous reservoirs are the most striking feature in the city of Dholavira. Steps down the side gave access to the water held in them. (Namit Arora)

significant extent by two modern villages. The settlement was probably founded in the late fourth millennium and, during the Early Harappan period, developed into a town with flourishing industries. The settlement greatly expanded in the Mature Harappan period when, it is thought, there were several walled residential areas with cardinally oriented streets. Mound 2, in the northwest of the site, was the high mound (citadel); part of a wall of mud brick faced with baked brick has been traced in its southeast corner, implying that it was separately walled. Within the citadel a platform with fire altars, pits containing cattle bones, and a well was found. Public and domestic drains and soakage jars (jars set in the ground that allowed liquid waste to drain away but retained solid waste), a storage facility, and a lapidary's workshop have also been discovered within the city and a cemetery outside it to the north.

Towns

Harappan towns were laid out like the cities with separate public and residential areas and cardinally oriented streets, but they had a more restricted role and served a smaller area. They were generally very small, around 4 to 16 hectares. While some towns had many functions—residential, industrial, religious, and administrative— and served their local area, others seem to have had a more focused role, related to external and internal trade. These were entry or transit points for goods and materials, located in key places with respect to resources and communications. Those at the interface with the outside world, in the Makran, in Gujarat, and perhaps on the margins of Baluchistan, had strong walls. Some also processed local raw materials on an industrial scale. Large-scale storage facilities are known from some of these settlements, such as Lothal and Kuntasi. Generally there was also an attached, unwalled suburban residential area, presumably housing workers and service personnel, while those responsible for running the establishment occupied housing on the citadel or in the walled town. The main role of these settlements would have been to acquire and, if relevant, process raw materials and finished goods from neighboring areas or overseas and to organize their distribution to other parts of the Indus realms or their dispatch as trade goods. Examples of this type of town include Lothal, Kuntasi, Shortugai, Sutkagen-dor, Gola Dhoro, and Surkotada. Sotka Koh, Desalpur, Pathani Damb, and a number of other sites that have seen little or no investigation may also have been such settlements.

Chanhu-daro (Sindh). Though now more than 10 miles (15 kilometers) from Chanhu-daro, originally the Indus flowed close to the town, which was about halfway between Mohenjo-daro and the Gulf of Kutch and therefore well placed in the communications network. Three mounds constitute the remains of the site today, but originally this formed a single mound of around 5 hectares. The town was constructed on mud brick platforms. Limited excavations exposed a single street with drains, brick-lined wells, and a number of houses with bathrooms, as well as a beadmaking factory. Other craft activities were also practiced in the town. Chanhu-daro conformed to Harappan norms: The street was oriented north-south, houses followed the usual courtyard model, and there are drains. No citadel was identified, however.

Nausharo (Kachi Plain). Settlement at Nausharo began during the Early Harappan period in the northern part of the mound. This was destroyed by fire and a new settlement was built farther south. In the Mature Harappan period, when the nearby town of Mehrgarh was abandoned, the remains of both earlier occupations were covered by a leveled layer of soil and debris on which a planned settlement was built. Detailed investigation of one area showed that the Harappan houses were arranged in blocks, separated by north-south and east-west streets; the houses were generally quite small, comprising a courtyard from which two or three rooms opened, one of which was generally a bathroom. Along the southern edge of the northern mound, part of a massive brick platform accessed by a stair was uncovered, but erosion made it impossible to gain information on the structures that had originally stood on it. South of this platform a potter's workshop was uncovered.

Kalibangan. A substantial parallelogram-shaped walled settlement existed at Kalibangan in the Ghaggar (Saraswati) Valley during the Early Harappan period. This was abandoned, perhaps due to an earthquake, but in the Mature Harappan period a new settlement was constructed, a citadel on the west being built over the remains of the earlier settlement and a separate walled lower town in the east. Parts of the earlier settlement's walls were reused, the east wall forming part of the west wall of the new lower town and the rest being incorporated into the citadel's walls. The streets of the lower town and the structures in the citadel were orientated north-south. There was therefore an uncomfortable mismatch between the parallelogram shape of the town conditioned by the refurbished walls and the cardinally orientated street plan dictated by Mature Harappan ideology.

The citadel was divided into two by a wall running east-west. Part of a street with houses was uncovered in the northern half, possibly elite residences. A gateway from here gave access to the southern part where there were a number of separate platforms, each accessed via a stair; one held seven fire altars. An impressive southern gateway with towers gave access from the plain to the southern half of the citadel: This may have been the public entrance. In the lower town there were four or five main streets running north-south and at least three running east-west between them, though frequently these were staggered. Unlike many settlements, Kalibangan did not have a regular system of drains. Fender posts at street corners suggest that carts were regularly brought into the town and the courtyards of the houses often had a wide entrance that would have allowed access for a cart; some courtyards had rectangular troughs constructed of mud bricks, probably to hold food or water for animals

To the east of the settlement, a small mound was found on which there was a single walled structure containing fire altars. A cemetery was found to the southwest of the settlement. There may also have been suburban occupation in the area south of the citadel.

Banawali. Founded in the Early Harappan period, Banawali was a walled town on a branch of the upper Saraswati River. An elevated citadel (Acropolis) was partitioned off from the rest of the town by an elliptical wall with bastions that joined the inside of the wall surrounding the town. A wide ramp, surfaced with baked bricks, linked the citadel with the lower town, and there was another entrance near the southeastern corner. The citadel was built on the remains of the earlier settlement, augmented by mud brick platforms. Houses built along a network of streets were uncovered in both the lower town and the Acropolis, the streets in the latter sometimes paved with bricks. Both the number of rooms in these houses and the objects found in them suggest that the town's inhabitants were prosperous. There seems little or no difference between the houses in the citadel and in the lower town. In the Late Harappan period, houses of packed earth were constructed in one part of the settlement and pits were dug in various places, including into the earlier town wall.

Balakot. The settlement of Balakot was located in the eastern Makran, originally on the coast, and its inhabitants combined marine fishing and shellfish procurement with the manufacture of shell artifacts. The mound was divided into two, with the higher citadel in the west. The main street on the citadel ran east to west and was flanked by large houses of mud brick, some with thinly plastered floors, associated with baked brick drains. Their kitchens had hearths and storage jars. In one house was a bathroom with a terra-cotta bathtub, a sunken water storage jar, and a hearth. The southern edge of the citadel mound was badly eroded, but part of a large building was recovered in which one room had a floor paved with clay tiles decorated with a pattern of intersecting circles. Another room, perhaps part of the same complex, had a fine lime-plastered floor with a central depression that had probably held a wooden column, and adjacent rooms seem to have been used for storage, since they contained large sunken jars. At a later stage, a room slightly to the north of these was paved with bricks and had a ceramic basin set in its center. Also on the citadel was a building with a large courtyard with pilasters in its wall. Working floors, where shell artifacts were made, were also located on the citadel. It is possible that the citadel was originally walled. Architecture in the eastern part of the mound (the Lower Town) was badly damaged by erosion, but in this area too there was evidence of a substantial nondomestic structure as well as houses. Kilns for firing pottery and terra-cotta figurines were found outside the settlement, indicating suburban occupation and industry.

Sutkagen-dor (Makran). The westernmost Harappan settlement, the port town of Sutkagen-dor was enclosed by natural ridges to north and south and walls made of large stone slabs set in clay mortar along the west and east sides. A gate flanked by two towers was identified in the southwest corner. A large mud brick and stone platform was built against the western wall, and there were traces of mud brick housing on stone foundations in the northern and eastern parts of the settlement. Traces of suburban settlement have been found outside the walls.

Shortugai. The Harappan outpost of Shortugai in Afghanistan was, despite its distance from the Indus, a typical settlement built of mud bricks in the usual 1:2:4 proportions. Inside the houses that have been exposed, there were internal partition walls of pisé (packed mud). One room was paved with bricks. Local copper was smelted and local lapis made into beads to be sent back to the Indus realms, while, conversely, beads were made of imported carnelian for local use and export.

Allahdino (Sindh). This tiny settlement (1.4 hectares) is extremely unusual and has been interpreted in various ways, for instance, as the residence attached to a rural elite estate, as a local administrative center, or as a storage and transit depot. It was situated on a tongue of land between rivers and had good alluvial land beside it.

The mound is unwalled and was centered on a courtyard on the summit, surrounded by small buildings separated by passageways. A stone well and a terra-cotta bathtub, decorated with intersecting circles, were found in one building, and a line of wells in another; in a third was a bathroom lined with stone. The largest building was built around an internal courtyard and included chambers containing storage jars. Another building was also used for storage in large jars. There was also a building housing ovens, apparently used for firing clay objects made there. At least some of these buildings are likely to have had a second story. A jar containing a hoard of jewelry made of gold, silver, and other valuable materials buried in one of the rooms suggests both the affluence of at least one of the residents and the sudden abandonment of the settlement in adverse circumstances.

Lothal. The town of Lothal in Saurashtra was a major center of trade and industry. Its walled area was approximately square, with one elongated and rounded corner. Along its east side ran the "dock" and associated quay. Adjacent to this in the southeast corner of the town was the Acropolis (citadel) built on a raised platform, while the rest of the walled area was occupied by a lower town with planned streets paved with mud bricks, blocks of housing, and numerous workshops related to a range of crafts, particularly in the north and southwest. Houses were also present on the citadel, and in both areas the streets were cardinally orientated. One block on the citadel had a row of twelve bathing platforms at the rear connected to a large drain, possibly a public facility used by citizens of Lothal or part of a row of small houses. There were a number of wells. A warehouse was also located on the citadel. In the uppermost levels, belonging to the Late Harappan period, brick-built houses were replaced by huts of wattle and daub. According to the excavator, S. R. Rao, the settlement experienced a number of episodes of flooding, a problem that the inhabitants attempted to counteract by constructing their houses and other buildings on individual platforms. A cemetery was located to the west, between the town and the river. Scatters of potsherds and brick south of the settlement suggest the existence of unwalled suburbs.

Brick platforms uncovered at Lothal were the base of a warehouse, probably with a light wooden superstructure. It was destroyed by fire, which baked (and therefore preserved) the clay sealings fastened to goods stored here. (Namit Arora)

Surkotada (Kutch). The small town of Surkotada, 1.4 hectares in extent, was roughly rectangular, divided by a wall into two equal parts, an eastern residential area and a western citadel raised on a one-meter-thick rammed earth platform. Single-story houses were excavated in both parts and were similar, though those on the citadel are said to be somewhat larger. There were also drains. Outside the walls lay the cemetery and, to the southwest, an industrial area where stone tools were made; to the southeast a very eroded mound may also have been the remains of extramural settlement, though little Harappan material has been found to support this interpretation.

Kuntasi (Bibi-no-Timbo). The port of Kuntasi near the northern coast of Saurashtra had two parts, a 2-hectare walled settlement and unwalled suburbs. A stone platform ran along the western side of the wall, and adjoining this inside the walled town were a substantial industrial complex and a number of storage facilities. A centrally placed house with a number of rooms, including a private kitchen, was thought by the excavator to have belonged to the person in charge of the complex. Other houses lay in the north and west of the walled area, mainly large rectangular buildings, sometimes subdivided and often with a veranda. They had stone foundations and walls of mud bricks in Harappan proportions but unusually large (9.5 by 19 by 38 centimeters). In the southwestern corner was a large isolated room identified as a kitchen serving most of the settlement. The buildings were arranged around a large open space, perhaps for public assemblies or for sorting out consignments of goods. From the residential area, a postern gate in the northern wall led to the flimsy suburban housing. Although Kuntasi was not laid out according to the cardinal directions, it appears to have been a planned settlement, organized for the production, storage, and movement of goods. In the Late Harappan period, the settlement declined, and only a small number of artisans still worked there, living in poor-quality houses of mud with thatched roofs.

Gola Dhoro (Bagasra). Situated at the head of the Gulf of Kutch, Gola Dhoro was an industrial settlement of just under 2 hectares. A massive wall surrounded the northern part of the town, enclosing an area of 0.25 hectare; the rest of the settlement, to the south, was unwalled. An area where fish and animals were butchered was uncovered in the latter and mud brick houses in both. Gola Dhoro specialized in the production of shell bangles and gemstone beads, as well as objects of copper and faience. While bead manufacture took place mainly in the unwalled area, faience was made only in the walled town, where shell was also worked and jasper and shell were stored for local working and onward distribution. Large blackware storage jars suggest the settlement engaged in overseas trade since such vessels were used for transporting goods to Magan (Oman).

Industrial Villages

The highly organized and integrated nature of Harappan industry is underlined by the existence of villages that specialized in the large-scale procurement and processing of particular raw materials, especially gemstones for beads and shells for bangles.

Padri (Kerala-no-Dhoro). An unwalled village on the southern coast of Saurashtra, Padri is thought to have specialized in the production of salt by evaporating seawater. This site was first occupied in the Early Harappan period when rectangular houses of wattle and daub were constructed. Later in this period, houses with a number of rooms began to be built and there were also workshops. Houses in the Mature Harappan period were generally built of mud with some mud brick, and their floors were plastered with lime and dung. They had storage facilities and hearths for cooking, either in the house or in the courtyard attached to the front or back of the house.

Nageshwar. Nageshwar, situated on a freshwater lake by the southern coast of the Gulf of Kutch in an area with very little arable land, was dedicated to the procurement and processing of marine shells. Concentrations of shellworking waste were located in various parts of the mound, each connected with a different activity. The area for processing *Turbinella,* an evil-smelling activity, was at some distance from the settlement. Pottery was also made in the village. The workers lived in rectangular houses of stone rubble with floors of rammed clay or in one case, of sandstone slabs. The settlement was constructed on ground that sloped gently toward the nearby lake; the Harappans leveled the ground before building on it, using clay from the lake bed.

Nagwada. The inhabitants of Nagwada, on the north Gujarat coast, engaged in beadmaking and shellworking using pre-prepared shells brought in from outside. Structures in the village were built of stone rubble or mud bricks of non-Harappan size and proportions (3 by 16 by 32), as well as bricks in the usual 1:2:4 proportions.

Rural Settlements

Although most known Harappan settlements were towns and cities, the bulk of the Harappan population must have been farmers and pastoralists, as well as fisherfolk and hunter-gatherers, living in villages, hamlets, and seasonal camps. Few such settlements have been found, though a number have been located in Gujarat; the majority of those that have been excavated apparently date from the early second millennium. In some sites the only traces of occupation were artifacts and rubbish located within ashy patches of soil, marking the interior of a temporary or flimsy hut; sometimes, as at Oriyo Timbo in Saurashtra, there were also hearths and storage pits. These were probably seasonal campsites, and they are known particularly from the sand dunes of north Gujarat, where grassland and waterholes were available for some months after the monsoon.

In other cases, postholes marked the edges of circular huts built of a post framework with walls of mud, wattle and daub, or reeds and mud tempered with cow dung. Sometimes there was also a central post to support the roof. Floors were generally of beaten earth. Similar huts in modern Gujarat have a life expectancy of around fifty years. Internal fixtures generally included a hearth. Some of these villages were as large as or larger than many towns. For example, Kanewal in southern Gujarat, whose economy was probably based on a mixture of farming, animal husbandry, and hunting, was 6 hectares. It contained circular huts of wooden posts, wattle, and daub. Large pottery jars were used for storage. Similar huts were excavated in the pastoral villages of Vagad in Saurashtra and Zekda (Jekhada) in north Gujarat; at the latter some of the houses had a large porch, and in a few there was a rectangular platform on which to stand pots. Occupation debris at Zekda formed a number of thin layers, indicating that this was a seasonal site to which people returned on an annual basis. Nesadi (Valabhi) in Saurashtra was another such pastoral village, 4 hectares in extent, occupied during the winter months when local grazing was good and deserted by the rainy season when the area was flooded.

The integration of these rural settlements into the Harappan communications and distribution network is shown by the discovery in them of a few exotic or valuable manufactured pieces, such as beads of lapis and faience. For example, the inhabitants of Kanewal had fine pottery and copper ornaments as well as everyday objects such as beads, figurines, and cooking pots.

Rojdi. The Saurashtran village of Rojdi is a striking example of a rural settlement. A stone wall surrounded the village and probably dates back to the original occupation of the mound around 2500 BCE, when the village was 2.5 hectares in extent. In the Late Harappan period, the village expanded to its south and north, tripling its size. A large building was put up at the northern end, and an enlarged wall, with bastions and a substantial gateway, was constructed around the entire settlement. All the structures uncovered belong to this period (period C, 1900–1700 BCE), though some fragments of earlier architecture were found: several floors, a hearth, some fragments of walls built of stones and boulders, and a number of shallow clay-lined bowl-shaped depressions. The Late Harappan houses had stone foundations, probably with upper walls of mud; no bricks were used. A number were uncovered on the main mound: These were small rectilinear structures, of one to three rooms, often adjoining a yard or open area. Some of the structures were animal barns or circular grain stores, and there were also paved threshing floors. The layout of the village was organic rather than planned, with domestic and other units built as and where required. In the south extension, the structures included a triangular building attached to a long yard, partially roofed with wooden beams. Like the buildings on the main mound, this provided separate accommodation for people and their domestic animals. Beneath the structures in the south extension were rubbish pits belonging to the early periods of occupation. The finds from the village, including copper tools and some gold and silver jewelry, underline the settlement's prosperity.

THE FEATURES OF URBAN CENTERS

Walls and Platforms

Major Indus settlements were generally surrounded by massive walls, constructed of baked bricks, mud brick, rubble, or stone, and, as Rojdi shows, even farming villages could be walled. The walls at Dholavira, for example, were 18 meters wide and at least 9 meters high. In many cases these were retaining walls for mud brick platforms, in others they were freestanding circuit walls, and they might be both. For example, the wall around Harappa mound E was a revetment in the northwest of the mound but a freestanding wall with gates around its south side. Frequently there were bastions and sometimes towers, and there were generally a number of imposing gateways.

The gateways were not designed primarily for defense, being typically a straightforward opening or passage, although strong wooden gates would have allowed them to be closed. The elaboration of gateways, for example with the addition of stairs or ramps, seems designed rather to increase the impressiveness and solemnity of the approach than to inhibit access or enhance defensibility. Side chambers often flanked the gateway, probably accommodating gatekeepers, who could monitor the flow of people into and out of the city. They may also, as Kenoyer (1998) has suggested, have collected taxes or customs dues on goods being brought into or out of the settlement. The large southern gateway of mound E at Harappa, though tall and imposing, was only

This northeastern corner of the citadel mound at Dholavira gives some indication of the massive scale of Harappan construction. (Namit Arora)

2.8 meters wide, enough to allow the passage of one cart at a time, and immediately inside the gate was a large open space where vehicles and people entering the city could be detained as required.

Gates also controlled access between parts of the settlement that were separately walled, such as the citadel, and ordinary residential areas. At Dholavira, a gateway with bastions and flanked by chambers gave access from the Lower Town to the Middle Town. A stone bar laid on the stone sill of the gateway contained slots thought to have been used to hold wooden planks to close the gate when required.

The settlement at Kuntasi had a double wall, made of boulders and mud, separated by a passage around 20 meters wide. In the southwestern corner was a tower, and in the east side a gate flanked by guard chambers, presumably the public access to the walled town. This contrasts with the small postern gate used by the residents of the unwalled suburbs.

A number of settlements, including Mohenjo-daro, Harappa, Chanhu-daro, Lothal, and Banawali, were wholly or partly founded on artificial platforms made of mud brick, earth, and rubble with substantial retaining walls, which gave some protection against flooding. These required enormous amounts of materials, time, and labor (calculated at around 4 million man-days for

Mohenjo-daro) and were therefore possible only where sufficient manpower could be deployed and the necessary organization existed. Flood damage has been reported at several Harappan sites, including Chanhu-daro and Lothal, confirming that flooding was a hazard endured by settlements located in the floodplains and in some other areas such as the Nal Depression. Jansen has demonstrated that the platforms at Mohenjo-daro, more than 6 meters high, raised the city above any possible floodwaters.

Suburbs

The evidence for suburban settlement is growing, and it seems likely that this was a feature of many Harappan towns and cities. Extramural architecture has been uncovered at Mohenjo-daro, Harappa, Balakot, and Kalibangan; mounds and scatters of Harappan material, including bricks, suggest that suburbs may also have existed around other settlements, including Lothal and Dholavira.

It is likely that suburbs often developed gradually as the area inside the walls became too small to accommodate all who wished to live in the town or city.

In some cases, areas of suburban development were later brought into the walled settlement by constructing additional walls: for example, mound ET at Harappa, and the successive additions of the Middle Town and the Lower Town to the walled area at Dholavira. In other cases, including Sutkagen-dor, Surkotada, Gola Dhoro, and Kuntasi, among others, the suburban area was not walled; it probably housed those connected to but excluded from residence in the fortified area. The suburbs are also likely to have been the locus for heavy industry and craft activities with noxious by-products, such as brick making. They may also have included gardens, fields, orchards, or grazing, as has been the case in the suburbs of many cultures.

"Citadels"

Discussions of Harappan urbanism always make reference to the so-called citadel. This is a culturally loaded term, implying defense, something that is not appropriate in the Harappan context, so some scholars eschew its use. It is, however, a term hallowed in its usage in the Harappan context and provides a useful shorthand by which to refer to the elevated or separately walled mound or sector commonly found in Harappan towns and cities. It is therefore employed here in this strictly limited sense, without any inherent implications about its cultural significance.

At Harappa, Mohenjo-Daro, and Kalibangan, the citadel took the form of a separate mound on the west of the settled area: Investigations at Mohenjo-daro have confirmed that there was no occupation to its west. Little can be said of the badly damaged citadel at Harappa. While the Mohenjo-daro citadel buildings are thought to have been planned as an integrated complex, the citadel at Kalibangan was divided into two contrasting parts, separated by a wall. Mohenjo-daro and Harappa were the first Harappan settlements to be investigated and seemed to set a pattern to which Kalibangan, excavated in the 1960s, appeared to conform, though already it was clear that the structures placed on the citadel varied from site to site. Later excavations have strengthened the picture of diversity. The citadels at Lothal and Banawali were a subdivision of the walled town. Surkotada in Gujarat was a walled settlement divided into two parts, the western half, built over a massive platform, being regarded as the citadel. At Dholavira, the citadel was a separately walled block surrounded by open spaces, subdivided into two halves: the Bailey and the Castle.

Kuntasi lacked a citadel, but there was a marked difference in function between the walled area and the surrounding suburbs, the latter being purely residential while the former included large-scale storage, an industrial complex, and organized accommodation. The situation at Gola Dhoro was similar, with walled and unwalled sectors.

In many cases the citadel was constructed over the remains of an earlier settlement: This is true, for example, of Banawali, Kalibangan, Dholavira, Lothal, and to some extent Harappa. This might suggest that the elevation of citadels resulted from the prior existence of a mound at the site: however, at settlements that were new foundations, including Mohenjo-daro, as well as in the settlements that had existed earlier, the construction of mud and baked brick platforms as the base for the citadel mound indicates that it was a deliberate policy to elevate citadels and the buildings they contained. Not all citadels were constructed on an elevation, but those that were not were still clearly separated from the rest of the settlement by an imposing wall that emphasized the distinctiveness and importance of the citadel and its structures. Although the location of the citadel varied (on the west in some, including Mohenjo-daro and Harappa; on the south in Dholavira and on the southeast in Lothal), in all cases the citadel was situated on one side of the settlement rather than at its heart. These regularities suggest that citadels were intentionally created to be a part of the settlement but separate and distinct. This meant that access could be controlled to the structures of the citadel, whether they were religious (such as the Great Bath at Mohenjo-daro), economic (for example, the warehouse at Lothal), political (the Pillared Hall at Mohenjo-daro, perhaps), or residential (for instance, the northern citadel at Kalibangan).

Access. Entry to the citadel and access to its various parts were on the one hand controlled and restricted and on the other made impressive by the way the entrances and their approaches were laid out. A partially investigated structure in the southeast corner of the citadel mound at Mohenjo-daro may have provided public access to the complex at its southern end, including the Pillared Hall. The entrance combined massive brick towers with a narrow gateway, later elaborated with further towers and a raised walkway with a parapet. Atre (1989) suggested that the layout of the southern complex may also have controlled the movement of people within its various parts. A gate on the western side of the citadel mound may have provided more restricted access to the Great Bath and to other structures in the north of the citadel via a substantial flight of stairs. At the top of the stairs, one passed through another gate into a bathing place where, it is thought, visitors would have been required to purify themselves before entering the sacred precinct. In the street between the Great Bath and the College, a platform of baked brick with sockets for wooden beams may be the remains of a gateway, perhaps preventing unauthorized personnel from entering the area north of the Great Bath.

At Dholavira, the citadel was divided into two separately walled parts, the lower Bailey and the higher Castle, around 18 meters above ground level. The latter had a gateway in each wall. The eastern gateway was flanked by a chamber, along the front of which were columns with stone bases. In the area around the gate were found several highly polished stone pillars, not known from any other Indus settlement and reminiscent of the famous Mauryan pillars fashioned two thousand years later. In the postearthquake period, the main, northern entrance to the Castle was elaborated. A gateway from the esplanade gave access to an approach ramp leading to a terrace in front of the north gate. This opened into a passage running the thickness of the wall, beyond which an L-shaped flight of stairs led up into the Castle. Two chambers flanked the passage, each fronted by a row of pillars on stone bases. Lying on the ground in one chamber were found the remains of what had once been a wooden signboard probably placed above the gateway, set with nine gypsum signs in the enigmatic Indus script, a unique object. At the other end of the esplanade, steps led to a terrace and a gate into the Bailey. A passage through the thickness of the Bailey wall, paved with stone flags, was also flanked by two chambers. Bailey and Castle were connected by a sloping passage through the thickness of the Castle's west wall, with a few steps at the Bailey end.

Access from outside the citadel at Kalibangan was through an impressive gateway in the south, flanked by towers, now badly disturbed but probably originally with steps. The excavator, B. B. Lal, noted a footing with holes to the east of the gate, which he thought might have held banners. From the northern portion of the citadel, entered by a simple gateway in the north wall, a path paved with mud bricks and a stair up the side of the internal wall led through a central gateway in the southern part. The two halves of the walled town at Surkotada were similarly connected by a passage through the internal wall. Each of the halves had a separate external entrance through the massive stone-faced mud and mud brick main town wall, that of the citadel being flanked by guardrooms. The design of the gates meant that no vehicles could enter either half of the settlement. In the final phase of occupation, the town wall was rebuilt in stone and the citadel gate was elaborated into an approach involving a stair, a ramp, and another stair. At Harappa, Wheeler excavated two or three entrances of different dates on the west side of the citadel mound, with gates, ramps, terraces, a bastion, a guard room, and stairs or a ramp climbing to the citadel. A century earlier, Cunningham mentioned flights of stairs on both sides of the citadel. A larger gateway with a ramp provided a link in the north between mound F and the citadel.

Architecture on the Citadels. It is hard to generalize about the diverse structures found on the citadels. However, elevation, enclosure within impressive walls, and control over access seem to imply that the citadel's structures served public functions. The citadels generally included some unusual buildings, which were rare in other parts of the settlement, although a few were located in the Lower Town at Mohenjo-daro and in mound F at Harappa. It is, therefore, likely that in general the citadel was the main location of official activity and public architecture. The data available are, unfortunately, quite limited. The most comprehensively explored and published remains are from Mohenjo-daro. Other sites have a much more restricted range of structures (such as those at Lothal), or they have not been explored or published in much detail (for instance, Banawali or Rakhigarhi), or the citadel deposits are badly disturbed or eroded (for example, at Harappa or Nausharo).

A few structures have been identified as religious installations, in particular the Great Bath at Mohenjo-daro and the platforms in the southern citadel at Kalibangan. A large reservoir and a rainwater collection system were uncovered on the citadel at Dholavira: In view of the strong link between water and Harappan ideology, these were perhaps related to religious practices. Large buildings are reported to have been uncovered in parts of the Dholavira citadel but published details are lacking. A large area in the northeast of the Mohenjo-daro citadel lies beneath the later Buddhist stupa, so it has not been excavated; however, architectural remains around its edge indicate that major buildings existed there. Much of the southern part of the mound was taken up by a large complex that included the Pillared Hall and perhaps a shrine; this complex seems to have had both public and residential areas. Residential buildings form a significant proportion of the structures found in all the excavated citadels; some were no different from the houses in the associated lower town, while others seem designed to accommodate large numbers of people.

Storage Facilities? Buildings identified as substantial storage facilities have been uncovered on the citadels of several settlements. Adjacent to the Great Bath in the northern part of the Mohenjo-daro citadel is a building that Wheeler thought to have been a granary, orientated east-west. A 6-meter-wide baked brick "loading platform" ran along the north side; this had many sockets for timbers, presumably supporting a roof. Toward the west end was a vertical-sided bay, which Wheeler interpreted as the place where bales were hauled up. The granary behind was a rectangular platform, 50 meters east-west by 33 meters north-south, bearing three rows of nine brick podia 1.5 meters high, separated by passages around 80 centimeters wide. The southern and central eastern blocks revealed rows of sockets that had held wooden timbers. Wheeler thought these had supported a ramp or flight of stairs, whereas Jansen (1979) suggested that each of these podia was covered by a light roof. Alternatively, the whole building may have had a massive wooden superstructure. Doubts have been cast on the building's interpretation as a granary since no grain was found during its excavation.

However, the Granary bears some similarities to the building at Lothal whose associated finds support an interpretation as a warehouse. The Lothal warehouse was constructed on a raised mud brick platform, with sixty-four mud brick blocks of which twelve have been uncovered, arranged in three rows of four separated by passages, and the building probably originally had a light superstructure. The finds from the building included numerous seals and sealings from bales of goods that had been packed in reeds, woven cloth, and matting. Storage facilities were provided in other settlements also. A granary with barley in one of its compartments was reported from the citadel at Rakhigarhi. Some of the buildings at Chanhu-daro may have been ware-houses. In the walled sector at Gola Dhoro, there were a number of clay-lined storage bins, some containing large quantities of jasper from Saurashtra. Whereas beads were made from the mottled jasper stored in these bins, larger pieces of a colored variegated jasper was not used at Gola Dhoro but stored for onward distribution.

The tiny settlement of Allahdino did not have a separate citadel (or it was all citadel), but its layout and buildings suggest that it fulfilled an administrative role. The north wing of the largest building had several chambers containing pottery storage vessels, and a separate smaller structure contained others. Sunken storage jars were found in some of the rooms in a large complex on the citadel at Balakot. The walled area at Kuntasi included a number of rooms used for storage, some with jars and clay bins, others themselves containers (strong rooms). These were similar to domestic storage facilities, for example in the houses at Banawali.

At Harappa, a large building in mound F, which lay between the river and the citadel, was originally identified as a granary. A large mud brick plinth supported a series of twelve compartments, arranged in two rows of six, pro-vided with sleeper walls to allow air to circulate beneath the floor. A wooden superstructure must originally have stood above this, probably a series of sep-arate rooms or halls, each accessed from the central passage by means of a stair, and separated from each other by narrow passages. The identification as a granary was largely based on its perceived resemblance to Roman grain stores; grain, however, was conspicuously absent among the finds from the building. It may have been used to store other goods and materials, though there is no report of sealings or other remains that might support this. Recent reinvestigation by the HARP team has not uncovered any new clues to its function, but the team suggests that it may have been a palace or public build-ing rather than a storage facility.

Residential Structures. Many of the buildings on Harappan citadels were resi-dential. In some cases these were houses, for example, those exposed in the northern part of the citadel at Kalibangan and in the citadels of Banawali and Surkotada. Although these are sometimes stated to be larger than those in the lower town, in other cases there seems to have been no difference in size or layout or in the quality of associated facilities and material.

Two other types of residential buildings have been found: These occur both in the citadel and in the lower town, though their function need not necessarily have been the same in each area. One is a building with a number of dupli-cated units, each comprising one or two rooms and a bathroom (referred to as a hostel); the other is a complex of courtyards and rooms, far in excess of the normal size and often with unusual architectural features (referred to as a palace). In some cases, the two are found together or combined. As with other structures, the majority come from Mohenjo-daro.

In the area to the north of the Great Bath at Mohenjo-daro, there was a block of eight bathrooms, arranged in two rows of four, each with a flight of stairs leading to an upper story. It has been plausibly suggested that this housed people (priests?) associated with the Great Bath. A nearby open courtyard may have been associated with the block but was separated from it by the street that ran between the east side of the Great Bath and a large complex known as the College. In the latter there were many small rooms, often faced with brick, and several courtyards, including a large one surrounded by a fenestrated walkway. At least seven entrances gave access to this complex, suggesting it was composed of a number of individual residences or fulfilled a number of functions, perhaps related to administration. Two flights of stairs in the complex show that the building had an upper story.

Farther south was a large hall with brick bases for four rows of five pillars, paved with baked bricks in patterns of unknown significance, though Kenoyer (1998) has suggested that they may indicate places where people were to sit during the activities that took place here. This building bore some resemblance to later public architecture in the subcontinent, such as the Mauryan pillared hall at Pataliputra and Buddhist monastic halls. It has been suggested that this hall was used for public gatherings. It formed part of a larger complex, reminiscent of Near Eastern palaces in the mixture of large courtyards and other public spaces, shrines, and residential quarters; these served both as centers of administrative, legal, economic, and political activity and as the residence of the rulers and their large households. A suite of rooms south of the Pillared Hall included an unusually high proportion of bathrooms; in the western block there were a number of small rooms probably for storage, a smaller hall with rectangular piers to support pillars, containing large-scale cooking facilities, and a long chamber adjacent to a large well. In a badly disturbed hall located farther west, the presence of ring stones suggests that there were wooden columns. One secluded room may have been a shrine. It is also noteworthy that three stone sculptures of people, a high proportion of the very few pieces of Harappan stone sculpture known, were found in parts of this complex.

The residential area on the citadel at Lothal includes twelve bathing platforms attached to a large drain that may have belonged to a row of single-roomed houses, though the architectural detail is uncertain. Nearby was a building that the excavator, S. R. Rao, suggested was the ruler's house. A large complex was partially uncovered on the citadel at Balakot, including courtyards and unusual architectural features such as a patterned floor.

Although structural remains have not demonstrated unequivocally that the citadels were the main location of public activities and the center of administration and government, they are at least consistent with such an interpretation.

The Lower Town

The citadel formed only a small part of most Harappan towns and cities, and the rest was taken up by the lower town, generally walled, and by unwalled sub-

Limestone ring stones were used to hold wooden pillars in some special structures, including gateways into the citadel at Dholavira and several pillared halls at Mohenjo-daro. (J. M. Kenoyer, Courtesy Department of Archaeology and Museums, Government of Pakistan)

urbs. The existence of a suburban area has only recently begun to be apparent; very few have been investigated at all and none to a significant degree, and in the majority of cases even the extent of such suburbs is unknown. Consequently, many aspects of Harappan urbanism and society are still unexplored or poorly known. The picture, probably skewed, provided by the investigated lower towns is of well-appointed housing, light industry, and high standards of civic architecture, including excellent provision of water and sanitation.

Street Planning. Straight cardinally orientated main streets generally divided Harappan towns and cities into residential blocks. The impression of the early excavators at Mohenjo-daro, reinforced by excavations at Kalibangan, was that settlements were laid out in a checkerboardlike grid pattern. Although more recent investigations have shown this to be untrue, the layout was nevertheless governed by precise criteria. The main streets ran north-south, diverging from this orientation by no more than 2 degrees. Holger Wanzke (1987) demonstrated that this cardinal orientation could have been achieved by aligning the streets with the setting point in the west of the bright star Aldebaran (Rohini), while the orientation of the Granary could have been aligned on the setting point of Procyon in the constellation of Canis Minor. The slight changes in orientation reflected the variation through time in the observed rising and setting position of the heavenly bodies on which the directions were based.

Though usual, cardinally orientated streets were not universal. At Dholavira, a straight main street ran west to east through the Middle Town and continued through a gate into the Lower Town, where it took a more crooked course. At Banawali, the grid pattern of streets was only loosely followed and in the smallest settlements, such as Allahdino and Kuntasi, the size of the settlement made streets unnecessary.

The main streets were often broad; for instance, First Street in Mohenjo-daro was 10 meters wide. Narrow lanes running off the principal streets often followed a crooked course; Wheeler suggested that this dog-leg arrangement would have broken the force of the prevailing wind. As in many modern Indian settlements, access to the houses was from these lanes, avoiding the dust of the main thoroughfares, where the houses that lined them presented only blank walls.

In some parts of Mohenjo-daro and Kalibangan, brick platforms stood outside the houses. These may have been places for people to sit and talk. Drains ran down the middle of the streets, part of the impressive system of sanitation. Numerous trees were probably planted along the streets; these would have provided shade and probably had a religious significance.

The planned layout, foreshadowed in the Early Harappan period at a few sites such as Harappa, Kalibangan, and Nausharo, was strictly maintained throughout the Mature Harappan period, with wide clear streets. The Late Harappan period, however, saw the abandonment of planning and the encroachment of buildings into the streets. The spacious courtyard houses were no longer built; in some cases, older houses were partitioned to provide small dwellings for a number of people, and in others they were replaced by closely packed collections of single-story houses, often built of recycled materials. In some cases, for example at Lothal, the houses were built of timber posts and mud daub, resembling Harappan and contemporary rural housing. Civic amenities were not maintained and unpleasant industries were practiced in domestic areas. Even the fine pillared hall on the citadel at Mohenjo-daro was subdivided by rough brick walls and part of the structure used for shellworking.

Public Architecture. In Harappan towns and cities, public secular and religious architecture is surprisingly elusive, in contrast to the prominent temples and palaces known from other primary civilizations. A rectangular area immediately in front of the citadel at Dholavira was paved and formed a stadium surrounded by seating, suggesting that it was the venue for public events or performances, and such facilities may have existed in other settlements: There is a suggestion that part of the citadel at Banawali was similarly an open area, and there is also a large open space in the center of Kuntasi, with a stone platform along one side.

An identification as a shrine or palace has been proposed for a few of the structures found in the Lower Town at Mohenjo-daro, on the basis of their unusual features or layout. Several large structures, such as houses XXX and L in the HR-B area, were very strongly built, with interior platforms, and they probably supported a monumental superstructure. Others contained a number of courtyards, such as House XVIII of HR-B and block 1 in the DK-G area, dubbed The Palace by Mackay. House V in the HR-B area was centered on a huge courtyard, and one of its rooms had a corbelled doorway and contained a number of ring stones and stone caps, suggesting that it had once had a row of columns constructed of stone and wood. The Granary at Harappa has also been suggested to have been a palace or administrative building.

One long building in the HR-B area at Mohenjo-daro comprised two rows of two-roomed units, with a bathing floor in one corner of each, a closed passage between them, a large internally partitioned room to their north, and several chambers in the south with wells and broken pointed-based goblets, possibly disposable drinking vessels. Immediately to the east of this complex was house XXX, one of those regarded as a possible palace or temple. This block may have served as accommodation for visiting merchants or officials given that the units were both small and well appointed, reminiscent of modern hotels with en suite bathrooms. At Harappa, south of mound E there was a complex of houses and bathing platforms that has also been interpreted as a caravanserai, and there may have been another in a nearby mound. Other possible candidates for interpretation as a caravanserai are the block with twelve bathrooms on the citadel at Lothal and the block in mound F at Harappa dubbed "coolie-lines" by Wheeler, two rows of structures consisting of one large and one small room. A hoard of gold jewelry was found buried beneath the floor of one of these buildings.

Houses

Although Harappan houses survive as bare brick walls with traces of plaster, it is likely that originally they were extremely colorful, the plaster being decorated with painted designs. Doorsteps, which raised the householder above the level of the lane, may have been decorated, as they often are today with auspicious designs in red and white. The upper floors probably had windows with wooden shutters so that they could be closed, and with wood or stone lattice grilles, or mats hung on the outside, to allow air into the house.

In the major settlements, especially Mohenjo-daro and Harappa, baked bricks were frequently employed for house construction, while in lesser settlements unfired mud bricks were more usual, and in some settlements, particularly in Gujarat, stone was also used. Baked bricks, however, were widely used for constructing wells, drains, and bathroom floors. The bricks were of uniform proportions (1:2:4) and usually of a standard size, 7 by 14 by 28 centimeters, though there was some variation (for example, at Banawali the bricks ranged in size from 6.5 by 13 by 26 centimeters to 8 by 16 by 32 centimeters). Wood was also employed, both structurally and for fixtures such as doors and their frames. Over time, the house walls were repaired and rebuilt in the same place, whereas internal walls might be moved to change the layout of the domestic space. Occasionally, however, single houses were divided into two, or two houses were amalgamated into one.

The houses, though they varied in detail, were similar in their general lay-out, with rooms around a courtyard and stairs to upper chambers. The en-trance usually gave on to a short passage or opened into a room, arranged so that the courtyard and house interior were not visible from outside, protecting the occupants from rubbish blowing in from the street and affording them pri-vacy. In some cases a small janitor's room faced directly on to the doorway so that the visitor was first confronted and checked out by a doorkeeper. The courtyard was the center of the household, as it is in modern South Asia. Here much of the day-to-day business of life took place for much of the year: preparing grain, fruit, and vegetables for storage or immediate consumption; washing and drying clothes; spinning, weaving, and sewing; cooking, eating, playing, and sleeping. In some houses at Nausharo, part of the courtyard was covered by a roof supported on posts or pillars.

Storage was provided in various forms, including jars, cylindrical clay bins, and small rectangular brick chambers without doors, probably accessed by ladder. Various rooms, generally including a bathroom, opened off the court-yard. At Kalibangan, Banawali, and Lothal, it has been suggested that the houses also included a room set apart as a domestic shrine.

In some cases there was a small kitchen with a hearth, where food and water could be heated. Hearths are rarely reported at Mohenjo-daro, though there were a few on brick platforms. This, combined with the evidence of house fires, has led to the suggestion that the hearths were located in the upper sto-ries, a dangerous practice given that the superstructures were of wood. However, in recent excavations at Harappa, some rooms were found to con-tain the lower part of large pottery jars that had been used as portable hearths. Similar facilities may have existed at Mohenjo-daro. At Nausharo there was usually a brick-built fireplace beside the eastern wall of the courtyard, with an attached brick compartment containing a jar or clay bin in which fuel was stored. Fire pits, with a central pillar made out of a brick coated in clay, are also known. Though generally for domestic use, some may also have been used for industrial purposes.

Floors were usually of beaten earth, but some were paved with bricks or tri-angular terra-cotta cakes. There is little evidence of furniture; some representa-tions on seals suggest that low stools were sometimes used, but it is likely that, as in modern times, people mainly sat on mats and cushions on the floor. One model bed of the Early Harappan period has been found at Kalibangan, though the details of its construction are obscured by a bedcover; beds may have resembled the modern charpoy, a wooden frame with a lattice of rope.

In many settlements, such as Mohenjo-daro, a stair led from the courtyard to one or occasionally two upper stories. In others, such as Kalibangan, houses had only a single story. Constructed of wooden beams covered by packed clay or matting and plaster, the roof provided an additional place for the household to sit, talk, and sleep.

Larger houses also included passages leading from the courtyard to addi-tional rooms, or they had several courtyards. These may have belonged to wealthy, elite households or to large extended families. Anna Sarcina, who has analyzed the houses at Mohenjo-daro, considers that most houses accommodated nuclear families. Some of the larger houses were surrounded by a number of smaller units, suggesting the quarters of families who depended on the central household. Houses were grouped together in blocks separated by lanes. Many houses show signs of frequent remodeling by adding or removing internal walls and by changing the location of the entrance, probably reflecting the alterations required when households changed in size or composition.

While courtyard houses of baked or mud bricks were the norm in towns and cities, in rural settlements, even those of some size such as Rojdi, houses were round or rectangular single-roomed structures built of packed mud or of wattle and daub. In some cases, a household might have several buildings, some accommodating animals, and a yard.

Water Supplies, Drainage, and Waste Disposal

Water played a vital part in the life of the Harappan people, and they were skilled hydraulic engineers. Michael Jansen has calculated that there were seven hundred or more wells at Mohenjo-daro, present in one in three houses. Those without a well of their own, however, were served by the public water supply, and the great wear around the rims of wells in houses suggests that they too were used by more than the immediate household. Grooves in the well curb show that water was drawn using containers, such as pots or wood buckets, attached to ropes. The huge number of wells at Mohenjo-daro indicates that the city was too far from the river for convenience; Jansen (1987) suggests that pits dug to extract clay for construction filled with rainwater and may been used as an additional water source for the city.

Other cities were less generously provided with wells but could draw water from nearby rivers, as at Harappa, which probably had fewer than thirty wells. Unlike those at Mohenjo-daro, all of which seem to have been created when the city was laid out, at least one of the wells at Harappa (on mound AB) was dug from an upper level. There may also have been a pool in the center of the city at Harappa. The area immediately inside the walls of the great settlement at Dholavira was taken up by at least sixteen enormous reservoirs that covered about a third of the enclosed area of the settlement. These were found to have been excavated down to bedrock and in some cases cut into the rock itself, and they were surrounded by embankments of earth faced with stone. Partly supplied by rainwater, they were mainly filled with water diverted, by means of a series of dams, from two seasonal streams that flowed past the settlement. A complex system of catchment areas and drains also collected rainwater from the citadel and channeled it into stone chambers. Two other reservoirs were constructed adjacent to the citadel, one of them more than 5 meters deep, with a flight of thirty-one steps allowing the inhabitants to descend to its foot. The reservoirs were carefully maintained by removing accumulated silt and reinforcing their walls. Satellite images indicate that there was an additional reservoir southwest of the city in the area of the cemetery.

One of the most impressive rooms of the Harappan house was the bathroom. Bathing would have followed the custom that is still used today, of pouring water over oneself with a small pot. In a few households, there may have been the refinement of a kind of shower: a small stair along one side of the bathroom allowing another person to ascend and pour water over the bather. The watertight bathroom floor was constructed sometimes of stone or of pottery sherds but usually of baked bricks, sawn and ground to achieve a perfect fit; the floor sloped slightly to allow the water to flow into one corner, where it ran away into the efficient drainage system that served the city, via terra-cotta drainpipes or drainage chutes. Drains from upper-story rooms were often built into the walls, so that they discharged near street level.

Private latrines were present in almost every house in Harappa and were probably common elsewhere. A large jar let into the floor provided the latrine itself: often just a squatting hole though some at Mohenjo-daro were furnished with seats. Some of these jars were connected by a drain to the city sewage system, and others had a small hole at the base to allow liquids to drain away. The latrine in one house in Banawali, which seems to have belonged to a prosperous family, was provided with a washbasin.

A view of a small part of the water supply and drainage system at Harappa. To the right is a well from which fresh water was drawn. A network of brick-lined drains criss-crosses the area, running along the lanes between buildings. (stock.xchng)

Wastewater was collected into small open drains in the lanes and flowed into the main drainage system. Drains, usually of closely fitted baked bricks, ran along the main streets, covered by large baked bricks or stone slabs. At intervals there were inspection covers so that the free flow of the drains could be checked and maintained. As the street level rose, the sides of the drains were also raised with additional courses of bricks, so that, over the life of the settlement, the drains might come to be several meters deep. Brick culverts on the outskirts of the city allowed the drains to discharge outside the walls; sometimes these had a sluice or grille, to catch solids or to prevent the use of these drains as illicit entrances into the city.

Such drains are a feature of many Harappan settlements but not of all. Kalibangan, for example, had no drains; instead sunken soakage jars along the streets were used. At Lothal there were both drains and soakage jars. Drains carrying rainwater were kept separate from those used for wastewater and sewage. The largest drains and culverts had corbelled roofs; a particularly impressive example is the drain running from the Great Bath at Mohenjo-daro.

At Harappa many of the streets had large jars half sunk into the ground along them, into which rubbish could be thrown; more than two hundred have been found. Immediately to the north of the Lower Town in Mohenjo-daro was a dump for domestic rubbish. Sump pits along the course of the drains allowed solids to collect so that the flow of water was unimpeded; these were regularly cleaned out. In the main north-south street in Mohenjo-daro, there were two brick cesspits, one of which had steps down into it to allow access for the cleaners. Civic standards were not always maintained; for example, there is evidence of a period of around fifty to a hundred years at Harappa when the drains overflowed and sewage ran into the streets before new drains were built and drain cleaning was resumed.

Industrial Activity

In most Harappan settlements there is some evidence of industry, both in individual houses and in areas of more concentrated activity. At Harappa, there were industrial quarters on the west side of mound E, in its center, and to the right of the southern gateway in mound ET. In mound F, near the river, there were circular working floors of baked bricks with central depressions that had once held wooden basins or mortars, each enclosed in a small building. Workshops are known from many parts of the Lower Town at Mohenjo-daro. Concentrations of debris from a range of industries, found along the eastern and southern periphery of the mound, reflect the existence of craft quarters; though the debris derives mainly from erosion and the dumping of rubbish, some industrial installations were located in situ in these areas.

One of the most impressive workshops was the beadmaking factory at Chanhu-daro, which included a furnace. Industrial quarters made up most of the limited excavated areas at this settlement and a major part of the towns of Kuntasi and Lothal. It is possible there were roofed open-air workshops around the periphery of mound II at Chanhu-daro.

A series of working platforms made of concentric circles of bricks, originally inside buildings, were uncovered in Mound F at Harappa. Material associated with one suggests that indigo dye was prepared here. (Harappa Archaeological Research Project, Courtesy Department of Archaeology and Museums, Government of Pakistan)

The majority of craft activities located in the towns and cities of the Mature Harappan period were light industry: making beads and faience and working in shell, stone, antler, bone, wood, metal, and steatite. Industries that created noxious fumes or other offensive by-products have seldom been located within the walled settlements; in most cases, the examples of such industries that have been found have either belonged to the period of urban decay or have been located in suburban areas, on the periphery of the residential area or in specialist industrial sites. For example, the malodorous activity of cleaning out shells took place on a separate suburban mound to the east of Mohenjo-daro's Lower Town; copper smelting may also have been undertaken there.

Cemeteries

Apart from skeletons deposited in disused streets or houses during the final occupation, no burials are known from Mohenjo-daro. At many of the other sites, however, cemeteries have been located outside the walled settlement. Like many other cultures, therefore, the Harappans kept their dead apart from areas of occupation or activity.

REFERENCES

Atre, Shubhangana. 1989. "Towards an Economico-religious Model for Harappan Urbanism." *South Asian Studies* 5: 49–58.

Bala, Madhu. 2004. "Kalibangan: Its Periods and Antiquities." In *Indus Civilization. Sites in India. New Discoveries,* edited by Dilip K. Chakrabarti, 34–43. Mumbai: Marg Publications.

Belcher, William R. 1997. "Ancient Harappa in 3-D." [Online article or information; retrieved 6/14/05.] www.harappa.com/3D/index.html.

Bhan, Kuldeep K. 1989. "Late Harappan Settlements of Western India, with Special Reference to Gujarat." In *Old Problems and New Perspectives in the Archaeology of South Asia,* edited by Jonathan Mark Kenoyer, 219–242. *Wisconsin Archaeological Reports.* Vol. 2. Department of Anthropology. Madison: University of Wisconsin Press.

Bhan, Kuldeep K. 1994. "Cultural Development of the Prehistoric Period in North Gujarat with Reference to Western India." *South Asian Studies* 10: 71–90.

Bhan, Kuldeep K. 2004. "In the Sand Dunes of North Gujarat." In *Indus Civilization. Sites in India. New Discoveries,* edited by Dilip K. Chakrabarti, 96–105. Mumbai: Marg Publications.

Bhan, Kuldeep, V. S. Sonawane, P. Ajithprasad, and S. Pratapchandran. 2005. "Gola Dhoro." [Online article or information; retrieved 7/5/05.] www.harappa.com/goladhoro/index.html.

Bisht, Ravi Singh. 1982. "Excavations at Banawali: 1974–77." In *Harappan Civilization. A Contemporary Perspective,* edited by Gregory L. Possehl, 113–124. New Delhi: Oxford & IBH Publishing Co.

Bisht, Ravi Singh. 1984. "Structural Remains and Town Planning of Banawali." In *Frontiers of the Indus Civilization,* edited by B. B. Lal and S. P. Gupta, 89–97. New Delhi: Books and Books.

Bisht, Ravi Singh. 1990. "Excavation at Dholavira, District Kutch." *Indian Archaeology—A Review 1989–90:* 15–20.

Bisht, Ravi Singh. 1991. "Excavation at Dholavira, District Kutch." *Indian Archaeology—A Review 1990–91:* 10–12.

Bisht, Ravi Singh. 1992. "Excavation at Dholavira, District Kutch." *Indian Archaeology—A Review 1991–92:* 26–35.

Bisht, Ravi Singh. 1993. "Excavation at Dholavira, District Kachchh (Earlier Kutch)." *Indian Archaeology—A Review 1992–93:* 27–32.

Bisht, Ravi Singh. 1999. "Dholavira and Banawali: Two Different Paradigms of the Harappan Urbis Forma." *Puratattva* 29: 14–37.

Bisht, Ravi Singh. 2002. "Dholavira Excavations: 1990–94." In *Facets of Indian Civilization. Recent Perspectives. Essays in Honour of Professor B. B. Lal,* edited by Jagat Pati Joshi, 107–120. New Delhi: Aryan Books International.

Bisht, Ravi Singh, and Shashi Asthana. 1979. "Banawali and Some Other Recently Excavated Harappan Sites in India." In *South Asian Archaeology 1977,* edited by Maurizio Taddei, 223–240. Naples: Istituto Universitario Orientale, Seminario di Studi Asiatici.

Bondioli, L., M. Tosi, and M. Vidale. 1984. "Craft Activity Areas and Surface Survey at Moenjodaro." In *Reports on Fieldwork Carried Out at Mohenjo-daro, Pakistan 1982–83 by the IsMEO-Aachen University Mission: Interim Reports I,* edited by Michel Jansen and Gunter Urban, 9–37. Aachen and Rome: RWTH and IsMEO.

Chakrabarti, Dilip K. 1997. *The Archaeology of Ancient Indian Cities.* New Delhi: Oxford University Press.

Chakrabarti, Dilip K. 1999. *India. An Archaeological History. Palaeolithic Beginnings to Early Historic Foundations.* New Delhi: Oxford University Press.

Cucarzi, Mauro. 1985. "Geophysical Investigations at Moenjodaro, 1985." *East and West* 35: 451–457.

Cucarzi, Mauro. 1987. "A Model of Morphogenesis for Mohenjodaro." In *Reports on Fieldwork Carried Out at Mohenjo-daro, Pakistan 1983–84 by the IsMEO-Aachen University Mission: Interim Reports II,* edited by Michael Jansen and Gunter Urban, 79–90. Aachen and Rome: RWTH and IsMEO.

Cunningham, Alexander. 1875. "Harappa." *Archaeological Survey of India: Report for the Years 1872–3* 5: 105–108.

Dales, George F. 1965. "New Investigations at Mohenjo Daro." *Archaeology* 18 (2): 1145–150. Reprinted 1979 in *Ancient Cities of the Indus,* edited by Gregory L. Possehl, 192–195. Delhi: Vikas Publishing House.

Dales, George F. 1974. "Excavations at Balakot, Pakistan, 1973." *Journal of Field Archaeology* 1 (1/2): 3–22.

Dales, George F. 1979. "The Balakot Project: Summary of Four Years Excavations in Pakistan." In *South Asian Archaeology 1977,* edited by Maurizio Taddei, 241–274. Naples: Istituto Universitario Orientale, Seminario di Studi Asiatici.

Dales, George F. 1982a. "Mohenjodaro Miscellany: Some Unpublished, Forgotten or Misinterpreted Features." In *Harappan Civilization. A Contemporary Perspective,* edited by Gregory L. Possehl, 97–106. New Delhi: Oxford & IBH Publishing Co.

Dales, George F. 1982b. "Adaptation and Exploitation at Harappan Coastal Settlements." In *Anthropology in Pakistan,* edited by Stephen Pastner and Louis Flam, 154–165. Ithaca, NY: Cornell University Press.

Dales, George F., and Jonathan Mark Kenoyer. 1993. "The Harappa Project 1986–9: New Investigations at an Ancient Indus City." In *Harappan Civilization,* 2nd ed., edited by Gregory L. Possehl, 469–520. New Delhi: Oxford University Press.

Dhavalikar, M. K. 1993. "Harappans in Saurashtra: The Mercantile Enterprise as Seen from Recent Excavation of Kuntasi." In *Harappan Civilization,* 2nd ed., edited by Gregory L. Possehl, 555–568. New Delhi: Oxford University Press.

Dhavalikar, M. K. 1996. *Kuntasi, a Harappan Emporium on West Coast.* Pune: Deccan College Post-Graduate and Research Institute.

Fairservis, Walter. 1982. "Allahdino: An Excavation of a Small Harappan Site." In *Harappan Civilization. A Contemporary Perspective,* edited by Gregory L. Possehl, 106–112. New Delhi: Oxford & IBH Publishing Co.

Flam, Louis. 1993. "Excavations at Ghazi Shah, Sindh, Pakistan." In *Harappan Civilization,* 2nd ed., edited by Gregory L. Possehl, 457–467. New Delhi: Oxford University Press.

Francfort, Henri-Paul. 1984. "The Harappan Settlement at Shortugai." In *Frontiers of the Indus Civilization,* edited by B. B. Lal and S. P. Gupta, 301–310. New Delhi: Books and Books.

Franke-Vogt, Ute. 1997. "Reopening Research on Balakot: A Summary of Perspectives and First Results." In *South Asian Archaeology 1995,* edited by Raymond Allchin and Bridget Allchin, 217–235. New Delhi: Oxford & IBH Publishing Co.

Hegde, K. T., K. K. Bhan, V. H. Sonawane, K. Krishnan, and D. R. Shah. 1992. *Excavations at Nageshwar, Gujurat. A Harappan Shellworking Site on the Gulf of Kutch.* Baroda, India: Department of Archaeology and Ancient History. M. S. University of Baroda.

Jansen, Michael. 1979. "Architectural Problems of the Harappa Culture." In *South Asian Archaeology 1977,* edited by Maurizio Taddei, 405–431. Naples: Istituto Universitario Orientale, Seminario di Studi Asiatici.

Jansen, Michael. 1981. "Settlement Patterns in the Harappa Culture." In *South Asian Archaeology 1979,* edited by Herbert Hartel, 251–269. Berlin: Deitrich Reimer Verlag.

Jansen, Michael. 1984. "Architectural Remains in Mohenjo-daro." In *Frontiers of the Indus Civilization,* edited by B. B. Lal and S. P. Gupta, 75–88. Delhi: Books and Books.

Jansen, Michael. 1987. "Preliminary Results on the 'Forma Urbis' Research at Mohenjo-Daro." In *Reports on Fieldwork Carried out at Mohenjo-daro, Pakistan 1982–83 by the IsMEO-Aachen University Mission: Interim Reports II,* edited by Michael Jansen and Gunter Urban, 9–22. Aachen and Rome: RWTH and IsMEO.

Jansen, Michael. 1993. *Mohenjo-daro: City of Wells and Drains.* Bergisch Gladbach: Frontinus-Gesellschaft e.V.

Jansen, Michael. 1994. "Mohenjo-Daro, Type Site of the Earliest Urbanization Process in South Asia: Ten Years of Research at Mohenjo-Daro, Pakistan and an Attempt at a Synopsis." In *South Asian Archaeology 1993,* edited by Asko Parpola and Petteri Koskikallio, 263–280. Helsinki: Suomalainen Tiedeakatemia.

Jansen, Michael. 2002. "Settlement Networks of the Indus Civilization." In *Indian Archaeology in Retrospect. II. Protohistory. Archaeology of the Harappan Civilization,* edited by S. Settar and Ravi Korisettar, 105–126. Indian Council of Historical Research. New Delhi: Manohar.

Jarrige, Catherine. 1994. "The Mature Indus Phase at Nausharo as Seen from a Block of Period III." In *South Asian Archaeology 1993,* edited by Asko Parpola and Petteri Koskikallio, 281–294. Helsinki: Suomalainen Tiedeakatemia.

Jarrige, Jean-Francois. 1986. "Excavations at Mehrgarh-Nausharo." *Pakistan Archaeology* 10-22: 63–131.

Jarrige, Jean-Francois. 1988. "Excavations at Nausharo." *Pakistan Archaeology* 23: 140–203.

Joshi, Jagat Pati. 1990. *Excavations at Surkotada 1971–72 and Exploration in Kutch. Memoirs of the Archaeological Survey of India.* SI 87. New Delhi: Archaeological Survey of India.

Kenoyer, Jonathan Mark. 1993. "Excavations on Mound E, Harappa: A Systematic Approach to the Study of Indus Urbanism." In *South Asian Archaeology 1991,* edited by Adalbert J. Gail and Gerd J. R. Mevissen, 165–195. Stuttgart: Franz Steiner Verlag.

Kenoyer, Jonathan Mark. 1996. "Around the Indus in 90 Slides." [Online article; retrieved 6/14/05.] www.harappa.com/indus/indus0.html.

Kenoyer, Jonathan Mark. 1998. *Ancient Cities of the Indus Valley Civilization.* Karachi: Oxford University Press and American Institute of Pakistan Studies.

Kenoyer, Jonathan Mark, and Richard H. Meadow. 1998. "The Latest Discoveries: Harappa 1995–98." [Online article; retrieved 6/14/05.] www.harappa.com/indus2/index.html.

Kesarwani, A. 1984. "Harappan Gateways: A Functional Reassessment." In *Frontiers of the Indus Civilization,* edited by B. B. Lal and S. P. Gupta, 63–73. New Delhi: Books and Books.

Lal, B. B. 1984. "Some Reflections on the Structural Remains at Kalibangan." In *Frontiers of the Indus Civilization,* edited by B. B. Lal and S. P. Gupta, 55–62. New Delhi: Books and Books.

Lal, B. B. 1997. *The Earliest Civilization of South Asia: Rise, Maturity and Decline.* New Delhi: Aryan Books International.

Mackay, Ernest J. H. 1938. *Further Excavations at Mohenjo Daro.* New Delhi: Government of India.

Mackay, Ernest J. H. 1943. *Chanhu-daro Excavations 1935–36.* New Haven, CT: American Oriental Society.

Marshall, John. 1931. *Mohenjo Daro and the Indus Civilization.* London: Arthur Probsthain.

Meadow, Richard, ed. 1991. *Harappa Excavations 1986–1990.* Madison, WI: Prehistory Press.

Meadow, Richard H., and Jonathan Mark Kenoyer. 1994. "Harappa Excavations 1993: The City Wall and Inscribed Materials." In *South Asian Archaeology 1993,* edited by Asko Parpola and Petteri Koskikallio, 451–470. Helsinki: Suomalainen Tiedeakatemia.

Meadow, Richard H., and Jonathan Mark Kenoyer. 1997. "Excavations at Harappa 1994–1995: New Perspectives on the Indus Script, Craft Activities, and City Organization." In *South Asian Archaeology 1995,* edited by Raymond Allchin and Bridget Allchin, 139–173. New Delhi: Oxford & IBH Publishing Co.

Meadow, Richard H., and Jonathan Mark Kenoyer. 2003. "Recent Discoveries and Highlights from Excavations at Harappa: 1998–2000." [Online article; retrieved 6/14/05.] www.harappa.com/indus4/e1.html.

Mehta, R. N. 1982. "Some Rural Harappan Settlements in Gujarat." In *Harappan Civilization. A Contemporary Perspective,* edited by Gregory L. Possehl, 167–174. New Delhi: Oxford & IBH Publishing Co.

Mehta, R. N. 1984. "Valabhi—A Station of Harappan Cattle-Breeders." In *Frontiers of the Indus Civilization,* edited by B. B. Lal and S. P. Gupta, 227–230. Delhi: Books and Books.

Mery, S. 1994. "Excavation of an Indus Potter's Workshop at Nausharo (Baluchistan), Period II." In *South Asian Archaeology 1993,* edited by Asko Parpola and Petteri Koskikallio, 471–481. Helsinki: Suomalainen Tiedeakatemia.

Millar, Heather M-L. 1994. "Indus Tradition Craft Production: Research Plan and Preliminary Survey Results Assessing Manufacturing Distribution at Harappa, Pakistan." In *From Sumer to Meluhha,* edited by Jonathan Mark Kenoyer, 81–99. *Wisconsin Archaeological Reports.* Vol. 3. Department of Anthropology. Madison: University of Wisconsin Press.

Momin, K. N. 1984. "Village Harappans in Kheda District of Gujurat." In *Frontiers of the Indus Civilization,* edited by B. B. Lal and S. P. Gupta, 231–234. New Delhi: Books and Books.

Nath, Amarendra. 1998. "Rakhigarhi: A Harappan Metropolis in the Sarasvati-Drishadvati Divide." *Puratattva* 28: 39–45.

Nath, Amarendra. 1999. "Further Excavations at Rakhigarhi." *Puratattva* 29: 46–49.

Nath, Amarendra. 2001. "Rakhigarhi: 1999–2000." *Puratattva* 31 43–45.

Possehl, Gregory L. 1979. "Lothal: A Gateway Settlement of the Harappan Civilization." In *Ancient Cities of the Indus,* edited by Gregory L. Possehl, 212–218. New Delhi: Vikas Publishing House.

Possehl, Gregory L. 1982. "Harappan Civilization: A Contemporary Perspective." In *Harappan Civilization,* edited by Gregory L. Possehl, 15–28. New Delhi: Oxford University Press.

Possehl, Gregory L. 1999. *Indus Age: The Beginnings.* New Delhi: Oxford University Press.

Possehl, Gregory L. 2002. *The Indus Civilization. A Contemporary Perspective.* Walnut Creek, CA: AltaMira Press.

Possehl, Gregory L. 2004. "Rojdi: A Sorath Harappan Settlement in Saurashtra." In *Indus Civilization. Sites in India. New Discoveries,* edited by Dilip K. Chakrabarti, 80-88. Mumbai: Marg Publications.

Pracchia, Stefano, Maurizio Tosi, and Massimo Vidale. 1985. "Craft Industries at Moenjo-Daro." In *South Asian Archaeology 1983,* edited by Janine Schotsmans and Maurizio Taddei, 207–248. Naples: Istituto Universitario Orientale, Dipartimento di Studi Asiatici.

Rao, S. R. 1973. *Lothal and the Indus Civilization.* Bombay: Asia Publishing House.

Rao, S. R. 1979 and 1985. *Lothal: A Harappan Town (1955–62).* 2 vols. *Memoirs of the Archaeological Survey of India.* SI 78. New Delhi: Archaeological Survey of India.

Ratnagar, Shereen. 2001. *Understanding Harappa. Civilization in the Greater Indus Valley.* New Delhi: Tulika.

Ratnagar, Shereen. 2004. *Trading Encounters. From the Euphrates to the Indus in the Bronze Age.* New Delhi: Oxford University Press.

Rissman, Paul C., and Y. M. Chitalwala. 1990. *Harappan Civilization and Oriyo Timbo.* New Delhi: Oxford & IBH Publishing Co. and American Institute of Indian Studies.

Sarcina, Anna. 1979. "The Private House at Mohenjo-daro." In *South Asian Archaeology 1977,* edited by Maurizio Taddei, 433–462. Naples: Istituto Universitario Orientale, Seminario di Studi Asiatici.

Sharma, Y. D. 1982. "Harappan Complex on the Sutlej (India)." In *Harappan Civilization. A Contemporary Perspective,* edited by Gregory L. Possehl, 141–165. New Delhi: Oxford & IBH Publishing Co.

Shinde, Vasant. 1991 "Excavation at Padri, District Bhavnagar." *Indian Archaeology— A Review 1990–1:* 8–10.

Shinde, Vasant. 1992a. "Padri and the Indus Civilization." *South Asian Studies* 8: 55–66.

Shinde, Vasant. 1992b. "Excavation at Padri, District Bhavnagar." *Indian Archaeology— A Review 1991–92:* 21–22.

Shinde, Vasant. 2004. "Saurashtra and the Harappan Sites of Padri and Kuntasi." In *Indus Civilization. Sites in India. New Discoveries,* edited by Dilip K. Chakrabarti, 64–70. Mumbai: Marg Publications.

Sonewane, V. H. 2004. "Nageshwar: A Center of Harappan Shell Craft in Saurashtra." In *Indus Civilization. Sites in India. New Discoveries,* edited by Dilip K. Chakrabarti, 71–79. Mumbai: Marg Publications.

Thapar, B. K. 1975. "Kalibangan: A Harappan Metropolis beyond the Indus Valley." *Expedition* 17 (2): 19–32. Reprinted 1979 in *Ancient Cities of the Indus,* edited by Gregory L. Possehl, 196–202. New Delhi: Vikas Publishing House.

Vats, M. S. 1940. *Excavations at Harappa.* New Delhi: Government of India.

Vidale, Massimo. 1989. "Specialized Producers and Urban Elites: On the Role of Craft Industries in Mature Harappan Urban Contexts." In *Old Problems and New Perspectives in the Archaeology of South Asia,* edited by Jonathan Mark Kenoyer, 170–181. *Wisconsin Archaeological Reports.* Vol. 2. Department of Anthropology. Madison: University of Wisconsin Press.

Wanzke, Holger. 1987. "Axis Systems and Orientation at Mohenjo-Daro." In *Reports on Fieldwork Carried out at Mohenjo-daro, Pakistan 1982–83 by the IsMEO-Aachen University Mission: Interim Reports II,* edited by Michael Jansen and Gunter Urban, 33–44. Aachen and Rome: RWTH and IsMEO.

Wheeler, R. E. Mortimer. 1968. *The Indus Civilization.* 3rd ed. Cambridge, UK: Cambridge University Press.

VIII

Social and Political Organization

INTRODUCTION

While the necessary reliance on archaeological evidence has ensured that many aspects of Harappan civilization, such as economic activities, settlements, industry, and biological anthropology, have been investigated as well as or better than those of literate civilizations, the absence of intelligible documentary material is a major handicap to understanding Harappan social and political organization and has put some aspects of Harappan life, such as the law, quite beyond cognizance. The situation is not entirely hopeless, however: There are many lines of evidence that may eventually result in a convincing reconstruction of how the Harappan polity worked.

CLUES TO SOCIAL ORGANIZATION

Archaeological studies of prehistoric social organization often focus on data in which differences and similarities between people, such as gender, social status, ethnicity, occupation, or cultural or religious affiliation, may be reflected, providing clues to the ordering of society. These include housing and the organization of settlements; personal appearance and access to valued objects and materials; funerary practices; and health and diet. Other clues to the nature of societies may lie in the organization of trade and craft production and the mobilization of labor for large-scale enterprises. Some of these avenues of inquiry are opened up by data from the Harappan civilization while for others there is little to go on.

Elites are generally thought to have had preferential access to both luxuries and basic productive resources. The population of the Harappan realms seems to have been well within the carrying capacity of the region, and their standard of living (reflected in housing, nutrition, and artifacts) seems generally to have been good. However, the Harappan elite may be expected to have had greater access to objects or materials of value, defined in terms of their expense of acquisition or manufacture, which would been used to display their status, for example when worn as jewelry; they may also have had closer access to the gods, which in the Harappan realms may have meant taking greater precautions to preserve ritual purity.

Personal Appearance

Many, if not indeed all, societies use features of personal appearance to make statements and to provide information about individuals and social groups. It should, therefore, be possible to glean some information about Indus social organization by examining variations in clothing, hairstyles, and personal ornaments. The many figurines supply much information on personal appearance, particularly that of women, and other clues come from the array of ornaments found on skeletons in burials. These data suggest some status differentiation among individuals, but not a markedly stratified society.

Jewelry. By analogy with other societies, the quantity and quality of jewelry worn may have indicated status. The Harappans' attitude to materials that were highly valued by their contemporaries was unusual. They made little use themselves of the lapis lazuli and turquoise that they obtained, with considerable effort, for export. Gold seems to have been valued no more highly than silver. Ivory was used like bone, for everyday objects. The Harappans mainly placed a high value on skill, on the investment of labor, and on the transformation of materials, creating such valuables as exceptionally long carnelian beads, steatite microbeads, and objects of faience and stoneware.

Bangles are an important element in traditional Indian female dress, offering symbolic protection, their types reflecting such things as membership of particular communities or marital status. Men may also wear bangles, the best-known example being the Sikh *kara*. Figurines and sculptures, such as the famous dancing girl, show that bangles were a common item of Harappan dress. Finds from burials confirm this: Women usually wore a number of bangles, either on both arms or on just the left, narrow ones around the wrist, and wider ones above the elbow.

The different materials from which these were made and their technological sophistication probably reflect status differentials in Harappan society. The majority were handmade of terra-cotta: These were probably for everyday wear, like the ubiquitous glass bangles worn today. Some were plain, others decorated with painted or incised designs. Some were made of finer clays. Less common but also widespread were shell bangles. Large sturdy bangles that could be worn even by women engaged in heavy manual work were known from many settlements but not in the graves at Harappa, where all the bangles found with women were of shell. These were a far more fragile type, thin kidney-shaped rings, a shape imitated in fine bangles made of faience. White or blue-green faience was also used for simple ring bangles decorated with chevrons. Other bangles were made of a copper or bronze rod bent round into a slightly open circle, while a few were manufactured from silver or from hammered gold sheet. Since faience, copper, silver, and gold bangles were far less common than those of terra-cotta or shell, their wearers are likely to have been members of the elite. Some of the latter also wore finger or toe rings of silver wire or copper.

The figurines show that women wore a great variety of jewelry, which might include ear ornaments, pendants, or anklets. Some had an ornament hanging over the forehead. A cylindrical or truncated conical amulet of black stone, or

A burial of a woman at Harappa. She is wearing shell bangles on her left arm, which was typical for women at the time. (J. M. Kenoyer, Courtesy Department of Archaeology and Museums, Government of Pakistan)

less commonly of serpentine, faience, or steatite, was worn by women buried at Harappa, suspended round the neck, and these amulets are common at other sites. Given their numbers, this may have been an ornament worn by women to indicate that they were married, like a number of the pieces of jewelry worn by Indian women today. Men were less frequently buried with jewelry: Among those at Harappa, one wore a shell bangle and a hair ornament of beads, steatite microbeads, and shell rings, while another had a necklace of three hundred and forty steatite beads and other jewelry using seven beads of gold, copper, and stone, including an onyx eye bead (a bead decorated with concentric circles or ovals that resemble the human eye). Male figurines were also generally unadorned, though a few had a neck ornament; in contrast, depictions of deities of either sex wore bangles the entire length of their arms and sometimes had enormous necklaces.

The prominence of beadmaking among craft activities indicates that beads played an important role in dress, and this is confirmed by figurines, which are often shown dressed in little else. Many wore neck chokers with pendant beads and single and multiple stranded bead necklaces of graduated lengths, virtually covering their chests. Others wore few or none, such as the models from Nausharo of women grinding grain and kneading dough. The Harappans made beads from a great variety of local and imported raw materials, including gold, silver, copper, agate, carnelian, jasper, and other gemstones, steatite, lapis, and shell, as well as manufacturing them from bronze, terracotta, and faience. Patterned stones such as banded agate were particularly prized, especially those that could be cut to show circles like eyes. Imitations of these natural eye beads were also made, in a variety of materials of differing worth: faience, "etched" carnelian, or painted pottery. Value was measured not only by the rarity of the raw material but also by the craftsmanship involved. Microscopic beads of steatite, only a millimeter wide, show extraordinary skill and patience in their manufacture. Necklaces and other jewelry made of thousands of these beads, such as the hair ornament found on a man buried at Harappa, must have been extremely valuable. Similarly skilled and labor-intensive was the production of very long carnelian beads, each of which took around two weeks to make. Cheap imitations of these were made in terracotta, known, for example, from Nausharo.

Hairstyles. Hairstyles may also have demonstrated the social standing of individuals. Female figurines often wear their hair either folded up over a pannier or fan-shaped frame or piled high on the top of their heads. Sometimes flowers or ornaments are worked in. A number are shown wearing a cone on their heads, and a few gold cones have been found at Harappan sites. Others have a simple bun or wear a turban. Elaborate and time-consuming coiffures suggest that the individuals wearing them had leisure and probably servants, suggesting high social status, and this is borne out by the heavy quantities of jewelry worn by such individuals.

Many figures on the seals, probably of both sexes, wear their hair in a long plait. While it is possible some of these figures are ordinary worshippers, ritually coiffed, they may all be deities, since no sculptures or terra-cottas depict people with their hair arranged in this way.

The less common male figurines and rare male statues generally wear their hair in a bun, divided horizontally by a headband, strongly reminiscent of a royal hairstyle in contemporary Sumer. A few gold fillets have been found, at Harappa, at Mohenjo-daro, and in the hoard at Alladino, with holes at the ends for fastening them with a cord. Sometimes Harappan men wore their hair short and combed straight, or covered by a turban. The majority of men were bearded.

Clothing. As well as jewelry, the Harappans wore clothes of cotton, leather, and probably wool, the latter probably imported from Mesopotamia, perhaps only for the elite. Here the artwork is less helpful, since most men and many of the women are depicted naked. The stone sculpture known as the Priest-King wears an elaborately decorated robe, draped to expose his chest and right shoulder. This was possibly a garment worn only by rulers or senior priests. Other, more complete stone statues show that this robe was worn over a garment resembling the modern dhoti, which is wound around the waist and frequently drawn up between the legs to tuck in at the back. The latter may have been common male dress, particularly as figures on seals, possibly of men, sometimes wear a skirt that could be the dhoti in the untucked state. Women appear to have worn a short skirt that covered the thighs and, in some cases, a substantial belt made of strings of beads.

One of the small number of Harappan stone sculptures, this male head shows the typical arrangement of the hair in a double bun, held in place by a thin fillet tied at the back. The pattern of hair on the top of the head suggests that it is braided. (J. M. Kenoyer, Courtesy Department of Archaeology and Museums, Government of Pakistan)

Burials

Few cemeteries have been discovered and only the one at Harappa has been extensively excavated; so there is at present only limited evidence from which to investigate status differentiation in burials. Harappans seem generally to have buried their dead wearing jewelry, but rarely with grave goods except for pottery. The number of vessels and the richness of the personal ornaments probably reflected an individual's status. Their jewelry indicates the high status of two men buried at Harappa. The few women who were interred with a copper mirror may also have been from the elite. Occasionally individuals were buried with other objects, such as a shell ladle or an animal or human figurine. People were never accompanied by seals or tools, perhaps indicating that their official role in life was not considered relevant in the next world.

While some individuals were placed in the grave directly on the ground surface, others were separated from it by a layer of pottery or clay, or their grave was lined with bricks. In a few cases traces have been found of a shroud, a wooden coffin, or sometimes both. One coffin was made of rosewood with a deodar lid; this contained a woman buried with thirty-seven pots. A burial of an elderly man at Kalibangan, in a brick-lined grave, was accompanied by more than seventy pots, some in a layer separating him from the ground surface. It is likely that individuals accorded these additional features were of a higher status, although there are other possible explanations, for example, related to religious beliefs.

The number of people buried in the known cemeteries represents only a fraction of the population. For example, at Kalibangan the cemetery contained the graves of fewer than ninety people, while the town itself accommodated somewhere around a thousand. It is therefore possible that only one section of society was buried, other members of the community being treated in some other way.

All the cemeteries that have been located lie outside the settlements. In contrast, toward the end of the Indus civilization when civic standards were breaking down, burials of a very different nature were made in the heart of Mohenjo-daro. Corpses were disposed of higgledy-piggledy in abandoned streets or empty houses: These are Wheeler's famous "massacre" victims. However, the bones bear witness to violence only in two cases, and in both the injuries predated death by several months. The largest group comprises thirteen adults and a child, found in a house of the HR-B area. Their bodies were placed or thrown there separately at different times, and associated finds show that they were wearing small amounts of jewelry. Two other groups were found—one of six individuals in the VS area and one of nine in the DK-G area—and there was also a single body in a street in the HR-A area. An ivory comb and a pair of elephants' tusks were found with one group, showing that grave offerings were sometimes made. The absence of animal damage to the bones implies that the bodies were deliberately covered with earth. If, as is likely, they were victims of disease, they may have been placed in deserted areas because they posed a health or ritual risk. Rather different were two people from the final period of the city's occupation who apparently died as they attempted to crawl up a stair from a well in the DK-G area: perhaps victims of disease or starvation who died a lonely death unnoticed by others.

Much has been made of the absence of royal burials from the archaeological record of the Harappans. While royal burials are among the best-known remains from a number of ancient societies, it is worth emphasizing how small a proportion of all the royal burials ever made have actually survived and been discovered. Many were robbed or looted in antiquity. The seclusion of the royal dead in a special place distant from settlements, a practice adopted by many societies, can be a major contributor to the failure to discover such graves. Nor need status necessarily be reflected in the elaboration of disposal, as is exemplified by the Saudi King Fa'ad's simple burial in an unmarked grave in 2005 (CE).

Housing

Differences in social status are often apparent from differences in the size and quality of houses. Evidence of this in the Harappan domains, however, is relatively limited. The majority of Harappan houses consisted of a courtyard surrounded by rooms. There was some variation in the number of rooms, and some larger houses had several courtyards. In some cases larger houses were surrounded by small ones, suggesting an elite household with those of

This grave at Harappa held the burial of a mother and her baby. The grave was disturbed when the body was still intact: she was turned over onto her front and her left arm was broken, perhaps by careless handling when removing the bangles she was likely wearing. The pottery vessels deposited with her were also disarranged. (J. M. Kenoyer, Courtesy Department of Archaeology and Museums, Government of Pakistan)

dependents. In some settlements, such as Mohenjo-daro, the houses had two or even three stories, whereas at Kalibangan, for instance, the houses had only one floor; this, however, may merely reflect the relative lack of space within the crowded cities, forcing householders to expand upward. At Banawali, the few excavated houses of the lower town seem prosperous, with storage chambers, an upper floor, and valuable artifacts. In mound E at Harappa, the main street leading from the gate was lined with houses whose contents included seals, stoneware bangles, and other inscribed material; unlike many houses in this walled area, these contained no trace of craft activity, suggesting their residents were probably from the literate elite. There was a noticeable difference in the small part of the settlement exposed at Dholavira between the straight cardinally orientated street in the walled Middle Town and the more crooked street of the Lower Town. Whether this difference was reflected in the size or quality of the housing in the two areas is not yet apparent. The investigation of Harappan suburbs might be revealing; however, one small excavation in a suburban area well outside the walled Lower Town at Mohenjo-daro suggests there was little difference in quality between housing in the city center and in the suburbs.

The architecturally flimsy housing outside the walled town at Kuntasi may have accommodated workers in the town's industries; alternatively, visiting pastoralists or hunter-gatherers bringing in goods and materials may have camped there. The residential buildings inside the walls comprised two large houses with their own kitchens, plausibly the residences of senior officials, and a number of smaller houses served by a separate communal kitchen, said by the excavator to resemble dormitories, which were probably the accommodation provided for staff employed in this trading and industrial center, such as craftspeople and lesser officials. Kuntasi is poorly located for agriculture, but the suburban areas of many towns probably housed the farmers, pastoralists, fishers, and hunter-gatherers whose produce sustained the settlement. These may also have resided within the walled area of some towns. The houses at Kalibangan were arranged so that animals and carts could be kept in the courtyard.

Analogies with other civilizations would lead one to expect palaces housing the rulers of the Harappan state, either on the citadel or in a segregated part of the lower town. Nothing certainly of this nature has been found. A small number of the buildings that have been uncovered may have included both residential and public rooms, such as the complex on the southern part of the citadel mound and House V in the HR-B area of the Lower Town at Mohenjo-daro, the "granary" at Harappa, the complex on the citadel at Balakot, and the buildings at Allahdino. These may have housed those in authority and their entourage.

Of considerable interest are the buildings in the northern part of the Mohenjo-daro citadel. Adjacent to the Great Bath is the College, a building that included a courtyard with a fenestrated walkway echoing that surrounding the Great Bath, several other courtyards, and a number of rooms, as well as a large number of entrances. North of the Great Bath, shut off from the outside world, was an accommodation block with bathrooms on the ground floor and presumably sleeping quarters above. Since the Great Bath was most probably a religious facility, it is likely that these nearby buildings provided the residential and administrative quarters of the priests who served here.

While houses uncovered on the citadel of Harappan settlements usually differ little from those in the associated lower town, in some cases they are said to be larger. There must in any case have been some significance to the difference in location, housing on the Indus citadels being associated with other structures that included both religious installations and probable administrative or public buildings.

Artifacts

Some clues to social organization can be gleaned from the types of artifact recovered from Harappan sites. Some tools were made in different materials, depending on the status of the owner: For example, high-status households may have used metal vessels for cooking and serving food, while other people had ceramic vessels of varying quality. Similarly, the elite may have had a higher proportion of their tools in metal rather than stone, although the abundance of copper and bronze tools found in Harappan settlements shows that few households had none. There is considerable evidence that good-quality materials were used by people in all the urban settlements and even in villages (for example, people in the small village of Kanewal owned copper ornaments and beads of faience as well as more ordinary shell and terra-cotta beads). The artifactual evidence, such as it is, therefore points to a widespread good standard of living and relatively little social differentiation.

Health and Nutrition

The physical examination of individuals from the excavated Harappan cemeteries indicates that the Harappans in general were well nourished and enjoyed good health, suggesting that social differences were not marked by differential access to adequate food and care. Admittedly these burials are only a sample of the population and not necessarily a representative one.

Around seventy skeletons from the R-37 cemetery at Harappa were examined: They were found to have been generally well fed and healthy, although three showed signs of arrested growth, due to childhood malnutrition or illness. Many individuals had, however, suffered from dental caries and other dental disease, due to a diet high in soft foods such as processed cereals. Women's teeth were worse than men's, suggesting that men had access to a more balanced diet: This may reflect cultural differences in the treatment of the sexes. Significantly, the occasional signs of childhood malnutrition were also found in female rather than male skeletons. Analysis of the animal bones from Dholavira showed that three-quarters of the bones from meat eaten by people in the Middle Town were from cattle or buffalo, while in the Bailey these accounted for only half the bones, with pig and caprines more important there than in the Middle Town. This may reflect some status differential in diet between the two areas, though data from other settlements are needed before any clear picture can emerge.

Some individuals suffered arthritis of the neck, probably due to stress from carrying heavy loads on their heads. One child who was buried at Kalibangan had suffered from hydrocephaly, and had undergone, and died from, trepanation, a dangerous operation in which a disc of bone is removed from the skull. Life expectancy seems to have been good: Nearly half the individuals studied from Harappa survived into their mid-thirties and almost a sixth lived beyond fifty-five.

Ironically the Harappans' obsession with water may have exposed them to disease, particularly at Mohenjo-daro. Seepage from the wastewater drains could easily have contaminated drinking water in the public wells. An outbreak of cholera in these circumstances could set in motion a vicious circle of contamination. While cholera is suspected but unproven, the presence of malaria has recently been demonstrated. Stagnant water, both inside the drainage system and in areas of flooded ground, provided the breeding ground for mosquitoes carrying the parasites that spread the disease. This situation would have been at its worst in the late period at Mohenjo-daro when civic standards were in decline. Many skeletons from Mohenjo-daro show signs of porotic hyperostosis, a thinning of the cranial bones probably due to anemia. Kennedy, a leading palaeoanthropologist, links this with the prevalence of malaria causing a high incidence of sickle-cell anemia (thalassemia), a debilitating genetically transmitted condition that, however, gives a degree of protection against malaria. In contrast, porotic hyperostosis was rare at Harappa.

Ethnicity and Kinship

The marked heterogeneity of some aspects of Harappan life, including such fundamental matters as religion, probably owes much to the diversity of cultural backgrounds from which its people sprang. In the centuries before the emergence of the civilization, these included indigenous hunter-gatherers and fishers, farmers and pastoralists of local stock, and others whose ancestors came from the Indo-Iranian borderlands, as well as those who still had their homes in the latter region. Differences in artifacts suggest that there were a number of distinct cultures within each of these broad economic and ethnic groupings. The universal adoption of the overarching Harappan ideology, most clearly shown by the widespread move during the Transition period to settlements constructed according to new principles, masks much of this heterogeneous background, but features of the regional groups that emerged after the collapse of Harappan urban culture in the early second millennium suggest that perceptions of ethnic and cultural identity were not entirely submerged by the shared experience of being Harappan during the Mature Indus period. Identifying ethnic groups has relied heavily on the indirect evidence from material culture. In Saurashtra various features including the pottery repertoire, which lacked many classic Harappan vessel forms, such as S-profile jars, and included distinctive local types, such as stud-handled bowls, led Possehl to identify a local variation of Indus culture which he called Sorath Harappan. A similar situation existed in the east where Sothi-Siswal pottery was used from the Early Harappan to the Posturban period and alongside Harappan pottery in the Mature Harappan period.

In the past many studies of human remains made broad racial attributions on the basis of a few physical features, such as skull shape; these gave too much weight to differences between populations and too little to the range of variation within them, producing results that had little meaning. In recent decades, however, much more sophisticated ways of assessing ethnic makeup have been developed, including genetics.

Studies of Harappan and other Indian skeletal material by Kennedy and others have yielded interesting results. The people buried in the cemetery at Lothal show a considerable degree of affinity to the local hunter-gatherer population: This would seem to fit with the deduction from artifactual evidence that the indigenous population of Gujarat had formed part of Harappan society since Early Harappan times. Regional diversity also characterizes the remains from Ropar and Kalibangan. Nevertheless, the human remains from Harappan sites exhibit a high degree of close biological affinity, showing that the members of the Harappan population were interrelated. The exception is Mohenjo-daro, where the human remains, which come from the late period of urban occupation, were significantly different and displayed a considerable degree of variability among themselves.

Genetic studies on the people buried at Harappa revealed that, while no strong genetic links existed among the men, the women displayed considerable similarities, indicating that many were related. This would seem to indicate that the marriage pattern in Harappan society was matrilocal, the man coming to live with his wife's family upon marriage and women continuing to live in or near their ancestral homes throughout their lives. Further studies are required to test whether this pattern was widespread.

Occupational Specialization

The great majority of the Harappan population must have been primary producers: farmers, pastoralists, fishers, or hunter-gatherers. Many, however, probably also engaged in other occupations during the periods in the year when there was time to spare from subsistence activities. The bulk of agricultural work took place during the winter months, allowing farmers to engage in other activities during the summer months, including craft production. When *kharif* (summer) cultivation of millets became important in Gujarat during the early second millennium, this may have changed. Marine fishing and shellfish collection also had seasonal periods of activity and slack periods in which other occupations could be followed, that of shellworking being particularly likely; river fishing was less seasonally dependent but could not be pursued during the annual inundation, at least in Sindh. Pastoralists and hunter-gatherers who moved between seasonal pastures and the localities where other resources were available at particular times of year also acted as carriers, moving raw materials and finished goods between producers and consumers. In addition hunter-gatherers, and perhaps pastoralists, could include in their seasonal round visits to places where other resources could be obtained, so they may have been largely responsible for mining gemstones and for quarrying flint in the Rohri Hills.

While many artisans may have practiced their craft on a part-time basis, there were also full-time specialists. These resided in the towns and cities, and many of them were highly skilled individuals producing special products, such as steatite seals, large storage jars, or the exceptionally long carnelian beads. Such skills required many years to perfect and were probably handed down from parent to child. Also resident in the urban settlements (though less visible archaeologically) were priests, officials, and other presumed members of the elite, as well as those who engaged in menial tasks such as cleaning drains. The arrangement of some houses to include a cubicle at the front door suggests that some households employed the services of a watchman. There may have been other full-time specialists, particularly in the cities, such as builders to maintain the wells and civic amenities, though these tasks might alternatively have been undertaken by citizens as corvée. It seems likely that the latter was also the means used to bring together the large teams required to construct major projects such as the platforms on which many towns and cities were built.

Merchants must have had their homes in the towns and cities, though their work would have taken them far afield. Overseas trade required skilled navigators and sailors. While conditions at sea limited sea voyages to certain times of the year, sea trade was probably a full-time occupation, involving long stays in foreign parts waiting for the right sailing conditions for the journey home. Repairs to vessels and the construction of new ones would have occupied the months back home and also involved specialist skills. River traffic, however, was possible for most of the year and may well have been conducted by people who lived in houseboats like those of modern river folk such as the Mohana, who are sailors and fishers.

CLUES TO POLITICAL ORGANIZATION

The nature of Harappan political organization has been endlessly debated. Evidence is extremely limited and open to many different interpretations. The highly organized system of craft production, the uniformity in artifacts, the planned layout of urban settlements, the well-attested overseas trade, and other distinctive aspects of Indus culture indicate the existence of occupational specialization and an overarching system of organization and control. However, many of the characteristic features of hierarchical states, such as palaces, rich burials, large-scale state storage facilities, and a military force for internal policing and external aggression, so visible in other civilizations, are apparently absent. What makes the situation even more puzzling is the sheer size of the Indus polity. In the face of this mystery, some scholars argue that the Indus civilization was not a state at all and seek other explanations for its striking uniformities.

Written Traces of Bureaucracy

Many civilizations have left ample evidence of bureaucracy in the form of written accounts. These are not available for the Indus civilization, and it is not known whether they existed in perishable form, such as palm leaves, cloth, or bark, or never existed. Nevertheless, the few inscribed materials that have been found offer some clues to Harappan sociopolitical organization.

Seals. Square stamp seals of steatite account for the majority of Harappan inscribed materials. Nearly all come from Mohenjo-daro or Harappa, but some are known from many towns and cities, including far-off Shortugai, and from some villages, such as Rojdi. Some have also been found abroad, in Sumerian cities, Susa, and the Gulf.

The seals have a perforated boss on the reverse, suggesting they were usually worn on a cord. Many of the known examples were lost when the boss broke away: Finds of these at Harappa occur generally along main roads, in certain workshops, and in houses in certain areas. Very occasionally, a seal has been recovered from a place of safety, for example, buried beneath a house floor, but far more common are broken seals that had been discarded. None have been found in burials. This distribution suggests that the seals were not personal possessions but objects related to some official role, disposed of when the holder left office.

The discovery of sealings at a few sites shows that the seals were used to stamp clay attached to packaging on goods or sealing jars. Almost all known sealings come from the warehouse at Lothal where they were fortuitously preserved by a fire: This suggests that sealings were in fact far more common than the meager number of finds would indicate. While some seals show signs of considerable wear, others were almost pristine, suggesting that the seals also served another function, most probably to identify the holder and to authorize certain activities that he (or she?) undertook.

A seal from Harappa. The design is the unicorn, the most common symbol, which I suggest showed that the holder represented the Harappan state in some capacity. Along the top is the inscription, written in reverse so that the impression it made would be in the correct direction to be read. This inscription begins with an oval with a curved line in each corner, thought by some scholars to represent the city, and ends with the "handled jar," a very common sign, usually placed at the end of an inscription or of a segment within it. The second sign, two short raised lines, is also in the place it generally occupies in inscriptions. (Harappa Archaeological Research Project, Courtesy Department of Archaeology and Museums, Government of Pakistan)

Harappan seals bore two things: a design and an inscription. The design could be recognized and its significance understood by anyone, while the inscription could be read only by the literate few. The Indus script is still undeciphered, so it is uncertain what these inscriptions said, but studies of seals from other cultures suggest they were probably personal names, titles, or both. On the stamp seals, the inscription was written in reverse, showing that it was usually read from sealings or impressions, not from the seal itself.

All but a few of the images on seals depicted a single animal, often with a feeding trough in front of it. The most common was the unicorn, a creature with a single horn combining elements of a humpless bull and an antelope. Unicorn seals have been found in most Indus towns and cities, particularly in Mohenjo-daro; more than a thousand are known, while fewer than a hundred have been found of any other individual design. Around fifty seals depict a zebu bull: These are almost all confined to Mohenjo-daro and Harappa, though one is known from Kalibangan. Zebu seals were generally large and beautifully executed, and they had short inscriptions. Other animals included the elephant, the rhino, the humpless bull, the tiger, the water buffalo, the sheep, and the goat, and were mainly wild creatures native to the Indus region. A very small number of seals bear scenes rather than individual animals. These seals were generally larger than average and must have had a special significance. While the depiction of the animals was standardized, with only small differences occurring in their detail, the scenes are unique, though some share a theme.

Interpreting the Seals. Many scholars consider that the animals depicted represented particular groups. Some see them as clan totems and argue that the unicorn was the sign of the dominant house, with other, less successful clans occupying positions of lesser status. Other scholars argue that the seal images were totems associated with individual cities, the unicorn representing Mohenjo-daro and its ubiquity reflecting that city's leading power in the organization of the civilization. Still others associate the different animals with individual social or occupational groups in the society, the rare zebu seals associated with the rulers themselves, the unicorn seals representing the elite or officials, and other animals or designs standing for lesser groups. Some scholars have seen evidence in the seal images of the existence of separate sociopolitical entities within the Indus region rather than a unified state. The standardized nature of the seals, however, favors the interpretation of the Indus realms as a single unified polity. Separate petty states would have been likely each to have its own distinctive style of seal. Rissman (1989), in a study of the unicorn seals, has shown that there were small stylistic variations and differences of detail among representations of the unicorn in different regions but general adherence to a standard iconography and execution, with all the main details being the same.

My own view is that the motif on the seals provided an easily recognized indication of the status or authority of the holder and of his (or perhaps her) field of operation. One might, on the basis of general distribution and ubiquity, suggest that the unicorn motif symbolized the Harappan state and its bureaucracy and that the bearer was on government business. It might have identified the bearer to individuals such as guards on city gates, workers in warehouses, or carriers, to expedite entry, ensure cooperation, or demonstrate the bearer's right to take delivery of goods. The majority of Harappan seals found in the Gulf and Mesopotamia bore the bull and manger motif, a common motif in the Indus realms too, and this perhaps denoted an individual authorized to engage in foreign trade. Perhaps this is supported by the fact that only humpless cattle were found overseas, in contrast to the local zebu. Other animal motifs would have represented other areas of state activity, while the unique seals with scenes or related images, which generally have a religious theme, could have been the personal emblems of those in the positions of highest authority, such as chief priest or king. Alternatively, the latter might have been represented by the beautiful zebu seals. A few seals are known that have the same inscription but different images. In this case, presumably, the bearer had authorization to operate in two different capacities.

Many of the seals that have been found were broken: It is quite likely that this was done deliberately when the seal ceased to be valid, for example, on the death of the authorized bearer. The discovery of heavily worn seals shows that they could continue in use for a long time, suggesting that a seal could have been issued to an individual for the duration of that person's working life.

Seals would have functioned somewhat differently when used to create sealings. These, placed on goods and materials in transit, conveyed information in the absence of the seal bearer. Goods and materials to be transported from one part of the Harappan realms to another would have been packed and a sealing affixed to ensure that the goods were taken to the appropriate destination and were not tampered with in transit. Sealings might also signify that a package had passed through the requisite official controls. One might surmise that the goods stored in the Lothal warehouse at the time of the fire were in transit: A unicorn seal on the packages allowed those handling them to recognize that these were intended for internal distribution, while those bearing an elephant seal might have been intended for use in the external exchange network. People in authority could read the name or title on the seals to provide them with the relevant information on the source of the goods or materials and thereby gain more detailed information on their destination or designated use.

Given that the majority of seals come from the places where they were lost or discarded rather than those in which they were used, the distribution of seals within settlements offers little information. However, in order to lose something in a place one must be there. It is therefore perhaps significant that at Harappa no seals were found in the area in the northwest of mound E where pottery, a commodity locally distributed, was made, whereas a number of inscribed objects came from the area where beads and bangles were made, these being goods that were widely circulated through the internal distribution network.

Stoneware Bangles. Small, very fine stoneware bangles of an exact standard size, whose production involved considerable skill and time, were manufactured at

Mohenjo-daro and probably Harappa. Each bore a short inscription. For firing, the bangles were sealed in a nest of containers, each sealed with clay on which Indus signs were incised, finishing with the impression of a unicorn seal on the outer covering of clay. In early civilizations, where literacy was confined to an often very restricted group, writing was used as a means of wielding spiritual or temporal control and power. The use of the Indus writing on the firing containers therefore implies official control of production.

The uniform narrow interior diameter of these stoneware rings, 5.5–6 centimeters, suggests that they may not have been worn as conventional bangles on the wrist or ankle, particularly if their wearers were men; instead they may have been sewn onto clothing or worn as a pendant or on a belt. The Priest-King statue, possibly a royal portrait, wears a circle in the center of his headband, and another on a band on his upper arm: if the statue were life-sized, these rings would match the stoneware bangles in size. (However, there are other possible interpretations of the rings worn by this sculpture: A gold bead with steatite inlay, found at Harappa, is also similar, though its proportions are different.) The stoneware bangles were produced in some quantity (ten in each container, and probably a number of containers in each kiln firing), suggesting that they were worn by more than one individual: It seems likely that they were badges of office held by leading members of the hierarchy. The fact that the bangles themselves were inscribed is also suggestive of an official function. Their use was almost exclusively confined to Mohenjo-daro and Harappa, regional centers of power and administration where one would expect to find symbolic objects that identified the holders of high office.

Other Inscribed Materials. Many of the inscribed objects from Harappan sites are likely not to have had any official significance. For example, small tablets of various materials were probably amulets, while tools with inscriptions may record the owner's name or a charm to ensure the tool's successful use. However, a number of pottery vessels, such as large jars or small drinking cups, bear a few signs impressed on them before they were fired—perhaps an indication of their contents or ownership. Graffiti, less formal and much less standardized than writing, were scratched on some vessels at some time after the vessel was fired— the personal mark of the owner or a check mark by an official, perhaps.

Settlement Hierarchy

The Harappan settlement pattern may offer some clues to the organization of society. The settlements fall basically into three categories. First there are a very few enormous settlements, the cities. These were at least 60 hectares in extent (Dholavira, which may actually be as much as 100 hectares) and could be as large as 250 hectares (Mohenjo-daro). Four (Dholavira, Mohenjo-daro, Harappa, and Rakhigarhi) have been investigated at least to some extent; Ganweriwala and perhaps others have been identified but require investigation to confirm their extent and nature. These cities were spaced fairly evenly throughout the Harappan realms and were separated from each other by somewhere between 280 and 600 kilometers. It is interesting to compare this arrangement with that in Sumer where the cities, which housed around 80 percent of the population, were far more numerous and were situated only about 20–60 kilometers apart, but distributed lineally since they were confined to the narrow floodplains of branches of the Euphrates. Harappan cities each served a huge domain of between 100,000 and 170,000 square kilometers, providing the full range of urban functions, including administration, social leadership, and specialist industries. Presumably, the cities also provided a religious focus, although it is only in the case of Mohenjo-daro that this is clear.

At the opposite end of the spectrum were rural settlements: farming villages, pastoralist and hunter-gatherer camps, and fishing villages. These could range in size from less than a hectare to 7 or 8 hectares. Their inhabitants were essentially primary producers of subsistence products who would also have undertaken domestic crafts such as weaving and woodworking. In addition, there were villages whose inhabitants were specialists, such as the shellfishers and shellworkers of Nageshwar. These settlements had none of the complexity of towns but were probably not self-sufficient in subsistence products like villages. They may have been occupied only seasonally by people who spent the rest of the year in primary production.

The third category, towns, is an amorphous catch-all, including a great diversity of different types of settlement. They were usually quite small, around 1 to 5 hectares, and, though some were larger, few exceeded 16 hectares. This figure does not include the suburbs that may have existed outside many towns; traces of suburban settlement have been reported outside a few and are suspected at others, but none has been properly investigated.

While towns resembled cities in that they housed officials, traders, and other occupational specialists and probably provided services for the people of their area, the majority were also specialist centers. Some, such as Balakot, were centers of craft production; others were ports, like Sutkagen-dor, or trading centers, like Shortugai. However, they shared certain features: They were all, to a greater or less extent, involved in craft production, usually of a specialist nature, making goods from local materials or materials brought there from a connected region, for distribution within the entire state and sometimes also for export; they all played some role in the internal distribution network, including storing goods and materials for onward transmission; and those on the periphery were located to fulfill a role also in the procurement of goods and materials from external regions. They were all small enough to be supported by the produce of their hinterland and probably all included primary producers, such as farmers and fishers, among their inhabitants, particularly in the suburbs from which these people could have easy access to their fields or to the rivers or coasts. The same is probably true of cities.

The settlement pattern seems to indicate that both towns and villages were tributary directly to their local domain capital (city), links between them being maintained by pastoralists and via water transport; towns also acted as funnels through which local goods were channeled toward the city.

The impression given by this settlement pattern is very different from the village-town-city hierarchy familiar from many cultures, in which villages looked to their nearest town for manufactured goods and services and local administration and in turn provided the town with subsistence products, while the city provided overall administration, specialist services, and specialist industries, whose products reached only the elite of the towns in its territory, from which it received subsistence produce. In states the apex of this food chain pyramid of replicated units was a capital to which all the rest of the settlements were politically, socially, and economically subordinate.

The Harappan state, in contrast, was more akin to a body: a single functioning entity composed of a number of different and complementary units, each with its own particular function within the whole. The head, limbs, organs, and other parts of the body equate to farming villages, pastoral camps, trade centers, hunter-gatherer camps, fishing villages, procurement centers, processing centers, and other types of Harappan settlement. As parts of the body are made up of cells, sharing the same basic biological elements but often specialized in function, so the Harappan settlements were made up of people who were occupational specialists, including officials and priests, as well as farmers, pastoralists, fishers, artisans, and traders, their composition depending on the function of the settlement. To continue the analogy, the internal distribution network was the circulation system that ensured that all the things necessary for life reached all parts of the body (state). Whether this had one head (Mohenjo-daro or Harappa), two, five or more is not yet apparent, but clearly this state was unusual for its time in how it operated.

The Organization of Craft Production

While some craft activities, such as spinning and weaving, took place within the home, many Harappan artifacts were made by professional artisans. Probably many rural artisans were part-time specialists, engaged in craft activities alongside subsistence production, during the slack period in the farming agricultural year, during the off-season for fishing, or as part of the seasonal round for pastoralists or hunter-gatherers. Some goods were manufactured close to the source of the appropriate raw materials, either in dedicated settlements, such as the shellworking village of Nageshwar, or in towns that specialized in their production, such as Balakot where fishing and shellworking were the major occupations. Raw materials might also be transferred to an industrial center, where a variety of raw materials from the local region were worked, as at Lothal, which had workshops making stone beads, objects of shell and ivory, and pottery as well as objects of copper from farther afield. Some raw materials were processed to reduce their bulk before being sent on to towns, where they were made into finished goods: For example, flint quarried in the Rohri Hills was knapped in situ to make flakes and blades that were turned into tools in the towns and cities. Major settlements were centers with many industries, using raw or partially processed materials sent on from their source areas, as well as manufacturing artificial materials such as faience. Here skilled artisans made specialized products such as seals, as well as ordinary objects like metal tools. Data from surveys in Cholistan suggest that many towns were surrounded by satellite industrial settlements; this may have been a more widespread pattern.

The material in the first phase of occupation at Nageshwar included none of the local Gujarat (Sorath) wares, suggesting its establishment as a shellworking settlement was centrally inspired rather than a local development, another indication of state involvement in craft production.

The distribution of craft-working debris, such as dumps of overfired pottery and vitrified kiln linings, discarded pieces of raw materials, and broken manufacturing tools, has been used to gain an insight into the organization of craft production within settlements. Small workshops for light industry were scattered throughout the city of Mohenjo-daro, each probably operated by a single family. Different crafts were often located side by side, rather than in quarters dedicated to particular crafts. But there were also a few larger-scale operations: factories rather than domestic workshops. It is likely that more of these were located in the city's suburbs, particularly those where the production process produced noxious fumes or other industrial pollution. This was true of the 4-hectare industrial site discovered east of the Lower Town, where shell processing and probably copper working took place. At Harappa the HARP team located an area in mound E that was devoted throughout the city's life to the manufacture of particular types of pottery. Other industrial areas and individual workshops were found in other parts of the city.

Although many of the artisans seem to have been involved in small-scale operations, clearly craft production was highly organized. The situation at Gola Dhoro is revealing: There the material for beadmaking was stored in the citadel, although the beads were manufactured in the unwalled settlement. This seems to imply official supervision of the issuing of raw materials and control over production. Individual workshops, both in small, specialized settlements and in major centers, often concentrated on producing particular products rather than a full range: For example, in the shell industry ladles might be made in one workshop, chank shell bangles in another, inlay pieces in a third. Often the debris from one manufacturing process was passed on to other specialists, to be made into smaller objects, such as beads and gaming pieces. In some cases, however, related industries might be grouped together in a single workshop, such as the beadmaking workshop at Chanhu-daro, where seals were also made. The distribution of different products depended on their nature and quality. For instance, fine chank shell bangles were widely distributed, reaching even Shortugai on the distant Amu Darya, but inferior bangles of clam shell were made at Balakot for distribution only in the Makran region.

The Organization of Distribution

For millennia pastoralists had played an important role in the movement of goods and materials throughout the regions bordering the Iranian plateau. One of the key factors in the emergence of the Indus civilization was the development of water transport, allowing goods to be moved over long distances in bulk and with relatively little labor input. Combined with pastoralist and hunter-gatherer carriers and short-distance transport in carts, water transport gave the Harappans a highly efficient internal distribution network and access to materials and goods from external sources.

A high degree of bureaucratic control is implied by the organization of craft production, with large quantities of goods being produced in stages in a series of different centers; by the efficient procurement of large quantities of raw materials (and probably Mesopotamian manufactured goods) from external sources; and by the distribution of these products throughout the civilization. Raw materials and manufactured goods were not the only commodities being distributed. For example, many bones of marine fish at Harappa show that dried fish from the coast were transported to the opposite end of the Indus realms in considerable quantities. Conversely, grain may have been transported from the plains to Gujarat, which may not have been agriculturally self-sufficient, a situation that was altered by the introduction of *kharif* crops in the early second millennium.

It is probable that the Harappan state had a number of officials, including traders organizing external procurement, overseers supervising craft production, and administrators organizing the collection, shipment or carriage, and redistribution of goods and materials. This was the context in which seals and sealings were used, providing a means of communicating authority in face-to-face situations, and long-range instructions on handling and destination. Seals are known to have been made at Mohenjo-daro, Harappa, and Chanhu-daro; their production was probably restricted to cities and major towns that were nodes in the administrative network. At Lothal, for example, there is no sign of the debris from seal making.

A major feature of the Harappan distribution network is that it did not involve the accumulation of large quantities of grain, raw materials, and manufactured goods in state stores. Storage facilities are known, such as the warehouse at Lothal and the bins and jars at Kuntasi and Gola Dhoro, and less certainly the Granary at Mohenjo-daro, but these are relatively small. This suggests that storage was temporary, providing a place where goods and materials could be kept and probably guarded while in transit between producer and consumer or between legs of their journey, for example, between water and land transport. This argues for an efficient and rapid turnover of goods and materials, one that involved a constant traffic in small quantities of commodities rather than bulk movement at certain times of year. If the state was financed by taxes of some kind, these must have been collected regularly in small quantities and quickly disbursed: This would fit the evidence of guard posts at city gates, which have been interpreted as collection points for tolls or customs' dues.

Some goods and materials would have been carried over long distances as intact packages, for example, being transported from the ports of the Makran to the towns of the Kachi plain by pastoralists moving to the summer pastures of the Baluchi uplands, then by others moving down to the Kachi plain in winter. The massive unexcavated site of Pathani Damb at the foot of the Mula pass may have been a city or at least a major town that was the gateway back into the Harappan realms at the terminus of this transport route. Generally, however, the consignments of goods and materials are likely to have been transported over short distances between nodes in the distribution network, where they were opened, sorted, and repackaged into different consignments for onward transmission to various destinations. At these nodes materials could also be distributed to artisans to be manufactured into blanks or finished goods, which would be collected and either distributed locally or packaged and sent on. The large quantity of copper tools found at Allahdino may reflect its functioning as such a collection, transit, and distribution node. Similarly, pieces of several types of jasper were brought to Gola Dhoro from Saurashtra 70 kilometers to the southwest: While the mottled variety was worked into beads there, the variegated jasper was not used at Gola Dhoro but rather stored for onward distribution.

The Mobilization of Labor

The power of the Harappan state to mobilize huge workforces is apparent in the construction of the massive platforms on which many of the towns and cities were built. Those at Mohenjo-daro are the most impressive feat: Jansen calculated that the platform underlying the citadel there would have required 300,000–400,000 man-days' labor to build. Equally impressive were the walls that surrounded many of the urban settlements, freestanding or as revetment for the platforms: These were in some cases more than 15 meters thick and could be as high as 9 meters, and they were furnished with elaborate gateways.

The sinking of wells was also a substantial undertaking: Mohenjo-daro is thought to have had around seven hundred, created during the foundation phase of the city's construction. Digging the reservoirs at Dholavira was also a vast project: At least sixteen in number, they together covered about 17 hectares and were excavated down to bedrock or in some areas cut down into it. Soil taken from them was built up into massive bunds (dykes), up to 7 meters wide and faced with masonry, running between the reservoirs. A number of dams were created on the two seasonal streams, running past the settlement to divert water into the reservoirs. In addition to the labor of their original construction, regular work was required to maintain the reservoirs and remove any accumulated silt. While not on the same scale, the Great Bath at Mohenjo-daro and the dock at Lothal were also considerable feats of hydraulic engineering.

The Harappans did not build monumental temples or tombs but these platforms, walls, and basins were similarly vast projects requiring the bringing together, feeding, and management of huge numbers of workers. While the work at Dholavira and Lothal may have been undertaken during the slack period of the agricultural year by the inhabitants of the city and its hinterland over the course of a number of years, the construction of the platforms and walls for the foundation of towns and cities were undertakings that had to be completed before the first houses could be built, and work could take place only during the winter months when the plains were clear of floods. Small huts found by the Aachen team when investigating the Mohenjo-daro citadel platform were probably occupied by the workforce.

Though on a smaller scale, there is evidence that suggests communities were organized to work together on a regular basis. In the Late Harappan period, after the breakdown of state control, individual households at Rojdi stored their grain in the ear (whole and unprocessed) and threshed it as and when they needed it. This contrasts to the situation during the Mature Harappan period when the grain was threshed and winnowed communally and stored as processed grain. Other substantial projects, such as the building and maintenance of the seagoing ships, have left no trace but must have taken place. Whether labor was also invested in digging and maintaining irrigation works is uncertain.

Uniformity and Standardization

The unity of the Indus civilization and the shared acceptance of an ideological system is demonstrated by the uniformity and standardization of many aspects of the Harappan material world. This is seen particularly in the layout of the towns and cities, which seem to have been conceived and built to a regular plan, following an accepted canon with variations as locally required.

Weights and Measures. The Harappans used a standardized system of weights and measures throughout their state; while only a few measuring rules have been found, weights are ubiquitous. Their conformity to a standard is highly significant. In Mesopotamia the early city-states used various systems, and it was not until the political unification of southern Mesopotamia under the Akkadian kings that a single standardized system came into use. With the collapse of the Akkadian empire, this system broke down and had to be reintroduced when southern Mesopotamia was reunified under the Ur III dynasty. In the Indus realms, however, standardized weights were present from the beginning of the Mature Harappan period, providing a strong suggestion that by the start of this period there was political unity. The use of standardized weights throughout the Harappan realms amply demonstrates the existence of a statewide system of organization that could dictate, monitor, and guarantee such uniformity. Regular checks must have been carried out by officials to ensure that these weights remained accurate: Very little deviation from the standard has been detected in the weights found.

The weights were found in all the settlements of the Harappan realms, but the full range of sizes was known only from the large urban centers while rural settlements had a limited range. The existence of standardized weights implies official control, centrally managed, over transactions involving the state, such as taxation; the issuing of materials for officially sponsored trade and receipt of materials resulting from such trade; the issuing or receipt of goods moving within the internal distribution network; the issuing of materials to artisans for the manufacture of goods and the checking of the resulting products; or the issuing of food rations for those engaged in state-sponsored activities.

At Harappa, a large number of weights were found immediately inside the city gates, which were designed to control and monitor traffic. This suggests that a toll was taken there on goods and materials entering or leaving the city.

Artifacts. The uniformity of Harappan artifacts must reflect an underlying ideology that dictated the "right" form for them to take, which was adhered to throughout the Harappan realms. Though some objects, such as shell bangles, could have been manufactured in relatively few workshops and widely distributed from these, the same was not true of pottery, required by every household, whose fragility made it impractical to transport in large quantities over long distances and which was probably manufactured in every town. Artisans therefore were manufacturing goods to a known template. This did not, however, mean that the repertoire of Harappan objects was unvarying: For example, scored goblets, used to contain liquids, were made with round bases for much of the Mature Harappan period but were eventually superseded by a pointed-based form, produced in huge quantities. The wider repertoire of forms (for example, in pottery) and of varieties of particular artifacts (for example, inscribed objects) that were found in Mohenjo-daro and Harappa may in some cases reflect the presence there of individuals or groups of people tasked with roles not required outside the cities, such as the senior positions in the bureaucracy. In other cases they may have been luxury products manufactured for the city-dwelling elite; to a considerable extent, the two groups are likely to have been the same people.

Warfare

Harappan Warfare? Wheeler's interpretation of his excavations at Mohenjo-daro and Harappa in the 1940s reflected a mind-set conditioned by active military service in two world wars and much archaeological experience with the Roman era. He therefore looked for, and believed he had found, evidence of Harappan militarism. The massive walls around the citadels were clearly defensive to Wheeler's eyes. Many Harappan artifacts could have been weapons, such as arrowheads, spearheads, and daggers, though to Wheeler's credit he admitted that these could have been used for other purposes such as hunting. In the streets of Mohenjo-daro, Wheeler reported evidence of a massacre: the last-ditch stand of the unfortunate inhabitants, slain in defense of the city.

In the years since Wheeler's investigations, this evidence has all fallen away. Wheeler's massacre victims seem more likely to have fallen to disease. None of the (admittedly few) excavated burials show signs of death by violence, except for a man from Kalibangan who suffered a fatal knee injury, quite possibly accidental. It has been shown that the city walls cannot have been constructed for defense. In particular, the gateways are not designed to impede the entrance of enemies or give military advantage to defenders. Instead the walls were often revetments for the platforms that provided defense against the constant threat of flooding, as well as demarcation for the principal areas of settlements, while the gateways enabled access to be controlled and probably tithes collected. The walls were probably also designed to impress.

The one area where town walls seem more convincingly defensive is on the west coast. Towns strongly fortified with stone walls, including Surkotada, Sutkagen-dor, and Kuntasi, may have been places of particular security, located where considerable quantities of valuables were stored when they entered or left the Harappan realms. Clay slingshot have been reported in the guardrooms flanking the gateway at Kuntasi (though they were also found in the village of Kanewal where they were probably used against animals that threatened the domestic herds). That it was property rather than people being defended by the stone walls is shown by the presence at all these sites of extra-mural settlement.

The Ubiquity of Warfare. That the Harappan civilization might have been a land without conflict is one of its most surprising aspects. A comparison with other civilizations shows how unusual and unexpected this is: For example, the texts of contemporary southern Mesopotamia are full of references to warfare, and there are numerous depictions of soldiers and battles. These civilizations often had periods of peace and strong government, but these were usually interspersed with fighting between rival groups.

Written sources attest to these struggles: Could they still be detected in the absence of literary evidence? This is a crucial question when considering the apparent absence of warfare in the Harappan state.

Social Control. The potential use of force as a sanction was one of the means by which rulers in the early civilizations could control their realms and their people. In its absence, what could have held together the Indus civilization and ensured cooperation among the members of society? In most civilizations, religion was a powerful force, and rule by religious authorities backed by reli-gious sanctions often preceded that of secular rulers backed by force. It may be suggested that the ideological basis of Harappan society made the need for physical deterrents unnecessary and that order was maintained by consent and the fear of offending against social and religious norms.

The Need for Warfare. The Harappans enjoyed an unusual situation when compared with other contemporary and later civilizations in that they lacked a natural enemy. The inhabitants of prosperous Mesopotamia were perpetually on the defensive against the mobile peoples of the desert and mountain re-gions that bordered their lands; the control of vital canal water for irrigation was a common source of friction between cities within Sumer and Akkad; and they were often competing with powerful neighbors, the state of Elam, and later others. Comparable problems were experienced by the Chinese, beset by Central Asian nomads; by the Greek city-states competing for control of lim-ited land and other resources; and similarly by others. The Harappans, in con-trast, were descended from the pastoral nomads of the mountain massif on their west and maintained good, probably kin-based, relations with them, even though the inhabitants of the northern part of the Indo-Iranian border-lands were not under Harappan political control and those of the Kulli culture in southern Baluchistan only loosely so. The presence of these well-disposed highland cultures on their border provided a buffer between the Harappans and their nearest civilized neighbors, the Helmand culture, and the mountains themselves were probably a sufficient deterrent to an armed invasion from the Iranian plateau. Within the Harappan realm, the diversity of resources and economic potential of the different regions and the great productivity of its lands and relatively low population meant that there was no spur to conflict and considerable benefits to be gained from cooperation among the inhabitants of the different regions. Population density in neighboring regions, such as the Aravallis, was even lower, and the benefits of peaceful cooperation even greater, given the relative technological levels of the Harappans and their neighbors. To the south was the sea, the only potentially hostile border, though Harappan shipping probably commanded the sea lanes, and the people of the nearest landfall, Magan, were in friendly collaboration with the Harappans. Nevertheless, pirates, acknowledging no political masters, the guerilla fighters of the seas, have always been a danger to shipping, which had to be countered by physical force and superior seamanship, and if the Harappans had any need to defend themselves against armed attack, it would have been here. It may be in this context that the strongly fortified towns of the coastal regions should be viewed.

Historical Clues

Given the strength of tradition within the subcontinent, later social and political systems may shed light on the Indus system, from which they may have sprung.

The caste system, fundamental to the structure of Indian society in later times, has its basis in the concept of ritual purity. Contact with many elements of organic life introduces ritual pollution, and bathing can remove this in many cases. As different activities convey different degrees of pollution, a hierarchy is created by the activities that individual groups can perform and by other related practices: For instance, vegetarianism is more pure than meat eating, and various types of meat, such as game, are less polluting than others. While the caste system is the product of millennia of evolution, its origins may well lie in the religious beliefs of the Harappans.

Kenoyer (1989, 188) singles out a number of features relating to a hierarchy based on ritual purity that would be visible in the material record: segregation of living areas; private water sources, drainage, and waste disposal; and distinct types of vessels for preparing, cooking, and serving food. He points to the existence of separate sectors in the Harappan settlements, such as the walled citadel (though he notes the absence of such divisions in some small sites such as Allahdino) and the emphasis on privacy in the home, exemplified by the arrangement of the entrance to prevent the direct viewing of or access to the interior courtyard; to this one can add the restrictions on access within areas of the settlements and even within some structures. There were private wells and well developed systems of drainage and waste disposal in many Harappan settlements.

While in other societies, the quality and material of artifacts may provide an indication of the wealth of different groups and their ability to command access to restricted resources, it is possible that hierarchy among the Harappans may have been organized along different lines. If ritual purity were the key factor in determining status, as it may well have been, those higher up the status scale would be identifiable by their possession of artifacts and materials

Jars for rubbish were a common feature of Harappan towns and cities: this example is from Dholavira. They formed part of a complex system of water supply and waste disposal; while this system obviously had a practical value, it may also reflect concern with ritual purity, a fundamental principle underlying later Indian religion, which may have its roots in the Harappan period. (Namit Arora)

thought to be more pure. In traditional South Asia, materials such as metal that can be purified after use are more pure than those that cannot, such as unglazed terra-cotta. Different styles of particular objects may also be associated with people in different ritual status groups, usable among themselves but liable to be polluted if used by individuals of lower ritual status: For example, at Mohenjo-daro Dales and Kenoyer (1986) identified five different varieties of cooking vessel that might have been used by different status groups.

Allied to the social structure dictated by caste is a redistributive mechanism known as the *jajmani* system. In this system, all members of the community have reciprocal obligations to provide the products of their labors and certain services to others with whom they have a formalized relationship that to some extent resembles kinship. Payment for these goods and services is made in kind and fixed by tradition. The payments take place at regulated intervals and often in the context of religious festivals or other special occasions. Underlying the system is the notion of ritual purity: Some activities are pure, others not, and the caste hierarchy, based on degrees of ritual purity, is reflected in the division of labor. Ritually pure individuals require the services of impure individuals to perform tasks that would pollute them.

Crosscutting this system, which operates at the level of the community, is a wider network that links all members of a particular caste (*jati*), wherever they live. All members of a caste group (often organized in historical times into guilds) would look after each others' needs while exercising considerable control over the activities of each individual within it.

Something akin to these two systems may have underpinned the organization of the Harappan state. Local officials and local priests, supplied by the official distribution system, may have provided goods that people required for social, economic, and ritual purposes, in exchange for subsistence products and various types of labor such as craft activities or public building works. Kinship ties could also have resulted in the movement of goods and the supply of foodstuffs between town and country through the medium of pastoral members of the extended family during their seasonal movements, and a tithe of these could have been extracted by the state upon their entering or leaving the town or city.

Shared Ideology

Two contrasting features characterize the Harappan civilization: very marked standardization of many aspects of life and very marked heterogeneity in others, some as fundamental as religious practices. It seems that the people of the Indus civilization, from different backgrounds, often with different beliefs, all subscribed to the overarching ideology of the Harappan state, which must have had a religious component reflected in the cardinal orientation of the settlements and the strong emphasis on water and purification. This was also apparent in the social and economic spheres, where the shared ideology was displayed in aspects of personal appearance, such as ornaments of beads and shell, and in the standardized forms taken by most artifacts, throughout the Harappan realms.

REFERENCES

Bhan, Kuldeep, V. S. Sonawane, P. Ajithprasad, and S. Pratapchandran. 2005. "Gola Dhoro." [Online article; retrieved 7/5/05.] www.harappa.com/goladhoro/index.html.

Biagi, Paolo. "The Rohri Flint Quarries." [Online article; retrieved 6/14/05.] www.harappa.com/rohri/index.html.

Bisht, Ravi Singh. 1984. "Structural Remains and Town Planning of Banawali." In *Frontiers of the Indus Civilization,* edited by B. B. Lal and S. P. Gupta, 89–97. New Delhi: Books and Books.

Bisht, Ravi Singh. 2002. "Dholavira Excavations: 1990–94." In *Facets of Indian Civilization. Recent Perspectives. Essays in Honour of Professor B. B. Lal,* edited by Jagat Pati Joshi, 107–120. New Delhi: Aryan Books International.

Bisht, Ravi Singh, and Shashi Asthana. 1979. "Banawali and Some Other Recently Excavated Harappan Sites in India." In *South Asian Archaeology 1977,* edited by Maurizio Taddei, 223–240. Naples: Istituto Universitario Orientale, Seminario di Studi Asiatici.

Chattopadhyaya, Umesh C. 2002. "Researches in Archaeozoology of the Holocene Period (Including the Harappan Tradition in India and Pakistan)." In *Indian*

Archaeology in Retrospect. II. Protohistory. Archaeology of the Harappan Civilization, edited by S. Settar and Ravi Korisettar, 365–419. Indian Council of Historical Research. New Delhi: Manohar.

Chitalwala, Y. M. 1984. "The Problem of Class Structure in the Indus Civilization." In *Frontiers of the Indus Civilization,* edited by B. B. Lal and S. P. Gupta, 211–215. New Delhi: Books and Books.

Clark, Sharri. "Embodying Indus Life: Terracotta Figurines from Harappa." [Online article; retrieved 6/14/05.] www.harappa.com/figurines/index.html.

Dales, George F. and Jonathan Mark Kenoyer. 1986. *Excavations at Mohenjo Daro, Pakistan: the Pottery.* Philadelphia: University Museum, Pennsylvania.

Dhavalikar, M. K. 1996. *Kuntasi, a Harappan Emporium on West Coast.* Pune: Deccan College Post-Graduate and Research Institute.

Dumont, Louis. 1980. *Homo Hierarchicus.* Rev. ed. Chicago: University of Chicago Press.

Dutta, Pratap C. 1982. *The Bronze Age Harappans. A Bio-anthropological Study of the Skeletons Discovered at Harappa.* Calcutta: Anthropological Survey of India.

Fuller, Dorian. 2001. "Harappan Seeds and Agriculture: Some Considerations." *Antiquity* 75 (288): 410–414. [Online article; retrieved 2/25/06.] www.ucl.ac.uk/archaeology/staff/profiles/fuller/pdfs/AntiquityWeber%20debate.pdf.

Gupta, S. P. 1984. "Internal Trade of the Harappans." In *Frontiers of the Indus Civilization,* edited by B. B. Lal and S. P. Gupta, 417–424. New Delhi: Books and Books.

Jansen, Michael. 1987. "Preliminary Results on the 'Forma Urbis' Research at Mohenjo-Daro." In *Reports on Fieldwork Carried Out at Mohenjo-daro, Pakistan 1982–83 by the IsMEO-Aachen University Mission: Interim Reports II,* edited by Michael Jansen and Gunter Urban, 9–22. Aachen and Rome: RWTH and IsMEO.

Jansen, Michael. 2002. "Settlement Networks of the Indus Civilization." In *Indian Archaeology in Retrospect. II. Protohistory. Archaeology of the Harappan Civilization,* edited by S. Settar and Ravi Korisettar, 105–126. Indian Council of Historical Research. New Delhi: Manohar.

Kennedy, Kenneth A. R. 1982. "Skulls, Aryans and Flowing Drains: The Interface of Archaeology and Skeletal Biology in the Study of the Harappan Civilization." In *Harappan Civilization. A Contemporary Perspective,* edited by Gregory L. Possehl, 289–295. New Delhi: Oxford & IBH Publishing Co.

Kennedy, Kenneth A. R. 1984. "Trauma and Disease in the Ancient Harappans." In *Frontiers of the Indus Civilization,* edited by B. B. Lal and S. P. Gupta, 425–436. New Delhi: Books and Books.

Kennedy, Kenneth A. R. 2000. *God-Apes and Fossil Men. Palaeoanthropology of South Asia.* Ann Arbor: University of Michigan Press.

Kenoyer, Jonathan Mark. 1989. "Socio-Economic Structures in the Indus Civilization as Reflected in Specialized Crafts and the Question of Ritual Segregation." In *Old Problems and New Perspectives in the Archaeology of South Asia,* edited by Jonathan Mark Kenoyer, 183–192. Department of Anthropology. *Wisconsin Archaeological Reports.* Vol. 2. Madison: University of Wisconsin Press.

Kenoyer, Jonathan Mark. 1994a. "The Harappan State. Was It or Wasn't It?" In *From Sumer to Meluhha: Contributions to the Archaeology of South and West Asia in Memory of George F. Dales, Jr.,* edited by Jonathan Mark Kenoyer, 71–80. *Wisconsin Archaeological Reports.* Vol. 3. Department of Anthropology. Madison: University of Wisconsin Press.

Kenoyer, Jonathan Mark. 1994b. "Experimental Studies of Indus Valley Technology at Harappa." In *South Asian Archaeology 1993*, edited by Asko Parpola and Petteri Koskikallio, 345–362. Helsinki: Suomalainen Tiedeakatemia.

Kenoyer, Jonathan Mark. 1995. "Ideology and Legitimation in the Indus State as Revealed through Symbolic Objects." *The Archaeological Review* 4 (1 and 2): 87–131.

Kenoyer, Jonathan Mark. 1998. *Ancient Cities of the Indus Valley Civilization.* Karachi: Oxford University Press and American Institute of Pakistan Studies.

Kesarwani, A. 1984. "Harappan Gateways: A Functional Reassessment." In *Frontiers of the Indus Civilization,* edited by B. B. Lal and S. P. Gupta, 63–73. New Delhi: Books and Books.

Lal, B. B. 1993. "A Glimpse of the Social Stratification and Political Set-up of the Indus Civilization." *Harappan Studies* 1: 63–71.

Lovell, N. C., and Kenneth A. R. Kennedy. 1989. "Society and Disease in Prehistoric South Asia." In *Old Problems and New Perspectives in the Archaeology of South Asia,* edited by Jonathan Mark Kenoyer, 89–92. *Wisconsin Archaeological Report.* Vol. 2. Department of Anthropology. Madison: University of Wisconsin Press.

Lukacs, John R. 1982. "Dental Disease, Dietary Patterns and Subsistence at Harappa and Mohenjodaro." In *Harappan Civilization. A Contemporary Perspective,* edited by Gregory L. Possehl, 301–307. New Delhi: Oxford & IBH Publishing Co.

Lukacs, John R. 2002. "Bio-archaeology of Ancient India: An Integrated Perspective on the Past." In *Indian Archaeology in Retrospect. II. Protohistory. Archaeology of the Harappan Civilization,* edited by S. Settar and Ravi Korisettar, 93–109. Indian Council of Historical Research. New Delhi: Manohar.

Momin, K. N. 1984. "Village Harappans in Kheda District of Gujarat." In *Frontiers of the Indus Civilization,* edited by B. B. Lal and S. P. Gupta, 231–234. New Delhi: Books and Books.

Murty, M. L. K., and Gunther D. Sontheimer. 1980. "The Prehistoric Background to Pastoralism in the Southern Deccan in the Light of Oral Traditions and the Cults of Some Pastoral Communities." *Anthropos.* 75: 163–184.

Parpola, Asko. 1994. *Deciphering the Indus Script.* Cambridge, UK: Cambridge University Press.

Patel, Ajita. 1997. "The Pastoral Economy of Dholavira: A First Look at Animals and Urban Life in Third Millennium Kutch." In *South Asian Archaeology 1995,* edited by Raymond Allchin and Bridget Allchin, 101–113. New Delhi: Oxford & IBH Publishing Co.

Possehl, Gregory L. 1992. "The Harappan Cultural Mosaic: Ecology Revisited." In *South Asian Archaeology 1989,* edited by Catherine Jarrige, 237–241. Madison, WI: Prehistory Press.

Possehl, Gregory L. 2002. *The Indus Civilization. A Contemporary Perspective.* Walnut Creek, CA: AltaMira Press.

Puskas, Ildiko. 1984. "Society and Religion in the Indus Valley Civilization." In *South Asian Archaeology 1981,* edited by Bridget Allchin, 162–165. Cambridge, UK: Cambridge University Press.

Ratnagar, Shereen. 1991. *Enquiries into the Political Organization of Harappan Society.* New Delhi: Ravish.

Ratnagar, Shereen. 2001. *Understanding Harappa. Civilization in the Greater Indus Valley.* New Delhi: Tulika.

Ratnagar, Shereen. 2004. *Trading Encounters. From the Euphrates to the Indus in the Bronze Age.* New Delhi: Oxford University Press.

Rissman, Paul C. 1989. "The Organization of Seal Production in the Harappan Civilization." In *Old Problems and New Perspectives in the Archaeology of South Asia,* edited by Jonathan Mark Kenoyer, 159–169. *Wisconsin Archaeological Reports.* Vol. 2. Department of Anthropology. Madison: University of Wisconsin Press.

Shaffer, Jim G. 1982. "Harappan Commerce: An Alternative Perspective." In *Anthropology in Pakistan,* edited by Stephen Pastner and Louis Flam, 166–210. Ithaca, NY: Cornell University Press.

Sharma, A. K. 1982. "The Harappan Cemetery at Kalibangan: A Study." In *Harappan Civilization. A Contemporary Perspective,* edited by Gregory L. Possehl, 297–299. New Delhi: Oxford & IBH Publishing Co.

Sharma, A. K. 1999. *The Departed Harappans of Kalibangan.* New Delhi: Sundeep Prakashan.

Steen, A-B. 1986. "The Hindu Jajmani System—Economy or Religion? An Outline of Different Theories and Models." In *South Asian Religion and Society,* edited by Asko Parpola and B. Schmidt Hansen, 30–41. Copenhagen: Scandinavian Institute of Asian Studies.

Vidale, Massimo. 1989. "Specialized Producers and Urban Elites: On the Role of Craft Industries in Mature Harappan Urban Contexts." In *Old Problems and New Perspectives in the Archaeology of South Asia,* edited by Jonathan Mark Kenoyer, 170–181. *Wisconsin Archaeological Reports.* Vol. 2. Department of Anthropology. Madison: University of Wisconsin.

Wheeler, R. E. Mortimer. 1968. *The Indus Civilization.* 3rd ed. Cambridge, UK: Cambridge University Press.

Wright, R. P. 1989. "The Indus Valley and Mesopotamian Civilizations: A Comparative View of Ceramic Technology." In *Old Problems and New Perspectives in the Archaeology of South Asia,* edited by Jonathan Mark Kenoyer, 145–156. *Wisconsin Archaeological Reports.* Vol. 2. Department of Anthropology. Madison: University of Wisconsin Press.

IX

CHAPTER 9

Religion and Ideology

INTRODUCTION

Of all the aspects of Harappan life that have been studied, religion and the un-deciphered script have attracted the greatest number of wild speculations, as well as sober hypotheses. The paucity of indubitably religious structures has concentrated investigations mainly on religious iconography, of which the most informative is that found on inscribed objects: for this reason many theories have embraced both fields, using religious inferences as clues towards deciphering the script and taking postulated decipherments as offering information on the religion. Because many aspects of South Asian life show continuity with the past, traditional South Asian religion has frequently been trawled for clues that may aid our understanding of Harappan beliefs and practices.

RELIGIOUS STRUCTURES

Religion has played a major part in all societies, and religious structures are generally a prominent feature of emerging civilizations. Each culture has its own distinctive form of shrine or temple, but in general it is possible to recognize religious buildings and to distinguish them from domestic architecture. Even in simpler societies, shrines can often be identified on the basis of differences from domestic structures in their form, internal layout, and contents. Attempts to find such clues in the Indus civilization, however, have met with only limited success; few structures suggest a religious function, and these differ from place to place, a strange contrast to the cultural uniformity indicated by so many other aspects of the Indus civilization, although this diversity is echoed in that of later Indian beliefs and practices.

Shrines?

The citadel mound at Mohenjo-daro is one of the few places where convincing religious structures have been uncovered. In the northern part of the mound was the Great Bath, and in the south there was a complex of halls and rooms. Some of these were residential but the complex also included one chamber (room 100) to which access was possible only via a long secluded corridor between two blocks, though accessible from both. This contained a sculptured female head and may perhaps have been a shrine. A number of other structures in the complex that may also suggest a religious function include three circular brick rings that probably surrounded sacred trees. The main feature of the complex, the pillared hall, is generally considered to have been a place for secular public assemblies, but its use for religious purposes cannot be ruled out.

House 1 in the HR-A area in Mohenjo-daro's Lower Town has been identified as a possible temple. A pair of doorways led from a large open space, probably a courtyard, into two passages, between two separate blocks of rooms that were not accessible from House 1, though they were probably related to it. At the end of the passages was a courtyard containing a brick ring that, like those on the citadel mound, may once have surrounded a sacred tree. From this courtyard two staircases, facing one another, led up to a second, raised courtyard from which opened a number of rooms, some leading into others. It is possible that the visitor followed a circular route, entering through one doorway, taking the corresponding staircase to the upper courtyard, and returning via the other staircase, passage, and doorway.

This complex is unusual in a number of ways, in addition to its unique layout. Nowhere within it was there a well, a real rarity in this city and one that may emphasize a nondomestic role. It contained several pieces of stone sculpture, one just a head, the other a seated man, broken into three pieces: Stone sculpture is extremely rare at Mohenjo-daro and almost unknown in other Harappan settlements. Other objects were not the usual range of domestic utensils: They comprised a large number of seals, all bearing the unicorn motif; many pottery vessels, including a number of miniature pots; terra-cotta figurines; and jewelry; all types of object that might have been offerings. Other explanations are also possible: for example, this could have been an administrative building. A burial was found, beneath the upper courtyard floor, of a man wearing a faience neck ornament and ivory bangles. This burial may have taken place sometime late in the city's history and was perhaps related to an episode in which the statues from the complex were smashed and the pieces scattered in the adjacent area. The building also belonged to a late period of the city's history, having being modified from earlier structures.

Houses XXX, XXIII, and L in the HR-B area and block 8A in the DK-G area at Mohenjo-daro were buildings with massive bases to support superstructures that are now gone, and the incompletely exposed Block 11 in the DK-G area contained three wells approximately in a line. All these are unusual and have therefore been suggested by various scholars as temples, though there is no evidence of ritual practices or objects to support this interpretation. Similar difficulties have been encountered in the attempt to identify Harappan temples in other cities and towns, difficulties compounded by the lack of concrete knowledge of the ritual practices or objects that one would expect to be associated with a Harappan shrine.

Atre (2002) points out the humble appearance of shrines in modern Indian villages, differing little from domestic huts, and it is worth noting that substantial temples do not feature in the early part of India's historical period and that, when rock-cut temples began to appear, the architectural detail shows that they were modeled on wooden structures. Worship was often focused on sacred objects, such as trees, pillars, or relic mounds, sometimes enclosed in shrines. Practices associated with such venues included the offering of fruit, flowers, or other things, as well as walking around the sacred object in a clockwise direction *(pradakshina)*. In addition, religious practices could involve contemplation, or they could involve listening to sermons within a pillared hall. Perhaps, therefore, we should not be looking for temples as such in the Harappan state, or, at least, not for imposing structures.

The Great Bath

The stair from the west ascending to the citadel at Mohenjo-daro had at its summit a bathroom where those entering the area were probably required to purify themselves. Beyond the Granary lay the Great Bath complex: Two doors led through an antechamber into the fenestrated courtyard with, at its center, the Great Bath, a large rectangular basin, carefully constructed so as to be watertight. Steps at each end of the bath led down to a narrow ledge from which the water could be entered.

Most scholars regard this as a religious structure, connected with ritual bathing, which has played an important role in Indian religion for at least two and a half thousand years. The colonnade probably enabled those not permitted to set foot inside the courtyard to observe ceremonies taking place in the Great Bath.

The Great Bath at Mohenjo-daro, looking in from the antechamber to the fenestrated colonnade surrounding the bath, which was undoubtedly a ritual facility. Beyond can be seen the ruins of a residential area with bathrooms, perhaps occupied by priests. (J. M. Kenoyer, Courtesy Department of Archaeology and Museums, Government of Pakistan)

A large well lay to the east of the colonnade, along with a series of bathrooms, presumably for participants to purify themselves before taking part in a ritual. The complex could also be entered from this side and from the north, from the secluded residential area probably housing its staff (presumably priests). The superbly constructed Great Bath was unique and suggests that Mohenjo-daro was the religious center of the Harappan state, if not its political capital too.

Ritual Purification

Though there is nothing comparable to the Great Bath in the citadels of other Harappan towns and cities, some had water facilities, such as bathing platforms at Lothal and Kalibangan. The recent excavations at Dholavira revealed a number of water facilities in the citadel. One of these, a small tank in the Castle, may have been used for bathing: It has steps down to its floor, where there is a cylindrical block as a seat. There were also a larger water tank and a well and there may have been associated bathrooms.

Fine bathrooms connected to an excellent and efficient drainage system were a feature of many Indus houses, far more sophisticated than the sanitary arrangements of civilizations contemporary with the Harappan. The strong emphasis on bathing and the separation of pure from impure materials, such as wastewater, suggest a concern with cleanliness that went beyond the needs of hygiene, an indication that the concept of ritual purity, so important in later Indian religion, was already present in the Harappan belief system.

Fire

Fire, an element of almost equal importance to water, has also played a major role in Indian religion, as an agent of ritual purification and as a means of transmitting offerings to the gods. While water seems to have had a religious significance throughout the Harappan realms, ritual installations involving fire are at present known only from the southern parts, along the Saraswati and in Gujarat. These fire altars were first uncovered at Kalibangan, where one of the platforms in the southern part of the citadel had a row of seven oblong clay-lined pits containing charcoal, ash, and terra-cotta cakes; such cakes were used in kilns to retain heat and perhaps had a similar function in these fire pits. In each pit there was also a cylindrical or faceted clay stele, perhaps representing the lingam (sacred phallus). A paved bathing platform and a brick-lined well were associated with these pits. On another platform, a single fire altar was found alongside a rectangular brick-lined pit containing antlers and cattle bones, presumably from animal sacrifices. The use of these pits for making burnt offerings therefore seems a reasonable supposition. There was also a mound with other fire altars to the east of the town. Many of the houses in Kalibangan's lower town are reported to have had a room containing a fire altar, set aside as a domestic shrine. Many Indian houses today likewise have their own shrine, where incense is burned and food and flowers are offered to the gods.

Fire altars were also found at Rakhigarhi and Banawali in the east and at Lothal and Vagad in Gujarat. One suggested example at Nageshwar was alternatively, and more convincingly, identified as an updraft kiln. There was some variation in the form taken by both the pit and the clay stele in these sites. Some examples in the houses at Kalibangan were lined with mud bricks. At Lothal the fire altars were placed within brick enclosures in the lower town; they continued to be constructed there into the post-Harappan period.

The distinction between fire altars and domestic hearths is not always clear. Excavations at Nausharo have uncovered similar structures in a domestic context where they are interpreted as hearths, albeit of an unusual type; these bore some resemblance to the hearths used by the later inhabitants of the Deccan, which sometimes had a central clay support for pots. This therefore begs the question whether the domestic "fire altars" were in fact ordinary hearths or, conversely, whether all domestic hearths could have been used in family worship as well as for cooking.

ICONOGRAPHY

Aspects of traditional Indian religion may shed some light on the practices and beliefs of the Harappans, and other clues may come from the religions of the Harappans' neighbors. The Hindu religion is many stranded and complex, and it has seen many transformations down the ages; so, though elements of later Indian religion were clearly present in Harappan times, one cannot assume that Harappan religion closely paralleled that of later times.

Household shrines today may contain an image of one of the gods, while temples house massive statues of the deity. However, Hindu religion does not regard these images as embodiments of the gods themselves but as a focus for devotions and a housing within which the god may choose to manifest him- or herself. This has much in common with the relationship between god and image in ancient Mesopotamia.

Attempts have been made to identify figures in Indus art as similar representations of deities. It is likely, however, that the stone sculptures represented people rather than deities, perhaps being portraits of rulers, and that many terra-cottas were toys. It is also probable that there was a significant difference in function or meaning between the extremely rare sculptures in stone or bronze and the ubiquitous terra-cotta figurines and seal motifs.

Sculpture

Of the very small number of pieces of sculpture, in stone or bronze, almost all come from Mohenjo-daro. Apart from the poorly preserved head from the citadel, which is thought to be female, the stone sculptures from Mohenjo-daro depict a male figure. The sculptures are generally incomplete, but when the body survives, it is clad in a robe that covered only the left shoulder, similar to the style of dress adopted by monks, ascetics, and other religious figures in later times. These figures are normally shown squatting on one heel, with the other knee raised and clasped by the corresponding arm, a position that may suggest reverence or supplication before a deity: It is matched by the position adopted by figures shown on seals making offerings. The surviving heads generally have a beard, though some may be clean shaven. The hair may be short and neat, or it may be tied in a bun and held in place by a fillet encircling the head. The fillet was probably of gold since thin gold bands with holes for a thread to fasten them have been found at Mohenjo-daro and elsewhere.

The finest example of this sculptural theme is the torso known as the Priest-king, found at Mohenjo-daro. He is a calm, austere figure, with short, neatly combed hair tied in a headband whose ribbons trail down his back. The back of his head is a flat, angled surface, suggesting that something was affixed to complete the image, perhaps a headdress. He is wearing a robe covered with trefoils that originally held a red paste. The garment this represents was probably of some fine material sewn with appliqués. Asko Parpola, who has studied Harappan religious iconography in great detail, believes these trefoils may have had many layers of religious significance: Parallels with Mesopotamian and Central Asian art and with later Indian traditions suggest their identification as stars on a sky-garment; the association of the trefoil at Mohenjo-daro and elsewhere with the color red links it with fire and the

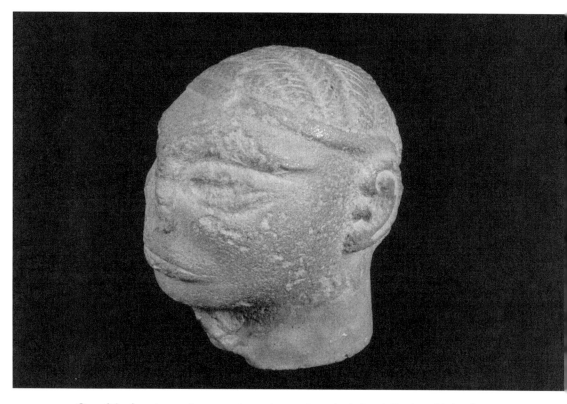

One of the few pieces of stone sculpture known from the Indus civilization, this head was probably part of a larger statue of a seated figure. Though similar in overall design, each figure is different, suggesting that they were portraits of individuals. (J. M. Kenoyer, Courtesy Department of Archaeology and Museums, Government of Pakistan)

hearth, which also later represents the yoni (vulva or womb), symbolizing rebirth in the heavenly realm. The yoni is the symbol of the goddess Durga and counterpart to the lingam (phallus), symbol of Shiva. In this context, trefoils decorate a finely polished red stone stand from Mohenjo-daro that may originally have supported a lingam. Parpola notes that the trefoil-shaped leaves of the bilva or wood-apple tree (*Aegle marmelos*) are traditionally used in the worship of the lingam. Similar trefoils decorate a number of (red) carnelian beads. Such speculations suggest valuable avenues for further investigation.

Two small sculptures from Harappa are very different in style. Each depicts a naked male torso; while the legs of both have broken off, dowel holes show that the arms and head were separately attached. One is in a posture that suggests he is dancing, the upper body swinging to one side while the left leg was originally raised in the opposite direction. The other figure, whose attribution to the Harappan period is not certain, also appears to be moving. Both are extremely naturalistic. Marshall compared the dancing figure to later images of Shiva Natraj (Lord of the Dance).

Two bronze figures have been found at Mohenjo-daro. Both depict young women, naked apart from a number of bangles and a necklace, and carrying something, perhaps a small bowl, in one hand. Though one is known as the Dancing-girl, the name refers to an assumption of her profession rather than to her stance since she is shown in a naturalistic, relaxed pose, one hand on her hip. The other figure stands more stiffly. A third bronze, from Chanhu-daro, is incomplete but is thought to depict a man, in the act of throwing something (perhaps a spear) overarm or dancing with a raised arm.

Terra-cotta Figurines

Numerous terra-cotta female figurines are known from Harappan sites. Many had panier-shaped headdresses, which may have served as lamps, probably in a sacred context, since some contained traces of a black residue, possibly burned oil. Some figurines at least probably served originally as votive offerings, though the great variety of places in which they have been found suggests that their role in ritual may have been confined to the ceremony in which they were offered and that they were then discarded, to be picked up and played with by children. Some female figures consisted of just a torso to which other features were later added. If the figures were acquired to be used as offerings, the additions may have defined aspects of the deity of particular relevance to the worshipper. Alternatively they may have been used as ex-votos in which the features selected related to the affliction suffered by the person who was making the offering, either in hope of or in gratitude for a cure.

Female figurines had been made by the cultures of the Indo-Iranian borderlands for thousands of years and continued to be popular in later millennia when they are often taken to represent Mother Goddesses. These play an important part in folk religion, being used in rituals connected with motherhood—to bring about conception, protect in childbirth, or guard the health of children. Some Harappan figurines similarly reflect such preoccupations, with their emphasis on generous breasts and wide hips, and their occasional depiction with a suckling baby. Female figurines are also used in a more general context, to ward off evil spirits and offer protection. However, many female figurines are not of the Mother Goddess type, and the latter have not been found throughout the Harappan realms but come mainly from sites in the Indus valley and the west. It is possible, as Marshall suggested, that these figurines were used as cult images in domestic shrines, though he preferred the idea that they were used as ex-votos. The less common male figures often emphasize the organs of generation, and there were also hermaphrodite figurines.

Representations of Animals

Some figurines may have been made specifically as toys. A number were jointed to allow their heads to bob or their limbs to move, and there were also model carts with moving wheels. However, animals played an important role in Harappan iconography, and many terra-cottas may have had a ritual use. Almost every creature that the Harappans were familiar with, from fishes and hares to elephants and rhinos, were depicted as terra-cotta figurines or as images on seals and other inscribed objects. Some terra-cottas may have been made for sacrifice, substituting for a live animal, a common practice in later times. Occasionally human or animal figurines were placed in burials. Small figurines, including squirrels, rams, and other animals molded in faience or carved in shell, may have been worn or carried as amulets.

Two miniature bronze animals are known from Mohenjo-daro: a beautiful water buffalo and a goat forming the end of a pin. There are also a few examples of animals sculpted in stone. Given the rarity of Indus sculptures, it seems likely that they had special significance, though this need not necessarily have been religious. Two stone figures of rams or bulls and a third of a composite beast are known from Mohenjo-daro. The latter has an elephant's trunk, ram's horns, and the body of a bull. Other depictions of hybrid animals occur, in terra-cotta and on seals, and, although none is exactly parallel to this one, a number of them use all these elements in different combinations, along with parts of tigers, water buffaloes, goats, and antelopes. In one example, the animal's tail is replaced by a cobra, a creature steeped in religious significance in India. Sometimes animals are shown with three heads, each from a different animal. Some also combine people and animals, particularly bulls, buffaloes, and tigers.

One seal depicts a pipal tree from whose trunk grow two unicorns' necks and heads. The unicorn is the most common image on seals. Although some scholars argue that this was a humpless bull shown in profile, it is more commonly thought that it represented a single-horned creature, combining features of both bull and antelope; a few figurines from Harappa, Chanhu-daro, and Lothal confirm this. It is clearly male, as are many other animals depicted on seals. Generally the unicorn is shown with a collar around its neck and a blanket across its frontquarters; often the blanket strongly resembles a pipal leaf. This is the most subtle version of the composite beast theme; the skillful blending of domestic and wild animals may have had iconographic significance, reflecting the integration of different ethnic groups or economic specialties into Harappan society.

Bulls and water buffalo played a major role in Harappan iconography. Massive bulls were a popular subject for figurines and were also shown on seals; the presence of cattle bones in the pit associated with a fire altar at Kalibangan and in another at Rakhigarhi indicates that cattle were chosen as sacrificial victims. Headdresses made from the horns of a buffalo or less commonly of a bull were worn by figures that seem to represent deities in mythological scenes on seals and in other contexts. Buffalo horns, often with pendant stars or associated with pipal leaves or flowers, also appeared on pottery from the Early Harappan period onward. A jar from Padri in Gujarat is decorated with a buffalo horn motif and with a large figure in a ragged skirt wearing an enormous pair of buffalo horns. Buffaloes frequently appear in scenes on seals or tablets, often in combat with humans. In some, a figure wrestles one or two animals; in others, a man stands with one foot on the animal's bowed head and pierces its body with a spear.

Scenes of combat between man and beast also feature tigers. In some, a male or female figure strangles two tigers; in others, a tiger is attacked by an individual with a bull's head. Some terra-cotta figurines depict tigers or other felines, and tiger stripes are shown on some of the figures identified as deities. In some scenes a stick figure sits in a neem tree, watched by a prowling tiger looking back over its shoulder. The figure balances on the tree branch with its legs in a similar posture to that of the stone sculptures, squatting on the heels with one knee raised; it is slender, wears neither clothes nor jewelry, and is apparently genderless. It seems that bovids and tigers, magnificent and powerful creatures, played a major and balancing role in the iconography of the Indus civilization, both individually and in combination. Both appear in later Indian religion, as vehicles for deities, as manifestations of gods in their more terrible forms, and as their opponents: for example, the goddess Durga riding a tiger and slaying the buffalo demon, Mahishasura. While the buffalo and bull, as well as the unicorn, are depicted as unmistakably male, tigers are not and may perhaps have been female, another significant duality.

The Harappans' concern with water is mirrored by the common occurrence of fish and gharials in their iconography. Parpola has convincingly argued that the fish sign in the Harappan script also represented stars, conceived to be swimming in the waters of the heavens. The words for "star" and "fish" are homonyms in the Dravidian languages (an early form of which might perhaps have been spoken by the Harappans), and Parpola has used this conjecture to identify the names of a number of constellations in the inscriptions on seals.

Sacred Trees

Nature plays an important part in mediating between the human and the divine in Indian religion, and so many plants and animals are venerated. Among these are trees, such as the pipal or *asvattha* (*Ficus religiosa*) and banyan (*Ficus indica*), the acacia (various species of *Acacia*), and the neem (*Azadirachta indica*). Often these are the abode of spirits, both benign and malevolent. From the

A cylindrical tablet showing a goddess fighting two tigers, with the sun above her and an elephant beneath. On the other face of this tablet is a scene in which a figure is spearing a water-buffalo, with his foot on its neck. Both scenes probably illustrate mythological themes. (J. M. Kenoyer, Courtesy Department of Archaeology and Museums, Government of Pakistan)

evidence of Harappan art it is apparent that these trees were already attracting such veneration. A number of tablets show an individual with a pot, apparently making an offering to a tree, usually a pipal. A few seals show figures that may be identified as gods and goddesses inside these trees, particularly the pipal, or under an arch of pipal leaves. These leaves had been a familiar decoration on pottery of the northwest since much earlier times; they were often combined with the horns of bulls or water buffaloes, and together they form headdresses worn by a number of deities. Sometimes the trees are shown standing in a pot or within an enclosure or a brick ring, as sacred trees were sometimes protected in later times. Several brick rings that may have protected such trees are known from Mohenjo-daro.

Possible Deities

Some Harappan inscribed objects bear scenes showing figures that display some of the features of later deities. Usually these figures, male or female, wear a horned headdress and bangles along the full length of both arms, and they may wear a hair braid or streaming scarf. Often elements of the figure, such as the feet, are those of an animal.

One famous seal, in which the figure is surrounded by wild animals, is thought to be the forerunner of Shiva Pasupati (Lord of the Beasts). On this seal the deity has two deer or antelope at his feet and is flanked by a buffalo, an elephant, a rhinoceros, and a tiger. This combination recurs and may have had a ritual significance; the four animals may be arranged to form a *mandala*, a cosmic diagram in which each represents one of the cardinal directions. On another the deity is associated with a pair of fish while on a triangular prism he is flanked by a gharial, snakes, and fishes. This deity also appears on a faience seal with cobras and a worshipper offering a pot. On a molded tablet from Harappa, the deity watches a man holding down a water buffalo by its horn while killing it with a spear. A gharial is shown above. All these creatures have their place in traditional Indian religion.

The seated deity is generally shown wearing buffalo's or bull's horns, often forming a three-pronged headdress with a pipal branch as the central part: This may be the origin of the *trisula* (trident), later an attribute of Shiva. The figure wears many bangles and, on the Pasupati seal, may have three faces (or four if there is one at the back, as in later Hindu iconography); another seal also shows him with three faces but without animals. Usually he is seated, generally on a low stool with bull's feet; in later Indian religion, such a seat indicated high rank. The figure adopts a yogic position, with the legs folded beneath the body and the feet pointing downward. Among his many roles, Shiva is later regarded as the lord of Yoga, a practice that employs discipline of the body, mind, and spirit to achieve union with the divine: it is possible that yogic practice and aims were features of Harappan religion. The later association of the yogic ascetic with meditative solitude in a forest retreat may perhaps be reflected in the depiction on two tablets from Harappa of the figure seated beside a reed hut or shrine.

On these seals the figure is shown with an erect phallus. Shiva's worship is intimately connected with fertility, and he is often represented by the lingam, which was probably an element of Harappan iconography. A few scholars, however, have suggested that the Pasupati seal actually depicts a goddess. The figure's body is slender and not distinctively of either gender, except for the phallus, which can alternatively be seen as the end of the waistband. His apparent beard has alternatively been interpreted as a tiger's mane, a possibility given that the face is not particularly human. A composite woman-tiger figure is shown on several seals, so this interpretation is not impossible.

Although it was only in the first millennium BCE that Shiva emerged as a major deity in literature, the features of the Harappan deity suggest that he was a precursor to Shiva and to other gods with whom Shiva is equated, including the South Indian pastoral deity, Murukan—in other words, that the worship of Shiva and these other deities developed, at least in part, out of a cult that was present in Harappan times. It is noteworthy that Shiva is traditionally associated particularly with cattle pastoralism, one of the main economic activities of the Harappans. The Tamil version, Murukan, had two wives, one from the settled community of farmers and merchants and the other from the mobile community of pastoralists and hunter-gatherers, reflecting the integration of these two ways of life, a further link with the Harappan period.

One unusual representation of a figure in the yogic pose is known from a faience tablet at Mohenjo-daro. Here the seated yogic figure does not wear any divine trappings, such as a horned headdress or bangles, but appears naked. On either side, however, is a human figure in an attitude of devotion and behind each a cobra rises up. The iconography is strongly paralleled in later Indian religion in scenes where the Buddha receives the homage of *nagas* (snake deities).

A female deity is also known from Harappan iconography. She is frequently depicted with a trisula headdress similar to that of the proto-Shiva, wears many bangles, and usually has her hair in a long plait or wears a streaming scarf. She often appears in the center of a tree, generally a pipal, or is associated with a tree or a tiger. On a seal from Kalibangan (unusually, this was a cylinder seal), a female figure stands between two men piercing each other with spears, either fighting over her or dueling and being separated by her. Elsewhere on the seal a female figure (the same one?) stands by, wearing her headdress, her body merged with that of a tiger. The goddess appears again in the latter form on a stamp seal, also from Kalibangan. Other representations of a female deity also include animal elements: On one seal she wears cow's horns, hoofs, and tail. She shares many features with the later goddess Durga, Shiva's consort. As with the proto-Shiva, one can suggest that the Harappans worshipped a female deity from whose cult that of Durga later emerged.

Lingam and Yoni

Marshall suggested the possible existence in the Harappan iconographic repertoire of representations of the classic Indian male and female symbols, the lingam (phallus) and the yoni (vulva or womb), associated in more recent times with the worship of the god Shiva. Some of his examples have been shown to have other functions. For example, many supposed lingams may have been gaming counters or pestles. Others, however, seem more convincing. These may include the clay stelae in the fire altars. A terra-cotta ladle was found near one of the Lothal fire altars, suggesting that the pouring of libations was part of the rites performed there, which may be echoed in the libations of milk, ghee, sacred water, and other substances poured over the lingam in the worship of Shiva. Several hemispherical stone stands with a central hollow must have held an upright stone or wooden post, plausibly creating a combination of yoni and lingam, a common symbol in later Hindu art. A complete example of this combination in terra-cotta is known from Kalibangan. A few stone cylinders were unmistakably phallic. A handful of terra-cottas depict an ithypallic male, and a number of divine figures on seals also seem to have an erect phallus. In addition, several seals have been interpreted as showing intercourse, in one case between a bull and a female, although these depictions are not clear and are capable of other interpretations.

Ring stones (stone spheres or truncated spheres, in various sizes, with a central hole) were originally identified as possibly yonis but were demonstrated to be pillar components by the discovery of examples in situ at Dholavira. While it is now clear that their use was architectural, a religious significance should not be ruled out on these grounds. Polished stone pillars with decorated capitals were erected as objects of devotion by the emperor Ashoka in the third century BCE, and it has been demonstrated that these were the climax of an earlier tradition of erecting stone and probably wooden pillars. Whether they symbolized the lingam and yoni or, as in later times, the World Axis, or some other sacred concept, it is entirely possible that stone pillars and ring stones holding a central wooden column had a sacred significance for the Harappans; this is underlined by their location in the gateways of the citadel at Dholavira, a liminal zone between the profane and sacred domains.

Asterisms

In his attempts to decipher the Indus script via plausible interpretations of some individual signs, Asko Parpola has studied the iconography of the Indus seals in great detail. Evidence that he has uncovered points to a strong interest by the Harappans in the stars, planets, and other heavenly bodies and their movements. Astral deities and mythology are a feature of later Indian religion. Comparison with the known movements of the stars and planets indicates that the traditional star calendar was in use in the twenty-fourth century BCE and was therefore that of the Harappans. Among the principal heavenly bodies that Parpola considered important to the Indus people were Saturn, Venus, the North Star, the Great Bear, and the Pleiades.

A famous seal from Mohenjo-daro allows Parpola to develop his theme in some detail. A goddess, her divinity indicated by her headdress, stands within a pipal tree. Before her kneels a male worshipper, also wearing a horned headdress and presenting an offering. This has often been identified as a severed human head although this is not entirely clear; the object may have two large animal ears rather than a double bun. An outsized ram with a human face stands behind him. Below them seven figures (probably female), with bangles, hair in plaits, and headdresses (probably of a pipal branch), walk in procession. Parpola identifies the goddess as Durga (seen in the heavens as Venus or Aldebaran), to whom human sacrifices were made until quite recently, and the kneeling figure as the youthful god known variously as Skanda, Rudra, or

A seal from Mohenjo-daro showing a ritual or mythological scene. A figure makes an offering to a deity in a tree, watched by a ram with a human face, while seven figures form a procession in the foreground. Asko Parpola has made a detailed interpretation of this scene, linking it to traditional Indian cosmology. (J. M. Kenoyer, Courtesy Department of Archaeology and Museums, Government of Pakistan)

Kumara, bound to the goddess in a sacred marriage that will culminate in his sacrifice. Rudra was nursed in his youth by the wives of the Seven Sages (who appear in the heavens as the stars of the Great Bear while their wives are represented by the Pleiades), and these may be the seven figures at the foot of the scene.

Such reconstructions may overstretch the evidence, but they provide a important first step in attempting to reconstruct something of the religious beliefs of the Indus people. Other scholars have interpreted this scene differently; for example, there is no agreement on the gender of the seven figures in the foreground. Processions of seven figures are known from other seals, and it is certainly probable that these seven figures had some religious significance. They all wear their hair in a braid, as do many figures on seals that seem to be divinities, and it is possible or even probable that this hairstyle was confined to deities. The braid appears in two forms: One, worn for example by these seven figures and by the female figure between two men with spears in one of the scenes already discussed, is a simple plait, shown as a ribbed line ending in a blob of loose hair or by a narrow pair of lines filled by diagonal hatching. The other is a great deal wider and may represent a scarf or streamer rather than hair; it seems in some instances to run continuously across the head as a head-band or hood. This is worn by a number of divine figures, such as the goddess with a tiger's body and the goddess within a tree, and it is also worn by the yogic figure with fish. In procession scenes, a similarly depicted streamer is carried attached to a pole.

Symbols

Abstract designs and other motifs are frequently found on copper tablets and a few seals, on pottery and other artifacts, or incorporated into the design of objects. The heart-shaped pipal leaf was particularly common, used to symbolize the pipal tree and in other contexts, for example in headdresses worn by deities, often combined with horns, as a blanket over the back of the unicorn on seals, and perhaps echoed in the heart- or kidney-shaped pieces of shell cut for inlay. Another motif, found particularly on copper tablets, is the endless knot, a design that has continued in use in the subcontinent, as has the swastika, also known from Harappan contexts, both of them auspicious signs. Overlapping circles formed a design used on pottery, occasionally on tiles, and on shell inlays, and echoed in eye beads; other designs, on pottery and elsewhere, included a regular fish scale pattern, circles with a central dot, and checkerboards. An circle or oval resembling a six-spoked wheel occurs in a number of contexts, especially as a sign in the script, written vertically. It is likely that it represented the sun disc since spoked wheels had not been invented by this time, and this is a way that many cultures have chosen to represent the sun. This interpretation is supported by the symbol's appearance above a scene on a cylindrical molded terra-cotta tablet showing a female deity wrestling two tigers; in this case it is shown horizontally, perhaps to indicate that it was not to be read as a script sign. Symmetry, geometric complexity, and order seem to have been key features of these motifs; the same guiding principles underlie many aspects of Harappan life, such as the cardinally orientated streets, the 1:2:4 proportions of bricks, the1:2 ratio of many citadels, or the layout of structures such as the complex of the Great Bath.

Numbers probably had ritual significance in Harappan as in later Indian religion. These included three, as in the three-lobed trefoil on the Priest-king's robe and elsewhere, and in the three-pronged headdress of deities (two horns and a branch). A number of scenes show seven worshippers, and seven is the number of fire altars on one of the platforms in the Kalibangan citadel. Thirteen is another number with later significance, for instance representing the number of lunar months in the year, and several images on tablets from Harappa show a deity under an arch with thirteen pipal leaves, while in another case the arch has seven leaves. Numbers had many astronomical links, possibly also reflected in Harappan iconography.

External Parallels

Some insights into Harappan religion may come from comparisons with the sacred imagery of contemporary West Asian cultures, especially Sumer and its neighbor Elam. A frequent scene in the artwork and iconography of this area is a hero or god wrestling two ferocious wild animals, lions or bulls. Similar contest scenes appear in Harappan iconography, but here the bulls are replaced by water buffaloes and the lions by tigers, and in some representations the human figure is female. This conflict scene has been interpreted by West Asian scholars as a representation of the eternal opposition between natural forces: between day and night, sun and moon, summer and winter, heat and cold, fire and water, life and death. In the Indian context, given the association of tigers with goddesses, buffaloes with gods, one might add the male and female principles to this list of binary cosmic oppositions. Similarly, the iconography of Greater West Asia includes a variety of imaginary beasts; in the Harappan realm, the constituent elements come from Indian creatures such as elephants. Many other shared iconographic elements are known, such as a sacred mountain and tree, sometimes being eaten by goats.

The occurrence of such parallels is not necessarily an indication of West Asian influence in the formation of Indus beliefs; it is more likely to relate to a common heritage that goes back many millennia, at least to the time of the first agricultural communities: long-range contacts linked West, South, and Central Asia and provided a channel for the sharing of ideas and beliefs.

RITUAL PRACTICES

Shamanism?

While terra-cotta and faience figurines include both wild and domestic animals of many sorts, those depicted on the seals are all large and powerful animals, the majority of which are wild. Frequently on the seals these animals are shown with a feeding trough in front of them, which may symbolize the making of real or symbolic offerings to them.

Ratnagar (2001) suggests that the emphasis on wild animals may reflect the practice of shamanism among the Harappans. Shamanism forms part of a belief system in which spirits are considered to be present in elements of the natural world, such as plants, animals, birds, and snakes and it is thought that they can be contacted by shamans, ritual practitioners who use various means to enter a trance in which they are believed to leave their bodies and enter the world of the spirits. By doing so, they are able to achieve certain results, such as curing the sick, counteracting natural disasters such as drought, or finding out the future. Assistants to the shaman from the spirit world are often visualized as animals or composite beasts. Such creatures occur in Harappan iconography, both on seals and on the copper tablets from Mohenjo-daro where they form part of a small repertoire of images that also includes a wild hairy man with horns, armed with a bow, the kind of form in which shamans crossing into the spirit world are often envisaged. Other images on these tablets are generally large wild animals, as on the seals, but also include the hare, rarely depicted elsewhere. It is possible that the perforated jars known from many Harappan sites were braziers used to burn incense or create smoke that would send a shaman into his trance (though there are other interpretations of these vessels, for example, as sieves or devices for catching fish); the brazier shown in front of the unicorn on seals might have served the same purpose. Drumming was another means used to induce a trance; a few figurines playing drums are known from Mohenjo-daro and Harappa, and the script also includes a sign that may be interpreted as a drummer. The possible link between the Harappan religion and shamanism was already suggested by During Caspers (1993).

Ritual Paraphernalia

A few objects seem likely to have been associated with rituals such as sacrifices and offerings. These include shell ladles, perhaps used for lustration, and chank shells from which libations may have been poured, a purpose for which they have been used traditionally. Chank shells are also used as trumpets, blown during ceremonies, and one example of such a trumpet is known from Harappa. A number of seals show jars being proffered to deities, probably containing liquids, grain, or other offerings.

Gaming equipment, such as boards, dice, and gaming pieces, are known from most Harappan sites. While these may have been used for games as pastimes, it is likely that, as in many cultures, they were also used in ritual contexts, for instance for divination. Ivory rods, with different numbers of concentric circles engraved on their sides, may also have been used as dice or in some ritual context, perhaps in divination or calendrics.

Unicorns, and occasionally other animals, were shown on seals facing a curious object consisting of a stick bearing a hemispherical bowl surmounted by a ridged cylinder. Sometimes the bowl is surrounded by droplets. This object also appears separately on faience and steatite tablets, on a gold headband, and as a three-dimensional model in ivory, and it was also depicted being borne aloft in processions. There has been much speculation about the identity of this object: Was it an incense burner, an offering stand, a sacred brazier? One intriguing suggestion is that it was a filter for preparing the sacred drink, soma, that is mentioned in the later Vedic texts. This substance also has not been satisfactorily identified, and it is not known whether it was made from a plant native to the subcontinent. Whatever the object was, it clearly had religious significance.

Although some narrative scenes appear on seals, they are more commonly found on small incised steatite or mold-made terra-cotta or faience tablets, found mainly at Harappa but also at Mohenjo-daro. Many identical copies of each are known, and they are often interpreted as amulets. On the reverse, many bear a few signs interpreted as numbers, often along with another sign, such as a U that probably represents a jar containing a votive offering since it is identical to the pots being offered to deities in some scenes. Parpola (1994,

A cubical die found among rubble at Harappa. Dice may have been used in divination, with the outcome of a throw of the die being interpreted to answer a question, predict a future event, or advise a particular course of action. (Harappa Archaeological Research Project, Courtesy Department of Archaeology and Museums, Government of Pakistan)

107–109) therefore suggests that these tablets may have been tokens issued when votive offerings were made, recording the quantity of the offering.

Public Events

Since there are few or no apparent Harappan temples, many religious ceremonies may have taken place in the open air. A few tablets show processions in which banners, braziers, and bull figures are borne aloft on poles, perhaps as part of religious festivals. Scenes probably from Harappan mythology are shown on a number of seals and on other inscribed objects, and such stories may have been acted out using models and masks of humans, animals, and composite creatures. Both full-sized terra-cotta masks and miniature masks that might have been finger puppets are known, as well as terra-cottas with a hole to allow them to be held on an stick. The latter include grotesque human and animal figures that may have provided light relief before or after the sacred dramas. Religious festivals may have been an important context within which goods circulated, people making offerings to the gods that were collected by the priesthood and redistributed to worshippers as sanctified objects and materials (like *prasad*).

THE TREATMENT OF THE DEAD

Burials are often an important source of inferences about religion, but the rarity of burials found at Harappan sites restricts the information available. In addition, it is by no means certain that inhumation in cemeteries was the only funerary rite practiced by the Harappans.

Harappan Burials

Excavations in Cemetery R-37 at Harappa have uncovered the largest corpus of Harappa burials, numbering nearly two hundred, and those undertaken by the HARP team in recent years have given a particularly thorough picture of Harappan burial rites. A few graves have been excavated at other sites.

Burials were generally placed in an oval or rectangular pit, sometimes lined with mud bricks or containing a wooden coffin, whose wood usually survives only as a stain. The body was laid fully extended on its back, with the head to the north, feet to the south, the direction associated in later Indian religion with the Land of the Dead. At Rakhigarhi, some unusual grave pits were undercut to form an earthen overhang beneath which the body was placed. The top of the pit was then filled in with bricks to form a vaulted roof for the chamber. At Kalibangan, a layer of clay was placed on the floor of the grave beneath the body. Sometimes the deceased was wrapped in a cloth or reed shroud, and generally individuals still had the ornaments that they had worn in life. A number of pots were buried with them, sometimes arranged beneath the body. Sometimes a copper mirror was buried with a woman; this was possibly an object used shamanistically to look into the spirit world. Three or four graves at Lothal contained the bones of two individuals: This is not, as has been suggested, likely evidence of *sati* (widow immolation) given that at least one of these examples was a pair of males.

In some cases, the graves were marked by a low mound of earth or stones or, in one instance, of mud bricks. At Kalibangan, the graves were neatly arranged in groups of six to eight, and each may have been associated with a "cenotaph," a rectangular pit that was left open and in which a number of pots were placed, perhaps an offering place belonging to an individual family.

In contrast, the arrangement of burials at Harappa and Lothal was much more haphazard, later burials often cutting into and disturbing earlier graves, something that was rare at Kalibangan. Scant respect seems to have been accorded to burials when they were disturbed; jewelry was sometimes removed and broken pottery, old bones, and half decomposed corpses thrown into nearby pits. Human bones and teeth have been uncovered as stray finds at a number of sites, such as Rojdi, where two infants were also found buried beneath a house floor. A single skull placed in a jar was found in mound II at Chanhu-daro. At Mohenjo-daro a basket of bones was reported from House XXVIII in the VS area and a single skull in House III in the HR-A area. In the final occupation of the city, perfunctory burials in deserted streets and houses reflect the crumbling of civic society.

In one grave at Ropar in the Himalayan foothills, an individual was buried with a dog, echoing a practice among the people of the Northern Neolithic in Kashmir; perhaps this individual had a link with that culture. In other respects, the burials at Ropar resembled those from Harappa R-37.

It is possible that Harappan funerary rites may also have included other methods of disposal, such as deposition in water, cremation, or exposure to allow excarnation. One grave at Kalibangan contained the fractional remains of several individuals, including three skulls, and a casket holding a child's

A miniature mask of terra-cotta, made in a mold, from Mohenjo-daro. Such masks, perhaps fastened to puppets, were likely used as props in public narrations or enactments of religious stories. (J. M. Kenoyer, Courtesy Department of Archaeology and Museums, Government of Pakistan)

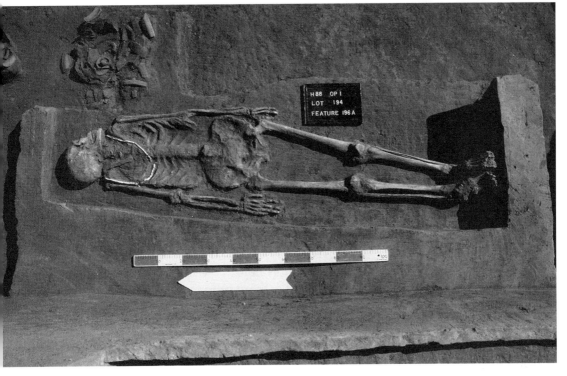

The burial of a man, probably an important individual judging by the fine necklace he was wearing and by the quality of his treatment: he was wrapped in a shroud and placed in a wooden coffin before being buried in a rectangular grave in the cemetery (R-37) at Harappa. (J. M. Kenoyer, Courtesy Department of Archaeology and Museums, Government of Pakistan)

tooth. In several cemeteries cenotaphs have been found, containing only pottery. In a part of Kalibangan's cemetery separate from the graves, pots were set in round pits with no associated human remains. Similarly, in the cemetery of cairns at Dholavira, four circular pits and two rectangular cists (pits lined with limestone slabs and probably once covered by capstones) contained pottery but no bones, though in one cist there was a clay structure resembling a coffin.

Charred patches of earth were noticed in the Kalibangan cemetery that may relate to cremation. Several hundred urns containing pottery, ash, and bones were reported at Harappa, but in only one was any human bone found; it is therefore unlikely that these were really burial urns. Each of two houses in the VS area at Mohenjo-daro yielded an urn containing cremated human remains, and a platform with the remains of five or more cremations was uncovered in a test excavation in the Mature Harappan site of Tarkhanwala Dera in the Saraswati Valley.

The practice of including cenotaphs in cemeteries has Early Harappan antecedents in Gujarat, where urn burials without bones and pits containing only pottery are known from cemeteries at Nagwada and at Surkotada; a grave with fractional inhumation and another with a tiny amount of cremated remains were also excavated at the latter, and an extended burial was found at the former. These practices contrast with those of the Indo-Iranian borderlands, where contracted inhumation had a long history, suggesting they may have had a local origin.

Burials and Beliefs

These burial practices have provided tantalizing clues about Indus religious beliefs. Individuals were carefully buried wearing the clothing and ornaments that distinguished their place in society, in separate cemeteries outside the bounds of the settlement. The pots accompanying burials included painted dishes on stands and S-shaped jars, as well as plain lotas, beakers, and dishes, all likely to be vessels used for serving food and therefore probably related to providing food in the afterlife; sometimes animal bones show that joints of meat were included. Where disease or civic breakdown disrupted life, the established rites might not be performed, but traditional extended burials continued at Harappa in the lower level of cemetery H, showing that the decline of the civilization did not universally affect burial practices.

Except in unusual circumstances, therefore, it was clearly important that the Harappan individual was laid to rest in the appropriate manner. In many cases this involved a physical separation between the body and the ground, by means of a shroud, coffin, or layer of pottery or clay; it is tempting to see in this an aspect of the concern with ritual purity.

Once these rites had been performed, however, it did not seem to matter what happened to the body and to its accompanying offerings, given the way bones, pots, personal ornaments, and even incompletely decayed bodies were treated when they were encountered in digging a new grave. Perhaps the Harappans believed that the transition to the afterlife required a rite of passage that involved burial (or other rites of disposal for which there is no evidence) but that, after this was performed, the soul had departed and had no further use for its bodily remains.

Diverse burial practices within the Harappan realms, of which only extended inhumation is well documented, may have reflected a number of different factors, such as social status, ethnic affiliation, or religious beliefs.

RECONSTRUCTING HARAPPAN RELIGION

Diversity characterizes Indian religion: the worship of Shiva and Vishnu in many forms, the philosophy of rebirth and the quest for nirvana, interwoven with a bewildering variety of local cults and practices. The subcontinent has seen many developments of indigenous inspiration, such as Buddhism and Jainism, while other strands have been added by the many groups of historically attested outsiders who have settled there. Practices, beliefs, and devotion to the worship of particular deities are often strongly linked to group identity. Going back into the Indus period, we should expect religious pluralism already to be present, given the multicultural background of the Harappans and their long-standing links with their many neighbors.

Though much about Harappan religion is obscure or speculative, the evidence that exists does allow something of the broad picture to be reconstructed. The abundance of water facilities in Harappan settlements and the Great Bath at Mohenjo-daro show that the use of water played a key role in religious practice, most probably being used in ritual purification, and the iconogaphy suggests that terrestrial waters, with their fish, were closely related in belief to the waters of the heavens in which swam the stars.

The Harappan seals were used in official contexts and should therefore reflect iconography of the official belief system shared by the people of the Harappan state. In this we see evidence of the worship of a male and a female deity, probably taking many forms, closely linked to the male and female principles and to the natural world, especially that of trees, particularly the pipal, and powerful animals, particularly the bull/water buffalo and the tiger. Animals not known in the real world also populated that of the gods, particularly the magnificent unicorn. Rites associated with the worship of these deities and spirits included processions, offerings, and probably shamanistic practices.

In addition there seem to have been lesser cults, practiced by certain groups within Harappan society or in certain regions, the latter in particular reflecting the differing cultural backgrounds of the Harappans' ancestors. In the Indus Valley, the ubiquity of female terra-cotta figurines, including Mother Goddesses, links to the long tradition of their manufacture by the people of the Indo-Iranian borderlands. In contrast, in Gujarat and the Sarawati Valley where many people were descended from indigenous hunter-gatherer stock, some rituals, probably both in public and in the home, involved sacrifices made through fire.

REFERENCES

Atre, Shubhangana. 2002. "Harappan Religion: Myth and Polemics." In *Indian Archaeology in Retrospect. II. Protohistory. Archaeology of the Harappan Civilization*, edited by S. Settar and Ravi Korisettar, 185–205. Indian Council of Historical Research. New Delhi: Manohar.

Bisht, Ravi Singh. 1984. "Structural Remains and Town Planning of Banawali." In *Frontiers of the Indus Civilization*, edited by B. B. Lal and S. P. Gupta, 89–97. New Delhi: Books and Books.

Bisht, Ravi Singh. 1993. "Excavation at Dholavira, District Kachchh (Earlier Kutch)." *Indian Archaeology—A Review 1992–93*: 27–32.

Bisht, Ravi Singh. 1999. "Dholavira and Banawali: Two Different Paradigms of the Harappan Urbis Forma." *Puratattva* 29: 14–37.

Bisht, Ravi Singh. 2002. "Dholavira Excavations: 1990–94." In *Facets of Indian Civilization. Recent Perspectives. Essays in Honour of Professor B. B. Lal*, edited by Jagat Pati Joshi, 107–120. New Delhi: Aryan Books International.

Bisht, Ravi Singh, and Shashi Asthana. 1979. "Banawali and Some Other Recently Excavated Harappan Sites in India." In *South Asian Archaeology 1977*, edited by Maurizio Taddei, 223–240. Naples: Istituto Universitario Orientale, Seminario di Studi Asiatici.

Clark, Sharri. "Embodying Indus Life: Terracotta Figurines from Harappa." [Online article; retrieved 6/14/05.] www.harappa.com/figurines/index.html.

Dales, George F. 1968. "Of Dice and Men." *Journal of the American Oriental Society* 88 (1): 14–23. Reprinted 1979 in *Ancient Cities of the Indus,* edited by Gregory L. Possehl, 138–144. New Delhi: Vikas Publishing House.

Dales, George F. 1984. "Sex and Stone at Mohenjo-daro." In *Frontiers of the Indus Civilization,* edited by B. B. Lal and S. P. Gupta, 109–115. New Delhi: Books and Books.

Dhavalikar, M. K., and Shubhangana Atre. 1989. "The Fire Cult and Virgin Sacrifice: Some Harappan Rituals." In *Old Problems and New Perspectives in the Archaeology of South Asia,* edited by Jonathan Mark Kenoyer, 193–205. *Wisconsin Archaeological Reports.* Vol. 2. Department of Anthropology. Madison: University of Wisconsin Press.

During Caspers, Elisabeth. 1993. "Another Face of the Indus Valley Magico-religious System." In *South Asian Archaeology 1991,* edited by Adalbert J. Gail and Gerd J. R. Mevissen, 65–89. Stuttgart: Franz Steiner Verlag.

Habib, Irfan. 2002. *The Indus Civilization: A People's History of India.* 2. Aligarh: Tulika/Aligarh Historians Society.

Huntington, Susan L. 1995. *The Art of Ancient India.* New York: Weatherhill.

Irwin, John. 1973–1976. "'Asokan' Pillars: A Reassessment of the Evidence." *The Burlingon Magazine* 115: 709; 116: 712–727; 117: 631–643; 118: 734–753.

Jansen, Michael. 1985. "Mohenjo-daro HR-A, House I, a Temple?—Analysis of an Architectural Structure." In *South Asian Archaeology 1983,* edited by Janine Schotsmans and Maurizio Taddei, 157–206. Naples: Istituto Universitario Orientale, Dipartimento di Studi Asiatici.

Kenoyer, Jonathan Mark. 1989. "Socio-Economic Structures in the Indus Civilization as Reflected in Specialized Crafts and the Question of Ritual Segregation." In *Old Problems and New Perspectives in the Archaeology of South Asia,* edited by Jonathan Mark Kenoyer, 183–192. *Wisconsin Archaeological Reports.* Vol. 2. Department of Anthropology. Madison: University of Wisconsin Press.

Kenoyer, Jonathan Mark. 1998. *Ancient Cities of the Indus Valley Civilization.* Karachi: Oxford University Press and American Institute of Pakistan Studies.

Marshall, John. 1931. *Mohenjo Daro and the Indus Civilization.* London: Probsthain.

Nath, Amarendra. 1998. "Rakhigarhi: A Harappan Metropolis in the Sarasvati-Drishadvati Divide." *Puratattva* 28: 39–45.

Nath, Amarendra. 1999. "Further Excavations at Rakhigarhi." *Puratattva* 29: 46–49.

O'Flaherty, Wendy Doniger. 1975. *Hindu Myths.* Harmondsworth, UK: Penguin.

Parpola, Asko. 1984. "New Correspondences between Harappan and Near Eastern Glyptic Art." In *South Asian Archaeology 1981,* edited by Bridget Allchin, 176–195. Cambridge, UK: Cambridge University Press.

Parpola, Asko. 1985a. "The Harappan 'Priest-King's' Robe and the Vedic Tarpya Garment: Their Interrelation and Symbolism (Astral and Procreative)." In *South Asian Archaeology 1983,* edited by Janine Schotsmans and Maurizio Taddei, 385–403. Naples: Istituto Universitario Orientale, Dipartimento di Studi Asiatici.

Parpola, Asko. 1985b. "The Sky-Garment. A Study of the Harappan Religion and Its Relationship to the Mesopotamian and Later Indian Religions." *Studia Orientalia* 57: 8–216.

Parpola, Asko. 1992. "'The Fig-deity Seal' from Mohenjo-daro: Its Iconography and Inscription." In *South Asian Archaeology 1989*, edited by Catherine Jarrige, 227–236. Madison, WI: Prehistory Press.

Parpola, Asko. 1994. *Deciphering the Indus Script*. Cambridge, UK: Cambridge University Press.

Pittman, Holly. 1984. *Art of the Bronze Age. Southeastern Iran, Western Central Asia, and the Indus Valley*. New York: Metropolitan Museum of Art.

Possehl, Gregory L. 2002. *The Indus Civilization. A Contemporary Perspective*. Walnut Creek, CA: AltaMira.

Puskas, Ildiko. 1984. "Society and Religion in the Indus Valley Civilization." In *South Asian Archaeology 1981*, edited by Bridget Allchin, 162–165. Cambridge, UK: Cambridge University Press.

Rao, S. R. 1979 and 1985. *Lothal: A Harappan Town (1955–62)*. 2 vols. *Memoirs of the Archaeological Survey of India*. SI 78. New Delhi: Archaeological Survey of India.

Ratnagar, Shereen. 2000. *The End of the Great Harappan Tradition. Heras Memorial Lectures 1998*. New Delhi: Manohar.

Ratnagar, Shereen. 2001. *Understanding Harappa. Civilization in the Greater Indus Valley*. New Delhi: Tulika.

Sharma, A. K. 1982. "The Harappan Cemetery at Kalibangan: A Study." In *Harappan Civilization. A Contemporary Perspective*, edited by Gregory L. Possehl, 297–299. New Delhi: Oxford & IBH Publishing Co.

Trivedi, P. K., and J. K. Patnaik. 2004. "Tarkhanewala Der and Chak 86 (2003–2004)." *Puratattva* 34: 30–34.

CHAPTER 10

X

Material Culture

WORKSHOPS AND FACTORIES

In Harappan towns and cities, there were both individual workshops operated by single individuals or families and a few larger industrial complexes (factories). These might be dispersed within the residential areas or clustered together. Some industries were also conducted in the citadels. For example, in the small town of Gola Dhoro, shellworking and faience manufacture took place in the citadel, while beadmaking was mainly undertaken in the residential area, though the raw material was stored in the citadel. In cities and some towns, specialists in a number of different crafts might work in adjacent workshops. Where the same skills or equipment were required for several different crafts, these might take place in a single workshop. Pottery firing and metalworking tended to be conducted in discrete areas, separate from other craft activities.

Much of the craft activity that took place may be undetected since regular or periodic cleaning would have removed the debris from workshops to dump areas, often at a distance. Many crafts using perishable materials, such as leatherworking, would have left no trace, except for tools whose functions are often not diagnostic. In other cases, only fixed equipment, such as a kiln, may survive to reveal the presence of craft activity in domestic workshops. In contrast, huge amounts of debris accumulated in areas of intense craft activity, making these easier to identify. Negative evidence does not preclude the presence of certain activities, although it can be suggestive; for example, the failure to detect metal smelting in the Harappan towns and cities suggests that this took place near the ore sources, though it might only reflect the siting of this activity in suburban or extramural quarters of settlements that have not been investigated.

Despite all these problems, however, intensive investigation at Mohenjo-daro and Harappa and studies of several other settlements have revealed much about Harappan craft production. Analysis of artifacts has been supplemented by technological experiments and studies of modern craft techniques, shedding much light on Harappan technology. At Mohenjo-daro, surface surveys used to map the distribution of debris from various manufacturing processes, such as sherds of misfired pottery and fragments of stone and shell, revealed a great concentration of industrial debris in the south and east of the Lower Town, especially in the Moneer area. A double row of workshops was also found to the east of the HR area. Dumps of material were found around the periphery of the

Moneer area from the periodic cleaning out of workshops; erosion of these dumps has deposited industrial waste over a considerable area. The industries in the Moneer area included beadmaking, the manufacture of stoneware bangles, steatite working, flint knapping, faience manufacture, shellworking, weight manufacture, and copper working. Pottery making was also attested to, but this was apparently confined to the latest period of occupation. Although these areas of the city seem to have been industrial quarters, they were composed mainly of small workshops, often arranged in a row, rather than large-scale operations. There were also many small craft workshops in individual houses scattered throughout the city, particularly concerned with specialist craft activities such as making beads, seals, shell inlays, and other small precious objects, and working silver and steatite. Facilities probably for dyeing also suggest the manufacture of cotton textiles. Many of the craft activities were highly specialized. Some were concerned with a particular stage of manufacture, such as the suburban site where chank shells were cleaned. Others produced a limited range of artifacts, such as two pottery-making sites in the Moneer area where pointed-based goblets were mass-produced. The sequence of activities in a group of houses in the Moneer southeast area shows that there was no long-term correlation between a single industry and a particular location at Mohenjo-daro: A number of steatite workshops were succeeded by one larger complex manufacturing stoneware bangles, which in turn was replaced by stoneworking and finally by pottery manufacture.

At Harappa, detailed investigations of workshop areas have shown that one in the northwest of mound E was devoted throughout the life of the city to the manufacture of particular types of pottery. Crafts were practiced in various parts of mounds E and ET, their products including shell objects, agate beads, flint tools, weights, seals, metal artifacts, and pottery. Wheeler excavated a large concentration of furnaces, probably for metalworking, north of the citadel in mound F; these belonged to the city's latest occupation.

Mohenjo-daro and Harappa housed workers in a number of highly specialized crafts as well as those producing everyday objects. Some operations that have not been detected, such as brick making and other industries that produced noxious fumes or by-products, may have taken place in the unexplored suburban areas. A few special types of artifact, such as stoneware bangles (which were produced under close official control) and inscribed copper tablets, were apparently made only at Mohenjo-daro and Harappa, though the other cities may have housed a similar range of craft activities.

Some towns were manufacturing centers, though the range of artifacts they produced was more restricted. Chanhu-daro may have been an exception, producing some specialist products, such as long carnelian beads, as well as more ordinary goods. The range of craft activities for which there is evidence included copper casting, beadmaking, stone weight manufacture, bone and ivory working, shellworking, faience manufacture, and perhaps pottery production. Some of these activities took place in small workshops around the edge of mound II, others in the houses excavated on mound I, which included a beadmaking factory. Raw materials and partially worked goods were also stored together in some of the rooms. The scale of craft production at Chanhu-daro seems much greater than that at Mohenjo-daro, perhaps taking up as much as half the town, probably reflecting the difference in emphasis between the industrial town and the residential heart of the much larger city, since in the latter much craft production was probably located in the as yet unexcavated suburbs. Settlements heavily involved in trade produced large quantities of a range of goods; for example, Lothal had pottery, bead, shell, and ivory workshops, as well as copper smithies, while at Kuntasi pottery and beads were made, including some of faience, and copper and steatite were worked. In the small settlement of Allahdino, there were ovens for firing terra-cotta objects, copper was worked, and large quantities of textiles were produced.

There was also, however, a great deal of specialization in Harappan craft activities. A number of towns and industrial villages worked local materials on an industrial scale, and their products were then distributed throughout the Harappan realms. For example, Balakot near the mouth of the Indus and Nageshwar in Gujarat were centers for processing shells obtained from the nearby coastal waters. Different parts of such sites were devoted to different stages in the production cycle. Separate parts of the process may have been the responsibility of different specialists. Workshops in the cities suggest that specialization was common; for example, the pottery area in the northwest of Harappa mound E made only certain types of ceramics. On the other hand, a single workshop might undertake several related activities, such as beadmaking and seal manufacture.

CONSTRUCTION

Building Materials

Clay. Bricks made of sun-dried or fired clay were the main material used in construction by the Indus people. Sun-dried bricks were used for both houses and town walls, though baked bricks were used in many of the buildings in Mohenjo-daro. Baked bricks were extensively used for constructing drains and bathroom floors; they were also used occasionally for other things such as the working platforms in mound F at Harappa and the dyeing vats at Mohenjo-daro. Bricks were generally made in two sizes: 7 by 14 by 28 centimeters for domestic structures and 10 by 20 by 40 centimeters for town walls and platforms. No brick-making sites have yet been found associated with Indus cities, but they would probably have been located in the suburbs or beyond; modern brick making takes place well away from towns and cities, but within a reasonable distance for transport. Brick making must have been a major activity in Indus times, given the volume of bricks used in urban construction. It used to be suggested that huge areas of forest had to be felled to to bake the great quantity of fired bricks used by the Harappans. However, more recent studies have shown that the scrubby natural vegetation of the Indus region would have provided perfectly adequate quantities of suitable fuel. Cow dung was probably also burned as fuel.

The techniques used in Harappan times are unlikely to have been very different from those of today. Bricks would have been made in molds, probably of wood. As well as the standard cuboid bricks, wedge-shaped bricks were made for building the numerous wells. Harappan bricks are rough on the lower face where they were in contact with the ground during drying and striated on the upper face where they were leveled with a piece of wood. After the bricks had set, the molds would be removed and the bricks left to dry. Mud bricks were now ready for use; those to be baked were stacked over a hearth, covered with fuel and fired. The stack would burn for days, sending off foul fumes. Since the only surviving trace would be the hearth, brickyards are likely to be hard to detect archaeologically.

Bricks were used occasionally to pave floors, for example in the pillared hall on the Mohenjo-daro citadel, or some streets, as in the citadel at Lothal. Clay was also made into terra-cotta drain pipes, triangular terra-cotta cakes, and overfired nodules. The cakes were used in some cases instead of bricks for paving in bathrooms or courtyards and were also employed as baffles to retain the heat in kilns and fireplaces. They have often been found in fire altars. Subspherical nodules of overfired greenish clay were used in construction, usually as a foundation layer under brick floors but also in masonry; these provided insulation and drainage.

Stone. Massive limestone rings found in the early excavations at Mohenjo-daro and Harappa remained a puzzle until the 1990s when they were uncovered in situ in the citadel gateway at Dholavira. Those with a large central hole were the base for wooden pillars, as were reel-shaped examples, while others, flattened spheres with a narrow central hole, were used to build stone columns, held together by a central wooden pole. Pillars of polished stone were also uncovered at Dholavira in and near the citadel. These monumental pillar bases and pillars may have had a religious significance as well as an architectural function.

Stone was occasionally used in houses, for example to floor a bathroom or as an elaborate version of wooden window grilles. Drain covers might be made of stone slabs. In Gujarat, however, stone was much more commonly used in construction, particularly of city and town walls. Often houses there had foundations and sometimes walls of stone rubble or dressed stone. At Dholavira, the bunds around the reservoirs were faced with stone, which was extensively used in the citadel, and in the nearby cemetery some grave pits were lined with stones.

Wood. Wood was also extensively used in architecture, though few traces have survived. Fragments of deodar, teak, and sissoo at Mohenjo-daro, Kalibangan, and Lothal show that wood was used for roof beams and rafters, doors and their jambs, and pillars. A few house models show that some Harappan houses had windows with a lattice grille and shutters, probably of wood in most cases. Wooden beams and timbers were also used to construct a number of large buildings, such as the so-called granaries at Mohenjo-daro, Harappa, and

Lothal. The complex in the southern part of the citadel at Mohenjo-daro included a large pillared hall and two smaller ones, all of which had originally had wooden pillars supporting their roofs.

Plaster and Mortar. Various materials were used for wall plaster, including clay. Early-third-millennium evidence from a failed bonfire firing of pottery at Mehrgarh shows that limestone cobbles were packed in beside the pottery and included in the firing, converting them to quicklime, which was then ground to powder on querns. It is probable that this practice continued in Harappan times. Lime was mixed with burned shell for use in plaster. Lime was also mixed with sand and water to make mortar, though mud mortar was more common. Cattle dung mixed with mud was applied as daub to the wattle walls of village huts; dung and mud or mud alone were also used to cover floors.

Construction Methods

Baked or mud bricks were often laid in what is known as English bond masonry, with alternating courses of headers and stretchers, an extremely strong construction method. Less commonly, Flemish bond masonry was employed, in which headers and stretchers alternate within each course. Masses of bricks were used, house walls at Mohenjo-daro being generally three to four bricks thick, while those at the smaller settlement of Banawali were two to four bricks thick.

Timber was used both for fixtures such as door and window frames and thresholds, and for ceilings and roof supports. Impressions of reed matting survive from the flat roofs, and thatch, packed earth, and wooden planks were probably also used in roofing. Wooden pillars were used in some buildings, to support internal balconies or external verandas; for example, the potter's workshop at Nausharo had a veranda whose posts were wedged in place with stones.

Many rooms had beaten earth floors, often covered with plaster or a thin layer of sand. However, bathroom floors were generally constructed of closely fitted sawn bricks, ground to ensure a close watertight fit. Courtyards at Mohenjo-daro were also often paved with bricks. Occasionally potsherds or tiles were used to cover a floor, and these might be decorated. At Lothal, floors were often paved with mud bricks.

City and town walls were constructed in a variety of ways. Frequently they had a mud or mud brick core enclosed in baked brick revetment walls. In Gujarat, the facing was more usually of rough or dressed stone. They were always extremely thick, ranging from around 4 meters at Surkotada to 14 meters at the base of the wall around the citadel at Harappa. Often their thickness was increased when further revetment layers were added during the history of the settlement.

The sophistication of Harappan construction techniques is visible in the Great Bath at Mohenjo-daro. This had a baked brick outer shell and inner wall, with mud brick packing between them. A thick layer of bitumen was spread as a seal on the inside, and within this the bath was constructed of closely fitted bricks placed on edge, the gaps between them filled with gypsum plaster.

A type of surveying instrument was found at Lothal, Mohenjo-daro, Banawali, and Pabumath. The example from Lothal was a hollow shell cylinder with four slits on each of its two edges. This could be used to determine alignments and lay out lines of buildings or streets at right angles. The one from Banawali was made from an animal vertebra and had two slits crossing at right angles.

Decoration

Although the brick buildings of Indus towns and cities now seem austere, it is probable that in Harappan times a variety of decorations made them far more attractive. Brick walls were generally plastered; for example, at Dholavira in the phases preceding the earthquake, both the city wall and the walls and floors of houses were covered with white and pink-red plaster. Walls may also have been decorated with textiles or other hangings. Some door frames had holes at the top from which curtains or matting may have been hung. The wooden structural elements and fixtures, such as door and window frames, may have been carved with designs that might invoke divine protection and ensure good fortune, as well as being decorative. House models show that some windows and internal partitions had intricately carved latticework grilles; a few examples made of alabaster and marble survive from Harappa and Mohenjo-daro.

ARTIFACTS

Salient features of Harappan crafts and craft production include the standardization, organized mass production, and widespread distribution of many artifact types. Jewelry, particularly bangles and beads, probably played an important role in identifying the social persona of individuals, so shellworking and beadmaking were major industries. While the Harappans often employed the same precious materials as their contemporaries, such as gold, they also placed a high value on artificially produced materials, such as faience, and on objects displaying the artisan's skill and virtuosity, such as long carnelian beads.

Ceramics

Workshops. Kiln bases, pieces of kiln lining, and scatters of misfired sherds are generally the only remaining evidence of pottery manufacture. However, one potter's workshop, a small structure with several rooms, was discovered in Nausharo at the foot of the wall surrounding the northern mound. Pots made there were stacked on shelves to dry; they and some tools were left in place when the workshop was suddenly abandoned. A later building, constructed over the earlier debris, was also a potter's workshop and included an area where the pottery was fired in a bonfire kiln. Sherds from misfired pots were used to surface the lane outside the workshop. Only some of the types of pottery used in the settlement were made in this workshop.

In the northwest corner of mound E at Harappa, there was a pottery-making area where several kilns were found. Tools such as bone spatulas and stone blades used in shaping the pottery and red ochre for painting the vessels lay scattered around them. Waste material deposited in a pit included a broken bat (clay disc) used when throwing pottery. This area produced a restricted range of vessels; terra-cotta cakes were made in another industrial area, on mound ET.

A number of kilns were found at Mohenjo-daro, in the HR, VS, and Moneer areas. All belong to the late period of occupation in the city; their location, on occasion, in former streets shows they were associated with the period of urban decay. It is probable that during the Mature Harappan period, pottery production took place away from the city center. This was the case at Kalibangan, where pottery waste was found in the unwalled area south of citadel.

A ceramic factory area was uncovered at Lal Shah, about a kilometer from Mehrgarh. This contained at least seven updraft kilns, and other debris from pottery manufacture, including stands and sherds used for smoothing the surfaces when finishing pots.

Clays. Fine textured clays for making pottery were available throughout the alluvial plains, and other suitable clays could be had in other areas; for example, there was excellent ball clay in Saurashtra, including near Kuntasi.

A variety of clays might be used to make different fabrics or for different sections of a vessel, as at Balakot, or this variation might be achieved by using different tempers, as at Mohenjo-daro. A considerable range of tempers was used, including organic material such as cow dung or straw, minerals such as sand, mica, or lime, and other materials such as grog. The clay was carefully levigated and was sieved when making fine wares.

Manufacture. Some pots were modeled by hand by coiling or were built up from slabs, but many were made partially or entirely on a potter's wheel. Although no wheels survive, as they were probably of wood, it is likely that they were similar to those used in the region today. These consist of a turntable, on which the clay is thrown, attached by an axle to a lower flywheel, which is set in a pit and turned with the foot. The wheel could be turned at different speeds, depending on the operations being undertaken, such as throwing on a fast wheel or trimming a vessel on a wheel turned slowly. A conical lump of clay with a depression in the top found at Nausharo had probably been set on the wheel to begin throwing when the workshop was suddenly abandoned. Often a bat was used; this was fastened to the turntable or firmly seated over it. The vessel was thrown on this, allowing it to be removed without the disturbance of cutting it from the wheel. This was particularly useful when a vessel was being constructed in several pieces. Simpler vessels were often cut from the wheel with a string on completion, and a number might be thrown from the same lump of clay in quick succession, a form of mass production for utilitarian wares. The lower part of some vessels was thrown in a mold, allowing vessels to be made in standardized sizes. A few flat-based

A revetment wall abutting the "granary" at Harappa illustrates both the arrangement of bricks in alternating courses of headers and stretchers, and the characteristic massiveness of Harappan walls, which were at least two bricks thick and generally more. (Ute Franke-Vogt)

molds, in different sizes, have been found at Nausharo and pieces of others at Mohenjo-daro and Balakot. The mold was attached to the wheel with chocks under the rim or with clay.

The wheel was used again to turn a vessel while removing excess clay or scraping it to make selected parts thinner. Tools found in the workshop at Nausharo included flint blades used to shape the vessel and terra-cotta scrapers. A wooden paddle and a stone or pottery anvil were used to create rounded bases on leather-hard pottery; rubbing stones found at Harappa and a pottery dabber from Nageshwar may have been such anvils.

Special wares included more complex shapes that required a high level of skill to produce, for example, the large storage jars. Their basal portion was thrown on the wheel, and the central portion was built up using slabs or coils of clay. These vessels were then turned on the wheel to trim the sides and shape the rim. After forming, cords were wrapped around them to ensure they kept their shape while drying.

Pedestaled vessels were also specialist products. These were made in two or three pieces. The flared base could be made in a mold or included in the making of the stem, which was thrown either freehand or round a central mold. This and the bowl or dish were separately thrown and left to dry to leather-hard before being assembled. The upper end of the pedestal and the base of the dish or bowl might be marked with a few short lines before semiliquid clay was applied to the one and soft clay to the other and the two parts joined. A thin coil of clay was then thrown around the join. Alternatively, the two parts might be brought together immediately after they were thrown; in this case an additional coil of clay was unnecessary but the top of the pedestal would broaden out.

Completed pottery was left to dry, like the twenty-five vessels abandoned on shelves at Nausharo. When it was leather-hard, it could be decorated in various ways. Some pots were returned to the wheel where horizontal grooves or combed lines were cut into the surface. Others were impressed with the edge of shells or with a pointed stick. Some were fluted or ribbed with the fingers. The inside of many pedestaled bowls was decorated with a series of concentric circles impressed with the end of a reed. A tiny central mark reveals that these circles were drawn first with compasses. Many vessels were coated in a red slip and some were burnished; both treatments reduced the vessel's porosity. Only a few types of pot had slip applied to the interior, including some large storage jars that were coated in a black slip inside and out. Some vessels, especially cooking pots, were partially coated with a sandy, gritty clay, which gave protection when the pot was heated on the fire. One particularly fine specialist ware, Reserved Slip ware, was coated first with a black and then a gray slip. The latter was then selectively removed to create combed patterns exposing the black surface beneath.

When the vessels were completely dry, they might be painted, usually with black made from a mixture of iron and manganese oxides or red from red ochre; occasionally white or very occasionally yellow, blue, or green was also used. Horizontal lines were applied while turning the piece on the wheel to create decorative zones within which, on some vessels, patterns were laid out using a grid. Plant and animal designs were included on many early painted vessels but these were rare later.

Firing. Pots might be fired in a simple bonfire kiln: these are still used in the subcontinent and had been for millennia by Harappan period. Fuel, such as cow dung, reeds, brushwood, or straw, was spread in a shallow pit or over sloping open ground, and the pots were stacked above it, in layers, facing in any direction except completely upright or upside down. Sherds were used to support unstable pots where necessary. To protect them during firing, particularly fragile pieces were placed inside a lidded jar (sagger), which was sealed with a mixture of straw and clay; some were found in the potter's workshop at Nausharo. Prefiring graffiti were perhaps used to identify vessels made by different potters when several shared a bonfire firing.

The pottery stack was covered with sherds and a layer of dust and ash, then more fuel, and finally a layer of clay spread over the top to seal in the bonfire, with the mouth of a broken jar set in the top to provide a smoke hole; others set around the edges enabled air to be drawn in and circulate inside the stack. At Nausharo, terra-cotta cakes may also have been used to cover the stack or protect its edges. After lighting, the bonfire kiln would be left for about eight to ten days: one to three days for the firing and about a week for the pots to cool. A small bonfire kiln site was associated with the pottery workshop at Nausharo, and it is possible that most pottery was fired in this way.

Other types of kilns are also known, however, perhaps reserved for firing small quantities of fine wares and other specialist products such as stoneware bangles since these allowed the firing conditions to be controlled. This was important, for example, in firing painted pottery. First the pottery was fired in an oxidizing atmosphere. Then the firing was completed in a reducing atmosphere by closing the air vents; this fixed the black color of the paint by sintering the pigment. Finally, the air vents were reopened to restore an oxidizing atmosphere in which the unpainted portions of the pottery returned to red.

The majority of kilns were of the updraft type, in which the round or oval clay-lined fire chamber was at the bottom, either constructed in a pit lined with clay or built of bricks and enclosed in an earthen bank. The pots were stacked on a perforated platform supported above the fire chamber on a pillar or tongue of bricks. A temporary domed roof was constructed over this for each firing and removed afterward; kilns were sometimes used and renewed over centuries. A funnel-shaped stoke hole at one side allowed the temperature of the kiln to be maintained by adding fuel and controlling the air flow. Terra-cotta baffles were used to prevent heat loss. Additional flues might be present on the other side to ensure that the air circulated fully causing the fuel to burn evenly throughout the kiln. Examples have been excavated at Harappa, Mohenjo-daro, Lothal, Lal Shah, Balakot, and Nageshwar. At other sites including Kalibangan, debris such as vitrified bricks or clay, ash, and sherds of misfired pottery (wasters) suggests the presence of kilns.

Pottery Types. Harappan pottery ranged from plain everyday pots, usually of a thick sturdy ware, to fine painted vessels. Generally Harappan pots were made of plain reddish orange ware, but a few types were black; painted examples were decorated in the contrasting color. A few early pots from Mohenjo-daro were of a grayish ware, and other wares are known from Gujarat, where they probably derive from earlier local pottery such as Padri ware.

The majority of pottery types were found throughout the Harappan realms; although there was some variation in domestic wares, there was great uniformity in more specialized products. Plain pottery included round-based cooking pots with a substantial rim for ease of lifting off the fire; medium-sized storage jars, often with pointed bases to be set in the floor; dishes and bowls for serving food; and beakers and cups to drink from. Specialist wares included fine pedestaled dishes and bowls, which may have been used for making offerings, and lavishly painted S-profile jars. Large black-slipped storage vessels were produced by skilled potters and perhaps only at Harappa. Other characteristic forms included jar stands, perforated jars that may have served as sieves or braziers, and pointed-based goblets, which were very common in the later levels at Mohenjo-daro and Harappa. In addition there were a few regional types used alongside standard Harappan wares in some areas, particularly Sothi-Siswal wares in the eastern province and Sorath wares in Saurashtra, which included distinctive stud-handled bowls.

The finer vessels were coated in a red slip and many were painted. In the early Mature Harappan period, the painted designs often included plant and occasionally animal motifs, such as peacocks or pipal leaves, as well as geometric designs, but later painted wares usually bore only the latter. These included various designs using intersecting circles, a distinctive fish scale pattern, and hatched squares or triangles.

Stoneware Bangles. Puzzling vitrified agglomerations of pottery, clay, and bangles found at Mohenjo-daro were subjected to detailed chemical and physical analyses and dissection by M. A. Halim of the Pakistan Department of Archaeology and Massimo Vidale of IsMEO, revealing that the debris resulted from the disastrous misfiring of an elaborate arrangement for firing stoneware bangles.

The stoneware bangles were a sophisticated product. The clay to make them was sieved and well levigated to produce a very fine paste. A thick hollow cylinder was thrown on the wheel and marked off into sections. After a few hours' drying this was cut, using a cord, into individual bangle blanks, which were then left to dry until hard. A central column was fastened to the wheel over which each bangle in turn was placed, allowing its outer part to be trimmed with a stone blade while the wheel revolved. The interior was also trimmed, either by hand or seated in a shallow bowl set on the wheel. The surface of the bangle was burnished with a stone and polished with a cloth. Finally a short inscription was scratched on the side with a burin.

By skillful throwing and careful control the bangles were made to an exact size, 5. 5–6 centimeters internal diameter after firing. The arrangements for

A distinctive Indus pottery type, the perforated jar; this example comes from Harappa. Such jars are usually found inside large bowls, a combination perhaps used as brewing equipment, with the perforated jar, wrapped in cloth, serving as a strainer. (J. M. Kenoyer, Courtesy Department of Archaeology and Museums, Government of Pakistan)

firing were complex. The bangles were usually placed in pairs in small, lidded bowls used as saggers, which were stacked in a column of around five and then coated in chaff-tempered clay. This stack was placed in a large, horizontally ribbed, clay-coated jar. A lid was placed over the jar and also coated in clay to seal it, effectively insulating the bangles from the air during firing. Finally a massive outer cap was placed over the top and impressed with a unicorn seal to ensure that the ensemble could not be tampered with. The sealed vessel was stably set on stacks of terra-cotta bangles in a kiln, which was fired at a high temperature.

The finished bangles were a mottled grayish black, resembling fine-grained metamorphic stone, and broken examples show that they were black right through. This was achieved in part by the reducing firing atmosphere, but the effect may have been enhanced by including some organic material within the nested containers; experiments showed that goat dung produced excellent results. These bangles were produced only at Mohenjo-daro and Harappa.

Terra-cottas. Terra-cotta rings were manufactured as the "cheapest" form of the bangles that were ubiquitous in the Indus civilization, and some of these had red-painted decoration. Other objects of terra-cotta included inscribed tablets, floor tiles, triangular cakes, and decorated cones whose function is uncertain. The most intriguing object was a birdcage found at Harappa, a globular vessel with horizontal and vertical slits in its walls, and a slotted terra-cotta door. But apart from pottery the most common objects of fired clay were human and animal figurines.

A unique terra-cotta object found in a late level at Harappa, thought to have been a birdcage. On the other side, not visible in this photograph, is a slot to take a sliding door. The top is missing. (Harappa Archaeological Research Project, Courtesy Department of Archaeology and Museums, Government of Pakistan)

The figurines were generally hand-modeled, although in later Mature Harappan times the heads of bull figurines were made in a mold, details, such as horns, being added by hand, along with the bodies. Studies of the female figurines found at Harappa revealed that many were made as separate left- and right-side halves, comprising head, torso, and legs, joined together before details were added; the latter included arms and thickened shoulders and accessories such as necklaces. Many of the features, such as noses, were pinched out by hand, while others, such as eyes and jewelry, were added as blobs and strips of clay.

The fabric of the terra-cottas was the same as that used for making pottery. Some bear slight surviving traces of paint. The vast majority of figurines were solid, but a few large animal figures were made of clay over a core of straw that burned out during firing, leaving a hollow interior. Kilns for firing terra-cottas were generally smaller than those for pottery; these are known, for example, from Balakot and Allahdino.

Stone

In the pre-Harappan period, metal objects were few in number and their repertoire quite restricted, whereas there were numerous stone tools of many types. In the Harappan period, the reverse was true, metal objects becoming common and the number and variety of stone tools relatively restricted. Nevertheless there were still many objects for which stone was the most appropriate material, such as grindstones, and others, such as drills and cutting tools, that were made both in stone and metal, either to be used on different materials or for use by different sectors of the population. Harappan stone artifacts included edge tools mainly of flint but also of jasper and chalcedony, weights, grindstones, seals, beads, and other small objects.

Hard Stone. Querns were made of granite, basalt, and other volcanic stone, often available as river pebbles. Quartzite or sandstone was used for grinding stone objects. Weights were manufactured mainly of chert, but felspar, chalcedony, carnelian, agate, jasper, and amazonite were also used. Marble, alabaster, and other attractive stones were made into gaming pieces, balls, and other small items, as well as small architectural components such as window grilles. Vessels such as jar stands might also be made out of stone. Small, perforated spherical objects of various sizes have been interpreted in a number of ways: as mace heads, digging stick weights, or bolas components.

Stone was dressed and shaped into artifacts by chipping and hammering with stones, using direct percussion, and finished by grinding and polishing with abrasive stones. Hollowed surfaces and perforations could be made in the same ways or worked with drills and abrasive sand. Sculptures were made by the same methods.

Flint. Pre-Harappan flint tools were generally made of different types of locally available flint. In contrast, those of the Harappans, including the residents of Shortugai in Afghanistan, were made almost exclusively from the brownish gray flint from the Rohri Hills in Sindh. This limestone plateau contains a substantial outcrop of very fine-quality flint that had been quarried since Palaeolithic times. Limestone, used for sculpture and for ring stones, was also available there. Many Harappan quarries were discovered along the plateau edges. These might be sunk more than a meter before a vein of flint was found.

The Indus stoneworkers swept aside the debris of earlier flint knappers to make cleared areas where they sat to work the flint. Debris defining one Harappan working floor comprised more than thirty-five thousand pieces of waste flint. First the flint knapper roughly shaped a suitable nodule using direct percussion with a hammerstone. This initial work generally took place near the quarry from which the flint had been extracted. The roughed-out precore was then worked into a shape suitable for striking blades, using a copper-tipped punch to remove flakes from its sides. Some prepared cores were taken to Harappan settlements such as Mohenjo-daro, where blades could be struck from them, though blades were also manufactured in the Rohri Hills factory site itself. The nearby town of Kot Diji was an important center for flint blade production.

The majority of Indus stone tools were made by using or modifying the long regular blades that were struck from the prepared core, using a copper-tipped tool that was pressed against the top of the core using the weight of the body. Often the core was heated before striking the blades because this enabled longer, smoother blades to be detached. Cores usually yielded several dozen blades before becoming too small. Tiny bullet cores, only about a centimeter in diameter, were made by specialists, and from these cores narrow microblades were struck, around 2–3 millimeters in width.

Most blades were used unmodified as cutting tools or were snapped into smaller segments. A few were used as blanks and shaped into other tools such as borers, scrapers for trimming pottery, and burins for incising shell. Leaf-shaped arrowheads were made by retouching blade segments, using pressure flaking with a soft hammer.

The Cambay Technique. Inverse indirect percussion may have been used, particularly to make objects with a square section, such as weights, drills, and beads. Known as the Cambay (Khambat) technique, this method of flint knapping is peculiar to South Asia, where it is attested to by the sixteenth century CE; although there is no indubitable proof that it was used in Harappan times, this is probable. The flint core was held against a stake tipped with copper or antler, while it was struck with a soft hammer made of wood, antler, or horn, detaching a long blade. The technique achieved the same results as normal indirect percussion but had the advantage, particularly useful when working small objects such as beads, that one hand was free to hold the object being knapped; in normal indirect percussion, the hands hold the hammer and the punch, so the object being knapped has to be held firm between the knees or feet.

Drills. Many of the drills used to perforate beads were made of phtanite, a type of green chert containing traces of iron oxide. These drills were made on small flakes that were retouched to form approximately square section bars; further chipping and polishing reduced them to tiny cylindrical drill bits with a slight depression in the tip. A few drill bits were made of an extremely hard stone that has been called Ernestite after Ernest Mackay who first identified its use. This was produced artificially by heating a rare type of fine-grained metamorphic rock containing titanium oxide until a change in its crystalline structure occurred, giving it exceptional hardness. Microdrills in flint were also made. The wear on flint drills suggests that they were not used for beadmaking but on softer materials, such as shell and leather.

Metalworking

Abundant copper and bronze tools and ornaments are known from all the Harappan towns and cities, and they occur even in small rural settlements. Evidence, such as copper prills and fragments of clay kiln lining and crucibles, and occasionally kilns, indicates the presence of metal workshops in many settlements.

Copper and Bronze. Analyses of Harappan artifacts suggest that almost all the copper used was either native copper or copper oxide ore, rather than copper sulphide ore, which is harder to work (though the latter is known in the early levels at Mohenjo-daro). Trace element analysis suggests that the Harappans obtained ore from several sources, notably the Aravalli Hills and Oman (Magan).

As yet, no definite evidence of copper smelting has been found in Harappan settlements; so copper was probably imported as smelted metal. This was certainly the case for copper from Magan, where copper was smelted, refined, and made into bun-shaped ingots at sites adjacent to the mines. Such ingots have been found at Lothal, Mohenjo-daro, and Chanhu-daro; however, this form of ingot need not be diagnostic since it is the shape produced naturally when smelted metal settles in the base of a bowl furnace, and it was therefore widespread in antiquity. Small square- and round-sectioned copper rods of refined copper may also have been ingots, in a form that could readily be made into artifacts by cold hammering; such rods are common at Mohenjo-daro.

It is assumed that Aravallis copper was also smelted near its source by the people of the Jodhpura-Ganeshwar culture. The traces of copper working kilns so far detected at Mohenjo-daro, Harappa, Kuntasi, and Lothal suggest that these were used for refining matte (roughly smelted copper still containing impurities) and for melting the metal for casting and alloying. Two types were used at Lothal: a circular kiln with a long flue for using bellows to circulate air and raise the temperature, and a rectangular type with a surround of baked bricks. A bowl-shaped crucible was also found there and a boat-shaped crucible at Dholavira.

However, polluting industrial activities such as smelting are likely to have been located on the outskirts of settlements or beyond, so they may still lie there undiscovered. It is possible that copper smelting occurred at Mohenjo-daro in an industrial area uncovered well to the east of the Lower Town, where chank shells were cleaned and where slag and fragments of furnace walls have been found. The possibility of smelting at Mohenjo-daro may be supported by the discovery in the DK area of a brick-lined pit in which copper oxide ore was stored.

Copper was used to make many everyday objects; since broken metal objects could be recycled, the examples discovered must represent only a fraction of those that were used. These included knives, daggers, razors, arrowheads, spearheads, axes, adzes, chisels, punches, barbed fishhooks, tubular drills, and various types of saws, including the true saw with teeth set alternately to left and right. Harappan copper/bronze saws could apparently cut shell as efficiently as the steel saws used today. There were also rings of copper wire, in a plain circle or a spiral, and copper beads and spacer beads. Most of these were of a very simple form that could be created by cold hammering and annealing or by casting in a one- or two-piece mold. Molds of sandstone and steatite have been found, for example, at Chanhu-daro. One cast copper axe from Mohenjo-daro was finished by dipping it into molten copper to give it a smooth outer shell. The straw-tempered crucibles used for heating metal were apparently heated from above, rather than from below, reducing the potential strains on them. Straw-tempered clay was also used to coat the walls of kilns for firing pottery and heating metal.

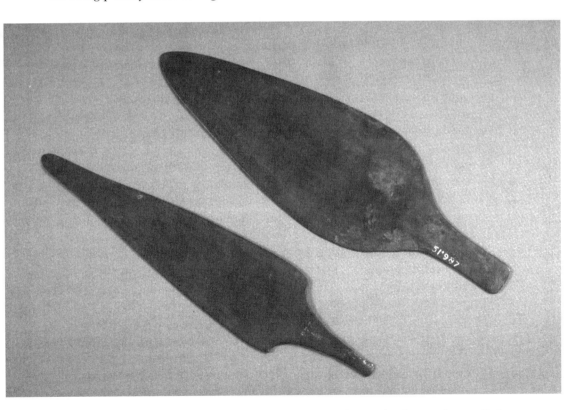

A dagger from Harappa (left) and a spearhead from Mohenjo-daro made of copper/bronze. Both are simple flat objects with no strengthening features such as a midrib, so they could not have been effectively used as weapons. They were, however, easy to manufacture and easy to repair. (J. M. Kenoyer, Courtesy Department of Archaeology and Museums, Government of Pakistan)

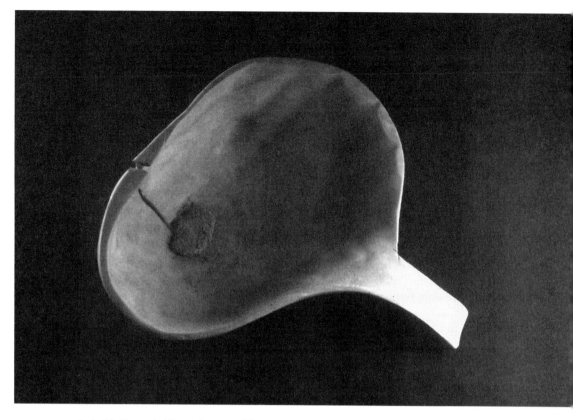

A shell ladle, probably used to pour libations in rituals. It was therefore a valuable object, thought worthy of repair. A lead rivet was inserted to mend a hole in its base. (The crack is more recent, due to the lead expanding and corroding.) (J. M. Kenoyer, Courtesy Department of Archaeology and Museums, Government of Pakistan)

Some objects such as metal vessels were made in several pieces that were joined by cold hammering. Stone anvils and hammerstones are known, for example, in the coppersmithing workshops at Kuntasi and Lothal. Other techniques used for joining included riveting and running on.

Many people have commented unfavorably on the technological simplicity of Harappan metal tools, pointing out, for example, that the Indus metalworkers were still making simple flat axes when their neighbors were making technically more advanced shaft-hole axes. It seems that the few shaft-hole artifacts found in Indus sites were all imports. Nevertheless, the use of simple technology was clearly a matter of choice since Harappan metalworkers also produced a range of sophisticated and complex products. These were made in specialist workshops in the cities, whereas the production of everyday objects was more widespread, with local metalworkers investing their time in mass-producing simple but practically efficient tools rather than turning out smaller numbers of more sophisticated products.

Bronze figurines show that the Harappans were masters of complex casting using the *cire perdue* (lost wax) technique. The most famous example is the Dancing-girl from Mohenjo-daro. Fine copper or bronze bowls and dishes were raised by beating a piece of copper over a bronze anvil, such as the snarling iron (a bronze bar with a convex surface at each end) identified at Chanhu-daro. This was found in a metalworking workshop along with several of the bowls that would have been raised on it and a number of other metal objects. In addition, there was a set of scale pans for weighing the metal. The opposite method, sinking, was also employed by the Harappans to make vessels. Copper wire was made, probably by drawing the metal through grooves cut in a stone block. A necklace made of tightly coiled wire was found at Harappa.

Although the majority of Harappan artifacts were of unalloyed copper, Harappan metalworkers made various alloys of copper, with tin, lead, arsenic, and even silver. Since tin was rare and had to be imported, it was used sparingly. Arsenic may have been deliberately alloyed with copper; however, arsenical copper ore was found in both Oman and the Aravalli Hills, so it is more probable that a natural alloy containing a low percentage of arsenic was deliberately selected because the Harappans appreciated its qualities. Arsenical copper was harder and stronger than pure copper though not as hard as tin bronze; the latter was also easier to cast. The alloys used were carefully matched to the purpose for which the artifacts were designed. Unalloyed copper was used for objects that did not have to stand up to hard use, but those, like knives, axes and chisels, that were for use against hard surfaces were made from copper alloyed with up to 13 percent tin: conventional bronze. The proportion of objects made with tin bronze increased during the Harappan period, presumably indicating an increase in the availability of tin. An alloy with much higher levels of tin, sometimes combined with lead, was used to make surfaces that would take a high polish for mirrors and attractive vessels.

Gold and Silver. Electrum was used by the Harappans: either natural electrum from South India or electrum produced by alloying gold and silver. These metals were also used separately. One possible silver workshop at Mohenjo-daro yielded a small crucible, a silver-lead ingot, and slag. Lead and silver may have been smelted there and at Harappa, though the evidence is slim. Objects of silver and gold have come mainly from Harappa and Mohenjo-daro; only a few are known from other sites, such as gold beads at Lothal and Banawali, and gold and silver objects in a jewelry hoard at Allahdino.

Gold was used mainly to make jewelry such as pendants, ear ornaments, cones, brooches, and beads. Bangles were made from hammered gold sheet, curved round into a hollow tube. A hoard found in the HR area at Mohenjo-daro included a necklace with gold spacer beads made by soldering a pair of disc beads edge to edge. Another necklace from Mohenjo-daro had spacers of strips of beaten gold, perforated to take six strings of beads. A Late Harappan hoard, accidentally discovered in 2000 CE at Mandi in Uttar Pradesh, contained a number of gold necklaces of paper-thin disc beads, spacer beads, and semicircular terminal beads, as well as tubular gold and silver bangles or anklets. Gold was hammered into sheets from which fillets, worn to secure the hair, were cut; these were burnished, erasing the hammer marks, and perforated at the ends. Gold sheet was also used to cover some terra-cotta beads found at Banawali, and several gold beads with a copper core and a button of gold sheet were found at Harappa. Gold beads and pendants were often combined with stone beads in necklaces and bracelets or anklets. Some more elaborate ornaments were also made by combining these materials. For example, two identical brooches found at Harappa had a gold base to which gold bands were soldered to form cells in a double-spiral pattern, which were filled with beads of blue-glazed steatite with gold ends, set in mastic.

Silver was also used to make jewelry. Silver wire and foil were made into bracelets, and silver wire was coiled into rings. A necklace of silver discs and spacer beads was among the jewelry in a hoard concealed in a jar at Allahdino, along with two or three necklaces of silver beads, several gold fillets, and other necklaces of stone and copper beads. Two seals made of silver were found at Mohenjo-daro, each bearing the common unicorn motif. However, silver was used mainly for vessels such as the elegant jars with lids found at Mohenjo-daro.

Many of the techniques used in working copper and bronze were also applied to gold and silver. In addition, Harappan jewelers used filigree and granulation in the production of their finest objects.

Other Metals. A number of lead ingots have been found but only a few objects of lead are known, for example, plumb bobs. A shell ladle from Harappa had been mended using a lead rivet. Lead was sometimes alloyed with copper, producing a more ductile though softer metal that was easier to cast.

It has been claimed that iron was produced in third-millennium South Asia, objects of iron being reported from Lothal and Chanhu-daro, as well as from Ahar in Rajasthan and Mundigak and a few other sites in the borderlands. It is possible that these objects were made from meteoric iron or were hammered from iron in slag produced either as a by-product of smelting iron-rich copper sulphide ore or when iron oxide was used as a flux in copper smelting. As in the contemporary Near East, iron would at this time have been a curiosity rather than a metal in regular use.

Shell

Seashells provided one of the main materials used for creating personal ornaments, particularly bangles, though they were also put to other uses. A few species were preferred, such as chank for bangles, but more than thirty different species are known to have been utilized, to a greater or lesser degree.

Workshops. While many shells were processed on or near the coast, in some cases intact shells were transferred to inland centers, such as Mohenjo-daro. The distribution of shellworking debris shows that different stages in the manufacturing process were often undertaken in different locations. This is particularly clear at the specialist shellworking settlement of Nageshwar. Here separate areas were given over to the evil smelling task of cleaning the shells, the production of bangles, the making of inlays, and the production of ladles.

In a workshop area in the citadel at Gola Dhoro were found three large heaps containing, respectively, unworked shells, shells discarded as too small or damaged by boring sea creatures, and roughed-out bangles, the latter evidently packed into a large square sack or bag of some perishable material, now gone. Whole shells were brought to Nageshwar and Gola Dhoro for processing; farther around the coast at Nagwada, the shell industry was based on pieces of chank shell that had already been prepared; these were used to make bangles, ladles, and inlay pieces, as well as a fine ball decorated with circles.

Large quantities of unworked shells, stored ready for use, at Gola Dhoro and Balakot and enormous heaps of waste material demonstrate the huge scale of production in sites like these. On the basis of the debris recovered, the volume of shells worked at Nageshwar was far higher than at Mohenjo-daro, though the picture might change if the city's suburban areas were explored. Evidence of shellworking was also found at Harappa in mound ET, at Lothal, and at Chanhu-daro, where bangles and ladles were made. At Mohenjo-daro, shell bangles seem to have been finished in many small dispersed workshops, whereas shell inlay manufacture was concentrated in a few larger working areas. Beads, ladles, and discs were also made in Mohenjo-daro's workshops, and in one house in the HR-B area, near a workshop making inlays, shell debris was burned to make lime for plaster.

In the Late period at Mohenjo-daro, a number of industrial activities, including shellworking, were undertaken in the pillared hall on the citadel mound. In contrast to earlier shellworking in the Lower Town, this workshop did not make bangles nor did it use chank, previously the most commonly used shell; instead it seems to have been concerned mainly with inlay production.

Procurement and Selection. The shells were gathered on the west coast where there were a number of settlements specializing in the processing of the shells, such as Balakot and Nageshwar. Chank (*Turbinella pyrum*), *Lambis truncata sebae,* and *Chicoreus ramosus* (spiny murex) shells were available along much of the Harappans' western seaboard, *Fasciolaria trapezium* was found in the Gulf of Kutch and off Oman, and other species, including the clam *Tivela damaoides,* could be caught off the Makran coast.

The pile of inferior shells at Gola Dhoro, discarded as unusable for bangle making, shows that selection was not always the job of those who procured the shells. In contrast, the debris at Nageshwar shows that the fishers who supplied the shells, who were perhaps themselves also the shell workers, took care to procure good-quality shells by catching them offshore where they were less exposed to boring organisms such as sponges.

Making Bangles. The majority of shell bangles were made from chank, which required metal tools to work. A hole was chipped in the shell's apex with a stone or bronze hammer, and the foul-smelling decayed remains of the mollusc removed. Segregated areas for this unpleasant task have been uncovered not only in the industrial village of Nageshwar and the town of Balakot, but also in an isolated quarter east of the Lower Town at Mohenjo-daro.

The columella and other interior portions were broken and removed using a hammer and metal punch or a pick. A chank shell might be made into a single bangle by diagonally removing the mouth and apex using a special thin convex bronze saw, leaving the wide central section: this produced a large sturdy bangle. Alternatively several finer shell rings could be sawn from a shell and ground to the required thickness and smoothness, using abrasive stone tools. This produced an elegant kidney-shaped bangle, circular with a slightly thickened portion at one side protruding a little into the center, a shape imitated in other materials. A decorative V was generally inscribed on the outside of the bangle to disguise the point where the whorls joined, using a metal file or flint blade.

While chank was the shell most commonly used for bangles, others were also used, including *Pugelina buchephala* and *Chicoreus ramosus.* Rather fragile bangles were made at Balakot from *Tivela damaoides* shells; this was laborious but required only stone tools. The shell was held on a stone anvil while it was chipped with a hammerstone, ground on a grindstone using wet sand as an abrasive, and filed with a stone rasp until the central portion of the shell was worn away and the edges smoothed to produce an almost circular bangle. Each shell of a *Tivela* bivalve produced only one such bangle, which could have been turned out in under two hours, though many may have broken during manufacture. These were worn only in the local region, along the Makran coast.

Other Shell Objects. The Harappans generally used the different types of shell available to them for different purposes, though not exclusively. Shells of the

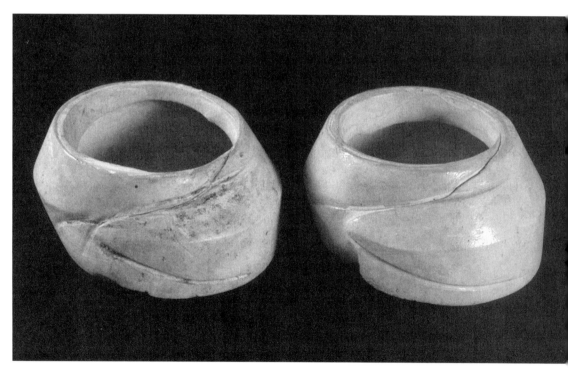

Two heavy bangles, each made from a single conch shell and decorated with a chevron motif over the natural suture. (J. M. Kenoyer, Courtesy Dept. of Archaeology and Museums, Government of Pakistan)

spiny murex (*Chicoreus ramosus*) were occasionally made into bangles (for example, at Chanhu-daro) but were mainly used to make ladles. Most ladles were of spiny murex, though at Nagwada they were made of chank. The ladles were roughed out in coastal sites such as Nageshwar and also at Chanhu-daro. The spines were sawn off and the shell sawn vertically to make two ladles, one smaller than the other. A right-angled piece was cut from either side to turn the narrower end into a handle. The ladle rough-outs were taken to the major centers, such as Harappa and Mohenjo-daro, where they were ground into their final shape and polished and where they would be used, probably in rituals.

Chank shells were sometimes, with great difficulty, hollowed out and the outside ground smooth, to made a vessel for pouring libations like those still used in India. Several chank shell libation vessels are known from Mohenjo-daro, and a similar vessel, made from a *Fasciolaria trapezium* shell, came from Chanhu-daro. At Harappa, a chank shell trumpet was found; this had a mouthpiece at the apex, formed by chipping. Like the libation vessel, the chank shell trumpet continued in ritual use through later times.

Several types of shell were used to make inlay pieces to decorate wooden furniture and occasionally sculptures. The body of the *Fasciolaria trapezium* shell was cut and ground into pieces, while *Lambis truncata sebae* shells were sawn into thick and thin sheets. Inlay pieces often bore incised designs; sometimes there are traces of red and black pigment along their edges or within the incised lines, showing that they were originally painted. Inlays were also made from the fragments of chank and spiny murex shell left from the manufacture of other objects.

Waste pieces and *Fasciolaria* and *Lambis* shells were also used to make small objects such as rings, cones, lids, gaming pieces, pendants, buttons, tiny figurines, and the caps used on beadmaking drills. Rings were generally made from the spire of the chank shell and perforated cylinders from the columella; other objects were made from any suitable shell. The tiny shells of some marine species were perforated and used as beads and pendants without further alteration. At Nageshwar in the bangle-making area, the debris was sorted and neatly stacked, ready to be taken by workers making inlays and other small shell objects in other parts of the site. The manufacture of such objects required a range of stone and metal tools, including a tubular metal drill to cut small circles and discs. Nothing needed to be wasted: small pieces of shell were made into beads or tiny inlay pieces such as the eyes of statues, which were fastened in place with gypsum mortar. Any remaining debris could be burned to mix with lime for making plaster.

Lapidary Work

Beadmaking had a long history in the subcontinent, but the Harappans developed a number of new and sophisticated tools and techniques for manufacturing more challenging types of bead, including drills capable of perforating long beads of hard stone. The Harappans were particularly fine lapidaries, making beads from a wide variety of semiprecious stones, particularly agate and carnelian but also amethyst, chalcedony, jasper, onyx, rock crystal, serpentine, and many others, as well as from gold, silver, copper, shell, ivory, faience, terra-cotta, and steatite. Surprisingly uncommon were beads of lapis lazuli or turquoise, beautiful blue stones from southern Central Asia that had been valued in the region since early times. In general the Harappans seem to have preferred stones like agate and chalcedony that were harder to work but that retained a high polish, in contrast to the softer lapis and turquoise; imitations were also made in faience.

Workshops. A number of Harappan settlements in Sindh and Gujarat (source of much of the stone) operated substantial beadmaking establishments ("fac-tories"). Beads were also manufactured in small workshops. The skills of the lapidary and the equipment used, including kilns, were equally applicable to the production of other objects in related materials, such as stone weights and amulets and steatite seals; these, therefore, were often made in the same workshops.

At Mohenjo-daro many workshops were found in individual houses throughout the city. In the Moneer area, one house yielded a large number of beads along with sixteen small weights and a set of copper scales. The dumps and eroded materials along the southeast edge of Mohenjo-daro's Lower Town contained a great deal of beadmaking debris including drills, grinding stones, and raw and worked pieces of many types of gemstone. Workshops making beads and other objects from steatite seem to have been separate from those making beads from other materials.

Large complexes included the beadmaking factory at Lothal, where a court-yard was the scene of the main manufacturing activities while accommodation and storage were provided by eleven small rooms that opened from it. Several jars set into the platform held beads in various stages of manufacture, and jars in the storerooms contained raw material. Another factory was found in the center of Chanhu-daro; this made a range of bead types and is at present the only workshop where the manufacture of the elongated carnelian beads is known to have taken place. A furnace with many flues is thought to have been designed for heating stone for beads and firing the steatite seals that were also made there.

Bead Manufacture. Different types of stone varied in their properties and therefore in the techniques by which they were worked. The quartz group, in-cluding the most commonly used stones such as agate, carnelian, and chal-cedony, was shaped by knapping, sawing, and grinding, whereas for the rarely used lapis lazuli, the groove-and-splinter technique was apparently employed.

Carnelian, the red stone of which many Harappan beads were made, was cre-ated from a yellowish chalcedony by heating it, in a closed pot packed with saw-dust, several times during the course of manufacture, gradually deepening its color. The fuel used was one that burned steadily at a relatively low temperature: this was probably charcoal mixed with reeds and cowdung. Heating also made the stone easier to work, and so other stones like agate were also often repeatedly heat-treated during manufacture. Even warming in the sun was effective. Several

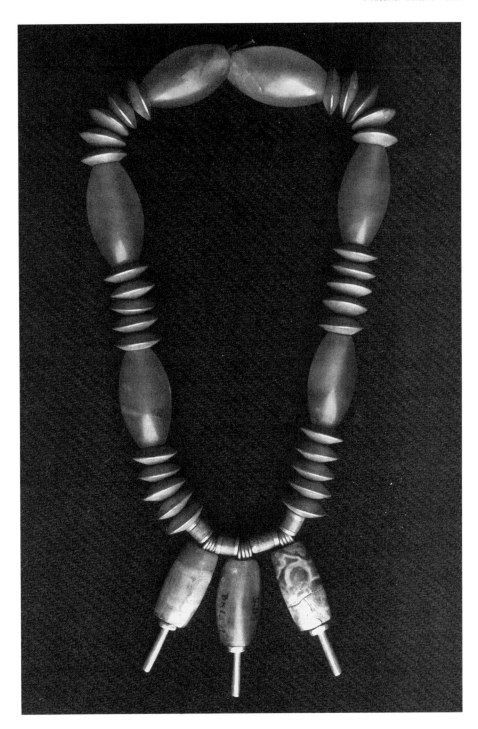

Part of a necklace found in a silver vessel at Mohenjo-daro. The necklace is composed of large beads of green stone separated by small gold beads, with pendant beads of jasper and agate separated by small steatite beads. Harappan lapidaries made extensive use of various types of chalcedony, such as agate, carnelian, and jasper, which could be highly polished, and of the versatile steatite, which was soft and therefore easy to work but could be hardened by heating. (J. M. Kenoyer, Courtesy Department of Archaeology and Museums, Government of Pakistan)

open-topped circular kilns used for this purpose were found at Lothal; these had linked flues and a shared stoke hole in an underground chamber.

The lapidary began work on a bead by removing a few chips from the raw nodule to assess the quality of the stone. From this he or she could determine the most appropriate way to work the nodule so as to achieve the most attractive design. The lapidary then chipped the stone into a bead blank: a rough cube for making spherical beads or a cuboid or triangular-sectioned shape for making long beads. This technique produced one bead from each piece of raw material. A number of small beads could be made from a single cobble by knapping it into a shape from which it could be struck into sections, each of which was shaped in the same way into a blank. An alternative, used for example in the bead factory at Chanhu-daro, was to cut the material into a blank using a copper saw, probably with abrasives. Some blanks might break during manufacture, particularly the banded varieties since their veins could vary in their response to the knapping blows.

Next the blank was knapped into a rough-out of the desired shape. This was then ground down into a bead shape by rubbing it against a groove cut into the abrasive surface of a sandstone or quartzite block, probably using a wooden board to press it down, as is done today.

A central perforation was made in short beads by chipping from both ends, creating an hourglass-shaped hole. Longer beads, however, were perforated using a microdrill whose head was made of hardened copper or phtanite. Often the tip of the drill was tubular, allowing it to hold a fine abrasive. Drill bits were made in the same workshops as the beads. The bit was mounted on a wooden rod that was rotated using a bow. A cap of stone or shell on the wooden shaft protected the hand as the beadmaker exerted pressure on the drill to keep it seated in the bead. Dripping water may have been used to prevent the bead and drill bit overheating. After drilling, more grinding put the finishing touches to the bead, before it was polished, probably by being tumbled in a bag with other beads and some fine abrasive.

Patterned Beads. Banded or variegated agate, jasper, and onyx were particularly prized, since they could be worked so as to expose bands around the bead or a series of circles over its surface; some had eye patterns of concentric circles. These beads were imitated in painted fired steatite, faience, etched carnelian, laminated shell, and painted terra-cotta. One eye bead from Harappa was of gold inlaid with a disc of steatite.

Carnelian. Carnelian beads were frequently decorated with designs in white or sometimes black. These often imitated the patterns on banded agate but also included trefoils or geometric patterns. These are generally erroneously described as etched carnelian beads. The designs were actually painted on with a bleaching agent; this may have been a solution of calcium carbonate or, as in modern times, a mixture of sodium carbonate and juice from the shoots of a caper bush (*Capparis aphylla*). The beads were allowed to dry and were then

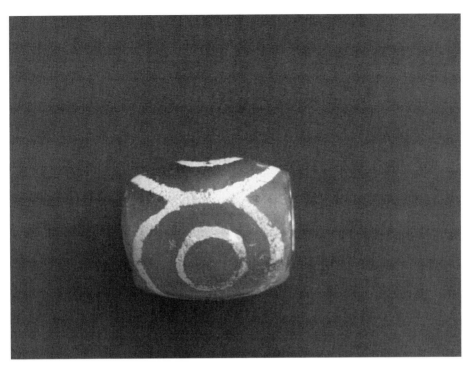

A carnelian bead decorated with an eye pattern in white. This was made by painting on a solution of a bleaching agent and then heating the bead, causing the painted area to lose its color. (Harappa Archaeological Research Project, Courtesy Department of Archaeology and Museums, Government of Pakistan)

heated, bleaching the surface where the paint had been applied. Over time the bleached area, which is weaker than the rest of the bead, has often eroded away, giving the impression of etching. Sometimes the whole bead was whitened in this way and designs were then painted on in black, possibly using a solution of copper nitrate or metallic oxide. Imitations of etched carnelian beads were made in painted steatite and faience.

Exceptional slender carnelian beads as much as 13 centimeters in length required extraordinary skill in their creation. Rectangular blanks for these beads were sawn from blocks of fine-quality, heat-treated raw carnelian and roughly shaped by indirect percussion. The beads were then ground into shape and special drills tipped with Ernestite bits in various sizes were used to create the long perforation. Many beads broke at this stage in their manufacture. The task was slow and hard, and it would have taken a lapidary about two weeks to manufacture a single such bead. An ornament made from these beads, such as the belt found in the Allahdino hoard, which contained thirty-six, could therefore represent the entire output of a skilled lapidary for a year or more. The manufacture of the Ernestite drill bits was also arduous, each one probably taking around a day's labor. Imitations were made of these beads in red-painted terra-cotta and were assembled into similar ornaments.

Steatite Microbeads. Equally amazing are the beautiful white steatite microbeads measuring only 1 by 1–3 millimeters. These were worn in long strings, each of which contained hundreds of beads, and have been found in a number of towns and cities. One man buried at Harappa wore a head ornament made from many strings of these microbeads. A cache buried in the rural settlement of Zekda in Gujarat numbered around thirty-four thousand beads, packed in ash inside two carefully sealed small pots. Clues revealed by examination under a microscope enabled three investigators, Hegde, Karanth, and Sychanthavong (1982), to reconstruct a possible method by which these beads may have been manufactured. They concluded that the raw stone, which is quite soft, was ground into a fine powder and mixed with water to make a paste. This was then extruded and cut into lengths. No suitable device for doing this is known; they suggested using a perforated copper disc with a fine copper wire soldered to pass centrally into each hole. Paste forced through the holes would emerge as tubes that could be cut into tiny lengths, perhaps using a hair. A tray of ash beneath to catch the beads would prevent them sticking to each other or getting damaged. The beads were fired at a high temperature, around 900 degrees Centigrade, converting them from the soft steatite paste to the extremely hard white material of the finished beads.

Another possible method, attested in the Moneer area at Mohenjo-daro and at Chanhu-daro, involved incredibly fine skilled working. A block of steatite was shaped into a tiny approximately cuboid shape that was perforated by drilling from both ends. This was then sawn into thin discs. Alternatively, as seems to have been the case at Harappa, thin steatite sheets were sawn and divided into roughly square discs that were then perforated. These discs were tightly strung together on a thread, so there was no possibility of lateral movement, and the string of bead blanks was rubbed against a grindstone until the beads were worn circular. The beads were then fired to whiten and harden them. It is incredible that it was possible to make such minute beads in this way and, given the hundreds used to make an ornament, also incredible that such a time-consuming process was undertaken.

Faience

By the early fourth millennium, artisans in the Indo-Iranian borderlands had devised a technique of coating steatite beads with a mixture of copper, lime, and clay before firing, to produce hard beads with a blue glaze. From this the Harappans went on to develop faience, using a different method to that employed in contemporary Mesopotamia and Egypt. This resulted in a stronger material that could be made into slender objects such as bangles. Much of the raw material used in making faience probably came from the waste from lapidary and seal-making workshops.

Harappan faience was manufactured in two stages. First rock crystal was ground to a powder and mixed with a flux and with the appropriate coloring material, of which the Harappans employed a considerable range, producing not only blue and blue-green but also white, red, buff, and brown faience. In some cases, two colors were used in the same object, as for example in some

A unique faience plaque found in a workshop at Harappa. On this face there is a four-sign inscription, beneath a box filled with dots; on the other a scene showing two bulls fighting beneath the spreading branches of a massive tree. The plaque was formed between two molds, probably carved from steatite. A mold and the fan-shaped faience tablet made in it were also recovered from this workshop, along with beads of agate and other types of stone, gold, and steatite, and miniature tablets and other objects of faience and steatite. (Harappa Archaeological Research Project, Courtesy Department of Archaeology and Museums, Government of Pakistan)

tablets and beads from Harappa. The mixture was melted at a temperature of 1,000–1,200 degrees Centigrade, producing a glassy material, which was again ground to a fine powder. This was mixed with a flux and some water to form a paste. Tiny pieces of bone consistently associated with, and embedded in, vitreous slag at Mohenjo-daro, Harappa, and Chanhu-daro suggest that calcined bone (containing calcium phosphate and calcium carbonate) may have been used as the flux in manufacturing faience.

The faience paste was shaped by hand or pressed into a mold to make small objects: beads and other jewelry such as bangles and ear ornaments, tablets, and charming little figurines that included monkeys and squirrels. A large number of molded miniature inscribed tablets, possibly amulets, are known from the later levels at Harappa. Tiny faience pots were made by molding the paste around the outside of a small bag filled with sand. Once formed, the sand was poured out and the bag removed. The faience objects were then dried in the air, allowing the flux to migrate to the surface. Finally they were again fired at a high temperature, around 940 degrees Centigrade, to produce the finished objects, which had a sintered interior and a glazed exterior.

Faience objects are widely known from Harappan sites, and they continued to be made in the Posturban period in the eastern region. Faience was produced at a number of sites; at Mohenjo-daro, Harappa, and Chanhu-daro, faience and steatite were often worked in the same workshops.

A further technological development is evidenced shortly after the Harappan decline: A bead dated around 1700 BCE was recovered from a hoard at Harappa and proved to have been made of brown glass, the earliest glass known in South Asia.

Steatite

Steatite is a soft material that was easily carved with tools of flint or copper, or possibly shell, but it becomes very hard when heated. It was used mainly for making seals and beads. At Harappa, one workshop in mound E manufactured faience and steatite beads and steatite tablets. Debris in the workshop included a steatite mold used to make fan-shaped molded faience tablets, and two discarded steatite tablets incised with the same poorly executed inscription, perhaps practice pieces.

Steatite's refractory properties also made it an ideal material for making molds for metal casting. At Harappa, a number of straw-tempered dishes were found, coated all over in steatite. Straw-tempered clay was used in pyrotechnological contexts, for example for crucibles; the steatite coating seems to have been put on to allow these dishes to withstand very high temperatures; however, their purpose is unknown. A series of small refractory bars, probably from a kiln or furnace, were found at Chanhu-daro; they had been made of clay mixed with a considerable amount of ground-up steatite.

Seals. The distinctive Indus seals were usually made of steatite, though other stones such as agate were sometimes used. Seal carving must have been a specialist skill since the seals are very small and the quality of workmanship and artistry high. Unfinished seals are widely known, showing that seals were manufactured at many centers, including Mohenjo-daro, Harappa, Chanhu-daro, and Lothal.

The seal maker first sawed a thick square block of steatite. He then roughly shaped the back by sawing off slices of steatite from each side, leaving a portion for the boss in the center. Next the front of the seal was carefully carved with a burin to produce an incised design, so that it would leave a design in relief when it was pressed into clay. A few unfinished examples suggest that a grid was drawn on the seal to allow the design to be properly laid out within the restricted space. An animal or scene was carved on the lower portion and a short inscription was added across the top; this may have been drawn by a literate specialist rather than the seal maker, since literacy is likely to have been confined to an elite few. The back was then completed, using a knife to form a hemispherical boss with a central groove over the outside from top to bottom. A hole was cut through the center of the boss by drilling from each side. This was the weakest point on the seal and was liable to break if the owner was unlucky. Finally a paste of powdered steatite and an alkaline flux mixed with water was spread over the surface of the seal and it was fired to harden and whiten it. The steatite paste fused to form a glazed protective surface over the seal.

Ivory, Bone, Horn, and Antler

Ivory, from wild or possibly domesticated elephants, was used for a wide range of small objects that were common in Indus towns, often outnumbering their counterparts in bone. These included sticks for applying makeup, carved cylinders, combs, pins, and beads. Inlays for boxes or furniture were also cut out of ivory. Small ivory representations of creatures such as fish and hares may have been amulets.

There were ivory-carving workshops in a number of towns and cities, including Lothal and mound ET at Harappa, where bone and antler were also worked. Unworked tusks are known from a few sites. These were probably sawn into sections using small, narrow-toothed metal saws and worked into the required shape with metal chisels, gouges, knives, and tubular drills. Pieces might be finished by polishing with an abrasive.

Bone was used for many everyday artifacts, such as handles for metal and flint tools, weaving equipment, beads, tools for smoothing and decorating pottery, awls, needles, and many other small objects. Unmodified bones were probably used as soft hammers for flint knapping. Horn and antler may have been used in similar ways, and antlers were also employed as picks or punches.

Gaming Equipment. Board games seem to have been popular among the Harappans. Most gaming boards were probably made of embroidered cloth, as they are today, but some were engraved on bricks or made of terra-cotta. The arrangements of boxes and lines suggest that there were a number of different games. Gaming counters and dice for use in these games were made of a variety of materials such as bone, shell, stone, or terra-cotta, those of ivory being the finest. There were various different pairings of the dots on the opposite faces of the cubical dice, including the modern arrangement in which the dots always add up to seven. Beautiful counters, thin rectangular rods engraved with dots and lines, their tops often in the shape of ducks, duck heads, or other animals or birds, were carved from ivory or bone.

Other Crafts

The Harappans must have practiced other crafts, but little is known of these because the objects themselves have disappeared. Instead, there are various indirect clues to what was made and how: traces left on other objects; tools and surviving elements in other materials; and information from modern practitioners of traditional crafts.

Wood. Small traces of wood found in various settlements show that the Harappans utilized timber from a variety of trees, including teak, sissoo, rosewood, deodar, pine, jujube, acacia, and elm, as well as bamboo. Wood was extensively used in buildings, both for structural elements and for fixtures, for

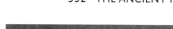

Three fine decorated rods carved from ivory, found at Mohenjo-daro. These may have been used as gaming counters or in divination. (J. M. Kenoyer, Courtesy Department of Archaeology and Museums, Government of Pakistan)

building many of the Harappan boats (although reeds may also have been used), and for making the carts so clearly depicted in models, which had a wooden frame and solid wheels constructed of planks.

Shell and ivory inlay pieces were used to decorate wooden furniture, such as the low stools sometimes depicted on the Indus seals. Shell inlay manufacture was among the crafts practiced in the final period of Mohenjo-daro's occupation, a counter to the usual picture of urban decline. Beds made of a wooden frame strung with a rope lattice in use today may have had their counterparts in Harappan times. Several terra-cotta model beds found at Kalibangan had corner posts, but the covers depicted on them concealed other details of their frames. Stains in the soil in Harappan graves occasionally show the use of wooden coffins; one at Harappa, of which fragments survive, was made of rosewood with a deodar lid.

Trees may have been felled with bronze flat axes or axes of stone, though the latter are rarely found. Timber was cut up with bronze saws and adzes, and carpentry and joinery work was executed with a range of metal tools, including chisels, gouges, drills, and knives. Stone blades were also used. Wooden surfaces could be smoothed on grindstones or with rasps made of cuttlefish "bones." The latter, known from the site of Othmanjo Buthi, could also be ground up to make an abrasive paste. A biconical terra-cotta pestle from Harappa has been identified as possibly a sander.

Though little evidence survives, it is likely that the Harappans used wood in many other ways, for example for household objects such as boxes or dishes and perhaps for figurines. One of the working platforms in mound F at Harappa had traces of a wooden mortar of jujube wood. The artistry displayed by the Harappans in other media suggests that many wooden objects would have borne carved or painted decoration.

Textiles. Most of the crafts discussed so far were practiced by specialists, producing goods for wide distribution. Textiles, on the other hand, were probably made in every home to meet the family's needs, though there may also have been larger-scale production. Spindle whorls have been found in many houses, their diversity of form a contrast to the more usual uniformity of Harappan artifacts, underlining the domestic nature of spinning. Possible loom weights suggest that some households may have used large upright looms to weave cloth (this seems unlikely since Barber [1991, 240–254] shows that upright looms were a European development, whereas the Near East and regions to its east used horizontal ground looms; the "loom weights" may have had other uses). A small backstrap loom was most probably used by many women, weaving narrow bands of cloth. Fairservis (2002) has suggested that many of the perforated rectangular clay objects usually identified as model cart frames (with holes into which wooden sticks could be slotted) may actually have been weaving shuttles; these have been found on many sites. At Allahdino hundreds were associated with perforated discs (probably spindle whorls rather than model cart wheels) and pillow-shaped clay objects with a central groove, which Fairservis interpreted as loom weights. It is therefore possible that Allahdino was an establishment particularly concerned with textile manufacture.

A small (broken) bone plaque from Ravi period Harappa with at least three lines of four holes may have been a device used to keep a number of separate strands from tangling, for example when warping a loom or when twisting cord. In the latter case either the strands or the plaque could be turned to ensure that the cord twisted evenly (Barber, personal communication).

A scrap of cloth from a bag was found at Mohenjo-daro, preserved in the corrosion products from two silver jars. This was made from cotton, a plant that had been cultivated in the subcontinent since the fifth millennium BCE. Evidence of cotton cloth similarly preserved on silver or bronze objects is also known from Harappa, Chanhu-daro, and Rakhigarhi and possibly from Lothal, where unidentified plant fibers were found on a piece of copper. Other traces of Indus textiles include the impressions of cotton fabric on the inside of faience vessels, the imprint of rougher cloth and of cord on the reverse of sealings that had been fastened on sacks, and marks on the base of pottery vessels (and in one case a brick) that had stood on cloth to dry before firing. These show that the Indus people were making cotton cloth of various grades, including very fine fabrics closely woven from thread so fine that it has been suggested that it was spun on a spinning wheel. The fabrics revealed by these data seem all to have been plain weave.

The exuberant geometric decoration on some pottery may reflect textile designs. Large jars set into the floor of one structure at Mohenjo-daro may have

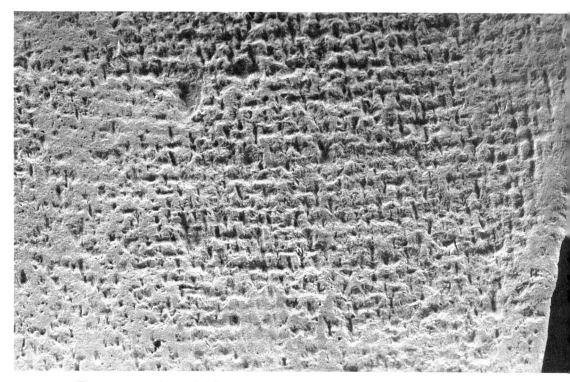

The impression of a textile left on the surface of a terra-cotta toy bed. The threads were finely spun and the cloth tightly woven in a plain weave, which was typical of Harappan cloth. (Harappa Archaeological Research Project, Courtesy Department of Archaeology and Museums, Government of Pakistan)

been for dyeing, and brick-built basins in other buildings there and in other settlements have also been identified as probable dyeing vats. The HARP excavations of one of the circular brick floors in mound F at Harappa revealed a deep depression containing greenish layers of clay; it is possible that this resulted from indigo dye preparation. It is likely that cloth was dyed various colors. At present the only surviving evidence of dyes comes from the cotton fragment found at Mohenjo-daro, which had been dyed red with madder root and fixed using alum as a mordant. However, other local plants such as indigo, found at Rojdi, and turmeric were probably also used for dyeing, producing blue and yellow respectively.

Cotton was certainly used for making cloth, but other textiles may also have been made. Wool and goat hair may have been used since the Harappans kept sheep and goats, although there is no evidence that they had woolly sheep. If woolen textiles were imported from Mesopotamia, it is possible, though less likely, that the Harappans also imported wool from which to weave woolen textiles themselves. Flax might have been used too, but at present the earliest evidence of its use in India comes some centuries after the Harappan period.

Silk is also a possibility. Although Chinese silk from the domestic silkworm was not traded to regions west of China until considerably later, India has several of its own wild species of moth that produce silk, including *Antheraea assamensis* (*maga*), *Antheraea mylitta* (*tussah*), and *Samia cynthia* (*eri*). This is inferior to Chinese silk, but it was extensively used in India in historical times. Like many forest products, the cocoons of these wild silkworms were collected in recent times by hunter-gatherers, who traded them with settled people. The Harappans could similarly have obtained supplies of raw silk from the hunter-gatherers with whom they traded various commodities. Currently the earliest evidence of silk in India is from the midsecond millennium BCE, but it is not unlikely that it was used by the Harappans.

Mats made from reeds and grasses and woven or coiled baskets have also left an impression on clay objects set down on them and on the clay floors on which they were set, as well as impressions of roof matting in surviving ceiling plaster. Floors or walls may have been covered with textiles: Kenoyer (1998, 159) has pointed out the similarity between a type of small curved knife made by the Indus people and knives used today to cut the pile of carpets, suggesting the possibility of carpet manufacture (although pile rugs would also have required wool).

Leather had probably been used for clothing in earlier times (as the evidence from Mehrgarh suggests) and may still have been so used in the Mature Harappan period by some sectors of the community or for some types of clothing. Leather would have had many other uses also, for buckets and other containers, for straps and belts, possibly for footwear, perhaps for sails, and for coverings; it was a substitute for cloth in many situations and could also be used to hold liquids.

ART

Fine arts are surprisingly poorly represented in the Indus civilization, with only a few known sculptures in bronze and stone; what does survive, however, includes some pieces of the highest aesthetic standard. Figurative bronze casting and stone carving, however, were by and large a relatively late development in India, sculpture until the late first millennium BCE being largely confined to exuberant modeling in terra-cotta. Lively terra-cotta figurines of people and animals attest to Harappan participation in a long-lived and vigorous folk art tradition, and other models were executed in ivory, shell, or faience. Painted pottery also continued earlier traditions, including both representational and geometric designs. There may have been painted designs on other media such as cloth wall hangings, and there were probably wooden carvings, though none survive. The artistic abilities of the Indus people are reflected best in the images on their seals.

Sculpture

Only a handful of stone sculptures have been recovered from Indus settlements, particularly Mohenjo-daro; most are of limestone though one is of alabaster. Some are unfinished and most are broken. These are all quite small: The famous Priest-king torso, for example, is only 17. 5 centimeters high. The usual subject of these sculptures is a half-kneeling male figure wearing a robe that leaves the right shoulder exposed. Where the head survives, the figures have almond eyes, widely spaced parallel lines on the chin representing a

The "Priest-king," the finest piece of Harappan statuary, was found at Mohenjo-daro. Though broken, it may originally have been a seated figure. Faint traces show that the trefoils on the figure's robe were originally filled with red pigment. The back of the head is cut away to form a flat surface where an elaborate headdress may have been mounted. (J. M. Kenoyer, Courtesy Department of Archaeology and Museums, Government of Pakistan)

beard, and braided or wavy lines showing the hair, short or in a bun, held in place by a headband. The finest example is the Priest-king, a calm, austere figure. The sculptures vary in quality and, although the posture is generally the same, the individuals' features and expressions all differ, perhaps suggesting that they were portraits of real people rather than images of idealized kings or divinities.

Two small incomplete sculptures from Harappa, in contrast, depict a naked male, carved in an extremely naturalistic style very different in feel from other Harappan art. It is thought possible that one (a red jasper torso) or both may be intrusive pieces of considerably later date. One, of dark stone, is clearly dancing, though only his torso and part of one leg, outstretched in front, survive. The other, of red jasper, broken off at the top of the legs, also appears to be slightly in motion. Both have dowel holes for the attachment of separate head and arms.

A recently discovered small wig, carved from black steatite, presumably formed part of a figurine, perhaps made of another type of stone or of wood.

Bronze sculptures are even rarer than those of stone. The best-known is the charming bronze figure from Mohenjo-daro known as the Dancing-girl, an extremely thin, unnaturally tall young woman with her hair in a bun, clad only in an armful of bangles and a small necklace. Her left hand holds something, while her right hand rests on her hip, and she is standing in a relaxed pose very true to life. Another figure with the same compositional features is far less convincing; she stands stiff legged with none of the insouciance of the Dancing-girl and has been humorously dubbed the Ugly Sister by Shereen Ratnagar.

The sculptures of animals also vary in artistic merit. An exquisite miniature model of a water buffalo tossing its head is extremely naturalistic, as is a beautiful stone ram, and a moufflon (probably Harappan though unprovenanced) is also skillfully modeled. In contrast, the composite beast from Mohenjo-daro, still integral with its plinth, is heavy and lifeless. Two other animals from Mohenjo-daro are also poorly defined and could be rams or bulls.

Figurines

The charming Harappan terra-cottas are very different from the sculptures. They are often quite crudely modeled, with tubular arms, pinched-out noses, and clay blobs and strips attached to represent everything from eyes and mouths to headgear, jewelry, or the markings on animals, but they are brimming with vitality.

Some are models from the real world: posed standing women or seated men in their finery or women engaged in everyday tasks; carts loaded with miniature pots, complete with driver and team of draft bullocks, among the most delightful of the Indus products; and a host of animals, particularly bulls, but also pets, domestic animals, birds, and wild creatures such as rhinos. A charming figurine from Harappa shows a dog in a decorated collar on its hind legs begging. Some had moving parts, such as bulls with a separate bobbing head or animals on wheels, and were presumably children's toys. While figurines of people were often scantily clad, great attention was paid to details of their often elaborate hairstyles, headdresses, and jewelry. Other figurines are caricatures of reality or perhaps characters from folktales; these include figures with animal heads and vaguely human potbellied bodies; one delightful example of the genre has a trumpet for a nose and is covering its face with both arms. Some of the animal figurines, however, are of a higher standard, very carefully modeled with attention to detail and quite true to life.

Possible Amulets. A number of tiny animals molded in faience or carved in shell or ivory may have been amulets. Often carefully modeled and realistic, they include creatures not known from the terra-cottas, such as fish, monkeys, hares, and squirrels.

Glyptic

Probably the finest examples of Harappan art occur on the seals, an extraordinary achievement since the majority are only a few centimeters across. The quality of the artwork depended to some extent on the design. Some of the scenes are rather schematic, incorporating a number of figures that crowd the

A seal found at Mohenjo-daro, with a convincing portrait of the dangerous and short-tempered rhinoceros. The seal is tiny, only 3.8 by 3.8 centimeters, making the mastery of the depiction all the more remarkable. (J. M. Kenoyer, Courtesy Department of Archaeology and Museums, Government of Pakistan)

composition and make it necessary to represent the people as stick figures or show their heads as ovals with a huge slit eye and three points for nose and lips. This is not always so: The figures in the scene of a half-bovid, half-woman deity fighting a horned tiger are lively and perfectly proportioned, their features completely naturalistic, and the composition well-balanced. The majority of the seals, however, show a single animal, sometimes accompanied by a manger or brazier. Here the artists were able to create miniature masterpieces: menacing rhinoceroses, short-horned bulls and water buffaloes with their heads down and one horn raised, majestic zebu bulls standing in calm contemplation. These are beautifully observed portraits of animals, true not only to the anatomical detail but also to the spirit of the beasts.

REFERENCES

Agrawal, D. P. 1970. "The Metal Technology of the Indian Protohistoric Cultures: Its Archaeological Implications." *Puratattva* 3 (1969–1970): 15–22.

Agrawal, D. P. 1982. "The Technology of the Indus Civilization." In *Indian Archaeology. New Perspectives*, edited by R. K. Sharma, 83–112. New Delhi: Agam Kala Prakashan.

Agrawal, D. P. 1984."The Metal Technology of the Harappans." In *Frontiers of the Indus Civilization*, edited by B. B. Lal and S. P. Gupta, 163–167. New Delhi: Books and Books.

Agrawal, D. P. 2002. "Archaeometallurgical Studies in India: A Review." In *Indian Archaeology in Retrospect. III. Archaeology and Interactive Disciplines*, edited by S. Settar and Ravi Korisettar, 423–442. Indian Council of Historical Research. New Delhi: Manohar.

Agrawal, D. P., K. Chattopadhyaya, R. V. Krishnamurthy, and Sheela Kusumgar. 1995. "The Metal Technology of the Harappa and the Copper Hoard Culture in the Light of New Data." In *Researches in Indian Archaeology, Art, Architecture, Culture and Religion*, edited by P. Mishra, 35–49. New Delhi: Sundeep Prakashan.

Audouze, F., and C. Jarrige. 1979. "A Third-millennium Pottery-firing Structure at Mehrgarh and Its Economic Implications." In *South Asian Archaeology 1977*, edited by Maurizio Taddei, 213–221. Naples: Istituto Universitario Orientale, Seminario di Studi Asiatici.

Bala, Madhu. 2002. "Some Unique Antiquities and Pottery from Kalibangan." In *Facets of Indian Civilization. Recent Perspectives. Essays in Honour of Professor B. B. Lal*, edited by Jagat Pati Joshi, 104–106. New Delhi: Aryan Books International.

Bala, Madhu. 2004. "Kalibangan: Its Periods and Antiquities." In *Indus Civilization. Sites in India. New Discoveries*, edited by Dilip K. Chakrabarti, 34–43. Mumbai: Marg Publications.

Banerji, Arundhati. 1994. *Early Indian Terracotta Art. Circa 2000–300 BC (Northern and Western India)*. New Delhi: Harman Publishing House.

Barber, Elizabeth J. W. 1991. *Prehistoric Textiles*. Princeton, NJ: Princeton University Press.

Bhan, Kuldeep, V. S. Sonawane, P. Ajithprasad, and S. Pratapchandran. 2005. "Gola Dhoro." [Online article; retrieved 7/5/05.] www.harappa. com/goladhoro/index. html.

Biagi, Paolo. 2005. "The Rohri Flint Quarries." [Online article; retrieved 7/5/05.] www.harappa.com/rohri/index.html.

Bisht, Ravi Singh. 1982. "Excavations at Banawali: 1974–77." In *Harappan Civilization. A Contemporary Perspective*, edited by Gregory L. Possehl, 113–124. New Delhi: Oxford & IBH Publishing Co.

Bondioli, L., M. Tosi, and M. Vidale. 1984. "Craft Activity Areas and Surface Survey at Moenjodaro." In *Reports on Fieldwork Carried Out at Mohenjo-daro, Pakistan 1982–83 by the IsMEO-Aachen University Mission: Interim Reports I*, edited by Michel Jansen and Gunter Urban, 9–37. Aachen and Rome: RWTH and IsMEO.

Bulgarelli, Grazia Maria. 1986. "Remarks on the Moenjodaro Lithic Industry Moneer South East Area." *East and West* 36: 517–520.

Clark, Sharri. "Embodying Indus Life: Terracotta Figurines from Harappa." [Online article; retrieved 6/14/05.] www.harappa.com/figurines/index.html.

Dales, George F. 1982. "Mohenjodaro Miscellany: Some Unpublished, Forgotten or Misinterpreted Features." In *Harappan Civilization. A Contemporary Perspective*, edited by Gregory L. Possehl, 97–106. New Delhi: Oxford & IBH Publishing Co.

Dales, George F., and Jonathan Mark Kenoyer. 1977. "Shellworking at Ancient Balakot, Pakistan." *Expedition* 19 (2): 13–19.

Dales, George F., and Jonathan Mark Kenoyer. 1986. *Excavations at Mohenjo Daro, Pakistan: The Pottery*. Philadelphia: University of Pennsylvania Museum of Archaeology and Anthropology.

Dales, George F., and Jonathan Mark Kenoyer. 1992. "Harappa 1989: Summary of the Fourth Season." In *South Asian Archaeology 1989*, edited by Catherine Jarrige, 57–67. Madison, WI: Prehistory Press.

Dales, George F., and Jonathan Mark Kenoyer. 1993. "The Harappa Project 1986–9: New Investigations at an Ancient Indus City." In *Harappan Civilization*, 2nd ed., edited by Gregory L. Possehl, 469–520. New Delhi: Oxford University Press.

Deo, Shantaram Bhalchandra. 2000. *Indian Beads. A Cultural and Technological Study*. Pune: Deccan College Post-Graduate and Research Institute.

Dhavalikar, M. K. 1992. "Kuntasi: A Harappan Port in Western India." In *South Asian Archaeology 1989*, edited by Catherine Jarrige, 73–81. Madison, WI: Prehistory Press.

Dhavalikar, M. K. 1993. "Harappans in Saurashtra: The Mercantile Enterprise as Seen from Recent Excavation of Kuntasi." In *Harappan Civilization*, 2nd ed., edited by Gregory L. Possehl, 555–568. New Delhi: Oxford University Press.

Dhavalikar, M. K. 1996. *Kuntasi, A Harappan Emporium on West Coast*. Pune: Deccan College Post-Graduate and Research Institute.

Fairservis, Walter A. 2002. "Views of the Harappans—The Transitional Years." In *Facets of Indian Civilization. Recent Perspectives. Essays in Honour of Professor B. B. Lal*, edited by Jagat Pati Joshi, 167–173. New Delhi: Aryan Books International.

Freestone, Ian C. 1997. "Vitreous Materials. Typology and Technology." In *The Oxford Encyclopedia of Archaeology in the Near East*. Vol. 5, edited by Eric M. Meyers, 306–309. Oxford: Oxford University Press.

Gupta, S. P. 1984. "Internal Trade of the Harappans." In *Frontiers of the Indus Civilization*, edited by B. B. Lal and S. P. Gupta, 417–424. New Delhi: Books and Books.

Halim, M. Abdul, and Massimo Vidale. 1984. "Kilns, Bangles and Coated Vessels. Ceramic Production in Closed Containers at Moenjodaro." In *Reports on Fieldwork Carried out at Mohenjo-daro, Pakistan 1982–83 by the IsMEO-Aachen University Mission:*

Interim Reports I, edited by Michael Jansen and Gunter Urban, 63–97. Aachen and Rome: RWTH and IsMEO.

Hegde, K. T. M., K. K. Bhan, V. H. Sonawane, K. Krishnan, and D. R. Shah. 1992. *Excavations at Nageshwar, Gujurat. A Harappan Shellworking Site on the Gulf of Kutch.* Baroda, India: Department of Archaeology and Ancient History, M. S. University of Baroda.

Hegde, K. T. M., R. V. Karanth, and S. P. Sychanthavong. 1982. "On the Composition and Technology of Harappan Microbeads." In *Harappan Civilization. A Contemporary Perspective,* edited by Gregory L. Possehl, 239–243. New Delhi: Oxford & IBH Publishing Co.

Hodges, Henry. 1988. *Artifacts.* Kingston, ON: Ronald P. Frye and Co.

Huntington, Susan L. 1995. *The Art of Ancient India.* New York: Weatherhill.

Inizan, M-L., and M. Lechevallier. 1997. "A Transcultural Phenomenon in the Chalcolithic and Bronze Age Lithics in the Old World: Raw Material Circulation and Production of Standardized Long Blades. The Example of the Indus Civilization." In *South Asian Archaeology 1995,* edited by Raymond and Bridget Allchin, 77–85. New Delhi: Oxford & IBH Publishing Co.

Kenoyer, Jonathan Mark. 1984a. "Shell Industries at Moenjodaro, Pakistan." In *Reports on Fieldwork Carried Out at Mohenjo-daro, Pakistan 1982–83 by the IsMEO-Aachen University Mission: Interim Reports I,* edited by Michael Jansen and Gunter Urban, 99–115. Aachen and Rome: RWTH and IsMEO.

Kenoyer, Jonathan Mark. 1984b. "Chipped Stones from Mohenjo-Daro." In *Frontiers of the Indus Civilization,* edited by B. B. Lal and S. P. Gupta, 117–132. New Delhi: Books and Books.

Kenoyer, Jonathan Mark. 1985. "Shell Working at Moenjo-daro, Pakistan." In *South Asian Archaeology 1983,* edited by Janine Schotsmans and Maurizio Taddei, 297–344. Naples: Istituto Universitario Orientale, Dipartimento di Studi Asiatici.

Kenoyer, Jonathan Mark. 1994."Experimental Studies of Indus Valley Technology at Harappa." In *South Asian Archaeology 1993,* edited by Asko Parpola and Petteri Koskikallio, 345–362. Helsinki: Suomalainen Tiedeakatemia.

Kenoyer, Jonathan Mark. 1996. "Ancient Indus: Introduction." [Online article; retrieved 1/8/05.] www.harappa.com/har/har1.html.

Kenoyer, Jonathan Mark. 1998. *Ancient Cities of the Indus Valley Civilization.* Karachi: Oxford University Press and American Institute of Pakistan Studies.

Kenoyer, Jonathan Mark, and Richard H. Meadow. 1998."The Latest Discoveries: Harappa 1995–98." [Online article; retrieved 6/14/05.] www.harappa. com/indus2/index.html.

Kenoyer, Jonathan Mark, and Richard H. Meadow. 2001. "Harappa 2000–2001." [Online article; retrieved 6/14/05.] www.harappa.com/indus3/index.html.

Kenoyer, Jonathan Mark, and Richard H. Meadow. 2003. "Mystery at Mound F. The Circular Platforms and the Granary at Harappa." [Online article; retrieved 6/14/05.] www.harappa.com/indus4/index.html.

Krishnan, K. 1992. "An Analysis of Decorative Pigments and Slips on Harappan Pottery from Gujarat." *South Asian Studies* 8: 125–132.

Krishnan, K., I. C. Freestone, and A. P. Middleton. 2005. "The Technology of 'Glazed' Reserved Slip Ware—A Fine Ceramic of the Harappan Period." *Archaeometry* 47 (4): 691.

Lal, B. B. 1993. "A Glimpse of the Social Stratification and Political Set-up of the Indus Civilization." *Harappan Studies* 1: 63–71.

Mackay, Ernest J. H. 1938. *Further Excavations at Mohenjo Daro*. New Delhi: Government of India.

Mackay, Ernest J. H. 1943. *Chanhu-daro Excavations 1935–36*. New Haven, CT: American Oriental Society.

Manchandra, Omi. 1972. *A Study of the Harappan Pottery*. New Delhi: Oriental Publishers.

Marshall, John. 1931. *Mohenjo Daro and the Indus Civilization*. London: Arthur Probsthain.

Meadow, Richard H., and Jonathan Mark Kenoyer. 1997. "Excavations at Harappa 1994–1995: New Perspectives on the Indus Script, Craft Activities, and City Organization." In *South Asian Archaeology 1995*, edited by Raymond and Bridget Allchin, 139–173. New Delhi: Oxford & IBH Publishing Co.

Mery, S. 1994. "Excavation of an Indus Potter's Workshop at Naushara (Baluchistan), Period II." In *South Asian Archaeology 1993*, edited by Asko Parpola and Petteri Koskikallio, 471–481. Helsinki: Suomalainen Tiedeakatemia.

Millar, Heather M-L. 1994. "Metal Processing at Harappa and Mohenjo-Daro: Information from Nonmetal Remains." In *South Asian Archaeology 1993*, edited by Asko Parpola and Petteri Koskikallio, 497–509. Helsinki: Suomalainen Tiedeakatemia.

Millar, Heather M-L. 1997. "Locating Ancient Manufacturing Areas: High Temperature Manufacturing Debris from Surface Surveys at Harappa, Pakistan." In *South Asian Archaeology 1995.*, edited by Raymond and Bridget Allchin, 939–953. New Delhi: Oxford & IBH Publishing Co.

Millar, Heather M-L. 2002. "Locating Indus Civilization Pyrotechnical Craft Production." [Online article; retrieved 12/10/06.] www.ioa.ucla.edu/backdirt/spr02/miller.html.

Pelegrin, J. 1994."Lithic Technology in Harappan Times." In *South Asian Archaeology 1993*, edited by Asko Parpola and Petteri Koskikallio, 587–598. Helsinki: Suomalainen Tiedeakatemia.

Pittman, Holly. 1984. *Art of the Bronze Age: Southeastern Iran, Western Central Asia, and the Indus Valley*. New York: The Metropolitan Museum of Art.

Possehl, Gregory L. 2002a. "Fifty Years of Harappan Archaeology: The Study of the Indus Civilization since Indian Independence." In *Indian Archaeology in Retrospect: II. Protohistory. Archaeology of the Harappan Civilization*, edited by S. Settar and Ravi Korisettar, 1–41. Indian Council of Historical Research. New Delhi: Manohar.

Possehl, Gregory L. 2002b. *The Indus Civilization: A Contemporary Perspective*. Walnut Creek, CA: AltaMira Press.

Pracchia, Stefano. 1985. "Excavations of a Bronze-Age Ceramic Manufacturing Area at Lal-Shah, Mehrgarh." *East and West* 35: 458–468.

Pracchia, Stefano. 1987. "Surface Analysis of Pottery Manufacture Areas at Moenjdaro: The 1984 Season." In *Reports on Fieldwork Carried Out at Mohenjo-daro, Pakistan 1982–83 by the IsMEO-Aachen University Mission: Interim Reports II*, edited by Michael Jansen and Gunter Urban, 151–167. Aachen and Rome: RWTH and IsMEO.

Pracchia, Stefano, Maurizio Tosi, and Massimo Vidale. 1985. "Craft Industries at Moenjo-Daro." In *South Asian Archaeology 1983*, edited by Janine Schotsmans and Maurizio Taddei, 207–248. Naples: Istituto Universitario Orientale, Dipartimento di Studi Asiatici.

Ratnagar, Shereen. 2000. *The End of the Great Harappan Tradition. Heras Memorial Lectures 1998.* New Delhi: Manohar.

Ratnagar, Shereen. 2001. *Understanding Harappa. Civilization in the Greater Indus Valley.* New Delhi: Tulika.

Ratnagar, Shereen. 2004. *Trading Encounters. From the Euphrates to the Indus in the Bronze Age.* New Delhi: Oxford University Press.

Rissman, Paul C. 1989. "The Organization of Seal Production in the Harappan Civilization." In *Old Problems and New Perspectives in the Archaeology of South Asia,* edited by Jonathan Mark Kenoyer, 159–169. *Wisconsin Archaeological Reports.* Vol. 2. Department of Anthropology. Madison: University of Wisconsin.

Roux, Valentine, ed. 1998. *Cornaline d'Inde. Des Pratiques Techniques de Cambay aux techno-systemes de l'Indus.* Paris: Editions de la Maison des Sciences de l'Homme.

de Saizieu, Blanche Bartelemy, and Anne Bouquillon. 1993. "Steatite Working at Mehrgarh during the Neolithic and Chalcolithic Periods: Quantitative Distribution, Characterization of Material and Manufacturing Processes." In *South Asian Archaeology 1993,* edited by Asko Parpola and Petteri Koskikallio, 47–70. Helsinki: Suomalainen Tiedeakatemia.

Shaffer, Jim G. 1982. "Harappan Commerce: An Alternative Perspective." In *Anthropology in Pakistan,* edited by Stephen Pastner and Louis Flam, 166–210. Ithaca, NY: Cornell University Press.

Shaffer, Jim G. 1984. "Bronze Age Iron from Afghanistan: Its Implications for South Asian Protohistory." In *Studies in the Archaeology and Paleoanthropology of South Asia,* edited by Kenneth A. R. Kennedy and Gregory L. Possehl, 41–62. American Institute of Indian Studies. New Delhi: Oxford & IBH Publishing Co.

Sonewane, V. H. 2004. "Nageshwar: A Centre of Harappan Shell Craft in Saurashtra." In *Indus Civilization. Sites in India. New Discoveries,* edited by Dilip K. Chakrabarti, 71–79. Mumbai: Marg Publications.

Srinivasan, S. 1997. "Present and Past of Southern Indian Crafts for Making Mirrors, Lamps, Bells, Vessels, Cymbals and Gongs: Links with Prehistoric High Tin Bronzes from Mohenjodaro, Taxila, South Indian Megaliths, and Later Finds." *South Asian Studies* 13: 209–225.

Tewari, Rakesh. 2004. "A Recently Discovered Hoard of Harappan Jewellery from Western Uttar Pradesh." In *Indus Civilization. Sites in India. New Discoveries,* edited by Dilip K. Chakrabarti, 57-63. Mumbai: Marg Publications.

Tripathi, Vibha, and Ajeet K. Srivastava. 1994. *The Indus Terracottas.* New Delhi: Sharada Publishing House.

Vidale, Massimo. 1984. "Surface Evaluation of Craft Activity Areas at Moenjodaro 1982–84." *East and West* 34: 516–528.

Vidale, Massimo. 1986. "Steatite Cutting on Glazing: Relational Aspects of Two Technological Environments in Harappan Urban Contexts." *East and West* 36: 520–525.

Vidale, Massimo. 1987a. "More Evidence on a Protohistoric Ceramic Puzzle." In *Reports on Fieldwork Carried out at Mohenjo-daro, Pakistan 1982–83 by the IsMEO-Aachen University Mission: Interim Reports II,* edited by Michael Jansen and Gunter Urban, 105–111. Aachen and Rome: RWTH and IsMEO.

Vidale, Massimo. 1987b. "Some Aspects of Lapidary Craft at Moenjodaro in the Light of the Surface Record of the Moneer South East Area." In *Reports on Fieldwork Carried out at Mohenjo-daro, Pakistan 1982–83 by the IsMEO-Aachen University Mission: Interim Reports II,* edited by Michael Jansen and Gunter Urban, 113–149. Aachen and Rome: RWTH and IsMEO.

Vidale, Massimo. 1989. "Specialized Producers and Urban Elites: On the Role of Craft Industries in Mature Harappan Urban Contexts." In *Old Problems and New Perspectives in the Archaeology of South Asia,* edited by Jonathan Mark Kenoyer, 170–181. *Wisconsin Archaeological Reports.* Vol. 2. Department of Anthropology. Madison: University of Wisconsin.

Vidale, Massimo. 1990. "Study of the Moneer South East Area. A Complex Industrial Site of Moenjodaro." *East and West* 40: 301–313.

Wright, R. P. 1989. "The Indus Valley and Mesopotamian Civilizations: A Comparative View of Ceramic Technology." In *Old Problems and New Perspectives in the Archaeology of South Asia,* edited by Jonathan Mark Kenoyer, 145–156. *Wisconsin Archaeological Reports.* Vol. 2. Department of Anthropology. Madison: University of Wisconsin.

Yule, P. 1988. "A Harappan 'Snarling Iron' from Chanhu daro." *Antiquity* 62 (234): 116–118.

XI

CHAPTER 11

Intellectual Accomplishments

NUMBERS, TIME, AND SPACE

The practical application of arithmetic and geometry in construction and measurement bear witness to the mathematical abilities and knowledge of the Harappans. By the Early Harappan period they were building with bricks made in the ratio 1:2:3 or 1:2:4, indicating that they were already working with numbers as an abstract concept; in the Mature Harappan period, the proportions of bricks became standardized to the efficient 1:2:4 ratio that was ideal for structural stability (as is shown by the walls still standing at Mohenjo-daro). Their engineering skills are also demonstrated by their sophisticated hydraulic constructions, including the enormous reservoirs at Dholavira, the Great Bath at Mohenjo-daro, and, in many towns and cities, the deep, brick-lined wells and networks of drains, sewers, and culverts, some with elaborate corbelled roofs.

Metrology

Remarkably accurate weights and measuring rules give some insight into the Harappans' numerical system. Four examples of graduated rules have been found: made of terra-cotta, ivory, copper, and shell, they came respectively from Kalibangan, Lothal, Harappa, and Mohenjo-daro. These were marked into divisions of about 1.7 millimeters, the largest unit marked on the Mohenjo-daro rule being 67.056 millimeters and others on the Lothal scale including 33.46 and 17 millimeters. The latter closely approximates the traditional unit of 17.7 millimeters known from the fourth-century BCE text *Arthashastra.*

The system of stone weights was similarly standardized throughout the Indus realms, and was also used overseas where it was known to the Mesopotamians as the standard of Dilmun, adopted as far away as Ebla. The weights were generally cubical, though truncated spheres also occur. The most common weight was equivalent to about 13.65 grams. Taking this as the basic unit, the Indus people also used smaller weights that were a half, a quarter, an eighth, and a sixteenth of this basic unit and larger ones that were multiples of 2, 4, 10, 12.5, 20, 40, 100, 200, 400, 500, and 800 times the basic unit.

It has been suggested that the basis for the weight system was the *ratti,* the weight of a seed of the gunja creeper (*Abrus precatorius*), equivalent to a 128th part of the Harappan basic unit, just over 0.1 grams. This is still used in India as a jeweler's weight and was the basis, among other things, for the weight standards of the first Indian coins in the seventh century BCE. The use of the *ratti* seed as the basis for the weight system may explain the endurance of the weight system through the period after the decline of the Indus civilization, when weights themselves disappeared.

Harappan Numbers. The weight and linear measurement systems and the probable numerals in the Harappan script seem to suggest that the Harappans used both a base-8 (octonary) and a base-10 (decimal) system in counting. Aspects of both have survived in later Indian mathematics and general use. For example, in the predecimal Indian coinage, the rupee was 64 paise or 16 annas, each divided into 4 paise; and the whole system of Arabic numerals, base-10 positional notation, and the use of zero derives ultimately from India.

Asko Parpola (1994) notes that a Proto-Dravidian root *en means both "eight" and "to count," a significant pointer to an octonary system if the Harappans spoke a Dravidian language (the question of language is discussed later in this chapter).

Astronomy

The layout of Harappan towns and cities provides evidence that the Harappans had a good knowledge of astronomy. The orientation of the main streets in cities and towns followed the cardinal directions. This may not be sufficient evidence of astronomy since a simple method of establishing an east-west line known from a later Indian text may have been employed in Harappan times. (A circle was drawn around a gnomon post, with its radius equal to the height of the gnomon. Markers were placed at the points where the gnomon's shadow touched the circle when exiting and reentering it; a line joining them would run exactly east-west.) However, Holger Wanzke's study (1987) of the orientation of Mohenjo-Daro's streets demonstrated that they deviated from the north-south line by 1–2 degrees. A slight divergence was also observed at other Harappan sites. Wanzke therefore proposed that the Harappans were establishing the cardinal directions by sighting on the stars, in the case of Mohenjo-daro using the profile of the Kirthar Mountains to the city's west as the horizon against which to record their movements. A star whose setting in the west would have been clearly visible to the inhabitants of Mohenjo-daro was Aldebaran (Rohini); its setting point, slightly north of cardinal west, exactly matched the orientation of the city's streets.

A star calendar based on an intimate knowledge of the movements of the heavens is recorded in later Indian literature. The relative position of the asterisms that compose this *nakshatra* calendar most closely match the arrangement of the heavens that was visible around the twenty-fourth century BCE, during the Harappan period, demonstrating that the calendar was devised by the Harappans. At this date, the North Star was not Polaris but Thubron (Alpha Draconis). The *nakshatra* calendar was composed originally of twenty-four asterisms, later increased to twenty-seven and then twenty-eight, selected from the fixed stars and constellations that appeared in the night sky during the course of one year. The sidereal year (the time taken for the stars to return to

A series of graduated cubical weights from Harappa. The smallest weighs 0.865 grams. At this end of the weight scale, each unit is double the weight of the one before. (J. M. Kenoyer, Courtesy Department of Archaeology and Museums, Government of Pakistan)

their starting point) and the solar year (the time taken for the earth to complete a revolution around the sun) differ in length by only 20 minutes, a discrepancy that had a minor cumulative effect on the calendar. Observation of the fixed stars therefore enabled the Harappans or their predecessors to establish the duration of a solar year and the timing of particular points within it, vital information for agriculture. During the Mature Harappan period, the beginning of the year was fixed by the heliacal rising of the Pleiades at the spring equinox: These events coincided exactly in 2240 BCE, and the Pleiades remained the constellation that rose closest to the equinox throughout the period 2720–1760 BCE. There is some evidence that originally the star used to mark the start of the year was Aldebaran, which rose heliacally at the spring equinox in 3054 BCE; as the position of the earth with respect to the fixed stars gradually changed, Aldebaran became unsatisfactory as the marker of the vernal equinox and was therefore replaced by the Harappans with the Pleiades sometime during the midthird millennium. Ashfaque (1989) suggests that the myth of the incestuous seduction of Rohini (Aldebaran) by her father Prajapati (Orion) reflects the observed rapprochement between these asterisms over time and the rejection of Aldebaran in favor of the Pleiades as the marker of the vernal equinox.

The Indian calendar, according to later texts, also made use of both the solar year, calculated at 366 days (the true length being around 365.25 days), and the lunar year of 354 days (composed of twelve cycles of the moon, each of around 29.5 days). The solar year was divided into twelve months each of thirty days, totalling 360 days, and the lunar year into twelve months alternately of twenty-nine and of thirty days. To bring these into line, both with the true length of the solar year and with each other, the calendar was reckoned over a five-year period, during which one intercalary solar month and two intercalary lunar months of thirty days were added.

In addition to the asterisms of the *nakshatra* calendar, Indian astronomers through the ages have shown particular interest in the planets, whose deities are considered to have a powerful and often malign influence. These numbered nine: the five planets visible with the naked eye (Mercury through Saturn), with the addition of the sun, the moon, the eclipse demon Rahu, and Ketu representing a comet or meteor. With the sun as the center, the planets also represent the cardinal directions and those between them (such as northwest). Worship of the planets is common in south India, particularly in conjunction with the worship of Shiva. Though the evidence is not conclusive, it is likely that all these astronomical aspects of Indian religion date back to Harappan times. Allchin and Agueros (1998) discuss the possible depiction of a comet on two seals, along with a man with a bow and in one case a stylized tree. Its identification as a comet is convincing, reflecting the Harappan interest in the heavens; it may, as Allchin and Agueros suggest, have been the comet Hale-Bopp, which was visible around 2000 BCE.

LANGUAGES

People and Language

The question of the ethnic, cultural, and linguistic identity of the Harappans has always generated debate, and in recent years the debate has been hijacked by groups determined to dictate a solution reflecting their own political or religious perspective rather than allowing the evidence to reveal the true picture.

A key point often overlooked in this debate is that languages, ethnic groups, and cultures are not and were not necessarily congruent. People from several ethnic groups may share a language, and, conversely, several languages may be spoken by people who are ethnically the same. Typically, when the speakers of two languages experience prolonged interaction and economic interdependence, there is a period of bilingualism during which each language influences and is influenced by the other. Eventually one language becomes dominant and the other may die out. Many factors may determine which language predominates; though numerical superiority may prevail, more usually it is the language of those who wield economic, political, religious, or military power that is adopted by those who wish to better their position.

Similarly, people of different ethnic backgrounds and speaking different languages may belong to the same cultural entity, while groups sharing a single ethnic makeup and speaking the same language may be culturally distinct. For example, there were many different ethnic and linguistic groups within the Roman Empire, all considering themselves to be Romans.

It is therefore a mistake to view South Asian prehistory as the story of monolithic blocks defined by the language they spoke. Over the millennia many languages have been introduced to the subcontinent and some have gained lasting currency; outsiders have arrived, both peaceful settlers and violent invaders, and have been assimilated; new cultural ideas have been introduced, some have been adopted from outside, and many more have developed within the subcontinent itself, among the rich mix of its peoples. The picture has always been a complex one in which perceived cultural identity crosscuts many underlying and interwoven strands of ethnicity, language, and religion.

The Languages of South Asia

The majority of languages spoken in modern South Asia belong to four major families. Most people in the north today speak Indo-European languages while those of the south are largely Dravidian speakers. The peoples of the Himalayan regions mainly speak Sino-Tibetan languages and in some tribal regions of India there are a small number of Austro-Asiatic speakers. In a few small isolated areas, people speak languages that have no known living relatives; once there were probably many more such languages.

Written sources provide some evidence of the languages spoken in the past. The earliest Dravidian literature, the *Sangam* poems, written in Old Tamil, comes from the south and dates from late BCE and the early centuries CE; the earliest Indo-Aryan inscriptions are a few centuries older but there is also a substantial body of earlier Indo-Aryan oral literature, faithfully preserved by exact repetition, and later written down. The earliest of these texts, the *Rigveda*, was composed during the second millennium BCE, beginning some time between 1700 and 1500 BCE.

Other information on languages spoken in early South Asia can be extracted by studying the ways in which languages have influenced each other and the relationships between South Asia's languages and those of other parts of Eurasia. Additional information can be gleaned from place-names and the modern distribution of the languages.

Indo-Aryan. The latest of these languages to arrive in South Asia was Indo-Aryan. By the late first millennium BCE, there were speakers of languages belonging to the Indo-European language family from Britain to Sri Lanka and Central Asia (although these regions were also inhabited by speakers of non-Indo-European languages). Much ink has been spilled on the question of how this wide distribution came about. The majority of scholars now accept that the Indo-Iranian branch of the family spread into eastern Iran and northern South Asia during the second millennium BCE, from regions farther to the north. This is supported by linguistic and textual evidence, the former including the relationship of the eastern, Indo-Iranian branch to other Indo-European languages, the close relationship of Old Iranian and Old Indo-Aryan (Sanskrit), the earliest Indo-European languages of eastern Iran and northern

South Asia respectively, and their subsequent divergence. Similarly the earliest extant religious texts of these two linguistic groups, the *Old Avesta* and the *Rigveda,* show striking cultural similarities, reflecting a close relationship between the groups, while the *Young Avesta* and later Vedic texts indicate growing cultural divergence. None of these texts can be closely dated, but most unbiased scholars assign dates in the range 1700–1000 BCE to the various parts of the *Rigveda* and around 1400 BCE to the earliest Avestan texts. Loanwords for a number of things related to agriculture and settled life, such as camels, canals, and bricks, present in both Indo-Aryan and Iranian, reflect a period before the two languages separated, when the speakers of Proto-Indo-Iranian were in close contact with the Bactria-Margiana Archaeological Complex (BMAC) in Bactria and Margiana, dated around 2100–1700 BCE. Although much of the detail has still to be established, it is clear that previously the speakers of Proto-Indo-Iranian had occupied an area to the north of the BMAC. As their descendants gradually migrated into Iran and northern South Asia during the second millennium, their languages diverged to form Iranian and Indo-Aryan. A small third branch, comprising the Nuristani (Kafir) languages, became established in the Hindu Kush but did not spread more widely.

The geographical information in the Indian sacred texts, particularly the *Vedas,* attests to the presence of Indo-Aryan speakers first in parts of Afghanistan, Seistan, Swat, and the Punjab and to their gradual spread south and east within the subcontinent. Gradually Indo-Aryan languages came to be spoken over most of the subcontinent except for the south, as well as in Sri Lanka. These included both Sanskrit, the educated language of the sacred texts, which remained relatively pure, and a variety of Prakrits, Indo-Aryan languages heavily influenced by the phonology of the Dravidian languages.

While it is possible that a few speakers of Proto-Indo-Iranian traveled to the Indus region during the third millennium, linguistic history firmly rules out any suggestion that an Indo-Aryan language was spoken by the Harappans. Furthermore, the Indo-Aryan texts reflect a society very different from that of the urban Indus civilization—small warlike groups of pastoral nomads to whom the domestic horse was supremely important; there were no horses in the subcontinent in the Harappan period.

Dravidian. The other main language family of the subcontinent is Dravidian. The majority of Dravidian speakers now live in the four southern states, forming the South Dravidian branch. Small groups in Maharashtra and Orissa, speaking Kolami, Naiki, Parji, and Gadaba, form the tiny Central Dravidian branch. Kurukh and Malto are spoken by groups in parts of eastern central India; according to their own traditions, they moved there in historical times from southern Gujarat, to which they had earlier migrated from the middle Ganges Basin. These languages belong to the Northern Dravidian branch, which also includes Brahui, spoken far to the north, in the Brahui Hills of southern Baluchistan. It is uncertain whether Brahui speakers are the last in situ remnants of a widespread Dravidian-speaking population that originally extended this far north or migrants into Baluchistan from Gujarat in historical times, though the latter alternative is thought more likely. There is good evidence that at some time Dravidian languages were spoken over most of western India and in much of Sindh as well as in the peninsula; this is shown by the distribution of Dravidian place-names and of certain shared features in the modern languages across these regions.

All these languages descend from Proto-Dravidian, which split first between North Dravidian and Proto-South-Dravidian. The latter separated into Central and South Dravidian probably by 1500 BCE. Finally, by around 1100 BCE, South Dravidian split in two: the southern branch (Kannada, Malayalam, Tamil, and a number of small languages) in Karnataka, Kerala, and Tamilnadu, extending into northern Sri Lanka; and the south-central branch, the majority Telugu speakers in Andhra Pradesh but with small groups speaking mainly Gondi in Maharashtra, Madhya Pradesh, and Orissa.

Austro-Asiatic. Some Indian communities still speak languages belonging to the Austro-Asiatic language family, which also includes the Mon-Khmer languages of Southeast Asia. Most—including the principal ones, Mundari and Santali—belong to the Munda group that is spread over much of Bihar, West Bengal, and Orissa but that is also spoken on the upper Tapti River in central India. The languages of the Nicobar Islands form a separate Austro-Asiatic branch. An extinct language, Para-Munda in the northwest, may represent a separate branch of Austro-Asiatic.

Sino-Tibetan. Another great language family that extends into the subcontinent is Sino-Tibetan, spoken from the Himalayas to China and Southeast Asia; the languages in South Asia belong to its Tibeto-Burman branch. Their present distribution in Tibet, Burma, and adjacent regions seems likely broadly to reflect that of the past.

Other South Asian Languages. In a few pockets, mainly in the mountains and in tribal areas, languages survive that have no known relatives, including Burushaski in the western Karakorum. Others are now extinct, including Kusunda in central Nepal, Vedda and Rodiya in Sri Lanka, and probably the original language of the hunter-gatherer Tharu in the Himalayan foothills. Nahali is spoken along the Tapti River and in the Aravalli and Vindhya Hills. This seems to have been a language isolate, overlain successively by Austro-Asiatic, Dravidian, and Indo-Aryan layers; about a quarter of its vocabulary derives from the original language.

It is likely that in the past many unrelated languages were spoken in different parts of the subcontinent. Work by Masica (1979) identified an unknown language, dubbed Language X, once present in Uttar Pradesh and Bihar. Words from this language that have entered the vocabulary of Dravidian and Indo-Aryan include the names of many indigenous flora and fauna, demonstrating that it was an earlier autochthone.

Neighboring Languages. Languages spoken in neighboring regions in Harappan times included those of the BMAC and Namazga cultures in Bactria, Margiana, and Turkmenia. Elamite was spoken in the west of the

Iranian plateau, and unrelated languages, about which nothing is known, were spoken in Marhashi and Aratta farther east—and there were probably many others. Elamite was probably a language isolate, although David MacAlpin put forward the theory, not widely accepted by linguists, that it shared a common ancestor, Proto-Elamo-Dravidian, with the Dravidian language family. Farther west, the people of southern Mesopotamia spoke Sumerian, another language isolate, and Akkadian, part of the large family of Semitic languages to which most present Near Eastern languages belong. The languages of the Gulf are unknown. Across the whole region, there were probably a large number of languages, including many that have now died out and some that had no living relatives even then.

Identifying the Harappan Language

Language Change. Languages spoken by groups who are in frequent contact influence each other in many ways. Changes generally take place in the context of bilingualism, when speakers of one language use the vocabulary of the other with the structures and sounds of their own. Evidence of such substrate influences can be traced in various ways, notably from the presence of loanwords and from the adoption of features of the phonology, grammar, and syntax of one language by the other. These data can be used to study past distributions of known languages and to detect the existence of languages that have otherwise completely disappeared. The chronological order of the languages in a region can be established by looking at loanwords, since incomers generally adopt the indigenous names for plants, animals, landscape features, objects, practices, and other things that are unfamiliar to them, and they often use or modify existing place-names. Loanwords can also give some idea of cultural and economic differences between the speakers of different languages.

The linguistic history of the Indo-Aryan languages has been intensively studied from the literary sources, and much work has gone into reconstructing the Proto-Dravidian language, but much less is known about the other languages of the subcontinent. Considerable work has been done on identifying the substrate influences on Indo-Aryan, far less on those affecting Dravidian and Munda.

Substrate Influences on Indo-Aryan. The Indo-Aryan language was the most recent to arrive, and the geography and relative chronology of substrate influences on it can be quite closely traced in its surviving oral literature. Around three hundred and eighty non-Indo-European words in the *Rigveda* reflect the early influence of a considerable number of languages, including Proto-Burushaski, Tibeto-Burman, Munda, Dravidian, and others. One feature that characterizes South Asian languages in general is the use of retroflex consonants; the Indo-Aryan languages are the only Indo-European group to include retroflex consonants in speech, and it is clear that this feature was acquired after Old Indo-Aryan entered the subcontinent.

Many linguistic features show an early substratum influence of Dravidian on Indo-Aryan, pointing to extensive contact between speakers of these languages during the Vedic period and suggesting that early Dravidian is the obvious candidate for the Harappan language. This, however, is challenged by Witzel (1999a), whose studies of the *Rigveda* lead him to identify three phases in the composition of its ten books. (Dating of the *Rigveda* is not precise but he suggests approximate dates for these of 1700–1500, 1500–1350, and 1350–1200 BCE.) In the first phase he identifies the main influence as coming from a non-Dravidian language, which was also the source of the majority of the loanwords acquired in the later phases. The word structure (particularly the use of prefixing) suggests this to have been an Austro-Asiatic language, which he calls Para-Munda; this reflects the existence of a hitherto unrecorded western branch of Austro-Asiatic, which he traces in the eastern Punjab, Haryana, and areas farther east. Loanwords also included some that probably came from Language X, spoken farther east in the Ganges Basin; these had probably been borrowed from this language into Para-Munda at an earlier date.

Though Para-Munda remained the major influence in Witzel's second phase, as the geographical horizons of the Indo-Aryan speakers broadened, a slight Dravidian substrate influence becomes apparent, probably acquired in Sindh, and this increased in his third phase. There were also loanwords from Language X, spoken in Uttar Pradesh and Bihar, and from Tibeto-Burman languages spoken along the Himalayan foothills. It is likely that the sacred Vedic texts were kept relatively free of "contamination" with non-Indo-Aryan language; the substrate influences apparent in the *Rigveda* must therefore reflect very considerable interaction and bilingualism between Indo-Aryan speakers and the indigenous population. Far more substrate influence is visible in the later *Vedas* and other early literature. Dravidian had a strong influence on later Indo-Aryan vocabulary, morphology, and syntax; most of the loanwords are South Dravidian.

Where Were the Dravidians? The prehistory of the Dravidian languages is not at all clear. Some information can be gleaned from the vocabulary of Proto-Dravidian, reconstructed on the basis of cognate words present in both a North Dravidian and a South and/or Central Dravidian language; these words must reflect something of the situation of Dravidian speakers before the branches separated. In contrast, although some developments that occurred after North Dravidian split off and before South and Central Dravidian separated may be reflected in cognates between nonadjacent members of the two branches, their proximity means that some of the shared words may be due to later contact.

Fuller (2007) has looked closely at the botanical vocabulary reconstructed for Proto-Dravidian and considers it to be characteristic of the Dry Deciduous forest zone of central and peninsular India, stretching from Saurashtra into the south and possibly extending into adjacent savannah regions. This, then, should represent the general area in which Dravidian speakers were living before the branches separated. According to Southworth (2005b), the Proto-Dravidian vocabulary indicates an economy with hunting, animal husbandry, and agriculture, including the use of the plow; though in general it seems to reflect a village existence, a few words suggest something more, including words for an upper story and for a beam, as well as others reflecting metallurgy, some degree of social stratification, trade, and some kind of payment of dues (perhaps taxes or contributions to religious ceremonies). These are not specific enough to pin down the Proto-Dravidian speakers, but archaeological communities that could be accommodated within it include the Neolithic/Chalcolithic cultures of western Rajasthan, the Deccan, and the peninsula in the third and second millennia, as well as the inhabitants of Harappan Saurashtra, who were part of the state but largely rural (Sorath Harappan). This is compatible with the evidence from the *Rigveda* on the chronology and geography of Dravidian influences on Indo-Aryan. The ancestors of the Proto-Dravidian speakers may therefore have been among the indigenous groups in these regions when pastoralists and farmers from the Indo-Iranian borderlands entered the Indus region.

An alternative, though perhaps less likely, scenario is that these colonists themselves were speakers of early Dravidian; Southworth does not rule out the possibility that ancestors of the Proto-Dravidian speakers could have come from outside the subcontinent. Not much substrate evidence survives in the *Rigveda* to indicate what language was spoken in Sindh in the second half of the second millennium, but on the basis of a few words Witzel suggests a language related to Para-Munda but with dialectal differences. This he calls Meluhhan, since that was the language spoken by the Harappans who traded with Mesopotamia, where it required a translator. He notes the presence of a number of Meluhhan words in southern Mesopotamian texts, none of which seem likely to have a Dravidian etymology. However, it is probable that sesame oil was among the Harappan exports to Mesopotamia; this oil was known as *ilu* in Sumerian and *ellu* in Akkadian, closely similar to a South Dravidian name for sesame, *el* or *ellu*, which may suggest that the oil was introduced under a Dravidian name; Witzel, however, points to the Para-Munda word for wild sesame, **jar-tila*, as a possible alternative source.

Parpola (1994) suggested that the name "Meluhha" might come from two Dravidian words signifying "highland country," though the term *mel-akam* itself is not attested to in any Dravidian language. Zvelebil (1972) provides evidence that may support this, showing that many Dravidian-speaking groups right across the subcontinent call themselves by names that mean something like "people of the hills." Variations on the name "Meluhha" reappear in Vedic and later literature, applied to communities not speaking Indo-Aryan. Particularly close is *milakkha*, in the Pali dialect spoken in western north India. Though the name might suggest a formative period in Baluchistan, there are suitable alternative mountain areas, such as the Eastern Ghats.

Other Languages. Substrate influences on Dravidian show that it arrived later in the subcontinent than Austro-Asiatic since many terms for native flora and fauna in Dravidian are loanwords, generally thought to come from Munda, though Para-Munda is now an alternative.

A few other words do not have etymologies traceable in any of the languages of the subcontinent. These include the word for wheat; this appears in Dravidian, Para-Munda, and Indo-Aryan in various forms, all of which can be derived from a Near Eastern original. It is therefore likely that this handful of foreign words came in with the Near Eastern domesticates (with or without associated settlers) in the eighth or seventh millennium BCE.

The Harappan Languages. The people of the Indo-Iranian borderlands were a major, and perhaps the predominant, component of the Harappan population. Biological evidence (discussed in Chapter 4) indicates that the population of the borderlands originally formed a biological continuum with other contemporary South Asians. Some biologically distinct individuals settled there sometime between 6000 and 4500 BCE, though cultural continuity was unbroken. Thereafter there was apparently no change in the population until the Post-Harappan period. It is possible that the fifth-millennium immigrants introduced a new language to the subcontinent; given that their biological affinities seem to have been with people living on the Iranian plateau, it is possible that their language was related to the pre-Iranian languages of this region. Some parts of Book 8 of the *Rigveda* relate to eastern Iran and Seistan, where names belonging to the pre-Iranian-speaking substrate sound like Dravidian. This may suggest that the new arrivals in the fifth millennium were early Dravidian speakers.

There are therefore several possible scenarios for the linguistic situation in the Indus region during the Harappan period. Para-Munda, spoken in the Punjab at the time when the Rigvedic Aryans arrived and seemingly also by the Late Harappan settlers who were moving eastward into the Ganges region, must have been in the subcontinent for a considerable period. If the area where it was spoken in the Pre-Harappan period included the Indo-Iranian borderlands, then it is likely that Para-Munda was the main Harappan language, at least in the Punjab and probably throughout the civilization, and that Dravidian was a language spoken by the indigenous inhabitants of the west, possibly as far northwest as Saurashtra. In this case the language of the Post-Harappans in Gujarat may have developed into the North Dravidian branch.

Alternatively Para-Munda may have been the language spoken by the hunter-gatherer-fisher communities that inhabited the Indus region before the people of the borderlands settled in the plains. If the newcomers to the region in the fifth millennium were Dravidian speakers, then it is possible that a Dravidian language was spoken by at least some of the farmers and pastoralists of the borderlands who settled in the plains and therefore by some Harappans but that Para-Munda remained the main language of many Harappan inhabitants of the Punjab.

Studies of the Harappan script indicate that it was used to write a single language. It seems plausible that the overarching cultural unity of the Harappans would be matched by the existence of an official language, used in writing and spoken as a lingua franca throughout the Harappan realms. Nevertheless, it is quite possible that one or several other languages were also spoken in the Harappan state, specific to different regions or occupational groups, reflecting the different communities that had come together in its formation. Prolonged bilingualism is known to have occurred in other areas, for example in Mesopotamia where Sumerian and Akkadian coexisted for many centuries: though they belonged originally to the south and north parts of southern Mesopotamia (Sumer and Akkad), educated people from both regions spoke both languages.

THE INDUS SCRIPT

Despite huge interest in its decipherment, the writing of the Harappans still cannot be read, for a number of reasons: the absence of bilingual inscriptions to provide a starting point, the stylized form of the signs, the very limited length and nature of the texts, ignorance of the language that the script was being used to record, and the fact that the script died out instead of giving rise to later scripts. In addition, the number of signs indicates that the script was probably logosyllabic; so the number of components to be deciphered and the complexities of their use and interrelations are much greater than they would be with a syllabic or alphabetic script.

The Development of the Indus Script

Scratched lines or other graffiti are known from earlier pottery in the greater Indus region, and graffiti continued to be used throughout the Mature Harappan period and into later times. There is no significant relationship between these and the signs of the Indus script, despite a few superficial resemblances; both include simple geometric marks that are common to all cultures and recur without any connection to the uses to which they are put. However, signs resembling distinctive Indus signs began to appear on pottery at Harappa during the late fourth millennium. In the following Early Harappan period, short sequences of two or three such signs began to be used there, often using the same sign order as that in the Indus script.

During the initial period of development, between 3200 and 2800 BCE, there was an Elamite presence at Shahr-i Sohta in neighboring Helmand, a town with which the cultures of the borderlands were in trading contact. The Elamites used a written accounting system with complex numerical notation and a script, Proto-Elamite, used mainly to write personal names and lists of commodities. It has not been deciphered, but the numbers and a few of the signs can be read, and there is considerable understanding of the structure of this script.

It is likely that the inhabitants of the Indus region and the borderlands were aware of the Proto-Elamite script and its uses; this knowledge may have encouraged them to develop their own script when the circumstances arose that made writing useful to them, even though they put it to different uses; similarly, although the Harappans developed completely different signs to those of Proto-Elamite, they may have drawn on the latter as a general model, borrowing some of its features. This is suggested by the fact that, of all the possible combinations of direction of writing and the use of space on their written media, the Harappans chose the same one as the Elamites: in lines from right to

The baffling though beautiful Indus script cannot be deciphered until it can be determined what language it was written in. This is as uncertain now as it was when the civilization was discovered more than eighty years ago. (Harappa.com)

left and from top to bottom. (For comparison, at much the same time, the Sumerians were writing in boxes arranged in columns.) The result of this influence was probably to kick-start the development of the Harappan script, which grew into a complete writing system during the Transition period. In contrast, the Proto-Elamite script disappeared.

Lack of Successors. When urban life declined in the early centuries of the second millennium, the script went out of use. A few Harappan signs occurred among the graffiti of the Posturban period, but these were rare and, when several were used, their order was random. Some signs resembling those of the Indus script continued to appear occasionally in later contexts; it is probable that these signs, while no longer encrypting speech, held a symbolic meaning for those who drew them, for example as auspicious or religious symbols or royal insignia.

Nothing links the Indus script with the Brahmi script that came into use more than a thousand years later. Brahmi derives from a north Semitic script first used somewhere in West Asia, one of the descendants of the consonantal alphabet invented in the Levant during the second millennium BCE. Another Indian script, Kharoshti, used for a while in the northwest, had a similar ancestry. The letters of the parent alphabet were adapted to form the basic consonantal signs of Brahmi; to these, diacritics were added to mark their combination with the different vowels. The direction of writing was from left to right, in contrast to that of the Harappan script. In the early first millennium CE, a modified version was created in south India to write Tamil. From Brahmi are descended more than two hundred modern Indian scripts, whose ancestry can be clearly traced.

Written Media

The majority (more than 80 percent) of Harappan inscribed objects, as well as the greatest diversity of them, come from the cities of Mohenjo-daro and Harappa. The rest, mainly seals and sealings, have been found widely distributed in Harappan towns and cities and in a few foreign locations.

Seals and Sealings. Most surviving Harappan inscribed materials are square stamp seals that bear an image and a short text. These are usually of steatite, though a few are made in other stones; two from Mohenjo-daro are of silver, presumably deluxe versions. The majority of images are of animals, especially the unicorn, but also bulls, elephants, and a number of other, mostly wild, animals; a few show scenes or composite animals. No link has been found between the images and the inscriptions on the seals. The seal texts are generally short, averaging four to five signs, and use a large repertoire of signs. The inscription was written in reverse so that it could be read correctly when impressed on sealings or elsewhere, for example occasionally on pottery. Clay sealings, of which relatively few have survived, might bear the impression of more than one seal or the same one several times. A small number of larger seals are known, all of an unusually high standard of workmanship.

Other types of seals occur in small numbers. These include a cylinder seal from Kalibangan and a few seals with inscriptions on both faces and no boss. A seal from Gola Dhoro took the form of a slim box with an inscribed face and an opening at one end, and several others are known from Mohenjo-daro. A few round Persian Gulf seals made by the people of Dilmun (see Chapter 6) also bear Harappan inscriptions. There were also long rectangular seals bearing only an inscription.

Miniature Tablets. From the upper levels at Harappa come many miniature tablets. These bear a short inscription on one face, written to be read directly from the tablet, and often a number on the other, sometimes accompanied by one or two other signs. The incised steatite examples often repeated the same inscription, while molds were used to produce multiple copies of the same design in faience or terra-cotta. Some bear a design as well as an inscription. These are often narrative scenes such as a deity watching a contest between two people; others had a single image, such as a tree inside a railing, or one or more auspicious symbols.

There are also inscribed cylinders from the later levels at Harappa; one is also known from Mohenjo-daro. These were made in two-piece molds. One side generally bears an inscription and the other a scene or an image with a religious theme.

The majority of these tablets come from Harappa, where they were probably all manufactured. Many have also been found at Mohenjo-daro, and they are also known from Dholavira, Lothal, Kalibangan, Chanhu-daro, and Ropar. Kenoyer (1998) suggests they may have been accounting tokens; a collection of thirteen tablets, nine with one design, four with another, was found together with weights, seals, and pendants in one location at Harappa. Others consider it more likely that they were votive offerings or amulets, perhaps bearing an auspicious message or prayer. On some tablets a jar sign forms part of the inscription or accompanies the number, and occasionally they also bear an image of an individual making an offering to a tree or seated deity; Parpola (1994) convincingly interprets these as records of offerings.

Perhaps related to these were a few triangular prisms, found at Harappa and Mohenjo-daro in the Indus realms and in Bahrein; a rather dissimilar example is also known from Maysar in Oman. These were of faience or terracotta and may have been made in a mold. One face bears a line of script, and the other two bear unusual images such as a houseboat or a procession in which individuals bear sacred images on poles, as well as more familiar themes such as the horned figure seated on a low throne.

At Mohenjo-daro, but at no other site, more than one hundred small engraved copper tablets have been found. These bear an inscription on one face and a design on the other. Generally a particular design is paired with a particular inscription, and the repertoire of inscriptions and pictures is quite restricted. Sometimes the image is replaced by another short inscription. The designs include composite animals, the endless knot motif, and a wild man with the hindquarters of a bull, armed with a bow and wearing a horned headdress—possibly a shaman or deity. These may have been amulets. A few quite different cast copper tablets with a raised design were found at both Harappa and Mohenjo-daro.

Inscribed Objects. Inscriptions were engraved or stamped on a number of other objects. These included ivory and bone rods that may have had some ritual significance and the stoneware bangles that may have been worn in a political or religious context. Inscriptions were impressed on many pots before firing or scratched on afterward, perhaps giving information on the designated contents, the capacity of the vessel, or its ownership. Large storage jars had an inscription in relief formed by incising the inscription into the mold used to shape their base section.

A number of small objects bear an inscription: bronze axes and chisels, gold jewelry from Mohenjo-daro, bone hairpins, painted terra-cotta bangles, and others. While in some cases these inscriptions may have denoted ownership, they are more likely in most cases to have been prophylactic charms to ensure the object's safe use or to protect the owner. Some objects, judged on their quality, seem more likely to have been votive than functional; on these the inscription may name the person or group dedicating the object or the deity to which it was being offered.

The Signboard. One other inscription is known that is at present unique. During their 1989–1990 season, the excavators at Dholavira uncovered a line of nine huge signs in the Indus script, made of a white crystalline material, lying in a side chamber of the North Gate to the citadel. The signs were about 37 centimeters high, and their widths ranged from 25 to 27 centimeters. They had probably originally been set on a board, probably of wood, displayed over the gate. Its location at the boundary between the citadel and the outside world suggests that the text probably had a religious significance, perhaps purifying or blessing those who passed under it. It is possible that comparable inscriptions existed in other cities and towns; given the fragility of the Dholavira lettering, the extant traces of this signboard clearly survived only by extreme good fortune.

Lost Media? The surviving inscribed objects served only some of the potential functions of writing, probably including personal or official identification (seals as badges), the marking of ownership (possibly names on artifacts), the prevention of tampering (sealings), the management of distribution (seals and sealings), and dedications, spells, prayers, or benedictions (miniature tablets, copper tablets, inscribed artifacts). Most literate societies also used their writing to record economic transactions and to glorify the deeds of their leaders. The Harappans seem to have had no interest in such propaganda, but it seems unlikely that the Harappan polity could have functioned as efficiently as it obviously did without using some kind of recording system. Viewed from another perspective, the literate Mesopotamians obsessively recorded everything and it is improbable that the Harappans, being intimately involved through trade with them, could have resisted the urge to use their own script in ways beyond the uses revealed by the surviving media. It therefore seems probable that the Harappans also used other media of which no trace remains.

In more recent times many perishable media have been extensively used in the subcontinent for writing: wood, cotton cloth, bark, palm leaves, and parchment, all of which, if used by the Harappans, would long since have decayed away. The absence from the Harappan repertoire of the clay tablets that were so much used in the Near East may well reflect the ready availability of these perishable media, which were more portable, easier to store, and less fragile than unfired clay. In Egypt, where a comparable writing medium was made from papyrus plants, it is only because the arid climate was favorable to its preservation that such texts have survived. Since the Harappans did not make monuments, there could be no monumental inscriptions in their realms.

In modern South Asia, children in school use wooden boards to write their lessons. These are covered in a white substance and can be wiped clean after use, ready for the next day's work. Two terra-cotta objects from Mohenjo-daro have exactly the same shape as these wooden writing boards, a rectangular surface with a short handle at one end; they may be models of wooden originals or may even have been used as writing boards themselves, covered with an appropriate writing surface. Two signs in the Indus script may represent such writing boards; these are composed of a square with a line rising from its top; one is blank and the other bears horizontal lines that may represent writing.

Arguing against the Harappan use of any lost media, Farmer and his collaborators (2004) point to the absence of any writing equipment such as ink and styli, though one may counter this by pointing to the absence also of the paints

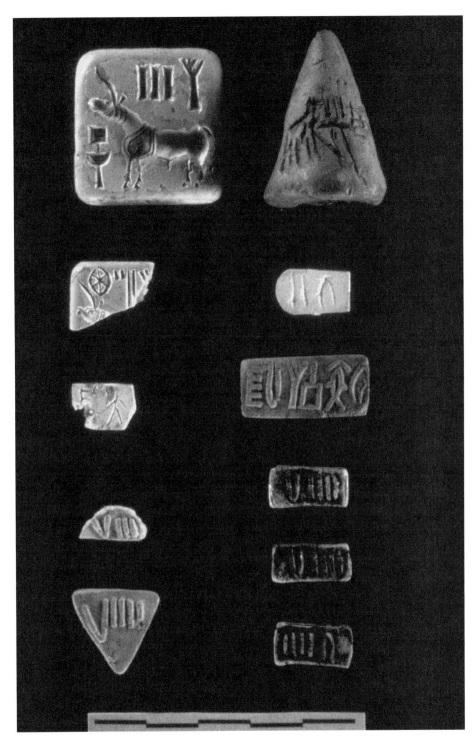

The inscribed materials from a single house in Mound E at Harappa illustrate some of the range of written media: these include a seal with a unicorn design (top left), with a broken seal beneath it; a terra-cotta sealing (top right) bearing two impressions of the same seal; beside it, two incised steatite tablets: and below, four faience tablets bearing short inscriptions, which were mass-produced in molds. (Harappa Archaeological Research Project, Courtesy Department of Archaeology and Museums, Government of Pakistan)

and brushes that were certainly used to decorate pottery and that could also have been used to write.

An Economic Argument. The Harappan state had an efficient internal distribution network and organized flourishing overseas trade, supplying goods from far and wide to people in every corner of their realms. The sealings that occasionally survive through being accidentally fired bear witness to the management of this distribution; their backs show they were attached to goods in transit packed in cloth bales, sacks, or jars, probably both to prevent unauthorized opening and for identification. The seals used to impress these sealings bore a design and an inscription, and they were carefully made objects for long-term use. The message they conveyed was therefore one that needed to be repeated unchanged, over a long period, as the wear on some examples shows. I argued in Chapter 8 that sealings both supplied general information, allowing packages to be correctly handled, and identified the sender. They would not have been used to provide the ephemeral information on the packages' contents, which were likely to vary in detail with each shipment even if the same types of goods were regularly dispatched, or the similarly variable instructions on what was to be done with the goods. This information might have been conveyed by word of mouth, but it is more likely that it was written down in an invoice that either accompanied the goods or was sent separately. Records of goods dispatched, issued, or received may have been less essential, but comparison with other early states suggests that these may also have been kept. The absence of any evidence for invoices or records seems more likely to reflect the use of perishable media than a Harappan failure to use such records at all.

An almost contemporary example may put this in perspective. A fantastically detailed picture of such a system in operation survives from the Near East, where the torching of the town of Kanesh in Anatolia around 1830 BCE caused the baking and therefore the preservation of the clay tablets recording a trading network operated by Assyrian merchants from Assur. These tablets, sent from Assur, include much information about private life and the circumstances in which the merchants were operating, but the vast majority of their contents are details about consignments: lists of what was being sent and by whom, the names of the carriers, and instructions about disposal on arrival in Kanesh, along with requests for particular goods to be sent back and minutiae on the payment of various local taxes and customs dues. The sender's seal was often impressed on the invoice or on its clay envelope, as well as on the sealings on the goods. The invoices were carefully stored in the trading quarter at Kanesh but were taken back to the home city of Assur at the end of a merchant's stay in Anatolia. Almost nothing related to this trade survives from Assur itself, and there would have been no evidence at all of this trade (which dealt in textiles, tin, and silver) had the Assyrians not used clay as their writing medium.

The Importance of Context

A great deal of valuable information can be extracted from the analysis of the various contexts of the Harappan inscriptions: These include the type of object on which they were inscribed, the placement of the inscription, the associated images, and the objects' place of discovery and distribution.

There are various types of inscribed material. Because the function of each type dictated the content of its inscriptions, it is essential to study the inscriptions associated with each as a separate group. For example, personal seals usually include some of the following information: the owner's name, patronymic, home town or place of origin, and title, as well as a dedication to a personal god and the name of the authority to whom the owner is responsible. Sign sequences that are frequently repeated or frequently substituted for each other on seals might therefore represent an official title or a personal name. Many texts in other cultures were bureaucratic records; the nature of the surviving Harappan inscribed media and the form of their texts preclude their use for this purpose. One possible exception is the small series of tablets that have a text on the front and a number on the back; these may have been used as sanctified receipts for offerings made to the gods or, more prosaically, as ordinary receipts for goods or taxes or as ration vouchers issued for work undertaken.

In some cases the placement of an inscription may be informative. For example, on some inscribed axes the text is placed where the haft would originally have covered it: in such cases it is unlikely that the inscription named the owner and more likely that it was a prophylactic charm, whose efficacy did not depend on its visibility.

Many inscribed objects also bear one or more images. Often, particularly on seals, there seems to have been no link between the inscription and the animal or scene depicted. It is, however, worth looking for regularities within groups; for example, the texts bearing the zebu motif may have been owned by rulers and might therefore include royal titles. In other cases, however, particularly the copper tablets, there is a close relationship between particular images and certain sign sequences; here the inscription may relate in some way to the content of the image.

Where an inscribed object was found may also be significant, and both the exact find spot and the general location are potentially revealing. Certain types of inscribed objects have a limited distribution, such as the stoneware bangles, which are known almost exclusively from the great cities of Mohenjo-daro and Harappa; they may therefore be badges of high office. Parpola (1994) noted that the sign | | / was found only at Chanhu-daro, where it occurred on eleven objects (around one-sixth of all Chanhu-daro's inscribed objects); he therefore suggested that the sign may represent the town's name. Exact findspots may provide little information if the inscribed object was accidentally lost. But in other cases, such as the burned warehouse at Lothal, there may be a great deal of useful information encapsulated in the associations between an inscribed object, other artifacts, and the structure in which it was found.

While contextual clues may not enable us actually to read the inscriptions, they may allow us to identify certain sequences as probably belonging to particular categories, such as names of individuals or deities or dedicatory formulas. These deductions should then feed into overall decipherment by pinning down the general meaning of certain signs or phrases that, in turn, can be used to check the credibility of suggested readings of these signs or sign sequences, perhaps also discouraging the adoption of absurd interpretations.

The Harappan Sign Repertoire

The Indus script uses a large number of signs. Some are unambiguously pictorial, such as the (headless) stick figure and the palm squirrel running headfirst down a branch. Many seem abstract, and many others appear to be pictorial but it is not clear what they show; for example, a sign that looks like a jar with handles might, alternatively, represent a cow's head. A few signs appear very frequently, with the most common twenty signs accounting for around 50 percent of the content of the inscriptions over the whole corpus. Some are known from only one occurrence (and are known as singletons), while many others occur only a few times.

An essential first step in studying the Indus writing system is to identify and count the repertoire of signs. This is far from straightforward.

Allographs. Many signs look similar. Some are likely to be allographs, that is, different accepted ways of writing the same sign. Others, however, must be different signs, with different semantic or phonetic values. The problem is to distinguish between these possibilities. If two similar signs behave in the same way, for example appearing interchangeably in sign sequences and forming ligatures with the same signs, they are likely to be allographs. In other cases, allographs of a sign form a cline, a series displaying a gradual shift in form. Even though the signs at either end of the cline look significantly different, each sign is close in form to its neighbor. Nevertheless, there are many ambiguities.

Ligatures. A related problem is that of ligatures. Ligatures are signs combined in various ways: by joining them with a line, by writing one inside another or one above another, or by superimposing parts of one sign on another (for example, the stick figure sign with the handled jar sign replacing the neck). Some ligatures are composed of more than two signs, sometimes as many as six. A ligature may also be formed of a sign and another element that does not appear as an independent sign. Establishing the boundaries of signs requires analysis of the sign sequences throughout the corpus, for example, to determine whether two parallel lines with a different sign between them represent three separate signs or a single ligature. Ligatures may be a space-saving device, allowing a complete word or phrase to be written as one, in which case they should be broken down into their separate components. Alternatively, the ligatured sign may express a meaning obliquely related to the sum of its parts or differing entirely from all of them, in which case such dissection is not helpful.

Sign Lists. A number of attempts have been made to establish a complete sign list, beginning with G. R. Hunter in 1934. Iravatham Mahadevan compiled one as part of his concordance published in 1977, and Asko Parpola included another in his 1994 volume. Most recently, a new sign list has been compiled by Bryan Wells (n.d.). These differ considerably in the number of signs they arrive at: Mahadevan distinguishes 419 signs, Parpola 386 plus twelve possibles, and

Wells 676. These numbers are the results of long considered decisions on the status of individual signs and potential allographs and ligatures. The sign lists form the basic tool when analyzing the texts to detect structure and eventually meaning, and many of the analyses use statistics; both lumping together signs that are different and separating out signs that are the same obviously affect the outcome of such analyses. It is an extremely difficult exercise, and new data necessitate constant revisions.

Corpora and Concordances. Detailed studies of the script depend on the availability of reliable published copies of all the inscribed objects (currently numbering around three thousand seven hundred) and their background information. Mahadevan (1977) compiled a concordance in which he listed all the texts then available, using a font generated to match his sign list. He accompanied this with background information on the settlement where each text was found and the design (or field symbol) on each seal, along with some analyses of the frequency and distribution of individual signs, within the texts and with respect to site and field symbol. Parpola and his collaborators produced several such concordances (Koskenniemi, Parpola, and Parpola 1973; Koskenniemi and Parpola 1979, 1982) but, dissatisfied with the quality and completeness of the data with which they were working, Parpola embarked on the mammoth task of producing a complete photographic record of all known inscribed Harappan material. Two volumes have now appeared (Joshi and Parpola 1987; Shah and Parpola 1991), and a third is expected soon. Wells has produced his own electronic corpus of the inscribed objects, along with much more detailed information on the find context of each; this is not yet publicly available.

All these corpora suffer from a major dilemma: The raw data from the inscribed objects have to be recorded in a manageable form before they can be analyzed, but this inevitably involves some loss of precision due to the decisions on sign identity taken by each scholar in compiling the sign list.

How Scripts Developed

A script is essentially a code whose meaning is accepted by those who use it, communicating a message between writer and reader. Most early scripts began with pictorial signs, but even for the most obvious pictograph the meaning represented was that agreed on by its users, which did not necessarily match its pictorial meaning. A pictograph might cover a range of related meanings (for example, a sign might mean both "legs" and "to walk"). Abstract signs might also be part of the initial sign repertoire (for example, the Sumerians used a circle quartered by lines to signify "sheep"), but pictographs predominated as new signs were added to the repertoire. Some new signs were made by modifying existing ones. When a new sign was introduced, it would be current among a limited group of people; some became more widely accepted and entered the standard repertoire, while others remained restricted or died out. Some signs also shifted their primary meaning through time. From an early stage, widely accepted conventions began to govern the use of signs, and a few signs were in frequent use over a wide area.

Initially the signs represented objects, but they soon came also to stand for sounds. The range of words that could be represented was now extended by punning (the rebus principle): using a pictograph to represent a homonym, a word that sounded the same (or almost the same) but had a different meaning (for example, "bee" for "be"). Further meanings could be achieved by ligatures (for example, "bee" plus "leaf" making "belief") or by modifying a sign (for instance, changing a jar sign in various ways to signify a jar of honey, beer, or milk).

Early scripts were devised to serve a restricted purpose or purposes, and it was adequate to use signs that just represented word stems or roots, with the appropriate form of the word being understood from the context. As the uses of the script diversified, the need to supply this information developed, and signs came increasingly to be used phonetically, often as single syllables, though logographic use also continued. Individual signs might by now have many possible semantic or phonetic values, so some scripts added extra, silent signs to aid identification of the value being used: semantic determinatives to indicate which of several alternative meanings was intended, and phonetic complements that reproduced part of the sound of the appropriate word. These developments took place in the Near East (including Egypt) from the late fourth through the third millennia, and later in China and Mesoamerica. In Mesopotamia, many modifications of the script, which had been developed to write the Sumerian language, took place as a result of the difficulties that arose when using it to write the quite differently structured Akkadian language.

At the same time the signs in the Sumerian script were simplified to make them easier to write, and the pictorial aspect was lost. The Egyptians maintained their pictorial hieroglyphic script for monumental inscriptions but developed a simplified hieratic (cursive) form for writing on papyrus.

While some scripts continued to be logosyllabic, by the late third millennium several scripts in the Near East used mainly syllabic signs. These allowed the sounds of speech to be reproduced more economically and efficiently. A further development took place during the second millennium BCE when Semitic speakers took the initial consonant of their own words for the pictorial meaning of a number of Egyptian hieroglyphs and assigned this consonantal value to a modified form of each sign, creating the first alphabet. From this developed all other alphabetic scripts of the world, including those of South Asia. (A roughly contemporary cuneiform alphabet, also devised in the Levant, was short-lived.) The Greeks developed a version more suited to their language in which vowels were also marked. In principle alphabetic scripts have a single sign for each phoneme (vowel or consonant), making it possible to write down any word so that its pronunciation is unambiguous; alphabetic scripts can therefore be adapted to render any language.

Analyzing the Indus Script

Understanding the Indus writing system depends on finding out as much about it as possible. Only then can meaningful attempts be made to decipher the script. Much has been revealed by detailed analyses of the text corpus, looking at features such as sign associations, frequency, and position.

Characterizing the Script. Alphabetic scripts can be recognized by the small number of different signs that they require, generally somewhere between twenty and thirty-five, and by the number of signs needed to make a word, which in English, for example, ranges from one to more than thirty. Syllabic scripts require a considerably larger number of different signs, generally in the range of a hundred to a hundred and fifty, but far fewer are needed to write a single word. Each sign represents a vowel (V) on its own or in combination with one or two consonants (C): V, CV, or CVC.

Logosyllabic scripts have a far larger sign repertoire, generally four hundred to seven hundred signs, though far fewer may be in regular use. The number of signs depends partly on the relative proportion of logographic and phonetic signs and on whether the latter are polysyllabic or monosyllabic. Words are typically around one to three signs long in logographic scripts.

The number of signs used in the Harappan script should reveal its nature. As well as being historically implausible, its identification as alphabetic or syllabic is ruled out by the number of its signs. While an exact number is not agreed, it lies somewhere in the range three hundred and fifty to seven hundred, of which about half were basic signs. This fits the number of signs expected in a logosyllabic script.

Text Length. The majority of Harappan texts are very short, around one to eight signs; fewer than one in a hundred has ten or more signs and quite a few have only one. The longest continuous text is seventeen signs; the longest text (on the faces of a triangular prism) is twenty-six signs but is probably composed of three shorter inscriptions. In part, this reflects the nature of the texts, most of which needed to convey very little information. Those on the seals probably gave brief information identifying the owner. Other objects might have borne the owner's name, a protective invocation or charm, or a dedication. The texts repeated on the mass-produced tablets seem likely to have been stock inscriptions, such as records of standard offerings or formula benedictions.

While this may provide an adequate explanation for the inscriptions' brevity, the latter could also be due to the use of many logographs and relatively few syllabic signs. This is probably consistent with the large number of rarely used signs in the script. Another possibility is that the use of ligatured signs, relatively common in the Indus script, reflects a tendency to agglutination, so that one ligatured sign may be composed of a number of morphemes, encoding a phrase or sentence.

Detecting Patterns. Attempts to understand the script's workings generally involve a detailed analysis of the full corpus of texts to reveal how the individual signs behave. Such laborious studies have been undertaken by a Russian team under Yuri Knorozov, the Finnish team under Asko Parpola, the Tamil scholar

Iravatham Mahadevan, and Bryan Wells, a Harvard scholar. One approach was to generate statistical information about the association of signs in pairs, with respect to the frequency of each sign in the inscriptions. This identified regularly associated pairs of signs that may reflect syntactical features of the script.

Some scripts mark word divisions, but the Indus script does not. It is therefore necessary to find other ways of determining where the divisions between words or phrases fall. Some texts have only one sign, which must represent a complete word. Many have two or three signs that must constitute a complete message, of one word or several. These sequences recur in some longer texts, and the remainder of such texts may then also represent self-contained segments. Where particular signs occur in a number of texts, they often occupy the same position: for example, the "handled jar" sign is placed at the end of many texts. This suggests that, when it appears within a text, the signs following it form a separate segment. The analysis of objects with more than one line of text shows that the line breaks almost always fall at points identified elsewhere as segment boundaries.

Various analyses of position and association allowed the identification of signs that behave in the same way and that may therefore be interchangeable within certain segments. For example, the "arrow" sign seems to have been interchangeable with the "handled jar" in the segment terminal position. For a while it was thought that these two signs might represent the dative and genitive markers, respectively. This theory is now discounted, but recently Mahadevan (2000) has suggested that they may instead mark person-number-gender (nominal-singular-male/nonmale, the gender distinction used in Dravidian).

Using a number of such clues and with immense labor, some characteristics of Harappan texts have been exposed. One is that a self-contained text segment is typically one to three signs long, matching the typical word length in logosyllabic scripts, particular those in which grammatical affixes are omitted. Another is that there is a definite pattern to many of the longer texts, which are made up of distinct sequences, each of which has a predictable composition. The behavior of many individual signs and sign sequences has been established, giving clues to morphology and syntax.

Farmer and his associates (2004), however, argue that the known third-millennium scripts include so many polyvalent signs and omit so much syntactic, semantic, and phonetic data that statistical studies of these sorts cannot identify any such features; this is probably an unduly pessimistic viewpoint.

Direction of Writing. Various lines of evidence have satisfactorily demonstrated that the Indus script was written from right to left, in rows from the top downward. (This is the direction of the text on tablets, objects, and sealings. The seals were cut the other way round so that they could be read in impressions on sealings and elsewhere; seal texts are therefore reversed before being studied.) Inscriptions that do not fill the whole upper line on a seal always begin on the right. Ones that run over on to another line generally start again on the right side, though a few run around onto the next line going left to right (backwards but continuous). Sometimes the writer started on the right using normal-sized signs but ran out of space toward the end and cramped the last few signs on the left or progressively reduced their size. In some instances, one sign overlapped its neighbor, the left-hand sign partially obliterating the previously written right-hand sign. One unusual inscription ran round three sides of a seal: The first line was complete; the seal was then rotated through 90 degrees clockwise, and the next line was written in the space remaining to the left of the first line; this was repeated, the third line finishing before the left edge of the seal.

Mahadevan (1977) used internal evidence to prove conclusively that the direction of writing was right to left. His studies had shown that certain signs regularly appear in a particular position in the inscriptions. Specifically, the "handled jar" sign is frequently at the left-hand end of the text, while certain others, such as the "chakra" (an oval divided by six lines), frequently appear at the right-hand end, and several regular combinations of signs are written to the right of the "handled jar," to the left of the "chakra," and together elsewhere.

By looking at the signs that were written on the second line when text was broken into two lines, Mahadevan was able to demonstrate that the "handled jar" comes at the end of texts and that the "chakra" and others from the right side come at the beginning.

Studying the Signs. The work undertaken by various scholars in compiling sign lists has established that there was a corpus of basic signs, numbering around one hundred and fifty to two hundred, and an equal or greater number of other signs, many of which are compounds of the basic signs.

Some of the signs are unambiguously pictorial. There can be no doubt, for example, that the stick figure is a person, though this figure may be male or genderless, human or divine. In a few cases, Harappan art confirms what appears to be the pictorial meaning of the sign: for example, the fish sign is identical to a fish shown in a gharial's jaws.

For many more signs, it is harder to identify their pictorial meaning: One scholar's crab is another's tongs; one sees a cobra where another sees a seated man; a vertical stroke with horizontal lines from it could be a comb or a harrow or even a tree. The art or script of other societies may helpfully suggest possible interpretations of signs: For example, a triangular sign with one extended arm bears a strong resemblance to a hoe used by the ancient Egyptians. These comparisons are useful but cannot have the compelling weight of images identified from Harappan art or later Indian symbolism that may be derived from Harappan iconography.

In some cases, suggested meanings can be ruled out on cultural grounds: For example, the oval or circle divided into six looks just like a spoked wheel, but this interpretation is impossible because the spoked wheel was invented centuries after the sign came into use and thousands of miles away; much more plausible is its interpretation as a *chakra*, a symbol that was part of later Indian iconography, representing royalty and divinity.

Many scholars have taken the pictorial signs as a starting point in their attempts at decipherment. Ideally these could yield words clustered around their pictorial meaning and one or several homonyms. It is always possible, however, that a sign was not chosen for its pictorial value, that it had shifted its logographic meaning through time, or that it had become a sign with a purely phonetic value. In addition, in logographic scripts there is often polyphony and polysemy (a number of different sounds and meanings represented by a single sign), so that even in scripts that have been deciphered there is often uncertainty about the selection of the appropriate value.

The problem of interpretation becomes even greater with compounds. These are often composed of two or more signs from the basic repertoire. Ideally, these should be words or phrases put together from their various parts, but experience of the way scripts behave shows that things need not be so straightforward. Wells has demonstrated a number of cases in which the compound behaves like neither or none of its components, suggesting that the compound is not the sum of its parts. He also identifies some cases in which two signs may be written either side by side or as a compound; these may be alternative ways of writing the same thing or may have entirely different meanings.

Other scripts show that there is a considerable range of possible interpretations of elements added to a basic sign, including grammatical or semantic affixes, indicating inflexion or agglutination, diacritics, phonetic complements, and semantic determinatives, not to mention the practice characteristic of evolving scripts of modifying existing signs to create new ones.

The decipherment of alphabetic or syllabic scripts, such as Linear B, is relatively straightforward, in that the range of possible values is limited and the discovery of some of the values assists in the interpretation of others, the results interlocking to reinforce each other. In contrast, logographic scripts are open-ended, with the discovery of some sign values providing little or no assistance in interpreting others. The recent decipherment of the Maya script, a logographic script of fiendish complexity, whose users delighted in employing a wide variety of different "spellings" (ways of expressing the same word), provides a beacon of hope that progress can be made in deciphering the Harappan script too.

Numerals. Numbers form an important subset of signs in scripts and have often proved the easiest type of sign to identify, using clues from their form and behavior. These, therefore, were looked for in the Indus script, and it seems likely that at least some of them have been identified.

Obvious candidates for numerals are three series of parallel strokes that vary in number: short strokes arranged in a single line; short strokes arranged in several parallel lines, each of up to five strokes; and long strokes. The probability of these representing numbers is supported by their consistent position in front of certain signs, coupled with the variation in their number in this position, apparently signifying $1x$, $2x$, $3x$, $3y$, $3z$, and so on. This seems extremely likely in the case of the short strokes, which number up to ten; the long strokes, on the other hand, do not behave quite as consistently, are less common, and only go up to five, so it is possible that they were not in fact numerals.

Not all such signs are likely to be numerals. Positional data show that twelve short strokes arranged in three rows of four, as well as one or two short strokes written in a raised position, seem not to behave like the numerals. In addition, in a number of contexts, numeral signs appear to have had a different significance, such as being read as phonetic signs. Wells argues that several other signs may have functioned as numerals, on the basis of their positions in texts and their frequent association with other numeral signs. Parpola identifies a different sign (semicircle) as a possible larger numeral, perhaps ten.

The Language of the Texts

Decipherment requires knowledge of the language that the script was used to write. A thorough understanding of the script's structure can assist in narrowing the field of possible candidates for the still-unknown Harappan language.

Global linguistic studies indicate that sentences may be constructed in a number of ways. The principal feature relates to the order of the basic elements, subject (S), verb (V), and object (O), particularly the latter pair; these elements, however, cannot yet be identified in the Harappan texts. However, many other features of word order are also significant. One is the respective order of nouns and qualifying numbers. The analysis of sign sequences and text segmentation in the Harappan script showed that the numeral signs always preceded the signs with which they were regularly associated; the word order was therefore number followed by noun. This tends to correlate with languages using the OV rather than the VO order, as do a number of other features: for example, in OV languages, titles follow names. This patterning offers clues to what may be looked for in the structure of Harappan texts, though, naturally, it is necessary to find independent evidence to demonstrate that these features have been correctly identified.

Evidence from the segmentation of the texts may also suggest that the Harappan language was agglutinative, using suffixes (like the Dravidian languages, including Proto-Dravidian), rather than inflected (like Latin and French), but this cannot be confirmed in the present state of knowledge. If the Harappan language should prove to have been of this type, this would strengthen the case for its identification as Proto-Dravidian, one of the main possibilities.

The analyses of the Harappan seal texts show that they follow a consistent structural pattern, regardless of where they were found in the Harappan realms. This indicates that a single language was used in writing throughout the state. Further confirmation comes from a number of Harappan seals found overseas, in Mesopotamia and the Gulf; these, in contrast, often bear sign sequences that are differently structured, suggesting that they were being used to write names, and perhaps other information, in a different language.

Experimentation. Another line of approach is to look at the signs that can be interpreted pictorially and assign plausible sound values to them from a candidate language. The words for the objects depicted should include some (probably many) that have homonyms in the chosen language. A sequence of signs that can be interpreted in this way should combine to form meaningful words, phrases, or sentences in the correct language, and gibberish in any other. Unfortunately this is a very hit-and-miss approach, given the great latitude available in the interpretation of the pictorial value of signs, and some would-be decipherers have used this to accord themselves so much freedom that they can interpret the script in any way they choose. In the early stages of decipherment—unfortunately still the point at which the Indus script is stuck—many plausible interpretations can be offered and justified. Through time, however, the correct path should become apparent, as further sign identifications using the correct language reveal themselves to be consistent with previously identified signs, and identifications in the wrong language prove inconsistent. At present, a number of convincing Dravidian-based identifications have been made that seem to provide consistent results, but they are too few to offer proof. A major drawback is that, apart from Proto-Dravidian, so little of any of the plausible candidate languages is known.

The Alternative: Not a Script at All?

Recently Steve Farmer, in collaboration with others (Farmer, Sproat, and Witzel 2004; Farmer 2006), proposed that the Harappan signs were not in fact a script but only a series of religious symbols. He argued that there were no lost manuscripts made of perishable materials and that what survives therefore represents the full range of uses of these signs. Various features led him to this conclusion. For a start, he points to the failure of the Harappan signs to evolve with frequent scribal usage as, for example, the Sumerian script developed from pictorial and geometric signs into highly abstract signs composed of a few wedges. However, Parpola (2005) notes that there was, in fact, some scribal simplification of Harappan signs. One may counter Farmer's argument by making a comparison with the Egyptian script: As with the formal carved or painted Egyptian hieroglyphic texts, with their highly conservative sign forms, the surviving Harappan inscriptions were mainly on finely made formal media where the signs were executed to a high standard; a cursive script—comparable to Egyptian hieratic, written at speed, and far less carefully rendered—could have existed for use on perishable media.

Farmer also draws attention to the absence of long Harappan inscriptions on potsherds. If the Harappan signs were a script, he contends, this absence would make it unique among the scripts of literate cultures, who all used potsherds, often like scrap paper. This need only imply, however, that the Harappans had other media that were easier to scribble on, such as cotton cloth or wooden boards, or that the writing medium was not well suited for use on sherds. Likewise, the absence of long monumental inscriptions seems significant to Farmer, but the Harappans did not create monumental art or architecture on which such inscriptions might have been written; the nearest they came to this is the Dholavira signboard, possibly the tip of an iceberg of now vanished public inscriptions. Again, Farmer points to the absence of representations of scribes in Harappan art or script, but in no branch of Harappan art are there portraits of occupational specialists, apart from a tiny number of figurines engaged in daily tasks, such as grinding grain or driving carts; the narrative

One of Farmer's main arguments against the Harappan signs representing a script is the absence of inscribed sherds (ostraca). This rare find from Harappa, however, contradicts this contention: it is a sherd which has been used as scrap on which to scratch a short message or temporary record. (Harappa Archaeological Research Project, Courtesy Department of Archaeology and Museums, Government of Pakistan)

scenes on a few seals are the closest the Harappans came to specifically themed art, and these are all concerned with religious subject matter.

The frequent singletons in the Harappan script strike Farmer as significant. These seem to increase in number with every new discovery of Harappan texts. This should not be the case with a true script, he argues; new discoveries should decrease the number by containing additional examples of previously unique signs. He also considers that the proportion of singletons and rare signs is unusually high; other scholars, such as Parpola (2005), demonstrate that this is not so, since in general logosyllabic scripts contain a small corpus of frequently used signs and a large number of much less common ones. Moreover, new signs are continuously added, even when the writing system is a fully developed one, something Farmer also denies. Statistically the Harappan script does not differ significantly in its sign proportions from other logographic scripts. A further point regarding the singletons is that Wells (n.d.) has demonstrated that many are variants or ligatures of basic signs, rather than completely different signs; again, this is something to be expected in a genuine script.

Conversely, Farmer points out that there is a high repetition rate of individual signs within texts in most scripts, something that is not apparent in Harappan texts. This, he suggests, indicates that the Harappan signs were not phonetic. However, the large number of signs suggests that the script used a considerable number of logographic signs, implying a lower proportion of phonetic sounds than in some logographic scripts. Perhaps more significantly, the brevity of the majority of Harappan texts (four to five signs, on average) makes it less likely that signs would repeat within them than it is in the longer texts with which Farmer compares them.

Farmer's arguments fail to account convincingly for the structural regularities that analyses have revealed in the use of the Harappan signs; these seem strongly to support the hypothesis that the Harappan signs represent a writing system. The theory put forward by Farmer and his collaborators has not been widely accepted, but it has been valuable in compelling scholars to look afresh at their assumptions about the script and in provoking a stimulating debate from which a deeper understanding of the script should emerge.

Decipherment

It is not certain that the surviving Harappan texts provide enough material for the script ever to be deciphered. Breaking the code of ancient scripts requires certain clues. The most helpful tool in decipherment is a bilingual text in which the same inscription is given in the undeciphered script and in a known script and language. For example, it was such an inscription, the Rosetta Stone, that enabled scholars to begin to decipher the Egyptian hieroglyphic script, but this was made possible by the fact that the underlying language (ancient Egyptian) was related to one that was already known (Coptic). It is impossible to decipher an ancient writing system if the language cannot be understood; for example, Etruscan is undeciphered because, although its script can be read, the language is an isolate and there is insufficient bilingual material to reconstruct it. In the Harappan context, if the language proves to be early Dravidian, there is hope that one day it can be deciphered; if it is Para-Munda, it is unlikely to be decipherable.

Jumping to Conclusions. Many attempts at decipherment made in the early decades after the discovery of the civilization (and, sadly, some recent attempts) have taken as their starting point untested assumptions and built elaborate interpretations upon these shaky foundations to claim a complete decipherment. These assumptions have involved identifications of the pictorial values of the signs, the underlying language, the general content of the texts, the type to which the script belongs, or its relationship to contemporary scripts or to later ones in the subcontinent, and many of the claimed decipherments involve several of these assumptions. Some have been wild fantasies, such as a link, based on superficial similarities in the form of some signs, between the Indus script and the very much later and geographically remote *rongo-rongo* of Easter Island (itself, unhelpfully, unreadable). Some have been less wild but still demonstrably wrong, such as those claiming a relationship between the

Indus and Brahmi scripts. Others have begun with reasonable and promising hypotheses which have initially yielded clear and meaningful results; these have then seduced the would-be decipherer into believing these hypotheses proven and making assumptions on the basis of them, assigning increasingly arbitrary semantic or phonetic values to individual Indus signs. This often results in a host of alternative sound values for each sign and a multitude of possible signs for each sound. The foolishness of this approach is reflected in the results: Despite the latitude in interpretation afforded by the final pack of assumptions, the readings obtained are generally extremely odd. These can be exemplified by the now infamous "translation" by Father Heras (1953, 97) of one seal text: "The mother of the middle of the year walking ant-like."

Each such claimed decipherment includes some readings that look superficially reasonable, accompanied by many more that are nonsensical; clearly a successful decipherment should yield consistent results across the corpus. To use Asko Parpola's analogy, they should interlock like the correct solutions in a crossword puzzle.

Systematic Approaches. Progress toward decipherment can be made only through proper scientific work in which hypotheses are put forward, explicitly as such, and tested against both internal and external evidence. Uncovering the internal evidence requires the painstaking analytical work that has characterized recent scholarly endeavors. These have provided such building blocks as the corpora, concordances, and structural information, which allow any interested scholar to progress further, unlike the assumption-based decipherments whose failures return the situation to its starting point. Further such groundwork will enable our understanding to continue to advance, step by step. Other data, from archaeology, linguistics, and philology, in the meantime, have helped to narrow down the range of possibilities in matters such as the identity of the Harappan language, the pictorial meanings of some of the signs, and the potential gist of the texts. Full decipherment requires the language to be known, but considerable progress can be made without this knowledge.

At some point in their work, however, individual scholars feel that they have amassed enough data to put forward plausible hypotheses. These also advance the cause of decipherment as long as they are presented as hypotheses and tested. Hypotheses that are consistent with all the known background data and that yield promising results invite further testing on more material; the results should intermesh, reinforcing the hypothesis, or throw up questions or problems that expose flaws in the hypothesis. Progress along these lines is painfully slow and limited, but it is solid. Taking an optimistic view, one day this progress may reach a tipping point where the accumulated mass of individual successful results is sufficient to cut a clear path through the problems that at present seem insurmountable.

Pictorial Bilinguals. Though no written bilinguals are at present available for the Indus script, in some cases, Harappan materials may act as their surrogates. At the simplest level, representations in Harappan art reveal or confirm the pictorial meaning of a few Harappan signs. One such sign is that shaped like a "U"; on a number of the miniature tablets, a figure is shown, half kneeling and half sitting, offering a jar exactly matching this sign to a tree or a seated figure, both of which probably represent deities. The sign must therefore represent a jar and probably a jar containing an offering. On the reverse of many of these miniature tablets, the sign is repeated, along with a series of short strokes; it is therefore plausible to read this as "one / two / three jars of votive offerings" and to interpret these tablets as records of an offering that had been made. A rare sign shows a stick figure in the same position, holding out a jar, and must therefore have the pictorial meaning of "devotee making an offering."

Priyanka (2003) takes this further. He suggests that the various standing stick figure signs represent deities, each with a different religious symbol. To support this, he draws several comparisons between art and signs: between a figure holding a club, arms akimbo, on an amulet from Harappa and a stick figure sign with arms akimbo and a slanting line over the shoulder that could represent a club; the archer figure on a number of Mohenjo-daro's copper tablets and a stick figure holding a bow; a stick figure sign with two strokes rising from the shoulders and the frequent representation of deities wearing horns. On some other seals, a deity is shown inside a tree, and Priyanka compares these to the stick figure enclosed between parallel straight or wavy lines. This leads him to interpret a sequence of signs on a tablet from Mohenjo-daro as recording a devotee making an offering to a horned tree deity.

Another type of pictorial bilingual may be offered by the copper tablets from Mohenjo-daro. These bear a limited range of texts, each coupled with a particular image on the reverse (a figure or an animal, probably representing a deity). In a few cases, however, the reverse bears a short inscription instead. Parpola (1994) suggests that this inscription may give the name of the deity it replaces.

Continuing Traditions. Another approach was adopted by Mahadevan (1972). Harappan seals most probably bore personal names, official titles, or both. Mahadevan tried to identify such titles, arguing that they were likely to have been paralleled by those used in later Indian society. He interpreted the sign of a stick figure carrying a yoke to mean "bearer" and suggested that two of its ligatures, with the "handled jar" sign and with the "arrow/lance" sign, could be read as titles that provided the inspiration for the dynastic names of later Deccan kings, Satavahana and Salivahana, meaning "jar-bearing" and "lance-bearing" respectively. Objections have been raised to this particular interpretation, but the general principle of the approach seems sound.

Mahadevan also argued that the sign resembling (but definitely not representing) a six-spoked wheel originally signified the sun; this sign was important in later Indian iconography as the chakra, symbolizing divinity, sovereignty, and dharma (moral or religious duty). Mahadevan suggests that the meanings may derive from a rebus in Dravidian: *vec/vey/ve-*, giving homonyms meaning the sun, god, and king. The chakra sign appears frequently in Harappan inscriptions. On several copper axes and a magnificent zebu seal, the same sequence of seven signs is inscribed, including a pair of chakra signs: Parpola (1994) suggests this may have been a royal title. A sequence of four signs on the Dholavira signboard partially matches this sign sequence, and, of the nine signs on the signboard, four are the chakra; in this case too, the meaning "god or king" is consistent with the inscription's likely content.

Language and Homonyms. Homonyms provide an important way of extending the meaning of signs. Unlike the pictorial meanings of signs, however, looking for homonyms requires an assumption to be made about the underlying language. Support for this assumption depends on finding suitable homonyms for many signs whose pictorial value is certain and producing credible readings from them. Promising results have been obtained using Dravidian as the suggested language, but they are at present far too few to provide conclusive support for this choice.

A painted wall with an accurate reproduction of the signs found in the gateway at Dholavira citadel. The sign sequence is seen in reverse so the signboard in which they were set must have been placed on the ground with its wooden back uppermost; this decayed away leaving the fragile signs lying face down. The inscription begins with the "chakra" sign, which is repeated several times in the inscription and probably signified royalty or divinity. (Namit Arora/Shunya.net)

Parpola (1994) argues that many Harappan names are likely to have been theophoric (that is, containing the name of a deity), as in classical India, and that deities would also be mentioned in other contexts on inscribed materials. He therefore looked for a set of sign sequences or ligatures that might plausibly be interpreted as divine names. His search focused on the commonly occurring fish sign, already identified by Father Heras (1953) as having useful homonyms in Dravidian: *min* = fish/shining/star. Fish seem unlikely subject matter for seal texts, so it is probable that in this context the sign is being used as a homonym; its reading as "star" parallels the apparent significance of fish as symbols in some Harappan iconography. Parpola identifies a number of ligatured fish signs and sequences containing fish signs. In a number of cases, the fish sign was paired with a numeral; Parpola demonstrates that in each case there is a matching asterism known from religious mythology and attested in Old Tamil. Thus a fish combined with the number six gives *aru-min* (six stars), the Dravidian name for the Pleiades, known in mythology as six of the wives of the Seven Sages. The Seven Sages themselves are represented in the heavens by the constellation of the Great Bear, whose Dravidian name *elu-min* (seven stars) matches the Indus fish sign combined with the number seven. *Mum-min* (three stars) is the name by which the asterism Mrgasirsa was later known. Both elements of the names are signs whose pictorial interpretation is secure, and the fact that there was a known asterism to match each of the fish-and-number combinations supported the interpretations, which have the approval of many scholars, including Mahadevan.

Mahadevan (1997) finds Parpola's other interpretations of fish sign combinations less compelling. In each of these, Parpola has attempted to match known asterism names with interpretations of the sign elements. For example, he identifies Vel-min (white star), the Dravidian name for the planet Venus, with a combination of the fish sign with a bracketing pair of long strokes, linking them through the homonym *vel* = white/*veli* = enclosed space, his interpretation of the significance of the parallel lines. Mahadevan points out that *veli* more accurately means "open space, exterior," which does not match the sign. The rejection of these additional readings does not undermine the overall thesis that fish combinations signify divinely linked asterisms; it merely emphasizes the importance of finding robust interpretations for the Harappan signs.

Despite the progress that has been made, it is likely that the Harappan script will continue to defy attempts at decipherment for the foreseeable future.

REFERENCES

Abhi. 2004. "The Indus Script: Was It Really a Script?" December 17. [Online article; retrieved 1/12/07.] www.sepiamutiny.com/sepia/archives/000834.html.

Allchin, F. R. and M. A. Agueros. 1998. "An Ancient Visitor Returns?" *South Asian Studies* 14: 155–159.

Ashfaque, Syed M. 1989. "Primitive Astronomy in the Indus Civilization." In *Old Problems and New Perspectives in the Archaeology of South Asia,* edited by Jonathan

Mark Kenoyer, 207–215. *Wisconsin Archaeological Reports.* Vol. 2. Department of Anthropology. Madison: University of Wisconsin.

Damerow, Peter. 2006. "The Origins of Writing as a Problem of Historical Epistemology." *Cuneiform Digital Library Journal* 2006 (1). [Online article; retrieved 1/12/07.] cdli.ucla.edu/pubs/cdlj/2006/cdlj2006_001.html.

Ehret, Christopher. 1988. "Language Change and the Material Correlates of Language and Ethnic Shift." *Antiquity* 62 (236): 564–574.

Fairservis, Walter A. 1984. "Harappan Civilisation According to Its Writing." In *South Asian Archaeology 1981,* edited by Bridget Allchin, 155–161. Cambridge, UK: Cambridge University Press.

Fairservis, Walter A. 1992. *The Harappan Civilization and its Writing.* New Delhi: Oxford & IBH Publishing Co.

Fairservis, Walter A., and Franklin C. Southworth. 1989. "Linguistic Archaeology and the Indus Valley Culture." In *Old Problems and New Perspectives in the Archaeology of South Asia,* edited by Jonathan Mark Kenoyer, 133–144. *Wisconsin Archaeological Reports.* Vol. 2. Department of Anthropology. Madison: University of Wisconsin.

Farmer, Steve. 2003. "Five Cases of Dubious Writing in Indus Inscriptions: Parallels with Vinca Symbols and Cretan Hieroglyphic Seals." [Online article; retrieved 1/12/07.] www.safarmer.com/indusnotes.pdf.

Farmer, Steve. 2006. "Lectures and Articles Online." [Online article; retrieved 1/12/07.] www.safarmer.com/downloads/.

Farmer, Steve, Richard Sproat, and Michael Witzel. 2004. "The Collapse of the Indus-script Thesis: The Myth of a Literate Harappan Civilization." [Online article; retrieved 1/12/07.] www.safarmer.com/fsw2.pdf.

Farmer, Steve, Steven A. Weber, Tim Barela, Richard Sproat, and Michael Witzel. 2005. "Temporal and Regional Variations in the Use of Indus Symbols: New Methods for Studying Harappan Civilization." *Electronic Journal of Vedic Studies* 11 (2): 19–57. [Online article; retrieved 8/20/06.] www.safarmer.com/downloads/abstract2.html.

Fuller, Dorian. 2007. "Non-human Genetics, Agricultural Origins and Historical Linguistics in South Asia." In *The Evolution and History of Human Populations in South Asia,* edited by Michael D. Petraglia and Bridget Allchin, 389–439. Netherlands: Springer.

Hemphill, Brian E., John R. Lukacs, and Kenneth A. R. Kennedy. 1991. "Biological Adaptations and Affinities of Bronze Age Harappans." In *Harappan Excavations 1986–1990: A Multidisciplinary Approach to Third Millennium Urbanism,* edited by Richard H. Meadow, 137–182. Madison, WI: Prehistory Press.

Heras, Henry. 1953. *Studies in the Proto-Indo-Mediterranean Culture.* Vol. 1. Bombay: Indian Historical Research Institute.

Hunter, G. R. 1934. *The Script of Harappa and Mohenjo-daro and Its Connection with Other Scripts.* London: Kegan Paul, Trench, Trubner & Co..

Joshi, Jagat Pati, and Asko Parpola. 1987. *Corpus of Indus Seals and Inscriptions. 1. Collections in India.* Helsinki: Suomalainen Tiedeakatemia.

Kenoyer, Jonathan Mark. 1998. *Ancient Cities of the Indus Valley Civilization.* Karachi: Oxford University Press and American Institute of Pakistan Studies.

Knorozov, Yuri. 1976. "The Characteristics of the Language of the Proto-Indian Inscriptions." In *The Soviet Decipherment of the Indus Valley Script: Translation and*

Critique, edited by Arlene R. K. Zide and Kamil V. Zvelebil, 55–59. Janua Linguarum, Series Practica, 156. The Hague and Paris: Mouton.

Konishi, Masatoshi A. 1987. "Writing Materials during the Harappan Period." In *Archaeology and History, Essays in Memory of A. Ghosh.* Vol. 1, edited by B. M. Pande and B. D. Chattopadhyaya, 213–217. New Delhi: Agam Kala Prakashan.

Koskenniemi, Kimmo, and Asko Parpola. 1979. *Corpus of Texts in the Indus Script.* Helsinki: Suomalainen Tiedeakatemia.

Koskenniemi, Kimmo, and Asko Parpola. 1982. *A Concordance to the Texts in the Indus Script.* Helsinki: Suomalainen Tiedeakatemia.

Koskenniemi, Seppo, Asko Parpola, and Simo Parpola. 1973. *Materials for the Study of the Indus Script, 1: A Concordance of the Indus Inscriptions.* Helsinki: Suomalainen Tiedeakatemia.

Lal, B. B. 2002. *The Saraswati Flows On. The Continuity of Indian Culture.* New Delhi: Aryan Books International.

Lubotsky, Alexander. 2001. "The Indo-Iranian Substratum." In *Early Contacts between Uralic and Indo-European: Linguistic and Archaeological Considerations,* edited by C. Carpelan, Asko Parpola, and P. Koskikallio, 301–317. Helsinki: Societo finno-ougrienne. [Online article; retrieved 4/6/07.] www.ieed.nl/lubotsky/pdf/Indo-Iranian%20substratum.pdf.

McAlpin, David. 1981. *Proto-Elamo-Dravidian: The Evidence and Its Implications.* Philadelphia: American Philosophical Society.

Mahadevan, Iravatham. 1972. "Study of the Indus Script through Bi-lingual Parallels." Paper read at the Second All-India Conference of Dravidian Linguists, Sri Venkateswara University. Reprinted 1979 in *Ancient Cities of the Indus,* edited by Gregory L. Possehl, 261–267. New Delhi: Vikas Publishing House.

Mahadevan, Iravatham. 1977. *The Indus Script: Texts, Concordance and Tables.* Memoirs of the Archaeological Survey of India 77. New Delhi: Archaeological Survey of India.

Mahadevan, Iravatham. 1982. "Terminal Ideograms in the Indus Script." In *Harappan Civilization. A Contemporary Perspective,* edited by Gregory L. Possehl, 311–317. New Delhi: Oxford & IBH Publishing Co.

Mahadevan, Iravatham. 1997. "An Encyclopaedia of the Indus Script." *International Journal of Dravidian Linguistics.* 26 (1): 110. [Online article; retrieved 1/27/07.] www.harappa.com/script/maha0.html.

Mahadevan, Iravatham. 1999. "Murukan in the Indus Script." *The Journal of the Institute of Asian Studies.* 16 (2): 21-39. [Online article; retrieved 1/27/07.] www.murugan.org/research/mahadevan.htm.

Mahadevan, Iravatham. 2000. "The Arrow Sign in the Indus Script." [Online article; retrieved 4/6/07.] www.harappa.com/arrow/1.html.

Mahadevan, Iravatham. 2002. "Aryan or Dravidian or Neither? A Study of Recent Attempts to Decipher the Indus Script (1995–2000)." *Electronic Journal of Vedic Studies* 8 (1): 3–21. [Online article; retrieved 4/6/07.] www.ejvs.laurasianacademy.com/ejvs0801/ejvs0801.pdf.

Mahadevan, Iravatham. 2006. "A Note on the Muruku Sign of the Indus Script in Light of the Mayiladuthurai Stone Axe Discovery." [Online article; retrieved 5/16/06.] www.harappa.com/arrow/stone_celt_indus_signs.html.

Mahadevan, Iravatham. 2007. "Agricultural Terms in the Indus Script." [Online article; retrieved 6/6/07.] www.harappa.com/arrow/indus-script-terms.html.

Mahadevan, Iravatham, and Omar Khan. 1998. "Interview." January 17. [Online article; retrieved 1/27/07.] www.harappa.com/script/mahadevantext.html#4.

Mainkar, V. B. 1984. "Metrology in the Indus Civilization." In *Frontiers of the Indus Civilization,* edited by B. B. Lal and S. P. Gupta, 141–151. New Delhi: Books and Books.

Mallory, J. P. 1989. *In Search of the Indo-Europeans. Language, Archaeology and Myth.* London: Thames and Hudson.

Masica, C. P. 1979. "Aryan and Non-Aryan Elements in North Indian Agriculture." In *Aryan and Non-Aryan in India,* edited by M. M. Deshpande and P. E. Hook, 52–151. Ann Arbor, MI: Center for South and Southeast Asian Studies.

Meadow, Richard H., and Jonathan Mark Kenoyer. 1994. "Harappa Excavations 1993: The City Wall and Inscribded Materials." In *South Asian Archaeology 1993,* edited by Asko Parpola and Petteri Koskikallio, 451–470. Helsinki: Suomalainen Tiedeakatemia.

Meadow, Richard H., and Jonathan Mark Kenoyer. 1997. "Excavations at Harappa 1994–1995: New Perspectives on the Indus Script, Craft Activities, and City Organization." In *South Asian Archaeology 1995,* edited by Raymond and Bridget Allchin, 139–173. New Delhi: Oxford & IBH Publishing Co.

Nissen, Hans J., Peter Damerow, and Robert K. Englund. 1993. *Archaic Bookkeeping.* Chicago: University of Chicago Press.

O'Connor, J. J., and E. F. Robertson. "Ancient Indian Mathematics." [Online article; retrieved 11/24/06.] www-history.mcs.st-andrews.ac.uk/Indexes/Indians.html.

Parpola, Asko. 1994. *Deciphering the Indus Script.* Cambridge, UK: Cambridge University Press.

Parpola, Asko. 2005. "Study of the Indus Script." [Online article; retrieved 1/18/07.] www.harappa.com/script/indusscript.pdf.

Possehl, Gregory L. 1996. *Indus Age: the Writing System.* New Delhi: Oxford University Press.

Priyanka, Benille. 2003. "New Iconographic Evidence for the Religious Nature of Indus Seals and Inscriptions." *East and West* 53: 31–66.

Robinson, Andrew. 2002. *Lost Languages. The Enigma of the World's Undeciphered Scripts.* New York: McGraw-Hill.

Shah, Syed G. M., and Asko Parpola. 1991. *Corpus of Indus Seals and Inscriptions.* Vol. 2: *Collections in Pakistan.* Helsinki: Suomalainen Tiedeakatemia.

Southworth, Franklin C. 1974. "Linguistic Stratigraphy of North India." In *Contact and Convergence in South Asian Languages,* edited by F. C. Southworth and M. L. Apte. Special publication of the *International Journal of Dravidian Linguistics* 3 (1–2): 201–223.

Southworth, Franklin C. 2005a. "Prehistoric Implications of the Dravidian Element in the NIA Lexicon, with Special Attention to Marathi." *International Journal of Dravidian Linguistics* 34 (1): 17–28. [Online article; retrieved 4/6/07.] ccat.sas.upenn.edu/~fsouth/DravidianElement.pdf.

Southworth, Franklin C. 2005b. *Linguistic Archaeology of South Asia.* London: Routledge-Curzon.

Southworth, Franklin C. 2006. "Proto-Dravidian Agriculture." In *Proceedings of the Pre-symposium of RIHN and 7th ESCA Harvard-Kyoto Roundtable,* edited by Toshiki Osada, 121-150. Kyoto: Research Institute for Humanity and Nature. [Online article; retrieved 2/12/07.] ccat.sas.upenn.edu/~fsouth/Proto-DravidianAgriculture.pdf.

Subramanian, T. S. 2006. "Significance of Mayiladuthurai Find." *The Hindu* May 1, 1.

Thapar, Romila. 1999. "The Aryan Question Revisited." Transcript of lecture delivered on October 11 at the Academic Staff College, JNU. [Online article; retrieved 1/31/06.] www.members.tripod.com/ascjnu/aryan.html.

Thapar, Romila. 2000. "Hindutva and History." *Frontline,* October 13. [Online article; retrieved 4/6/07.] www.safarmer.com/frontline/horseplay.pdf.

Veenhof, Klaas R. 2000. "Kanesh: An Assyrian Colony in Anatolia." In *Civilizations of the Ancient Near East,* edited by Jack M. Sasson, 859–872. Peabody, MA: Hendrickson Publishers. (Reprint of 1995 edition. New York: Scribner's).

Wanzke, Holger. 1987. "Axis Systems and Orientation at Mohenjo-Daro." In *Reports on Fieldwork Carried out at Mohenjo-daro, Pakistan 1982–83 by the IsMEO-Aachen University Mission: Interim Reports II,* edited by Michael Jansen and Gunter Urban, 33–44. Aachen and Rome: RWTH and IsMEO.

Wells, Bryan. 1998. *An Introduction to Indus Writing.* MA thesis, Department of Archaeology, University of Calgary, Calgary, Alberta, Canada. [Online article: retrieved 3/6/07] www.collectionscanada.ca/obj/s4/f2/dsk2/ftp03/MQ31309.pdf

Wells, Bryan. No date. Unpublished doctoral dissertation. Department of Anthropology, Harvard University.

Witzel, Michael. 1999a. "Substrate Languages in Old Indo-Aryan (Rgvedic, Middle and Late Vedic." *Electronic Journal of Vedic Sanskrit* 5 (1): 1–67. [Online article] users.primushost.com/~india/ejvs/ejvs0501/ejvs0501article.pdf.

Witzel, Michael. 1999b. "Early Sources for South Asian Substrate Languages." *Mother Tongue,* Special Issue. October: 1–70. [Online article; retrieved 4/6/07.] www.people.fas.harvard.edu/%7Ewitzel/Substrates_MT1999.pdf.

Witzel, Michael. 2000. "The Home of the Aryans." In *Anusantatyai,* edited by A. Hintze and E. Tichy, 283–338. Dettelbach, Germany: J. H. Roell. [Online article; retrieved 4/6/07.] www.people.fas.harvard.edu/~witzel/AryanHome.pdf.

Witzel, Michael, and Steve Farmer. 2000. "Horseplay in Harappa." *Frontline,* October 13. [Online article; retrieved 4/6/07.] www.safarmer.com/frontline/horseplay.pdf.

Zide, Arlene R. K., and Kamil V. Zvelebil, eds. 1976. *The Soviet Decipherment of the Indus Valley Script: Translation and Critique.* Janua Linguarum, Series Practica, 156. The Hague and Paris: Mouton.

Zvelebil, Kamil V. 1972. "The Descent of the Dravidians." *International Journal of Dravidian Linguistics* 1 (2): 57–65.

PART 3

Current Assessment

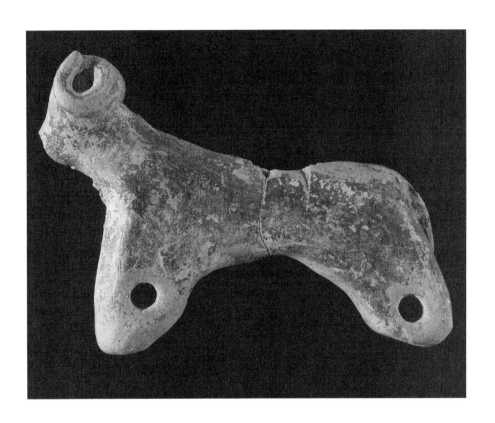

XII

CHAPTER 12

The Indus Civilization Today

The Indus civilization has challenged scholars' understanding since its discovery some eighty years ago, and in recent years the application of systematic and problem-orientated research, coupled with much new and unexpected data, has overturned many previous interpretations.

The early picture of the Indus civilization was largely based on what was revealed by excavations in the two great cities of Mohenjo-daro and Harappa. Other cities have since been discovered and those at Dholavira and Rakhigarhi investigated; the known extent of the civilization has been greatly extended by discoveries in Gujarat, the Indo-Gangetic divide, and the Saraswati Valley; and there is now a greater knowledge of the diversity of Harappan culture. Nevertheless, data from Mohenjo-daro and Harappa still provide a large part of what is known about the civilization, reflecting their evident importance, and recent work in the cities, using many modern archaeological methods, has continued to advance knowledge and understanding of the civilization. The HARP excavations have established the chronology of development at Harappa, and the sequence of development is known at a few other sites, including Dholavira. However, developmental history within the Mature Harappan period as a whole is still little known.

The early concentration on towns and cities has been counterbalanced in recent decades by the investigation of a number of rural settlements, including specialist industrial villages such as Nageshwar. Field surveys, notably in Bahawalpur and Gujarat, have greatly advanced knowledge of the extent and diversity of Harappan settlement. Interdisciplinary studies, including archaeobotany, zooarchaeology, and ethnoarchaeology, have yielded much new information, as have experiments, particularly those designed to investigate Harappan technology. Recent studies in other parts of the subcontinent and in adjacent Oman, Iran, and Afghanistan have broadened understanding of the context in which the Harappan civilization emerged, flourished, and declined.

These data still provide only partial answers to the major questions about the Harappan civilization: What brought about the development of civilization in the Indus region? Who ran the Harappan state, and why did it disintegrate?

THE EMERGENCE OF HARAPPAN CIVILIZATION

Investigations of primary (also known as pristine) states around the globe have identified various prime movers that may have both exerted pressure toward the development of greater social and economic complexity and enabled this development to occur, leading to the emergence of civilization.

A view of the citadel mound at Mohenjo-daro, looking across to the building housing the Great Bath and behind it the "granary." Data gathered at Mohenjo-daro and Harappa still dominate what is known of the Indus civilization. Though this is partly because these two cities are the most intensively investigated of Indus sites, it probably also genuinely reflects their preeminence in the Indus state. (Corel)

These include population growth, high agricultural productivity, environmental challenges, resource imbalance, and technological innovation. Other factors such as competition, craft specialization, and religion are also generally implicated in this development.

It is still not clear exactly what happened in the Transition period (ca. 2600–2500 BCE) to transform the regional traditions of the Early Harappan period into the unified Mature Harappan state and to cause the majority of Early Harappan settlements to be abandoned or destroyed and new settlements built in their place or in other locations. Many key developments must have begun during the Early Harappan period; others probably occurred only after the beginning of the Mature Harappan period.

Population Growth and Distribution

The prehistory of the Indo-Iranian borderlands shows a steady increase over time in the number and density of settlements based on farming and pastoralism. In contrast, the population of the Indus plains and adjacent regions lived mainly by hunting and gathering; the limited traces suggest their settlements were far fewer in number, and were small and widely scattered, though to some extent this apparent situation must reflect the difficulty of locating hunter-gatherer settlements. The presence of domestic animals in some hunter-gatherer settlements attests to contact with the people of the borderlands, probably in the context of pastoralists' seasonal movement from the hills into the plains. The potential for population expansion in the hills was severely limited, and so, from the fourth millennium into the third, settlers moved out from the borderlands into the plains and beyond into Gujarat, the first being pastoralists, followed later by farmers. The enormous potential of the greater Indus region offered scope for huge population increase; by the end of the Mature Harappan period, the Harappans are estimated to have numbered somewhere between 1 and 5 million, probably well below the region's carrying capacity.

The circumscribed mountain valleys of the borderlands, linked by a few routes, limited the potential for large political groupings to develop. In contrast, the wide plains had few physical barriers and were linked by waterways and relatively unrestricted land routes, encouraging the development of larger communities than before, better developed social networks, and wider political groupings; the response to this potential is reflected in the emergence of regional cultures marked by differences in material such as pottery. At the same time, although links between highland and lowland communities were maintained during the Early Harappan period, the contrasting potentials for integration in the lowland and highland regions probably meant that they were already developing in different directions. As a result, the people of the borderlands did not become part of the Mature Harappan state, though those of the southern borderlands (the Kulli region) enjoyed a special relationship with the Harappans.

The need for mechanisms of social control to manage relations within the larger, denser societies of the Early Harappan period must have led to the development of greater social and political complexity. Harappa was already a substantial town in the Early Harappan period, eventually covering around 25 hectares; this was probably the chief settlement of its region and may already have provided political leadership as well as goods and services for the region's rural inhabitants. Developments at Harappa may well hold the key to the emergence of the state.

Intensive Agriculture

High agricultural productivity was a necessary precondition for the development of civilization. The ability to produce an agricultural surplus allowed a population to grow and some portion of their society to specialize full-time in craft production or the exercise of power. Often the area of high agricultural productivity was environmentally circumscribed, restricting expansion outside the areas suited to the culture's agricultural practices.

The people of the Indo-Iranian borderlands evolved an economy that combined pastoralism, involving seasonal movement, with arable agriculture in the relatively restricted areas of suitable land. Limited rainfall encouraged the early development of methods of irrigation and water conservation. Colonization of the Indus region brought the major challenge of developing ways to cope with the opposite problem, an excess of water. Early settlements on the plains avoided the active floodplains, and it was probably not until the Mature Harappan period that the technology and the labor were available to tackle the problems of flooding by constructing settlements on massive platforms. It is still uncertain whether irrigation was needed for agriculture in the plains, but the preexisting knowledge of hydraulic engineering was essential for creating the wells, water tanks, and drainage systems needed by the Mature Harappan towns and cities.

The mountains to the north and northeast and the desert to the south formed natural barriers to agricultural expansion. The Greater Indus region was open at both ends, in Gujarat leading to the Deccan and in the east leading into the Ganges-Yamuna doab. However, given the crops and animals of the Early Harappans, neither the Deccan nor the doab offered anything like the potential of the Indus region, and there can have been little incentive to expand further at this stage.

Resource Imbalance and Trade

Civilizations often developed in areas where huge agricultural potential was balanced by a scarcity of important raw materials. Surplus agricultural produce could be used for external trade and channeled into supporting craft production, manufacturing goods also for trade. The need to organize these different economic sectors in order to obtain foreign goods and materials was often one of the main catalysts to the emergence of civilization. Most societies participated in trade networks that eventually brought in the resources of distant lands, but the mechanisms involved, such as gift giving between kin or exchanges between trading partners along an extended chain of neighboring communities, did not provide either the required volume of goods and materials or the necessary reliability of their supply; new and more organized mechanisms of trade and resource procurement had therefore to be developed.

The people of the Indo-Iranian borderlands and their neighbors in the greater Indus region had for millennia been part of networks that enabled materials to travel between the seacoast and the mountains and as far as Turkmenia. In the fourth millennium more organized trade networks developed across the Iranian plateau, from Mesopotamia to the Indus, with the growth of towns such as Shahr-i Sokhta that procured, processed, and moved desirable raw materials. The Early Harappans participated in these networks, but their widening settlement horizons brought them into contact with new communities and sources of material to the south and east. In particular, they gained access to the abundant copper ores of the Aravalli Hills, vitally important to a society that increasingly used metal artifacts. New sources close at hand lessened their involvement with the Iranian plateau trade network, though this continued at a low level. With the emergence of the lowland state, however, ties with the borderlands weakened and the trade route into Seistan ceased to be used.

The Early Harappans occupied a land that held many of the resources they required, while others could be obtained by trading with neighbors with whom they had long enjoyed cordial relations, such as the hunter-gatherer communities of Rajasthan, or to whom they had kinship ties, notably the communities still living in the borderlands. On the other hand, resources were not evenly distributed within the greater Indus region, and as communities spread toward the edges of the region, the managerial requirements of the trade increased. This situation is reflected at Harappa, where in the period just before the Transition materials from the south begin to appear in the settlement, reflecting a broadening of trade relations. Some materials were required for tools and everyday needs, while others, particularly those used for jewelry, had a symbolic significance, indicating social status or serving ideological or religious needs. It was therefore the need to organize resource procurement within the greater Indus region that was a key factor in the emergence of the Harappan state, rather than the need for an external trade network.

The Role of Navigation. The demands of the growing Early Harappan population for raw materials and other goods stimulated improvements in communications, drawing on the accumulated aquatic knowledge, expertise, and technology of the hunter-fisher-gatherer inhabitants of the Indus plains and coasts. The foundation of settlements in the Indus floodplains probably reflected the growing importance of river transport. Jansen (2002) argues that this was the case with Mohenjo-daro given that its location was otherwise unsuitable for settlement, at great risk from flooding by the nearby Indus. This pristine settlement was founded in the key central location midway between Harappa and the mountains on the one hand and Dholavira and the sea on the other, where the great highway of the Indus met a major route into the mountains via the Kachi plain and the Bolan pass. The enormous amount of labor involved in the creation of Mohenjo-daro's flood defense platforms (calculated at around 4 million man-days) indicates the existence of an authority able to plan the construction and to mobilize and feed the requisite labor force.

Though foreign trade played little part in the emergence of civilization in the Indus region, growing confidence in maritime technology and navigation soon enabled the Harappans to engage in seafaring, accessing the copper ores of Oman and subsequently the textiles and other desirable manufactured goods of Mesopotamia. By the late twenty-fourth century BCE, if not before, Harappan ships were docking in Sumerian ports. Settlements were founded in the Makran to extend the season when safe maritime transport was possible. Outposts were founded to procure raw materials, including Shortugai in Afghanistan. Dholavira thrived as the city controlling overseas trade; Mohenjo-daro enjoyed a preeminent role as the hub of the whole network, the point of intersection of all the routes, and Harappa flourished as the control center for the lucrative trade from the north.

High-Risk Lands

Unpredictable and unreliable climatic or environmental features, particularly those affecting the water supply vital for agriculture and life, often encouraged early societies to rely on religious leaders credited with the power to placate the gods and control events. A knowledge of astronomy could provide the vital calendric information needed to time the crucial activities of the agricultural year; often this knowledge was confined to the religious authorities, enhancing their power.

When people from the borderlands settled on the plains in the fourth millennium, they had to adjust to a very different environment from the one they knew. The Indus Valley was a highly productive agricultural region but one that was extremely unpredictable: The extent and location of the annual floodwaters were very variable and the river prone to shifting its channels. The need to control the uncertainties of this new life must have increased reliance on the religious leaders. The extent of Harappan astronomical knowledge is revealed by the cardinal orientation of the streets of later Harappan towns. This knowledge may have been developed in response to the need for ways to determine the timing of the seasons and the natural cycles dependent on them. The *nakshatra* star calendar appears to go back at least to the late fourth millennium, when the heliacal rising of the star Aldebaran marked the beginning of the year at the vernal equinox. Aldebaran became progressively less satisfactory as a marker, and, from around 2700 BCE, the Pleiades became the constellation whose heliacal rising came closest to the spring equinox.

During the Transition period most Early Harappan settlements were abandoned and some were destroyed by fire, perhaps to ritually purify the site. New settlements were constructed that followed certain principles, such as cardinal orientation and the provision of systems for removing wastewater, suggesting the widespread adoption of a new ideology. It is tempting to associate this with the major calendric change from Aldebaran to the Pleiades as the marker of the spring equinox, some time in the period 2700–2500 BCE: such a change, relating as it did to the organization of the agricultural year, was likely to have been made within a strong ideological setting. Whether this was the case or not, it still seems probable that the emergence of the Harappan state took place in the context of the widespread adoption of a unifying ideology, linked to religion, that specified the proper way to do things. Such an ideology dictating uniformity would have been a powerful means of uniting a society whose composition was heterogenous, as was that of the Indus region.

Harappa may have been the first city of this civilization. The city developed organically and without the marked and sudden transformation that characterized so many other settlements. It is at Harappa that evidence of the early development of writing has been found, as well as an Early Harappan stone weight. In the early Mature Harappan period, both mound AB and mound E were walled, and in some parts platforms were constructed. It may have been in this region that the idea of the Harappan urban form developed, including platforms and walls, cardinally orientated streets, hydraulic engineering and the importance of water, houses constructed of bricks of uniform size and proportions, and a walled subsection of the settlement that probably housed public buildings of various sorts, as well as standards for the form and decoration of artifacts, and the correct materials to be used for making particular objects, especially those with a symbolic significance. Harappa was the major settlement of the Kot Diji regional tradition, the largest of the Early Harappan groups. From there, the ideology may have spread out like a wave into the neighboring cultural areas, influencing new construction and reconstruction.

Conflict

In many of early civilizations, competition among communities for resources, becoming scarce as the population continued to rise, spiraled into warfare. Power came to rest in the hands of those who could mobilize force to defend their own community and to expand its resources at the expense of its neighbors. This led to the emergence of territorial states that were unified by military force and within which there were social inequalities reflecting differential access to resources. Defense was also required against the inhabitants of neighboring regions where resources were restricted.

The Indus civilization seems to have been exempt from this move toward conflict and militarism. One reason was that the abundant resources of the Indus region seem to have been more than adequate for the Harappan population, so there was no intercommunity competition. Another was the absence of envious neighbors: The people of the Indo-Iranian borderlands were related by past kinship ties and some probably still descended to the plains to pasture their animals in the winter months and engaged in mutually beneficial trade. Similarly, the hunter-fisher-gatherer and farming communities of adjacent regions, including the Aravallis and the Himalayas, had more to gain by peaceful cooperation than by raiding. Militarism therefore played no part either in the emergence of Harappan civilization or in its continued cohesion. Instead, the state seems to have been held together by ties of economic cooperation and shared ideology.

THEORIES ON THE SOCIOPOLITICAL ORGANIZATION OF THE INDUS STATE

The nature of Harappan political organization is still unclear, though much debated, and there is not even agreement on whether it was a single state.

Toward a Model of Harappan Society

Accepting the Harappan ideology gave a sense of unity to the participating communities, but this was a matter of choice rather than compulsion; the political organization of the state therefore involved the willing participation of communities that had a stake in its running. This fits Possehl's (2002) suggestion that the state was a heterarchy, with shared power and collective responsibility. This would mean that the organization was bottom-up rather than top-down; rather than having a strong central authority appointing officials to control the regions and the subdivisions within them, those in authority would have been locally appointed, perhaps by a council of tribal or local elders, to manage the participation of the local community in the larger network. Alternatively, this responsibility might be vested in the community's religious leaders. Such a system would still require a degree of hierarchy and centralization of authority, though this could have been relatively weak. The great differential in size and complexity between the cities and the other settlements, the small number of the cities, and their even distribution demonstrate that they had a major political role as regional administrative and organizational centers.

State or Federation?

A number of scholars have suggested that the Indus civilization was not actually a state, but a federation made up of smaller units that shared a common material culture and a common ideology. The great uniformity of Indus artifacts and other aspects of Indus life masks smaller cultural groupings and cultural differences, making it hard to identify regional entities. However, these existed before the emergence of the civilization and reemerged after its demise, suggesting that they continued, unmarked, throughout the time of the civilization. The diversity of religious practices also points to some multiculturalism in Indus society. However, the existence of a number of smaller city-states would probably have led to competition and conflict, something for which there is no evidence. The degree of specialization and the huge scale of production of objects such as shell bangles or beads in particular areas also argues against the existence of regional states; such operations seem unlikely to have been undertaken by individual states relying on interregional trade to dispose of their products. Specialist settlements such as Nageshwar and Lothal served the entire Indus region rather than just Gujarat, and production was integrated, with some objects processed on the spot and others sent inland to be completed. An integrated state therefore seems a more probable interpretation of the evidence.

Priest-kings?

The suggestion that the Harappan state was a theocracy seems particularly apt in the Indian context, where the highest status in the ideological hierarchy is accorded to the priestly caste, which often enjoyed temporal power. Many scholars are nevertheless unhappy with this theory.

In some ways, however, the dichotomy between temporal and religious authority is a false distinction. In all ancient civilizations, whatever the form of government, the rulers governed through divine sanction. The gods were always the ultimate authority in society, and the rulers the channel through which their will was done. In this sense every society was a theocracy. What is in dispute, therefore, are the means by which those in power controlled society; the sanctions at their disposal; the mechanisms by which people were impelled to share the fruits of their labors with others and by which they could be assured a supply of other people's produce; the means by which the huge labor forces required to construct and maintain the settlements' flood defense platforms could be mobilized, inspired, and fed, as well as the smaller numbers of laborers needed to maintain and clean the complex waste-disposal system and other regular civic tasks. To my mind, the model of a society in which power was vested in the priesthood fits the Harappan evidence.

The elusive trappings of power, the emphasis on the use of water for purification, and the suggestion of segregation rather than glorification all accord better with a spiritual than with a temporal elite and head of state. The absence of overt evidence of the use of force as a sanction for unacceptable behavior suggests that the intangible threat of divine punishment was the main sanction that kept potential wrongdoers in line and ensured conformity with the requirements of the social order. Communities are generally very effective in administering and policing such a system themselves, without the need of intervention by the state.

Shared ideology was a major integrating mechanism. Religion would have played a regulatory role, individuals performing their obligations, making their offerings and supplying their labor to please the gods, and avoiding wrongdoing for fear of divine retribution. In many societies large-scale construction was of massive monuments, such as temples or tombs, but, given the astronomically linked orientation of the settlements and the link between astronomy and religion, the building of city platforms might well have been seen in a similar light as a construction that honored the gods.

Kinship Ties

Kinship may also have underlain the organization of the Harappan state. The historical integration of arable agriculture and transhumant pastoralism as activities practiced by members of the same family, maintained when the people of the Indo-Iranian borderlands colonized the plains, provided a mechanism by which people were linked and related to each other over wide areas, with systems of mutual obligation. Similar networks characterize hunter-gatherer societies such as those of the greater Indus region, with whom the people of the hills already had ancient connections on a small scale. The peaceful integration of the incomers and indigenes further strengthened a system of mutual interdependency, with rights and obligations that spread goods and services through communities, a forerunner of the *jajmani* system.

Some states are territorial in nature, their citizens owning land or being tied in some relationship to those who do. Such states have as their basis sedentary agriculture, and their people see their identity in terms of place. Power is therefore exercised through the control of territory, and often the ruler or the deity of the land is nominally owner of it all. Other states are based on control of people rather than territory and are more likely to be associated with economies in which pastoralism is important. These are characterized by hierarchies in which individuals owe service to their superiors in the state, to whom they often have a theoretical kin relationship; the land is not owned, only the rights to exploit it; and there is a complex network of rights and obligations. In such states loyalty was not to place but to people (the ethnic group or tribe), and identity was expressed in terms of kinship. Though the Harappans practiced agriculture as well as pastoralism, it is more likely that the Harappan state was of this second type. Pastoralism remained a major component of the economy, as did hunter-fisher-gathering, and, though permanently cultivated fields were possible in some regions, in many others, due to the vagaries of the rivers, cultivable areas were liable to change from year to year, making it inappropriate to have ownership ties to any particular piece of land. This social system, in combination with something similar to the *jajmani* system, would have enabled kin or occupational groups to be integrated into a single functioning whole.

State Management

The development of the state strengthened the system of interdependency and added to it some official backbone and order as well as stepping up the scale at which it operated. A managerial class emerged whose role was to facilitate and organize the circulation of goods and materials. Economies of scale developed, with dedicated centers of craft production where materials were processed for distribution throughout the Harappan realms; trade missions were dispatched overseas; and a few resource procurement colonies were established even in Mesopotamia and Afghanistan.

Towns developed at communications nodes or in locations well-placed to procure resources. Rural and town craft production could have been sustained by local agriculture. Some villagers practicing farming or fishing for most of the year may have moved into satellite industrial villages during the slack part of the year to undertake such activities as beadmaking or shellworking. Artisans and state functionaries in the towns and cities may have been sustained by agricultural produce collected as taxes, probably at the city gate, where weights are often found, suggesting the weighing of goods or materials in order to deduct a fixed proportion.

Goods and materials may also have been collected as compulsory offerings, owed to the gods at appropriate times and seasons, and perhaps surrendered in the context of religious festivals. In the same context, other goods and materials may have been issued by the religious authorities, their value enhanced by having passed through the temporary ownership of the gods. In Indian tradition, nonfixed payments and services are made within the *jajmani* system at such times, and this may well also have been the case in the Harappan period.

The movement of goods and materials from other regions of the state or from overseas would probably have been bureaucratically controlled, but their distribution could also take place in the same contexts. Goods in transit or awaiting distribution would probably only have required temporary storage and in relatively small amounts; there seems unlikely to have been any of the stockpiling that characterized many states.

A Line of Kings?

The stone sculptures of seated men from Mohenjo-daro may be portraits or stock representations of rulers or important individuals (for example, saints or religious leaders). All come from late levels at Mohenjo-daro, and all are broken. They may have been deliberately vandalized, though the damage could be due merely to accident and weathering. A tempting reconstruction, though one for which there is at the present no supporting evidence, is that they are the portraits of a ruling dynasty, deliberately broken when the dynasty was overthrown. If so, the absence of such sculptures at an earlier date may mean that the existence of a line of kings at this time represented an unwelcome break with tradition.

Few Harappan stone sculptures are known, but the majority of those found are figures of seated men and were found at Mohenjo-daro. All of these came from late levels and all were broken. It is tempting to see them as the smashed portraits of a line of hated rulers. (J. M. Kenoyer, Courtesy Department of Archaeology and Museums, Government of Pakistan)

INDUS COLLAPSE

The final centuries of the Harappan civilization in the early second millennium saw a decline in civic standards in many settlements, including the cities of Harappa, Mohenjo-daro, and Dholavira. Drains were not maintained and inferior houses were put together, often from salvaged bricks. Heavy industry, including pottery kilns and metal furnaces, appeared in what had formerly been residential houses, and the Pillared Hall on Mohenjo-daro's citadel was divided into workshops. The breakdown of civic life seems particularly marked at Mohenjo-daro, where dead bodies were given perfunctory burial in disused houses or streets. In many settlements, concealed hoards of valuables whose owners never returned to reclaim them reveal a climate of insecurity.

The internal distribution system that had integrated the state began to break down, each region gradually coming to rely on its own resources and local trade networks. Regional cultures emerged, with many material similarities to the local Early Harappan cultures of half a millennium before; some regions flourished while others, notably Sindh, declined further. Writing and weights no longer served a purpose and were abandoned. Gujarat continued overseas trade but was linked internally with western India instead of with the Harappan realms. In the east, the Saraswati Valley was becoming depopulated as settlers spread toward the Ganges-Yamuna doab.

The disintegration of the Indus civilization, the abandonment of settlements in some areas, and the subsequent disappearance of its culture are in stark contrast to other early civilizations, which were generally replaced by their rivals or developed new foci but rose again. When civilization reemerged in India, it was in quite a different area, on the Ganges, where civilizations continued to rise and fall for the rest of South Asia's history. The causes of the Indus collapse are still not completely known but some possible factors have been isolated.

Health

One reason for the urban decay at Mohenjo-daro was probably the poor health of its residents. Skeletons from the upper levels, deposited in abandoned houses or streets, were in the past interpreted as victims of warfare (identified by Wheeler as Indo-Aryan raids), but studies have shown their fate to have been quite different. No traces of violence were found on the bones of these famous "massacre victims," with two exceptions, and in both cases the injuries were suffered well before death. Instead, the skeletons showed signs that many individuals had suffered from malaria, spread by mosquitoes probably breeding in flooded land near the city. Mohenjo-daro's residents may also have suffered from cholera. Seepage of wastewater from the drains may have contaminated drinking water in the numerous wells, and a few cases could have escalated rapidly into a major epidemic.

Environmental Problems

Many possible natural and humanly induced disasters have been suggested to account for the collapse, some of them sudden and dramatic, others long-term and insidious. For example, it is possible that the monsoon winds may have shifted slightly southward, decreasing critical rainfall in some areas, causing drought, and increasing it in others, causing flooding. Opinions and evidence on this matter, however, ebb and flow with the years, and we still cannot say for certain whether such a change took place and, if it did, whether it contributed to the Indus decline.

Climate Change. The late third millennium BCE saw a global increase in aridity that had a serious impact on the civilizations of Egypt and Mesopotamia and on the Harappans' neighbors in Seistan. The effect in the Indus region was to decrease the reliability of the summer monsoons, and, paradoxically, to increase winter rainfall, neither of which had a serious impact on Harappan agriculture, although it may have encouraged diversification. Nevertheless, recent studies of soil samples from Harappa suggest that this global dry period had a longer-term effect on vegetation and landscape in the region, possibly contributing to population decline and the abandonment of settlements in the period 1900–1600 BCE.

Environmental Degradation. It has been suggested that firing the huge number of baked bricks used in Harappan settlements would have entailed massive deforestation. However, recent investigations have shown that the scrubby vegetation of the Indus Valley would have been a sustainable source of fuel adequate for this purpose. Perhaps more serious was the quantity of fuel used in industry, especially metalworking, but also making pottery and faience. An unknown volume of timber was also felled for domestic construction and for export. Agriculture may also have taken its toll. Limited evidence of environmental degradation exists in some areas such as Gujarat, where the shift to scrubby acacia wood and dung for fuel in the Late Harappan period implies significant earlier deforestation.

The Coastline. Sea levels began falling in the late third millennium, leaving Harappan ports in the Makran high and dry. This must have had a major impact on trade passing through the Makran. In Saurashtra, Lothal lost its access to the sea, and the port of Kuntasi was abandoned around 1700 BCE. On the other hand, a new port was established at Bet Dwarka on the northern peninsula of Saurashtra, a spot exposed by the receding coastline (and today again under water).

The Gujarat coastline was also affected by the deposition of enormous volumes of silt by the Indus and other rivers then debouching into the Ranns of Kutch, transforming them gradually from open water to salty marsh, though the extent to which this had occurred by the last centuries of the Mature Harappan culture is unknown. It is likely to have been enough by that stage to cause inconvenience to shipping, creating hazardous stretches of shallow water and forcing the closure of some established sea lanes. It is possible that the vicissitudes of Dholavira (which was temporarily abandoned in the twentieth century BCE) were attributable to difficulties of access by sea.

The Indus River. The Indus region is prone to earthquakes and their effects have been observed in several settlements, including Mature Harappan Dholavira and Early Harappan Kalibangan. No major earthquake damage, however, has been noted in settlements around the time that the decline set in. Eruptive mud from tectonic activity has in recorded times occasionally dammed the Indus, causing massive but short-lived ponding and flooding. However, there is no convincing evidence that Mohenjo-daro experienced major and prolonged flooding in the critical period.

The Indus has changed its channels many times, and sometimes there has been a major shift in its course; the river today flows much farther east than in the Harappan period. However, major flooding and river course changes in the Indus plains were a regular hazard of life, with which the Harappans had learned to cope when they first colonized the plains: Major settlements were constructed on massive platforms, while villagers in the floodplain may have managed by occupying houseboats for all or part of the year.

The Saraswati Valley. In contrast, changes taking place in the Saraswati Valley in the early second millennium were probably a major contributor to the Indus decline. In Harappan times, the Saraswati was a major river system flowing from the Siwaliks at least to Bahawalpur, where it probably ended in a substantial inland delta. The ancient Saraswati River was fed by a series of small rivers that rose in the Siwaliks, but it drew the greater part of its waters from two much larger rivers rising high in the Himalayas: the Sutlej and the Yamuna. In its heyday the Saraswati appears to have supported the densest settlement and provided the greatest arable yields of any part of the Indus realms. The Yamuna, which supplied most of the water flowing in the Drishadvati, a major tributary of the Saraswati, changed its course, probably early in the second millennium, to flow into the Ganges drainage. The remaining flow in the Drishadvati became small and seasonal: Late Harappan sites in Bahawalpur are concentrated in the portion of the Sarawati east of Yazman, which was fed by the Sutlej. At a later date the Sutlej also changed its course and was captured by the Indus. These changes brought about massive depopulation of the Saraswati Valley, which by the end of the millennium was described as a place of potsherds and ruin mounds whose inhabitants had gone away. At the same time new settlements appeared in the regions to the south and east, in the upper Ganges-Yamuna doab. Some were located on the palaeochannels that mark the eastward shift of the Yamuna. Presumably many of the Late Harappan settlers had originated in the Saraswati Valley.

Changing Agricultural Regimes

During the Mature Harappan period, the staple crops—wheat, barley, and many pulses—were winter sown. Rice, a summer crop, was known but apparently little used until the early second millennium. Native millets, also grown in summer, were the main crops in Saurashtra but were low yielding. However, in the early second millennium much higher-yielding African millets (sorghum, finger millet, and pearl millet) were introduced and began to be cultivated. These new crops now made it economical to invest time and effort in summer *(kharif)* cultivation.

During the Mature Harappan period, Gujarat was an area of low agricultural productivity, and many of its inhabitants engaged part- or full-time in other activities such as trade by land and sea, shellworking and beadmaking, fishing, and salt making, supplying goods and materials to other Harappan realms and receiving the means of subsistence. The cultivation of African millets, by greatly increasing productivity, brought about an agricultural revolution on Saurashtra during the early second millennium, with a massive increase in the number of settlements; some, such as Rojdi, were far larger than before. The new prosperity of Saurashtra offered Gujarat a local market, weakening its need to be integrated into the Harappan internal distribution system. Gujarat's opting out would have had serious repercussions for the organization of the state.

At the cost of an increase in labor, two crops could now be raised each year in areas where both the old and the new crops could be grown. These included the Kachi plain, where rice now became an important crop. Since rice required irrigation, this implies a considerable labor investment in the creation of permanent irrigation systems. The millets were tolerant of arid conditions and were therefore well suited for cultivation in marginal areas that had previously only provided rough grazing. The millets could be used both as human food and as fodder for domestic animals.

Rice also began to be grown in the eastern Indus zone. This proved important in facilitating the gradual spread of farming communities into the northern part of the Ganges region.

Outside Contacts

Sea Trade. The importance of overseas trade to the Harappans is uncertain. It has been suggested that the disruption of direct trade with Sumer due to political changes there around 2000 BCE may have had an impact on the Harappan state. This, however, seems unlikely since trade continued, albeit on a reduced scale, through the entrepot of Dilmun until the mideighteenth century BCE, when Sumer suffered economic collapse, by which time the Harappan state was itself already in decline. The loss of the Makran ports, due to the falling sea level, and the collapse of the Harappan state put sea trade into the hands of the Late Harappans in Gujarat, who continued to profit by some trade with Dilmun and Magan until at least 1600 BC.

Overland Traders, Raiders, and Settlers. In the early second millennium, people from the BMAC in Bactria and Margian expanded into adjacent regions, including Seistan, from where they penetrated the Indus region or traded with its inhabitants. This took place, however, after the Indus decline had begun: BMAC material occurs in Baluchistan, in Pirak and other sites on the Kachi plain, alongside Cemetery H material at Harappa and Jhukar material in Sindh, and in the Gandhara Graves in Swat, as well as much farther south at Gilund in Rajasthan. The physical diversity of the skeletons from the final period at Mohenjo-daro suggests that some were outsiders. Burned settlements in Baluchistan suggest that the newcomers came as raiders rather than as traders, though there is little evidence that this was also the case in the Indus region.

Linguistic evidence indicates that Proto-Indo-Iranians, pastoral nomads from the steppe, spent some time in contact with the BMAC. Later groups of their Indo-Aryan-speaking descendants began to appear in the northern part of the subcontinent, including Swat. The most apparent archaeological trace of their arrival is the appearance, for the first time in the subcontinent, of domestic horses. They began to penetrate the Punjab some time between 1700 and 1500 BCE, well after the disintegration of the Harappan state.

Summary

The decline of Harappan urbanism probably had many contributing factors. The shift to a concentration on *kharif* cultivation in the outer regions of the state may have seriously disrupted established schedules for craft production, civic flood defense, building and drain maintenance, and other publicly organized works on which the smooth running of the state depended. The reduction in the waters of the Saraswati and the response of its farmers by migrating into regions to the east tore apart the previous unity of the Harappan state, disrupting its cohesion and its ability to control the internal distribution network. At the same time, Gujarat may have been asserting its independence. The poor state of health of Mohenjo-daro's citizens can have done nothing to improve the situation: decline there would have seriously affected the management of the internal communications networks, particularly along the Indus. The state organization crumbled away, leaving behind a series of flourishing regional communities in Gujarat, the Kachi plain, and the Punjab/eastern region, but undermining the infrastructure that had held together the urban way of life.

REFERENCES

Agrawal, D. P., and J. S. Kharakwal. 2003. *Archaeology of South Asia. II. Bronze and Iron Ages in South Asia.* New Delhi: Aryan Books International.

Chakrabarti, Dilip K. 1997. *The Archaeology of Ancient Indian Cities.* New Delhi: Oxford University Press.

Dales, George F. 1964. "The Mythical Massacre at Mohenjo Daro." *Expedition.* Vol. 6: 36–43. Reprinted 1979 in *Ancient Cities of the Indus,* edited by Gregory L. Possehl, 293–296. New Delhi: Vikas Publishing House.

Fuller, Dorian Q. 2007. "Non-human Genetics, Agricultural Origins and Historical Linguistics in South Asia." In *The Evolution and History of Human Populations in South Asia,* edited by Michael D. Petraglia and Bridget Allchin, 389–439. Dordrecht, Netherlands: Springer.

Jacobson, Jerome. 1986. "The Harappan Civilization: An Early State." In *Studies in the Archaeology of India and Pakistan,* edited by Jerome Jacobson, 137–173. New Delhi: Oxford & IBH Publishing Co.

Jansen, Michael. 2002. "Settlement Networks of the Indus Civilization." In *Indian Archaeology in Retrospect. II. Protohistory. Archaeology of the Harappan Civilization,* edited by S. Settar and Ravi Korisettar, 105–126. Indian Council of Historical Research. New Delhi: Manohar.

Kennedy, Kenneth A. R. 1984. "Trauma and Disease in the Ancient Harappans." In *Frontiers of the Indus Civilization*, edited by B. B. Lal and S. P. Gupta, 425–436. New Delhi: Books and Books.

Kennedy, Kenneth A. R. 2000. *God-Apes and Fossil Men: Palaeoanthropology of South Asia*. Ann Arbor: University of Michigan Press.

Kenoyer, Jonathan Mark. 1994. "The Harappan State. Was It or Wasn't It?" In *From Sumer to Meluhha: Contributions to the Archaeology of South and West Asia in Memory of George F. Dales, Jr.*, edited by Jonathan Mark Kenoyer, 71–80. *Wisconsin Archaeological Reports*. Vol. 3. Department of Anthropology. Madison: University of Wisconsin.

Kenoyer, Jonathan Mark. 1998. *Ancient Cities of the Indus Valley Civilization*. Karachi: Oxford University Press and American Institute of Pakistan Studies.

Kenoyer, Jonathan Mark, and Richard H. Meadow. 1998. "The Latest Discoveries: Harappa 1995–98." [Online article; retrieved 6/14/05.] www.harappa.com/indus2/index.html.

Lawler, Andrew. 2007. "Climate Spurred Later Indus Decline." *Science* 316: 979.

Meadow, Richard H., and Jonathan Mark Kenoyer. 2003. "Recent Discoveries and Highlights from Excavations at Harappa: 1998–2000." [Online article; retrieved 6/14/05.] www.harappa.com/indus4/e1.html.

Misra, V. N. 1984. "Climate, a Factor in the Rise and Fall of the Indus Civilization—Evidence from Rajasthan and Beyond." In *Frontiers of the Indus Civilization*, edited by B. B. Lal and S. P. Gupta, 461–489. New Delhi: Books and Books.

Misra, V. N. 1994. "Indus Civilization and Rgvedic Sarasvati." In *South Asian Archaeology 1993*, edited by Asko Parpola and Petteri Koskikallio, 511–526. Helsinki: Suomalainen Tiedeakatemia.

Misra, V. N. 1995. "Climate Change and the Indus Civilization." In *The "Lost" Saraswati and the Indus Civilization*, edited by S. P. Gupta, 125–163. Jodhpur, India: Kusumanjali Prakashan.

Mughal, M. Rafique. 1984. "The Post-Harappan Phase in Bahawalpur District, Pakistan." In *Frontiers of the Indus Civilization*, edited by B. B. Lal and S. P. Gupta, 499–503. New Delhi: Books and Books.

Possehl, Gregory L. 1990. "Revolution in the Urban Revolution: The Emergence of Indus Urbanization." *Annual Review of Anthropology* 19: 261–282.

Possehl, Gregory L. 1999. *Indus Age: The Beginnings*. New Delhi: Oxford University Press.

Possehl, Gregory L. 2002. *The Indus Civilization. A Contemporary Perspective*. Walnut Creek, CA: AltaMira Press.

Raikes, R. L. 1984. "Mohenjo Daro Environment." In *Frontiers of the Indus Civilization*, edited by B. B. Lal and S. P. Gupta, 455–460. New Delhi: Books and Books.

Ratnagar, Shereen. 2000. *The End of the Great Harappan Tradition: Heras Memorial Lectures 1998*. New Delhi: Manohar.

Singh, Gurdip. 1971. "The Indus Valley Culture (Seen in the Context of Post-glacial Climate and Ecological Studies in North-west India)." *Archaeology and Physical Anthropology in Oceania* 6 (2): 177–189.

Yash, Pal, B. Sahai, R. K. Snood, and D. P. Agrawal. 1984. "Remote Sensing of the "Lost" Saraswati River." In *Frontiers of the Indus Civilization*, edited by B. B. Lal and S. P. Gupta, 491–497. New Delhi: Books and Books.

Glossary

ACACIA *Acacia* spp, a shrubby tree that thrives in drier regions of northern South Asia and has many uses.

AGADE Capital of the Akkadian empire. Ships from Meluhha were said to dock at its quays.

AHAR-BANAS CULTURE A Chalcolithic culture in Rajasthan, contemporary with the Harappan civilization but probably not directly in contact with it.

AKKAD The northern part of Babylonia (southern Mesopotamia).

AKKADIAN EMPIRE The first state uniting the lands of southern Mesopotamia (Sumer and Akkad), founded by Sargon of Akkad in 2334 BCE and enduring until 2193 BCE.

ALLAHDINO A small (1.4-hectare) but highly organized settlement in Sindh, probably concerned with textile production and the distribution network.

ALUM A white mineral, aluminium potassium sulphate, used as a mordant to stabilize some dyes.

AMAZONITE A type of pale blue-green stone used for making beads and possibly coming from Karnataka or the Himalayas.

AMRI A settlement in Sindh occupied in the Early Harappan period. It was destroyed by burning in the Transition period before being rebuilt in the Mature Harappan period.

AMRI-NAL PHASE The Early Indus period in Sindh and southern Baluchistan, named after Amri in Sindh and Nal in the adjacent mountains.

AMU DARYA A river in southern Central Asia and northern Afghanistan, also known as the Oxus.

ANATOLIA Asiatic Turkey.

ANTELOPE Antelope hunted in the Indus region included blackbuck, four-horned antelope or chausingha, and nilgai.

ARAVALLIS A range of hills running south of the Thar Desert in Rajasthan, an important source of minerals, particularly copper.

ARD A primitive form of plow that cut through the soil, breaking it up and creating a furrow, but not turning the soil.

ARTHASHASTRA A text in which Kautilya, minister to the first Mauryan emperor, Chandragupta, gave advice to his king on statecraft. In its practical but ruthless suggestions, it has been compared to Machiavelli's *The Prince*.

ARYANS *See* Indo-Aryans.

ASSYRIA Northern Mesopotamia.

AUSTRO-ASIATIC A language family now comprising the Mon-Khmer languages of Southeast Asia and the Munda languages, spoken by a small number of tribal people in India. Munda was probably more widely spoken in antiquity, and there may have been another branch, currently known as Para-Munda, now extinct but possibly spoken by at least some Harappans.

AVESTA   The sacred books of the early Iranians, comprising the *Older Avesta* and the *Younger Avesta*.

BABYLONIA   Southern Mesopotamia (Sumer and Akkad).

BACKSTRAP LOOM   A loom in which the warp threads are tied to a rod at one end, with their other ends attached to the weaver's waist. The rod can be fastened to a post or tree or held in tension by the weaver's feet. Very easy to use and portable, it has the disadvantage that only narrow strips of cloth can be woven on it.

BACTRIA   A region in northern Afghanistan between the Amu-Darya and the Hindu Kush.

BACTRIA-MARGIANA ARCHAEOLOGICAL COMPLEX   *See* BMAC.

BACTRIAN CAMEL   The two-humped camel (*Camelus bactrianus*), domesticated in southern Central Asia during the third millennium, when it was present at Shahr-i Sokhta. It was probably brought into South Asia by BMAC traders and raiders in the early second millennium, when it was present at Pirak.

BADAKSHAN   A district of northern Afghanistan including the Kokcha gorge, source of lapis lazuli in antiquity.

BAGASRA   *See* Gola Dhoro.

BAGOR   A campsite near the Arawalli Hills, occupied from around 5000 BCE onward by hunter-gatherers, who also raised domestic animals. In the second period, from around 2800 BCE, a few copper tools were in use there.

BAHAWALPUR   The western part of the lost Saraswati system, along the dry beds of the Hakra-Ghaggar River.

BAJRA   Pearl or bulrush millet (*Pennisetum typhoides*), introduced from Africa during the early second millennium.

BALAKOT   A small (2.8-hectare) town in eastern Makran concerned mainly with fishing and shell bangle making.

BALATHAL   A major settlement of the Ahar-Banas culture.

BALUCHISTAN   The mountainous region to the west of the Indus Valley, which forms the eastern end of the Iranian plateau.

BANAWALI   A 16-hectare town in the eastern region.

BANYAN   The Indian fig (*Ficus indica*), famous for its aerial roots. It was venerated in South Asia probably from early times.

BARASINGHA   The swamp deer, *Cervus duvauceli*.

BARU GRASS   *Sorghum halepensis*, a tall grass with a tough tubular stem that grows in Gujarat and is used for constructing small seaworthy craft resembling reed boats.

BAT   A clay disc seated on the potter's wheel, on which the pot was thrown. The bat was then lifted off with the vessel on it, minimizing the risk of damaging the vessel when removing it from the wheel.

BER   *See* Jujube.

BET DWARKA   A Post-Harappan port established in Saurashtra after the sea level fell around 2000 BCE.

BITUMEN   Natural asphalt, used particularly as an adhesive and a waterproofing material.

BLACKBUCK   An antelope (*Antelope cervicapra*).

BLACK COTTON SOILS   Volcanic lava soils found in the Deccan, Kutch, Saurashtra, and some parts of mainland Gujarat, on which cotton is often grown. They are fertile and water retentive. Their tendency to crack during the dry season causes a certain amount of mixing of the upper soil layers; they are therefore said to be self-plowing.

BMAC The Bactria-Margiana Archaeological Complex, which occupied northern Afghanistan in the late third and early second millennia BCE, and colonized Seistan. Its people were in contact with the Late Harappan and other Chalcolithic cultures of northern South Asia.

BOLAS A weapon, used particularly in the ancient Americas, for catching animals. It consisted of one or several lengths of rope to which stone balls were attached, and was thrown to entangle an animal's legs, bringing it down. It has been suggested that the Harappan perforated balls, which are usually called mace heads, may have been part of such a device.

BRAHMI The alphabetic script developed in the later first millennium BCE from a West Semitic script, ancestral to all later Indian scripts.

BRAHUI An isolated Dravidian language spoken in southern Baluchistan.

BREAD WHEAT Free-threshing wheats suitable for making bread because of their high gluten content: *T. aestivum vulgare*, clubwheat (*T. aestivum compactum*), and shot wheat (*T. aestivum sphaerococcum*), the latter being the variety most used in South Asia.

BRISTLEY FOXTAIL MILLET A small millet (*Setaria verticillata*), probably cultivated in Mature Harappan Saurashtra.

BROOMCORN MILLET Common or broomcorn millet (*Panicum miliaceum*), probably introduced from the Namazga area, possibly via Shortugai, though it was not certainly cultivated in Harappan times.

BROWNTOP MILLET A native millet (*Brachiaria ramosa*), cultivated in Mature Harappan Saurashtra.

BUND A small dam or wall, usually constructed of earth and rocks, built to retain water, generally for irrigation. The gabarbands of Baluchistan, which may have been built from pre-Indus times onward, sometimes involved a stepped series of small *L*-shaped platforms, the long side stretching out into the stream to divert a portion of the water and suspended alluvium on to a small field in the base of the *L*.

BURIN A sharp instrument, usually a flint blade, with an angled cutting edge, typically used for engraving.

BURUSHASKI A language isolate, spoken in the Western Karakoram region of the Himalayas.

BURZAHOM A settlement of the Northern Neolithic culture.

CAMBAY TECHNIQUE A method of working stone by inverse indirect percussion, peculiar to South Asia and particularly used by beadmakers. The object to be knapped was held against a sharp point embedded in the ground and was hit with a soft hammer, detaching a flake.

CAMEL *See* Bactrian Camel; Dromedary.

CARNELIAN Also known as sard, a distinctive red stone favored by the Harappans for making beads. Naturally occurring carnelian is rare. To produce it artificially, yellow chalcedony containing iron oxide was repeatedly heated to alter its color. This could produce a range of shades from orange to deep red.

CEMETERY H The cemetery associated with the Late Harappan period at Harappa. The lower level shows continuity of local practices, while there are marked changes in the upper level.

CEMETERY H CULTURE The culture of the Late Harappan period in the Punjab and areas to its north and east, named after the later cemetery at Harappa.

CEMETERY R-37 The cemetery at Harappa belonging to the Mature Indus period.

CHAGAI HILLS A mineral-rich area in western Baluchistan exploited particularly by the people of Seistan.

CHANDRAGUPTA MAURYA A great emperor (ca. 320–292 BCE), founder of the Mauryan dynasty, who united most of the subcontinent.

CHANHU-DARO A small (4.7-hectare) town located on the Indus River about halfway between Mohenjo-daro and the sea. Certain features, such as its baked brick architecture and heavy involvement in industrial activities, including the manufacture of some very specialist products such as long carnelian beads, make the town seem like an industrial and administrative satellite of Mohenjo-daro. Like the latter, it was probably founded in the context of communications along the Indus River highway.

CHANK A shellfish (*Turbinella pyrum*). Chank shells were mainly used for making bangles, but also libation vessels and trumpets.

CHAUSINGHA The four-horned antelope (*Tetracerus quadricornus*).

CHAUTANG *See* Drishadvati.

CHINKARA The Indian gazelle (*Gazella bennetti*).

CHITAL The spotted deer (*Axis axis*).

CHLORITE A form of steatite, used particularly to manufacture fine bowls that were widely circulated during the third and early second millennia. The *série ancienne* bowls were manufactured at Tepe Yahya and probably at Jiroft on the Iranian plateau, and at Tarut in the Gulf. These are also known as the Intercultural Style of vessels because they enjoyed a very wide distribution. Later styles were mainly manufactured in Oman.

CHOLISTAN The region in which the western part of the lost Saraswati system lies.

CIRE PERDUE Also known as lost-wax casting, a technique for casting metal (mainly copper or bronze) objects in complex shapes. A full-scale model of a desired object is made in wax, then coated in clay and fired. The wax runs out, leaving a mold in which the metal object is cast. Usually the mold is smashed to remove the object.

COPPER HOARDS Hoards of very distinctive copper artifacts, including antenna-hilted swords, found in the Ganges-Yamuna doab and Rajasthan. It took archaeologists many decades to discover the evidence that linked these hoards with the makers of OCP (Ochre-Colored Pottery) and to establish that the culture they represented dated to the earlier second millennium.

CORVEE Days of labor performed as a duty to the state, the religious authorities, or other official bodies, as a form of tax. Although unpaid, corvée was often recompensed by the issue of rations.

COTTON Used for making thread by the end of period I at Mehrgarh (sixth millennium BCE), cotton (*Gossypium arboreum*) was domesticated in the subcontinent and probably cultivated as a perennial shrub.

CROCODILE *See* Gharial; Mugger.

CYLINDER SEAL A cylinder, usually of stone inscribed with a design and written text that could be endlessly reproduced by rolling it across wet clay. Cylinder seals were the characteristic product of Mesopotamia, contrasting with the square stamp seals of the Indus.

DAIMABAD   A Chalcolithic settlement in Maharashtra, where there is evidence for the presence of Late Harappan people, probably from Gujarat.

DAIMABAD HOARD   Four bronze sculptures accidentally discovered near Daimabad. They have been attributed to the Harappans or their descendants, but there is no stylistic or technological evidence to support this identification, and no contextual data to support this period attribution.

DAMB SADAAT   A settlement in central Baluchistan that gives its name to an Early Harappan culture related to Kot Diji.

DANCING-GIRL   A famous bronze statuette discovered by Mackay at Mohenjo-daro depicting a naked girl in a loose-limbed and provocative pose. This stance led to her being known as the Dancing-girl (nautch-girl), though she is not dancing but standing.

DEER   Deer hunted by the Harappans included Kashmir stag, hog deer, chital, barasingha, and sambhar.

DEODAR   The Himalayan cedar (*Cedrus deodara*), a tree that grows in the mountains of the northwest, at elevations above 1,200 meters. Its aromatic wood is extensively used in the construction of buildings and boats and for making coffins.

DHAND   A lake created or enlarged by seasonal rainfall or flooding. Dhands include seasonal lakes in the Thar Desert, most of which become saline as their waters evaporate; lakes in Sindh and the Indo-Gangetic doab, forming after the inundation in parts of old levees and in dried-up or abandoned river beds; and pools and lakes in depressions forming after the inundation or the monsoon, including the Nal Lake in Gujarat, but also Lake Manchar and other perennial lakes that expand and contract annually.

DHOLAVIRA   The Harappan city in Gujarat, founded in the Early Harappan period and occupied for more than a millennium, though it declined in the Late Harappan period and was eventually abandoned. It is best known for its signboard, its remarkable citadel, and its impressive water tanks.

DHOLE   The ferocious cuon or red dog (*Cuon alpinus*), native to peninsular India and as far north as Kashmir.

DILMUN   The name by which Bahrain and adjacent areas were known to the Mesopotamians in the third millennium; it also referred to Failaka in the early second. Dilmun was an important entrepot, trading with Mesopotamia, Magan (Oman), and the Harappans.

DK AREA   A residential area in the northeast of Mohenjo-daro's Lower Town, excavated by K. N. Dikshit from 1924.

DOAB   The area between two rivers, a term used particularly of the land between the Ganges and the Yamuna, but also more generally. The areas between the rivers of the Punjab are also named doabs, of which the Sindh-Sagar doab between the Indus and the Jhelum is the largest.

DRAVIDIAN   The language family to which belong the languages of South India and a few in other parts of the subcontinent. It is possible that some Harappans spoke a Dravidian language.

DRISHADVATI   The modern Chautang River, one of the main rivers contributing its waters to the Saraswati system in the Harappan period when what is now the Yamuna flowed in its bed. Later the Yamuna changed its course, leaving the Drishadvati/Chautang as a small river with only seasonal flow along much of its course.

DROMEDARY The one-humped Arabian camel (*Camelus dromedarius*) was domesticated in Arabia sometime during the second or possibly third millennium, probably for its milk; its use for riding came later, around 1000 BCE.

DURGA The principal Hindu goddess, consort of the god Shiva. In Hindu mythology, she rides a tiger and slays the buffalo demon Mahishasura. Among her many roles is Mother Goddess.

EARLY HARAPPAN The period preceding the Harappan civilization, circa 3200–2600 BCE, also known as Early Indus. It comprises four regional traditions: Amri-Nal, Kot-Diji, Sothi-Siswal, and Damb Sadaat.

EARLY INDUS *See* Early Harappan.

EASTERN NARA A branch of the Indus flowing parallel to the Indus to its east.

ELAM The region to the east of Babylonia, in southwestern Iran, comprising both highland and lowland zones.

ELAMITE A language spoken by the people of southwestern Iran, the inhabitants of Elam; it possibly shared a common ancestor with Dravidian, Proto-Elamo-Dravidian.

ELECTRUM A natural alloy of gold and silver.

"ERNESTITE" A very hard stone, made by heating a rare type of fine-grained mottled metamorphic rock that contained titanium oxide. This was employed by the Harappans to make bits for the microdrills used to perforate beads of hard stone and in particular the exceptionally long carnelian beads. This stone has been named after Ernest Mackay, who made a detailed study of bead production, based on material from his excavations at Chanhu-daro.

ESHNUNNA A city on the Diyala in northeast Babylonia.

"ETCHED" CARNELIAN BEADS Beads made of carnelian bearing a design that falsely appears to have been etched. In fact, the design was created by bleaching the surface, which weakened the bleached areas, causing them eventually to erode away.

EYE-BEAD A bead made generally from patterned stone, such as banded agate, cut so as to create concentric circles or ovals on the surface, resembling an eye. Imitations of these were also made of other materials, such as painted terra-cotta.

FABRIC A term used when describing pottery in the finished state, referring to the material of which it is made and reflecting details of its composition, structure, surface treatment, hardness, color, texture, and other physical features.

FIELD SURVEY A method of archaeological exploration that involves, among other things, the systematic traversing of a large area, collecting material from the surface to obtain information on the archaeological material that lies beneath, an exercise known as fieldwalking. Field survey also includes reconnaissance techniques such as aerial photography.

FINGER MILLET *See* Ragi.

FIRE ALTAR A rectangular clay-lined pit containing a clay stele, filled with ash, charcoal, and often terra-cotta cakes. In some cases there are associated animal bones suggesting that these were involved in a sacrificial ritual. The stele is thought perhaps to represent a lingam.

GABARBAND *See* Bund.

GANDHARA GRAVE COMPLEX A second-millennium culture in Swat, with a range of distinctive funerary practices and material reflecting both local and intrusive cultural features, including the presence of horses.

GANESHWAR A settlement of the Jodhpura-Ganeshwar culture.

GANGES The holy river of India, which rises in the Himalayas and flows south and east to a great delta in the Bay of Bengal.

GANGES-YAMUNA DOAB The area between the Ganges and Yamuna Rivers.

GAUR The Indian bison (*Bibos gaurus*), native to peninsular India but probably found as far north as Gujurat and possibly the Indus Valley in Harappan times. It may be among the animals depicted in Indus figurines and seals, or these figures may represent humpless cattle (*Bos taurus*).

GHAGGAR A river, now dry, located in India, and formerly part of the western course of the lost Saraswati; known as the Hakra in Pakistan.

GHARIAL The fish-eating crocodile (*Gavialus gangeticus*), common in the Indus, a dangerous beast that can grow up to 6 meters (19 feet) long.

GILUND A major settlement of the Ahar-Banas culture.

GOLA DHORO (Bagasra) A small (1.92-hectare), unwalled town in Gujarat with a walled citadel; it seems to have been a center for trade and industry.

GROG Finely crushed potsherds, used as a temper in making pottery.

GRUNT A species of marine fish (*Pomadasys hasta*) whose bones are numerous in the Harappan coastal settlement of Balakot.

GUFKRAL A settlement of the Northern Neolithic culture.

GUJARAT The region southeast of Sindh, comprising Kutch, Saurashtra, and the North Gujarat plain to their east, as well as the smaller region of South Gujarat.

HAKRA A river, now dry, in Pakistani territory, formerly part of the western course of the lost Saraswati; known as the Ghaggar in India.

HAKRA PERIOD The period circa 3800–3200 BCE when people from Baluchistan began settling in the Indus region.

HARAPPA Situated on the River Ravi in the Punjab, Harappa was one of the two first cities of the Indus to be discovered and the source of much that is known about the civilization, though many parts of the city were badly damaged by brick robbing. Occupation at the site began in the fourth millennium and continued till around 1300 BCE. *See also* Mound AB; Mound E/ET; Mound F.

HARP The joint American-Pakistani Harappa Archaeological Research Project, begun in 1986.

HELMAND CULTURE The third-millennium culture on the Helmand and Argandab Rivers and the large Hamun-i Helmand lake in Seistan. The culture depended on irrigation agriculture and trade. Its main settlement was the city of Shahr-i Sokhta.

HOG DEER *Axis porcinus*.

HR AREA A residential area in the west of Mohenjo-daro's Lower Town, excavated by H. Hargreaves from 1925.

HYACINTH BEAN An East African pulse (*Lablab purpureus*), introduced in the early second millennium BCE.

INDIGO A plant (*Indigofera tinctoria*) from whose leaves a blue dye is extracted. It is known from Rojdi.

INDO-ARYAN An Indo-European language, descended from Proto-Indo-Iranian.

INDO-ARYANS The speakers of Indo-Aryan who entered the subcontinent during the second millennium BCE.

INDO-EUROPEAN The large and widespread language family to which Indo-Aryan belongs.

INDO-GANGETIC DIVIDE The area between the catchment basins of the Indus and Ganges Rivers.

INDO-IRANIAN The branch of the Indo-European language family that comprises the Iranian, Nuristani, and Indo-Aryan languages. These shared a common ancestor in Proto-Indo-Iranian, from which Old Iranian and Old Indo-Aryan diverged during the second millennium BCE.

INTERCULTURAL STYLE *See* Chlorite.

ISMEO The Italian Istituto Medio e Estremo Oriente.

JAJMANI SYSTEM A traditional Indian redistributive mechanism, related to the caste system, in which all members of the community have reciprocal obligations to provide the products of their labors and certain services to others with whom they have a formalized relationship. Payment for these goods and services is made in kind at regulated intervals, often in the context of special occasions such as religious festivals.

JALILPUR A fishing settlement in the Ravi Valley occupied during the Hakra and Early Harappan periods.

JHUKAR A town in Sindh, occupied from the Early Harappan period to the period of decline, in the early second millennium, to which it gives its name.

JHUKAR CULTURE The Late Harappan culture in Sindh and adjacent areas, marked by severe urban decline leading to the abandonment of many settlements.

JIROFT A recently discovered third-millennium state in the Halil River valley in southeast Iran.

JOB'S TEARS A millet (*Coix lacrima-jobi*) with hard white shiny seeds that were used as beads.

JODHPURA-GANESHWAR CULTURE A hunter-fisher-gatherer culture in the Aravalli Hills, who mined and smelted the region's copper ore from the late fourth millennium BCE.

JOWAR Sorghum (*Sorghum bicolor*), an African millet introduced after 2000 BCE and grown in Saurashtra.

JUJUBE Known in South Asia as *ber*, a tree (*Zizyphus jujuba*) that grows in Baluchistan and other parts of the northwest. It yields an edible berry, gathered since early times, being known, for example, in the first period at Mehrgarh. Its timber was used by the Harappans; a wooden mortar at Harappa has been identified as jujube wood.

KACHI PLAIN An area protruding into Baluchistan and running north from Sindh, through which flows the Bolan River. The Bolan pass is one of the main routes into the hills of Baluchistan. Mehrgarh, situated on the Bolan River, is the earliest known farming settlement in the subcontinent.

KALIBANGAN A town situated at the confluence of the Saraswati and Drishadvati Rivers.

KASHMIR STAG The hangul, a variety of deer (*Cervus affinis hanglu*, formerly *Cervus elaphus hanglu*) whose antlers were used by the Harappans.

KAUTILYA Adviser to the Mauryan emperor Chandragupta Maurya and author of the *Arthashastra*.

KAYATHA CULTURE A Chalcolithic farming culture in Madhya Pradesh who traded with the Harappans.

KECHI BEG PERIOD The period 3800–3200 BCE in Baluchistan, contemporary with Hakra on the Indus plains.

KHARIF The wet season, from late May to September, when summer crops such as rice and millet are grown. During this period, heavy rains are brought to many regions of the subcontinent by the prevailing southwest monsoon winds.

KISH An important northern Sumerian city.

KODON Kodon or Kodo millet (*Paspalum scrobiculatum*), native to southern India and introduced to the Indus region in the early second millennium.

KOKCHA A river tributary to the Amu Darya; Shortugai was located near the confluence. The Kokcha gorge was probably the main source of lapis in antiquity.

KOT DIJI A settlement of the Early and Mature Harappan periods situated near the important flint source of the Rohri Hills.

KOT DIJI PHASE The most extensive Early Harappan regional culture, occupying an area including northern Baluchistan, Cholistan, and the Punjab. Though it developed into the Mature Harappan civilization on the plains, in the northern borderlands it continued throughout the later third millennium as the Late Kot Diji culture.

KULLI CULTURE A culture in southern Baluchistan contemporary and closely associated with the Harappan civilization.

KUNTASI A small port and industrial town in Saurashtra.

KUTCH The northwest lobe of Gujarat, now divided from the mainland by the marshy Ranns of Kutch, but in Harappan times an island.

LAGASH An important Sumerian city-state, prominent in the period between the Akkadian and Ur III empires.

LANGNAJ A long-lived hunter-gatherer camp in North Gujarat, whose inhabitants probably acquired domestic animals as well as some small manufactured goods from the Harappans.

LAPIS LAZULI A beautiful and highly valued blue stone, mined in Badakhshan in Afghanistan; its supply was controlled by the Harappans in the later third millennium. A stone similar in appearance was available in the Chagai Hills in western Baluchistan.

LATE HARAPPAN PERIOD The Post-urban or Late Harappan period, from around 1900 BCE. It saw the disintegration of the Harappan state and the decay and abandonment of cities and towns. The effects were most marked in Sindh, the Makran, Kutch, and Cholistan. *See also* Cemetery H Culture; Jhukar Culture.

LATE KOT DIJI *See* Kot Diji Phase.

LITTLE MILLET An important crop (*Panicum sumatrense*) in Mature Harappan Saurashtra. It may also have been grown near Harappa. It was superseded by the more productive African millets in the early second millennium.

LINGAM The sacred phallus representing the god Shiva.

LOGOGRAM A sign representing a word. This has the same meaning in different languages but a different spoken form.

LOST WAX CASTING   *See* Cire Perdue.

LOST SARASWATI   *See* Saraswati.

LOTHAL   An important trading and manufacturing town in Gujarat, established on the southern Harappan border, at the interface with lands inhabited by hunter-gatherers and rich in gemstones such as agate and carnelian. A brick basin interpreted as a dock may reflect involvement also with the overseas trade network.

LOTESHWAR   A hunter-gatherer camp in Gujarat perhaps occupied by the sixth millennium and certainly by the fourth when, as well as hunting game, the inhabitants kept domestic animals acquired from their farming neighbors and made their own styles of pottery.

MADDER   A perennial herb (*Rubia tinctorum*) with lanceolate leaves producing a red pigment used for dyeing linen, wool, cotton, and leather, using alum as a mordant. The hue produced can be varied from brown through red to violet by adding different metals. Its use is attested to at Mohenjo-daro.

MAGAN   The name by which the Oman peninsula was known to the Mesopotamians. Its inhabitants mined the substantial deposits of copper ore in its interior and traded with Mesopotamia, Bahrein, the Indus, and probably southern Arabia and East Africa.

MAKRAN   The inhospitable coastal region between the Arabian Sea and Baluchistan. Its main attraction is its good anchorages.

MANCHAR   A large lake in Sindh, massively extended annually by the floodwaters of the Indus.

MANDA   An outpost settlement on the Chenab River in the Himalayan foothills, probably situated to manage the export of Himalayan timber downriver.

MARGIANA   The region of the Murghab River in northern Afghanistan.

MARKHOR   A species of wild goat (*Capra falconeri falconeri*) native to Baluchistan.

MATURE HARAPPAN PERIOD   The period circa 2500–1900 BCE when the Indus civilization was at its height.

MATURE INDUS PERIOD   *See* Mature Harappan Period.

MAURYAN EMPIRE   The state that unified most of South Asia, founded by Chandragupta Maurya in 322 BCE. It reached its height under his grandson, Ashoka, and ended in 185 BCE.

MAYSAR   A major copper processing center in Oman in the third millennium BCE.

MEGASTHENES   A Greek envoy to the court of the Mauryan emperor Chandragupta Maurya, whose account of what he saw there is an important source on early Indian history.

MEHRGARH   A long-lived settlement in the Kachi plain, founded around 7000 BCE. It is the only early farming site of this antiquity known in South Asia. It was abandoned in favor of Naushotro in the Mature Harappan period.

MELUHHA   The name by which the Indus civilization was known to the Mesopotamians.

MESOPOTAMIA   The lands watered by the Tigris and Euphrates, now lying mainly in modern Iraq but also including parts of Syria. It was divided into a northern part, Assyria, and a southern, Babylonia, the latter divided into

Akkad in the north and Sumer in the south. It was in Babylonia that civilization emerged in the late fourth millennium.

MIANWALI An outpost settlement located just south of the Salt Range, probably established to manage the supply of salt down the Indus to the Harappan heartlands.

MICROBEADS Tiny steatite beads 1–3 millimeters in diameter.

MILLET A general term for a large number of genera of small-seeded cereals. Some were native to India and were domesticated there; many of these also occurred in Southeast and East Asia. Others were introduced from Africa or Arabia around 2000 BCE. *See* Bajra; Jowar; Ragi; Kodon; Broomcorn Millet; Foxtail Millet; Bristley Foxtail Millet; Browntop Millet; Little Millet; Job's Tears.

MOHENJO-DARO One of the two great cities of the Indus, first discovered and excavated in the 1920s, situated beside the Indus in Sindh. Among its unique features is the Great Bath. *See also* Moneer Area; DK Area; HR Area; VS Area.

MONEER AREA A section of Mohenjo-daro's Lower Town (also known as DK-I), excavated by Q. M. Moneer and K. N. Puris in 1933–1938 but unpublished until the area was reinvestigated by the Aachen team in the 1980s. Situated in the southeast of the mound, the Moneer area has proved to be a major industrial quarter of the city.

MORDANT A chemical added to a dye to make it colorfast.

MOUFFLON A wild sheep (*Ovis orientalis*) found in the high mountains of northern South Asia.

MOUND AB The badly damaged citadel mound at Harappa.

MOUND E/ET The main residential and industrial area excavated at Harappa. Early settlement in mound E expanded to the east to form mound ET.

MOUND F The area between the citadel mound and the river at Harappa. Its architecture included the so-called granary.

MUGGER A freshwater crocodile (*Crocodylus palustris*), native to the rivers of the Indus region and found particularly in slow-moving watercourses such as canals. It grows up to 12 feet (4 meters) long and generally avoids people, though it can be dangerous.

MUNDA A branch of the Austro-Asiatic language family. Its languages are now spoken only by tribal groups in central India.

MUNDIGAK A town in the Kandahar region of northern Baluchistan, situated at the intersection of a number of important routes. Around 2600 BCE it became incorporated into the Helmand culture.

NAGESHWAR An industrial village in Gujarat where shell was worked.

NAGWADA A village in Gujarat where beadmaking and shellworking took place. Early Harappan burials are also known there.

NAKSHATRA The Indian star calendar, dating back to around 2300 BCE.

NAL A settlement in southern Baluchistan of the early third millennium.

NAL CULTURE *See* Amri-Nal Phase.

NAMAZGA CULTURE A culture flourishing in southern Turkmenia contemporary with the Harappans. Harappan material has been found at Altyn-depe, one of its principal towns.

NAUSHARO A town in the Kachi plain that flourished through the Early and Mature Harappan periods, superseding Mehrgarh.

NILGAI An antelope (*Boselaphus tragocamelus*), also known as blue bull.

NORTHERN NEOLITHIC A farming culture in Kashmir contemporary with the Early and Mature Harappans, with whom they traded. There is some evidence suggesting that they also had distant trading links with China.

OCP   A culture of the second millennium, in part a successor to the Jodhpura-Ganeshwar culture, characterized by Ochre-Colored Pottery and also responsible for depositing hoards of copper artifacts. *See* Copper Hoards.

OLD INDO-ARYAN   A descendant of Proto-Indo-Iranian, the language of the *Rigveda*.

ONAGER   The wild steppe ass (*Equus hemionus*), locally known as the khur, native to northwest South Asia, including Gujarat. It is likely that the equids identified at a number of Indus sites were hunted onager, not domestic horse as has often been claimed.

OXUS   *See* Amu Darya.

PADRI   A settlement originally of the local inhabitants of Saurashtra, later becoming part of the Harappan civilization.

PARA-MUNDA   An extinct language known only from loanwords in the *Rigveda*. It probably belonged to an extinct branch of the Austro-Asiatic language family and may have been spoken by the Harappans.

PASUPATI   Lord of the Beasts, an epithet of Shiva. While now this refers specifically to cattle, in the past it seems to have referred particularly to wild animals.

PATHANI DAMB   A large unexplored settlement in the Kachi plain near the Mula pass.

PHTANITE   A hard green chert containing traces of iron oxide employed by the Harappans for the microdrill bits used to perforate beads.

PIPAL   The *asvattha*, or Bodhi tree (*Ficus religiosa*), a tall tree with heart-shaped leaves, which has had a religious significance in South Asia probably from pre-Harappan times.

PIRAK   An important settlement founded on the Kachi plain around 1700 BCE.

POSTURBAN HARAPPAN PERIOD   *See* Late Harappan period.

PRADAKSHINA   Clockwise circumambulation, a form of worship.

PRASAD   Gifts offered to the gods, redistributed to worshippers after they had been sanctified by the gods' use of them.

PRE-HARAPPAN PERIOD   An alternative, but less satisfactory, term for the Early Harappan period.

PRIEST-KING   The famous stone sculpture from Mohenjo-daro, the broken torso of a robed male.

PRIMARY STATE   Also known as a pristine state, one of the small number of states that emerged first in their region and without the influence of prexisting states: these are usually listed as Mesopotamia (Sumer), Egypt, the Indus, China, and the civilizations of Mesoamerica and the Andean region.

PROTO-ELAMITE   The script briefly used by the Elamites circa 3200–2800 BCE, a period when they were active in the Iranian plateau.

PULSES   Also known as legumes; a large range of crops, including various peas, beans, and lentils. The Harappans grew both native species, such as green gram and black gram, and pulses introduced from West Asia and Africa.

PUNJAB   The region of five rivers (Jhelum, Ravi, Chenab, Sutlej, and Beas) that are tributaries of the Indus, flowing west from the Himalayas.

QALA'AT AL-BAHRAIN   A major trading settlement on Bahrain.

RABI   The dry season, from October to late February, during which winter crops such as wheat are grown.

RAGI Finger millet (*Eleusine coracana*), an African millet introduced during the early second millennium.

RAKHIGARHI A settlement established in the Early Harappan period, which became the city of the eastern region in the Mature Harappan period.

RANNS The Great Rann and Little Rann, an area of seasonally flooded salt flats on the north and east of Kutch. In Indus times these were open water.

RA'S AL-JUNAYZ (Ra's al-Jinz) A fishing village on the south coast of Magan (Oman peninsula), which traded extensively with the Indus civilization.

RAVI PHASE The earliest period of occupation at Harappa, corresponding to the Hakra phase in Cholistan.

REHMAN DHERI An important town in northern Baluchistan during the Early Harappan period.

RIGVEDA The earliest of the collection of sacred texts making up the *Vedas*, dating from around 1700/1500–1000 BCE.

RING STONE A large stone ring, used as part of a pillar.

ROJDI A prosperous farming settlement in Saurashtra that tripled in size in the Late Harappan period.

ROPAR (Rupar, Rupnagar) An outpost settlement on the Sutlej River in the Himalayan foothills, probably situated to manage the export of Himalayan timber downriver.

ROSEWOOD A tree (*Dalbergia latifolia*) growing in peninsular India and in parts of the north and west. It yields a hard, fine-grained blackish wood used particularly for making furniture. It was identified at Harappa as the wood from which a coffin had been made.

SAAR An important third-millennium settlement in Dilmun (Bahrain).

SAGGER A lidded ceramic vessel used to contain fragile or particularly fine pieces of pottery during firing, protecting them from direct contact with flames or fuel, which could discolor them or fire them unevenly, and from damage by other vessels in the kiln. Sealed saggers could also be used to fire pieces in a reducing (oxygen-free) environment, generally to create a dark surface color.

SAL A tree (*Shorea robusta*) that grows in thickets in northeastern regions of the subcontinent and that is used for timber.

SAMBAR A deer (*Cervus unicolor*).

SANSKRIT The language of the early sacred texts, the *Vedas*.

SARASWATI A river of great importance in Harappan times, flowing from the Siwalik Hills, either to an inland delta in the Derawar region or, less probably, to the sea. The Saraswati dried up during the second millennium, and the name now belongs only to a small seasonal river.

SARGON OF AKKAD (2334–2279 BCE) Founder of the Akkadian empire.

SAURASHTRA The southern peninsula of Gujarat, also known as Kathiawar. In Harappan times it may have been divided from the mainland by perennial water in the Nal Depression.

SEMITIC LANGUAGES The group of languages spoken by most of the peoples of the Near East, ancient and modern.

SHAHR-I SOKHTA A major town on the Helmand River south of the Hamun-i Helmand in Seistan, founded around 3200 BCE, particularly involved in the lapis trade. By 2400 BCE, Shahr-i Sokhta was a city of about 150 hectares, but it declined from 2200 BCE.

SHIVA One of the principal Hindu deities, associated both with destruction and with fertility.

SHORTUGAI Established 1,000 kilometers from the Harappan heartlands to control the supply of minerals from the Amu Darya-Kokcha Valleys of northern Afghanistan, especially lapis but probably also tin and possibly gold.

SINDH The region of the lower Indus, east of Baluchistan.

SISSOO A tree (*Dalbergia sissoo*) found both in the Indus Valley and in the surrounding mountains, used as timber for construction, furniture, and tools.

SLOW WHEEL An early device that aided pottery production, also known as the tournette or turntable. This was a flat disc set on a pivot or spindle, which was turned by hand, allowing pottery to be rotated during its manufacture or decoration. It could not, however, be used for throwing pottery; this was only possible with the more sophisticated fast wheel (or potter's wheel), a later invention.

SOTHI-SISWAL PHASE The Early Harappan period in the eastern region. Pottery of the Sothi-Siswal types continued in use throughout the Mature Harappan period and into the Posturban period, a fact that makes it difficult to date sites in this area from surface collected material alone.

SOTKA KOH A town in the Makran, probably a Harappan port. It has not been excavated, but exploration has revealed the remains of many houses and kilns in an unwalled settlement. A possible wall suggests that there was also a fortified settlement.

SPINY MUREX A shellfish (*Chicoreus ramosus*). Its shells were used by the Harappans mainly to make ladles.

STEATITE Soapstone. It was used by the Harappans particularly for making seals, but also for making inscribed miniature tablets and beads.

STELE A freestanding stone post or pillar.

STONEWARE BANGLES Small, very finely made ceramic bangles imitating mottled stone. The managed conditions of their firing suggest they were official insignia of some kind.

SUKKUR HILLS A limestone outcrop in Sindh, divided from the Rohri Hills by a gorge through which the Indus now flows.

SUMER The southern part of Babylonia, home of the first city-states.

SURKOTADA A fortified Harappan town in Kutch, probably with unwalled suburbs. Early Harappan burials were also found there.

SUSA An ancient city, capital of Elam.

SUTKAGEN-DOR The westernmost Harappan settlement in the Makran, probably a port, important for trade through the Gulf.

SURVEY *See* Field Survey

SWAT The mountainous region north of Punjab and west of the Indus through which runs the Swat River, later known as Gandhara. The inhabitants of this region had links with those on the Indus plain, but their culture was often very different.

TAMARISK A scrubby tree (*Tamarix* spp) that can grow on sandy and saline soils and is found in Gujarat and the Indus Valley. Used by the Harappans for fuel, it yields a wood that can also be made into building fixtures such as doors, tools, and other objects.

TANK   An artificial pool or cistern created to retain water for irrigation and other purposes, including drinking water.

TEAK   A tall tree (*Tectona grandis*) that grows in Gujarat and in other western regions of the subcontinent. Its oily timber is resistant to fire, termites, and water, making it prized for building ships and furniture.

TEPE YAHYA   A town in the Kerman region on the Iranian plateau, a participant in the trade networks, particularly involved in the manufacture of bowls and other goods from the locally abundant chlorite.

TERRA-COTTA CAKES   Triangular objects of well baked clay. For a long time their function was a puzzle; it seems now that they were used both for retaining heat in kilns and hearths and for paving.

THAR   The Great Indian Desert, which forms the southern boundary of the greater Indus region.

THARPARKAR   An area of seasonal grassland linking Sindh with Gujarat.

TIBETO-BURMAN   A group of languages spoken in much of the Himalayan region, belonging to the Sino-Tibetan language family.

TOURNETTE   *See* Slow Wheel

TRISULA   The trident associated with the god Shiva.

TURKMENIA   The area of Central Asia to the west of the southern half of the Caspian Sea. It was occupied in Harappan times by the Namazga culture.

TURNTABLE   *See* Slow Wheel

UMM-AN-NAR   A settlement in Magan (Oman) whose inhabitants lived by fishing and by trading copper ore from the interior with people from Mesopotamia and Dilmun, either in situ or by traveling to those countries. This site gives its name to the local culture of the later third millennium.

UR   One of the principal cities of Sumer, a major port in the third millennium.

UR III EMPIRE   Established in 2112 BCE, the Ur III empire incorporated Sumer and Akkad and a large area to the east, reaching its peak under Shulgi (2094–2047) and declining under later kings until 2004, when the Elamites sacked Ur.

URIAL   The wild sheep (*Ovis vignei*) native to the Indo-Iranian borderlands and regions to the west and north. It was not ancestral to the domestic Ovis aries.

VEDAS   Four books of Indo-Aryan religious texts that are the earliest extant Indian literature. They were transmitted orally by faithful repetition and committed to writing only around 1000 CE. Strict Brahminical tradition dictated that the *Vedas* be memorized perfectly and transmitted without the slightest change. The oldest book is the *Rigveda*.

VS AREA   A residential area in the southwest of Mohenjo-daro's Lower Town, excavated 1923–1926 by M. S. Vats, who also excavated at Harappa, 1926-1934.

WATER BUFFALO   The wild *Bubalus arnee* and the domestic *Bubalus bubalis* were probably both exploited by the Harappans, particularly for their rich milk.

WESTERN NARA   A branch of the Indus currently flowing to its west.

ZAGROS   A mountain range to the east of Mesopotamia.

ZEBU   *Bos indicus*, the humped cattle of the subcontinent, probably domesticated from the now extinct wild *Bos namadicus*.

ZIZYPHUS   *See* Jujube.

REFERENCES

Barber, Elizabeth J. W. 1991. *Prehistoric Textiles*. Princeton, NJ: Princeton University Press.

Chakrabarti, Dilip K. 1997. *The Archaeology of Ancient Indian Cities*. New Delhi: Oxford University Press.

Chakrabarti, Dilip K. 1999. *India: An Archaeological History. Palaeolithic Beginnings to Early Historic Foundations*. New Delhi: Oxford University Press.

Huntington, Susan L. 1995. *The Art of Ancient India*. New York: Weatherhill.

Parpola, Asko. 1994. *Deciphering the Indus Script*. Cambridge, UK: Cambridge University Press.

Possehl, G. 1999. *Indus Age: The Beginnings*. New Delhi: Oxford University Press.

Ratnagar, Shereen. 2000. *The End of the Great Harappan Tradition*. Heras Memorial Lectures 1998. New Delhi: Manohar.

Ratnagar, Shereen. 2001. *Understanding Harappa: Civilization in the Greater Indus Valley*. New Delhi: Tulika.

Ratnagar, Shereen. 2004. *Trading Encounters. From the Euphrates to the Indus in the Bronze Age*. New Delhi: Oxford University Press.

Roaf, Michael. 1990. *Cultural Atlas of Mesopotamia*. New York: Facts on File.

Chronology

Before 7000   *Cultural Periods in the Greater Indus Region and Baluchistan*
Mesolithic

Cultural Developments in the Greater Indus Region and Baluchistan
Development of postglacial hunter-gatherer communities

Neighbors and Developments in South Asia
Development of postglacial hunter-gatherer communities

Relevant Developments outside South Asia
Beginning of sedentism, arable farming, and animal husbandry in parts
of the Near East and their gradual spread into adjacent regions

7000–6000   *Cultural Periods in the Greater Indus Region and Baluchistan*
Aceramic Neolithic (Possehl's Kili Ghul Mohammad phase)

Cultural Developments in the Greater Indus Region and Baluchistan
Farming community established at Mehrgarh (period I)

Relevant Developments outside South Asia
Near East: beginning of pottery making and metallurgy; Turkmenia:
farming communities by 6000

6000–5000   *Cultural Periods in the Greater Indus Region and Baluchistan*
Aceramic and Ceramic Neolithic (Possehl's Kili Ghul Mohammad phase)

Cultural Developments in the Greater Indus Region and Baluchistan
Granaries constructed at Mehrgarh; trade links as far as Turkmenia.
Beginning of pottery making at Mehrgarh (Mehrgarh II). Possibly
additional farming settlements in Baluchistan such as Kili Ghul
Mohammad

Relevant Developments outside South Asia
Farming communities in Iranian plateau and Turkmenia.

5000–4300   *Cultural Periods in the Greater Indus Region and Baluchistan*
Neolithic. (Possehl's Burj Basket-marked phase)

Cultural Developments in the Greater Indus Region and Baluchistan
Farming settlements in Baluchistan; pottery; small-scale irrigation;
copper smelting. Hunter-gatherers of lowlands acquiring domestic
animals

4300–3800 *Cultural Periods in the Greater Indus Region and Baluchistan*
Chalcolithic (Possehl's Togau phase)

Cultural Developments in the Greater Indus Region and Baluchistan
Many farming settlements in Baluchistan; wheel-turned pottery; glazed
steatite; copper casting; some immigrants from Iranian plateau

3800–3200 *Cultural Periods in the Greater Indus Region and Baluchistan*
Chalcolithic. Kechi Beg (Baluchistan). Hakra (plains). Ravi (Harappa
area, 3300–2800)

Cultural Developments in the Greater Indus Region and Baluchistan
Increasing number of farming settlements in Baluchistan, some large;
pastoralist camps established in the plains especially Cholistan; Harappa
founded; local hunter-fisher-gatherer communities keeping some
domestic animals and making pottery

Relevant Developments outside South Asia
Iranian plateau: development of trading towns and trade networks from
Mesopotamia to Turkmenia and Baluchistan; settlement in Seistan and
foundation of Shahr-i Sokhta

3200–2600 *Cultural Periods in the Greater Indus Region and Baluchistan*
Early Harappan: Amri-Nal (Sindh, S. Baluchistan); Kot Diji (Punjab, N.
Baluchistan); Damb Sadaat (C.Baluchistan); Sothi-Siswal (eastern region);
local traditions in Gujarat: Anarta, Padri, and other wares

Cultural Developments in the Greater Indus Region and Baluchistan
Baluchistan: bunds and other irrigation works constructed. Spread of
farming communities into the lowlands, including Gujarat and the Indo-
Gangetic divide; walls and flood defenses; Dholavira and Rakhigarhi
founded. Some towns including Harappa, Mehrgarh, and Rehman Dheri;
uninscribed stamp seals; protoscript at Harappa; copper trade with
Aravallis; some craft specialization

Neighbors and Developments in South Asia
Jodhpura-Ganeshwar culture in Aravallis; Ahar-Banas in Rajasthan;
Northern Neolithic in Kashmir, related settlements in Swat and northern
Punjab

Relevant Developments outside South Asia
Mesopotamia: city-states emerging in Sumer and Elam; Sumerian and
Proto-Elamite scripts; trade networks across Iranian plateau flourishing.
Seistan: 3200–2800 Elamite presence at Shahr-i Sokhta; after 2800 Shahr-i
Sokhta important in lapis trade. Fishing communities in Oman and
Makran probably in contact.

2600–2500 *Cultural Periods in the Greater Indus Region and Baluchistan*
Transition period (Harappa phase 3A, 2600–2450)

Cultural Developments in the Greater Indus Region and Baluchistan
Many settlements in the plains destroyed or abandoned, some rebuilt, many new settlements founded, probably including Mohenjo-daro; cultural integration; growing craft specialization; emergence of writing

Neighbors and Developments in South Asia
Jodhpura-Ganeshwar culture in Aravallis; Ahar-Banas in Rajasthan; Northern Neolithic in Kashmir, related settlements in Swat and northern Punjab

Relevant Developments outside South Asia
Mesopotamia: Royal Cemetery at Ur ca. 2600–2450 includes Harappan material; Namazga V–VI culture in Turkmenia

2500–2000   *Cultural Periods in the Greater Indus Region and Baluchistan*
Mature Harappan (Harappa phase 3B 2450–2200; 3C 2200–1900)

Cultural Developments in the Greater Indus Region and Baluchistan
Cultural unity in Indus plains from Gujarat to northern Ganges-Yamuna doab; separate but related Kulli culture in southern Baluchistan; separate Late Kot-Diji culture in northern Indo-Iranian borderlands; well integrated internal distribution network; external trade with neighbors, Gulf and northern Afghanistan where Shortugai is founded; towns and cities; writing; craft specialization and industrial villages

Neighbors and Developments in South Asia
Jodhpura-Ganeshwar culture in Aravallis; Ahar-Banas in Rajasthan; Northern Neolithic in Kashmir; Kayatha culture in Madhya Pradesh; farming communities in middle Ganges; Southern Neolithic in south India

Relevant Developments outside South Asia
Seatrade: with Umm-an Nar culture in Magan (Oman) and with Dilmun (Bahrain); Mesopotamia 2334–2193; Akkadian empire 2193–2112; city-states 2112–2004. Ur III empire: trading with Harappans, some Harappans resident there; Helmand culture in Seistan no longer trading with Indus and declining after 2200; Namaza V–VI culture in Turkmenia, declining from 2200; BMAC established in Northern Afghanistan

2000–   *Cultural Periods in the Greater Indus Region and Baluchistan*
1900/1800   Late Mature Harappan (Harappa Phase 3C to 1900)

Cultural Developments in the Greater Indus Region and Baluchistan
Decline in many towns and cities, especially in Sindh and Cholistan; flow reducing in Saraswati River; introduction of African millets; summer cultivation of rice and millets increasingly important

Neighbors and Developments in South Asia
OCP/Copper Hoards culture in Aravallis; Ahar-Banas in Rajasthan; Northern Neolithic in Kashmir; Gandhara Grave culture in Swat; Malwa

culture in Madhya Pradesh; Savalda culture in Deccan; Southern Neolithic

Relevant Developments outside South Asia
Isin-Larsa period in Mesopotamia: Harappan trade now through Dilmun; relations with Wadi Suq culture in Oman still flourishing

From 1900/1800

Cultural Periods in the Greater Indus Region and Baluchistan
Posturban Harappan/Late Harappan: Late Harappa/Cemetery H 1900–1300 in Punjab; Jhukar in Sindh; Late Harappan in Gujarat; Sothi-Siswal, Late Harappan and OCP/Late Harappan in eastern region; Pirak from 1700

Cultural Developments in the Greater Indus Region and Baluchistan
Distintegration of Indus polity; abandonment of most urban centers in Sindh, Kutch, Makran, and Cholistan; strong regional cultures in Gujarat, interacting with neighbors to south and west, in eastern region, expanding into Ganges-Yamuna doab, and in Kachi plain; destruction and abandonment of settlements in Baluchistan

Neighbors and Developments in South Asia
OCP/Copper Hoards culture in Aravallis; Ahar-Banas in Rajasthan; Northern Neolithic in Kashmir; Gandhara Grave culture in Swat; Malwa culture in Madhya Pradesh; Late Harappan then Malwa culture at Daimabad in Deccan; Southern Neolithic

Relevant Developments outside South Asia
Mesopotamia no longer trading through Gulf; BMAC abandoning northern Afghanistan, but settled in Seistan and in contact with Indus region and beyond

Resources for Further Study

GENERAL

Chakrabarti, Dilip K. 1999. *India: An Archaeological History—Palaeolithic Beginnings to Early Historic Foundations.* New Delhi: Oxford University Press.

Habib, Irfan. 2002. *A People's History of India. 2: The Indus Civilization.* Aligarh: Tulika and Aligarh Historians Society.

Jansen, Michael, Maire Mulloy, and Gunter Urban, eds. 1995. *Forgotten Cities on the Indus.* Oxford: Oxford University Press.

Joshi, Jagat Pati, ed. 2002. *Facets of Indian Civilization. Recent Perspectives. Essays in Honour of Professor B. B. Lal.* New Delhi: Aryan Books International.

Kenoyer, Jonathan Mark, ed. 1989. *Old Problems and New Perspectives in the Archaeology of South Asia. Wisconsin Archaeological Reports.* Vol. 2. Department of Anthropology. Madison: University of Wisconsin.

Kenoyer, Jonathan Mark, ed. 1994. *From Sumer to Meluhha. Wisconsin Archaeological Reports.* Vol. 3. Department of Anthropology. Madison: University of Wisconsin.

Kenoyer, Jonathan Mark. 1998. *Ancient Cities of the Indus Valley Civilization.* Karachi: Oxford University Press and American Institute of Pakistan Studies.

Lal, B. B. 1997. *The Earliest Civilization of South Asia.* New Delhi: Aryan Books International.

Lal, B. B., and S. P. Gupta, eds. 1984. *Frontiers of the Indus Civilization.* New Delhi: Books and Books.

Possehl, Gregory L., ed. 1979. *Ancient Cities of the Indus.* New Delhi: Vikas Publishing House.

Possehl, Gregory L. 1993. *Harappan Civilization.* 2nd ed. New Delhi: Oxford University Press.

Possehl, Gregory L. 2002. *The Indus Civilization. A Contemporary Perspective.* Walnut Creek, CA: AltaMira Press.

Ratnagar, Shereen. 2001. *Understanding Harappa. Civilization in the Greater Indus Valley.* New Delhi: Tulika.

Settar, S., and Ravi Korisettar, eds. 2002a. *Indian Archaeology in Retrospect. II. Protohistory. Archaeology of the Harappan Civilization.* Indian Council of Historical Research. New Delhi: Manohar.

Settar, S., and Ravi Korisettar, eds. 2002b. *Indian Archaeology in Retrospect. III. Archaeology and Interactive Disciplines.* Indian Council of Historical Research. New Delhi: Manohar.

HISTORY OF DISCOVERY

Chakrabarti, Dilip K. 1988. *A History of Indian Archaeology.* New Delhi: Munshiram Manoharlal.

Lahiri, Nayanjot. 2005. *Finding Forgotten Cities. How the Indus Civilization Was Discovered.* London: Seagull Books.

Mughal, M. Rafique. 1973. *The Present State of Research on the Indus Valley Civilization.* Karachi: Department of Archaeology.

Roy, T. N. 1961. *The Story of Indian Archaeology: 1784–1947.* New Delhi: Government of India.

INDUS ANTECEDENTS

Jarrige, Catherine, Jean-Francois Jarrige, Richard H. Meadow, and Gonzaque Quivron. 1995. *Mehrgarh: Field Reports 1974–1985, from Neolithic Times to the Indus Civilization.* Karachi: Department of Culture and Tourism of Sindh, Department of Archaeology and Museums, French Ministry of Foreign Affairs.

Possehl, Gregory L. 1999. *Indus Age: The Beginnings.* New Delhi: Oxford University Press.

Shaffer, Jim G. 1978. *Prehistoric Baluchistan.* New Delhi: B. R. Publishing Corporation.

THE INDUS CIVILIZATION IN SOUTH ASIAN CULTURE

Allchin, Bridget, and Raymond Allchin. 1982. *The Rise of Civilization in India and Pakistan.* Cambridge, UK: Cambridge University Press.

Bag, A. K., ed. 1997. *History of Technology in India.* New Delhi: Indian National Science Academy.

Huntington, Susan L. 1995. *The Art of Ancient India.* New York: Weatherhill.

Lal, B. B. 2002. *The Saraswati Flows On: The Continuity of Indian Culture.* New Delhi: Aryan Books International.

Schwartzberg, Joseph E., ed. 1992. *A Historical Atlas of South Asia.* 2nd ed. New York: Oxford University Press.

NEIGHBORS OF THE INDUS CIVILIZATION

Crawford, Harriet. 1998. *Dilmun and Its Gulf Neighbours.* Cambridge, UK: Cambridge University Press.

Dani, A. H., and V. M. Masson, eds. 1996. *History of Civilizations of Central Asia. 1: The Dawn of Civilization: Earliest Times to 700 BC.* Paris: UNESCO.

Neumayer, E. 1983. *Prehistoric Indian Rock Paintings.* New Delhi: Oxford University Press.

Possehl, Gregory L. 1986. *Kulli: An Exploration of Ancient Civilization in South Asia.* Durham, NC: Carolina Academic Press.

Postgate, J. N. 1992. *Early Mesopotamia. Society and Economy at the Dawn of History.* London: Routledge.

Potts, Daniel T. 1999. *The Archaeology of Elam. Formation and Transformation of an Ancient Iranian State.* Cambridge, UK: Cambridge University Press.

Potts, Daniel, Hasan Al Naboodah, and Peter Hellyer, eds. 2003. *Archaeology of the United Arab Emirates. Proceedings of the First International Conference on the Archaeology of the U.A.E.* London: Trident Press. [Online information; 4/4/07.] www.kenzay-training.com/uae/download/archeology/000contents.pdf.

Sasson, Jack M., ed. 2000. *Civilizations of the Ancient Near East.* 4 vols. Peabody, MA: Hendrickson Publishers. (Reprint of 1995 edition. New York: Scribner's.)

Settar, S., and Ravi Korisettar, eds. 2002. *Indian Archaeology in Retrospect. I: Prehistory. Archaeology of South Asia.* Indian Council of Historical Research. New Delhi: Manohar.

Sherratt, Andrew. 2006a. "Altyn Depe, Turkmenistan." *ArchAtlas,* 2nd ed. [Online information; retrieved 1/1/07.] www.archatlas.org/NearMiddleEast/AltynDepe.php.

Sherratt, Andrew. 2006b. "Anau and Namazga, Turkmenistan." *ArchAtlas,* 2nd ed. [Online information; retrieved 1/1/07.] www.archatlas.org/NearMiddleEast/AnauNamazga.php.

Sherratt, Andrew. 2006c. "Shahr-i Sokhte, Iran." *ArchAtlas,* 2nd ed. [Online information; retrieved 1/1/07.] www.archatlas.org/NearMiddleEast/ShahrISokhte.php.

Stacul, Giogio. 1987. *Prehistoric and Protohistoric Swat, Pakistan (c. 3000–1400 BC).* Rome: IsMEO.

THE END OF THE INDUS CIVILIZATION AND THE POST-HARAPPAN PERIOD

Allchin, F. R. 1996. *The Archaeology of Early Historic India.* Cambridge, UK: Cambridge University Press.

Gupta, S. P., ed. 1995. *The "Lost" Saraswati and the Indus Civilization.* Jodhpur: Kusumanjali Prakashan.

Jarrige, Jean-Francois, and Marielle Santoni. 1979. *Fouilles de Pirak.* Paris: Diffusion de Boccard.

Lahiri, Nayanjot, ed. 2000. *The Decline and Fall of the Indus Civilization.* New Delhi: Permanent Black and Orient Longman.

Mallory, J. P. 1989. *In Search of the Indo-Europeans. Language, Archaeology and Myth.* London: Thames and Hudson.

Mallory, J. P., and Douglas Q. Adams, eds. 1997. *Encyclopedia of Indo-European Culture.* London: Routledge.

Ratnagar, Shereen. 2000. *The End of the Great Harappan Tradition. Heras Memorial Lectures 1998.* New Delhi: Manohar.

Thapar, Romila. 1990. *From Lineage to State.* New Delhi: Oxford University Press.

ECONOMY, TRADE, AND FOREIGN RELATIONS

Chakrabarti, Dilip K. 1990. *The External Trade of the Indus Civilization.* New Delhi: Munshiram Manoharlal.

Fuller, Dorian. A number of recent papers. [Online articles; retrieved 4/9/07.] www.ucl.ac.uk/archaeology/staff/profiles/fuller/

Lahiri, Nayanjot. 1999. *The Archaeology of Indian Trade Routes up to c.200 BC. Resource Use, Resource Access and Lines of Communication.* New Delhi: Oxford University Press.

Olijdam, Eric, and R. H. Spoor, eds. 2005. *Intercultural Relations between South and Southwest Asia. Studies in Commemoration of E. C. L. During Caspers.* Oxford: Archaeopress.

Ratnagar, Shereen. 2004. *Trading Encounters. From the Euphrates to the Indus in the Bronze Age.* New Delhi: Oxford University Press.

Ray, Himanshu Prabha. 2003. *The Archaeology of Seafaring in Ancient South Asia.* Cambridge, UK: Cambridge University Press.

Weber, Steven A. 1991. *Plants and Harappan Subsistence. An Example of Stability and Change from Rojdi.* New Delhi: Oxford and IBH Publishing Co. and American Institute of Indian Studies.

INDUSTRY, TECHNOLOGY, AND SCIENCE

Agrawal, D. P. 2000. *Ancient Metal Technology and Archaeology of South Asia. A Pan-Asian Perspective.* New Delhi: Aryan Books International.

Chakabarti, Dilip K., and Nayanjot Lahiri. 1996. *Copper and Its Alloys in Ancient India.* New Delhi: Munshiram Manoharlal.

Dales, George F., and Jonathan Mark Kenoyer. 1986. *Excavations at Mohenjo Daro, Pakistan: The Pottery.* Philadelphia: University of Pennsylvania Museum of Archaeology and Anthropology.

Manchandra, Omi. 1972. *A Study of the Harappan Pottery.* New Delhi: Oriental Publishers.

Roux, Valentine, ed. 1998. *Cornaline d'Inde: Des Pratiques Techniques de Cambay aux techno-systemes de l'Indus.* Paris: Editions de la Maison des Sciences de l'Homme.

Tripathi, Vibha, and Ajeet K. Srivastava. 1994. *The Indus Terracottas.* New Delhi: Sharada Publishing House.

Tripathi, Vibha, ed. 1998. *Archaeometallurgy in India.* New Delhi: Sharada Publishing House.

Vidale, Massimo. 2000. *The Archaeology of Indus Crafts. Indus Craftspeople and Why We Study Them.* Rome: ISIAO.

THE HARAPPAN PEOPLE

Dutta, Pratap C. 1982. *The Bronze Age Harappans. A Bio-anthropological Study of the Skeletons Discovered at Harappa.* Calcutta: Anthropological Survey of India.

Kennedy, Kenneth A. R. 2000. *God-Apes and Fossil Men. Palaeoanthropology of South Asia.* Ann Arbor: University of Michigan Press.

Sharma, A. K. 1999. *The Departed Harappans of Kalibangan.* New Delhi: Sundeep Prakashan.

SOCIAL AND POLITICAL ORGANIZATION

Malik, S. C. 1987. *Indian Civilization: The Formative Period.* Shimla and Delhi: Indian Institute of Advanced Study and Motilal Banarsidass.

Ratnagar, Shereen. 1991. *Enquiries into the Political Organization of Harappan Society.* New Delhi: Ravish.

SETTLEMENT AND SETTLEMENTS

Casal, Jean-Marie. 1964. *Fouilles d'Amri.* Paris: Klincksieck.

Chakrabarti, Dilip K. 1997. *The Archaeology of Ancient Indian Cities.* New Delhi: Oxford University Press.

Chakrabarti, Dilip K., ed. 2004. *Indus Civilization. Sites in India: New Discoveries.* Mumbai: Marg Publications.

Dhavikar, M. K. 1994. *Cultural Imperialism—Indus Civilization in Western India.* New Delhi: Books and Books.

Dhavikar, M. K. 1996. *Kuntasi, a Harappan Emporium on West Coast.* Pune, India: Deccan College Post-Graduate Research Institute.

Francfort, Henri Paul. 1989. *Fouilles de Shortugai.* Paris: Diffusion de Boccard.

Hegde, K. T., K. K. Bhan, V. H. Sonawane, K. Krishnan, and D. R. Shah. 1992. *Excava-*

tions at Nageshwar, Gujurat. A Harappan Shellworking Site on the Gulf of Kutch. Baroda, India: Department of Archaeology and Ancient History, M.S. University of Baroda.

Jansen, Michael. 1993. *Mohenjo-daro: City of Wells and Drains.* Bergisch Gladbach: Frontinus-Gesellschaft e.V.

Jansen, Michael, and Gunter Urban, eds. 1984. *Reports on Fieldwork Carried out at Mohenjo-daro, Pakistan 1982–83 by the IsMEO-Aachen University Mission: Interim Reports I.* Aachen and Rome: RWTH and IsMEO.

Jansen, Michael, and Gunter Urban, eds. 1987 *Reports on Fieldwork Carried out at Mohenjo-daro, Pakistan 1983–84 by the IsMEO-Aachen University Mission: Interim Reports II.* Aachen and Rome: RWTH and IsMEO.

Joshi, Jagat Pati. 1990. *Excavations at Surkotada 1971–72 and Exploration in Kutch. Memoirs of the Archaeological Survey of India.* 87. New Delhi: Archaeological Survey of India.

Marshall, John. 1931. *Mohenjo Daro and the Indus Civilization.* London: Arthur Probsthain.

Mackay, Ernest J. H. 1938. *Further Excavations at Mohenjo Daro.* New Delhi: Government of India.

Mackay, Ernest J. H. 1943. *Chanhu-daro Excavations 1935–36.* New Haven, CT: American Oriental Society.

Meadow, Richard, ed. 1991. *Harappa Excavations 1986–1990.* Madison, WI: Prehistory Press.

Mughal, M. Rafique. 1997. *Ancient Cholistan: Archaeology and Architecture.* Lahore: Ferozsons.

Possehl, Gregory L. 1980. *The Indus Civilization in Saurashtra.* New Delhi: B. R. Publishing Corporation.

Possehl, Gregory L., and M. H. Raval. 1989. *Harappan Civilization and Rojdi.* New Delhi: Oxford & IBH Publishing Co.

Rao, S. R. 1979 and 1985. *Lothal: A Harappan Town (1955–62).* 2 vols. *Memoirs of the Archaeological Survey of India.* SI 78. New Delhi: Archaeological Survey of India.

Rissman, Paul C., and Y. M. Chitalwala. 1990. *Harappan Civilization and Oriyo Timbo.* New Delhi: Oxford & IBH Publishing Co. and American Institute of Indian Studies.

Suraj Bhan. 1975. *Excavations at Mitathal (1968) and Other Explorations in the Sutlej-Yamuna Divide.* Kurukshetra, India: Kurukshetra University.

Vats, M. S. 1940. *Excavations at Harappa.* New Delhi: Government of India.

LANGUAGE, WRITING, AND SEALS

Farmer, Steve. A number of recent papers. [Online articles; retrieved 4/9/07.] www.safarmer.com/

Joshi, Jagat Pati, and Asko Parpola. 1987. *Corpus of Indus Seals and Inscriptions. 1: Collections in India.* Helsinki: Suomalainen Tiedeakatemia.

Mahadevan, Iravatham. 1977. *The Indus Script: Texts, Concordance and Tables. Memoirs of the Archaeological Survey of India* 77. New Delhi: Archaeological Survey of India.

Parpola, Asko. 1994. *Deciphering the Indus Script.* Cambridge, UK: Cambridge University Press.

Parpola, Asko, B. M. Pande, and Petteri Koskikallio, eds. In press. *Corpus of Indus Seals and Inscriptions. 3: New Material, Untraced Objects and Collections outside India and Pakistan.* Helsinki: Suomalainen Tiedeakatemia.

Possehl, Gregory L. 1996. *Indus Age: The Writing System.* New Delhi: Oxford University Press.

Shah, Syed G. M., and Asko Parpola. 1991. *Corpus of Indus Seals and Inscriptions. 2: Collections in Pakistan.* Helsinki: Suomalainen Tiedeakatemia.

Southworth, Franklin C. A number of recent papers. [Online articles; retrieved 4/9/07.] ccat.sas.upenn.edu/~fsouth/

Southworth, Franklin C. 2005. *Linguistic Archaeology of South Asia.* London: Routledge-Curzon.

Witzel, Michael. A number of recent papers. [Online articles; retrieved 4/9/07.] www.people.fas.harvard.edu/~witzel/

Zide, Arlene R. K., and Kamil V. Zvelebil, eds. 1976. *The Soviet Decipherment of the Indus Valley Script: Translation and Critique.* Janua Linguarum, Series Practica, 156. The Hague and Paris: Mouton.

USEFUL WEB PAGES

pubweb.cc.u-tokai.ac.jp/indus/index.html
Indus Civilization. (Japanese website that includes 3-D reconstructions of Dholavira)
www.harappa.com
Information and photos, mainly from Harappa but also from Mohenjo-daro, Lothal, Gola Dhoro, and elsewhere, discussions on the script, and a portal to Indus material.
www.shunya.net/Pictures/Highlights/LostCities-India.htm
Excellent photographs of Dholavira and Lothal.

JOURNALS AND OCCASIONAL PUBLICATIONS

East and West
Indian Archaeology—A Review
Man and Environment
Pakistan Archaeology
Puratattva
South Asian Archaeology (The proceedings of the biennial Conference of South Asian Archaeologists in Western Europe)
South Asian Studies

Index

About the Author

Jane McIntosh is a native of Scotland. She studied archaeology at the University of Cambridge, from which she also received her doctorate and where she taught for a number of years. She has traveled widely, taking part in excavations and other fieldwork in Iraq, Cyprus, India, and Britain. Since 1995, she has worked full-time as a writer of books, articles, and multimedia on a range of archaeological subjects. She is a widow with one son.